MOZART

HIS CHARACTER, HIS WORK

FACSIMILE OF FRONTISPIECE TO *Mozarts Leben*

Mozart

HIS CHARACTER HIS WORK

ALFRED EINSTEIN

TRANSLATED BY

Arthur Mendel and Nathan Broder

DOMI NVS ILLV MINA TIO MEA

OXFORD UNIVERSITY PRESS

London · New York · Toronto

1945

TO MY 'THREE LADIES'
HERTHA, EVA, BERTHA

Preface

ÖREN KIERKEGAARD wrote concerning *Don Juan:* 'What I can offer has a meaning only for those who have heard, and who keep on hearing. To such I may be able to give a suggestion here and there for renewed hearing.' The present volume is not an introduction to Mozart's life and music. It addresses itself to readers who already know and love at least some of his works.

Over a long period I have occupied myself with Mozart intensively, most recently in the work, lasting many years, on the Third Edition (1937) of Köchel's *Chronological-Thematic Catalogue*—the book that has given Mozart's works the numbers by which they are customarily identified. In the course of this work I had to investigate not only the externals of every Mozart manuscript and edition, but also the bearing and style of every work. It was inevitable that in doing this I should arrive at new results, and it is perhaps understandable that in the end I have felt impelled to present these results not only in the dry form of a catalogue, but also in a more connected and more personal one.

I have made no effort to retell in all its details the story of Mozart's life, for which new sources of information have flowed but sparsely in the last few decades. What I have sought to do is to draw as sharply defined a picture as I could of his character and of the personalities and events that exercised a decisive influence upon it. The works that are mentioned are not described, but characterized from the point of view of their time and—so far as possible—of our relation to them. This seems to me the only possible approach to the task of portraying a great musician.

From the large field of Mozart literature, I am deeply indebted to many works, both to those with which I agree and to those with which I do not. I should like to acknowledge a special debt to three fairly recent works. Most of all I owe to the four volumes of Théodore de Wyzewa and Georges de Saint-Foix, *Wolfgang Amédée Mozart* (Paris,

vii

1912, 1936, 1939, Desclée de Brouwer & Cie)—the first two volumes being the product of both men, and the second two by Monsieur de Saint-Foix alone. May he, despite everything that has taken place, be able to publish the fifth and concluding volume! Then there is the penetrating monograph, *Mozart et ses concertos pour piano*, by C. M. Girdlestone (Paris, 1939, Librairie Fischbacher); and finally the masterful little popular book *Mozart* by Eric Blom, in the Master Musicians Series (London, 1935, J. M. Dent & Sons; New York, 1935, E. P. Dutton & Co.). My special thanks go to the publishers of Miss Emily Anderson's complete translation of the *Letters of Mozart and His Family* (London, 1938-9, Macmillan & Co.), for permission to quote it extensively. The only separately published article that has been taken over into this book is the one on Mozart's Choice of Keys, which originally appeared in the October 1941 issue of *The Musical Quarterly*, published by G. Schirmer, Inc., to whom I am indebted for their friendly permission to reprint it.

Where a question of fact was involved in the translation (as, for example, in the rendering of the word *clavier* usually by *piano*) I was consulted and the decisions are mine.

ALFRED EINSTEIN

Northampton, Massachusetts
1 July 1944

Contents

I. THE MAN

II. THE MUSICIAN

III. THE INSTRUMENTAL WORKS

IV. THE VOCAL WORKS

V. OPERA

Plates

I. THE MAN

1. *The Traveler*

*T*HERE is a strange kind of human being in whom there is an eternal struggle between body and soul, animal and god, for dominance. In all great men this mixture is striking, and in none more so than in Wolfgang Amadeus Mozart.

As an artist, as a musician, Mozart was not a man of this world. To a certain part of the nineteenth century his work seemed to possess so pure, so formally rounded, so 'godlike' a perfection that Richard Wagner, the most violent spokesman of the Romantic Period, could call him 'music's genius of light and love'; and this without contradiction, for in such a view Wagner was in full agreement even with the opponents of his own art—with Robert Schumann, who called Mozart's G minor Symphony a work 'of Grecian lightness and grace' (*Griechisch schwebender Grazie*), or with Otto Jahn, Mozart's biographer, who partly unconsciously and partly intentionally overlooked all the darker dissonances in his life and work. We know that intention entered into Jahn's attitude because, unlike Wagner and Schumann, he knew most of Mozart's letters; and these letters reveal Mozart so completely 'a man of this world,' in all his warm, childlike, childish, human personality, that at least in Germany no one has ever dared to publish them without omissions, and either his widow or other well-meaning persons made certain passages, even in the letters of his last years, forever illegible.

Thanks to these letters—the liveliest, least dressed-up, most genuine letters ever written by a musician—we really know Mozart the man. There are several intervals in his short life, such as the Salzburg years 1775-6, or the time between his return from Paris and *Idomeneo*, or the year 1789 in Vienna, that are shrouded in darkness. But to make up for this we have more exact and intimate information about other days, months, and years of his life than about those of any other great musician of the eighteenth or even the nineteenth or twentieth century. Our information is so exact that sometimes the picture that emerges of the man seems no longer to agree with our conception of the musician. In reality, however, there is a glorious unity. The young man who wrote the high-spirited letters to his sister and the obscene 'Bäsle' letters, and who found pleasure in canons on texts completely unsuited to the drawing-room, was also the author of the G minor Symphony. In the *Musikalischer Spass* we find his love of horse-play expressed in music itself; but the horse-play has a background of deep theoretical knowledge, to which Mozart at one time wished to give literary form. And the unity of the man and the creative musician becomes clearest when we contemplate its two aspects in Mozart the uncannily sharp, pitiless, and incorruptible judge of human nature, and in Mozart the great dramatist. His music speaks of secrets of the heart that both the man and the artist well understood.

But to a certain extent it is true that Mozart was only a visitor upon this earth. Mozart as a man was nowhere truly at home: neither in Salzburg, where he was born, nor in Vienna, where he died. And between the periods of residence in Salzburg and Vienna he made journeys to all points of the compass, journeys that filled a considerable portion of his life. For Mozart never 'deliberated' over undertaking a journey, and if he returned to settled habitation in one place it was only on compulsion—or at least with reluctance.

'My heart is completely enchanted with all these pleasures, because it is so jolly on this journey, because it is so warm in the carriage, and because our coachman is a fine fellow, who when the road gives him the slightest chance, drives so fast,' he writes home on his first trip to Italy (Wörgl, 13 December 1769). How he envies Gyrowetz, who is off to Italy (1786). 'You lucky man! O, if I could only go with you, how happy I should be!' This is the year at the end of which he feels a strong urge to go to England again, and proposes that his old father should take charge of his two children—a proposal that the father 'very emphatically' rejects. He must have remembered that three years earlier Mozart's first child had died while in the care of a wet-nurse with whom he had been put out to board in Vienna while the parents were visiting in Salzburg. Leopold Mozart had ample grounds for suspecting that these two other children would probably have remained in his care longer than he desired. For what do children mean to Wolfgang Amadeus when traveling is in prospect? They are forgotten: it is his work that matters. And travel does not interrupt Mozart's creative activity; it rather stimulates it. When long journeys are out of the question, as for example during the last ten years in Vienna, he is constantly changing his residence—never really a home—from one apartment to another, from the town out into the suburbs, and from the suburbs back again into town. Not even Beethoven changed his living quarters so often, and Beethoven usually moved for very substantial reasons. But Mozart is animated by an inner urge to gain stimulation from a new environment. He accepts the discomforts of moving: they merely take the place of the discomforts of the stagecoach.

Mozart began to travel early in life. On 12 January 1762, Leopold took the boy, not quite six years old, to the Electoral Court at Munich, and until 1773 Wolfgang was completely under the direction of his father. Because of this fact, and also because the personality of Mozart must be viewed not only in itself but as the fruit of the Mozart family tree, we must leave the main path of our discussion for a moment to discover something about the father.

Leopold Mozart is remembered by posterity as the father of his son. If he had not been connected with Wolfgang Amadeus, his name would be no more significant than that of any one of the hundred other honest musicians of the eighteenth century, pursuing their goals at the many little ecclesiastical and secular courts of South Germany; and his name would not even have been the first within his own narrow circle, since he never even became first Kapellmeister.

But he was the father of his son, and as the father of such a genius, he understood his mission. Without the influence of the father, reflected both in the son's submission and resistance to it, Wolfgang would never have achieved the character and the greatness that he did. Leopold stands in the circle illuminated by his son, and without that illumination he would have remained in obscurity. But the light of his son's genius and fame does reveal him: not always a completely attractive personality, often a very questionable one, but clearly outlined as a plastic and living figure. Although his talent does not lift him far above his many contemporaries, his ambition, his will, and his energy do. He was no mere *Musikant*. The literary evidence he left—the *School of Violin-Playing*—assures him in any case of a small place in every history of instrumental music. Even without Wolfgang's fame, Leopold would always have been known as the author of this *Versuch einer gründlichen Violinschule*, which he was writing at about the time of the birth of his son.

During the first year of Wolfgang's life, Leopold wrote a short autobiography for F. W. Marpurg's *Historisch-kritische Beyträge zur Auf-nahme der Musik,* which contains a 'report on the present state of the music of His Princely Grace, the Archbishop of Salzburg, in the year 1757.' In it is a sketch of the life and works of the 38-year-old musician:

Mr. Leopold Mozart of the Imperial city of Augspurg. First violinist and leader of the orchestra. He composes both sacred and secular music. He was born 14 November 1719, and, soon after finishing his studies in philosophy and law, entered the Princely service in the year 1743. He has made himself known in all forms of composition, but has not yet printed any music, although in the year 1740 he himself engraved on copper 6 sonatas à 3—mostly in order to study the art of engraving. In June 1756, he published his School of Violin-Playing.

Of the manuscript works of Mr. Mozart which have become known, the ones principally to be noted are many contrapuntal and other sacred pieces; also a large number of symphonies, some only à 4, and some with all the usual instruments; further, more than 30 grand serenades, in which solos for various instruments occur. He has also written many concertos, especially for transverse flute, oboe, bassoon, horn, trumpet, etc., innumerable trios and divertimenti for various instruments; also 12 oratorios and a great number of theatrical pieces, including panto-mimes; and especially occasional compositions such as: military music for trumpets, timpani, drums, and fifes in addition to the usual instru-ments; a Turkish music; a piece including a steel clavier [a kind of celesta]; and finally a sleigh-ride piece with 5 sleigh bells; not to speak of marches, so-called *Nachtstücke,* and many hundred minuets, opera dances, and similar pieces.

We may amplify this information somewhat. Leopold Mozart was the eldest of six sons of the Augsburg bookbinder Johann Georg Mozart, whose paternal ancestors can be traced back to the seventeenth and per-haps to the sixteenth century. The name, which has become a symbol of grace, sometimes took on rougher forms (e.g. Motzert) and rough doubtless were those who bore it—artisans and peasants. Leopold's mother, née Anna Maria Sulzer, the bookbinder's second wife, was also a native of Augsburg. She outlived her husband, who died at the age of fifty-seven on 19 February 1736, by more than thirty years. She seems to have been in comfortable circumstances, for at the time of the creation of the *School of Violin-Playing* Leopold was active in an effort not to receive less than his many brothers and sisters from the estate; each of them had already received an advance of 300 gulden.

Leopold did not become an artisan like his brothers Joseph Ignaz and Franz Aloys, who were both bookbinders. His godfather, the canon Johann Georg Grabher, got him appointed as *discantist* in the choir of the church of the Holy Cross and St. Ulrich—and of course a church singer could easily become a clergyman. He learned not only singing but also organ-playing. In 1777 Wolfgang made the acquaintance in Munich of a former fellow pupil of Leopold's who clearly remembered the forceful and individual organ-playing of the young musician in the monastery of Wessobrunn.

Upon the death of his father, Leopold was sent to Salzburg and received financial support on the assumption that it would be used for theological studies. But he was already a young diplomatist. Secretly, he cherished quite other plans and meanwhile he 'hoodwinked the clerics about becoming a priest.' After two years at the university of Salzburg he was no longer studying theology at all, but logic instead, and, as he claimed, jurisprudence. Consequently the financial help from Augsburg presumably stopped, and Leopold was forced to give up his studies. He became a domestic in the service of the President of the Chapter of the Salzburg Cathedral—Count Johann Baptist Thurn, Valsassina, und Taxis (the name Thurn und Taxis is world famous as that of the hereditary postmasters of the Holy Roman Empire).

That is about all we know concerning the first twenty years of Leopold's life. Who his teachers in organ playing and in composition were remains obscure; what he sang as a member of the Augsburg cathedral choir, on the other hand, is easier to establish. The music consisted of the *concertante* church works of South-German and Italian masters, of whom the most brilliant and historically most influential was the Imperial Kapellmeister J. J. Fux. The free city of Augsburg, which included both Roman Catholics and Protestants within its walls, contributed to Leopold's personality a certain tolerance, perhaps, or, more accurately, a certain critical attitude towards everything clerical, which kept him from becoming a priest. Further, it made his taste in church music solid and somewhat provincial, and in secular music gave it a typically South-German sturdiness. The clearest documentary evidence we have of this South-German taste is contained in Valentin Rathgeber's *Augsburger Tafel-Confect*—a lengthy collection in four volumes, containing folksongs, songs of the peasants and burghers, choruses, quodlibets, and instrumental pieces, all published in the years 1733 to 1746 by Leopold's Augsburg publisher, Lotter, and all full of the broad, easy, often rough humor typical of Bavaria and Swabia. These pieces played a great role in the Mozart family, and without them neither Leopold's *Sleigh-Ride* and *Peasant Wedding* nor Wolfgang's youthful *Galimathias Musicum* would have been conceivable. Leopold had a very poor opinion of the people of his native Augsburg, and Wolfgang a much poorer one still; nevertheless, this South-German heredity was in their blood.

We do not know what led Leopold to Salzburg and why he should have passed over, on his way from Augsburg, a cultural center like Munich. Ingolstadt, the Electoral University of Bavaria, was much closer to the people of Augsburg, and would have offered just as much as Salzburg a strictly orthodox education for the young theologian. Perhaps the canons of St. Ulrich recommended that Leopold go to Salzburg, for St. Ulrich was one of the Benedictine monasteries that had once contributed to the founding of the University there, and some of the canons of St. Ulrich (e.g. Dietrichstein and Waldstein) were also canons of Salzburg. However that may be, fate led Leopold to the Salzach—a circumstance that was not without consequences either for Leopold or for Salzburg. His study of *Logica* had important effects upon his thinking, both good and bad. He became an 'educated' musician, who had ideas not only about the world and his fellow-men, but also about the rules of his art. He interested himself in Rubens's pictures, in literature, and in all phases of the politics of the princes of his time, both great and small. He understood Latin fairly well, and knew how to handle his own language—handled it, in fact, with extraordinary skill and liveliness, employing many robust, South-German folk-expressions, which give his style a particular charm. Anyone who has read the descriptions in his letters from Paris and London, or in those to his son in Mannheim, knows how vividly and graphically Leopold Mozart could write. When he describes his feelings on the morning of the departure of his wife and son for Paris—a fateful moment, for he was never to see his wife again—the truth and realism of his description rise to the level of the unconsciously poetic (letter of 25 September 1777):

After you both had left, I walked up our steps very wearily and threw myself down on a chair. When we said good-bye, I made great efforts to restrain myself in order not to make our parting too painful; and in the rush and flurry I forgot to give my son a father's blessing. I ran to the window and sent my blessing after you: but I did not see you driving out through the gate and so came to the conclusion that you were gone already, as I had sat for a long time without thinking of anything. Nannerl wept bitterly and I had to use every effort to console her. She complained of headache and a sick stomach and in the end she retched and vomited; and putting a cloth round her head she went off to bed and had the shutters closed. Poor Bimbes [the Mozarts' little dog] lay down beside her. For my own part, I went to my room and said my morning prayers. I then lay down on my bed at half past eight and read a book and thus becoming calmer fell asleep. The dog came to my bedside and I awoke. As she made signs to me to take her for a run, I gathered that it must be nearly noon and that she wanted to be let out. I got up, took my fur cloak, and saw that Nannerl was fast asleep. The clock then showed half past twelve. When I came in with the dog, I waked Nannerl and ordered lunch. But she had no appetite, she would eat nothing and went to bed immediately afterwards, so that, when Bullinger had left, I passed the time lying on my bed, praying and reading. In the evening she felt better and was hungry. We played piquet and then had supper in my room. After this we had a few more games and, with God's blessing, went off to bed. That is how we spent that sad day which I never thought I should have to face . . .

There is no harm in the fact that Leopold, ever the diplomatist, wished in writing this naive description to make an impression upon his son, who for his part was in the best of moods: '. . . All will yet be well,' he had written two days earlier. 'I hope that Papa is well and as happy as I am . . .'

The intellectual superiority of Leopold, enhanced, in the course of the many journeys he made, by experience and increased knowledge of the world, was not an unmixed blessing. For it made him feel superior to his colleagues, and critical of those placed above him. It isolated him professionally and contributed greatly to his unpopularity. His 'diplomatic sense' caused him to suspect behind the words and actions of his fellow-men even more hidden malice than was actually there, and led him not only into keen observation but also into mistakes of decisive importance. But who could blame him for warning Wolfgang, in a letter dated 18 October 1777: 'Hold fast to God, I beg you, who will see to everything. For all men are villains! The older you become and the more you associate with people, the more will you realize this sad truth.' Had Leopold read Machiavelli's *Il Principe*?

For of men it may generally be affirmed that they are thankless, fickle, false, studious to avoid danger, greedy of gain, devoted to you while you are able to confer benefits upon them, and ready . . . while danger is distant, to shed their blood, and sacrifice their property, their loves, and their children for you; but in the hour of need they turn against you.

This pessimism is balanced by Leopold's affection for his family and his care for them in all details of daily life, a care that showed itself strikingly on journeys. For in 1760 it was an adventurous undertaking to travel all over Europe with a wife and two delicate children, and to act as travel agent and impresario combined. And to the favorable side of the scales we must also add his uprightness as a citizen and as a professional musician. It is true that he considered his colleagues mere hacks and drunkards, and that he saw in his archiepiscopal patron not only the patron but also the cruel tyrant, and accordingly felt there was no harm in occasionally pulling the wool over his eyes. (Unfortunately, the Archbishop did not relish being taken in.) But all Leopold's weaknesses were atoned for in the tragic bitterness of his fate, which he keenly felt. He saw in his child the sun and light of his life, and he believed that under his direction Wolfgang would attain the peak of human success. Yet he had to watch his son slip away from him; and he died a lonely man to whom nothing remained but his correspondence with his daughter and his joy in a little grandson, whose first apparent musical stirrings he observed with delight— although actually this grandson did not inherit even the palest reflection of the brilliance of his family.

But we have anticipated, and must return to Leopold's character. His service as a domestic in the household of the capitular canon, Count Thurn und Taxis, was obviously only a station or a detour on Leopold Mozart's path to music as a career. In 1740 he dedicated to his patron his first work, six church and chamber sonatas for two violins and bass, of which he had engraved the musical portion himself; in the dedication he calls the prelate, in baroque style, the 'fatherly sun, whose beneficent influence has brought him out of the bitter darkness of all his misery and set him upon the path to all his good fortune.' One of these sonatas has been reprinted in the *Denkmäler der Tonkunst in Bayern* (ix, 2, ed. M. Seiffert). It exhibits a curious mixture of old-fashioned stiffness with a few freer features of the *galant* style. Leopold's development as a musician came in those difficult decades in which the noble and elegiac elements of the old Classic style—embodied, for example, in Corelli, Bach, Handel, and Vivaldi—were becoming rigid and inert, while the new *galant* style inspired by the spirit of the *opera buffa* was just taking root. Leopold never succeeded in achieving a complete reconciliation of these two elements.

But this fact did not hinder him from plunging at once into the surging stream of the musical life of Salzburg. Salzburg reverberated with the sound of music: music in the cathedral and the many other churches of this archiepiscopal seat; instrumental music written for the drawing-rooms of the prelates and nobles of the Court; and music composed for the dramatic performances of the schools and the university, as well as for oratorios and occasionally even for the opera. That all this was very provincial, Leopold did not notice until after his travels—that is after 1762. Thus, soon after his arrival in Salzburg he wrote for Lent, 1741, an oratorio-like cantata, *Christus begraben*, for three voices, with recitatives, arias, a duet, and a final chorus. (Only the text survives.) In 1742 he composed for the smaller auditorium of the University the music for a school play *Antiquitas personata*, which has the flavor of antiquity, but with an edifying moral. And in 1743 he wrote another passion cantata, *Christus verurtheilt*, this time for four voices and chorus.

Such labors smoothed his path into the archiepiscopal Court *Kapelle*, as the assembly of vocal and instrumental musicians was called. As early as 1743 he became a violinist in the orchestra, and in 1744 he was entrusted with the instruction of the boys of the *Kapelle* in violin playing —evidence of the early development of his pedagogic talent—and named court-composer. Now he could consider setting up a household. He must have become acquainted soon after his arrival in Salzburg with Anna Maria Pertl, daughter of the superintendent of a clerical institution at St. Gilgen on the Wolfgang-See. For on 21 November 1772 he wrote to her from Milan: 'It was twenty-five years ago, I think, that we had the sensible idea of getting married, one which we had cherished, it is true, for many years. All good things take time!'

This remark, in its dryness as well as in its affectionate character, is typical of both husband and wife, upon whose marital happiness we may be sure that no shadow ever fell. Anna Maria Mozart, who was a year younger than her husband, having been born on 25 December 1720 at Schloss Hüttenstein near St. Gilgen, and who had been an orphan since early childhood, always recognized Leopold's superiority. She was a good woman of definite limitations, undoubtedly an excellent mother and housewife, very receptive to all the gossip in Salzburg, and very much interested in all the events and personalities of the little capital, which she judged with an eye just as friendly as her husband's was critical and sarcastic. It was from her that Wolfgang, who loved her dearly and had not the slightest respect for her authority, inherited all his naive, gay, childish traits—everything in his character that we think of as typical of Salzburg.

For during this period the inhabitants of Salzburg enjoyed throughout the Empire no particular reputation for seriousness, brilliance, or wisdom; on the contrary, they were considered to be very devoted to all earthly pleasures, and very disinclined towards all spiritual ones. They embodied all the characteristics that are attributed to the comic protagonists of the South-German *Hanswurst* comedy. Casperl Larifari is a true native of Salzburg, for he combines elements that come from Munich, from Vienna, and even from Venice, and Salzburg lies near the center of the triangle formed by the three cities. Wolfgang knew the qualities of the residents of Salzburg very well; he hated them, and at the same time it amused him to share them a little.

Leopold and Anna Maria had seven children, of whom only two lived to maturity: the fourth, Maria Anna Walpurga Ignatia, known as Nannerl, born 30 June 1751, and the seventh and last, Wolfgang Amadeus, born 27 January 1756.

The first signs of musical talent in Wolfgang completely changed the direction of Leopold's life and thought. From the moment of their appearance, he lived and thought only in relation to his son. Until 1762, it had been his ambition to achieve the leading position in the Court *Kapelle*—an ambition thwarted by the presence of the Kapellmeister Johann Ernst Eberlin. Eberlin far surpassed Leopold as a creative musician, and Leopold himself recognized Eberlin as the model 'of a thorough and completely finished master,' and of wonderful ease and fertility in artistic production. But when Eberlin died, in 1762, Leopold was on tour with his children, and he considered this activity far more important than his official duties in Salzburg, both as a moral obligation and as a financial investment. (The proportions of obligation and investment are not easy to determine.) With some pains, and not without veiled threats to turn his back entirely on Salzburg, he achieved on 28 February 1763 the post of Vice-Kapellmeister, while Giuseppe Francesco Lolli, an insignificant musician who had been Vice-Kapellmeister under Eberlin, was named the latter's successor.

Leopold never rose above the rank of Vice-Kapellmeister. In 1772

came the death of the Archbishop Sigismund von Schrattenbach, who
had reigned in a rather easy-going and patriarchal spirit for eighteen
years (1753-71) and was well disposed towards the Mozart family. His
successor, Hieronymus Colloredo, was the son of the Viennese Imperial
Vice-Chancellor under Francis I, just forty years old, an admirer of
Rousseau and Voltaire, in the grip of the Emperor Joseph's zeal for
reform, and hated by the inhabitants of Salzburg. He was so much less
willing to accept without question the absences of his Vice-Kapellmeister Leopold Mozart and his Concertmaster and court organist,
Wolfgang Amadeus, that a conflict was unavoidable. This conflict had
historical significance and has achieved world fame, and here again it
is difficult to weigh the opposing forces accurately. It is certain, however, that the fault was not all on the side of authority. In any case,
Leopold was continually slighted. From the year 1773 on, he had two
superiors: Lolli and Domenico Fischietti; from 1777 on, Fischietti and
Jacob Rust. When Rust left Salzburg, Leopold was really in line to
become Kapellmeister, and in August 1778 he swallowed his pride to
the extent of 'laying himself most humbly at the feet of his patron'
and of recalling that he had 'been serving this worthy Archbishopric
for thirty-eight years, and that since the year 1763, that is, for fifteen
years, [he had] been performing as Vice-Kapellmeister most of the
services required, and indeed nearly all of them, without any blame.'
But this self-abasement was in vain. The Archbishop granted Leopold
an increase in salary, but not the appointment, and Fischietti was succeeded in 1783 by another Italian: Lodovico Gatti. Leopold remained
Vice-Kapellmeister until his death.

About his having 'performed nearly all services without blame,' there
is room for doubt. For if one adds up the durations of all the journeys
Leopold Mozart made from 12 January 1762 to 13 March 1773, his
absences from Salzburg amount to something like seven years; and the
Archbishop was certainly not unjust in withholding Leopold's salary
while permitting the journeys. It was generous enough of him to hold
open Leopold's position in the *Kapelle*. And it was soon felt in Salzburg that when Leopold returned to his provincial home from such
journeys, which broadened his horizon greatly, he was a changed man.
He became more critical than ever of conditions and of his colleagues;
he performed his duties less wholeheartedly than ever. His prime concern was and remained the development of his son. Wolfgang de-

scribed his father's position well when he wrote to Padre Martini in Bologna (4 September 1776):

He has already served this court for thirty-six years and as he knows that the present Archbishop cannot and will not have anything to do with people who are getting on in years, he no longer puts his whole heart into his work, but has taken up literature, which was always a favorite study of his . . .

In actual fact Leopold did not concern himself with literature, but only with his son. Even in the years of almost complete estrangement —the years after 1782—Wolfgang occupied the central point in his father's thoughts and feelings—even when Leopold referred to him in the letters to Nannerl only as 'your brother,' and when the correspondence between father and son was becoming ever more sporadic and, on the father's side, at times was taking on harsh and unpleasant forms. Leopold's last great joy was his stay in Vienna in February, March, and April 1785, during which he could observe his son's mature genius and external success. The climax of his life was perhaps that Saturday evening in February when Mozart's three String Quartets, K. 458, 464, and 465, were played for the first time, and Haydn, to whom they were dedicated, said to Leopold: 'Before God and as an honest man, I tell you that your son is the greatest composer known to me either in person or by name. He has taste and, what is more, the most profound knowledge of composition.'

What a testimonial from the mouth of the one great musician who was in a position to evaluate Mozart's greatness accurately! Genius and art combined; the *galant* and the 'learned'—the two extremes into which music during this period threatened to split—re-united. We shall see in a later chapter that this was the most profound comment that could be made about Mozart. Leopold perhaps did not altogether understand it, in its historical sense, but it crowned his whole work of educating his son, and justified his whole existence.

Leopold's attitude towards Salzburg was critical; Wolfgang began early in life to make fun of his native city and later, from 1772 on, hated it with all his soul. Now, it is hard to hate Salzburg when one thinks of the architecture of the town and of its position in the landscape: the majestic cathedral, the noble Residenz, the prevailingly gay and theatrical baroque architecture; the gardens with their southern fragrance, the river flowing swiftly and brightly down from the mountains to the Bavarian plateau between the Capuzinerberg and the Veste Hohensalzburg, which gloriously dominates the town and landscape; in the distance the mountains, meadows, forests, rocks, and snow; and over all the blue that reminds one of Italian skies and makes one long for Italy. Comparisons have not been lacking between Mozart's music and this landscape, and it is certainly not difficult to relate his melody, his sense of form, the deep and serious harmony of his work, to these amiable surroundings, which seem doubly amiable against their somber background. But one cannot avoid the thought that if Mozart had been born in Augsburg, Munich, Bozen, or Würzburg, similar comparisons could be made with equal ease.

Probably Mozart never saw all this beauty; probably it had no effect upon him even unconsciously. Neither the city nor the landscape awoke in him any feeling of home. From his sixteenth year on, Salzburg represented to him only the town in whose archiepiscopal palace a spiteful patron resided, and in which also lived some ten thousand provincial, small-town inhabitants. Amid all the gay scenery he saw the boorishness and the dirt that were always there, and that can still be seen. He was no lover of hunting and fishing, like Haydn, or of tramping through the woods, like Beethoven; he could never have written the *Midi* and *Soir* symphonies, or *The Seasons*, or a *Pastoral Symphony*. He traveled in a tightly closed coach, and the view through the tiny windows interested him very little. Friedrich Rochlitz reports, allegedly from information furnished him by Constanze: 'When Mozart traveled through beautiful landscapes with his wife, he looked around him observantly and silently. His expression, which was usually somber and introspective rather than gay and open, gradually brightened, and then he would begin to sing or rather to hum.' But this is just a well-meaning but irresponsible hoax, like the other anecdotes this inventive chatterer of Leipzig put into circulation after Mozart's death. For when did Mozart travel with Constanze 'through beautiful landscapes'? I can think only of the journeys from Vienna to Salzburg in the summer of 1783 and of the two trips to Prague in 1787 and 1791; and on the Prague trips Mozart was extremely busy. For he composed and 'speculated' in the coach. His music needed no visual stimuli; it was self-contained; it followed its own laws and was not influenced by the appearance of the real sky above, whether fair or cloudy.

Mozart's first journey was, as we have mentioned, to the Court of the Elector Maximilian III in Munich. He was hardly six years old, and presumably remembered little about it. But he had already developed from a little virtuoso into a little composer when, slightly more than half a year later, in the autumn of 1762, he went to Vienna with his mother and father and his sister, and exhibited his musical precocity in the palaces of the nobles and at the Imperial Court. They arrived on 6 October. The first performance of Gluck's *Orfeo ed Euridice* had taken place on the preceding evening, and it is not unlikely that Mozart saw and heard one of the subsequent performances—doubtless, despite all his precocity, without the maturity necessary for an understanding of this work, which harks back to the spirit of antiquity. But he had another experience in Vienna that was an effective means of hastening his maturity: a severe illness, the fateful scarlet fever that was perhaps partly responsible for his early death. After his recovery, the family went to Pressburg for a seven weeks' stay, and thus Mozart came to know a little bit of Hungary. But he was not tempted by this acquaintance to make further journeys to the southeast. The only places that interested him were those where there was music—art-music, not the folk-music which interests us so much today. He found his stimuli not in primitive or folk material, but in material already formed. Towards folk-music he maintained to some extent the attitude of the Renaissance, which saw in all the expressions of the people, including the musical ones, something comic and suited only to parody.

On 9 June 1763, the Mozart family set out on the long trip to France and England, from which they were not to return until 30 November 1766, and in the course of which they passed through not only a number of South- and West-German cities—Munich, Ludwigsburg, Schwetzingen, and Frankfurt—but also Catholic Belgium and Protestant Holland, southeastern France, Switzerland, and Leopold's native city, Augsburg. The literary reflections of this long excursion are contained in the letters already mentioned, of Leopold to his Salzburg friend, landlord, and financial adviser, Lorenz Hagenauer. Of these letters, only those parts have been published which deal with Wolfgang and the personal and musical experiences of the family. But a knowledge of the whole contents of the letters produces an ever new astonishment at the breadth of Leopold's interests, his power of observation, his keen judgment of men and circumstances, obscured only when the estimate of his children's success is concerned. Leopold occasionally had an eye for the character of cities and landscapes, too, although his judgment of them never went beyond the limitations of his period.

Even on the first visit to Vienna he took little Wolfgang into the Joseph-Stadt and to the Carls-Kirche; the latter, which is in the true spirit of Salzburg, must have made a great impression on Leopold. But read his description of Ulm (11 July 1763):

Ulm is a horrid, old-fashioned, and . . . tastelessly built place . . . Just picture to yourself houses in which the whole structure and wooden framework of the building and the way it is laid out have to show on the outside, and of which, when special effort has been made to beautify them, the framework is painted in color, while the walls remain lovely and white; or in which every brick is painted in its natural color, so that the walls and the framework may be seen all the more clearly. And that is the way Westerstetten, Geislingen . . . Göppingen, Plochingen, and much of Stuttgart look . . .

The lovely Neckar region, on the other hand, pleases both him and Frau Mozart:

But I must tell you that Württemberg is a very beautiful district. From Geislingen to Ludwigsburg you will see nothing to left or right but water, woods, fields, meadows, gardens, and vineyards, and all these at once and mingled in the most charming fashion.

He compares Heidelberg with Salzburg, and indeed there is a certain similarity as far as the relation of the town to the *Burg* is concerned, or that of the *Veste* to the town and the river, though it does not apply to the rest of the landscape. Leopold is interested in castles, sights of the town, pictures: the *Descent from the Cross* by Rubens, in the cathedral at Antwerp, fills him with extraordinary enthusiasm. On the other hand, of Ghent we read (19 September 1765) only: 'Ghent is a large but not a populous town.'

It is only with the visits to Italy, during which his mother and sister had to stay home in Salzburg, that Wolfgang's own observances about people and the world began. From the very beginning, he viewed men with an uncanny penetration, especially when they were concerned with music and drama. At the age of fifteen, he described to his sister the leading figures of the opera of Verona, as he had observed them in a *Ruggiero*, the music presumably by Pietro Alessandro Guglielmi (letter of 7 January 1770 *):

* The original whimsical mixture of German and Italian may be reproduced as follows:

'Oronte, il padre di Bradamante, è un principe (fa il signor Afferi), un bravo cantante, un baritono, ma forced when he sings falsetto, but not as much as Tibaldi

Oronte, the father of Bradamante, is a prince (sung by Signor Afferi), a fine singer, a baritone, and forced when he sings falsetto, but not as much as Tibaldi in Vienna. Bradamante, daughter of Oronte, in love with Ruggiero (she is to marry Leone, but she does not want him), is sung by a poor Baroness who has had some great misfortune, I do not know what. She appears under an assumed name, but I do not know it, has a passable voice, and her stage presence would not be bad, but she sings off pitch like the devil. Ruggiero, a rich prince, in love with Bradamante, is a castrato, sings a little in the manner of Manzuoli, and has a most beautiful strong voice, and he is an old man already, he is 55 and has a flexible throat . . .

Or hear Mozart describe à *la Rabelais* a Dominican monk of Bologna:

. . . who is regarded as a holy man. For my part I do not believe it, for at breakfast he often takes a cup of chocolate and immediately afterwards a good glass of strong Spanish wine; and I myself have had the honor of lunching with this saint who at table drank a whole decanter and finished up with a full glass of strong wine, two large slices of melon, some peaches, pears, five cups of coffee, a whole plate of cloves, and two full saucers of milk and lemon. He may, of course, be following some sort of diet, but I do not think so, for it would be too much; moreover he takes several little snacks during the afternoon . . . [letter of 21 August 1770]

That is the fifteen-year-old boy who is later to be the creator of Osmin and Monostatos. In the Mozart household, despite all the external maintenance of pious forms, there was not the slightest awe of priests, potentates, or celebrities; the Mozarts had seen them too much behind the scenes. How discreetly Goethe, on his visit to Naples, treats Their Serene Majesties, Caroline, that daughter of Maria Theresa so unlike her mother, and her Polichinelle of a king: 'The King is off hunting, the Queen is of good hope, and thus things cannot be better.' Leopold, on the other hand, wrote home on 26 May 1770: '. . . I only wish that the natives [of Naples] were not so godless and that certain people [namely, the King and Queen], who do not for a moment

in Vienna. Bradamante, figlia di Oronte, innamorata di Ruggiero (she is to marry Leone, but she does not want him), fa una povera Baronessa, che ha avuta una gran disgrazia, ma non so che. Recita under an assumed name, but I do not know it, ha una voce passabile, e la statura non sarebbe male, ma distona come il diavolo. Ruggiero, un ricco principe, innamorato di Bradamante, un musico, canta un poco in the manner of Manzuoli ed ha una bellissima voce forte ed è già vecchio, ha cinquantacinque anni ed ha una flexible throat . . .'

imagine that they are fools, were not so stupid as they are.' And Wolfgang, on 5 June, wrote without the slightest reverence: 'The King has
had a rough Neapolitan upbringing and in the opera he always stands
on a stool so as to look a little taller than the Queen . . .'

When, in Vienna, Wolfgang renewed his acquaintance with the
Archduke Maximilian—the youngest brother of the Emperor, once an
agreeable young fellow, who had in the meantime become Archbishop
of Cologne—he wrote (17 November 1781):

When God gives a man a sacred office, He generally gives him understanding; and so it is, I trust, in the case of the Archduke. But before
he became a priest, he was far more witty and intelligent and talked
less, but more sensibly. You should see him now. Stupidity oozes out
of his eyes. He talks and holds forth incessantly and always in falsetto—
and he has started a goitre. In short, the fellow seems to have changed
completely . . .

Or take the description of a European celebrity, the poet Wieland,
who had to come to Mannheim for the performance of an opera based
on his *Alceste* (27 December 1777):

I had imagined him to be quite different from what I found him.
He strikes you as slightly affected in his speech. He has a rather childish
voice: he keeps on quizzing you over his glasses; he indulges in a sort
of pedantic rudeness, mingled occasionally with a stupid condescension.
But I am not surprised that he permits himself such behavior here, even
though he may be quite different in Weimar and elsewhere, for people
stare at him as if he had dropped from Heaven. Everyone seems embarrassed in his presence, no one says a word or moves an inch; all listen
intently to every word he utters; and it's a pity they often have to wait
so long, for he has a defect of speech that makes him speak very slowly
and he can't say half a dozen words without stopping.

But he adds at once:

Apart from that, he is what we all know him to be, a most gifted
fellow. He has a frightfully ugly face, covered with pockmarks, and he
has a rather long nose. In height he is, I should say, a little taller than
Papa . . .

One may look through all the Memoirs of the classic Weimar period
and all the literature about it, without finding another description of
Wieland as alive and keen as this.

But the accounts in Mozart's letters of impressions of landscape are

as rare as his descriptions of people are plentiful; and about art he did
not express himself at all. A travel diary of Marianne's, dating from
the grand tour of 1763 to 1766, shows that the children's attention was
drawn by their father above all to the sights. In Heidelberg they in-
spected 'the castle, the tapestry and silk factories, the famous "Heidelberg Tun," ' and the well where 'the ladies and gentlemen have the
water fetched'; in London, 'I saw the park and a young elephant, a
donkey that has white and coffee-colored stripes, so even that they
could not be more so if they were painted'; but Marianne also referred
to Greenwich and the British Museum. Leopold described the environ-
ments of Naples in true tourist-guide style, and disposed of them with
similar dispatch. For a *Baedeker* he carried with him the dry volume
Neueste Reisen durch Teutschland . . . Italien, published in 1740
(Leopold's edition was perhaps that of 1752) by Johann Georg Keyssler
(1693-1743), and he referred his wife frequently to this book. It was a
work after Leopold's own heart, full of critical remarks, full of interest
in the sights of the town, and not lacking in joy in the court gossip: a
true book of the eighteenth century, with no interest in real beauty.
Bozen, visited in the most beautiful season, although in the rain, was
described by Leopold (28 October 1772) as 'dreary Bozen,' and Wolfgang agreed entirely with his father: 'Bozen—this pigsty. Here is a
poem about someone who became wild and enraged with Bozen:

> 'If to Bozen I must come,
> Faith, I'd rather cut my thumb.'

The Mozarts came from the gay town of Salzburg, where there were
no dark arcades and the principal church was not Gothic; Bozen's loca-
tion, the Dolomites, the jagged cliffs of the Schlern in the moonlight,
meant nothing to either father or son. Compare their impression with
that of Goethe, who was interested in mountains chiefly as a mineralogist, geologist, or meteorologist, but who fifteen years later could
write:

In the hot sunshine I arrived at Bozen. The mass of merchants' faces
pleased me. One feels the expression of a purposeful, well-ordered
existence. In the square sat the fruit-women, with round, flat baskets,
more than four feet in diameter, on which peaches lie side by side so
as not to press upon each other. Pears, too . . .

Goethe's eye is 'bright, pure, and clear.' Mozart's is sharp and incorruptible, but only where people—and striking events—are concerned

(30 November 1771): 'I have seen four rascals hanged here in the Piazza del Duomo. They hang them just as they do in Lyons.'

Leopold had a good word to say for the situation of Florence (3 April 1770): 'I should like you to see Florence itself and the surrounding country and the situation of the town, for you would say that one should live and die here.' And when he took leave of Italy—forever— he wrote on 27 February 1773: 'Indeed I find it hard to leave Italy,' and in his sadness there was more than just the thought of returning to the yoke of his hated Salzburg patron. Wolfgang saw the Capitol and the other six hills of Rome, but his short description would not be complete without its jokes (14 April 1770):

I only wish that my sister were in Rome, for this town would certainly please her, as St. Peter's church and many other things in Rome are *regular*. The most beautiful flowers are now being carried past in the street—so Papa has just told me . . .

The most beautiful flowers did not interest him, for he was sitting at home covering paper with music. 'Naples is beautiful . . .'; 'Venezia mi piace assai' (13 February 1771); this is all he finds to say. Leopold seems to have visited the sights of Venice alone, for he wrote (1 March 1771) that upon his return home he would 'tell you in detail how I liked the Arsenal, the churches, the ospedali, and other things, in fact Venice as a whole.' But when later, in February 1783, Wolfgang wrote a pantomime and acted it out with his sister-in-law, his brother-in-law, and a few friends, he showed how accurately he had observed the figures of the Venetian carnival twelve years earlier, and how exactly he remembered them. It is an eternal loss to art that this masterpiece of the commedia dell'arte survives only in sketches and fragments.

His later travels to Mannheim and Paris in 1777 and 1778, begun with his mother but completed alone, and to Munich for the completion and performance of *Idomeneo*—made him thoroughly mature as a human being, and sharpened his consciousness of the deep-seated provincialism of Salzburg. Every little Italian village seemed superior to his native city in taste and culture, not to speak of Mannheim, which at this time was a center of civilization and progress. In Paris all he noticed was the worsened and more restless mood of a nation that he found thoroughly uncongenial—mainly because he found its music uncongenial.

To Vienna, too, early in 1781, Mozart came as a guest and traveler.

He did not yet know that, as a result of the break with his archiepiscopal patron, it was to become his permanent residence. And when
he had moved there for good, he greeted every change and every departure with eagerness. If he could not travel, at least he could change
his dwelling—sometimes voluntarily, often rather involuntarily. In the
summer of 1788, he moved (involuntarily this time) to a garden dwelling in Währing, and wrote to Puchberg (17 June):

We are sleeping tonight, for the first time, in our new quarters, where
we shall remain both summer and winter. On the whole the change is
all the same to me, in fact I prefer it. As it is, I have very little to do in
town, and as I am not exposed to so many visitors, I shall have more
time to work . . .

It is clear that he would rather be in town, and is only trying to make
his exile to the country seem palatable to himself and to his friend.
A letter to his father (13 July 1781), from Reisenberg, near Vienna,
seems to reflect real joy in the landscape:

I am writing to you at an hour's distance from Vienna, at a place
called Reisenberg. I once spent a night here, and now I am staying for
a few days. The little house is nothing much, but the country—the
forest—in which my host [Count Cobenzl] has built a grotto which
looks just as if Nature herself had fashioned it! Indeed that's magnificent and very delightful.

Actually, it was not his feeling for nature that was touched so much
as his feeling for comfort, his need for cheerful surroundings.

The contrast he draws between two South-German cities in a single
letter to his wife (28 September 1790) is very characteristic: 'We break-
fasted at Nuremberg, a hideous town. At Würzburg, a fine, magnificent town, we fortified our precious stomachs with coffee.' The Gothic
and what he considered the small-scale Renaissance style of the old
Free City did not appeal to him; the bright and cheerful Baroque of
the episcopal town, on the other hand, in whose castle Tiepolo had
finished his frescoes barely forty years earlier, made him feel thoroughly
at home.

Eleven times within a period of nine or ten years Wolfgang and his
wife changed their residence in Vienna—sometimes after as little as
three months. Their life was like a perpetual tour, changing from one
hotel room to another, and the hotel rooms were soon forgotten. In
one of the handsomer dwellings, Schulergasse 8, at that time Grosse

Schulerstrasse 846, the ceiling of Mozart's workroom had fine plaster ornamentation with sprites and cherubs. I am convinced that Mozart never wasted a glance on it.

He was ready at every instant to exchange Vienna for another city or Austria for another country. Leopold was quite right in his misgivings about the possible duration of the projected journey to England in 1787; it could easily have turned into a permanent settlement there. In 1789 or 1790 Mozart acquired a book, the purpose of which is all too revealing—Geographisches und Topographisches Reisebuch durch alle Staaten der österreichischen Monarchie nebst der Reiseroute nach Petersburg durch Polen.* He was thinking of a trip to Russia, doubtless as a result of conversations with the Russian ambassador in Dresden, Prince Bieloselski, at whose home Mozart played a good deal in April 1789. But he had to be satisfied with smaller journeys, and with 'journeys' within Vienna. At the end of September 1790, he took a new apartment in the Rauhensteingasse, without suspecting that it was to be his last. Or did he suspect it, and was that the reason he stayed in it for such an unusually long time, feeling that moving was no longer worth the trouble? For in December 1791, he was to move into a permanent dwelling, one designated by Constantin von Wurzbach, who was the first to attempt the compilation of a complete list of Mozart's dwelling-places, as 'the last and the smallest in the graveyard of St. Mark's.'

* Geographical and Topographical Guide to All States of the Austrian Monarchy, with the Traveler's Route to Petersburg through Poland, Vienna, 1789.

2. *Genius and Human Frailty*

WOLFGANG MOZART was a child-prodigy. As soon as Leopold recognized the unusual musical gifts of the boy he sought to develop them, 'even while the child was at play,' as it is put in the most reliable source about Mozart's youth—Schlichtegroll's necrology of 1792, based on information furnished by Mozart's sister Marianne and by the Court Trumpeter Andreas Schachtner, a family friend of the Mozarts.

Mozart the son was about three years old when his seven-year-old sister began to receive clavier lessons from her father. Already at this time the boy showed his extraordinary talent. He entertained himself often for long periods at the keyboard by hunting out the thirds, which he then always sounded, and showed his pleasure at having discovered this harmony.

Now, such activities may be observed in many another child, who later turns out to be anything but a second Mozart. But more revealing are the additional facts reported by Marianne and Schachtner:

In his fourth year, his father began to teach him some minuets and other pieces on the clavier, an occupation just as easy and pleasant for the teacher as for the pupil. For a minuet he needed half an hour, and for a longer piece an hour, to learn it and then play it perfectly, cleanly, and with the steadiest rhythm. From this time on he made such progress that in his fifth year he already composed little pieces, which he played for his father so that the latter could put them on paper.

Behind this simple report (in which the only slips are that Nannerl was eight years old in 1759, and that Mozart's first compositions date from his sixth year) lie many things that were important for Wolfgang's future. Leopold has been reproached with having forced his son's talent like a plant in a hothouse, and for having commercialized it. But Leopold was not being altogether hypocritical, or indulging solely in secret self-justification, when he emphasized repeatedly that he held it to be his duty before God and the world to further the inconceivable talent of Wolfgang as a gift sent from above. It is fairly certain that without the early travels, with their hardships and exposure to infection—to all of which Wolfgang fell a victim: scarlet fever, small-pox, etc.—he would have lived much longer. But his development would also have taken place at a different tempo. And Leopold was justified by the great willingness of the child, the boy, and the youth. Mozart was twenty-two years old before he slipped out from under his father's control.

In these years [i.e. between his sixth and tenth] he was very teachable. And whatever his father prescribed he worked at for a time with the greatest industry, so that he seemed to forget everything else, even music, for a certain period. When, for example, he was learning arithmetic, the table, the chairs, the walls, and even the floor were covered with figures written in chalk. In general he was full of enthusiasm and was very easily attracted to any subject; he would thus have been in danger of going off into harmful by-paths, if his excellent training had not protected him from doing so.

The pleasure in playing with figures remained with Mozart all his life long. Thus he once took up the problem, very popular at that time, of composing minuets 'mechanically,' by putting two-measure melodic fragments together in any order. And we possess a page of musical sketches on which he had begun to figure out the sum which the chess-player would have received from the King, in the famous Oriental story.

What has been said about Mozart's latent immoral tendencies is true of every man of creative imagination, and particularly of the dramatic genius. Goethe stated that he had within him the potentiality of committing every crime, and the story that Shakespeare was a poacher, even if it were not true, and though entirely harmless, is at any rate well conceived. Men of such tremendous fantasy and suggestibility sublimate these dangerous tendencies in their art, and create figures like Lady Macbeth, Mephisto, and Don Giovanni.

But among all things it was music, after all, which filled his soul, and with which he occupied himself constantly. He progressed in it with giant strides, so that even his father, who was of course with him daily, and could observe every step of his education, was often surprised and astonished as by a miracle . . . He had progressed so far in his art that it would have been wrong of his father not to have wished to let other towns and countries witness this extraordinary talent . . .

Leopold rose in authority from *pater familias*, to instructor in music and in the humanities (Wolfgang never had any other teacher and never went to school), then to that of impresario and Master of Travels, only to sink finally to be the servant of his son. Mozart was by the very fact of his towering genius unsuited for this life, and Leopold made him still more so.

Although he [Wolfgang] received every day new evidence of the astonishment and admiration of men for his great talent and ability, this did not make him in any way self-seeking, proud, or self-willed, but, on the contrary, he was a thoroughly obedient and good-natured child. He never showed any displeasure with a command given by his father, and even if he had had to let himself be heard the whole day long he was still perfectly ready to play for anyone the minute his father wished him to. He understood and obeyed every gesture of his parents, and he pushed his dependence on them to the point of not taking it upon himself without their permission to eat or accept the slightest thing that was offered to him.

It is understandable that a person who for so long was denied all self-sufficiency, all initiative, all action, who lived entirely in his musical imagination, should do all sorts of foolish things as soon as the paternal reins were broken. And it is understandable that the father should be astonished, frightened, and beside himself at seeing this happen, without suspecting that he himself had laid the foundation for his son's inability to behave sensibly and realistically in this world.

This inability has sometimes been doubted. There is a theory of genius, according to which the direction taken by talent is more or less accidental and determined by events and experiences. Thus it is believed that a great poet might instead have become a great statesman, a great painter, or a great philosopher. But even if Goethe in his ministerial capacity had had more important affairs to decide than those of Weimar, he would hardly have influenced the history of Europe more profoundly than he did; and if Eugène Delacroix had painted less, and written more on the theory of art, he would still never have become a philosopher. What Goethe says about the state he says as a poet; when Delacroix discusses art, he speaks as a painter.

Mozart's sense of superiority arose from his understanding of music; he knew just how great a distance separated him from his composer contemporaries, with the single exception of Joseph Haydn. It is evidence at once of his greatness, of his knowledge of himself, and of his lack of diplomacy that he showed his consciousness of superiority in his actions, and expressed it openly. An example of this lack of diplomacy is related by Mozart himself. He attributed one of his failures in Paris to the Italian composer Giovanni Giuseppe Cambini, whom he suspected of having put obstacles in his way with Le Gros, the director of the Concerts Spirituels (letter of 1 May 1778):

I believe . . . that Cambini, an Italian maestro here, is at the bottom of the business. For in all innocence I swept the floor with him at our first meeting at Le Gros' house. He has composed some quartets, one of which I heard at Mannheim. They are quite pretty. I praised them to him and played the beginning of the one I had heard. But Ritter, Ramm, and Punto, who were there, gave me no peace, urging me to go on and telling me that what I could not remember I myself could supply. This I did, so that Cambini was quite beside himself and could not help saying: 'Questa è una gran testa!' *

'Questa è una gran testa!' Exceptional gifts automatically make their owners hated by the mediocrity, and Mozart was not careful enough, or worldly-wise enough, to avoid arousing this hatred. He was in fact not worldly-wise in any way, and in many conclusions and opinions he was far surpassed by lesser men. Like all great men, he was 'ein Mensch mit seinem Widerspruch' (a man with a man's contradictions), and not a book, calculated and consistent. To the end of his life his character continued to exhibit not only childlike aspects, but childish ones, too. Leopold, in one of his most serious and despairing letters, refers to this dualism in his son's character (16 February 1778):

My son! You are hot-tempered and impulsive in all your ways! Since your childhood and boyhood your whole character has changed. As a child and a boy you were serious rather than childish and when you sat at the clavier or were otherwise intent on music, no one dared to have the slightest jest with you. Why, even your expression was so solemn that, observing the early efflorescence of your talent and your ever grave and thoughtful little face, many discerning people of different countries sadly doubted whether your life would be a long one. But now, as far as I can see, you are much too ready to retort in a bantering tone to the first challenge—and that, of course, is the first step towards undue familiarity, which anyone who wants to preserve his self-respect will try to avoid in this world. A good-hearted fellow is accustomed, it is true, to express himself freely and naturally: none the

---

* 'He's a first-rate fellow!'

less, it is a mistake to do so. And it is just your good heart which prevents you from detecting any shortcomings in a person who showers praises on you, has a great opinion of you and flatters you to the skies, and who makes you give him all your confidence and affection; whereas as a boy you were so extraordinarily modest that you used to weep when people praised you overmuch.

But actually, on one occasion Leopold had reported of the seven- or eight-year-old boy, in a letter written on tour (Frankfurt, 20 August 1763): 'Wolfgang is extraordinarily jolly, but a bit of a scamp as well.' The contrast is seen strikingly in two early portraits, one that can be dated exactly (6-7 January 1770), made by the painter Cignaroli at the direction of the Venetian Tax-Collector-General, Pietro Luggiati, and the less well-authenticated one by Thaddeus Helbling, painted a few years earlier, when Mozart was about ten years old—for who should this child be, with genius radiating from his eyes (though they are brown, not blue), if not Mozart? In the Venetian portrait, the fresh, impudent boy, ready for any mischief; in the Helbling painting, the genius just waking from his deep absorption in music and, with his hand still resting on the keyboard, trying to get his bearings in the world again.

It is this dualism that explains, too, the letters that Mozart sent from his Mannheim-Paris tour to his 'Bäsle' (the daughter of his uncle) in Augsburg, of which the originals have never been published in full, and which are to be found unexpurgated only in the courageous translation of the English edition of Emily Anderson. This suppression is not an exercise of the same prudence that banishes the erotic etchings of Rembrandt to the secret drawers of the cabinet, and a few of the Roman Elegies of Goethe to 'scientific editions.' Of course, the prudery of the nineteenth century is involved, which is responsible for the emasculated biographies of the great masters and their idealized heads in plaster. But there is also a certain not incomprehensible embarrassment. It is difficult to understand how a young man of twenty-two or twenty-three, and above all a Mozart, could write such childish obscenities, such ill-smelling bouquets, to a young girl. But we must accept the fact that Mozart did find genuine amusement in writing them.

It must not be forgotten that in the eighteenth century all human and animal functions took place more publicly than in our more civilized and hygienic days, and that unembarrassed reference to matters of an intimate nature was not confined to the lower or middle classes.

One need only read the letters of 'Madame,' Elisabeth-Charlotte, sister-in-law of Louis XIV, to learn some amusing things about occasional 'princely conversations' among husband, wife, and son. Things were called by their right names, and when Wolfgang reported to his father about the good health of his first-born he did so in just as plain fashion as Leopold himself later reported to his daughter on the health of her first-born, whom the grandfather had taken into his house. *Naturalia non sunt turpia*. Until the end of his life Mozart preserved his capacity for enjoying word-distortions, childish nicknames, exuberant nonsense, and humorous obscenity—a trait of South-German gaiety which has never been understood and will never be understood in the less uninhibited regions north of the Main. Certain unspeakable expressions used by Mozart in the letters to his 'Bäsle' return word for word in the texts to some of the Viennese canons. Mozart was not thinking of eternity either in the letters or in the canons, or of the possibility that some day professors of Leipzig or Berlin would concern themselves with them. He was a child and always remained one; childishness is sometimes necessary to a creator for purposes of relaxation, and to conceal his deeper self. With others, this necessity takes itself out in rudeness, as with Brahms; and still other great men (we are considering musicians only), who do not possess such weapons of self-defense, perish—like Chopin and Schumann, both lyricists. But a dramatist like Mozart must work among men, and in order to get along with men needs humor, the weapon of wit, and sometimes even cruder aids.

We must accept the fact that Mozart was 'a man with a man's contradictions' and that with all his keenness of observation of men and circumstances, and all his insight into the essence of characters and affairs, he never learned how to deal with the world. Schlichtegroll's necrology states that fact categorically:

For just as this rare being early became a man so far as art was concerned, he always remained—as the impartial observer must say of him—in almost all other matters a child. He never learned to rule himself; for domestic order, for sensible management of money, for moderation and wise choice in pleasures, he had no feeling. He always needed a guiding hand, a guardian, to take care of domestic affairs for him, since his own mind was always occupied with an abundance of quite other conceptions, and in its absorption in them quite lost its capacity for serious reflection in other fields. His father recognized this lack of self-control very clearly, and accordingly, when his own duties kept him in Salzburg, sent his wife along to Paris to act as her son's companion.

Mozart's widow was so displeased with this (and many other statements) in Schlichtegroll that she bought up a whole Graz reprint (1794) and made the offending passages illegible. But the first Mozart biography of any length, the one by the good professor of Prague, Franz Niemtschek, which was written under Constanze's influence, says that 'it will not alienate the student of human nature to see that this man, so exceptional as an artist, was not equally great in the other affairs of life,' and that 'the nature of his upbringing, the irregularity of his life on tour, during which he lived solely for his art, made a true knowledge of the human heart impossible for him . . . To this lack must be ascribed many of the unwise actions of his life.'

'A true knowledge of the human heart'? No one had a truer and deeper knowledge than Mozart. But the insight of a genius into the essence of a man is something quite different from worldly wisdom. It is just because Mozart very quickly recognized this essence that he made mistakes in his dealings with the men he came in contact with, and fell into their traps.

He understood the character of the encyclopedist and journalist Melchior Grimm—who for a time was a very helpful patron of the child-prodigy, but whose protection of the youth in Paris in 1778 was of a most humiliating nature—much more profoundly than Leopold, who could only remember the friend of 1764. But Grimm portrays one side of Wolfgang's character accurately, when he tells Leopold (Leopold's letter of 13 August 1778):

He is too good-natured, not active enough, too easily taken in, too little concerned with the means that may lead him to good fortune. Here, in order to break into the world, one must be crafty, enterprising, bold. To get ahead I could wish that he had only half as much talent and twice as much ability to handle people, and then I would not worry about him.

This is very well said, and worthy of a contemporary of Voltaire and Diderot. Mozart was the opposite of 'crafty, enterprising, and bold.' When other men had such characteristics, he was defenseless against them.

The whole undertaking of the tour to Mannheim and Paris, on which, at the age of twenty-two, he had to take his mother along more or less as a nurse, and yet during which he was expected to show that he had become a man, was simply beyond him. It was a failure from beginning to end. Undertaken in the spirit of the proverb *Aut Caesar, aut nihil*, it ended in the humiliating return to the slavery of Salzburg—and without his mother, who lay buried in Paris. Then, in the most fateful year of Mozart's life, Leopold confirmed Grimm's characterization of Wolfgang in an even more accurate formulation (letter to Baroness Waldstädten, 23 August 1782):

On the whole, I should feel quite easy in my mind, were it not that I have detected in my son an outstanding fault, which is, that he is far too *patient* or rather *easy-going*, too *indolent*, perhaps even too *proud*, in short, that he has the sum total of all those traits, which render a man *inactive*; on the other hand, he is too *impatient*, too *hasty*, and will not abide his time. Two opposing elements rule his nature, I mean, there is either too *much* or too *little*, never the golden mean. If he is not actually in want, then he is immediately satisfied and becomes *indolent* and *lazy*. If he has to bestir himself, then he realizes his worth and *wants to make his fortune at once*. Nothing must stand in his way; yet it is unfortunately the most capable people and those who possess outstanding genius who have the greatest obstacles to face.

Leopold, too, is no mean psychologist. It is impossible to reject the testimony of two men who knew Wolfgang so well.

The proportions of happiness and unhappiness in the life of a human being are determined more than half by his own character. Every man has typical experiences, which, if he does not learn through misfortune, continually recur. Mozart's typical experiences are his failure in quest of a position and his failure in his relation to women.

The refrain that rings in Mozart's ears as he struggles to obtain a position is: 'There is no vacancy. If only there were a vacancy!' Not that Mozart lacked positions. But he never obtained a post really worthy of him. There was justice in Leopold's lack of success. He was, so to speak, a born Vice-Kapellmeister; he would have attained the office of Kapellmeister, even in Salzburg, only by seniority, like so many other mediocrities; and it is only with the thought of these mediocrities in mind that his anger is understandable and justified.

Wolfgang never attained the leading position because he was much too big for it.

For we must supplement what we have said by stating that the grounds for Mozart's lack of success did not lie entirely in his character but also in his historical position. It is impossible not to smile at the thought that Beethoven once wanted to go as Court-Kapellmeister to King Jérôme in Cassel. Fortunately, nothing came of the project. Imagine Beethoven as Kapellmeister, in daily contact and friction with singers and orchestral musicians, straightening out administrative matters! It seems altogether fitting that the Royal Saxon Court-Kapellmeister, Richard Wagner, became a revolutionary just because he had held an official position so long (six or seven years were a long time in Wagner's life!), as well as that the composer of *Tristan* could hardly accept a regular post any more, or even the title of *Generalmusikdirektor*. Thus it was fortunate for Mozart that he had only subordinate functions to perform in Salzburg, those of Concertmaster and organist.

Mozart could attain his due position only in the role of creator: as 'Court Composer'; as a musician receiving commissions to compose specific works—operas, symphonies, quartets—and having the leisure to do so.

Nevertheless both father and son always exerted themselves to obtain a position, the more strongly when their relations with Hieronymus Colloredo, the successor of the patriarchal Prince-Bishop Schrattenbach, made their work more and more unpleasant, and made them look upon it as drudgery. But even before Colloredo's reign began, Leopold was casting his eyes towards Milan in behalf of his son. Mozart had written the second opera—the serenade *Ascanio in Alba* (first performed 17 October 1771)—for the celebration of the wedding of the Archduke Ferdinand, Governor of Lombardy, the third son of the Empress. Leopold must have found an opportunity to propose humbly that the young Archduke, who was only a year and a half older than Wolfgang, engage his son. The Archduke, trained in obedience to his mother, asked her advice. She answered:

You ask me about taking into your services the young Salzburg musician. I do not know in what capacity, believing that you have no need for a composer or for useless people. If, however, it would give you pleasure, I do not wish to prevent you. What I say is intended only to urge you not to burden yourself with useless people, and not to give such people permission to represent themselves as belonging in your service. It gives one's service a bad name when such people run about like beggars; he has, besides, a large family.*

The docile Archduke naturally thought no more of engaging Mozart, and did not confer any title upon him. If Leopold had had any idea what Maria Theresa, the kindly Queen who had once presented his children with the cast-off clothing of her royal children, really thought about him and Wolfgang ('useless' people—bohemians—bothersome folk!), his loyalty would have suffered a bit.

Unsuspecting, however, he made another attempt with Maria Theresa's second son, the Archduke Leopold of Tuscany, later Emperor Leopold II, who was on the Imperial throne at the time of Mozart's death. He pursued the matter from Milan, assiduously and in great secrecy, for he knew very well that the new Archbishop would make short work of him if he heard anything about negotiations on the part of his Vice-Kapellmeister with the Court of Tuscany.

Leopold's efforts were unsuccessful, despite the fact that in December 1772 and in the first months of 1773 he repeatedly put off his return to Salzburg on their account. 'I hear from Florence that the Grand Duke has received my letter, is giving it sympathetic consideration and will let me know the result. We still live in hopes,' he wrote home in the childish code-writing of the Mozart family on 9 January 1773. And on 16 January:

There is little hope of what I wrote to you. God will help us. But do save money and keep cheerful, for we must have means, if we want to undertake a journey. I regret every farthing which we spend in Salzburg. Up to the present no reply has come from the Grand Duke; but we know from the Count's letter to Troger that there is very little likelihood of our getting work in Florence. Yet I still trust that at least he will recommend us.

Finally, after waiting in despair (27 February): 'As for the affair you know of, there is nothing to be done.' What the obstacles were that stood in his way is not known; I have looked in vain in the archives at Florence for Leopold's letters and the drafts of the Court Marshal's answers.

In the summer of 1773 father and son returned to Vienna; on New Year's, 1775, they were off to Munich for the performance of *La Finta*

* 12 December 1771; cf. A. Ritter von Arneth, *Briefe der Kaiserin Theresia an ihre Kinder und Freunde*, Vienna, 1881, I, 93.

giardiniera; and it may safely be assumed that Leopold Mozart industriously used the opportunities to put out feelers in both places, to
discover where a favorable position for his son might be found. But no
such positions offered themselves. For Vienna, Wolfgang was no longer
young and yet was not old enough; and *La Finta giardiniera* was simply
a local event in Munich, without consequences.

But the increasingly strained relations with the archiepiscopal patron
were moving towards a decisive change. It is difficult to apportion the
blame justly between Hieronymus Colloredo and the Mozarts, father
and son. Colloredo bears the blame before posterity for having treated
badly one of the greatest geniuses of humanity—even for having abused
him—and no one can acquit him entirely of this accusation. But we
have concerning his behavior only the one-sided testimony of the two
plaintiffs, Leopold and Wolfgang, and for the last part of the story
only that of Wolfgang, who wished, in his letters to his father, to present the figure of Colloredo in the most unfavorable light. The testimony of impartial witnesses concerning the personality of Colloredo
is quite different. Colloredo's position among the inhabitants of Salzburg, as successor to the easy-going Schrattenbach, was a difficult one.
The populace, having witnessed in the year 1732 the banishment of
Protestant peasants who had been faithful to their belief, were not at
all disturbed by the fact that under this same Schrattenbach there was
in the southern part of the Archdiocese the citadel of Werfen, into
which unbelievers and doubters could be thrown for life. On the contrary: unbelievers and doubters, they felt, could not be treated badly
enough. But Colloredo, who was still only forty, was received with
suspicion by the populace and with fear by the Chapter. The suspicion
of the populace developed into lasting hatred, and the Chapter's fear
led eventually to a lawsuit. In Colloredo's study there hung pictures of
his admired Rousseau and Voltaire. It is this fact, perhaps, that explains the passage in which Wolfgang reports from Paris on the death
of Voltaire, with a spitefulness that is a stain upon his letters (3 July
1778): '. . . that godless arch-rascal Voltaire has pegged out like a dog,
like a beast! That is his reward!' In actual fact, Voltaire, as his last good
joke, had died in the bosom of the Holy Catholic Church, revered by
his whole nation. On 15 July 1782, Colloredo issued a pastoral letter,
of which the purpose was 'the abolition of unnecessary church expenses,
recommendation of Bible reading, and the introduction of a new song-

book, and a series of improvements in the guidance of spiritual care.' *
This could hardly please the Mozarts, for elaborate church music was
one of the 'unnecessary church expenses,' and the two simple German
Kirchenlieder (K. 343), which Mozart presumably composed for the
projected songbook, with their whiff of Protestantism, consort oddly
with his Latin Masses.

The judgment of history upon this Prince of the Church is that he
did not recognize, or did not wish to have it recognized, that he had
a genius in his service. This, however, constitutes not a sin, but simply
a lack of insight or of good will—to be regretted but not condemned.
Salzburg was too small a place for a genius who wished, among other
things, to write operas. These he could write only for other places—
Munich, Vienna, Milan, or Venice. What Colloredo needed, on the
other hand, was not a genius, always wanting to go on leave, but a con-
scientious musician, faithful to his duties. Thus on his side cold un-
friendliness gained the upper hand, and on the Mozarts' side a feeling
of injury and of hatred, which steadily grew because it had to be suppressed.

The Mozarts decided, after the failure to obtain anything in
Munich, to write a letter to the influential Padre Martini in Bologna—
the letter already quoted on page 14, in which a desire for recommendation is easy to read between the lines, and which well describes
the situation (4 September 1776):

The regard, the esteem, and the respect which I cherish for your
illustrious person have prompted me to trouble you with this letter and
to send you a humble specimen of my music, which I submit to your
masterly judgment. I composed for last year's carnival at Munich an
opera *buffa, La Finta giardiniera*. A few days before my departure the
Elector expressed a desire to hear some of my contrapuntal compositions. I was therefore obliged to write this motet in a great hurry, in
order to have time to have the score copied for His Highness and to
have the parts written out and thus enable it to be performed during
the Offertory at High Mass on the following Sunday. Most beloved
and esteemed Signor Padre Maestro! I beg you most earnestly to tell
me, frankly and without reserve, what you think of it. We live in this
world in order to learn zealously and, by interchanging our ideas, to
enlighten one another and thus endeavor to promote science and art.

* Thus described in *Geschichte der deutschen Höfe*, by Ed. Vehse, VI, 12, 2,
page 157.

Oh, how often have I longed to be near you, most Reverend Father, so that I might be able to talk to and reason with you. For I live in a country where music leads a struggling existence, though indeed apart from those who have left us, we still have excellent teachers and particularly composers of great wisdom, learning and taste. As for the theater, we are in a bad way for lack of singers. We have no *castrati*, and we shall never have them, as they insist on being handsomely paid; and generosity is not one of our faults. Meanwhile I am amusing myself by writing chamber music and music for the church, in which branches of composition we have two other excellent masters of counterpoint, Signori Haydn and Adlgasser. My father is in the service of the Cathedral and this gives me an opportunity of writing as much church music as I like . . . Alas, that we are so far apart, my very dear Signor Padre Maestro! If we were together, I should have so many things to tell you! I send my devoted remembrances to all the members of the Accademia Filarmonica. I long to win your favor and I never cease to grieve that I am far away from that one person in the world whom I love, revere and esteem most of all . . .

But this letter, too, was without result, and meanwhile the tension between master and servants became unbearable. In March 1777, Leopold, referring to the 'unhappy circumstances' of his family, asked for leave to go on tour, but to this request Colloredo seems to have returned not even an unfavorable answer—simply none at all. He forestalled a further attempt on Leopold's part by requiring his *Kapelle* to be in full readiness for a visit of the Emperor Joseph, who was to pass through Salzburg. When, after this visit, Leopold tried once more, he received a simple refusal with the remark that Wolfgang, as 'only a half-time servant anyway, could be permitted to travel alone.' But when Wolfgang wanted to follow this suggestion, the Archbishop raised new objections. What was left but revolt? On 1 August 1777, Wolfgang asked for his dismissal, formulating his reasons in an unfortunate statement that in every word smacks of Leopold's style:

. . . Most Gracious Prince and Lord! Parents endeavor to place their children in a position to earn their own bread; and in this they follow alike their own interest and that of the State. The greater the talents which children have received from God, the more are they bound to use them for the improvement of their own and their parents' circumstances, so that they may at the same time assist them and take thought for their own future progress. The Gospel teaches us to use our talents in this way. My conscience tells me that I owe it to God to be grateful to my father, who has spent his time unwearyingly upon my education, so that I may lighten his burden, look after myself and later on be able to support my sister . . .

Whereupon the Archbishop, who did not pay too much attention to God and the Gospel, eight days later wrote the dry and biting comment: 'Referred to the Chancellery with the [decision] that father and son, in accordance with the Gospel, have permission to seek their fortune elsewhere.' It is certainly not unfavorable evidence of the Archbishop's character that he later cancelled the dismissal of Leopold, apparently of his own accord, and without subjecting Leopold to any further humiliation.

On 23 September 1777, Mozart, in fine spirits, set out with his mother, who was to take his father's place in watching over him a bit, on the grand tour to Mannheim and Paris, which was supposed to bring him fame and employment. In January 1779, completely beaten, laden down with a series of failures in his attempts to find an appropriate position, having suffered his deepest disappointment in love, and having lost his mother, he returned to Salzburg, and placed himself again under the yoke of the Archbishop Hieronymus Colloredo. We may imagine his feelings when, in the first days after his return, he wrote the following note:

Your Grace,
    Most worthy Prince of the Holy Roman Empire!
    Most Gracious Prince and Lord!
After the decease of Cajetan Adlgasser Your Grace was so good as to take me into your service. I therefore humbly beseech you to grant me a certificate of my appointment as Court Organist.

On 17 January, Colloredo most graciously issued the certificate. But that was not what Wolfgang had hoped for, when, a year and a half earlier, he had withdrawn from the Archbishop's service. His first hopes had been directed towards Munich, and not without reason. In Munich there reigned a music-loving and benevolent sovereign, the Elector Max Joseph III, who played the viola da gamba with skill and even tried his hand at composition. (His favorite pose for his portrait was with a gamba in his hand, and surrounded by his family and court circle.) It was in his reign that the opera house was opened (1753), a jewel among all the opera houses of the world. This is the house that still exists as the Residenztheater; here Mozart's *Idomeneo* was produced for the first time; and this house later became a center for the cultivation of Mozart's operas. Now, this Elector was not served by outstanding musicians. Skilful as Ferrandini, Bernasconi, Tozzi, Michel may have been as opera craftsmen, they could not in any way be compared with Graun in Berlin, Hasse in Dresden, or Jommelli in Stuttgart. Mozart, who from the time of *La Finta giardiniera* on had known the musical and operatic situation in Munich very thoroughly, would undoubtedly have been the right man for the place, and in addition he had friendly and powerful advocates. Yet he failed; and this first failure is specific and symbolic. Here is the conversation that took place in the Elector's residence in Munich, according to Mozart's own account of it, in which again we may observe his dramatic gift (letter of 29/30 September 1777):

Count Seeau [the Intendant of the Munich Court Opera] went by and greeted me in the most friendly fashion, saying: 'How do you do, my very dear Mozart!' When the Elector came up to me, I said: 'Your Highness will allow me to throw myself most humbly at your feet and offer you my services.' 'So you have left Salzburg for good?' 'Yes, your Highness, for good.' 'How is that? Have you had a row with him?' 'Not at all, your Highness. I only asked him for permission to travel, which he refused. So I was compelled to take this step, though indeed I had long been intending to clear out. For Salzburg is no place for me, I can assure you.' 'Good Heavens! There's a young man for you! But your father is still in Salzburg?' 'Yes, your Highness. He too throws himself most humbly at your feet, and so forth. I have been three times to Italy already, I have written three operas, I am a member of the Bologna Academy, where I had to pass a test, at which many maestri have labored and sweated for four or five hours, but which I finished in an hour. Let that be a proof that I am competent to serve at any court. My sole wish, however, is to serve your Highness, who himself is such a great—' 'Yes, my dear boy, but I have no vacancy. I am sorry. If only there were a vacancy—' 'I assure your Highness that I should not fail to do credit to Munich.' 'I know. But it is no good, for there is no vacancy here.' This he said as he walked away. Whereupon I commended myself to his good graces.

Exactly the same thing happened in Mannheim, and the disappointment was even greater, since Mozart had made more prolonged and more serious efforts to achieve success there—more serious efforts, because Mannheim was at that time, thanks to its famous orchestra, the leading musical city of the entire Empire. Mozart himself praises the quality and strength of this musical organization in a letter of 4 November 1777:

The orchestra is excellent and very strong. There are ten or eleven violins on either side, four violas, two oboes, two flutes and two clarinets, two horns, four violoncellos, four bassoons and four double basses, also trumpets and drums.

But this brilliant situation has its darker side, too, for he continues:

They can produce fine music, but I should not care to have one of my masses performed here. Why? On account of their shortness? No, everything must be short here too. Because a different style of composition is required? Not at all. But because, as things are at present, you must write principally for the instruments, as you cannot imagine anything worse than the voices here . . . The reason for this state of affairs is that the Italians are now in very bad odor here. They have only two *castrati*, who are already old and will just be allowed to die off. The soprano would actually prefer to sing alto, as he can no longer take the high notes. The few boys they have are miserable. The tenors and basses are like our funeral singers . . .

In the opera house of Mannheim, too, the situation was not what Mozart would have wished. The inhabitants of the Electoral town were riding the wave of nationalism, and were seeking to replace the Italian opera *seria* with 'German Opera.' These were the years in which the attempt was being made to set up *Günther von Schwarzburg* by the old Kapellmeister Ignaz Holzbauer, and Wieland's *Rosamunde* and *Alceste* with music by Schweitzer, in competition with the opera *seria* of Metastasio and the innovations of Gluck. And Mozart, at least at this time, was much more interested in writing Italian opera than German—*seria* or *buffa*, it was all the same to him.

But he was willing to accept what did not suit him. The irreligious and immoral atmosphere, in which Mannheim sought not unsuccessfully to rival Paris, did not trouble him particularly. He could overlook such things when he had a good reason to do so. The aging Elector Carl Theodor was a man for whom almost no expense for luxury in general and for musical luxury in particular was too great. Mozart went every day to see Christian Cannabich, the 'real musical director' of the *Kapelle*, who seems not to have behaved in a particularly friendly manner on the occasion of the Mozarts' first visits in Schwetzingen, in

1763, for Mozart writes: 'He is quite a different person from what he used to be and the whole orchestra say the same thing.' He gave lessons to Cannabich's daughter Rose, 'who plays the clavier quite nicely' and even portrayed her in a Sonata (K. 309). He played at court, and there ensued a second conversation with an Elector, unlike the first one in Munich only in that this Prince put Mozart off with false hopes. But in the end the result was exactly the same (letter of 8 November 1777):

After the concert Cannabich arranged for me to speak to them. I kissed the Elector's hand. He remarked: 'I think it is about fifteen years since you were here last.' 'Yes, your Highness, fifteen years since I had the honor of—' 'You play admirably.' When I kissed the Princess's hand she said to me: 'Monsieur, je vous assure, on ne peut pas jouer mieux.' I went yesterday with Cannabich on the visit Mamma has already referred to and there I talked to the Elector as to an old friend. He is a most gracious, courteous gentleman. He said to me: 'I hear that you have written an opera at Munich.' 'Yes, your Highness,' I replied, 'I commend myself to your Highness's good graces. My dearest wish is to write an opera here. I beg you not to forget me utterly. Thanks and praise be to God, I know German, too,' and I smiled. 'That can easily be managed,' he answered. He has a son and three daughters. The eldest girl and the young Count play the clavier. The Elector put some questions to me in confidence about his children, and I expressed myself quite frankly, but without disparaging their teacher . . . *

Only gradually did Mozart perceive, or rather did he admit to himself, that he was only being put off with fine words (letter of 29 November 1777):

Last Tuesday week, 18 November, the day before St. Elizabeth's Day, I went to Count Savioli in the morning and asked him whether it was not possible that the Elector might keep me here this winter? I would like to instruct the young Count. He said: 'Yes, I will suggest it to the Elector; and if it rests with me, it will certainly be arranged.' In the afternoon I was at Cannabich's. As I had gone to the Count on his advice, he asked me at once whether I had been there. I told him everything. He then said: 'I should very much like you to stay with us for the winter, but I should like it still more if you could get a permanent post.' I replied that it was my dearest wish to be near them

---

* The mother of the four natural children was the actress Josephine Seyffert, whom Carl Theodor later created Countess Heydeck; the son, born in 1769, and thus only nine years old at the time of Mozart's visit, became Prince Carl von Bretzenheim, prominent in the Napoleonic-Bavarian troubles.

always, but that I really did not know how it would be possible for me to be so permanently. I added: 'You have two Kapellmeisters already, so I don't know what I could be. I shouldn't like to be subordinate to Vogler!' 'That you shan't,' he rejoined. 'None of the musicians here are subordinate to the Kapellmeister, or even to the Intendant. Why, the Elector could make you his chamber-composer. Just wait, I shall discuss it with the Count.'

And then there were repeated the importunate inquiries by Mozart and polite excuses by Savioli. For the Elector was quite willing that Mozart should stay for the winter, instruct his natural son in clavier-playing, and compose something for his illegitimate daughter. But he did not at all wish to take him into his service, and still less did Cannabich wish to conjure up a dangerous competitor, whose superiority to his own wretched talents he knew only too well. For his playing at court, Mozart received a gift (letter of 13 November 1777):

It was just as I had expected. No money, but a fine gold watch. At the moment ten carolins would have suited me better than the watch, which including the chains and the mottoes has been valued at twenty. What one needs on a journey is money; and, let me tell you, I now have five watches. I am therefore seriously thinking of having an additional watch pocket on each leg of my trousers so that when I visit some great lord, I shall wear both watches (which, moreover, is now the 'mode'), so that it will not occur to him to present me with another one.

In his inmost soul, Wolfgang had acknowledged the hopelessness of his sojourn in Mannheim, but he stayed on and heeded only too willingly the advice of his acquaintances in the orchestra (letter of 26 November 1777): 'Where will you spend the winter then?—It's a very bad time of the year for traveling. Stay where you are.'

For meanwhile he had fallen in love, with a violence that robbed him of any possibility of judging his position objectively. He had made the acquaintance of the Weber family, the head of which was the former official of the barony of Schönau, Fridolin Weber, now, thanks to the bohemian streak that ran through all the family, in reduced circumstances and employed in the mean position of musician, singer, and copyist in the Mannheim *Kapelle*. The fatal effect of Mozart's acquaintance with this family on his whole life is pointed out by Emil Karl Blümml, one of the best authorities on Mozart's Vienna period, in his sketch of Maria Cäcilie Weber in *Aus Mozart's Freundes- und Familien-Kreis:* *

According to an old German folk-legend, a fairy appears at the birth of every child and lays in his cradle two gifts, one of joy and one of sorrow; and the relative size of these gifts determines the favorable or unfavorable course of the child's life. A good fairy stood at Mozart's cradle. If she gave the little mortal eternal fame, unshakeable cheerfulness, a childlike spirit, and, in the shape of his father Leopold, a good angel to accompany him and to start him on the steep path to fame and glory, it was in the Weber family that she embodied the evil and demoniac element which he could never escape; which would never loosen its hold upon him; which worked against him even after his death and caused his grave to be forgotten. The leading factor in this gift of misfortune was Maria Cäcilie Weber, née Stamm, of Mannheim, whom fate had ordained to throw a dark shadow on Mozart's destiny as his mother-in-law and evil spirit . . .

The only exception I would take to this statement is that the activity of the good fairy at Mozart's cradle is painted in too rosy colors, for the eternal fame of Mozart was dearly bought, the 'unshakeable cheerfulness' was based on a profound fatalism, the 'childlike spirit' was mated to a gift of keen observation and healthy skepticism, and we have seen that the 'good angel,' Leopold, although he always had good intentions, by his very intentions nearly always achieved bad results.

The Weber family consisted of the poor devil of a father, who did not have much to say, the sinister mother, and six children—at least Mozart (letter of 17 January 1778) speaks of 'five girls and one son'; the only children we know of otherwise are four daughters: Josefa, Aloysia, Constanze, and Sophie. The bait that Madame Weber threw out to catch Mozart was her second daughter, Aloysia, at that time fifteen years old.

The bait was effective. The condition of a man in love used to be described in old German by the expression *am Narrenseil laufen*, literally: 'to walk the fool's tight-rope,' and the term was still in use in the Mozart household. Mozart walked the fool's tight-rope as if possessed. Aloysia infatuated him not only by her youth and femininity but also by her gifts as a singer, which alone he correctly judged: 'She sings most excellently my aria written for De Amicis . . . she sings admirably and has a lovely, pure voice . . .' We shall consider the course

* Vienna, 1923, Ed. Strache, p. 10.

of this love affair in our next chapter. Here we need only say that it led Mozart to lose sight entirely of his immediate task—the search for an honorable and lucrative position—and to make instead the most adventurous plans. While still in Munich he had had adventurous schemes, which he attributed to his landlord, Albert (letter of 29-30 September 1777):

Since my arrival Herr Albert has thought out a scheme, which, I believe, would not be impossible of execution. It amounts to this. He wants to collect ten good friends, each of whom would fork out one ducat a month, thus making ten ducats or fifty gulden a month, or 600 gulden a year. Then if I could get 200 gulden a year from Count Seeau, I should have 800 gulden. Now what does Papa think of this idea? . . .

Papa quite rightly thought absolutely nothing of this idea, which would have made Mozart dependent on unreliable Munich patrons and is reminiscent of La Fontaine's fable of Perrette, the milk-maid with her pitcher. Not even Beethoven, whose ability to stand up for his rights was of quite a different calibre from Mozart's, and who dealt with quite different and much more powerful patrons, was entirely successful with a similar plan.

In Mannheim, Wolfgang conjured up other Utopias. He treated a rumor that there were prospects for him in Vienna so lightly that it is clear he did not take it altogether seriously (letter of 10/11 January 1778):

I know for a fact that the Emperor is proposing to establish German opera in Vienna and that he is making every effort to find a young Kapellmeister who understands the German language, is talented, and is capable of striking out a new line. Benda of Gotha is applying, but Schweitzer is determined to get it. I think it would be a good thing for me—provided, of course, that the pay is good. If the Emperor will give me a thousand gulden, I will write a German opera for him: if he won't have me, it's all the same to me . . .

But only four weeks later (4 February), upon his return from a visit to a Princess of Orange in Kirchheimbolanden, he came out with his real plans. During this excursion the Weber family had been sponging on him and, in return, its female members had been darning his stockings and keeping his clothes in order:

I have become so fond of this unfortunate family that my dearest wish is to make them happy; and perhaps I may be able to do so. My advice is that they should go to Italy. So now I should like you to write to our good friend Lugiati, and the sooner the better, and enquire what are the highest terms given to a prima donna in Verona . . .

He wanted of course to go with them, and to write arias (and, wherever possible, operas) for Aloysia:

I will gladly write an opera for Verona for 50 zecchini, if only in order that she may make her name; for if I do not compose it, I fear that she may be victimized. By that time I shall have made so much money on the other journeys we propose to undertake together, that I shall not be the loser. I think we shall go to Switzerland and perhaps also to Holland . . . If we stay anywhere for long, the eldest daughter will be very useful to us; for we could have our own ménage, as she can cook . . .

It is quite understandable that Leopold, at the thought of his son's wandering through the world in the role of musical gypsy and composing factotum for a budding prima donna, almost went out of his mind. On 5 and 12 February 1778, he wrote two serious and despairing letters, which sought to open his son's eyes to circumstances at home and to the senselessness of his Italian plans, and which do honor equally to Leopold's understanding, his character, and his power of expression. The letters culminate in the command:

Off with you to Paris! And that soon! Find your place among great people. *Aut Caesar aut nihil.* The mere thought of seeing Paris ought to have preserved you from all these flighty ideas. From Paris the name and fame of a man of great talent resounds throughout the whole world. There the nobility treat men of genius with the greatest deference, esteem, and courtesy; there you will see a refined manner of life, which forms an astonishing contrast to the coarseness of our German courtiers and their ladies; and there you may become proficient in the French tongue.

It was Wolfgang's character that made Leopold wrong in his estimate of Paris and the Parisian nobility. For Wolfgang was no conqueror and he could not have conquered Paris even if he had wanted to. One need only think for a moment of how Gluck laid Paris at his feet. The reason was not that Gluck was more than forty years older than Mozart, but simply that Gluck was Gluck and Mozart was Mozart—the younger man infinitely superior to the older in native,

God-given talent, in real genius, but incapable of imposing his personality upon society and the world.

Both were Knights of the Order of the Golden Spur, a decoration the Pope awarded as lightly as other sovereigns made presents of golden snuff-boxes or diamond-studded shoe-buckles. Gluck had received his in 1756; Mozart was awarded the order as a boy of fifteen, on 8 July 1770. By this time the order in itself had become cheap and ridiculous. The title of 'Chevalier' lent Gluck a dignity that made him feel, like Bismarck, that wherever he sat was 'the head of the table.' But when Mozart wore the order in Augsburg, he made himself the butt of the stupidly proud and boorish patricians to such an extent that he never wore it again. Only one portrait shows him wearing it, that made for Padre Martini in 1777.

How carefully Gluck's conquest of Paris had been prepared! Not only ambassadors and queens but the entire public took part in these preparations. Gluck played on the instrument of propaganda with the mastery later displayed by Meyerbeer or of some twentieth-century virtuoso of the baton. At the time of Mozart's arrival, the strife between the Piccinnists and the Gluckists was at its height. It was only a few months since the first performance of Gluck's *Armide* (23 September 1777), and a few weeks since that of Piccinni's *Roland*, which had been presented on Mozart's twenty-second birthday. No day of Gluck's stay in Paris passed without publicity, and when, on his way home to Vienna, Gluck visited old Voltaire in Ferney, the meeting was like that of two reigning princes. Meanwhile Mozart slipped into Paris, quietly and unobserved, an unprepossessing young man like hundreds of others, accompanied by his mother, who had had to come along to keep an eye on him.

The period from his arrival in Paris, on 23 March 1778, to his return to Salzburg in January 1779 was one of the low points in Mozart's life. He had entered upon the journey unwillingly, since it separated him from Aloysia. He thought constantly of her, instead of attending to his success. He composed little; hated Paris, its nobility and its bourgeoisie; found Friedrich Melchior Grimm—the patron upon whom Leopold had set his highest hopes, because he held the keys to public acclaim in his hand—insufferable, because he himself was ill-tempered and insufferable. And on top of all that came the illness and death of his mother, whom he had to bury in foreign soil. It was a dark hour when, on 4 July 1778, he had to beg the old family friend in Salzburg, Abbé

Bullinger, to prepare his father for the news of the death of his wife. 'Mourn with me, my friend! This has been the saddest day of my life— I am writing this at two o'clock in the morning. I have to tell you that my mother, my dear mother, is no more!'

Still darker must have been the hours during which he had sat at her bedside, knowing that she was beyond hope. After her funeral, he returned remarkably quickly to his own affairs, and it is not easy to decide to what extent the Catholic faith in which he had been brought up helped him to 'resign himself to the will of God.' The beginning of a letter to his father, two days later (18 July) is almost wounding in its abruptness:

I hope you have safely received my last two letters. We will not talk any more about their chief contents. It is all over now; and were we to cover whole pages, we couldn't alter it!

Mozart was a strange being, full of contradictions. He had undoubtedly been writing eager letters to his Aloysia, and one in Italian (30 July) has been preserved; whether she answered them with equal eagerness we do not know. There survives also a long letter dated 29 July to Fridolin Weber—one of several letters obviously concerned with the death of the Elector of Bavaria, Max Joseph III, and the removal of the Electoral Court to Munich. For Carl Theodor was Max Joseph's closest descendant in the male line, and he lost no time in taking possession of his rich heritage—threatened by the Habsburgs as it was— despite all his reluctance to leave Mannheim. The removal of the court reduced Mannheim forever to the rank of a provincial city, at least as far as opera and concert music were concerned. Only in the field of German drama was Mannheim to have another flowering, thanks to Wolfgang Heribert von Dalberg, the producer of Schiller's first dramas. Now, in this letter Wolfgang assumed the role of patron and adviser of the Weber family; he played the part of Leopold; he spoke of plans for having the father and daughter come to Paris, and for looking out for their support; he gave prudent and diplomatic advice concerning Aloysia's appearing and not appearing in public; he counseled against an engagement with the theatrical company of Seyler; he suggested applying to Mainz, where possibly he, too, might be engaged; and so on.

How the Weber family must have smiled at their twenty-three-year-old friend and patron, who did not even know how to get along himself. They knew very well how to take care of themselves. A few weeks later, in September, Aloysia was engaged as a singer in Munich; her father was perforce taken along, and there was no further need of Mozart's protection.

Mozart himself described his situation in Paris quite openly:

I must now tell you something about my own affairs. You have no idea what a dreadful time I am having here. Everything goes so slowly; and until one is well known—nothing can be done in the matter of composition. In my previous letters I told you how difficult it is to find a good libretto. From my description of the music here you may have gathered that I am not very happy, and that . . . I am trying to get away as quickly as possible . . .

He was completely lost in the midst of the intrigues and court politics of the metropolis and was exploited from the beginning by those in power and by so-called 'friends.' He composed choruses, ensembles, and arias, and eight lengthy pieces for a *Miserere* by Holzbauer, which was to be performed at the Concerts Spirituels—*gratis,* for the director of these concerts, Le Gros, had asked him for them. We should gladly exchange all of Holzbauer's works for these eight pieces, if they had only been preserved. For the four wind-players from Mannheim who were in Paris at the same time, he wrote a *Sinfonia concertante* (for flute, oboe, horn, and bassoon)—again for nothing, in two senses: for Le Gros did not even once bring this work before the public. This piece, too, has been lost, at least it does not survive in its original instrumentation. Mozart indulged the hope of being entrusted with the composition of an opera through the famous Noverre, the theorist of the ballet, who pretended to have influence with De Vismes, the director of the Grand Opera. Accordingly Mozart wrote for Noverre the music to a ballet, *Les petits riens,* consisting of thirteen orchestral pieces, some of them lengthy—once again for nothing. The ballet was produced six times, but neither the announcement nor the newspapers mentioned Mozart's name.

In St. Germain, where he met his old London friends Johann Christian Bach and the *castrato* Tenducci, he wrote for the latter a scena with clavier, oboe, horn, and bassoon, in the hope of getting into the good graces of Tenducci's patron, the Maréchal de Noailles. But he actually had little hope, as is evident from his letter of 27 August:

I shall not gain anything here, save perhaps a trifling present; at the same time I shall not lose anything, for this visit is costing me nothing; and even if I do not get anything, I shall still have made a very useful acquaintance . . .

The scena has been lost, and—it almost goes without saying—nothing more was ever heard about the Maréchal de Noailles. Mozart composed for the Duc de Guines, who played the flute, and for that prince's daughter, who played the harp 'magnificently,' a concerto for the two instruments. Four months later the Duke had not yet paid him for it. And in the composition lessons he gave the daughter, which were presumably also very tardily paid for, Mozart suffered all the torments of the impatient teacher (letter of 14 May):

She is . . . extremely doubtful as to whether she has any talent for composition, especially as regards invention or ideas . . . Well, we shall see. If she gets no inspirations or ideas (for at present she really has none whatever), then it is to no purpose, for—God knows—I can't give her any.

He composed for Le Gros one or two symphonies, and was satisfied if they pleased Le Gros and the Parisian public, which he scorned. Indeed, he composed for the first of these symphonies (K. 297) a second Andantino, since the first 'has not had the good fortune to win his approval; he declares that it has too many modulations and that it is too long.' What a connoisseur of music, the director of the Concerts Spirituels!

Once, a real chance offered itself (letter of 14 May):

Rodolphe [Jean-Josephe Rodolphe, an influential and, so far as we know, reliable man who had been since 1770 a member of the French Royal Chapel] is in the Royal service here and is a very good friend of mine; he understands composition thoroughly and writes well. He has offered me the post of organist at Versailles, if I will accept it. The salary is 2000 livres a year, but I should have to spend six months at Versailles and the other six in Paris, or wherever I like.

From the very beginning, Mozart was not inclined to accept the offer. He did not take into consideration the invaluable proximity to the Royal family, or the lightness of the service required, which would have left him plenty of time for composition in the six months' annual leave. He declined because he was thinking of Aloysia and because he did not like French music:

After all, 2000 livres is not such a big sum. It would be so in German money, I admit, but here it is not. It amounts to 83 louis d'or, 8 livres a year—that is, to 915 gulden, 45 kreutzer in our money (a considerable sum, I admit), but here worth only 333 thalers, 2 livres—which is not much. It is frightful how quickly a thaler disappears here. I am not at all surprised that so little is thought of a louis d'or in Paris, for it really does not go far. Four of these thalers or one louis d'or, which is the same thing, are spent in no time . . .

It is idle to imagine what the course of Mozart's life and what the history of French music would have been if he had accepted the offer.

At the beginning of September 1778, Mozart decided, although very reluctantly, to return to Salzburg. He made the conditions that he should no longer be burdened with the duty of playing the violin in the Archbishop's service, but that he should conduct and accompany arias at the keyboard, for he wished to be sure of the succession to the post of Kapellmeister. He knew exactly what he was facing (letter of 15 October):

Still, I must frankly confess that I should arrive in Salzburg with a lighter heart, did I not remember that I am to be in the service of the court. It is that thought which is intolerable to me. Consider it yourself—put yourself in my place! At Salzburg I never know how I stand. I am to be everything—and yet—sometimes—nothing! Nor do I ask so much nor so little—I just want something—I mean to be something! In any other place I should know what my duties were. Everywhere else, whoever undertakes the violin, sticks to it, and it is the same with the clavier, etc. But no doubt all this can be arranged.

In his heart, however, he knew that it could not all 'be arranged,' and that he would never again be able to fit himself really into the Salzburg situation. In a letter to the Abbé Bullinger—a letter to which we shall return later—he showed much greater skepticism.

It is characteristic that now when he was about to return home, Mozart began to think better of his prospects in Paris, and was sure he would succeed completely if he were only to stay there a few years longer; characteristic, too, that he now appeared to have an opportunity to compose a French opera, towards which he suddenly no longer showed any disinclination. Now he would have been glad to remain in Paris despite his misunderstandings with Grimm, who was pressing him to depart. He did not even have time to oversee the engraving of his six sonatas for violin and clavier, Op. I; he had to deliver them to the consort of Carl Theodor in Munich just as the publisher Sieber had drawn them from the plates. They had netted him 15 louis d'or—much less than he had originally asked for.

On 26 September he left Paris in a hackney-coach, making as little haste as possible to see the cupola of the Salzburg cathedral again. He stayed for a few weeks in Strassburg, where, for a few louis d'or, he made the inhabitants of the town a present of his art in the form of several concertos. And he stayed an even longer time in—Mannheim, of course, to which town he did not hesitate to make the necessary detour, although he no longer found the Weber family there. Indeed, he would have prolonged his stay in Mannheim for another two months, if he had succeeded in arriving at an understanding with Baron Heribert von Dalberg. Dalberg had written the text of a monodrama in the style of the *Ariadne* and *Medea* of Georg Benda, and a 'musical drama' entitled *Cora* in the style of the *Alceste* by Wieland and Schweitzer. Mozart offered to supply the two works with music for 25 and 50 louis d'or respectively, provided only that he should be assured of receiving his honorarium for the monodrama at the end of the two months. This was in spite of the fact that his father at home was awaiting his return with painful impatience. For Leopold had already had the provisional decree for Wolfgang's appointment in his hands for four months, and he feared that the Archbishop would eventually find out that the man who was about to be appointed court organist was making a fool of him, and would withdraw the decree. But Baron Dalberg evidently could not or would not give this assurance, and Mozart had after all learned something from his Parisian experiences. So he went on to Munich, where he was to have the last and bitterest disappointment of this tour so full of disappointments—the one to be discussed in the next chapter. His spirits were so heavy that he found it impossible to open his heart to his father, and he saved his confession to be delivered orally. As he wrote in a letter of 29 December 1778, 'today I can only weep. I have far too sensitive a heart.'

A reference by his father in a letter of 28 December to Wolfgang's 'gay dreams,' meaning the fantasies he had entertained in connection with Aloysia and the Weber family, brought the irritated answer three days later:

A propos; what do you mean by 'gay dreams'? I do not mind the reference to dreaming, for there is no mortal on the face of this earth

who does not sometimes dream! But *gay dreams!* Peaceful dreams, re-
freshing, sweet dreams! That is what they are—dreams which, if realized,
would make my life, which is more sad than cheerful, more en-
durable . . .

This passage reveals the whole state of his soul, compounded equally
of sorrow and fatalism.

Now he was back in Salzburg, a duly installed official in the *Kapelle*
of the Prince-Bishop. And this was the culmination of the high-flown
dreams with which his father had sent him forth a year and a half
earlier, and with which he himself had set out! He felt the contrast
deeply, for no one knew his exceptional gifts better than he himself.
And these gifts he must waste on a purposely uncomprehending patron
and on Salzburg. His genius demanded the best means of performance, the most perfect execution, and what of all that could he find in
Salzburg? The letter to Abbé Bullinger already mentioned (7 August
1778) foresees all this in an ironic description, and this letter is so
revealing and so little known that it deserves quotation:

Now for our Salzburg story. You, most beloved friend, are well aware
how I detest Salzburg—and not only on account of the injustices which
my dear father and I have endured there, which in themselves would
be enough to make us wish to forget such a place and blot it out of
our memory forever! But let us set that aside, if only we can arrange
things so as to be able to live there respectably. To live respectably and
to live happily are two very different things, and the latter I could not
do without having recourse to witchcraft—indeed if I did, there would
have to be something supernatural about it—and that is impossible, for
in these days there are no longer any witches. But, stop, I have an idea.
There are certain people born in Salzburg—indeed the town swarms
with them—you would only have to alter the first letter of their true
name [*Fexen*=fools] and then they could help me [*Hexen*=witches].
Well, happen what may, it will always be the greatest pleasure to me to
embrace my very dear father and sister, and the sooner the better. Yet I
cannot deny that my joy and delight would be doubled if I could do so
elsewhere, for I have far more hope of living pleasantly and happily in
any other place. Perhaps you will misunderstand me and think that
Salzburg is too small for me? If so, you are greatly mistaken. I have
already given some of my reasons to my father. In the meantime, content yourself with this one, that Salzburg is no place for my talent. In
the first place, professional musicians there are not held in much consideration; and, secondly, one hears nothing, there is no theater, no

opera; and even if they really wanted one, who is there to sing? For the last five or six years the Salzburg orchestra has always been rich in what is useless and superfluous, but very poor in what is necessary, and absolutely destitute of what is indispensable; and such is the case at the present moment. Those cruel French are the cause of the orchestra's having no Kapellmeister. I feel assured therefore, that quiet and order are now reigning there! That, of course, is the result of not making provision in time. Half a dozen Kapellmeisters should always be held in readiness, so that if one drops out, another can instantly be substituted. But where, at present, can they get even one? Yet the danger is pressing! It will not do to allow order, peace, and intelligence to gain the upper hand in the orchestra, or the mischief will spread still further and in the long run become irremediable. Are there really no ancient periwigs with asses' ears, no lousy heads available, who could restore the concern to its former disabled condition? I shall certainly do my best in the matter. Tomorrow I intend to hire a carriage for the day and drive round to all the hospitals and infirmaries and see if I can't find some Kapellmeister for them. Why were they so careless as to let Misliveczek give them the slip?—and he was so near too! He would have been a fat morsel for them. It would not be easy to get someone like him and someone moreover who has just been discharged from the Duke Clement's Conservatorio. He would have been the man to terrify the whole court orchestra by his presence. Well, we need not be uneasy—where there is money, there are always plenty of people to be had. Only my opinion is that they should not postpone action too long, not because I am so foolish as to be afraid that they might not get anyone at all—I know only too well that all these gentlemen are longing for a Kapellmeister as eagerly and hopefully as the Jews are awaiting their Messiah—but simply because in the present circumstances things are unendurable. It would be more useful and profitable, therefore, to look around for a Kapellmeister, as they really have none at present, rather than to be writing in all directions (as I have been told they are doing) in order to secure a good female singer. But I can scarcely believe this! A female singer! When we have so many already! And all admirable singers! If it were a tenor, I could more easily understand it, though we do not require one either. But a prima donna! When we now have a castrato! It is true that Mme Haydn is in poor health. She has overdone her austere mode of living. There are few of whom this can be said. I am surprised that she has not lost her voice long ago by her perpetual scourgings and flagellations, her hair-shirt and her unnatural fasts and night prayers! But she will long retain her powers and, instead of becoming worse, her voice will improve daily. When at last

God places her among the number of His saints, we shall still have five
singers left, each of whom can dispute the palm with the other. So you
see how superfluous a new singer is! But just let me argue from an
extreme case. Suppose that, apart from our weeping Magdalene, we
had no other female singer, which, of course, is not the case; but suppose
that one were suddenly confined, the second were imprisoned, the third
were whipped to death, the fourth had her head chopped off, and the
fifth were perhaps whisked off by the devil, what would happen? Nothing!—For we have a castrato. You know what sort of animal he is? He
can sing high treble and can thus take a woman's part to perfection.
The Chapter would interfere, of course. But, all the same, interference
is better than intercourse; and they wouldn't worry him to any great
extent. Meanwhile let Ceccarelli be sometimes man, sometimes woman.
Finally, because I know that in Salzburg people like variety, changes,
and innovations, I see before me a wide field, the cultivation of which
may make history. As children, my sister and I worked at it a little bit,
and what would not grown-ups be able to do? Why, if one is *généreux*,
one can get anything. I have no doubt (and I would even undertake to
arrange it) that we could get Metastasio to come over from Vienna, or
that we could at least make him an offer to write a few dozen opera
texts in which the primo uomo and the prima donna would never meet.
In this way the castrato could play the parts of both the lover and his
mistress and the story would be even more interesting—as people would
be able to admire that virtue of the lovers which is so absolute that they
purposely avoid any occasion of speaking to one another in public.
There is the opinion of a true patriot for you! Do your best to find an
arse for the orchestra, for that is what they need most of all! They have
a head indeed, but that is just their misfortune! Until a change has been
made in this respect, I shall not go to Salzburg. When it has been
made, I am willing to come and to turn over the page whenever I see
V. S.

'There is no theater, no opera.' In the Salzburg years of 1779 and
1780 Mozart wrote two Masses and two vespers as well as church
sonatas, symphonies, serenades, concertos, and sonatas; and he began
a *Singspiel* (dubbed *Zaide* in the nineteenth century), which remained
unfinished—perhaps Mozart thought it tailored to altogether too modest
circumstances. He needed opera on the grand scale. Symphonic and
chamber music and compositions for the church seemed to him trifles
and minor works in comparison with anything connected with the
stage. As early as 28 May 1764, when Wolfgang was only eight years
old, his father had written from London: 'He has now continually in

his head an opera which he wants to produce there with several young people.' This urge to write opera continued throughout his life—big opera with a large orchestra. And Italy had taught him that opera constituted the highest ecstasy of art: all the forms and devices of music culminating in the most beautiful of instruments, the human voice, and dramatic passion transfigured in a magic medium of expression. In order to compose an opera, Mozart made every sacrifice, and even overcame his aversion to the French language, French singers, and the French public. He would compose in every form: *opera seria* or *opera buffa*, *Singspiel* or 'machine'-opera, in either German or Italian; and to counterbalance his letter to Professor Anton Klein in Mannheim (dated 21 March 1785), in which he offers himself with so much patriotism and pathos to the task of creating a national German opera, there are passages from a dozen other letters in which he demands just as emphatically Italian and only Italian opera.

At the end of 1780 this latter wish was fulfilled. He received a commission to write a grand *opera seria* for Munich, and composed his *Idomeneo*, a work unique among his creations. At last he had all the required means at his disposal: the combined orchestras of Mannheim and Munich, excellent singers (with one exception), and a highly discriminating court as an audience. In his intoxication at having these forces to command, he so overburdened the opera with music that its dramatic effectiveness would have been lost even if their possibilities had been greater than they were, and even if it had not belonged to a species that was becoming extinct. (Mozart was conscious of the unique qualities of this opera; he always loved it, and later tried vainly to get it produced in Vienna.) The hopes he had entertained with respect to Carl Theodor again remained unfulfilled.

It is easy to understand that after this experience a break was bound to come between Mozart and Salzburg. In retrospect he acknowledged that he had felt cramped by the provincialism of his native city (letter of 26 May 1781):

I confess that in Salzburg work was a burden to me and that I could hardly ever settle down to it. But why? Because I was never happy. You yourself must admit that in Salzburg—for me at least—there is not a farthing's worth of entertainment. *I refuse to associate with a good many people there*—and most of the others do not think me good enough. Besides, there is no stimulus for my talent! When I play or when any of my compositions are performed, it is just as if the audience were all tables and chairs. If only there were even a tolerably good theater in Salzburg! For in Vienna my sole amusement is the theater.

Thus he received as a sign from heaven the command to join the suite of the Archbishop, after the performance of *Idomeneo*, in a journey from Munich to Vienna (same letter): 'It seems as if good fortune is about to welcome me here, and now I feel that I *must* stay. Indeed, I felt when I left Munich, that, without knowing why, I looked forward most eagerly to Vienna . . .'

From the very beginning, he looked around for opportunities that might make it possible for him to break with the Archbishop. When the latter conferred upon him the honor of being allowed to live in the palace, while the *castrato* Ceccarelli and the violinist Brunetti were quartered elsewhere, Mozart was amused: 'Che distinzione!' The Archbishop was proud of his court music, and showed it off in several great houses, among others that of his old father, the Imperial Vice-Chancellor; but Mozart looked upon such activities as infringements upon his right to earn money privately. The Archbishop at first refused him permission to appear at the Tonkünstler Societät, which threw Mozart into a rage. But the postscript of the same letter that contains the expression of his fury announces that the Archbishop has reluctantly given his consent. Mozart's place at table is between the personal valets and the cooks, rightly shocking both to him and to us. But Mozart's rank as court organist was actually that of a personal servant, and according to eighteenth-century etiquette, which knew nothing of special treatment for genius, this seating at table was formally correct. Referring to the Archbishop as the *Erzlümmel* (Archbooby), Mozart writes to his father on 4 April 1781: 'I shall certainly hoodwink the Archbishop, and how I shall enjoy doing it!'

There can hardly be any doubt that Colloredo, under whose very eyes, so to speak, such letters were written, did in fact read them. He saw clearly that Mozart was fighting a delaying action, and reproaches followed, which deeply hurt Mozart's pride as an artist. Finally, at the beginning of May, when Mozart presented a childish and imaginary excuse—in plain words, a lying one—for not returning from Vienna to Salzburg on a certain day, because of some supposedly important errand, there was an explosion. Colloredo scolded his court organist roughly, and told him in anger that he could go to the devil. Mozart took that as a formal invitation to ask for his dismissal; but his request was not accepted by Count Karl Arco, the son of the court-chamberlain. Mozart insisted, despite the anxious remonstrances of his father, who liked to play politics and spin his secret webs, but who feared the consequences of open indignation. On the occasion of one attempt to get his memorandum accepted—it was the third he had written— Mozart was literally kicked out the door by Count Arco. But no formal dismissal from the archiepiscopal service ever came to him. And thus, in the spring of 1783, when he thought of visiting his father and sister, with his young wife, he voiced the fear that Colloredo would take revenge on him. It is another point in the Archbishop's favor that he never thought of such a thing, as well as that he never made Leopold suffer for the behavior of his son.

Colloredo lived to know the world-fame of his former court-organist. In 1803, after the secularization of the diocese of Salzburg, he moved to Vienna. He lived until 1812, reaching the age of 80. In all probability the memory of his relation to his former servant, Wolfgang Amadeus Mozart, never gave him a moment's concern. But it is a misfortune for his reputation that he ever had anything to do with the Mozarts.

Count Karl Arco, who has suffered a notoriety similar to that of Colloredo for having kicked Mozart, uttered a prophecy in a conversation that preceded that final interview. He urged Mozart's return to Salzburg, pointing out the fickleness of the taste of the Viennese (Mozart's letter of 2 June 1781):

Believe me, you allow yourself to be far too easily dazzled in Vienna. A man's reputation here lasts a very short time. At first, it is true, you are overwhelmed with praises and make a great deal of money into the bargain—but how long does that last? After a few months the Viennese want something new . . .

This was an observation the truth of which Mozart had to acknowledge with some limitations (same letter):

It is perfectly true that the Viennese are apt to change their affections, *but only in the theater;* and my special line is too popular not to enable me to support myself. Vienna is certainly the land of the clavier! And, even granted that they do get tired of me, they will not do so for a few years, certainly not before then. In the meantime I shall have gained both honor and money. There are many other places; and who can tell what opportunities may not occur before then?

As far as the first four or five years are concerned, Mozart's prophecy turned out to be quite correct, but not in respect to the later years. For the moment, it was not too important that his efforts to become the clavier teacher of the Princess Elizabeth von Württemberg, the fiancée of the Russian Archduke, were unsuccessful:

I know that my name is in the book which contains the names of all those who have been chosen for her service. [31 August 1782] . . . Well, the distinguished clavier teacher for the Princess has at last been appointed. I need only mention his pay and you will easily estimate the competence of this master—400 gulden. His name is Summer. [5 October 1782]

Mozart would not have sold his services for 400 gulden, and that fact helped him to swallow his disappointment. He actually succeeded in establishing himself as what later came to be called a free-lance artist. He gave 'academies'—that is, concerts—which were more than sold out, and to which all the music-loving families of Vienna subscribed. He published a few works, some of which were well paid for, as for example the six quartets dedicated to Haydn, for which Artaria paid 100 ducats. He gave lessons in clavier playing and in composition, which were financially profitable. Leopold, when he visited Vienna in the spring of 1785, saw the high-water mark of his son's success. He reported to his daughter, after a careful survey of the situation (19 March 1785): 'If my son has no debts to pay, I think that he can now lodge two thousand gulden in the bank. Certainly the money is there, and so far as eating and drinking is concerned, the housekeeping is extremely economical.' These 2000 gulden were only about four times what Mozart usually took in at one of his subscription concerts in the *Mehlgrube*.

But Leopold was sadly mistaken if he believed that Wolfgang was thinking of depositing money in the bank. Whether Mozart at this time was already in debt we do not know, but it is clear that only a short time later he did not know which way to turn. As a free lance he was a complete failure after only a few years. *Die Entführung aus dem Serail* (1782) was an immense success, for which Mozart, according to the custom of the time in respect to authors' rights, received nothing but a fee for the composition; even the proceeds of the clavier reduction were stolen from him by a publisher in Augsburg, who got ahead of Mozart's own reduction. *Le Nozze di Figaro* (1786) and *Don*

Giovanni (1787) were partial or total failures in Vienna. Between 1787 and 1790 (*Così fan tutte*), there were no commissions for operas. It became constantly more difficult to produce subscription concerts. The three great symphonies of 1788, presumably composed in Vienna with an eye to the future, were perhaps never performed under his direction. Pupils became scarcer and scarcer, so that a year before his death he had to beg his friend and fellow-Mason, Puchberg, to let people know that he could accept more pupils—actually, he had only two left. His compositions were bought by publishers at ridiculous prices, for he had to let them go quickly in order to get his hands on immediate cash. To seek his fortune elsewhere was impossible. The projected visit to England was made impossible by his father's refusal to take the grandchildren into his house. Munich, Dresden, Stuttgart, Berlin—the only possible places—were out of the question. The offer that is supposed to have been made to him during his stay in Berlin, in the spring of 1789, to leave the service of the Emperor for that of the King of Prussia, belongs in the realm of invention, just as does the alleged sentimental reason for his refusal: 'that he, Mozart, could not leave his good Emperor!' Such sentimentality was quite foreign to Mozart; moreover, he had little reason to feel attached to his Emperor, for Joseph II had always shown only very limited understanding of his art.

Nevertheless, Joseph did give Mozart a position. On 15 November 1787, Gluck had died, and on 7 December the Emperor named Mozart Royal and Imperial Court-Composer, with a yearly salary of 800 gulden. Mozart writes his sister the news on 19 December, and thinks she 'will be pleased to hear it.' But she must have expressed her astonishment at the small salary (presumably she knew that Gluck had received 2000 florin), for Mozart replies (2 August 1788): 'I now have a permanent appointment, but *for the time being* at a salary of only 800 gulden. However, no one else in the household is drawing *so large a sum* . . .' It was a sort of honorary stipend, which Mozart was not obliged actually to earn in any way—at least we know of no work that he can have been obliged to write on Imperial command (except possibly *La Clemenza di Tito*). So it is quite believable that Mozart should have written on a tax return, in mentioning the sum: 'Too much for what I do; too little for what I could do!'

In 1790 Joseph II died, and the Archduke Leopold in Florence, to whose services Leopold Mozart had once made such efforts to have his son appointed, succeeded to the Imperial throne. Mozart cannot have been entirely unknown to him. He knew at least *Le Nozze di Figaro*, which had been performed in Florence in the spring of 1788. And Mozart entertained new hopes. He entered his application to the Emperor for the post of second Kapellmeister, as he informed his friend Michael Puchberg in a letter of 17 May 1790:

I now have great hopes of an appointment at court, for I have reliable information that the Emperor has not sent back my petition with a favorable or damning remark, as he has the others, but has retained it. That is a good sign . . .

How greatly he deceived himself! He was only building castles in the air for his friends, his fellow-Masons, and his creditors. The Emperor Leopold was the husband of the Empress Maria Ludovica, the same lady who is supposed to have described Mozart's last opera, commissioned and written for the coronation ceremonies in Prague—*La Clemenza di Tito*—as 'porcheria tedesca' (German rubbish). It was pure indifference, if not worse, that made the Emperor delay action on Mozart's application. Mozart attempted to set his cause in motion by writing to the Archduke Franz, who was later to become Emperor. We do not know whether the letter was ever actually sent; only the draft survives:

I make so bold as to beg your Royal Highness very respectfully to use your most gracious influence with His Majesty the King with regard to my most humble petition to His Majesty. Prompted by a desire of fame, by a love of work, and by a conviction of my wide knowledge, I venture to apply for the post of second Kapellmeister, particularly as Salieri, that very gifted Kapellmeister, has never devoted himself to church music, whereas from my youth up I have made myself completely familiar with this style. The slight reputation which I have acquired in the world by my pianoforte playing, has encouraged me to ask His Majesty for the favor of being entrusted with the musical education of the Royal Family . . .

What a humble and humiliating letter, even including an obeisance before Salieri, in whom Mozart must have seen a deadly enemy! (Salieri himself was out of favor at the time.)

But the instruction of the Imperial Family was not to be entrusted to a musician about whose ruined circumstances, both financial and domestic, there were the most serious rumors. The good Niemtschek, Mozart's first biographer, tells us:

Mozart's enemies and vilifiers, particularly just before and after his death, became so wicked, and so loud in their slanders, that many an evil story about Mozart rose actually to the ears of the Monarch himself. These rumors and lies were so shameless and so shocking that the Monarch, who never heard the other side of the story, was enraged. Not only were all sorts of shameful and exaggerated dissipations attributed to Mozart, but it was claimed that he had left debts of not less than 30,000 gulden—a sum that startled the Monarch.

The widow had the idea of asking the Monarch for a pension. A noble friend and excellent pupil of Mozart [Frau von Trattner?] informed her of the slanders of her husband that had circulated at court, and advised her to enlighten the kindly Monarch as to the truth.

The widow soon had the opportunity of following this advice.

'Your Majesty,' she said proudly, when she was received in audience, 'every man has enemies; but no one has ever been persecuted and slandered by his enemies more violently and more persistently than my husband, simply because he was such a great talent. They have dared to tell Your Majesty much untruth about him; they have exaggerated *tenfold* the debts he left. I will stake my life that I could pay all his debts with a sum of about 3000 gulden. And he did not contract these debts wantonly. We had no secure income; my frequent confinements, and a grave and costly illness of a year and a half which I underwent, will serve as an excuse to the friendly and understanding heart of my King.'

'If that is the way things are,' said the Monarch, 'then there is surely a way out. Give a concert of the works he left, and I will support it.'

He graciously accepted her memorial, and a short time later she was granted a pension of 260 fl., which in itself is small enough, but since Mozart had been in the Imperial service only three years, and his wife was accordingly not really entitled to a pension yet, it was an act of kindness.

Everything Constanze told the Emperor was true, although it was not the whole truth. We know with certainty only that at the death of the Royal and Imperial Court-Composer Wolfgang Amadeus Mozart, in the first hour of 5 December 1791, all he left was cash in the amount of about 200 gulden, miserable house furnishings, musical instruments, and a small library appraised at 23 gulden 41 kreuzer. This was the material, worldly result of Mozart's life. But his own manuscripts were still there, more or less complete, as the pledge of his immortality.

3. *Mozart and the Eternal Feminine*

NO BIOGRAPHY of Mozart would be complete without a chapter on 'Women in Mozart's Life,' any more than a biography of Goethe, or Byron, or Wagner could pass over this *punctum puncti*. This aspect of life may not be important when the subject is a philosopher like Kant, or some other great man in the field of abstract knowledge; but it is of the essence with a great dramatist. The dramatist Mozart—who created figures like Constanze and Blonde; Susanna and the Countess; Donna Anna, Donna Elvira, and Zerlina; Fiordiligi and Dorabella; Pamina and Papagena—knew as much about women as Shakespeare, and his achievement in opera can in fact be compared only with that of Shakespeare, who gave his characters the reality of living human beings: eternal types, and yet completely living embodiments of those types. Just as Olivia, Rosalind, and Katharina, although they still have something to do with the stock comedy figures of the virtuous lady, the disguised shepherdess, and the shrew, live in Shakespeare's comedies as real women—so although Susanna has something of Colombina in her, she is wholly herself, a living and individual being, and we know every fiber of her heart.

Mozart's knowledge of woman was not derived from any actual success with women. Casanova had considerable success with women, but his knowledge of woman, astute as it sometimes is, is one-sided. Byron may have had great success with women, despite his club-foot; but he was a romantic poet, a romantic hero, extraordinarily rich, and a peer—and in Italy especially peers were held in great respect in those days. Mozart had no club-foot, but he was small, delicate, unprepossessing, and poor. Thus his relations with women formed a chain of inadequacies, and in them we have further evidence that he was not fitted to deal with the actualities of life.

As a child-prodigy in Vienna, Paris, and London, he was naturally pampered by women. As a boy, whose senses were already awakened, he was often rewarded for his playing or for a composition by a kiss from a lovely lady. While he was in Italy or in Vienna, he always had a flame back in Salzburg to whom he sent messages and greetings through his sister, who acted as his confidante and *postillon d'amour*. Salzburg, where as in all of southern Bavaria the erotic has always been treated more lightly and more naturally than in the Protestant north, was the right place for flirtations by the score, and Mozart himself once declared in later years that he would have been a husband a hundred times over if he had had to marry every girl with whom he had flirted on occasion. The most grateful object of these flirtations he found in Augsburg in 1777—his cousin, Maria Anna Thecla Mozart, the daughter of Leopold's younger brother Franz Alois. His 'Bäsle' dressed up for him once in French style, and then of course she was a thousand times prettier than in her native Augsburg costume. The flirtation of the two cousins was continued in the notorious 'Bäsle' letters, which with their indecencies and double meanings were intended to call forth blushes. These may very well be called disguised love letters, for bantering and love-making are very closely allied. No doubt 'Bäsle' also set certain hopes upon her cousin. But after the experience with Aloysia, although Mozart did indeed take 'Bäsle' along from Munich to his parents' house in Salzburg, the tone of his letters to her became steadily more serious. Maria Anna consoled herself in thoroughly South-German fashion. Leopold Mozart, who from the first judged the character of his niece better than Wolfgang, refers to it in a letter to his daughter (dated Vienna, 21 February 1785):

The story of your cousin in Augsburg you can easily imagine—a gentleman of the cathedral has made her happy. As soon as I have time I will write the devil of a letter from here to Augsburg, as if I had heard about it in Vienna. The funniest part of it is that all the presents she received, which the whole world admired, came from her uncle in Salzburg. What an honor for me!

But why 'the devil of a letter'? A contemporary observer, Professor August Ludwig Schlözer of Göttingen, who passed through Augsburg on a trip to Italy in 1781-2, explained what Leopold knew better than many another: 'The freedom of most of the citizens of Augsburg is as cheap as the virginity of their daughters, who are bought in dozens every year by the gentlemen of the cathedral here.' In the year 1793 'Bäsle' bore a natural daughter, christened Maria Anna Victoria, who in 1822 married the bookbinder and night-watchman Franz Fidelio Pümpel, resident in Feldkirch in Vorarlberg, and died in 1857.

If 'Bäsle' ever had hopes of Wolfgang, they were lost the instant he set eyes on Aloysia Weber, in Mannheim. Aloysia possessed every quality needed to capture him: youth—she was barely sixteen years old; beauty—she was of the slender, proud, queenly type; and musical gifts— her voice and her singing were of excellent quality, although she never became what Mozart in his lover's blindness expected of her. True coquette that she was, she encouraged Mozart only as far as her mother permitted, and only as long as he seemed a good matrimonial prospect. We may learn something about her from the fact that she did not consider it worth while to save the letters Mozart wrote her from Paris; chance has preserved one, in Italian, containing the most loving suggestions for her development as a singer. When he passed through Munich in December, on his way home from Paris, Aloysia, now that her father was engaged at a salary of 600 florin, and she herself at 1000 florin, made it unmistakably clear to Mozart that he had become superfluous. He kept his outward composure—it is related that he went to the clavier and relieved his feelings with a rough, South-German expression whose equivalent can hardly be printed in English. But in his heart he was a broken man.

Later he saw through Aloysia and was even unjust to her—and he had opportunity enough to observe her from close by. For, to his misfortune, the Weber family had preceded him to Vienna by a year and a quarter, arriving in September 1779—Aloysia as a singer in the Deutsche Oper, and her father Fridolin as a box-office employee in the National Theater. The father died a few weeks after their arrival, leaving nothing but a small chest with a little linen in it. At least that is what his widow managed to tell the probate court. Aloysia was the support of the family. And she became so in even greater degree when, on the last day of October 1780, in the Stefanskirche, she became the wife of Joseph Lange (1751-1831), painter and actor in the Court Theater. Mozart was completely wrong when he wrote to his father as follows (9 June 1781; Leopold had apparently reproached him for leaving his family in the lurch, like Aloysia, although he owed his entire education to them):

Your comparison of me to Madame Lange positively amazed me and made me feel distressed for the rest of the day. That girl lived on her parents as long as she could earn nothing for herself. But as soon as the time came when she could show them her gratitude (remember that her father died before she had earned anything in Vienna), she deserted her poor mother, attached herself to an actor, and married him—and her mother has never had a farthing from her.

This was Mother Weber speaking through him, and Mother Weber was lying, because her evil and hysterical nature was such that she could not help lying. In actual fact, Aloysia was not taken from the Weber household without compensation. Lange had obligated himself to contribute 600 florin annually to the Weber household, as long as he and Aloysia should both be earning. This did not prevent Mother Weber from intriguing against their marriage, or from attempting to separate the couple. Lange had to appeal to the office of the Chief Court-Marshal for consent to the marriage. At the hearing in this office, he raised his offer of support from 600 to 700 gulden, and he obligated himself to pay that amount annually to his mother-in-law throughout her life. But he never found happiness with Aloysia. He was 'a jealous fool'—at least so Mozart terms him—and he doubtless had reason enough to be jealous, for Aloysia seems to have made eyes even at Mozart again:

Even now I feel that she is not a matter of indifference to me; it is, therefore, a good thing for me that her husband is a jealous fool and lets her go nowhere, so that I seldom have an opportunity of seeing her . . . [letter of 16 May 1781]

An opportunity did present itself, however, in the first Vienna years: in 1782 and 1783 Mozart wrote four big arias for her. Then there came a pause, and not until April 1788 did he again supply her with a brilliant aria, the last one. It is possible from the arias he wrote for her between 1778 and 1788 to obtain a picture of her voice and ability, or rather to see what picture Mozart had of them. The arias he wrote in Mannheim are full of warmth; in the ones that date from the Vienna period, Mozart was thinking chiefly of how best to exhibit her exceptional vocal technique—for by now he knew how cold was the heart of Aloysia Lange, his sister-in-law.

Yes, Aloysia Lange, née Weber, was his sister-in-law. For on 4 August 1782, Mozart had married Aloysia's younger sister Constanze, and the events that led up to this fatal step are too characteristic to be passed over. The relation of the Weber family to Mozart, of which Carl

Maria von Weber was so proud, cost Mozart very dear. We have hinted above that in Mozart's life Maria Cäcilie Weber was the evil genius. There is, as we have said, an evil genius that shadows many men's lives, which they can no more escape than a fly can keep out of the spider's web.

Mother Weber, after the death of her husband, had quite purposefully taken the rudder of the family into her own hands. There were four daughters to be taken care of, and the younger ones were just reaching marriageable age. Maria Cäcilie decided to rent rooms. She abandoned the little dwelling on the Kohlmarkt, from which her husband had been buried, and moved to the *Auge Gottes*, taking a fairly large apartment on the third floor, where she rented rooms to young men. Aloysia very soon left her mother's home; and there remained Josefa (the eldest daughter), Constanze, and Sophie. The first lodger to walk into the spider's web, on 2 May 1781, was Wolfgang Amadeus Mozart, who was in the midst of his quarrel with the Archbishop. A week later he reported quite naively to his father:

. . . old Madame Weber has been good enough to take me into her house, where I have a pretty room. Moreover, I am living with people who are obliging and who supply me with all the things which one often requires in a hurry and which one cannot have when one is living alone . . .

His father smelled a rat at once, and must have written warning after warning, in letters which, it goes without saying, were later destroyed by Mozart's widow. But they did not help:

Believe me when I say that old Madame Weber is a very obliging woman and that I cannot do enough for her in return for her kindness, as unfortunately I have no time to do so.

But he had time enough to joke and banter with the second of the three remaining daughters, Constanze. Josefa was already a little too old for him and Sophie a little too young. Meanwhile, Mother Weber took care that there should be talk in Vienna—which in those days and for a long time afterwards remained a small town as far as gossip and slander were concerned—about the fact that Wolfgang and Constanze were in love and were going to be married. Too late she gave him the insincere advice to move out, in order to silence such talk. Mozart took the advice and left the Weber apartment in September

1781, but only to return for daily visits. And it was only a few months later that he had to ask his father, to whom he had so long painted his relations with the Weber family as quite harmless, for permission to marry Constanze Weber.

For in the meantime Mother Weber, believing that she had taken sufficient steps to compromise her second daughter with Mozart, had been pulling other strings. In doing so, she hid behind an accomplice, an accomplice thoroughly worthy of her, Johann Thorwart, the man appointed by the Court Marshal as guardian of her four daughters. This Thorwart had pushed his way up from the position of house-servant and hair-dresser to Prince Lambert, to that of auditor in the National Theater. He was a crude climber, who, as the factotum of the Gentleman-Intendant, Prince Franz von Orsini-Rosenberg, had his chief in his pocket; and it was with Thorwart that Mozart had to reckon when he wanted to accomplish anything in the theater. Thorwart had become rich, obviously through adroit peculations that could never be definitely traced to him, or at least never were. How much Maria Cäcilie gave him or promised him is not known. At any rate, he played his part well, and acted as if Mother Weber had had nothing to do with the whole affair. Mozart quite unjustly suspected others, such as the composer Peter Winter (letter of 22 December 1781):

Certain busybodies and impudent gentlemen like Herr Winter must have shouted in the ears of this person [Thorwart] (who doesn't know me at all) all sorts of stories about me as, for example, that he should beware of me—that I have no settled income—that I was far too intimate with her—that I would probably jilt her—and that the girl would then be ruined, and so forth. All this made him smell a rat—for the mother, who knows that I am honorable, let things take their course and said nothing to him about the matter. For my whole association with her consisted in my lodging with the family and later in my going to their house every day. No one ever saw me with her outside the house. But the guardian kept pestering the mother with his representations until she told me about them and asked me to speak to him myself, adding that he would come some day to her house. He came— and we had a talk—with the result (as I did not explain myself as clearly as he desired) that he told the mother to forbid me to associate with her daughter until I had come to a written agreement with him. The mother replied: 'Why, his whole association with her consists in his coming to my house, and—I cannot forbid him my house. He is too good a friend—and one to whom I owe a great deal. I am quite satisfied. I trust him. You must settle it with him yourself.' So he forbade me to have anything more to do with Constanze, unless I would give him a written undertaking. What other course was open to me? I had either to give him a written contract or—to desert the girl. What man who loves sincerely and honestly can forsake his beloved? Would not the mother, would not my loved one herself place the worst interpretation upon such conduct? That was my predicament. So I drew up a document to the effect *that I bound myself to marry Mlle Constanze Weber within the space of three years and that if it should prove impossible for me to do so, owing to my changing my mind, she should be entitled to claim from me three hundred gulden a year.* Nothing in the world could have been easier for me to write. For I knew that I should never have to pay these three hundred gulden, because I should never forsake her, and that even should I be so unfortunate as to change my mind, I should only be too glad to get rid of her for three hundred gulden, while Constanze, if I know her, would be too proud to let herself be sold. But what did the angelic girl do when the guardian was gone? She asked her mother for the document, and said to me: 'Dear Mozart! *I need no written assurance from you. I believe what you say*,' and tore up the paper.

With which noble gesture Constanze only enmeshed the fly more securely in the web. Thorwart had given his word of honor never to breathe a word of the whole story, not even on his deathbed, but (letter of 16 January 1782) 'notwithstanding his word of honor he has told the story to the whole town of Vienna, which has very much shaken the good opinion I once had of him . . .' Mozart goes on to defend, though a bit weakly, the blackmailer and her accomplice:

Herr von Thorwart did not behave well, but not so badly that [as the enraged Leopold seems to have proposed] he and Madame Weber 'should be put in chains, made to sweep streets, and have boards hung round their necks with the words *seducers of youth.*'

But soon his eyes were opened to the true nature of his future mother-in-law and sisters-in-law. Mother Weber's next attempt was to induce her daughter and future son-in-law to lodge with her. In her eyes, Mozart must have taken on more and more the character of a very promising object for exploitation. When both Mozart and Constanze declined the invitation, she began to make life miserable for her daughter, in order to get her out of the house, being ably assisted in this project by her other daughters. Only Constanze was an angel (letter of 15 December 1781):

> In no other family have I ever come across such difference of character. The eldest is a lazy, gross, perfidious woman, and as cunning as a fox. Mme. Lange is a false, malicious person, and a coquette. The youngest—is still too young to be anything in particular—she is just a good-natured, but feather-headed creature. May God protect her from seduction! But the middle one, my good, dear Constanze, is the martyr of the family and, probably for that very reason, is the kindest-hearted, the cleverest, and, in short, the best of them all . . .

Things came to a point where Constanze left her mother's dwelling and moved to the home of a patroness of Mozart, Baroness von Waldstätten—which was little help to Constanze's reputation, for the Baroness was a very broad-minded woman, and her own reputation was none too good. Mother Weber then wanted to have her daughter brought home by the police. Nothing was left but to marry quickly. The fourth of August 1782 was the fateful day; symbolically enough, Leopold's consent did not arrive until the day after.

When one looks back upon the whole dreary story of Mozart's marriage, his inability to break out of the web that was spun around him is very hard to understand. For Mozart could be very rough in dealing with women who had designs upon him. For example, there was the daughter of the court baker in Salzburg, the one with the lovely big eyes, 'who danced with him at the Stern, who often paid him friendly compliments, and who ended by entering the convent at Loreto' (letter of Leopold, 23 October 1777). When she heard that Wolfgang planned to quit Salzburg, she left the convent, hoping to keep him from going. It is a story of hopeless love, which one cannot hear without being touched. Mozart's reply to Leopold (25 October) was embarrassed but at the same time flippant. It is clear that he felt badly about the affair, but he tried to get it out of his head.

During his first years in Vienna, Mozart became the object of another one-sided love affair, with the pianist Josephine Aurnhammer. In a letter dated 22 August 1781 he describes her with gruesome realism:

> If a painter wanted to portray the devil to the life, he would have to choose her face. She is as fat as a farm-wench, perspires so that you feel inclined to vomit, and goes about so scantily clad that really you can read as plain as print: 'Pray, *do look here.*' True, there is enough to

see, in fact, quite enough to strike one blind; but—one is thoroughly well punished for the rest of the day if one is unlucky enough to let one's eyes wander in that direction—tartar is the only remedy! so loathsome, dirty, and horrible! Faugh, the devil!

The fact is that Constanze had just won her game.

What sort of woman was Constanze Weber? She owes her fame to the fact that Wolfgang Amadeus Mozart loved her, and in so doing preserved her name for eternity, as a fly is preserved in amber. But this does not mean that she deserved either his love or the fame it brought her. Schlichtegroll's necrology has this to say of her:

> In Vienna he married Constanze Weber and found in her a good mother for the two children she bore him, and a worthy wife, who sought to restrain him from many follies and dissipations . . .

Was it shame at such a perversion of the truth that impelled Constanze to make this passage illegible in the Graz edition of the necrology?

Mozart—follies and dissipations! Mozart died in his thirty-sixth year; yet he went through all the stages of human life, simply passing through them faster than ordinary mortals. At thirty he was both childlike and wise; he combined the highest creative power with the highest understanding of his art; he observed the affairs of life and he saw behind them; and he experienced before his end that feeling of imminent completion that consists in the loss of all love for life (letter from Frankfurt, dated 30 September 1790):

> If people could see into my heart, I should almost feel ashamed. To me everything is cold—cold as ice. Perhaps if you were with me I might possibly take more pleasure in the kindness of those I meet here. But, as it is, everything seems so empty . . .

And even more unmistakably five months before his death (7 July 1791):

> I can't describe what I have been feeling—a kind of emptiness, which hurts me dreadfully—a kind of longing, which is never satisfied, which never ceases, and which persists, nay, rather increases daily . . .

It was certainly not longing for his wife—as he tried to make her believe, and perhaps believed himself—that made him feel 'a kind of emptiness,' 'a kind of longing.' It was the presentiment of death. Did Constanze understand this? No—she was not fitted to follow Mozart into such regions. She was not even a good housewife. She never looked ahead, and instead of making her husband's life and work easier by providing him with external comforts she thoughtlessly shared the bohemianism of his way of living. Mozart, on the other hand, tried to make her life as pleasant as possible by his tender care for her—care that, with her numerous confinements, she certainly needed. She bore six children between June 1783 and July 1791, four boys and two girls, of whom only the second and fourth sons survived. Mozart was tied to her by a physical attraction to which a few of his last letters give striking testimony; other such bits of evidence have been destroyed or made illegible.

From her father, Constanze had inherited a slight musicality. Mother Weber was completely unmusical; Mozart once remarked, when he was taking her to a performance of *Die Zauberflöte* (October 1791): 'In her case what will probably happen will be that she will *see* the opera, but not *hear* it.' Constanze's musical gifts were not very considerable as expressed either in her singing or in her understanding of music, and the fact that Mozart never finished any of the compositions intended for her is significant.

She was wholly uneducated, and had no sense of the fitness of things. To try to gain the affections of her future father-in-law and sister-in-law, she sat down on 20 April 1782 and wrote the following postscript to a letter of her betrothed, which must be reproduced in the German original * in order to indicate the intellectual and cultural level of the writer:

Wertheste und schätzbahreste freundin! Niemals würde ich so kühn gewesen seyn, mich so ganz gerade meinem triebe und Verlangen, an sie, wertheste freindin, zu schreiben, zu überlassen, wenn mich dero Hr. bruder nicht Versichert hätte dass sie mir diesen schritt, welcher

* It contains awkwardnesses and mistakes in orthography impossible to reproduce in translation.

'Dearest and most precious friend! Never would I have been so bold as to abandon myself wholly to my impulse and longing to write to you, dearest friend, if your esteemed brother had not assured me that you would not take amiss such a step, which results from too great a desire to converse at least in writing with a person still unknown to me but made very precious by the name of Mozart. Would you be angry if I dared to tell you that I prize you above everything, just as the sister of so worthy a brother, even without knowing you in person and—love you—and dare to ask for your friendship. Without being proud I may say that I have half earned it, and to earn it wholly will be the object of my striving! May I offer you mine in return (in my heart I have long since given it to you)? Oh, yes! Indeed I hope so. And in this hope I remain, dearest and most precious friend,

your most obedient servant and friend

Constanze Weber

Please give my greeting to your esteemed papa!

aus zu grosser begierde mich mit einer obschon unbekannten, doch durch den namen Mozart mir sehr schätzbahren Person wenigestens schriftlich zu besprechen, geschieht, nicht übel nehmen werden.—sollten sie böse werden wenn ich mich ihnen zu sagen unterstehe, dass ich sie, ohne die Ehre zu haben sie von Personn zu Kennen, nur ganz allein als schwester eines—ihrer so würdigen bruders, überalles Hochschätze und—liebe—und es wage—sie um Ihre freundschaft zu bitten.—ohne stolz zu seyn darf ich sagen dass ich sie halb Verdiene, ganz—werde ich mich sie zu Verdienen bestreben!—darf ich ihnen die meinige (welche ich ihnen schon längst heimlich in meinem Herzen geschenkt habe) entgegen anbieten?—o ja! ich Hoffe es.—und in dieser hofnung Verharre ich

werteste und schätzbahreste freundin

dero

gehorsamste dienerin
und freundin
Constanze Weber

bitte meinen handkuss an dero herren papa!—

It is easy to picture the shrug of the shoulders with which Leopold must have read this diplomatic message. The superficiality that Mozart saw in the youngest sister was present to a quite sufficient extent in Constanze herself. A letter is well known in which Mozart, on 29 April 1782, three months before the wedding, made Constanze the gentlest and at the same time most serious reproaches about her thoughtless behavior in playing a game of forfeits:

. . . the least acknowledgment of your somewhat thoughtless behavior on that occasion would have made everything all right again; and if you will not make a grievance of it, dearest friend, everything will still be all right. You realize now how much I love you. *I do not fly into a passion as you do. I think, I reflect, and I feel. If you will but surrender to your feelings,* then I know that this very day I shall be able to say with absolute confidence that Constanze is the virtuous, honorable, prudent, and loyal sweetheart of her honest and devoted

Mozart

A passage in a letter written from Dresden on 16 April 1789 suffices in itself to document fully all Mozart's care and concern:

Dear little wife, I have a number of requests to make. I beg you
1) not to be melancholy,
2) *to take care of your health and to beware of the spring breezes,*

3) not to go out walking alone—and preferably not to go out *walking at all*,

4) to feel absolutely assured of my love. Up to the present I have not written a single letter to you without placing your dear portrait before me.

5) I beg you in your conduct not only to be careful of your honor and mine, but also to consider appearances. Do not be angry with me for asking this. You ought to love me even more for thus valuing our honor.

6) and lastly I beg you to send me more details in your letters. I should very much like to know whether our brother-in-law Hofer came to see us the day after my departure? Whether he comes very often, as he promised me he would? Whether the Langes come sometimes? Whether progress is being made with the portrait? What sort of life you are leading? All these things are naturally of great interest to me.

In nothing could Mozart really rely upon Constanze. Even in the very last period, he had to warn her, whose behavior was all-important to him, against bad company (summer of 1791):

. . . please do not go to the Casino.
Primo, the company is—*you understand what I mean*—
Secondo, you can't dance, as things are—and to look on . . . ?
Why, you can do that more easily when your little husband is with you.

He was not at all sure of her fidelity, and in this connection an anecdote that has come down to us deserves to be believed, and to be taken as not altogether harmless:

In the summer of 1791 the young lieutenant von Malfatti was taking the cure near by in Baden, in order to recover fully from wounds received in the last Turkish war; and, since he limped, he had to spend the greater part of his time in his ground-floor room. He sat in his window reading, and often enough raised his eyes from his book to glance across the way to the slender, dark-haired young woman who occupied another one of the rented lodgings on the ground floor. One day, towards evening, he saw a little man creep up to the house, look around carefully in all directions, and act as if he were going to climb in the lady's window. The lieutenant quickly hobbled over to the defense of his pretty neighbor and grasped the little man by the shoulder:
'What do you want here, Sir, that is not the door!'
'Well, I guess I may climb in my wife's window!' was the answer. It was Mozart himself, who had returned, no doubt unexpectedly, from Vienna to visit his 'Stanzerl' [as he nicknamed Constanze], and who

wanted, in characteristic fashion, to surprise her doubly by letting her find him sitting in her room in the evening, when she returned from her evening 'constitutional,' before any one knew he was there.*

We may read a good deal between the lines when he writes to Constanze at the spa (25 June 1791): 'Beware of the baths! And do sleep more—and not so irregularly, or I shall worry—I am a little anxious as it is . . .'

But Constanze knew how to turn things around to make it appear that she had had to overlook her husband's little escapades and affairs with chambermaids. There is not the slightest evidence to justify any such insinuation. Not even the so-called Hofdemel affair offers any testimony against Mozart. The Court-Attaché Franz Hofdemel, formerly private secretary of one Count Seiler, was a lodge-brother of Mozart's. He was married to the daughter of the Kapellmeister Gotthard Pokorny, Magdalene, to whom Mozart gave lessons. Hofdemel was one of Mozart's creditors. Mozart had asked him several times for loans, as is evidenced by a letter (April 1789) in which Mozart alludes to the approaching reception of Hofdemel into the lodge. Five days after Mozart's death, Hofdemel attempted to kill his wife, who was expecting a child, slashing at her face and throat with a razor, and then committed suicide. The deed was attributed to a fit of jealousy—but cases of unwarranted jealousy are not unknown. The widow received a pension of 560 gulden from the Emperor Leopold. The public scandal impelled her to leave Vienna for her father's home in Brünn, where she gave birth to a son, Johann Alexander Franz. Whether the boy was Mozart's or Hofdemel's we cannot know; he bore the first names of both.†

The only woman of whom Constanze would really have had a right to be jealous, a woman who had more than a mere physical attraction for Mozart, was Anna (Nancy) Selina Storace, his first Susanna. She was born in 1766 in London, of an Italian father, the contrabass player Stefano Storace, and an English mother. Her brother Stephen was a composition pupil of Mozart's, and by no means an unworthy one, as his most popular *opere buffe* show. She studied singing under Rauzzini and then went to Italy where she completed her vocal studies at the Ospedaletto in Venice. From 1780 on, she appeared in public in Flor-

---

* Cf. H. Rollett, 'Mozart und Baden,' *Mozarteums-Mitteilungen* ii, 4; August 1920.

† Mozart was christened Johann Wolfgang Amadeus.

ence, Parma, and Milan, and in 1783 she came to Vienna. Her marital history, like Mozart's, was not very happy. In 1784 she was stupid enough to marry her countryman John Abraham Fisher, twenty-two years her senior, a violinist, composer, and bachelor and doctor of music of Oxford, who was passing through Vienna on a concert tour. He so mistreated her that the indignant Emperor banished him from the Imperial domains. Anna Selina resumed her maiden-name, and always kept her marriage a secret in her native country.

Between Mozart and her there must have been a deep and sympathetic understanding. She was beautiful, attractive, an artist, and a finished singer, whose salary at the Italian opera in Vienna attained a figure at that time unheard of. The scena and aria *Ch'io mi scordi di te* (K. 505) for soprano, obbligato clavier, and orchestra, is dedicated to her. In Mozart's thematic catalogue it is labelled 'Für Mselle Storace und mich'; the autograph reads: 'Composto per la Sig^{ra}. Storace dal suo servo ed amico W. A. Mozart Vienna li 26 di dec^{bre} 1786.' It is an accompanied duet for voice and clavier, a declaration of love in music, the transfiguration of a relation that could not be realized except in this ideal sphere. Fortunately, Constanze had no ear for such things. It was with Miss Storace, her brother, and the tenor Michael Kelly that Mozart planned in 1787 to visit London—a plan his father upset, as has been mentioned. But he remained in correspondence with Anna Selina. What happened to these letters is a mystery. Anna Selina certainly treasured them, but perhaps before her death, which occurred in Dulwich in 1817, she destroyed them as not intended for the eyes of an outsider.

Constanze's behavior upon the death of Mozart, and after it, has been criticized with varying degrees of severity. She was ill and beside herself, and she could not prevent Mozart's 'patron,' the Imperial Court Librarian Gottfried van Swieten, from having Mozart's body buried in a pauper's grave, for reasons of economy. Later, she could not visit the grave, or bedeck it with flowers, or erect a tombstone— and this has also been the basis of stupid reproaches—simply because the grave could not be found. Not until years later (1808 or 1809) did she ride out to the graveyard of St. Mark's in search of the spot. But she was told that pauper's graves were left intact for only seven years. Under the date of her husband's death she wrote in his album, beneath an entry which Mozart had written for his friend Dr. Sigmund Barisani:

What once thou hast written upon this page for thy friend, that do I now, deeply bowed in sorrow, write for thee, dearly beloved husband! O Mozart, whom neither I nor all Europe can ever forget, now is it well with thee—forever well.

At one o'clock in the morning between the fourth and fifth of December of this year he departed, in his thirty-sixth year—alas, all too soon!—this good but ungrateful world. O God—for eight years we were joined by the tenderest bond, on earth unbreakable! Oh! could I but soon be joined with thee forever, thy most deeply troubled wife,

Constanze Mozart, née Weber.

I see no reason to doubt that this entry was made on 5 December, but it seems very unlikely that the year was 1791. In 1791 Constanze had no idea that 'all Europe could never forget' her husband. Only the growing world-fame of Mozart awakened her gradually to the realization of the nature of the man who had once led her forth from the Auge Gottes, and with whom she had lived for nine or ten years. What contributed most to this realization was the growing material value of his unpublished manuscripts, of which she still possessed a great number (not more than 70 of his more than 600 works had been published during his lifetime), and which she accordingly kept together very carefully.

Now we are almost ready to take leave of Constanze Weber—almost, because there are still a few words in her favor left to say. For after Mozart's death she exhibited certain better qualities, among which, ironically, we find even a marked native business sense, which she had lacked completely during his lifetime. A few weeks after his death she sold eight manuscripts to the King of Prussia for 800 ducats, i.e. about $1500; she produced concerts in memory of Mozart as benefits for herself; and she carried on negotiations concerning a few of his works. Like her mother before her, she began to rent rooms. The counselor of the Danish legation, Georg Nikolaus von Nissen, born in 1761, an admirer of Mozart, took lodgings with her. He became her friend and adviser: all the letters she wrote to the publisher André in Offenbach about the sale of Mozart's manuscript remains show Nissen's influence, in both thought and style. When Nissen was called back to Copenhagen in 1809, he legitimized his relation with Constanze, and from that time on she signed herself in letters as '*Constanze Etatsräthin von Nissen, gewesene Witwe Mozart*' (Constanze, wife of the State Counselor von Nissen, formerly Widow Mozart). Under Nissen's influence she even became a good mother to her two sons, Karl Thomas and Franz Xaver Wolfgang. For ten years, from 1810 to 1820, she lived with Nissen in Copenhagen; then, strangely enough, the couple moved to Mozart's birthplace, since Nissen wished to settle near Bad Gastein, and doubtless also wished to be near the sources for the story of Mozart's early life. Constanze remained in Salzburg even after Nissen's death in 1826, and thus there lived in Salzburg two old women who in their youth had been the closest companions of Wolfgang Amadeus— his sister Marianne and his wife Constanze; but they had very little to do with each other. In 1828, Constanze published the first big biography of Mozart, prepared by Nissen. This gives only a conventional idea of Mozart's greatness, and limits itself mainly to biographical matter; and even here, there are omissions, suppressions, and even misrepresentations. But it was the first biography, and even today it is not without a certain value, since it reproduces many documents which have since disappeared. After Nissen's death, Constanze took into her house her younger sister, Sophie Haibel, who had also lost her husband; and eventually Aloysia Lange, too, came to spend her last days in Salzburg. Constanze departed from this group of ghosts in 1842, having outlived Mozart by fifty years. A series of her letters, principally to her sons, are preserved, as well as a diary of the years 1824-37. The letters are chiefly a reflection of Nissen's views. They are conventional and insignificant, with never a word of wit, magnanimity, or humor. In the diary platitudes alternate with observations that show a sense of business. Constanze is taking the baths in Gastein, as once she took them in Baden-bei-Wien:

Today, being the 18th of September, 1829, I had the good fortune to take my seventh bath, I took my coffee as usual at half past five, after I had washed my face and my mouth I went to visit Mr. Rösiger at the baths, but found instead of him a stranger, who had just come from London and told me much about it, and who will take some letters there for me. I do not know his name yet. A very nice man. Then I went to my room, got my bath linen, and when the bath was free I went in with Mona and let her bathe for a good quarter of an hour with me, but I stayed a whole hour, after which I went to bed again to rest a little, and then took half a cup of camomile tea and then I sat here to write all this down, and now Dr. Storck has just come and praise God has found me well—so much till 11 o'clock, the rest will follow—at half past eleven I went out to take a little walk in front of the house.

4. Catholicism and Freemasonry

HE RELATION of educated Catholics to their religion in the seventeenth and eighteenth centuries was once very neatly described by 'Madame'—Elisabeth-Charlotte—writing in 1691 about her husband, the brother of Louis XIV, who denied that he was *dévot* (at the Parisian Court it was sometimes stylish to play the free-thinker): 'Between you and me he really is *dévot* for that gives him considerable diversion, and since he loves ceremony, he is diverted by everything that is connected with devotion . . .'

The Mozart family could not permit itself such an aristocratic point of view. For them religion was a serious matter—more than a mere 'diversion.' And so Leopold Mozart insisted with both his wife and his children upon fairly strict obedience of the requirements of the Church: regular attendance, fasting, and prayer. But he was far too rationalistic and acute not to allow himself a certain freedom of thought, to which he felt entitled by the very fact that he and his family carefully observed all the ceremonial of religion. Leopold, who was to have become a priest, was willing to hoodwink his priestly patrons, perhaps because he had observed them behind the scenes in Augsburg and Salzburg. And if he ever had been a bigot, he certainly returned from the grand tour of 1763-6 with a definitely freer outlook, as is clearly evidenced by his letters. Especially in Italy, the Mozarts could not fail to observe the profoundly irreligious temper of the time, revealed rather than hidden by the gay ceremonial of the church. And their disagreement with their patron contributed still further towards making them draw an increasingly sharp distinction between God and his earthly representatives. In Mozart's letters there is not a word of respect for these representatives, with the exception of the worthy Padre Martini in Bologna, in whom Leopold and Wolfgang honored chiefly the musician and musical scholar rather than the Franciscan monk.

Nevertheless the Mozart household was a sincerely Catholic one.

Religion was an honorable convention, and a pledge of decent behavior. During Wolfgang's long journey, when he was no further away than Augsburg, Leopold sent him exhortations to fulfil his religious obligations, and these urgings became particularly insistent when he suspected that his son was wasting time in Mannheim. Wolfgang's reassurances were frequently repeated (letter of 25 October 1777):

Papa must not worry, for God is ever before my eyes. I realize His omnipotence and I fear His anger; but I also recognize His love, His compassion, and His tenderness towards His creatures. He will never forsake His own. If it is according to His will, so let it be according to mine. Thus all will be well and I must needs be happy and contented.

This sounds like a quotation from the catechism. But soon to this faith in God there was added a fatalism not at all to Leopold's taste (letter of 26 November 1777): 'What is the use of needless speculation? What will happen we know not—and yet we do know! It is God's will . . .' This did not quiet Leopold's anxiety, for he favored active attempts to influence God's will. He tried to bring Wolfgang to reflect more about his own character, by reminding him of the confessional (15 December 1777):

Is it necessary for me to ask whether Wolfgang is not getting a little lax perhaps about confession? God must come first! From His hands we receive our temporal happiness; and at the same time we must think of our eternal salvation. Young people do not like to hear about these things, I know, for I was once young myself. But, thank God, in spite of all my youthful foolish pranks, I always pulled myself together. I avoided all dangers to my soul and ever kept *God* and my *honor* and the consequences, the *very dangerous consequences* of foolishness, before my eyes . . .

But Wolfgang thought of God as an arbiter of destiny, whose decisions and verdicts must be accepted with fatalistic resignation. This became particularly clear at the death of his mother: it had to be; God could have preserved her, but now He had taken her away, and there was nothing to do but bow to His inscrutable will. When the performance of one of his symphonies at the Concerts Spirituels was a success, 'I went off to the Palais Royal, where I had a large ice, said the rosary as I had vowed to do—and went home . . .' (letter of 3 July 1778)—for how could one have known beforehand? The Parisian public is an unpredictable animal!

In Vienna, the break with the Archbishop seems to have led Wolfgang to speak rather freely about the requirements of the church, and the substance of his remarks was reported to his father. Wolfgang defended himself in a letter of 13 June 1781:

My chief fault is that—*judging by appearances*—I do not always act as I should. It is not true that I boasted of eating meat on all fast-days; but I did say that I did not scruple to do so or consider it a sin, for I take fasting to mean abstaining, that is, eating less than usual. I attend Mass every Sunday and every holy day and, if I can manage it, on weekdays also, and that you know, my father . . .

But there is no denying the fact that he relied on religion a good deal during this period, when he was trying to emphasize his obligation to marry Constanze. After the marriage, he had a genuine spell of religious devotion (letter of 17 August 1782):

I forgot to tell you the other day that on the Day of Portiuncula my wife and I performed our devotions together at the Theatines. Even if a sense of piety had not moved us to do so, we should have had to do it on account of the banns, without which we could not have been married. Indeed for a considerable time before we were married we had always attended Mass and gone to confession and taken communion together; and I found that I never prayed so fervently or confessed and took communion so devoutly as by her side . . .

Just as in Paris he had vowed to say a rosary if his symphony was a success, so now he had vowed the composition of a mass for a favorable outcome of his engagement. This was the great C minor Mass, which remained unfinished.

This brings us to the question of Mozart's church music. Is it really Catholic? Is it sincere? Is it appropriate to the Church? There has been in the past, and still is, an attitude in favor of austerity in church music —a movement that would reject as unliturgical and secular the greater part of the sacred music of the seventeenth and eighteenth centuries, including the masses, litanies, and motets of Mozart and Haydn. This movement accepts for the liturgy only music that is 'unobjectionable.' Its ideal is the passionless—that is, apparently passionless—polyphony of the *a cappella*-music of the sixteenth century. But would not such an attitude require the abandonment of Michelangelo's Basilica of St. Peter's, Vignola's Church of Sts. Ignatius and Xavier in Rome, and the Karlskirche in Vienna?

A further comparison with architecture will help us in understanding this question. South Germany and Austria are full of eighteenth-century churches, quite lacking in austerity or mystic quality—full, rather, of festive gaiety. The columns rise in serpentine spirals, the altars gleam in purple and gold, and in the bright ceiling paintings the Holy Trinity is surrounded by throngs of saints and cherubs. From those churches, somewhat peasant-like in character, to those that are miracles of the most refined art, like the Wallfahrts-Kirche at Wies, in Upper Bavaria, none are 'secular'; on the contrary, they are of a childlike piety that is no less truly devout than the purest Gothic, or the best imitations of Gothic produced in the nineteenth and twentieth centuries. The musical counterparts of these churches are the masses, litanies, and hymns—the *Sancta Maria* and the *Ave verum*—of Mozart. Whether or not he had periods of critical thinking in his relation to the Roman Catholic faith, in his church works he was definitely religious. These works are religious in the deeper sense. They are completely rounded works of art, without the slightest skepticism or break with convention. We shall have more to say about this question when we deal with Mozart the musician. But even now we may think for a moment of Beethoven, who in his *Missa Solemnis* is certainly Catholic, but who is critical as well. Beethoven's faith was not arrived at without inner conflict, and his prayer for peace is not without its memories of internal and external strife. With Mozart everything connected with the church is a matter of unshakable faith and—in art—of utter security. In this respect he still belongs to those ages in which the individual did not think of trying to come to a personal understanding of the divine. God was the Father, Mary the Virgin Mother, to whom one could turn with an intimate intensity. The very uttering of the prayer insured that it was heard. If ever a great musician was a Catholic composer it was Mozart.

On 4 April 1787, Mozart wrote to his father:

This very moment I have received a piece of news which greatly distresses me, the more so as I gathered from your last letter that, thank God, you were very well indeed. But now I hear that you are really ill. I need hardly tell you how greatly I am longing to receive some reassuring news from yourself. And I still expect it, although I have now made a habit of being prepared in all affairs of life for the worst. As death, when we come to consider it closely, is the true goal of our existence,

I have formed during the last few years, such close relations with this best and truest friend of mankind, that his image is not only no longer terrifying to me, but is indeed very soothing and consoling! And I thank my God for graciously granting me the opportunity (you know what I mean) of learning that death is the key which unlocks the door to our true happiness. I never lie down at night without reflecting that—young as I am—I may not live to see another day. Yet no one of all my acquaintances could say that in company I am morose or disgruntled. For this blessing I daily thank my Creator and wish with all my heart that each one of my fellow-creatures could enjoy it. In the letter which Madame Storace took away with her, I expressed my views to you on this point, in connection with the sad death of my dearest and most beloved friend, Count von Hatzfeld. He was just thirty-one, my own age. I do not feel sorry for him, but I pity most sincerely both myself and all who knew him as well as I did. I hope and trust that while I am writing this, you are feeling better. But if, contrary to all expectation, you are not recovering, I implore you by . . . not to hide it from me, but to tell me the whole truth or get someone to write it to me, so that as quickly as is humanly possible I may come to your arms. I entreat you by all that is sacred—to both of us.

What had happened? Although in this letter Mozart speaks of God, the spirit of the letter would hardly have given pleasure to a priest. The thought of death does not bring the feeling of repentance, or a fear of dying in a state of sin, or any desire to prepare for death by confession and absolution; on the contrary, it suggests living more intensely and with more gaiety than ever. Mozart and his father had become Freemasons. Wolfgang had been the first to join, at the end of 1784, becoming a brother in one of the smaller of the eight lodges of Vienna, the one called *Zur Wohltätigkeit* (Benevolence), and Leopold had followed his example on 6 April 1785, during a visit to Vienna. When an imperial decree early in 1786 ordered the merger of these lodges into three larger ones, the Benevolence lodge combined with the *Gekrönte Hoffnung* (Crowned Hope) to form the *Neugekrönte Hoffnung* (Newly Crowned Hope).

Did membership in the order of Freemasons represent for Mozart any contradiction of his religion? The question cannot be answered with a simple yes or no. In those days a good Catholic could perfectly well become a Mason. Of course only an 'enlightened' Catholic would have done so, and he had to run the risk of being looked upon with some misgiving and suspicion by the Church. Mozart was a passionate, convinced Freemason, unlike Haydn, who also became a Freemason in name, but after his reception into the order never was an active member of any lodge and never wrote a single Masonic work. Mozart wrote a whole series of significant works for Masonic ceremonies, and the consciousness of his membership in the order permeates his entire work. Not only *Die Zauberflöte* but many others of his works are Masonic, even though they reveal nothing of this quality to the uninitiated.

No, Mozart was no longer what a gloomy or fanatical priest would call a good Catholic. The history of Freemasonry in Austria is very curious. Francis of Lorraine, later the consort of Maria Theresa, had been admitted to the Order at The Hague, in 1731, through Lord Chesterfield, the English ambassador. His young wife permitted him to remain a member—presumably she regarded this 'escapade' of her husband with fewer misgivings than she did his occasional philanderings with beautiful ladies of the court. The Emperor's membership in the Order actually prevented the publication of the bull against Freemasonry that Clement XII had already prepared (23 April 1738). In 1764, however, Maria Theresa formally suppressed the Order throughout her possessions; it could continue only in secret. Her death, in 1780, seemed to augur a re-birth of Freemasonry in Vienna and in Austria in general. While Joseph II was not himself a lodge member, the efforts and aims of the Order seemed to conform so closely to his ideas that its members confidently expected to make progress, and deceived themselves about Joseph's true attitude, which was one of distrust, even derision, documented in the bureaucratic measures he proceeded to take. And when Joseph died, the Catholic clergy, especially the monks, began again to storm against the lodges—with great success, as is known. The mere fact of membership in a lodge constituted a protest against the Church. One of the writings of the mineralogist Ignaz von Born, the spiritual head of the Vienna lodges—his *Monachologia*—was a satire on monasticism. Moreover, in the 1780's Austrians had an excellent opportunity to observe the fate of a related order, the so-called 'Illuminati,' in near-by Bavaria. In 1776, one year before the death of the devoutly Catholic but sympathetic Elector Max Joseph, this Order had been established in Ingolstadt, up to that time a bastion of Jesuitism, by the youthful Adam Weishaupt, professor of natural and canonic law, the first secular teacher in a university that had been dominated entirely by Jesuits up to 1773. Weishaupt was a muddle-headed idealist, as may be seen from his sketch of the statutes of the Order:

The secret society has for its aim the uniting in a single, lasting group, by means of a given higher interest, of men of independent mind from all parts of the world, men of all conditions and all religions, without prejudice to their freedom of thought, and despite their differences of opinions and emotions; to arouse in them a burning desire for this higher interest and such a responsiveness to it that they will behave though away as if they were present; though subordinate, as equals; though many, as one; that they will do of their own accord, from true conviction, that which no overt force, since the beginning of the world and men, has been able to make them do. The Order that has this secret goal divides into three classes. The first class consists of the Training-School; the second of Freemasonry, the hitherto existing Lodge; but the third and highest class consists of the Mysteries. In the first class, the Training-School, the candidate rises from novice to *Minervalis*, from *Minervalis* to *Illuminatus minor*, and finally to Magistrate. In the second class, Freemasonry, the degrees are *Illuminatus major* or Scottish Novice, and *Illuminatus dirigens* or Scottish Knight. Finally in the third and highest class, the Mysteries, there are four degrees . . .

This sounds somewhat fantastic; but Weishaupt had learned something from the Jesuits: the will to power, the urge to increase the number of his followers, and the demand for absolute obedience by the members. And the Order gained adherents and influence in many places in Germany—among princes, such as the Duke of Gotha; among the clergy, such as Carl von Dalberg, the famous Coadjutor of the Archbishopric of Mainz; and among men of culture, such as Baron von Knigge in Hanover. Internal quarrels weakened the Order; and the dual activity of officials who were both servants of the state and members of the Order was distrusted by the government and led to the dissolution of the Order at the place of its origin. On 24 June 1784, Carl Theodor decreed a general prohibition of all secret societies; Freemasons in Bavaria and the Palatinate obeyed at once, and the Illuminati were compelled to follow suit a year later. Weishaupt fled to his protector in Gotha, and in Bavaria that darkness set in again which serves every despotic government as the most favorable pre-condition for its rule. Carl Theodor, the prototype of the Queen of the Night! Recollection of the fate of Freemasonry in the neighboring land played its part in the growth of *Die Zauberflöte*. The aggressive stand taken by

Masonry against the superstition practiced by the Church and the ignorance on which it thrived is not to be denied.

And yet, Mozart either was not aware of the contrast, or he bridged it over. In the year of his death he wrote the Masonic *Zauberflöte* at the same time that he began to set to music the liturgical text of the Requiem. Can it be that Masonic elements infiltrated into the setting of the funeral rites of the Church? This is a question we shall have to answer later, by considering the character of the music. How different Mozart is from Gluck and Haydn! There is no church music at all by Gluck; there is religious music, to be sure, like the *De profundis*, but there are no masses, no litanies, no hymns. I do not know whether Gluck was a Freemason, but it does not matter. He was a man of the world; membership in a lodge would have meant no more to him than membership in any other society, such as the 'Arcadians,' to which he actually belonged. Haydn *was* a Freemason; but even if he had been a less indifferent and unenthusiastic 'brother' than he was, the spiritual and musical character of his work would have remained completely uninfluenced by the Masonic ideal of humanity. Towards the end of his creative activity he again wrote quite ingenuous masses, more mature and greater than the earlier ones, but not essentially different; and he composed joyful and devout oratorios that breathe a new feeling for nature—but no new feeling for mankind. For Mozart, Catholicism and Masonry were two concentric spheres; but Masonry—the striving for moral purification, the labor for the good of mankind, the intimacy with death—was the higher, broader, more comprehensive of the two. It is worth stressing also that artistic natures like Mozart's were susceptible to the attractions of the fully developed symbolism of Masonry. The symbolism and the ceremonial of the Catholic Church were familiar to him; the mysterious symbols of the Lodge were new. It is entirely characteristic that he at once began to poke fun at certain peculiarities of lodge-procedure. The Illuminati, like the 'Arcadians' in Rome, were given special names—not fantastic shepherd-names, however, but ancient or Biblical ones. The Duke of Gotha was called 'Timoleon'; Prince Ferdinand of Brunswick, 'Aaron'; the Coadjutor of the Archbishopric of Mainz, 'Crescens'; Baron von Knigge, 'Philo.' On 15 (14) January 1787, Mozart wrote from Prague to his young friend Gottfried von Jacquin, in Vienna:

Now farewell, dearest friend, dearest Hikkiti Horky! That is your name, as you must know. We all invented names for ourselves on the

Painted by Thaddeus Helbling

THE BOY MOZART (1767)

journey. Here they are: I am Punkitititi. My wife is Schabla Pumfa. Hofer is Rozka Pumpa. Stadler is Notschibikitschibi. My servant Joseph is Sagadarata. My dog Goukerl is Schomanntzky. Madame Quallenberg is Runzifunzi. Mlle Crux is Rambo Schurimuri. Freistädtler is Gaulimauli. Be so kind as to tell him his name.

The name 'Gaulimauli' even found its way into a canon by Mozart. It would be labor lost to try to penetrate into the deeper meaning of the names of this brother- and sisterhood; but inventing them must have been a cause of endless delight to Mozart, a joy explainable only by their parodistic intent. A few weeks and months after this, Mozart wrote the A minor Rondo for piano and the G minor Quintet.

Perhaps he was driven into the Lodge also by his feeling of profound loneliness as an artist and his need for unreserved friendship. In the Lodge, he, who had been admonished by a kick from Count Arco and treated as a servant by Archbishop Colloredo, was, as a man of genius, on an equal footing with the nobility, and had the same privileges. He wrote the funeral music 'for the death of Brothers Meklenburg and Esterházy'—that is, for Duke Georg August zu Mecklenburg Strelitz and for Franz Count Esterházy von Galantha, not as a musician composing to order, for money, but as a brother for the brothers. It must be added—and this has already been observed by others—that he had no friend among musicians, at least no intimate friend. The only exceptions, aside from the beloved, fatherly Johann Christian Bach and Joseph Haydn, were perhaps Hoffmeister, whose loans Mozart repaid by means of compositions (for Hoffmeister was not only a composer but also a publisher), and honest old Albrechtsberger, later Beethoven's teacher. Mozart was by no means a good colleague. One is continually astonished and often distressed to encounter in the letters—private utterances, it is true—the most merciless reports about musical contemporaries like Jommelli, Michael Haydn, Beecké, Abt Vogler, Schweitzer, Clementi, Fischer, Hässler, and many others. Praise for musicians, even for those to whom Mozart owed much—Gluck, Boccherini, Viotti, Misliveczek—is scanty; against Gluck both father and son harbored a lifelong personal distrust. In matters of art Mozart admitted no compromises; and his gift of clear observation, which was like a child's, led him to discover the ludicrous and weak sides of a man rather than his worthier qualities. And this is a trait that cannot remain concealed in life, in personal intercourse. It is the only explanation for the animosity, concealed under extreme polite-

ness, of a Salieri, or the raw spitefulness of a Leopold Anton Kozeluch—
not to mention the many mediocrities in whom immeasurable, un-
attainable spiritual superiority is itself enough to arouse implacable
hatred for the person possessing it. But Mozart was really not successful
enough to arouse such hatred. His wicked tongue was not unknown. In
1791 Joseph Haydn heard in London that Mozart had made uncom-
plimentary remarks about him. 'I forgive him,' he said. Although the
rumor was surely not true, it is distressing that Haydn could assume
that it was.

5. *Patriotism and Education*

MOZART was not interested in politics. He was born a subject of the Archbishop of Salzburg, and he died an official
in the service of the Holy Roman Emperor; but we have seen that
loyalty in general was not one of the virtues of the Mozart family, and
that, as far as Colloredo was concerned, Wolfgang entered into open
rebellion. Nor did he develop any attachment for Joseph II; and he
had much too keen an eye for all the human frailties of potentates like
the luxury-loving Elector of the Palatinate, Carl Theodor, or the Duke
of Württemberg, Carl Eugen the jailer of Rieger, Moser, and Schubart—to entertain even respect for such rulers. One need only read
how he reported the arrival of Paul I, Grand Duke of Russia (24 November 1781): 'The Grand Duke, the big noise, has arrived . . .' There
was no trace of servility in Mozart; in that respect he was a quite modern, democratic man. Gluck, on the other hand, with all his personal
pride, always felt himself to be in the service of the Habsburgs, and
Haydn never completely doffed the lackey's uniform he was obliged to
wear in the service of the Esterházys. Mozart was too widely traveled
not to be able to see beyond frontiers of rank as well as country. Thus
he became on occasion a German patriot, as is shown by the oft-quoted
letter (21 March 1785) to Anton von Klein, Professor of Poetry in
Mannheim. Klein, who furnished the libretti for the 'German Opera'
under Carl Theodor, had written a *Kaiser Rudolf von Habsburg*, and
offered it to Mozart. But Mozart hesitated to commit himself, requested
more definite information about the possibilities for performance of
such a work, and described all the uncertainties and inadequacies that
the cause of German opera was encountering in Vienna.

Were there but one good patriot in charge—things would take a
different turn. But then, perhaps, the German national theater which
is sprouting so vigorously would actually begin to flower; and of course

that would be an everlasting blot on Germany, if we Germans were seriously to begin to think as Germans, to act as Germans, to speak German and, Heaven help us, to sing in German!!

It is remarkable how similar this letter is to another one, also addressed to an inhabitant of the Rhineland—the one written on 13 July 1787, by Emperor Joseph II to Dalberg, the Coadjutor of Mainz (quoted in Vehse, II, 8, p. 235): he is 'proud to be a German . . . If our good German compatriots could give themselves at least a patriotic way of thinking, if they had neither Gallomania, nor Anglomania, nor Prusso-mania, nor Austromania, but a view of their own, not borrowed from others . . .' Presumably, Joseph II could conceive of a united Germany only under Habsburg hegemony. Mozart's patriotic exclamation fortu-nately did not prevent him from composing *Figaro*, *Don Giovanni*, and *Così fan tutte*. And, just as fortunately, he never composed a patriotic German opera like *Günther von Schwarzburg* or *Kaiser Rudolf von Habsburg*; instead, he wrote the fairy-tale *Singspiel*, *Die Entführung aus dem Serail*, with its unexpected, human dénouement in the closing scene, and *Die Zauberflöte*, on the surface a suburban machine-comedy, but in reality a piece for all mankind. One need only compare Mozart's supernational human Germanness with the Teutonism of the *Singspiel*-composers of the time—Hiller, Neefe, Benda, Wolf—and their attempts to imitate 'nature' not only in the opera but also in the song; their patriotic satire 'on the bombast and empty tinkle of many Italian arias,' * their derision of 'our Italianized German composers.' Mozart might have considered himself one of the targets of this deri-sion, for he was one of those Italianized German composers; but he was far above any cheap German chauvinism.

Mozart preferred some countries to others. He did not like French music, and his experiences in Paris set him against the French people, at least the Parisians, who seemed to him much changed (1 May 1778): '. . . the French are not nearly as polite as they were fifteen years ago; their manners now border on rudeness and they are detestably self-conceited . . .' There is not a word in his letters, or in the accounts of him in the reminiscences of those who knew him, about the French Revolution, which began while he was still alive; it did not touch him. On the other hand, from his childhood days on, he was especially fond

* J. F. Reichardt, in the *Briefe eines aufmerksamen Reisenden* (Letters of an Observant Traveler), II, 1776, p. 101.

of England and the English; and two Englishmen—Stephen Storace and Thomas Attwood—were among the pupils whom he loved and who were devoted to him. He even wrote a composition about a heroic English action—Elliot's defense of Gibraltar and the attack by 'Black Dick' (Admiral Richard Howe). The fortress had been besieged for several years by the French and Spaniards when Howe, by a surprise attack, brought fresh supplies to the garrison and thus forced the enemy to raise the siege. A Hungarian lady living in Vienna commissioned Michael Denis, ex-Jesuit, poet, and admirer of Milton and Ossian, to celebrate the heroic act of the British in an ode, and, at the end of 1782, Mozart began to set the ode to music. We shall shortly see why he did not finish it.

Occasionally he sent his father reports of curious political occurrences, for he knew that Leopold was fond of commenting sagely on world events. A few examples of this trait of Leopold's are found particularly in the last part of his correspondence with his daughter, and Leopold was very pleased when Marianne remarked wonderingly that the world had lost a great statesman in him. When Elector Max Joseph of Bavaria died suddenly on 30 December 1777, leaving no direct issue, Emperor Joseph would have snatched the prize had not Carl Theodor, next in line of succession, arrived in Munich so quickly, and had he not been backed by powerful protection—the grenadiers and cannon of the Prussian king, 'Old Fritz.' Joseph was too late, and Wolfgang sent his father (7 February 1778) the rhymed satire on the Emperor, in the last couplet of which the Imperial wolf doffs his sheep's clothing:

> Bayern! seyd ruhig! ich komme zu schützen,
> —Und das Geschützte zu besitzen.*

Wolfgang agreed wholeheartedly with Leopold on one important subject: aversion to militarism. In Ludwigsburg Leopold had occasion to remark the costly military games of Duke Carl Eugen of Württemberg, who maintained in that small land a militia of 15,000 troops—a militia supported at the price of corruption and misery throughout his domain, and one, moreover, that fled immediately when the country was invaded by the French revolutionary army. Leopold writes (11 July 1763):

Ludwigsburg is a very queer place. It is a town. Yet more than hedges and garden-trellises the soldiers form the walls of this town.

---

* Bavaria, keep calm! I come to defend,
—But what I defend, I'll have in the end.

When you spit, you spit into an officer's pocket or into a soldier's cartridge-box. In the streets you hear nothing but perpetual: 'Halt! *Quick march! Right, Left,'* etc., and you see nothing but arms, drums, and war material. At the entrance to the castle there are two grenadiers and two mounted dragoons, with grenadier caps on their heads and cuirasses on their breasts, naked swords in their hands and overhead a fine large tin roof, instead of a sentry-box. In a word it would be impossible to find greater accuracy in drilling or a finer body of men. You see only men of the grenadier type, and every sergeant-major draws forty gulden a month. You will laugh; and really it is laughable. As I stood at the window, I thought I was looking at soldiers about to take their parts in some play or opera. Just picture them to yourself. They are all exactly alike and every day their hair is done, not in ringlets but just as any petit maître does his own—in innumerable curls combed back and powdered snow-white, with the beard greased coalblack.

And Wolfgang echoes him when he reports from the Bavarian *Kaisersheim* (18 December 1778): 'What appears to me truly ridiculous is the *formidable military organization*—I should like to know of what use it is. At night I hear perpetual shouts of "Who goes there?" and I invariably reply "Guess!"' What would the Mozarts, father and son, have said of the militarized nineteenth and twentieth centuries, militarized because of the incurable stupidity of this *race méchante!* For the rest, they found themselves in complete agreement with Vittorio Alfieri, the great Italian contemporary, who visited Berlin in 1769.

When I entered the kingdom of Frederick the Great [wrote Alfieri in his autobiography], which appeared to me just one continuous corps of guards, my feeling of horror at this infamous military profession was redoubled and tripled; the sole and infamous base of arbitrary authority, which is always the fruit of having so many thousands of paid satellites . . . I came out of this universal Prussian barracks . . . abhorring it as much as it deserves.

Much more than in world events Mozart was interested in small political affairs, for these concerned people he knew. On 11 September 1782 he wrote to his father:

The Jewess Eskeles has no doubt proved a very good and useful tool for breaking up the friendship between the Emperor and the Prussian court, for the day before yesterday *she was taken to Berlin* in order that the King might have the pleasure of her company. She is indeed a sow of the first order. Moreover, she was the whole cause of Günther's misfortune, if indeed it be a misfortune to be imprisoned for two months in a beautiful room (with permission to have all his books, his pianoforte, and so forth) and to lose his former post, but to be appointed to another at a salary of 1200 gulden; for yesterday he left for Hermannstadt. Yet an experience of that kind always injures an honest man and nothing in the world can compensate him for it. I just want you to realize that he has not committed a great crime. His conduct was due entirely to étourderie, or thoughtlessness, and consequently lack of discretion, which in a Privy Councillor is certainly a serious fault. Although he never divulged anything of importance, yet his enemies, chief of whom is the former Stadtholder, Count von Herberstein, managed to play their cards so cleverly that the Emperor, who formerly had such immense confidence in Günther that he would walk up and down the room arm in arm with him for hours, now began to distrust him with an equal intensity. To make matters worse, who should appear on the scene but that sow Eskeles (a former mistress of Günther's), who accused him in the most violent terms. But when the matter was investigated, these gentlemen cut a very poor figure. However, the affair had already caused terrific commotion; and great people never like to admit that they have been in the wrong. Hence the fate of poor Günther, whom I pity from my heart, as he was a very good friend of mine and, if things had remained as they were, might have rendered me good service with the Emperor. You can imagine what a shock and how unexpected it was to me and how very much upset I was; for Stephanie, Adamberger, and I had supper with him one evening and on the morrow he was arrested.

Mozart was quite wrong (as G. Gugitz has shown in the *Mozarteums-Mitteilungen* III, 1921, pp. 41-9) in his apportioning of guilt and innocence in this scandal, which stirred up so much dust that some of it blew as far as Salzburg. Johann Valentin Günther, a Freemason and ten years older than Mozart, had been an officer but later became, as private secretary, the trusted favorite of the Emperor, although, or perhaps because, he was a man of limited abilities who agreed with everything his patron said. He maintained a liaison with Eleonore Eskeles, the divorced wife of a man named Fliess, and daughter of a rabbi. She was accused, quite unjustifiedly and with a complete lack of proof, of having coaxed state secrets from Günther and of having turned them over to two Prussian spies. Günther was overthrown, but fell into a sinecure—the position of functionary at the War Office at Hermannstadt in Siebenbürgen, where he was welcomed with open arms by the Freemasons of the place. Joseph vented all his rage on the Jewess, who, despite her proved innocence, was exiled from the country. After Joseph's death, Leopold II rehabilitated her, with a great to-do, but she did not choose to return to Vienna until 1802; she died there highly esteemed in 1812, and was honored by an obituary in the form of a letter—by Goethe. Mozart himself was anything but an enemy of the Jews, nor had he any reason to be one. He chose, though somewhat unwillingly, his Jewish landlord, Baron Raimund Wetzlar von Planken-stern, one of his patrons and supporters, as godfather to his first son, Raimund Leopold; and the names of many Jewish families appear on the very informative list of subscribers to his concerts that he sent to his father on 20 March 1784. It is not known whether the Viennese usurers into whose hands he fell during the last years of his life were Jewish or not.

It has sometimes been said that Mozart underwent his great cultural experiences only in the field of music. Like so many other general state-ments about him, this one, too, is only partly true. It is true that every-thing he heard in music was either rejected or so thoroughly assimilated that it became a part of him. His growth as a creator was like that of a rare and precious plant, whose innermost secret remains a mystery, but which is nourished by sun and rain and hindered by unfavorable weather. We know many of the sunny and rainy days that influenced the growth of Mozart's music. This growth is shown in his work as a whole, which is not capricious but logical and continuous, and so crystal-clear and unified, when one knows all the circumstances, that it seems to lead its own life independently of its creator. From this point of view, one could say that Mozart the man was only the earthly vessel of his art; indeed that the man was sacrificed to the musician. But every great artist obsessed with his art is sacrificed, as a person, to that art.

What Mozart seemed like to his contemporaries, or at least to many of them, is very crassly expressed by Caroline Pichler, daughter of the Viennese Privy Councilor Franz von Greiner, at whose house Mozart had quartets performed in his last years. She is deeply convinced of the 'lack of education' of great musicians in general and of Mozart, Schubert, and Haydn in particular; to her, only Weber and Cherubini are exceptions. She represents the point of view of the nineteenth century when she writes in her Memoirs, printed in 1844:

Mozart and Haydn, whom I knew well, were men who showed, in their personal associations with others, no other outstanding spiritual force and practically no sort of learning or higher culture. An everyday turn of mind, insipid jokes, and, as regards the former composer, a thoughtless way of life, were all they displayed in their associations.

And she is being very gracious when she adds: 'And yet what depths, what worlds of fantasy, harmony, melody, and emotion lay concealed behind these unprepossessing exteriors!'

But Mozart was much more than a mere professional musician. Just as he saw through people, despite the fact that he was continually taken in by them, so his deep intuition pierced the cultural tendencies of his time, without the help of a single lecture on esthetics. Although he had no eye for landscape, or for architecture, sculpture, or painting, he had as a dramatist the finest sense for poetry, both lyric and dramatic. He must have read a great deal—the only point on which he and Beethoven resembled each other. His library contained books on travel, history, and philosophy; poetical works such as those of Metastasio and Salomon Gessner; Molière's comedies, which he had received as a gift from Fridolin Weber; Wieland's *Oberon*; and the lyrics of Gellert and Weisse. Whether he actually read all this, nobody knows; but we do know that he read Metastasio and Gellert. He also knew Fénélon's *Télémaque* and Tasso's *Aminta*; he found amusement in the tales of *The Thousand and One Nights*; and above all he knew a large part of the boundless Italian libretto literature, having followed it closely and with a highly critical eye from his twentieth year onwards. On 7 May 1783, he writes: 'I have looked through at least a hundred libretti and more, but I have hardly found a single one with which I am satisfied . . .' He was looking for something new, something not just half-way usable but completely adapted to his dramatic requirements, and he finally settled upon Figaro. Only when one considers this fact does one fully realize what the meeting with Lorenzo da Ponte meant to him. He himself commented prophetically on the importance of this meeting in a letter to his father, dated 13 October 1781, in which he summed up his operatic esthetics:

Why do Italian comic operas please everywhere—in spite of their miserable libretti—even in Paris, where I myself witnessed their success? Just because in them the music reigns supreme, and when one listens to it all else is forgotten. Why, an opera is sure of success when the plot is well worked out, the words written solely for the music and not shoved in here and there to suit some miserable rhyme (which, God knows, never enhances the value of any theatrical performance, be it what it may, but rather detracts from it)—I mean, words or even entire verses which ruin the composer's whole idea. Verses are indeed the most indispensable element for music—but rhymes—solely for the sake of rhyming—the most detrimental. These high and mighty people who set to work in this pedantic fashion will always come to grief, both they and their music. The best thing of all is when a good composer, who understands the stage and is talented enough to make sound suggestions, meets an able poet, that true phoenix; in that case no fears need be entertained as to the applause even of the ignorant.

This is just the opposite of Wagner's principle of opera and to some extent of Gluck's also. Mozart's letter testifies to the complete independence of his thought and the sureness of his esthetic feeling, for he had certainly read and considered the dedication of Calzabigi and Gluck in the score of *Alceste*.

He showed the same independence in regard to the new currents that heralded the approach of the nineteenth century, the period of Romanticism whose full flowering he might well have lived to witness. Anything that belonged simply to change or transition did not concern him. He was completely a child of the eighteenth century, perhaps, but also of the twentieth; which is another way of saying that he belonged to the eternity of art, and was in no sense a 'forerunner.' Beethoven found a great deal in Haydn that he could take as a point of departure, but very little in Mozart. How should one try to continue Mozart's work? It was possible to strive for perfection on another level, and perhaps even to achieve it; but Mozart's perfection could not be surpassed on its own level. With Haydn, on the other hand, one could in many respects compete on his own terms. Now, Mozart lived in the middle of the period of *Sturm und Drang*, the age of 'sensibility,' the age of Jean-Jacques Rousseau. Mozart never mentions Rousseau, although he composed a *Singspiel* on Rousseau's *Devin du Village*, and he must have heard Rousseau's name often enough in Paris. Presumably he would have had no use for the philosopher and musical amateur of Geneva, whose call 'Back to Nature' would have meant very little to him. Mozart was on the side of Voltaire, in spite of the ill-tempered words he pronounced upon the sage of Ferney as an obituary. Voltaire, too, belongs to the eighteenth century and to eternity; and he has the same power of dry and pitiless observation, the same irony, the same fierce satire, and the same profound fatalism. Between *Candide* and the G minor Symphony there is a real kinship.

Sturm und Drang is a far too superficial and a far too formless movement for an artist like Mozart. To him 'sensibility' was a passing fashion, and he made fun of it. It has often been said that as a musician he was a disciple of Philipp Emanuel Bach, that master of sensibility *par excellence*. In the second part of this book we shall have to inquire whether and to what extent this assertion is justified. Gluck set odes of Klopstock to music, and wanted to write music for that work of Teutonic patriotism *Hermanns Schlacht*. Mozart parodied a famous ode of Klopstock (*Edone*) in one of the 'Bäsle' letters, the same ode later set to music by Zumsteeg. With his exuberant sense of humor, he set his finger at once on the comic element in Klopstock's sentimental exaggeration. For the poem represents a North-German sentimentality that is repellent to a South German (although this fact did not prevent Klopstock from being enthusiastically imitated in Vienna). At the end of 1782, Mozart had the commission we have mentioned, to set to music a poem in the style of Klopstock or Ossian: the Ode on Gibraltar by the former Jesuit Denis, or, as he called himself, 'Sined, the Bard.' But Mozart could not bring himself to finish it (letter of 28 December 1782):

. . . I am engaged in a very difficult task, the music for a bard's song by Denis about Gibraltar. But this is a secret, for it is a Hungarian lady who wishes to pay this compliment to Denis. The ode is sublime, beautiful, anything you like, but too exaggerated and pompous for my fastidious ears. But what is to be done? The golden mean of truth in all things is no longer either known or appreciated. In order to win applause one must write stuff which is so inane that a fiacre could sing it, or so unintelligible that it pleases precisely because no sensible man can understand it . . .

Mozart added that he would like to write a short introduction to music, with musical examples, to make clear his esthetic ideal: the golden mean, avoiding both the trivial and the precious. His opinions sound like those of an old man, singing the praises of bygone days. But they are the views of a musician of eternity.

To obtain a still clearer view of Mozart's South-German naturalness and his inability to be 'sensitive' in the sense of the second half of the eighteenth century, we need only contrast him with his contemporaries, such as Johann Friedrich Reichardt, from the Prussian town of Königsberg, who was hardly four years older than Mozart. Reichardt was the prototype of the Berlin intellectual who can approach art only on the side of *raisonnement*. He was a zealous partisan of the art of Gluck, apparently so reasonable and rationalistic, and he was highly critical of Haydn and Mozart, both of whom he outlived. The evil corollary of intellectualism is always 'sensibility.' Reichardt felt a literary urge very early in life and published at the age of twenty-four his *Briefe eines aufmerksamen Reisenden*, a mixture of superficial reasoning and critical impudence. In Berlin he heard a performance of Handel's *Judas Maccabaeus*. Of the chorus:

> For Sion lamentation make
> With words that weep, and tears that speak,

he writes: 'Every sensitive listener must draw a heavy sigh in listening, and even now tears obstruct my writing . . .' Such exaggeration—assuming that it was sincere and not mere play-acting—would have made Mozart laugh. This was the period of the 'original genius' in German poetry, and in German music, too, there were many who would have been delighted to play the role of 'original genius,' if only music had been as easy a medium to handle as words. Mozart never desired to be 'original'—unique as his music often is. We shall have more to say on this point when we compare him with the 'revolutionary' Haydn. At the same time, the mere rules of convention meant nothing to him. On one occasion, in a letter to his father dated 13 October 1781, he speaks of the inability of librettists to get away from their conventional routine: 'Poets almost remind me of the trumpeters with their professional tricks.' (Trumpeters in Mozart's time were still united in a guild, and they jealously preserved the ancient guild customs.) 'If we composers were always to stick so faithfully to our rules (which were very good at a time when no one knew better), we should be concocting music as unpalatable as their libretti.' Mozart was in fact a powerful innovator, and his contemporaries recognized him as such. But he never set out to be original.

Every sort of exaggeration and extravagance as well as of bungling, not only in music but in other fields as well, aroused his mockery. On 14 August 1773, he apostrophizes his sister:

I hope, my queen, that you are enjoying the highest degree of health and that now and then or rather, sometimes, or, better still, occasionally, or, even better still, *qualche volta*, as the Italians say, you will sacrifice for my benefit some of your important and intimate thoughts, which ever proceed from that very fine and clear reasoning power, which in addition to your beauty, and although from a woman, and particularly from one of such tender years, almost nothing of the kind is ever expected, you possess, O queen, so abundantly as to put men and even greybeards to shame. There now, you have a well-turned sentence. Farewell.

Wolfgang Mozart

He wrote this highfalutin nonsense from Vienna, where he was passing the summer, and where he must have seen one of the bombastic and swollen pieces that helped to fill up the repertory at the time; I am afraid, indeed, it may have been Gebler's *König Thamos*, for which he was furnishing the music. Gebler was a patron of his, but even for patrons he had no respect when they sponsored tasteless nonsense.

For many people, Mozart has been and still remains the true musical representative of the Rococo, of the anacreontic grace of the *ancien régime*—presumably because as a child he wore pig-tails and the jewelled dagger that was the emblem of gallantry. But this conception fits neither Mozart's nature nor his external appearance, as may be seen merely by looking at the four portraits that are relatively the most faithful: the one in the Salzburg family picture, the Bologna portrait, Lange's sketch in oils, and the pencilled profile by Doris Stock. Mozart's charm and grace are not anacreontic, and they are not merely representative of the eighteenth century.

The poet Wieland played a major role in the literary culture of the Mozart household. The Mozarts knew his *Abderiten* and his *Oberon*, and we have already read the word-portrait of the poet which Mozart sent his father in a letter, knowing how much it would interest him. Many things in Wieland—such as the *Musarion*, for example—are masterpieces of charm and playful humor; but his 'philosophy of free spirits,' his play upon Grecian gaiety, and his prurient half-revelation of feminine charms have nothing at all to do with Mozart's sturdy strength, his seriousness, and his transcendent power and perfection. Listen to Wieland's conception of love:

Ich liebe dich mit diesem sanften Triebe
Der, Zephyrn gleich, das Herz in leichte Wellen setzt,
Nie Stürm' erregt, nie peinigt, stets ergetzt:
Wie ich die Grazien, wie ich die Musen liebe,
So lieb' ich dich.
　　　　　　　　　　—*Musarion*, Book iii *

Wieland has no other conception of love. Now compare this with
Mozart's conception of Constanze, Zerlina, Pamina, not to mention
figures like Donna Anna or Donna Elvira, or declarations of love such
as that in Don Giovanni's Drunken Aria or Tamino's *Dies Bildnis*.
Mozart is never just lovable—never 'cute.' He belongs to the eighteenth
century to this extent: that he still looked upon art as an integral part
of life, not yet subject to the questionings brought about by Romanticism or civilized barbarism. But he is also timeless.

In a letter of Mozart's to his father, from Munich, dated 29 November 1780—the period of the conception and preparation of *Idomeneo*—
there is a strange remark in criticism of *Hamlet*. In *Idomeneo* the solution of the conflict—if one can speak of a conflict in an opera seria—is
brought about by the solemn tones of a mighty and divine voice sounding from the depths. This effect must not last too long, Mozart feels:

Tell me, don't you think that the speech of the subterranean voice is
too long? Consider it carefully. Picture to yourself the theater, and
remember that the voice must be terrifying—must penetrate—that the
audience must believe that it really exists. Well, how can this effect be
produced if the speech is too long, for in this case the listeners will
become more and more convinced that it means nothing. If the speech
of the Ghost in Hamlet were not so long, it would be far more effective . . .

Mozart saw *Hamlet*, and perhaps *Macbeth*, too, and it is not improbable that in the last weeks of his life he may have toyed with the idea
of setting an adaptation of Shakespeare's *Tempest* to music. Salzburg
in the late 'seventies was a theater town. During the years of Mozart's
grand tour, Salzburg was host to the troupe of the impresario Nössel—
a troupe that Leopold considered 'mediocre,' but that numbered in its

---

* I love thee with that soft and gentle pleasure
　That blows upon the heart as zephyrs on the waves,
　And, without storm or cloud, the spirit sweetly laves.
　As I the Graces, as I the Muses treasure,
　So do I love thee.

ranks Franz Xaver and Caroline (Reiner) Heigel, who were later to achieve great fame in Munich. In the season of 1779 to 1780 there was a visit from the Böhm troupe; but in September 1780 Emanuel Schikaneder's company arrived and thus began the acquaintance that was to be renewed in Vienna and was to lead to collaboration in *Die Zauberflöte*. From the middle of September until the beginning of November, Mozart and his father and sister missed none of Schikaneder's offerings, which were presented four times a week. The entrance to the theater was just across the Hannibal-Platz. The list of the pieces presented is preserved: it consists mostly of worthless things, including a few *Singspiele*, monodramas, and occasional ballets. But on 26 September, Mozart saw Lessing's *Emilia Galotti* and Anton Leisewitz's *Julius von Tarent*, on 11 October, Beaumarchais' *Barbier de Seville*, and on 13 October, *Hamlet, Prinz von Dänemark*, in the adaptation of F. W. L. Schröder. Among the ballets, we must attribute a certain importance to the one given on 8 October, *Die belebten Statuen* (The Animated Statues), since it treated the same subject matter as *Don Giovanni*. The performance of these pieces was anything but 'classic' in style. Schikaneder was already fond of effect, picturesque costumes, and glitter in general, and the favor of the inhabitants of the Salzburg region would surely not have been won by subtlety or refinement. But Mozart took it all in with passionate interest and in Munich he even reread one of the plays, a German adaptation of Carlo Gozzi's *Le due notti affannose*, and wrote an interpolation for it (now lost). 'The comedy . . . is charming,' he writes on 13 December 1780; and indeed the play does have, for its time, a vein of strong and pure passion, even in the wretched German version.

We know that when Mozart first lived in Vienna he was an enthusiastic theater-goer, although we have almost no account of his impressions. We do not know just what he saw, but it is clear that his literary interest was concentrated on the drama, for he was a born man of the theater. Thus in a deeper sense it makes no difference exactly what dramas he knew, since a genius of such calibre gains both stimulus and experience even from mediocre or poor plays. In the Vienna of this period, moreover, the quality of the works produced was not of the greatest importance, since attention was focussed upon the actors. Nor is it of much consequence that Mozart's knowledge of the drama must have had considerable gaps—he was not an 'educated' man like Schumann and Wagner, who knew Shakespeare, Schiller, and Goethe. In another domain, however, his knowledge was comprehensive and quite without gaps: the domain of the opera in all its species from the *opera seria* and the *opera buffa* to the German *Singspiel*, the French *opéra-comique*, the *festa teatrale*, the *serenata teatrale*, the pantomime, and the ballet. Only the combination of spoken drama and descriptive instrumental music—the monodrama or duodrama—was new to him when he visited Mannheim, and he was at first quite *surpreniert* by its effect. During twenty-five of his thirty-six years he had to do with theater music. We should have to say that opera in all its forms represented the culmination of his life's work, and that he was an opera creator above all—if he had not reached an equal peak of achievement in the field of instrumental music. But to these questions we shall have plentiful occasion to return.

II. THE MUSICIAN

6. Universality

MOZART once wrote to his father (7 February 1778): 'As you know, I can more or less adopt or imitate any kind and any style of composition.' He meant the Italian, the French, and the German also. And he was right, but this accounts not for the universality we have in mind here but only for his supernationality: his strange position in musical history as neither an 'Italian' nor a 'German' composer, and least of all a 'French' one, but as just Mozart, who stands far above all national boundaries and limitations. It was not Italian or German music that determined his musical character—he is Italian or German only in externals; it was he who determined the character of Italian or German music.

His universality becomes clear when one asks oneself whether he is greater as a vocal composer or as an instrumental composer, whether *Le Nozze di Figaro* or *Don Giovanni* ranks higher or lower than the C major Symphony, or the C minor Piano Concerto, or the C major Quintet. It would be idle to rack one's brains over this question; perfections in various fields do not lend themselves to comparison. In respect to universality Mozart may be compared only with other great masters; and in our comparisons we shall limit ourselves to the eighteenth and nineteenth centuries. Nearest him, perhaps, is Handel, the master of the cantata, the opera, the oratorio, the concerto grosso, the sonata—but we are stopped short already. Did not all this flow from one unified, mighty source, Italian vocalism, the *bel canto* of the monumental aria? Is Handel, as heir to the forms of the sixteenth and seventeenth centuries—the fugue, the *ricercar*—equal to his contemporary, Johann Sebastian Bach? And was Bach universal? To be sure, he left no corner uncultivated in the fields of instrumental and vocal music, either sacred or secular, not even the opera, if we may regard his secular cantatas as operas. Actually, however, all this, too, grows from one root—instrumental music; more specifically, even, from the polyphony of the organ, which determines even Bach's vocal themes. One could say, very mistakenly and yet justifiably, that Bach was not a vocal composer at all, that even his recitative, vivid and plastic as it is, has fixed, instrumentally determined form.

As for Gluck, his one-sidedness and lack of universality are quite indisputable. True, he wrote some instrumental pieces and a handful of songs, but he was an opera composer first and always, Italian for the first half of his life, up to *Paride ed Elena*, and French for the second half, from *Iphigénie en Aulide* on. It has been said, not entirely without justification, that it was actually because of his one-sidedness that Gluck attained greatness, that he became the reformer of the *opera seria*. The abundance of musical invention that pours forth in all forms was denied him; his pathos forced him into the field of musical drama, of opera; and a great, power-seeking, logical brain like his made virtues even of his limitations. The statement that Haydn and Beethoven were one-sided, that they were essentially instrumental composers, will be more vehemently contested. What, the master of *The Creation*, the composer of *Fidelio* and the *Missa solemnis* not vocal composers? And yet it cannot be denied: both Haydn and Beethoven are cramped by the word, they speak most freely in the instrumental fields—Haydn in that of the quartet and the orchestra, Beethoven in that of the piano also. Neither Haydn nor Beethoven is a master of the song, although both composed songs. And this would bring us to Schubert, the composer of the 'Unfinished' and the D minor Quartet, and of hundreds of perfect songs, the only one who could be compared to Mozart, if it were not that, although he wrote operas too, the dramatic, the scenic, the feeling for the stage, were denied him.

The heyday of one-sidedness begins in the nineteenth century. Weber composed church music, operas, and instrumental music; but his instrumental works, of which only those for the piano still live to some extent, are based on the formula of 'brilliance,' and of his operas only *Freischütz* has national validity. Mendelssohn and Schumann lack the dramatic vein; Wagner, again an 'international' master, becomes weak and helpless when he lacks the stimulation of the scenic word, of the mental picture of the stage. Verdi achieved international importance as an opera composer, since Italian opera is indeed an international export, and particularly since, thanks to his humanity, he grew far above the national; but to him was denied the symphonic, upon which depend almost all Wagnerian effects.

When one considers the somnambulistic surefootedness and grace
with which Mozart masters the vocal and the instrumental, mass and
opera, quartet and concerto, one's admiration grows immeasurably at
the phenomenon of his uniqueness as a universal musician. It grows
still more, if one considers the historical and national problems implicit
in his situation. To the historical problems we must devote a special
chapter. They arise from the fact that Mozart was born into a *galant*
era of music, an era in which expression by means of polyphony was
no longer natural and fitting. Only as a result of a serious crisis was he
able to overcome this difficulty also. The national problems become
apparent if one considers that, as a German musician, he had to compose Italian opera, and that he was too great or too individual to become entirely an Italian composer—or rather, to remain one. This was
not a problem for other German musicians—Hasse, and Graun, and
many others; they belong entirely to the history of Italian opera.
Is it not a significant indication of the uncomplicated and unprob-
lematic character of Italian opera between 1720 or 1725 and 1775,
that in Italy there is practically no literature of an esthetic nature on
the question of national opera? There is, to be sure, much writing on
the opera as a form, in its relation to the drama, above all to the ancient drama. By contrast, the chain of such literature is hardly ever
broken in France, where the opera was always menaced by Italy; and
in Germany the theorists concerned themselves not only with the opera
but with musical style in general. Mozart had no influence at all on the
Italian opera *buffa*, although the greatest masterpieces of the form are
his; and it would be very interesting to know what musicians like
Paisiello, Sarti, Cimarosa said or thought about *Figaro* or *Don Giovanni*.

Of Paisiello we know at least what he thought about the difference
between Italian and German music in general. Questioned about this
by a pupil, Giacomo Gotifredo Ferrari of Rovcredo, he replied:

I'll tell you. If two masters studied in the same school, there would
be no difference [in style] at all, would there? But the Italians generally
begin without finishing, and the Germans finish before they begin: I
do not know whether I express myself clearly. In Italy we attach value
only to melody; whether by nature, or whether because of the harmonious effects our voices and our manner of singing produce in us; and we
make use of modulations only to strengthen the expression of the word.
In Germany, however, whether for other reasons or because the German

musicians feel themselves inferior to us in singing, they attach little value to melody and employ it only very sparingly; thus they are obliged to avail themselves of a studied harmony, in order thereby to make up for the lack of melody and of the magic of a beautiful voice.*

Paisiello admits a few exceptions: on the German side, Hasse, Handel, and Gluck (!), on the Italian side, Padre Martini, Durante, and Valotti. But, aside from the fact that this conversation took place on 21 November 1784, before *Figaro* and *Don Giovanni* were written, how superficial and primitive is this instruction! Neither the problem of the 'national in music' nor the problem of Mozart can be handled with intellectual tools of this sort. Rossini did express the greatest admiration at least for *Don Giovanni*, but without allowing himself to be influenced in the slightest degree by the 'transalpine' master.

Another threat to Mozart's universality has been indicated, with sensitive understanding, by Wyzewa and Saint-Foix—Mozart's predominantly instrumental education by his father. How did Mozart elude this danger? In a way, it is to be wondered at, that Mozart became a great vocal composer also. He avoided the threat more successfully and completely than Beethoven, who never quite escaped it. Mozart and Beethoven were both brought up as pianists—at least the piano was their instrument, which influenced them, even as composers. But the mind of Mozart the creator soon functioned quite independently of the keyboard, and the vocal principle became for him a law, first for vocal music, then for instrumental music also.

Problems similar to those in the field of the opera arose for Mozart as an instrumental composer. For Joseph Haydn the situation was much simpler. It was easy for Haydn, indeed he was positively forced, in his isolation, to become 'original.' Italian, French, Viennese, Czech influences touched Haydn too, but from a distance; he worked in the silence of Weinzierl, Lukavec, Eisenstadt; he did not make his first long journey until he was almost sixty and had already dictated his

---

* 'Ti dirò. Se i due professori avessero studiato nello stesso modo, non vi sarebbe differenza alcuna: capisci? Ma gl'italiani incominciano generalmente senza finire, e i tedeschi finiscon prima d'incominciare: non sò se mi spiego. In Italia non facciam caso che della melodia; sia per natura, o per gli effetti armoniosi che le voci e la maniera di cantare ci producono; nè usiam modulazioni che per rinforzare l'espressione della parola. In Germania, poi, sia per altre ragioni o perchè i tedeschi si veggono inferiori a noi pel canto, essi non si curan della melodia, ne l'usan che pochissimo; ond'è che sono obbligati di servirsi di un'armonia ricercata, per supplire in tal guisa alla mancanza e alla bellezza magica della voce.'

personal style to the whole musical world. Mozart, taken at the age of seven or eight upon his first journey, turned out into the world, was subjected to every musical influence. It is astonishing enough that he did not succumb, that he did not lose his talent at sixteen, as is the rule with child prodigies; that his personality, his powers of resistance were strong enough to enable him to assimilate only what truly suited him. He could easily have become an Abbé Vogler, or, to name a pupil of Abbé Vogler, a Meyerbeer: an international monster who with great talent brings into the world the style-monstrosity of 'grand opera.' But he became Mozart.

7. *Mozart and His Contemporaries*

(Imitation and Affinity)

*I*T HAS BEEN SAID that the musical, the spiritual, development of Mozart ran its course quite independently of his personal fate, in a closed and inaccessible sphere, above all everyday experience. This is quite true; it is, in fact, the rule with the great masters. Art, and especially music, is not a reflection of the biographical, but follows its own law. The two tombs of the Medici in San Lorenzo at Florence have nothing to do with the Republic's loss of freedom, despite their creator's famous verses on the 'Night'—as sculpture they are not affected by any poetical interpretation; such an interpretation would render them neither more nor less perfect; but they have, of course, a great deal to do with the mighty soul of their creator, turbulent with dark and powerful emotions. It is actually fortunate, in an artistic sense, that we know so little about the life of Johann Sebastian Bach— that the composition of the C minor Passacaglia or the Chaconne, of the B minor aria for alto from the St. Matthew Passion, of the three-part Sinfonia in F minor, and so on, cannot in any way be connected with a biographical date. Enough mischief has been created already with the little we do know—for example, with the melodramatic as well as unmusical association of Bach's last organ-chorale, Vor *deinen Thron tret' ich hiemit* (in G major), with the *Kunst der Fuge* (in D minor). So far as musical comprehension is concerned, it has been a misfortune that we know so many details of Beethoven's career, that documents like the 'Heiligenstadt Testament,' or the knowledge of his deafness and of his sufferings because of a spoilt nephew, have falsified or at least beclouded the image of his music. Beethoven's work too is shaped and completed in a region that has indeed much to do with suffering and happiness, with a great man's capacity for suffering and happiness, but has no relation to everyday events. With Mozart especially the relation between life and art-work is quite obscure and mysterious. There is therefore no special merit in the fact that no writer has yet tried to connect the composition of the D minor String Quartet (K. 421) with Constanze's giving birth to her first son, which took place while the quartet was being written down—although (I speak ironically) the minor mode might easily have been seized upon as a point of contact. And the fact that Mozart composed the G minor Symphony in the summer of 1788, when he was making the most touching appeals to his friend Puchberg for help, is also, fortunately or unfortunately, not a plausible excuse for claiming 'reciprocity between art and life'—for, if matters indeed went very badly for Mozart before 25 July, when he finished this symphony, did they go very well before 26 June and 10 August, when the E-flat major and C major Symphonies were completed? Mozart was again in a desperately bad situation in the last months of 1789, and yet it was at this time that he composed *Così fan tutte*, a work of purest happiness and creative bliss.

The 'splendid isolation' of Mozartean music from the standpoint of biographical interpretation caused this music to be explained, in a period of romantic afflation, as academic in form, cold, empty, frivolous, superficial. Its depth, however, is not 'poetic' but musical and personal. This is not contradicted in the least by the fact that Mozart's work, with very few exceptions, is occasional work, that it is music written to order, that it still belongs entirely to that era in which operas, symphonies, chamber music, were not composed out of 'inner impulse,' that is, at random. Mozart wrote his early Italian operas for Milan, his *Idomeneo* for Munich, because he received the *scritture*, the commissions to write these operas. That *La Finta semplice* was not performed in Vienna was because of a particular mischance; and it is rare and puzzling when a work clearly ordered for a specific occasion does not seem to have attained performance, like the oratorio *La Betulia liberata*. Mozart refused, politely but firmly, to compose the *Rudolf von Habsburg* of the Court Councilor Klein before a performance was assured; and he composed no opera between 1787 and 1789—to the misfortune of posterity—because none was ordered from him: he was out of fashion. Opera was always composed for a special occasion and for particular singers; the choice of singers influenced the vocal style and other characteristics as well. Never did Mozart write 'for eternity,' and it is precisely for that reason that much of what he wrote is for eternity.

This is true not only of his operatic and church music but also of the instrumental works. Only the few that were published were an appeal to the greater public of music-lovers—but what could one publish in the eighteenth century? Sonatas for clavier with accompanying violin (Opp. I, II, III, IV of the child-prodigy; then the new Op. I of 1777-8, and the Sonata in A); sonatas, rondos, and variations for the clavier; string quartets (the last ten); clavier trios, clavier quartets, a few songs and dances—in all no more than 18 opus numbers. Only very few of Mozart's symphonies and piano concertos were printed during his lifetime, and those only in parts, none, with the possible exception of K. 318, in score. 'Publication' meant dissemination in manuscript copies. Mozart *must* write a great deal of all sorts of music to satisfy daily demands. And although he must proceed from principal work to secondary work, from secondary work again to principal work, the unity of his product as a whole, its logic, its consistency, its progress, continue from modest beginning to magnificent end.

Mozart began as a child-prodigy, presented to the world not merely as a virtuoso on the clavier (and as a violinist), but also as an improviser and precocious composer; child-prodigies must always be abreast of the times. And Mozart complied with this demand by means of his astonishing capacity for imitation, assimilation, and elaboration of whatever suited him. His education came through his travels, his visits to Munich and Vienna, his long stay in Paris and London—two places with an equal hankering for the latest novelties. He heard there such a quantity of music and received such a quantity of changing impressions that one continues to marvel equally at his receptivity and at his powers of resistance—his talent for appropriating what was congenial and rejecting whatever was opposed to his nature. He found congenial material in lesser contemporaries, uncongenial material in greater contemporaries, and vice versa. Many impressions left him indifferent.

The most important contemporary for him was at first his father, Leopold Mozart. And the law of attraction and repulsion showed itself at once in connection with this composer. All the paternal authority cannot cause Wolfgang to take more out of Leopold's music than he can use. And here, to be sure, the fact that Leopold belongs to a quite different generation is of importance also. He had grown up in the era of *basso continuo*, and was still stuck fast in the declining thoroughbass period, which the son parodied so deliciously in his song, *Die Alte*. Leopold's Opus I, the sonatas for two violins and figured bass of 1740, engraved by himself, still treats the bass entirely in the old way as a mere harmonic support, as the lackey of the composition. These sonatas are shallow, spent, the last stragglers of the epoch of Legrenzi and Corelli. Ten years later Leopold writes a trio in the most modern style, a trio for clavier, violin, and violoncello, in which the clavier is the leading instrument and the two strings have so little to say that they could be omitted without great harm to the composition. Leopold tries painfully to become a modern, *galant* composer; even more than in the clavier trio, this endeavor is shown in the three clavier sonatas that the Nuremberg publisher J. Ulrich Haffner—judging from his Christian name, perhaps a fellow countryman of Leopold's—printed in 1762 and 1763. They are typically lacking in *chic*—behind them hides a provincial schoolmaster trying to appear fashionable. One would never imagine that five years previously a master of the clavier style had died, one Domenico Scarlatti! But the transition in style from 1740 to 1760, in which neither Scarlatti nor Bach and Handel had been obliged to participate, had probably been a painful experience for Leopold. If we try to listen to these sonatas of Leopold's with the ears of the young Wolfgang, a few similarities in the works of both remain in our memory: successions of measures in the high register of the instrument; the minuet episode interpolated in the finale of a sonata, that in F major; cadences like the following (Andante of the B-flat major Sonata):

Ex. 1   LEOPOLD MOZART

Little Mozart heard such things not only in his father's work; they belong to the *galant* idiom of the period. But it was his father's work in which he first encountered them and in which they surely impressed him most. For the rest, however, the dispositions of father and son were as different musically as personally. The law of musical heredity fails so strikingly in this case that Mother Mozart has been made responsible for the contrast; but Mother Mozart might as well have been accused of adultery with the god Apollo. For Leopold is an Augsburg or Salzburg composer, half rationalist, half 'popular,' while Wolfgang is never rationalistic and never popular, but godlike, regal, and aristocratic. The Salzburg quality in Leopold does not consist merely in the fact that he wrote pieces for the *Hornwerk* (a mechanical organ), known to every visitor, on the Veste Hohensalzburg—pieces 'of which one is played daily . . . morning and evening.' The Salzburg character and the Augsburg are closely related, and both cities probably enjoyed the coarse naturalistic or realistic works by which Leopold made himself best known in his time: the *Sleigh Ride*, the *Peasant Wedding*, the *Hunt*, the *Sinfonia burlesca*, the *Divertimento militare*. These pieces have their Augsburg precursors in the compositions previously mentioned, published anonymously under the title *Augsburger Tafelconfect*, between 1733 and 1746, probably by a Frankish monk, Peter Valentin Rathgeber—compositions full of Bavarian-Swabian coarseness and popular humor, songs, duets, trios and quartets with accompaniment; especially rude quodlibets, a *Bettel-Zech* (Beggars' Drinking Bout), a vulgar *Juden-Leich* (Jewish Funeral), scenes of tippling and gorging, etc. This was the realism that fascinated Leopold; and anyone who knows his thoroughly respectable letters would never conclude from them that the same man, as composer, enjoyed such trivialities.

How different Wolfgang! A reminiscence of the Augsburg traits in Rathgeber and Leopold is found only in the early work written for entertainment at the Court of The Hague or Donaueschingen—the *Galimathias musicum*. Leopold yields completely to the 'popular'; for Wolfgang the Salzburg character in particular and the popular in general is always an *object*, now of fun-making, now also of greater seriousness. He never allows it to become a part of his invention, as Haydn does; he is never 'folky.' There is always a wide cleft here, a dualism: on one side the aristocratic Wolfgang Amadeus; on the other, the rustic child or country maid, to whom the cavalier condescends, as the knight to the shepherdess in the times of knightly love-poetry. Mozart has been called an indoor composer, in contrast to Haydn, the hunter and fisherman and musical child of nature; he is really an aristocrat, who knows the people well, but does not mingle with them. Mozart expressed his attitude towards the 'popular' in a description of the first three Vienna piano concertos (28 December 1782):

These concertos are a happy medium between what is too easy and too difficult; they are very brilliant, pleasing to the ear, and natural, without being vapid. There are passages here and there from which connoisseurs alone can derive satisfaction; but these passages are written in such a way that the less learned cannot fail to be pleased, though without knowing why . . .

Leopold undoubtedly felt that to be regarded in earnest as a 'serious' composer, he lacked the most essential quality: the impulse, the divine spark. He knew that at best he could serve as a model only in slight degree; so he sought elsewhere for models. And he did this in a pedagogical way: in 1762 he put together for Wolfgang an album containing pieces that he had arranged in 25 suites, many quite short, consisting only of an aria and *musette*, others longer, like the fourteenth, for example: *Aria—March—Menuet—Gigue—Polonaise de Mons. Hasse*. Each suite begins with an aria, to which Leopold always adds an edifying or moral text, usually from the *Neue Sammlung geistlicher Lieder* (New Collection of Sacred Songs) of Count Heinrich Ernst zu Stolberg-Wernigerode. The North-German character of this collection (in which the composers named for the instrumental works are Telemann and Philipp Emanuel Bach of Hamburg, Hasse of Dresden, Gottfried Kirchhoff of Halle, Balthasar Schmidt of Nuremberg; the songs are all by Graefe and Hurlebusch of Brunswick) has occasioned surprise, as has the 'unmodernity' of the little pieces, many of which were almost thirty years old. But new pieces in the latest fashion, with *galant* and 'slovenly' basses, were to be met with aplenty in Salzburg and in the Mozart house; there was no need to collect them; and there is something rather credulous about the assumption that the album now became young Mozart's sole musical nourishment. No, its contents were models of a style of melodic solidity and a sound combination of melody and bass, with, for amusement, a few dances, murkies,* a 'smith's courante,' a horn piece. In emulation of these examples Mozart wrote his first little clavier pieces, naive and yet so serious, in which the bass progresses so surely—minuets, an Allegro, the beginning or rather first part of an Andante, which is already more an independent reverie of the boy than an exercise.

But as early as the Salzburg period, before the start of the grand tour, such exercises in a style of the preceding generation mingle with *galant* movements, in which the basses are a succession of broken chords, a sparkling sea on which the boat of equally *galant*, pointed, brilliant melody is tossed. The sojourns in Munich, Ludwigsburg, Mannheim, Brussels, and Paris were not needed to acquaint Mozart with music of this sort. In Paris, to be sure, the boy encountered a series of musicians who offered him something new, and with whose works he had to occupy himself very seriously. Leopold has named them for us and has described, with considerable historical accuracy, the musical situation in Paris (letter of 1-3 February 1764):

* Clavier pieces in which the bass progresses in broken octaves.

There is a perpetual war here between the Italian and the French music. The whole of French music is not worth a sou.* But the French are now starting to make drastic changes, for they are beginning to waver very much; and in ten to fifteen years the present French taste, I hope, will have completely disappeared. The Germans are taking the lead in the publication of their compositions. Amongst these Schobert, Eckardt, Honnauer for the clavier, and Hochbrucker and Mayr for the harp are the favorites. M. Le Grand, a French clavier-player, has abandoned his own style completely and his sonatas are now in our style. Schobert, Eckardt, Le Grand and Hochbrucker have all brought us their engraved sonatas and presented them to my children.

'At present four sonatas of M. Wolfgang Mozart are being engraved,' Leopold continues. And it is obvious that M. Wolfgang Mozart too was obliged to offer the latest thing in Parisian taste—that is to say, to imitate these German-French or Franco-German musicians. How and to what extent he did this may be studied in detail by the interested reader in the work on Mozart by Théodore de Wyzewa and Georges de Saint-Foix, with which our book will not and cannot compete: a work of the bulk of the present one would be needed to substantiate agreement or disagreement. Perhaps their work—which imbued Mozart research with new life after it had been led astray by Jahn and, after Jahn, had languished—is conceived in too rationalistic a spirit. Mozart heard and assimilated and rejected far more than we know; his mind was too active, lively, creative in the act of listening, for us to be able to retrace in detail the process of its formation. What concerns us is the character of its formation and education in general: the congeniality or uncongeniality of the models, the growth under favorable or unfavorable circumstances; the force and tempo of this growth; the flowers and fruits.

Of the models Leopold names, Wolfgang was most deeply and enduringly affected by the works of the very man for whom Leopold expresses the strongest personal antipathy—'this mean Schobert' who 'cannot conceal his envy and jealousy' of poor Nannerl, who allegedly played the most difficult pieces by Schobert and Eckardt as well as these virtuosi themselves. Mozart's first two opera, each comprising two sonatas for clavier and violin—the latter part not really obbligato, having been composed later—follow in their outer vestment as well as

* Leopold expresses himself still more forcefully: 'Keinen Teufel wert' of which perhaps a closer English equivalent would be 'not worth a damn.'

in their essence Schobert's example above all. But the imitation befits Wolfgang's age; it is naive and sincere, it abjures certain virtuoso traits and extravagances of Schobert. And Schobert was more than a Parisian composer of fashion. To be sure, he offered what the Parisian of 1760 demanded—'taste,' grace; grace in melodic invention, taste in figuration, as for example in the distribution of triplets and sixteenth-notes, in the variants in *Redicten* (echo-like repetitions). But his music contains more than this, namely, true passion, seriousness, fatalism. A sonata that begins in D minor (Op. XVI, 4) also ends in D minor: this is an affinity that first comes to light in the later Mozart, just as the memory of the beginning of a clavier quartet by Schobert (Op. VII, 1) enriches Mozart's fantasy years later.

Just as here, about twenty years later, Mozart surpasses Johann Schobert a hundredfold in tension, energy, and force, so he remains, as a child, a hundredfold inferior. Schobert's art has depths and surprises that a child of eight could not understand and imitate; and Schobert comes from the Polish border, he is a Silesian, and so he often writes polonaises—usually as middle movements—which have a national charm to which the young Mozart can oppose only his *cantabile* but melodically neutral minuets. At times, to be sure, Mozart too writes a movement, like the Adagio of the D major Sonata (K. 7), that flows out of his innermost soul: over a quietly moving bass the clavier sings a dreamy melody, triplets throb lightly in the singing 'cello register, and the violin tosses caresses into every measure. And the last of these four sonatas, that in G (K. 9), already shatters, in the development section of the first movement, the scheme drawn from the model.

Schobert's image was overshadowed, for a time, when Mozart came to London. London was then, in the field of the symphony and the clavier concerto, the domain of two German masters, Karl Friedrich Abel (1725-87) and Johann Christian Bach (1735-82), both in the service of Queen Charlotte, and together the founders of subscription concerts, which introduced the most important events in the musical life of London between 1764 and 1782. We have evidence of how much Abel interested young Mozart, in the E-flat major Symphony that formerly was considered an early work by Mozart himself (K. 18), but—thanks to Wyzewa and Saint-Foix—was revealed as a copy of Abel's Op. VII, No. 6; and, what is more, the boy set it in score before its publication, from the manuscript. But Abel's influence quickly faded before that of Johann Christian Bach, who seems to have interested himself personally also in the young composer, and indeed to have loved him dearly. And Mozart returned this love. Johann Christian is the only musician—perhaps with the exception of Joseph Haydn— about whom not a harsh word appears in Mozart's letters. Mozart made a new setting, for Aloysia Weber, his beloved, of the text of an aria composed by Johann Christian, and wrote (28 February 1778):

For practice I have also set to music the aria 'Non sò d'onde viene,' etc. which has been so beautifully composed by Bach. Just because I know Bach's setting so well and like it so much, and because it is always ringing in my ears, I wished to try and see whether in spite of all this I could not write an aria totally unlike his. And, indeed, mine does not resemble his in the very least . . .

A few months later, when Mozart was in Paris, Johann Christian Bach arrived also, to prepare an opera (*Amadis*), and Mozart wrote home (27 August 1778):

Mr. Bach from London has been here for the last fortnight. He is going to write a French opera, and has only come to hear the singers. He will then go back to London, and compose the opera, after which he will return here to see it staged. You can easily imagine his delight and mine at meeting again; perhaps his delight may not have been quite as sincere as mine—but one must admit that he is an honorable man and willing to do justice to others. I love him (as you know) and respect him with all my heart; and as for him, there is no doubt but that he has praised me warmly, not only to my face, but to others also, and in all seriousness—not in the exaggerated manner which some affect . . .

And after Johann Christian's death in London on 1 January 1782, Wolfgang wrote from Vienna the following brief but for him very significant obituary (10 April 1782): 'I suppose you have heard that the English Bach is dead? What a loss to the musical world!'

The 'English' or 'London' or 'Milan' Bach was the eleventh and youngest son of the great Johann Sebastian, and, as the contemporary admirers of Johann Sebastian and the older sons, Wilhelm Friedemann and Carl Philipp Emanuel, believed, a 'black sheep.' For when he, his father's favorite, outgrew Philipp Emanuel's disciplinary rod in Berlin and Potsdam, he went to Italy in the service of a Conte Litta in Milan, studied counterpoint—no longer Johann-Sebastian counterpoint!—with Padre Martini in Bologna, and became at twenty-five organist at the cathedral in Milan, which would have been impossible without his having become a Catholic. The son of the Thomas-Cantor a Catholic! The son of the creator of the *Kunst der Fuge* and the St. Matthew Passion a *galant* composer, writing Italian *opere serie*, cantatas, canzonettas, symphonies, sonatas for dilettantes—not, like his brother Philipp Emanuel, 'for connoisseurs and amateurs'—and becoming altogether a fashionable composer! For such he was and remained, when in 1762 he turned towards London and began to support the English and French engravers with an immensely wide output.

Despite this, or rather precisely because of it, he made the deepest impression on the young Mozart, a much deeper one than did his older and more serious brother, Philipp Emanuel. (Friedemann affected Mozart but little, and then only in the Vienna period.) Niemtschek, Mozart's first biographer, said: 'Emanuel Bach, Hasse, and Handel were his men; their works his incessant study!' Now, as far as Hasse is concerned, this is true at best of the 'Italian' Mozart, the Mozart of the early masses and the Milan operas; and, as regards Handel, it is true only of the late, the 'Vienna' Mozart, who had to put Handel's oratorios into shape for performance, for Baron van Swieten. But, as concerns Philipp Emanuel, it is true only in a most superficial sense. To be sure, Mozart arranged a piece from Philipp Emanuel's *Musicalisches Mancherley* (1762-3) as a finale for a clavier concerto (K. 40), as he did with similar pieces by Eckardt, Schobert, Raupach, Honauer; and at the end of his life he made a new instrumentation of an aria by Philipp Emanuel. But Philipp Emanuel's art as a whole must have been repugnant to his inmost soul. For Philipp Emanuel is the true musical representative of the period of 'sensibility.' 'It seems to me that music must above all move the heart, and this is never achieved by a clavier-player by mere pounding, strumming and playing of arpeggios, at least not for me,' said Philipp Emanuel in his autobiographical sketch.* By itself, this utterance could have come from Mozart; but the point is the *presentation* of the 'moving of the heart,' the *manner* in which it manifests itself musically. With Philipp Emanuel this emotion is an unrestrained exhibition of his own feelings in the slow movements, and, in the rapid ones, an exhibition of the witty, the pithy, the surprising. This is not an attempt to make a formula for Philipp Emanuel's art out of these two tendencies alone; there is no formula for so remarkable and versatile a musician—one whose work, in a time of revolutionary transition, extends over a period of more than fifty years; or for so conscious a master, who never forgot that he was the son of the great Johann Sebastian. But both tendencies were antipathetic to Mozart. The older Mozart grew—and he grew old very early, since he must die early—the more closely did he veil his feelings, the less was he prepared to sacrifice the logic of form for the sake of a witticism, a surprise, as Philipp Emanuel so often did. Once, in his later work, he imitated Philipp Emanuel, in the Rondo K. 485, which, significantly, he did not list in his thematic catalogue. A sly trick is concealed in this well-known piece, so completely outside the frame of Mozart's work. For in it Mozart united the brothers Johann Christian and Philipp Emanuel. The theme is found in Johann Christian's Quintet in D, Op. XI, No. 6, dedicated to the Elector Carl Theodor (c. 1775), at a striking place, namely as second subject:

But Mozart treated it entirely in the manner of the rondos that Philipp Emanuel had published in 1780 and 1783 in his *Clavier-sonaten und Freye Fantasien nebst einigen Rondos fürs Fortepiano für Kenner und Liebhaber* (Clavier Sonatas and Free Fantasies together with Some

---

* In the German edition of Charles Burney's *Musical Travels*, Hamburg, 1773, p. 209.

Rondos for the Fortepiano for Connoisseurs and Amateurs). But he gave Philipp Emanuel a lesson—or rather he was unable, it was contrary to his nature, to follow Philipp Emanuel in all the surprises, expectant pauses, piquancies, sentimental coquetries of these rondos. He is full of wit, but he does not love witticism; and even in this little piece à la Philipp Emanuel he reveals, rather, his love for the inventor of the theme, Johann Christian. Philipp Emanuel's true imitator or adept among the members of the so-called Viennese Classical School is not Mozart but Joseph Haydn, and even he only in some of his clavier sonatas—almost never in the quartets or in the symphonies.

On the other hand, there exists between Johann Christian Bach and Mozart, to use lightly a term from Leibniz's philosophy, a pre-established harmony, a wondrous kinship of souls. Also a similarity of education, the mixture of northern and southern elements. It is indeed not an accident that neither Friedemann nor Philipp Emanuel went to Italy, as did Johann Christian, and afterwards Mozart. Mozart felt the spell of this mixture before he himself went to Italy. Johann Christian became completely an Italian, and if one were obliged to choose between calling him the 'Milan' or the 'London' Bach, the former would be preferable by far, for he imported the Milanese quality, the lightness, the *buffo* character in instrumental music, the sweetness of melody, into England, which, conservative as it was, still found nourishment in the early classical style of Corelli, Veracini, Geminiani, Handel. But in spite of having become so completely Italianized, Johann Christian is yet of a different calibre from the Milanese, Venetians, and Neapolitans. This is not to be imputed to the school of Padre Martini, who could teach only 'learned' counterpoint, not living polyphony, even though he understood the living polyphony of the Palestrina period also. But one is not Sebastian's son, Philipp Emanuel's pupil, with impunity. Johann Christian's *galanterie* is not always—indeed not often—shallowness. He has been called 'a Mozart without a soul,' with as much right as one might call Perugino 'a Raphael without a soul.' Just as Schobert was obliged to work for the Parisian salon, so Johann Christian had to work for the English drawing-room, and he had even less liberty to overstep a certain boundary of passion or seriousness than Schobert. Leopold once hinted at this when he demanded of his son that he compose something 'practical' for the Parisian taste— this would be no abasement of art (13 August 1778):

. . . let it be something short, easy and popular . . . Do you imagine
that you would be doing work unworthy of you? If so, you are very
much mistaken. Did Bach, when he was in London, ever publish anything but such-like trifles? *What is slight can still be great*, if it is written in a natural, flowing, and easy style—and at the same time bears the
marks of sound composition. Such works are more difficult to compose
than all those harmonic progressions, *which the majority of people cannot fathom*, or pieces which have pleasing melodies, but which are
difficult to perform. Did Bach lower himself by such work? Not at all.
Good composition, sound construction, *il filo*—these distinguish the
master from the bungler—even in trifles . . .

With these lines Leopold characterized Johann Christian perfectly.
He is wrong only in calling Johann Christian's Opus V—six clavier
sonatas that appeared during the Mozarts' stay in London (more accurately, at the end of their stay)—'trifles.' For then he would have to
designate as trifles all of his son's clavier sonatas composed before
1777. The example of these sonatas by Johann Christian is always
present in Mozart's mind, and it is not only the similarity of melodic
invention, perhaps of Johann Christian's Op. V, No. 3, say:

or still more of Op. XVII, No. 4, published about 1778:

with the beginning of K. 333:

but the deep inner spiritual and musical relationship: in charm, which however is not entirely devoid of deeper feeling; in the gentle power of the progressions away from the theme and of the return to it; in the natural growth of one idea out of another, well designated by Leopold as *il filo*, a succession that never becomes coquettish or piquant, as with Philipp Emanuel. In a C minor Sonata (Op. V, No. 6) Johann Christian even attempted to solve a problem which, about 1766 and 1767 and for a long time thereafter, lay far beyond the boy Mozart's horizon: the combination of the 'learned' and *galant* styles, in a series consisting of an Introduction (Grave), a completely elaborated fugue, and, despite the minor tonality, a graceful gavotte—a kind of blending of Italian, German, French *goûts*. (We do not by any means wish to imply that Wolfgang was not already familiar with the fugue: in 1767 he had to compose 'fugues for the clavier,' and the scholar Daines Barrington has informed us that upon one occasion, when Johann Christian broke off a fugue in the course of its improvisation, Mozart took it up and completed it.)

Young Mozart felt that Johann Christian had traversed a path that he himself should follow: from a northern region to a southern—to Italy—and from the southern back again to a northern. That path led to a new, ideal land, in which only men of harmonious disposition felt at home. It was easier for Johann Christian Bach than for Mozart to settle in the new land, for Johann Christian did not possess the younger man's irritable, fatalistic temper; on the other hand, the fact that Mozart found in Johann Christian a predecessor of the same disposition made it easier for him than it would otherwise have been. A predecessor, moreover, who was almost as universal as he was himself, for Johann Christian was a model for him not only in the instrumental field—the field of the clavier sonata, the sonata with violin, the clavier trio, the clavier concerto, the symphony, but also in the vocal field—that of the aria, the *opera seria*. But perhaps we ought not to say 'model.' Even if Mozart had the intention of imitating Johann Christian, the result was bound to be something quite different from imitation. When Mozart allowed himself to fall completely under the spell of Johann Christian Bach in London, he had already come into contact with Schobert's more passionate soul; and so the six sonatas, Op. III, which he dedicated to the English Queen Charlotte in January 1765, not only show the mixture of influences derived from Schobert and Johann Christian, but they reveal, more and more, Mozart himself.

Mozart used his models as a kind of springboard—he soared higher and farther than his predecessors. Mozart is not unique in this; Bach and Beethoven did the same. Bach, particularly, had an inclination not to 'invent' for himself, but to borrow a theme of a predecessor or contemporary and transplant it in his polyphonic soil. What with Albinoni, Legrenzi, Corelli became only a shrub, or with others—say, J. C. F. Fischer—only a blossom, became with Bach a huge tree, whose mighty trunk supported branches laden with leaves and fruit stretching wide on all sides. Beethoven's fondness for a 'springboard' arose from his delight in competition and from exuberance, and the object of his exuberance was usually Joseph Haydn, less often Mozart. Nevertheless traces of this longing for 'rivalry' exist in the relation between the finale of the Eighth Symphony and that of Mozart's Salzburg symphony of 1779, K. 319, or, to mention a universally known example, between Beethoven's Piano Quintet, Op. 16, and Mozart's Piano Quintet K. 452—even though Beethoven generally avoided such contests with Mozart, because he felt that nothing Mozart did could be surpassed. Between Beethoven and Haydn, however, such relations abound, and connect even such disparate works as the 'Eroica' and the 'Schoolmaster' Symphonies.

Mozart's temperament preferred a different procedure. He yielded to an influence quite ingenuously, quite in feminine fashion. He strove least of all for originality, because he was entirely certain of the Mozartean, personal stamp of his product. *Facile inventis addere* cannot apply to him; this adage applies indeed only to science or technique. What he derived from others was for him a fertilization, which eased the course of the spiritual and musical pregnancy and birth. We are inclined to regard with some reserve or misgivings a part of the musical examples in the Appendix of Jahn's biography—there Mozart's *Misericordias* (K. 222) is juxtaposed with its model, the *Benedixisti Domine* of the Salzburg master, Eberlin; the Spanish fandango from *Figaro* with a ballet-piece from Gluck's *Don Juan*; the utterance of the ghost of the Commendatore with the oracle in Gluck's *Alceste*; the duet of Donna Anna and Don Giovanni with the corresponding duet from Gazzaniga's *Convitato di pietra*. But Mozart used such 'springboards,' if not wholly naively, nevertheless quite unconcernedly. Why begin anew, if another has already gone over a good part of the ground? Mozart was a traditionalist; it did not occur to him to do something new at all costs. He wanted to do it not differently, but better.

Nothing throws more light on the principle of musical attraction and repulsion as exemplified in Mozart than his relation to Gluck. The personal attitude of the Mozart family to Gluck was one of distrustful aloofness. When, in the summer of 1768, obstacles arose to prevent the performance of Wolfgang's *La Finta semplice* in Vienna, the father saw in Gluck one of those chiefly responsible (30 July 1768): '. . . all the composers, amongst whom Gluck is a leading figure, undermined everything in order to prevent the success of this opera . . .' Apparently Leopold had a preconceived opinion of Gluck as a great intriguer; but Gluck was only a great diplomatist, and assuredly saw no harm in the performance of a boy's *opera buffa*—a field he himself did not cultivate at all. We have already mentioned that during the stay in Paris Leopold expressly forbade his son all intercourse with Gluck. In Vienna Gluck actually chanced to thwart Wolfgang's plans: the preparations for *Alceste* and *Iphigenie auf Tauris* at the end of 1781 prevented a performance of *Idomeneo* in Vienna, a performance Mozart was contemplating and for which he would have arranged the work 'more in the French style,' that is, in the style of Gluck. And the performances of those same operas by Gluck delayed the completion of *Die Entführung*. Mozart did not harbor resentment against Gluck for this; it is true that he did not go to the actual performance of *Iphigenie*, but he attended almost all the rehearsals; and when Gluck expressed pleasure in *Die Entführung*, Mozart showed his gratitude by improvising variations (*Unser dummer Pöbel meint*, K. 455) on a theme from Gluck's *Pilger von Mekka*. On 11 March 1783, Gluck attended Aloisia's concert, at which Mozart had her sing, among other things, the aria *Non sò d'onde viene* and resurrected his Paris symphony, and Gluck was so enchanted that he invited both couples, the Mozarts and the Langes, to dine with him the following Sunday. It was a memorable repast. And Mozart's feelings towards Gluck had surely changed since the day when he dryly wrote to his father (27 June 1781): 'Gluck has had a stroke and his health is in a very precarious state.' He was not so stupid as not to perceive and acknowledge the greatness of the personality of that mighty man.

Nevertheless he remained essentially quite untouched by the essence of Gluck. He borrowed from him certain effects of *opera seria*; he recognized the strength and power of Gluck's choral scenes; and he admired him as a melodist: the fandango in *Figaro* is not the only evidence that he knew Gluck's *Don Juan* very well; the finale of the

D minor String Quartet, too, is a flower from a melodic seed in Gluck. Of Mozart's work as a whole, the 'most Gluckish' composition is *Bastien und Bastienne*—that *Singspiel* written when he was a boy and affected by the *opéra-comique* cultivated by Gluck, though not by a specific work of Gluck in this form. And it is obvious that there is some relation between Gluck's 'Turkish opera,' *Die Pilger von Mekka*, and *Die Entführung aus dem Serail*.

But a true comparison between Gluck and Mozart is possible only in the field of *opera seria*. And there we find that Gluck and Mozart are fundamentally not comparable. For Mozart the dramatist is at his greatest not in the domain of *opera seria* but in that of the Italian *dramma giocoso*—and this domain was completely closed to Gluck. I have attempted elsewhere to indicate why it was closed to him: * he did not have the ability to carry the action forward—in ensembles, in *introduzioni* and finales—to color the characters with a light stroke of the brush, to invest them in a flash with sensuous reality—an ability that Mozart possessed in the highest degree. Gluck's procedure was rationalistic; he presented in one aria only a single essential character-trait, another in another aria, and it was only the sum of these traits that yielded the full, rounded portrait. And he became a 'reformer' of *opera seria* perhaps precisely because he lacked the 'safety-valve' of *opera buffa*; he wished, he needed, to simplify and humanize the action in the domain with which he was most concerned, to set into new motion all the musical parts—arias, choruses, ballet-movements, overture, and interludes—and to bring them into new relationship. And at the same time the relations of words and tones, of drama and music, were altered also. Gluck's statement, that before beginning the composition of an opera he first forgot that he was a musician, is not quite true. He meant by it only that for his work he could not use music's rich store of sensuous appeal, its dominating quality, which would have smothered his operatic-dramatic plan. And, great diplomatist that he was, he made a virtue of one of his weaknesses, of the slenderness of his musical resources, of the exertion it cost him to overcome the monumental style of his generation, in the interest of a more active, more fluid style. The rationalistic spirit of the time, with its purist ideal of Classical Antiquity, demanded the reform of the opera; Gluck was pre-destined to satisfy this demand.

* In my small book on Gluck, published in London by J. M. Dent in 1936.

Mozart had not the slightest urge to 'reform' the opera, to change the relation between drama and music. Of the boy, no such urge could be expected. He accepted the libretti of his first *opere serie*, of *Mitridate* and *Lucio Silla*, as well as the festival play *Ascanio in Alba*— all sailing in the wake of Metastasio—just as they were furnished him, and composed them without the slightest misgiving, without a thought of *Orfeo* or *Alceste*, both of which he knew. Nor had he any misgivings about composing the next dramatic works written for special occasions —*Il Sogno di Scipione* or *Il Re pastore*. But even *Idomeneo* is not Gluckish, despite its choruses and oracle. This is precisely the opera that Mozart invested most with music, with an overwhelming abundance of sensuous reality expressed by means of music. We have just seen, in his letters to his father, that he did not hesitate to allow this opera to vie with Gluck's *Alceste* or *Iphigénie*, that he wanted only to make it a little less Italian, more like Gluck in style: sung in German instead of Italian, the role of Idomeneo given to a bass instead of a tenor; and with 'some other alterations,' but untouched at the core. His conception of dramatic truth was different from Gluck's. For Mozart it is music that is of first importance; the poet is there only to serve the musician. The relation, the balance, between drama and music with him is quite different from what it is with Gluck—it is a merging into a single stream, and often the fullness of the music's power is so great that the current bears the operatic vessel along even when the action temporarily fails. More will have to be said about this in connection with *Don Giovanni*. Mozart was able to mix opera seria and opera buffa without troubling about the esthetics of such a procedure: does anyone, in listening to *Don Giovanni*, bother to notice that the murder of the Commendatore is followed by a *buffo* dialogue, that an aria in seria style like *Non mi dir* is followed by the finale *Già la mensa è preparata*; or that in *Figaro*, on the other hand, unashamed, genuine passion is shown, as in the Count's *Vedrò, mentr'io sospiro?* With Gluck, tragedy is completely absent from the *Singspiel* and humor from the *opera seria*; in this respect it is he who is much 'purer in style' than Mozart.

At the end of his life Mozart reverted to 'purity of style' in the sense of opera seria—in *La Clemenza di Tito*. Gluck's entire struggle was directed against the Metastasian opera and its court conventionality; but Mozart, for a court festivity, chose once more a libretto of Metastasio's. This libretto was revised, to be sure, by the poet to the Saxon court, Caterino Mazzolá, into 'a true opera'—a vera opera, as Mozart put it in his thematic catalogue. Not, however, into a 'reform opera.' Mozart had no interest in revolution. He had confidence in his ability to say the last word, to do the right thing, within a given pattern. He avoided violence. And violence was one of the fundamental characteristics of Gluck.

The contemporary master from whom Mozart learned most, after Johann Christian Bach, was the elder of the brothers Haydn—Joseph Haydn. Mozart was much stimulated by the younger brother, Michael, also. In 1762 Michael became director of the archiepiscopal orchestra in Salzburg, and later concertmaster and organist at the Cathedral, and his wife, Maria Magdalena Lipp, must often enough have participated in performances of young Mozart's works. The Mozart family looked askance at the private life of Michael Haydn and his wife; the letters are full of disparaging remarks about Madame Haydn's tendency to fall into debt, and about Michael's great fondness for beer and wine, and about his peasant ways (though Wolfgang finds him 'dry and smooth')—for example Leopold remarked on 29 June 1778, when Michael, while playing the organ in the Cathedral during a solemn *Te Deum*, had been slightly tipsy: '. . . Haydn would drink himself into dropsy in a few years, or at any rate, as he is now too lazy for anything, would go on getting lazier and lazier.' This did not prevent the Mozarts, father and son, from entertaining the greatest respect for Michael Haydn as a musician; it did not prevent Wolfgang, while still a child, from taking an interest in Michael's vigorous, 'German' minuets, or from participating in the performance of Haydn's quintets in Munich, or Leopold from praising unreservedly Haydn's *entr'acte* music for Voltaire's *Zaïre*; nor did it prevent Wolfgang from furnishing a symphony by Haydn with an introduction and performing it, or, finally, from composing for him the two duos for violin and viola (K. 423 and 424) during the visit to Salzburg in 1783, these duos giving us the best information concerning his artistic relations with Michael. It was as a composer of church music, as a contrapuntist, that Michael Haydn was especially esteemed by father and son; and in Wolfgang's report to Padre Martini about musical conditions in Salzburg, he praises Haydn and Adlgasser as 'due bravissimi contrapuntisti.' Wolfgang retained this high regard until the first years in Vienna, when he became acquainted with still better counterpoint, or rather with true polyphony, namely that of Johann Sebastian Bach.

The symphony to which Mozart supplied an introduction is not the only evidence, however, that he followed Michael's work with keen interest. It is perhaps to the stimulation received from Michael that we owe the origin of Mozart's triad of great symphonies of 1788. For the G minor Symphony, to be sure, not only is there no model, there is not even a 'springboard,' except in Mozart himself. But, as regards the E-flat Symphony, it was probably the beginning of a symphony by Michael of 14 August 1783—Mozart was then in Salzburg and may have become acquainted with the work—that supplied the stimulus for the first Allegro:

Similarly with the *Adagio affettuoso* of the Haydn work and Mozart's *Andante*. And it is quite certain that we would not have possessed the finale of the 'Jupiter' Symphony in its particular form, in its contrapuntal texture, had it not been for the finale, entitled *Fugato*, of a C major symphony of Michael's, dated 19 February 1788. Here no doubt is possible:

And if this should still be thought an accident, there is the rhythmic motive, which appears at first in the horns:

or a counter-motive to the principal theme:

Ex. 10

—further, the play of syncopation, the introduction of groups of rapid eighth-notes; the juxtaposition of all these motives. Of course these are only stimuli, nothing more. The two movements are worlds apart: Michael Haydn's, the 'learned' if also the forceful and healthy work of an honest master who knows his craft; Mozart's, a miraculous blending of styles, but beyond that the crowning of a life of symphonic work—triumph and self-justification in a sphere inaccessible to all that is earthly. In a deeper sense, Mozart had nothing to learn from Michael Haydn.

Mozart's relation to the older and greater brother of Michael Haydn was quite different. Externally much could be learned from Michael Haydn, and he could provide a series of models for Mozartean works. Joseph Haydn, however, was one of the great musical personalities of the time; he had to be reckoned with and he was able to exert a deep personal and musical influence upon Mozart. Moreover it must not be forgotten that Haydn, although a quarter-century older than Mozart, developed slowly and late; while Mozart was a child-prodigy. Haydn came into public notice scarcely five years before Mozart did, and he must be considered a contemporary and successor of Mozart rather than a precursor.

But for Mozart himself, Haydn was the most important contemporary. It is striking and significant that in the correspondence between father and son Haydn's name does not appear before the Vienna period. But this by no means indicates that Leopold and Wolfgang did not follow attentively the productions of the quiet master in Estoras or Eisenstadt. In the domain of opera, to be sure, he had nothing to tell them; he had so much the more, on the other hand, to tell them in the domains of chamber music, the symphony, and perhaps church music also. As early as the visit to Vienna of 1768 Mozart must have become acquainted with some of Haydn's symphonies, which had found their way to that city; and a few years later Wolfgang was deeply impressed by Haydn's six quartets, Op. 20, which appeared in 1771—he imitated them forthwith in the six quartets, K. 168-173, composed at Vienna in August and September 1773. And ten years later Mozart imitated Haydn again—another Haydn, who had meanwhile made the great stride from the half *galant*, half 'learned' quartet style to the *quatuor dialogué*, in his 'Russian' quartets of 1781. Between 1783 and 1785 Mozart wrote his six great quartets, Op. X, and dedicated them 'to his dear friend Haydn,' from whom he said he had first learned the art of quartet-writing. He loved and commended the new quartet style even in Haydn's pupils—Ignaz Pleyel, for instance, whose newly published quartets he called to his father's attention (24 April 1784) with the remark: 'Well, it will be a lucky day for music, if later on Pleyel should be able to replace Haydn.' (It was not Pleyel who did so, of course, but Beethoven.) In his first years at Vienna he noted down the themes of three symphonies by Haydn (Nos. 47, 62, and 75), either to perform them or to examine them more closely—they are, incidentally, three symphonies of particularly songful character.

Much will be said in the course of this book about details of Mozart's relation to Haydn; at this point we shall restrict ourselves to a general discussion of their very different personalities. Mozart was a hothouse fruit. And the most prodigious thing about the child-prodigy is that he developed into Mozart the great, harmonious creator. Haydn was anything but a child-prodigy, and it is most extraordinary that the well-thrashed choir boy of St. Stephen's, the valet of Nicola Porpora, the poor and humble Viennese 'occasional' composer, became, not a hack musician or, at most, a choir-leader in one of the numerous churches in Vienna, but the musician we know as Haydn. Mozart had experienced a thousand musical stimuli in France, England, Italy; Haydn's fate led him from Vienna first to the rural seclusion of Lower Austria, and then from a corner in Bohemia to one in Hungary, whence he seldom ventured forth. Visits to Vienna became important events. Haydn drew entirely upon his own resources. He became 'original' long before 'original genius' appeared in the poetry of the time.

Mozart, the greatest master of style, or rather of all musical styles, had to come to an understanding of Haydn and his 'originality.' Originality is absence of style. It exists in Haydn not because he tossed into his compositions the undeveloped material of what we call folklore but because he invented folklike melodies in the carefree manner of a composer of folksongs. He was a revolutionary. His earliest quartets, Opp. I, II, and III, show that he was well acquainted with the charm and sweetness of Italian melody; but he did not concern himself with *galanterie* for any length of time. From Pergolesi's time on, the *buffo* spirit had penetrated even into Italian chamber music and symphonic music; but Haydn rejected this always *galant* cleverness too, and substituted for it his own wit, which is robust, healthy, jolly, and yet subtle. His minuets are not elegant but peasant-like, strong, and natural. The music falls out of its stylistic frame, sometimes with a great din. This trait in Haydn greatly annoyed many of his contemporaries, especially the Berliners, who spoke of the 'degradation of art,' and referred to Joseph Haydn as the 'buffoon.' The criticism irritated Haydn but did not prevent him from continuing along his way.

Mozart was not at all annoyed by Haydn; he was too much of a South German himself not to understand Haydn's grand unconcern with 'style' and the taste of the time. But he accepted from Haydn only what was suited to his own musical nature. His mission was one of fulfilment, not of revolution. We shall see later, in a special chapter, how differently these masters conceived tonality: the circle of 'possible' keys is much narrower for Mozart than for Haydn, but though these keys are numerically few, each is a much more extended, richer, more fruitful field, and has much wider boundaries. And so Mozart becomes the more daring and sensitive harmonist: Haydn commands all seven colors of the rainbow, but not the iridescent palette of Mozart. Haydn is a lover of nature; he draws inspiration from moving about in the open air; he eavesdrops on peasants at their festivities; *The Creation* and *The Seasons* are full of observations and impressions that could be gained only by a person living in the country. Mozart could never have written such works as these two. As has been said above, he was an 'indoor' composer, whose music was stimulated only by music itself. At the same time his music was not alone spirit made flesh but also flesh made spirit. From this standpoint his contact with Haydn only made his music that much more Mozartean.

Thus Mozart was not understood by his contemporaries, while Haydn, also frequently misunderstood, nevertheless lived to see his own popularity and triumph. We have documentary evidence of this in the so-called Old Lexicon of Ernst Ludwig Gerber, chamber musician to the Prince of Schwarzburg-Sondershausen and court organist at Sondershausen, an intelligent and amiable man. He praises Haydn the symphonist very beautifully:

Everything speaks when his orchestra begins to play. Each subordinate voice, which in the works of other composers would be merely insignificant, often becomes with him a decisive principal part. He commands every harmonic refinement, even if it comes from the Gothic period of the gray contrapuntists. But as soon as he prepares it for our ear it assumes a pleasing character in place of its former stiffness. He possesses the great art of making his music oftentimes seem familiar. Thus, despite all the contrapuntal refinements that may be found therein, he becomes popular and pleasing to every amateur . . .

Mozart, on the other hand, was unfortunately not 'popular.' He never won the palm, even as a clavier-player or clavier-composer. Gerber considers the probable successor of the greatest master of the clavier of his time to be his fellow-countryman, Johann Wilhelm Hässler—in reality a pleasing talent, but no more to be compared with Mozart than, say, Czerny with Beethoven. It is not uninteresting to read Mozart's own frank opinion of Hässler, whom he met at the Russian Embassy at Dresden in the spring of 1789, on the trip to Berlin (16 April):

You must know that a certain Hässler, who is organist at Erfurt, is in Dresden. Well, he too was there. He was a pupil of a pupil of Bach's. His forte is the organ and the piano. Now people here think that be cause I come from Vienna, I am quite unacquainted with this style and mode of playing. Well, I sat down at the organ and played. Prince Lichnowsky, who knows Hässler very well, after some difficulty persuaded him to play also. This Hässler's chief excellence on the organ consists in his foot-work, which, since the pedals are scalewise here, is not so very wonderful. Moreover, he has done no more than commit to memory the harmony and modulations of old Sebastian Bach and is not capable of executing a fugue properly; and his playing is not thorough. Thus he is far from being an Albrechtsberger. After that we decided to go back to the Russian ambassador's, so that Hässler might hear me on the fortepiano. He played too. I consider Mlle Aurnhammer as good a player on the fortepiano as he is, so you can imagine that he has begun to sink very considerably in my estimation.

But compare Gerber:

Hässler (Joh. Wilhelm), Music Director at concerts and organist at the Barfüsserkirche at Erfurt, was born there 29 March 1747. This countryman of mine, of whom I am proud, is at present undeniably one of our greatest and strongest clavier and organ players in Germany. The skill with which he performs at sight, without any preparation, not only his own works but any other composition, is astounding. He becomes even more enchanting when, at the clavier or organ, he gives

full rein to his fantasy and leads his listeners, by means of endless figures, imitations, and passages, through the whole vast field of harmony.
His wit, his ardor, and the unbounded power of his two hands over the
entire keyboard, are then incomparable. With all these arts he combines,
in both hands, a clarity and a precision of expression which bring out,
by means of accented notes, the smallest and most insignificant figures.
But as nimble as his hands are on the keys and as powerfully as the
instruments often resound under them—just as pleasantly is he able to
surprise the hearer by his lovely and tender tenor voice, which he not
only employs at the clavier but by means of which he can portray complete roles, in the most affecting manner and with the strictest expression. But this still does not exhaust the list of his talents. Even by
those who have never had the opportunity to marvel at his playing,
he must be esteemed, through his works as a composer. And his youth
gives us the right to see in him an eventual replacement for the loss of
our great clavier composer, Emanuel Bach. Even now, in his more
recent clavier works, he combines in a happy manner the style of Bach
with that of Haydn. How can anything in his clavier pieces remain to
be desired by music and clavier lovers, if he continues along this path?

He believes that Mozart, on the other hand, pursues a dangerous course:

This great master, because of his early acquaintance with harmony,
has come to know it so deeply and inwardly that the unpracticed
ear has difficulty in following him in his works. Even practiced ones
must hear his pieces several times. It is fortunate for him that, though
still young, he has preserved his perfection despite the obliging and
playful Viennese muses; otherwise the same fate could easily have be-
fallen him as befell the great Friedemann Bach, whose flights could be
followed by the eyes of only a few other mortals. The reader will not
need to be told that he still belongs among our best and most skilled
clavier-players now living.

And this was printed in 1790, one year before Mozart's death, and
written by a man who understood music. There is some excuse for the
more distant contemporaries, if not for the Viennese, since they knew
little about Mozart's most important works: not a single one of his
piano concertos, for example, became generally known during his lifetime. Only his early death, and the growing fame of *Die Zauberflöte*
(which is reflected in Goethe's *Hermann und Dorothea*) and of *Don
Giovanni,* contributed to the appreciation of the instrumental works
also. And so the article on Mozart in Gerber's New Lexicon (1813) is

quite different from that in the old. However, Mozart is still considered revolutionary:

These merits of Mozart had their basis in part in his extreme sensibility and in his innate, extraordinary musical talent. By means of these natural gifts and his unceasing studies at the clavier and on paper his power of imagination became in time great and inexhaustible, while he acquired a skill for which difficulties no longer existed. Thus arose the boldness with which he wove rare melodies over and through each other, created new harmonies, and filled his music with so powerful a spell that it seems as if, in a period of a few years, he accelerated the progress of musical taste by more than half a century. This power of imagination and great virtuosity raised him far above the average to the rarest melodies and harmonies, which, introduced with deep insight, never failed to make a great and profound effect. The richness of his ideas is reflected delightfully in the brilliance and blooming vitality of the instrumental parts of his vocal works, in which his music was always very well thought out and characteristic.

One can scarcely refrain from the seemingly paradoxical remark that Mozart appeared on the scene too soon and left it too soon. He had not yet shown us, in their full development, all the beauties that, so to speak, lay hidden in the folds of his genius when he died. And yet what he vouchsafed us in his brief sojourn on earth was great and lofty enough to border often upon the inconceivable. He was a meteor on the musical horizon, for whose appearance we were not yet prepared; we were still climbing up the mountains that obstructed our musical course, when he leaped over them with giant strides, left us behind, and revealed to us from afar, as it were, the perfection towards which we, still in vague expectation of the future, were developing in Nature's slowest manner. The perfections and beauties that we perceived in his art-works enchanted and enraptured us to such a degree that our taste for other, less inspired music was almost spoiled, and many, in their enthusiasm, began to forget the great and treasurable things that Hasse, Graun, Hiller, Benda, Schulz, and other masters had accomplished in their way. Artists were calmly proceeding, industriously and actively, along the sure and direct road of art and approaching their fulfilment, according to the laws of Nature—slowly, yet all the more surely and effectively; when suddenly *Mozart* appeared, and by the force of his genius brought about a general revolution in artistic taste. To sum up briefly a situation rich in overtones of feeling: With a power of imagination that pursued each individual emotion to its most imperceptible nuance, and supported by a genius that not only organized these ideas, but also, with the aid of an all-embracing practical knowledge and skill in art, mastered the whole domain of the tone-system so that he was able to express ideas with the same perfection with which his own feeling and imagination had presented them to him, with these means, I say, he produced art-works that seemed to differ widely from everything that had heretofore been heard and seen in the way of practical application of the laws of art. They were filled with a richness of invention, an abundance and power in execution, which produced a beauty that only a few could elucidate and analyze artistically—the majority could only feel it.

No biography should fail to reproduce, however—as evidence of contemporary presumption, especially characteristic of Berlin—the dictum of an anonymous writer who was moved by an enthusiastic description of *Don Giovanni* by Bernhard Anselm Weber in the *Musicalisches Wochenblatt* of 1792 to the following reprimand:

His report of Mozart's *Don Juan* is highly exaggerated and one-sided. No one will misjudge Mozart, the man of great talents and the expert, prolific, and pleasing composer. Yet I do not know any well-grounded connoisseur of art who considers him a correct, not to say finished, artist; still less will the critic of sound judgment consider him, in respect to poetry, a proper and fine composer.

8. *The Fragments and the Process of Creation*

HE FACT that so many fragments and 'incipits' by Mozart survive has some connection with his habitual preference for using a 'springboard.' The fragments are presumably only a small fraction of those he wrote down, but even so they amount to more than a hundred. They have been woefully misunderstood. Constanze, the widow, began the round of misunderstandings; she believed that Mozart had noted down, for later use, a number of melodic 'ideas' and had then abandoned them for some reason or other—that they needed only 'to be developed and completed by a master's hand' to become lucrative material for publication.

Now there is, indeed, a series of works by Mozart that, for external reasons, he simply did not finish. The best-known is the great Mass in C minor, for whose unfinished state several reasons can be advanced. It owed its origin to a solemn vow by Mozart that he would write a mass when he had led his Constanze to the altar—and Mozart already had his Constanze. It was composed at a time when Mozart was beginning to take an interest in Freemasonry; and at a time of crisis in Mozart's creative activity—the years between 1782 and 1784. At no other time did fragments accumulate to such an extent—beginnings of fugues and fugati, and of other contrapuntal experiments. They will be discussed in a special chapter.

But there are also enough examples to show that Mozart would abandon a *galant* work because the external motive for finishing it had vanished. One of those to be regretted most is the *Sinfonia concertante* for violin, viola, violoncello, and orchestra (K. Anh. 104), presumably sketched for three players of the Mannheim-Munich orchestra who by about 1779 were no longer together. Similarly with the Concerto for Clavier and Violin (K. Anh. 56), which was begun in November 1778 for the violinist Fränzl and the composer, but which, since a few weeks later the Mannheim orchestra no longer existed, remained a noble torso. We already know why Mozart did not complete the *Ode to Gibraltar* (K. Anh. 25): he could not persuade himself to clothe with his music the 'exaggerated and pompous' text.

Most of the incipits, however, consist of 'springboards' or 'trial runs,' later discarded. It is noteworthy that comparatively few of them date from the first two decades of his creative activity. During that period he used the works of other masters for such purposes; and his father's teaching had inculcated the habit of finishing whatever had been begun. He needed only the beginning: his imagination and unerring taste provided the appropriate continuation, the *filo* of ideas, the choice of the character of additional movements. For the *concertante* Sonata for Two Pianos (K. 448)

Ex. 11 *Allegro con spirito*

K.448

Mozart undoubtedly remembered the incipit of Johann Christian Bach's Clavier Concerto, Op. XIII, No. 2, published in 1777:

Ex. 12 *Allegro con spirito*   JOH. CHRISTIAN BACH

The very fact that he avoided the dualism in Bach's announcement of the theme, expressed by means of *f* and *p*—a dualism of which he was himself very fond (compare, for example, the announcement of the theme in the Clavier Sonata, K. 309, of November 1777)—is evidence of their relation. Or consider the Violin Concerto in D major (K. 218) and its relation to a violin concerto, also in D major, by Boccherini, which Mozart may have heard in Florence, in 1770, through his youthful friend, Thomas Linley. The themes as well as much of the figuration lay dormant in his subconsciousness and were resurrected in Mozart's mind five years later. The best-known example of all is the fugue subject of the Overture to *Die Zauberflöte*. Mozart must have heard it in the contest that took place between him and Clementi in December 1781 or January 1782, before the Emperor in the Palace at Vienna. He may also have remembered it from a quartet in Piccinni's

Barone di Torreforte, cited by A. della Corte.* Mozart himself reports (16 January) that Clementi, who played first, 'improvised and then played a sonata.' And Clementi substantiated the connection in the first edition of his sonata: 'Cette sonate, avec la toccata qui la suit, a été jouée par l'auteur devant Sa Majesté Joseph II en 1781, Mozart étant présent.' ('This sonata, with the toccata that follows it, was played by the composer before his Majesty Joseph II in 1781, Mozart being present') and emphasized his priority, not without bitterness, in later editions: 'tulit alter honores.' Now in this case Mozart used much more of Clementi's first movement than the incipit—an indication of how attentive he had been and how well his memory functioned; and yet Mozart's 'plagiarizing' shows even more clearly than do most such examples the unreality of the concept of plagiarism. For what with Clementi was nothing more than a striking idea—striking both intrinsically and historically, since it is a belated *canzon francese*-theme— is filled by Mozart with meaning: it becomes by means of polyphonic treatment and polyphonic experience highly symbolic and significant, and rises into the realm of eternity.

But in the last decade of Mozart's life and creative activity, he relies in general upon his own ideas as 'springboards.' He writes them down as the beginning of a work or a movement; but soon they no longer satisfy him—sometimes while he is still writing them down, sometimes after 16 or 32 measures, sometimes not until after 100 measures or more. Nowhere is there a better opportunity to gain an insight into the mystery of his creative activity—which remains, of course, essentially an impenetrable and eternal mystery. Mozart, of course, made more or less extensive changes in completed compositions also. The six quartets dedicated to Haydn are especially rich in such alterations; not only does the manuscript display many corrections but there are changes also in the printed parts—all brought about by Mozart himself. Several improvements have become well known, as for example the little stroke of genius in Donna Anna's *Or sai chi l'onore*, in which, by the exchange of two notes, a conventionality becomes a wild threat; or the one in the finale of the D major Quintet (K. 593), where the theme, which originally scrambled down a chromatic scale, gains, through a slight change, its whole naturalness and charm.

Such strokes are found in every composer. But Mozart and Bee-

* *Piccinni*, Bari, 1928, p. 54.

thoven have their special, characteristic methods. For Beethoven it is practically a rule not to be satisfied with the first idea of a motive or theme. The most characteristic example is the beginning of the song cycle *An die ferne Geliebte*, where endless transformations are required before the theme appears in its final form. Beethoven's first idea is usually too simple, too raw, like a half-hewn stone; it requires further treatment, chiseling, polishing, in order to gain all its characteristic and expressive traits. Mozart's procedure is different. If he begins a movement on too low a level of invention, he does not embark on a long process of molding the theme, but commences anew on a higher level. Sometimes he notices the mistake after the very first measure, as for instance in the slow movement of the D minor Quartet (K. 421), where he begins:

Ex. 13

only to start anew at once:

Ex. 14

Nothing remains but the meter, register, and homophonic character or the beginning. The quartets, indeed, contain several examples of this sort. The clavier concertos, however, are particularly important with respect to 'first and second thoughts.' Mozart originally began the Larghetto of the C minor Concerto (K. 491) as follows:

Ex. 15

This did not please him; the idea had to become simpler, more restful, more stable, in order to provide contrast to the powerful, daemonic opening and closing movements:

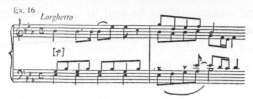

Ex. 16 *Larghetto*

Sometimes it takes him a long time to become aware of his 'error.' He begins the finale of the E major Piano Trio (K. 542) as follows:

Ex. 17 [*Allegro*]

and continues for 65 measures. He starts twice and reaches a *fugato* before he notices that the movement is becoming too restless, that it will not serve to conclude and round off the work sufficiently; and, without troubling to strike out the work that has reached such an advanced point, he begins anew:

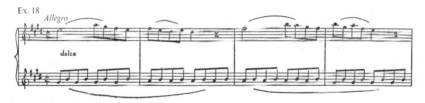

Ex. 18 *Allegro*

dolce

with an almost childlike theme, through whose development, however, the work attains its stability and unity. Beethoven's second and third thoughts are usually finer, more complicated; Mozart's almost always simpler. There are some instances, it is true, in which he leaves a piece ostensibly a torso, with the intention of returning to it and completing it at a later and more favorable time. This seems to be the case with the G major String Trio (K. Anh. 66), which he worked out as far as the tenth measure of the development section. For us this is the beginning of a masterwork; we cannot conceive why Mozart did not bring himself to finish it, a task that would have taken him only a few hours. But it is likely that he abandoned it in favor of the E-flat major Divertimento (K. 563), one of his noblest works; by the time the later work was completed, the dimensions of the earlier had become too small for him, and he had said everything he had to say in this form and for this combination of instruments.

When Mozart found the right beginning he was certain of the right continuation and the right conclusion. An 'idea' of the whole work—we trust it not necessary to emphasize the fact that we mean a *musical* idea, not a 'program'—is present in his mind, half consciously, half unconsciously, whether he is dealing with a sonata, a mass, or an opera. The unity of a work by Mozart is musical, not programmatic. And with him a sonata, a quartet, or a symphony is not put together out of individual movements, but united by means of a hidden logic, which we immediately sense and agree with. There are no instances of Mozart's exchanging movements, as Beethoven did, for example in the 'Kreutzer' Sonata, of which the last movement originally belonged to another sonata, in A (Op. 30), and of which the variations likewise spring from a region quite different from that of the incomparable first movement. Nor does Mozart take a slow movement out of a sonata and then send it out into the world as a more or less homeless *Andante favori*, as Beethoven did in the case of the 'Waldstein' Sonata. (We do not mean to imply by this that it was not precisely the new slow movement through which the 'Waldstein' Sonata attained its compelling unity, its inner perfection.) Only the D major Minuet, K. 355, which wanders about, homeless, in Mozart's work, may have belonged originally to another composition; it may have served as the third movement of Mozart's last piano sonata (K. 576), and—who knows?—perhaps actually without a trio.

The mystery of mysteries in Mozart's instrumental works, however, is the unity of the individual movements—what Leopold called *il filo*, the 'thread,' the succession and connection of the ideas. This connection is less obvious than with most of the other great composers—for example with Beethoven, who employs contrast much more than Mozart does, and whose movements and successions of movements much more frequently grow out of a single germinal motive. Beethoven and his predecessor Haydn—both in a certain sense revolutionaries—had much more need than Mozart to give their works a perceptible, demonstrable unity; their work had to carry with it its own clear justification. Mozart was a traditionalist. One does not wholly understand him, his grace, his humor, his daring, if one is not aware of his relation to tradition, if one does not know where he follows it, where he toys with it, and where he departs from it. It was his good fortune, historically as well as personally, that he was still at liberty to move within a given frame, that he employed organic forms, not arbitrarily made ones, forms that had grown naturally, not those violently called into existence. An aria is an aria; a sonata is a sonata; a sonata movement has its definite law, which Mozart would never break. The forms differ according to the performing media; a clavier concerto will never have more or less than three movements, just as a full-grown string quartet or string quintet must have four movements with a minuet, and a divertimento two minuets. Why not make the most of such given conditions, why tear down such barriers, if one can move freely within them? It is only when these given conditions are known and felt that the spirit, the 'originality'—and in this sense one may venture to speak of originality in connection with Mozart also—the personality, and the daring of Mozart become manifest.

Every instrumental work of the mature Mozart—and how early he matures!—might serve as an illustration; but we choose one of the most unpretentious ones, the Clavier Sonata, K. 332, composed in the summer of 1778 at Paris, and known to every child who studies the piano:

Ex. 19 *Allegro*

August Halm, one of the musicians who, after a period of 'poeticising' preoccupation with musical works in Germany, concerned themselves with music again, said of this theme, after calling it 'irresolute, to be sure,' but nevertheless 'good music':

It is pretty, and agreeable in an unassuming and refined way. It is aware of its limitations and does not aspire to be more than it is, and consequently it is not windy or hollow. But lacking intrinsic structure, not being devised in answer to a definite need, the theme and its wanderings to and fro have the effect of an almost accidental design. Its contrasts in direction do not accomplish anything; they indicate neither a controlled energy nor even a sub-conscious one, and therefore no energy at all.*

But why reproach Mozart for not having invented any Beethovenian themes? And why must a theme be 'devised in answer to a definite

* *Von zwei Kulturen der Musik*, 1913, p. 224.

need' and 'accomplish anything'? The charm of this sonata-beginning lies in the fact that it is not like a beginning, but like a second theme, lyrical and songful, as if fallen from heaven. It is followed by an after-section that is like a lovely sound of nature, with the horn-like fifths in the left hand, and only then by what analytical editions call the 'epilogue'—a menacing section in D minor, full of the tension of the minor, out of which the second theme unfurls like a luminous phe-nomenon, one of Ariel's company. Idea springs from idea; the develop-ment section again begins with a new, 'unthematic' theme, and in the recapitulation the whole 'energyless' succession is repeated on a new plane of enchanting loveliness. No one can fathom how one melodic blossom is connected with another in this movement. Yet everyone will feel their naturalness and necessity, and the inevitability of their growth. Nor is anything to be gained here by searching for a model, for none will be found, either in Germany, or in Italy, or in Paris; either in Philipp Emanuel or Johann Christian Bach or Wagenseil, or in Rutini or Galuppi, or in Schobert or Raupach. Beethoven felt deeply the charm of beginning this way, with something drawn out of the air, and he made use of the same procedure even into his later years—as in the first movement of the 'Waldstein' Sonata; in the E-flat major Sonata, Op. 31, No. 3; and in the A major Sonata, Op. 101, which opens the cycle of the five 'Last Sonatas.'

The *filo*, the 'thread' that Mozart follows, is so dependent upon the right beginning; the beginning must be 'the very best.' Mozart has this *filo* in his head before he starts to write: all witnesses of Mozart at work agree that he put a composition down on paper as one writes a letter, without allowing any disturbance or interruption to annoy him—the writing down, the 'fixing,' was nothing more than that—the fixing of the completed work, a mechanical act. Mozart's procedure during this process is easily followed, thanks to his frequent changes to fresh-cut quills and the varying colors of his ink, which evidently thickened quickly and had to be thinned out or freshened very often. Mozart never writes out parts or sections of a movement, complete in all voices, but always a *whole*. Sketch and final form blend into one act of writ-ing; he does not make rough drafts. In an opera score, for instance—not merely in an aria or a short ensemble, a quartet or a sextet, but even in an extended finale—he writes out the first violin, the voices and the bass from beginning to end; only then does he fill in the sub-ordinate parts, and one can trace stroke by stroke how even during such half-mechanical labor the joy of inventing details, of 'inspiration,' never forsakes him. (Of course, where the orchestral part contains solo passages for the wind-instruments, these are included in the first writing.) In a work of chamber music, or a symphony, he fixes first the principal voices, the melodic threads, from beginning to end, leaping as it were from line to line, and inserting the subordinate voices only when he 'goes over' or 'overhauls' the movement in a second stage of the procedure.

It is his desire to carry out without inner hindrance this first process of fixing a whole—and yet there are places in the first and last movements of sonatas that even a Mozart cannot glide over as one writes a letter. These are, in the sonata form, the development sections, and, in the rondo form, the passages of contrapuntal complexity from which the rondo theme is to detach itself as a fresh surprise. If all of Mozart's fragments of instrumental compositions should ever become available in published form, it would be seen that most of them break off before the development section (like K. Anh. 80, a string quintet in B-flat major) or during it, because Mozart had neglected to prepare for the surmounting of this obstacle by making a contrapuntal sketch. Learning by experience, however, he did often prepare one. Only a few of these sketches have come down to us; but this is no indication that many did not exist. Only recently one has come to light in which Mozart worked out the contrapuntal combination of the Allegro of the so-called 'Prague' Symphony, before he approached the task of writing out the score. Is it really believed that a movement like the *finale* of the 'Jupiter' Symphony could have been set down in score without thorough preparation, not only in the imagination but also, for some passages, on paper? There is enough to marvel at.

Mozart had begun as a *galant* composer, and the assimilation of counterpoint was laborious for him. Twice, in connection with the composition of string quartets, he speaks of 'wearisome labor'; he gives the lie to the naive notion that he extemporized his works. Mozart and Counterpoint, Mozart and Polyphony—these are subjects for a separate chapter.

9. *Mozart and Counterpoint*

*M*OZART was born into a *galant* period of music, a period that had completed a break with the past, begun more than a hundred and fifty years earlier, when a number of esthetes and musicians, whose spokesmen were the so-called *Camerata fiorentina*, declared war on counterpoint in defense of verbal clarity, and inaugurated 'monodic' vocal and instrumental music. Composers began to write cantatas and operas, solo and trio sonatas, in which the voice-leading grew out of an awareness of *harmony*. The principle of polyphony was transformed into the principle of emphasizing the solo element. But polyphony, counterpoint, the combination of independent voices are eternal principles of music. Composers did not stop writing 'fugally,' and towards the end of the seventeenth century came the birth of one who fused the 'harmonic' and 'polyphonic' types of thinking into a unity, and on the basis of a thorough knowledge of all the laws of harmony brought polyphony to its highest point: Johann Sebastian Bach.

Bach was, to be sure, what might be called a posthumous musician. All about him—in Germany, Italy, and France—the schism between styles had long been consummated, the *galant*, homophonic, *concertante* style had triumphed, and polyphony, the stricter counterpoint, had become not only old but old-fashioned. Polyphony became an archaism. When a modern composer—Alessandro Scarlatti, say, to name one of the most influential—wished to write a mass, he had the choice of casting it entirely in the *galant* style; or writing entirely in the 'old' style—that is, that of the Palestrina period (or what the seventeenth and eighteenth centuries considered the Palestrina style); or mixing the two. A composer who did not write for the church could go through life without concerning himself with the stricter style at all. Gluck was such a composer; we possess no fugues, either vocal or instrumental, by Gluck, and what we call 'free imitation' scarcely existed for him. And he was quite right, from his standpoint, not to trouble himself with the strict style. For what his time and surroundings could have offered him was no longer a true, living polyphony but an artefact, a congealed and rigid product of textbooks. The most famous and most modern of these was itself a product of 'posthumous' thinking: the *Gradus ad Parnassum* of 1725, a textbook written in the form of a dialogue, by the Imperial Court Kapellmeister Johann Joseph Fux. About ten years later, in 1735 or 1736, a sickly, crippled Negroid musician in Naples by the name of Pergolesi wrote the *duetto spirituale* that achieved unexampled fame and dissemination in the eighteenth century. This was the *Stabat Mater*, which already shows the dualism, the schism between styles, in its pure state: Jacopone da Todi's strophes are divided into a dozen arias and duets, the purest operatic or even *buffo* style being mixed with the conventional and anemic 'polyphony' of movements like the *Fac, ut ardeat* or the *Amen* of the *Quando corpus morietur.*

Now this mixture of the *galant* and the 'learned' remained the guiding principle for the whole eighteenth century, especially in church music. It is true that instrumental fugues continued to be written, here and there, in Germany and Italy. But, except for the unobtrusive man in Leipzig and his sons and pupils, no one was really aware of what was involved in the invention of a true fugue-subject and its legitimate development. In church music, however, it became a tradition to treat certain sections of varying length 'polyphonically' or 'fugally'—in the mass, for example, the *Et vitam venturi* and *Cum sancto Spiritu*, sometimes the *Patrem* or *Dona* also; in the *Te Deum* the *In te Domine speravi*; in the litany the *Pignus*, in the *Magnificat* the *Sicut erat in principio*, and so on. Every composer for the church had to have a thorough knowledge of what was called the 'strict style.'

Leopold, in educating his son, took due account of this state of affairs. In 1767 he had him write 'fugues for the clavier,' which are now lost; two years previously, in London, Wolfgang had written for the British Museum a short four-part chorus (K. 20), which can be said to display polyphonic character; for to write polyphonically was the best proof of the precocity of a child-prodigy. The *Galimathias musicum*, written in 1766, had closed with a fugue, the theme of which was taken from the song *Willem van Nassau*. In as early a work as the G major Cassation of the spring of 1769 Mozart wrote a minuet in which the basses follow the rest of the strings canonically at the distance of one measure—in exact imitation of a minuet from Joseph Haydn's G major Symphony of 1764 (No. 23), which Mozart had probably heard in Vienna.

And a similar little exhibition of artistry may be found in the minuet of the G major Symphony composed in Salzburg in July 1771; only here the voice imitating in canon follows at the fifth below—the freedom of the treatment already displays a higher level of skill. For in the interim Mozart had occupied himself with older, stricter polyphony, when he visited Bologna and Padre Giambattista Martini in the spring and autumn of 1770. Martini had set him to do canonic studies in the style of the somewhat colorless canons that he himself had inserted as vignettes in his history of music. The old Franciscan had sought to acquaint Mozart with an older polyphonic vocal style of which perhaps he himself alone in the eighteenth century still had a full and true conception. In Florence, after the first visit to Bologna, Wolfgang encountered the most petrified counterpoint in the world in a *Stabat Mater* by the Grand Ducal Superintendent of Music, Marchese di Ligniville; and he was so industrious or impressed that he copied out of the printed work no less than nine movements, just as he also copied and solved several puzzle canons out of Padre Martini's *Storia della musica.*

The exercises imposed by Padre Martini were a preparation for Mozart's frequently mentioned admission to membership in the famous Accademia Filarmonica of Bologna on 10 October 1770. The requirements for admission were strict. The candidate was given a piece of Gregorian chant (in Mozart's case it was an antiphon melody), to which, while shut up in a room alone, he had to compose three upper voices in the strictest style, 'in istile osservato.' Now Mozart failed completely. All of Leopold's boasts about Wolfgang's glorious solution of the problem have turned out to be a fraud. In the archives of the Accademia Filarmonica and the Liceo Musicale at Bologna may be found all three of the documents for the affair: Mozart's original work, completed in seclusion; Padre Martini's corrections; and Mozart's copy embodying these corrections, which was then presented to the jury. Despite the assistance of the good Padre, the verdict was not an enthusiastic one: 'At the end of less than an hour [Leopold always speaks of half an hour] Signor Mozart brought his essay and in view of the special circumstances it was adjudged sufficient.' * This is a mild and humane judgment, disclosing sound instinct—it was later to be justified by Mozart. The Accademia Filarmonica need boast of no greater member, there is no prouder name on its list than that of Wolfgang Amadeus Mozart.

He quickly forgot this experience in Bologna. Nothing connected with sixteenth-century style, whether authentic or anachronistic, had any interest for him: he, who was able to imitate all styles and composers, never felt the need of imitating Palestrina, at least not directly. In Salzburg, after his return from traveling in Italy, he sought to deepen his *galant* style of church music by the study of contrapuntal models. The evidence for this is contained in a notebook of more than 150 pages, in which Mozart copied works in the strict style—masses, sections of masses, motets, offertories, graduals—by the Salzburg masters J. E. Eberlin and Michael Haydn. This conception of the serious ecclesiastical style guided him for the next six or seven years. It was as a matter of fact a not unworthy conception, being rich in harmony, plentifully supplied with suspensions, chromatically enlivened, and provided with earnest and somewhat provincial and 'home-made' themes treated in fugal style. He imitated one of these 19 pieces, Eberlin's *Benedixisti Domine*, and developed the fugue-subject into a contrapuntal display-piece, the offertory *Misericordias Domini*, written in Munich in January or February 1775, the period of *La Finta giardiniera*. Straining passionately for release from Salzburg, he wrote it to demonstrate his skill in the strict ecclesiastical style for the Elector of Bavaria, and sent the score to Padre Martini 5 March 1775. Martini's opinion was significant. He replied that he found in the motet all the

---

* 'Nel termine di meno d'un'ora ha esso Sr. Mozart portato il suo esperimento, il quale riguardo alle circostanze di esso lui è giudicato sufficiente.'

qualities 'che richiede la musica moderna, buona armonia, matura modulazione, moderato movimento de Violini, modulazione delli passi naturale, e buona condotta' ('that modern music demands, good harmony, rich modulation, moderate movement of the violins, and natural and good voice-leading'). *La musica moderna!* For Padre Martini's sensitive ear, schooled in the polyphonic masterworks of the sixteenth century, this was modern music, while Mozart thought he had created church music in the authentic old strict style. He can scarcely have understood Martini's opinion; at least he must have felt it to be very reserved.

His conception of the strict ecclesiastical style, as it appears not only in the *Misericordias* but in all the 'worked out' parts of his masses, litanies, and mass-sections, remained unaltered until after he settled in Vienna. There he chanced to become a member of the coterie of Baron Gottfried van Swieten, a patron and friend of music and a man of varied interests. Van Swieten, a son of the Empress's personal physician, was born in 1734, and from the end of 1777 onward was Director of the Imperial Court Library. He played an important part in the lives of all three of the musicians who comprise what is called 'the Vienna Classical School': it was through him that Beethoven became acquainted with Handel's oratorios and the works of Shakespeare and Homer, and Beethoven's First Symphony is dedicated to him; if it had not been for van Swieten Haydn would never have written *The Creation* or *The Seasons*. But contact with this controversial figure— who was indisputably a fearful pedant and a miserable skinflint—was even more important for Mozart than for the others. Van Swieten had organized private concerts in his home 'which were not intended for audiences. A string trio formed the basis, being occasionally extended, by the attendance of Haydn or another composer, to a quartet. Other regular visitors were the Court Kapellmeister Starzer and the Court Secretary Karl von Kohaut . . .'* Mozart's entrance into this circle supplied the clavier-player and score-reader. The group met every Sunday between 12 and 2 o'clock in the Baron's house, and Mozart came to know, from English scores that van Swieten had acquired during his stay in England in 1769, *Judas Maccabaeus, Joseph, Samson, The Messiah, Alexander's Feast, Acis and Galathea,* the *Ode to St. Cecilia, Heracles, Athalia,* the Funeral Anthem, the Utrecht *Te Deum,*

---

* R. Bernhardt, 'Gottfried van Swieten,' in *Der Bär*, 1930, p. 140.

and smaller works of Handel; much of this music, of course, he may have heard when he was a boy.

The style of these works was not entirely new to him. And so he considered the Salzburg church music not unsuited for these meetings at van Swieten's. He requested (4 January 1783) that the notebook with pieces by Eberlin and Michael Haydn be sent to him: '. . . there are a few counterpoint works by Eberlin copied out on small paper and bound in blue,' and he even asked for some of his father's own church music, but Leopold, wisely self-critical, refused. Whereupon Wolfgang answered (12 April 1783):

When the weather gets warmer, please make a search in the attic under the roof and send us some of your own church music. You have no reason whatever to be ashamed of it. Baron van Swieten and Starzer know as well as you and I that musical taste is continually changing— and, *what is more*, that this extends even to church music, which ought not to be the case. Hence it is that true church music is to be found only in attics and in a worm-eaten condition . . .

But this is just politeness. For on 20 April 1782 he had already written his father:

If Papa has not yet had those [instrumental] works by Eberlin copied, so much the better, for in the meantime I have got hold of them and now I see (for I had forgotten them) that they are unfortunately far too trivial to deserve a place beside Handel and Bach. With due respect for his four-part composition I may say that his clavier fugues are nothing but long-drawn-out voluntaries . . .

With the mention of Bach and Handel the cat is out of the bag. And Handel's name belongs here only for historical reasons. Bach is the important event in Mozart's life about 1782. On 10 April of that year he wrote his father, after asking him to send the toccatas and fugues of Eberlin referred to above, and six fugues by Handel (which we thus know to have been available in the Mozart home): 'I go every Sunday at twelve o'clock to Baron van Swieten, where nothing is played but Handel and Bach. I am collecting at the moment the fugues of Bach—not only of Sebastian, but also of Emanuel and Friedemann . . .'

Great events in music history sometimes depend upon accidents. It was an accident that Mozart entered van Swieten's immediate circle; it was an accident that the music-enthusiast or dilettante van Swieten was Imperial chargé d'affaires at the Prussian court from 1770 to 1777, that is, the intermediary between Count Kaunitz and Frederick the Great. It speaks well for the wisdom of the Count that, in the eternally tense relations between Berlin and Vienna, he sent to the old King, who was a match for any rogue (even the brothers Casanova), not a diplomatic fox but the worthy baron with his musical and literary leanings. Since the King himself had given up music, van Swieten moved mostly in the musical circle of Her Highness, the King's sister, Princess Amalie, who was hostile to Gluck and a patroness of Marpurg and her Kapellmeister Kirnberger. In this circle only 'strict' music was indulged in.

Nevertheless it was the King himself who directed van Swieten's attention to Johann Sebastian Bach. The evidence for this may be found not in musical literature but in the appendix to Arneth's *Geschichte Maria Theresia's* (VIII, p. 621), where it has slumbered for 65 years. In a confidential letter (26 July 1774) to Count Kaunitz concerning an audience with the King, van Swieten relates:

He spoke to me among other things of music, and of a great organist named Bach, who lived for a while in Berlin. This artist is endowed with a talent superior, in depth of harmonic knowledge and power of execution, to any I have heard or can imagine, while those who knew his father claim that he, in turn, was even greater. The King is of this opinion, and to prove it to me, he sang aloud a chromatic fugue-subject which he had given this old Bach, who on the spot had made of it a fugue in four parts, then in five parts, and finally in eight parts.

It is clear that van Swieten had never heard a word about Johann Sebastian Bach before that July day in 1774, and that he had slightly misunderstood the King. When the King mentioned the name Bach, van Swieten had presumably thought of Philipp Emanuel, whereupon the King had emphasized the surpassing greatness of Johann Sebastian and recalled that visit of the greatest of all masters which had led to the birth of the *Musikalisches Opfer*. But van Swieten's interest was aroused. He procured Bach's works. He seems to have visited Philipp Emanuel in Hamburg, within the same year; the result was a correspondence and the purchase of some of Johann Sebastian's works. Van Swieten brought to Vienna not only a few printed compositions by Bach, including the *Art of the Fugue*, but also manuscript copies of the *Well-Tempered Clavier*, the organ trios, and perhaps some of the great preludes and fugues for organ as well—works that were completely unknown in Vienna at that time.

For Mozart the encounter with these compositions resulted in a revolution and a crisis in his creative activity. This crisis may perhaps be compared only with that experienced by an artist in another field— Albrecht Dürer—as a result of his journeys in Italy, especially the second, in the years 1505-7. His encounter with Mantegna and Bellini completely altered the outlook of this Northerner and pupil of Michael Wolgemut. He created works against his own nature, in which he was no longer entirely himself, and yet he never attained the calm security, the natural sweetness of his Venetian models. Still if it had not been for this crisis we would not have possessed the two pairs of apostles painted in 1526—a synthesis of North and South, the personal and the general, the pinnacle of everything a great artist learned in the course of a lifetime. We shall find this synthesis in Mozart too. (If we had any desire to join in the popular game of drawing parallels between artists in different fields of endeavor, we would say that Mozart could be compared only with Dürer. Nothing is more superficial and wrongheaded than to compare Mozart with Raphael, who was a great 'learner' in a quite different sense, since he never had to come to terms with a much older style.)

Not that Mozart was the only one who felt the dangers of the division between the *galant* and the 'learned.' Carl Philipp Emanuel Bach, in his autobiography (in Bode's translation of Burney's *Travels*, III, p. 201), deplores the decline of music that set in after his father's death:

. . . who does not know the epoch in which, as regards music in general as well as specifically its most accurate and refined interpretation, a new period began, in which the art climbed to so great a height, from which, however, I fear that in a way much has already been lost. I believe, with many intelligent men, that the present love for the comic accounts for this more than does anything else. Without mentioning men who might be reproached with having written either nothing or very little of a comic nature, I shall name one of the greatest living masters of the comic—Signor Galuppi, who in my house in Berlin completely agreed with me, and told on that occasion of some very amusing experiences he had had, even in some Italian churches . . .

But Philipp Emanuel and Baldassare Galuppi could only lament the decline, the dualism between *galant* and 'learned,' the crisis in the music of their time, or poke fun at themselves about it. Only Haydn and Mozart overcame it, each in his own way.

Van Swieten induced Mozart to apply himself thoroughly to the music of Sebastian Bach. For his patron's string trio he first arranged three fugues from the *Well-Tempered Clavier*, one from the *Art of the Fugue*, and one from an organ sonata (No. II), as well as a fugue by Wilhelm Friedemann Bach. He provided preludes in slow tempo for four of them, while for the other two he used movements from Bach's organ sonatas. For van Swieten's quartet—in which he himself presumably took over the viola—there are autograph arrangements of five fugues from the *Well-Tempered Clavier*; there were originally probably six or more. And then began for Mozart, with Constanze's pleased encouragement (it is the only indication that she may have been really musical), a period of fugue-composition, the grandest traces of which appear in the C minor Mass. It is significant that only a portion of these fugues were completed. Mozart began to write a fugue as the finale of a violin sonata in A (K. 402), but it remained unfinished for two reasons: it was composed for Constanze, and it was a fugue. And those that were completed have a curious, archaic flavor. Why is it that the fugue of K. 394, of April 1782, though masterly in itself, cannot compete with a Bach fugue—for example, that in C minor from the *Well-Tempered Clavier*, Book I, after which it appears to be patterned? Because, despite all the art in the handling of augmentation, diminution, and *stretto*, the theme:

Ex. 21   *Andante maestoso*

is too 'learned,' too neutral, not Mozartean enough, while Bach's fugues are always Bachian and have, in addition to the augmentations, diminutions, and *stretti*, a personal character, peculiar to them. The same is true in still greater degree of the fugue in the Suite 'in Handelian style,' K. 399:

Ex. 22   *Allegro*

The most remarkable thing about this knotty fugue in A minor is its function as a transition from an Overture in C major to an *Allemande* in C minor.

We need not trace here in detail Mozart's difficulties in connection with Bach or with polyphony. It need only be emphasized that they were real difficulties, a true crisis of creative activity. Mozart was too great and fine a musician not to feel deeply and painfully the conflict produced when his habit of thinking in terms of *galant* and 'learned' music was shaken by the encounter with a living polyphonic style. Bach did not live to experience the musical dualism of the second half of the eighteenth century. The smallest gavotte, the shortest *passepied* from one of his clavier suites, though it may appear *galant*, is in reality as polyphonic in feeling as one of the organ chorales or the *Kunst der Fuge*. Can it be believed that Mozart was not deeply aware of the superhuman grandeur of this music, as an overpowering quality that was not to be found in the work of any of his contemporaries? Where in contemporary music were there compositions with the free logic of voice-leading, the scope and consistency of structure of Bach's organ trios? Mozart was never completely finished with this experience, but it enriched his imagination and resulted in more and more perfect works. The first is a *Menuetto in canone* in the Serenade for eight wind-instruments (K. 388, July 1782), with the *trio al rovescio*—an artful piece in which he is still influenced more by Joseph Haydn than by Johann Sebastian Bach. The second is perhaps the Fugue for Two Claviers in C minor (K. 426), which he himself later dignified by arranging it for string orchestra and furnishing it with an introductory Adagio (K. 546). And the crown of his labors with the fugue is found in the Fantasy in F minor for an organ-mechanism in a clock, dating from the last year of his life, or the Adagio and Allegro for a similar instrument (K. 594), finished a few months before. Here his mastery achieved full freedom in the conquest of the 'strict style'; and it is the more remarkable because he wrote the Adagio and Allegro with extreme unwillingness ('. . . as it is a kind of composition which I detest . . .') 'for the watchmaker,' namely Count Deym, who had commissioned the piece as commemorative of the death of a hero, Field Marshal Laudon.

After 1783 or 1784 Mozart composed no more fugues merely for the sake of writing fugues. The finale of the G major String Quartet (K. 387) or of the C major Symphony surely ought not to be regarded as fugues. These movements represent something different and new, in the creation of which Mozart was assisted by Haydn's 'dialogued' quartets and by his development sections. Mozart learned from Haydn to handle polyphony or counterpoint lightly, as a playful exercising of humor and wit, though also, to be sure, as an object of the greatest seriousness. Although before 1780 Haydn had sometimes treated the finales of his quartets and symphonies fugally, he did not do so in a single one written after that date. And when, as for instance in the String Quartet Op. 76, No. 5, he wrote a minuet in canon form, it was as a grim joke. For Mozart, counterpoint always remained a very serious matter. The only instance in which he may be said to parade his counterpoint is in the minuet of the G minor Symphony, where one thinks one hears four or five voices, though there are only two:

Ex. 23

Mozart prefers to hide his counterpoint, to conceal his 'art'; it must not appear as artificiality. This is part of his nature. Did he not once write about the violinist Fränzl's playing (Mannheim, 22 November 1777): 'He plays difficult things, but his hearers are not aware that they are difficult . . .'? So in the works written after 1783 one hears 'difficult' things without noticing them, because the difficulty is overcome with the ease of child's play. And to know what Mozart thought about 'learned' music pure and simple, one need only read his report of a concerto for two flutes by the Augsburg Kapellmeister Friedrich H. Graf (14 October 1777):

This is what I think of it. It is not at all pleasing to the ear, not a bit natural. He often plunges into a new key far too brusquely and it is all quite devoid of charm. When it was over, I praised him very highly, for he really deserves it. The poor fellow must have taken a great deal of trouble over it and he must have studied hard enough . . .

Here are Mozart's esthetics in a nutshell. Music must not 'sweat,' it must be natural, though controlled with the highest art. And so we find passages like the A-flat major canon—*E nel tuo, nel mio bicchiero* —in the second finale of *Così fan tutte*, the most comic of all his comic operas; the 'ordinary' listener scarcely notices a passage like this, but for the discerning listener it has a double function: it is a lyric point of repose in the whirl of this finale, and it allows pure beauty to shine forth as a symbol that everything in this drama is only a pretense; it gives one a sweet and aching feeling of the unreality of the events on the stage.

Other passages of this sort include the complex beginning of the Allegro of the 'Prague' Symphony, which Mozart had to plan for himself by means of a sketch. Almost a dozen motives are combined here, but the listener is immediately convinced of the naturalness of the structure, it no longer 'smells of the lamp.' There is nothing like this in Haydn, who loved to begin as simply as possible, to make his group of themes as unpretentious as possible, in order to show later, in a long, witty, and often also fiery development section, what could be made out of such simplicity. He is a musician of surprises. Mozart is not that at all. With Haydn the recapitulation is almost always the result of a dramatic process; it leaps out as lightning out of a cloud. With Mozart the development section almost always leads into the recapitulation, or the recapitulation makes its appearance almost imperceptibly, as in the first movement of the G minor Symphony. Wyzewa and Saint-Foix have deplored the brevity of Mozart's development sections as an inheritance from his father (Vol. 1, 8-9). An inheritance from the father from whom the son learned so little? Why did he not prolong his developments after he came to know Haydn? And is brevity a fault? Does the 'Prague' Symphony, complex as it is, require a longer development? Is not this development section in fact an intensification of concision to still greater tightness, still greater concentration?

The 'Prague' Symphony contains, in its slow movement, a further example of the marvelous fusion of the *galant* and 'learned' that Mozart attained at the end of his life. Here the unison motive that appears in the exposition:

Ex. 24

continues at once in a canonic dialogue between violins and basses, with a simple filling-in of the harmony by the other strings and the horns. In the development, however, not only does this canon itself become more aggressive chromatically, but the 'filling-in' becomes richer and more agitated, especially in the second violin:

Ex. 25

There are hundreds and thousands of such passages; they are evidence of that 'second naïveté' for which only a few masters in all the arts were pre-destined and which actually presuppose a long life—in Mozart they are the more miraculous since he lived to be only thirty-six. Sometimes he displays his art somewhat more openly, at the end of a movement—now humorously, as in the finale of the E-flat major String Quartet (K. 428), where he adds a new 'counterpoint' to the thematic material:

now with deepest feeling, as when in the *Andante cantabile* of the C major Quartet (K. 465) he adds a coda in which the first violin openly expresses what seemed hidden beneath the conversational play of the subordinate theme. Compare such passages with the ostentatious polyphony of the Prelude to *Die Meistersinger*, and what is meant will become clear.

10. Mozart's Choice of Keys

A GERMAN SCHOLAR named Gustav Engel, who was at the same time a singer and philologist, once undertook, on the occasion of the hundredth anniversary of Mozart's *Don Giovanni*, a harmonico-mathematical analysis of that opera. He therein demonstrated that the whole work not only set out from D and returned to D, but that when all its intervals were measured according to just rather than tempered tuning, it was found to return to exactly the same pitch from which it started. For the purposes of this calculation, the recitatives were left out of consideration, for their inclusion would have meant that the opera, performed with perfect pitch accuracy, would end about a fourth lower than it began. And even so, the neatness of the result obtained was possible only by considering the great *recitativo accompagnato* of Donna Anna in the first act to be in A-sharp rather than in B-flat major.

There have been and still are people who consider this attempt of Engel's as one of the foolish aberrations of musicology. (Brahms so considered it.) But it is possible also to take it as the painstaking proof that even on the acoustical side Mozart's house is in perfect order. It confirms the fact that for Mozart an astonishingly narrow choice of tonalities suffices for an opera that explores the extreme limits of emotion and the deepest recesses of the soul. On the flat side, *Don Giovanni* does not go beyond E-flat, in the numbers in 'closed' forms; on the brighter side, A major is touched only twice, and E major only once, in the graveyard scene. We may really take D major or D minor as the main key of *Don Giovanni*, surrounded only by its most closely related keys. But what an A major we have here! Consider the seduction duet, *Là ci darem la mano*, and the trio of temptation, *Ah taci, ingiusto core!* This music is full to the brim with sensuousness; another drop and it would overflow. And what an E major, in the graveyard scene! It is the very embodiment of the cold, clear—uncannily clear—

moonlight. And the eerie shift to C major is already an unmistakable warning of the downfall of our *cavaliere estremamente licenzioso*. Greater expression could not be attained, or with smaller means. A message of revolutionary import is made explicit without overstepping the boundaries of the inconspicuous.

Let it not be objected that Mozart was confined to such modest limits by the limitations of his orchestra, especially of his horns and trumpets. Elvira's aria 'in Handelian style' (*Ah, fuggi il traditor*) is accompanied only by strings. Mozart was not compelled by any external circumstance to reconcile the intensity of the emotions in the work with his key scheme. Yet he stays in D. That key suffices; nay, it is the only possible medium to match the force and impressiveness of this warning with adequate stability. No; Mozart's seeming restraint has deeper roots.

It informs all his works. There are masses, litanies, and other church works by him that remain within C, D, F, or E-flat, and even in his symphonies and concertos he never goes outside the domain bounded by A and E-flat. Here, too, it might be maintained that these limits were set for him by the use of natural horns and trumpets. But he practices the same moderation, with few exceptions, even in those groups of works in which it would not have been in any way obligatory: in the quartets, quintets, trios, and sonatas for piano or for violin. It is as if the *Well-Tempered Clavier* had not existed for him, although he had in fact known it since 1782, and, as we have seen, had transcribed a series of fugues from it for string trio and string quartet, though not without transposing those that were originally in the more distant, 'more difficult' keys into 'simpler' ones.

It would not be accurate to say that in this limitation Mozart was no different from his contemporaries. It was not only the so-called Mannheim School that went somewhat further than he did; not only the Vienna symphonists—we need but remember the Symphony for strings in B major by G. M. Monn (1717-50)—not only Michael Haydn, who composed an E major Symphony; even Johann Christian Bach, Mozart's beloved model, wrote a Symphony in E major. The most progressive of all was Joseph Haydn, and not in his later years, either. Haydn had written before 1773 symphonies in E major and E minor, B major, F minor, F-sharp minor (the 'Farewell' Symphony), and quartets in E major and F minor; while in 1781 he had used B minor, a key that Mozart approached only with the greatest caution. The contrast is even more striking if one compares the internal key-relations of the works of the two men, and their differing conceptions of modulation within a movement. To speak first of the relations between the keys of different movements, consider Haydn's clavier trios. In Mozart the slow movement is always in a key closely related to that of the opening and closing movements: the dominant, the sub-dominant, the mediant, or there is an interchange between a related major and minor. In Haydn's Trio with the *Rondo all'ongarese* (G major), the middle movement is in E; in the Trio with the *Finale alla tedesca* (E-flat) it is in B; in No. 24 (Breitkopf and Härtel), which is in A-flat, it is, similarly, in E; the E-flat Trio (Peters) has a middle movement in G. A trio in F-sharp minor has its middle movement in F-sharp major (this is the same movement that recurs, in another key, in one of the London Symphonies). Haydn's last Trio, dating from 1795, is in E-flat minor. Not much is gained by speaking of 'subjectivity' or even of 'Romanticism' in this connection, for these are concepts that one cannot be too careful in applying to Haydn and Mozart. Nor would it be correct to attribute this supposed subjectivity or Romanticism specifically to Haydn's clavier music. (The Trios are hardly more than clavier sonatas with more or less obbligato accompaniment.) For although Haydn's real clavier sonatas are somewhat more varied in their choice of key than Mozart's, they are—those of them that have more than two movements—quite normal in the relations of the middle movements to the opening and closing movements. An exception is the Sonata in E-flat major, Op. 82, published in 1798, in which the Adagio is in E major. In the string quartets, too, Haydn is freer than Mozart. In Op. 17, No. 4 (1771), in C minor, the Minuet is in C major and the slow movement in E-flat. And, to consider a later period, we need only think of the so-called 'Rider' Quartet, Op. 74, No. 3, in G minor, with an Adagio in E, or of Op. 76, No. 5, in D, with the wonderful Largo in F-sharp. What is the explanation for this idiosyncrasy of Haydn's? The most obvious thing to do would be to explain it on grounds of 'originality,' for which, in turn, there is no explanation. There is an impulse of the spirit to rise suddenly into a richer and more emotional sphere, a flight that the often earthy Haydn needed, far from the domain of humor, of play, of a too robust health.

For the aristocrat Mozart, this is unthinkable. He does not imitate it, although he must have noticed it. But he tacitly rejects it, as he does the Scherzo that Haydn employs in place of the Minuet, or the Scherzando into which he transforms it. Haydn does this most strikingly in the Russian quartets of 1781—works that in so many other characteristics served Mozart as models. But Mozart holds fast to the minuet. Indeed one might say that his minuets now become more definitely minuets than ever. One need only think of the Minuets of the three great symphonies of 1788, in all of which the minuet character is emphasized. Young Mozart, with his respect for inherited forms and a deep feeling for their inner laws, sticks closer to tradition than old Haydn.

But this is only apparently true. One may preserve all the forms and yet in essentials be much more independent than any revolutionary. Mozart drinks deep of Tradition, and chooses the simplest and least striking points of departure, only to arrive at the furthest and most undreamed-of destinations. The concept *key* had for him a significance quite different from what it had for Bach, Beethoven, and many other masters, including Haydn. Every sensitive musician has no doubt observed that in the works of these men particular types of melody and figuration are associated with particular keys. In Bach, for example, G major is often a key of 6/8 chain rhythms, and D minor of a sensitive type of figuration, combined with chromaticism. In Beethoven, C major has a specific brilliance, combined with a chordal type of figuration. No one can mistake, for example, in the Allegro of the C minor Sonata, Op. 111, the *involuntary* reminiscences of the 'Waldstein' Sonata—a sort of return, in spirit, to a period of more youthful and more carefree expression—or listen to these echoes without being deeply moved by them. These are examples of a kind of idiosyncrasy that brings about with the choice of certain keys the exclusion of certain types of melody and the preference for others. In this connection we leave out of consideration the question of the character of keys, for this is a question that has no generic answer. With each composer one must consider the character of *his* keys, and for this consideration not only psychology but history is necessary. Thus the close relation between chromaticism and the key of D minor dates from before the introduction of equal temperament for keyboard instruments, when the only available chromatic tones, C-sharp, G-sharp, F-sharp, B-flat, and E-flat, were most conveniently obtainable in the Dorian mode. Even Mozart wrote a chromatic *fugato* in D minor, in the finale of the String Quartet K. 173, on a theme found dozens of times in the seventeenth century—note for note, for example, in a fugue by Johann Pachelbel. Mozart was anchored in tradition more firmly than he himself knew.

In Mozart, the keys are more neutral in character, carefully as he chose them for each work. His C major, D major, and E-flat major are richer, broader domains than those keys are to his contemporaries— more fertile soil, in which not only roses may grow, but cypresses. Only very rarely does he use a key for the sake of its special character. Thus A minor, the strange, and A major, the boisterous, characterize the *Alla Turca*, while B minor is to him exotic, as is shown by Pedrillo's Romance in *Die Entführung*—a piece that is not exactly in B minor, but shimmers between F-sharp major and D major. The neutrality, or rather the many-sided, iridescent quality of the keys for Mozart is to be seen not so much in his development sections—where he is often more conservative than Haydn, but when the occasion requires goes far beyond him, as for example in the opening and closing movements of the G minor Symphony, in which he penetrates to the farthest regions—as in his expositions. He cannot do enough to confirm the tonality of an exposition, and the more mature he grows the truer this becomes (consider the 'Jupiter' Symphony). That he considered the failure to do so a capital one may be seen at the beginning of his *Musikalischer Spass*, where the leading tone of the dominant is heard far too soon. (The *Musikalischer Spass* provides, in fact, a negative key to Mozart's whole esthetics.) But at the same time his suggestion of darker regions is one of his most characteristic traits, and the passing modulations that he makes in those directions serve to confirm the key. Consider the C major String Quintet, with its turn towards A-flat (measure 47), and the tensions that this creates towards the resolution on the six-four chord of C. Thus C major, the plainest of all the keys, becomes a shining goal, a glorious revelation. Nor is this effect something Mozart mastered only in maturity. We see it fully developed in K. 338, the last of the symphonies written in Salzburg. There Mozart, in the exposition, tints the light of C major and G major with prismatic flashes of F major, F minor, G minor, D major, and E minor. The road from the tonic to the dominant is not straight; it is full of incidents, and the key of C major is not an 'easy' key like that of the *Sonata facile*. The most beautiful balance is achieved by the establishing of the key and then by its confirmation through the richness of its relations, in the Piano Concerto K. 467. Here Mozart cannot do enough to show how beautiful C major and G major are; he is forever departing from them and returning to them.

What is true of C major is true also of D major and E-flat major,

Mozart's most 'neutral' keys; less so of F major, A major, or G major, which have for him a more specific coloring. B-flat stands in the middle. To cite but one example: how brief, concentrated, and of almost Schubertian abundance of melodic invention is the *tutti ritornello* in the Piano Concerto in G major, K. 453! It springs from depths of agitation; the invention of the motives and the choice of key are two aspects of the same creative act. F major, on the other hand, is for Mozart a quieter key than C major; more naive, and not without a certain pastoral character. In his later symphonies, Mozart no longer made use of either G major or F major. He chose only C, D, E-flat, and, for an exceptional work, G minor. The 'neutrality' of the key gave him greater freedom—a longer radius.

Thanks to this neutrality, the relation of a modulation to the main key is more important in Mozart, and every deviation is consequently more telling than in Haydn. Haydn does not hesitate, especially in his clavier sonatas and clavier trios, to use long passages (often introduced by enharmonic changes) with a key-signature different from the main one of the movement. He does not care if the feeling of tonality is weakened by this procedure. But this sort of thing is never found in Mozart, who believes that modulatory freedom and the expansion of the tonal domain must be treated with discretion. An excursion into a remote region of tonality and of feeling as we find in the slow movement of the E-flat major Piano-and-Violin Sonata (K. 481) is the exception that proves the rule. When Donna Elvira sings the aria 'in Handelian style' mentioned above, it must be in the 'stablest' key, D major, and never leave it for a measure; that is, it must move within the narrowest circle. When, in *Le Nozze di Figaro*, Barbarina is looking for the lost pin, it is the choice of key that gives the tiny cavatina its humor: F minor, the key of sombre-hued pathos, employed for a trifle—the concern of a naive (though no longer wholly naive) girl.

Mozart belongs, like Bach, to the rare species of the conservative revolutionaries, or the revolutionary conservatives. We have seen that in the days when oblique parallels between music history and the history of the pictorial arts were favored, Mozart was compared with Raphael. But this is one of the most oblique of all parallels. For what Michelangelo said of Raphael is true: one sees in this young man what study can accomplish. Raphael's is an ideal, calligraphic, soaring perfection in which the soul is not involved. Mozart, too, was a great learner, but his soul was never uninvolved. He took over a complete language, and used it in new combinations, giving its words new meanings, to say things that were at once old and new, unknown and thrice known. Thus a great poet uses but the twenty-six letters of the alphabet, and without devising a single new word gives voice to thoughts undreamed-of.

III. THE INSTRUMENTAL WORKS

11. Chamber Music for Strings

HERE are two ways of examining Mozart's instrumental and vocal works in detail. Both ways have advantages and disadvantages. By proceeding chronologically from work to work, from the earliest minuets to the Requiem, without separating the different categories, one may observe a steady growth from the seed to the fruits of the wide-spreading tree; and one may appreciate the noble unity of the work as a whole, despite occasional failures or incomplete successes, harkings backward, and gaps—for we do not by any means possess Mozart's complete works. But this manner of presentation is apt to become too dependent upon biographical matters; it incurs the risk of rationalizing on the one side and confusion and lack of perspective on the other.

Separation into categories involves another danger. It divides things that belong together; for vocal music is often influenced by instrumental music and vice versa—Die Zauberflöte and the pieces for a mechanical organ have certain points of style in common—not to mention works belonging to similar fields but written for different purposes, like Die Zauberflöte and the Requiem. Sometimes works that lie far apart have to be connected, like the first String Quintet, written in Salzburg, and the five or six masterworks of the last years in Vienna. Yet we have chosen this procedure. For Mozart's work is not only universal but consistent in each field. Mozart did indeed leap from one work to the next, but he discriminated with increasing care among the various categories, even though he sometimes writes a work that is quite personal, quite sui generis. In La Clemenza di Tito the opera seria became more completely opera scria, in Così fan tutte the opera buffa more completely buffa, and in Die Zauberflöte the Singspiel more completely a Singspiel, a 'German opera.' This process of enhanced differentiation may be seen still more clearly in the instrumental music. A divertimento became more thoroughly a divertimento, a quartet more characteristically a quartet; towards the end of his life he preferred to write a divertimento for only three stringed instruments, lest, by writing it for four, he risk its being mistaken for a true string quartet. When he began to write instrumental music he found the whole field of symphonic and chamber music in a state of some confusion, and at first he shared in this confusion. But with each passing year his taste became finer, his feeling for the requirements and capacities of the different categories became more discriminating.

Our course is set. We must first of all separate Mozart's music for clavier, and for all instrumental combinations including the clavier, from the rest of the chamber music, which may be lumped together only by reason of the fact that the clavier plays no part in it. The chamber music, in turn, separates itself from the symphonic music, in which the wind-instruments become ever more essential. There is still another category contrasting with that of chamber music—the serenades and cassations, intended for performance in the open air, and differing to some extent from the chamber divertimenti also. Chamber music for strings alone is more serious than chamber music with clavier—a statement paradoxical from the standpoint of the nineteenth and twentieth centuries but from that of the eighteenth self-evident. A string quartet moves on a higher level, in a more earnest sphere, than, say, a clavier trio. The reasons for this are historical. Anyone who gives the matter some thought will admit that it is true not only in Haydn and Mozart but in a certain sense even in Beethoven. But Mozart had begun as a clavier-player and he would not have been Mozart if he had not apotheosized his instrument. Chamber-music elements unite and blend with the symphonic and pianistic elements in his piano concertos, the pinnacle of his instrumental achievement. We shall not go astray if we consider first the chamber music and the symphonies, then the works for clavier alone and in combination with other instruments, and finally, in a separate chapter, the synthesis of all these—the clavier concertos.

When Mozart wrote his first string quartet, on the evening of 15 March 1770, in the inn at Lodi on the first journey to Italy, that form had only a comparatively short history behind it—a history that badly needs clarification. No one has yet been able to describe in detail how it happened that the *basso continuo*—performed by a keyboard instrument—the indispensable servant of all orchestral and chamber music, was relieved of its duties or bondage and the modern symphony and string quartet came into existence. Conservative nations long retained this old lackey, without which no cantata of Bach's, no oratorio of Handel's, no concerto of Vivaldi's is conceivable: in the early 1790's in London Haydn still had to 'accompany' his symphonies at the cembalo, although he had long since ceased to write symphonies that contained anything requiring accompaniment; and even in 1820, when Louis Spohr became the first man to 'conduct' the London Philharmonic, a piano was still in use.

It is certain, however, that what we should call today 'open-air music' played a decisive part in the disappearance of the *basso continuo*. Since Italy, Vienna, and Bohemia were places where the practice of music was not confined to the living room, and where there were warm, amorous nights, and palaces with magnificent inner courts and loggias, they may share equally in the honor of having given birth to this type of music, which influenced the subsequent course of composition. And it is certain that 'chamber' music started out as anything but music to be performed in a chamber. There was no room in a Venetian gondola for a cembalo. When a group of street musicians—four string-players and two horns—forgathered in Vienna or Prague, they did not drag with them a big box with wire strings, on which the *basso continuo* was to be performed with the left hand and the 'harmony' filled in with the right. And that fact altered the whole structure of this branch of music. The middle voices suddenly became alive. In the thorough-bass period, upper voice and bass formed opposite poles: at the top were one or two *concertante* voices; below, a more or less accompanying or supporting bass, participating more or less in the thematic activity. The trio-sonata—two competing violins and a cembalo (with violoncello)—was the ideal form of the time. Now four stringed instruments became the accepted norm, and while the first violin still led, and the violoncello still supported, the second violin and the viola also were given their little something to say.

To tell the truth, it was not much, at first. A serenade, small or large, or a cassation must be simple and popular: the individual movements must be short, no complicated movements in sonata or rondo form, a sensuously appealing adagio or andante, and two minuets. The strings were often doubled or tripled, and technical difficulties had to be avoided. But soon—doubtless as early as the 1750's and perhaps even in the 1740's—music was written that was too fine, too vital, too rich in invention, to be condemned to a fleeting life as open-air music. It

wandered into the auditorium, into the 'chamber.' The forms inter-
mingled, just as the styles did—we shall find in Mozart works in which
the symphonic style is grafted onto the *concertante*—and no hard and
fast distinction was made between orchestral and chamber-music forms.
There are serenades out of which symphonies or divertimenti may
easily be made, merely by omitting movements, in the one case, or by
reducing the number of performers, in the other. There is no reason
why Mozart's *Kleine Nachtmusik* may not be performed either orches-
trally—with double basses—or as chamber music. The style, the inner
bearing, determines whether such works belong to chamber music or
the symphony, to the divertimento or the string quartet.

We know how long the distinction took to crystallize in Joseph
Haydn, how many quartets he wrote before he became a true quartet-
composer. His first three or four *opera* for string quartet are wholly or
partly divertimenti, and whether they are to be performed as chamber
music is by no means definite: we know that the fifth quartet of Op. 1,
in B-flat, is simply a symphony—an Italian symphony—without winds;
string quartets like this may easily be altered into symphonies or serenades by adding two oboes and two horns. In discussing early Haydn
and early Mozart one would really have to treat symphony and chamber
music simultaneously. The slow, intimate movements especially are
scarcely to be distinguished in style and content and would be inter-
changeable without harm. Nevertheless a distinction is gradually
achieved. In Haydn it is completed with Op. 9, written at the end of
the 1760's, and the quartet ends its singular travels by returning to the
chamber, which it had once left as an untamed revolutionary. It has
become true chamber music. It has parted from open-air music. It needs
no listeners, only players, and this determines its style, just as the style
of vocal chamber music in the sixteenth century—of the Italian madrigal
above all—was determined by the fact that it was primarily music for
singers, and required no audience. Music history too often forgets that
'analysis,' with its talk about tonic and dominant, and its separation
of exposition, development, *fausse reprise*, and recapitulation, is not
enough; that music once was a living thing, created for a definite purpose, and that such music is explainable only by the conditions of its
origin. All music of the past may be divided into such as existed for
players and singers alone and such as was intended to be listened to;
the preludes and fugues of the *Well-Tempered Clavier* into those that
can be played for oneself and those that can be played for others;

Beethoven's sonatas into the intimate and the *concertante*. How bar-
barous our concert-life has become is shown principally in the fact
that we no longer feel such distinctions.

Mozart's first quartet is undoubtedly not yet a quartet, and shows
very clearly the transitional character of quartet production about 1770.
It stands alone. It shows clearly enough that it came into being in
Italy, in the neighborhood of Milan; for the influence that glimmers
through is not that of Haydn—Mozart at that time either did not yet
know the quartets of Op. 9 or in this case did not wish to know them—
but that of Giambattista Sammartini, the then 70-year-old Milanese
master, who had at one time been more a colleague than a teacher of
Gluck—the same man whom Haydn once called a 'scribbler' (there is
indeed a great difference between Haydn's and Sammartini's styles in
the quartet and symphony). For Sammartini is only *galant*, and nothing more. While he produced some works with the melody and spirit
of the old classical style his contribution consists in the fact that he
helped to give Italian instrumental music freedom, freshness, spontaneity, the finest folk-quality, the *buffo* and the sensitive—sometimes,
too, the shallow and the noisy. Mozart follows him pretty faithfully.
He begins with a delicate Adagio, follows it with a noisy Allegro, and
closes with a worked-out minuet, that is, a minuet with a trio in a new
key—and this is typically Milanese. The Allegro movement could form
part of a symphony; and the first movement could easily be altered into
a trio-sonata in the old style, with two dialoguing violins and *basso
continuo*, for the violoncello is somewhat passive and uninterested and
the viola is very timid. The Salzburg origin of the young composer is
shown only by his beginning the development section of the Allegro
with a turn to the 'learned':

Ex. 27

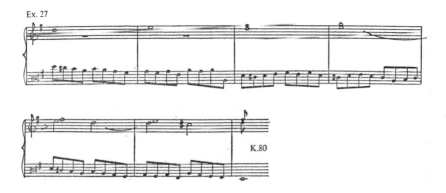

K.80

a passage that could also form part of a stiff old trio-sonata. Strangely enough, Mozart retained a certain fondness for his first quartet. At the end of 1773 or the beginning of 1774 he added to it a rondo, in itself a charming piece, whose gavotte-like theme recalls an arietta from Gluck's *L'Île de Merlin:*

But it belongs to a quite different style from that of the first three movements, for it is already an authentic, chamber-music quartet movement. Goethe would have called the work in its four-movement form a *tragelaph.*

Between 1770 and 1774 Mozart became a quartet-composer. His work as such is easy to survey. It falls into two sharply defined groups: the fifteen early quartets, K. 136-138, 155-160, and 168-173, all from the beginning of the 1770's; and the ten celebrated 'great' quartets— the six of Op. X, the 'Hoffmeister' Quartet, and the three last, 'Prussian' quartets, Op. XVIII—beginning in 1783 with the G major Quartet, K. 387.

The three early groups vary greatly. The quartets K. 136, 137, and 138, written in Salzburg in the first months of 1772, are called 'divertimenti' on the manuscript, but this designation cannot possibly have come from Mozart himself. For a divertimento should have two minuets, and these three works have no minuets at all. Each contains three movements; in two of the works the slow movement is in the middle, in one it is at the beginning. They are simply symphonies for strings alone, without oboes and horns; or rather they tend towards the symphonic style in the same degree that Mozart's first quartet had tended towards the chamber-music style. I believe that Mozart wrote them in preparation for the last Italian journey, in order not to be disturbed during the composition of *Lucio Silla* if symphonies should be demanded of him, and that he would then have added wind-instruments to the outer movements on the spot in Milan, according to need and feasibility. The keys chosen are evidence for this supposition. There is nothing of chamber music in the first 'quartet,' in D: the first movement is rather a virtuoso piece for the violins, which play somewhat in the manner of a *concertante* duet; the second movement is graceful and 'tender,' quite in the Italian fashion; and the last, while not a rondo, has a low specific gravity, the beginning of the development being characterized by a bit of counterpoint. The same is true of No. 2, in B-flat, although the 'tender' movement comes first; the *Allegro di molto* that follows is even quite plainly designed in the *al fresco* manner, and the rapid last movement has the *buffo* character of a symphonic finale, not the wit or cleverness of chamber music. Only in the last of these three 'divertimenti,' that in F, is any dualism noticeable: the first movement is purely symphonic, but both the Andante and the final, very aggressive *Presto*—in this case a rondo with an episode in minor à la Johann Christian—are more delicately formed, but still suitable for performance by an orchestra. These are not opera-sinfonias but Italian symphonies for use at concerts, written for the salon of Count Firmian, the Governor-General of Milan.

It is in the quartets K. 155-160—all six written at the end of 1772 on the journey to Milan or in Milan itself—that the shift to chamber music is definitely made. If the three divertimenti be counted as chamber music, then it must be said that Mozart made incredible strides as a quartet-composer in half a year. There is a connection between these two groups of works. The opening movement of the first quartet, written in 'dreary Bozen,' still toys with symphonic theme-invention, but the roles of second violin and viola are quite different from what they ever were in the symphony, and in the development (again emphasized by imitation) it is the second violin that has a charming and piquant *cantabile* melody in B minor, of the type that could not lightly be entrusted to ripieno players. This D major Quartet is related, both in spirit and in its external shape, to the first of the 'Prussian' quartets, K. 575, the beginnings of the first and second movements of which recall these days of happiness and sunshine in Milan. The finale is a bit Haydnish, in the sense that the later Haydn once more wrote and developed such short-legged rondo themes and virtuoso episodes for the first violin.

The opening movement of the second of these quartets, K. 156, in G major, also has the character of early Haydn, but the work as a whole reflects bluer skies than can be found in any of Haydn's compositions. It is perfect of its kind, and one hesitates to commend it to a period that is perhaps no longer capable of appreciating so fleeting and yet at the same time eternal a moment of joy. This time the development is no longer pointed up 'learnedly.' It bears indeed no relation to the themes of the exposition; but can it be called *galant*? Nothing like this can be found in any other composer:

Ex. 29

K.156

The autograph of the Adagio, in E minor, shows Mozart wise in matters of art at an early age: a first draft is discarded, because, with its *cantilena* in the first violin and the inferior role of the three 'accompanying' instruments, it is much too serenade-like, too 'Italian.' So Mozart writes a second, of the finest chamber-music construction, a first adumbration of later movements drawn from a deeper well of emotion. And in the *Tempo di Minuetto*, the finale, appears a motive familiar to us from *Così fan tutte*—in his last opera *buffa* Mozart's memory must have turned once more to this, his most Italian quartet.

Foreshadowings of the 'great' string quartets are found everywhere in these quartets by the seventeen-year-old Mozart; nor are they mere foreshadowings—is spring only a foreshadowing of summer? In the first movement of the C major Quartet we find already the firmness and grace that combine so readily in this key in Mozart's later works; the rondo-finale already contains a closing 'witticism'; and the slow movement, in C minor, is full of an Italian poignancy and pathos. In the F major Quartet, K. 158, the beginning of the development section of the first movement introduces a singular anticipation of the opening of the second part of the minuet in the great E-flat major Quartet:

Ex. 30 [Allegro]

[Allegro]

—although it is otherwise not at all minuet-like, but, on the contrary, capricious and playful. How widely the pendulum of feeling swings in these quartets may be seen in the Andante, in A minor (the relative minor of the dominant), full of melancholy and emotional unrest. The same strong contrast marks the next Quartet (K. 159, in B-flat major), where a grandiose, dark, and passionate Allegro in G minor stands between a very restrained and yet individual Andante and a rondo (Allegro grazioso) full of sensuous beauty. The last Quartet in this group (K. 160, in E-flat) is again more conventional and 'symphonic' in style; and if we did not possess rather definite information concerning the time of its origin, we should be inclined to count it among the orchestral quartets, K. 136-138.

In Köchel numbers and in date the next group of Mozart's string quartets, K. 168-173, is not widely separated from the preceding group, K. 155-160; but there is a definite gulf between them, nevertheless. These are no longer Italian or Milanese, but Austrian, Viennese, quartets: Mozart wrote all six in the late summer of 1773. The sojourn in

Vienna in 1773 played a decisive part in his development. It marked the end of his boyhood, of his career as a child-prodigy; it confronted him, after he had become more discerning (he had visited Vienna previously), with a fresher, less conventional art—for operatic and instrumental music in Italy had been purely conventional; and it brought about his acquaintance with Joseph Haydn, the revolutionary—specifically, with the six quartets, Op. 17, which appeared in 1771, and the six quartets, Op. 20, the so-called 'Sun Quartets,' which appeared in 1772. This encounter sharply deflected him from his course, just as did the encounter with the works of Johann Sebastian Bach about ten years later. Just as at this later period he was to write a series of somewhat uncomfortable fugues, so he now wrote a series of highly uncomfortable movements for string quartet, which stand too close to their model and yet do not attain their goal. For Mozart here only imitates that which the older, more mature Haydn had worked out. The quartet-series Opp. 17 and 20 were products of a crisis in Haydn's creative career. Haydn, approaching his fortieth year, was tired of the *galant* style; he felt the necessity of deepening his work, of infusing it with greater seriousness, greater intimacy. For the time being, he could think of nothing better than to revert to 'learnedness,' to counterpoint, to polyphony. Not to strict polyphony—he had much too much taste to incorporate actual fugues, for example, in a quartet. If he proudly entitles the finale of his C major Quartet, Op. 20, No. 2, *Fuga a quattro soggetti*, or that of Op. 20, No. 6, in A major, *Fuga a tre soggetti*, this is a playing with the technical possibilities afforded by the fugue, in answer to a feeling of compulsion to give all four voices—even the viola and the violoncello—the utmost independence. And if, at the end of the finale of Op. 20, No. 5, a *Fuga a due soggetti*, he has the first violin and violoncello imitate each other in *stretto*, this is a bit of playful ostentation. But how personal a matter the apparent reversion to the old classical style was to him is indicated by the either bitter or humorous remark at the end of the C major fugue: 'Sic fugit amicus amicum.' Nevertheless one feels a break in style, a dualism, in these works; they oscillate between the *galant* and the 'learned'; virtuosity in the first violin part, utmost robustness, as in some of the minuets, the exotic (as in the 'gipsy minuet' in Op. 20, No. 4), the employment of instrumental recitative—all these disparate things jostle against one another.

Mozart was no match for this. Once more he imitated only that which suited him, but he was unable to make it wholly his own. The imitation is quite obvious. For the first time (in K. 170) he writes variations as a first movement, as Haydn did in Op. 17, No. 3; for the first time he too suddenly writes fugues as finales (K. 168, 173), and without feeling Haydn's need to seek this way out. Accordingly, these two fugues do not have, either in their invention or in their working out, the personal quality, the humor, of Haydn's fugue-finales. We have seen that the D minor fugue employs a chromatic theme that was common property. Involuntary reminiscences set in. The beginning of the first movement of K. 168 is like an echo of Haydn's Op. 17, No. 3, in the same key; one of the fugue themes from Haydn's Op. 20, No. 5, returns in Mozart as an Andante (K. 168):

Since Haydn reverts in some slow movements to the serenade-type—broad *cantilena* in the first violin, with accompaniment—Mozart is encouraged to do likewise (in K. 169 and more pronouncedly in K. 170 and K. 172). Haydn's sublime heedlessness misleads Mozart into combining, in the first movement of K. 171, an *Introduzione* (Adagio) with an Allegro that begins fugally; the *Introduzione* is also employed as a conclusion or rounding-off. But adumbrations of a new style, like the combination of first and second themes in Haydn's C minor Quartet, Op. 17, No. 4, escape him. The minuets become rhythmically more irregular and capricious; and only the four finales that are not fugal are truly Mozartean, if also sometimes (as in K. 171) again too symphonically conceived.

Mozart was, so to say, confused by Haydn. And though Haydn himself was a bit confused, Mozart failed by far to achieve the originality, the independence of convention, the discursive voice-leading, the combination of the popular and the intellectual, of his model. One is tempted to believe that these six quartets owe their existence to a command from Leopold. When the publisher Torricella brought them out in manuscript copies at the end of 1785, after the publication of the six great quartets dedicated to Haydn, they aroused considerable aston-ishment among amateurs and occasioned an exchange of asperities be-tween Torricella and Artaria that must have been disagreeable to Mozart.

For ten years, from 1773 to 1783, a very long period for Mozart's brief lifetime, he did not write any more string quartets. The period between, more particularly the years of the journey to Mannheim and Paris (1777-8) and the stay at Munich, did see the composition of some quartets—four with flute and one with oboe—but these belong to a different category of chamber music from that of the string quartet, an older and 'lighter' one, with lower specific gravity. Three of the flute quartets, K. 285, 285a, and *Anh*. 171, were commissioned by a Monsieur de Jean in Mannheim, a rich Dutch amateur, and Mozart wrote them with the greatest unwillingness and without feeling im-pelled to any high flight of the imagination. He then had some diffi-culty in obtaining full payment from de Jean. This is understandable, for only the first, in D, gave full value, either in its style and content or in its length—it comprises three movements while the other two con-tain only two each. It is somewhat *concertante*; the flute predominates—without, however, entirely subordinating the violin or even the viola; and, as an introduction to the Rondo, there is an Adagio in B minor of the sweetest melancholy, perhaps the most beautiful accompanied solo ever written for the flute. The Rondo itself is of the most delight-ful gaiety, full of charming melodic invention and lovely sound—no one would suspect that it was not written *con amore*. The other two quartets, in G and C, not only revert to some extent to Johann Chris-tian Bach by having only two movements; they are in good style and 'tender,' nothing more, and the finale of the second is remarkable only for the fact that it contains what is presumably the original version of the *Tema con variazioni* of the Wind Serenade, K. 361. The last of the four flute quartets (K. 298, in A), composed in Paris, can be re-garded only as a joke or an act of exuberance—Mozart himself let the cat out of the bag with the inscription over the last movement: *Ron-dieaoux—Allegretto grazioso, ma non troppo presto, però non troppo adagio. così—così—molto garbo ed espressione.* But *garbo* (elegance) and *espressione* unfortunately cannot be applied to the theme, which was borrowed from a melody of Paisiello's with the text *Chi mi mostra, chi m'addita dove sta il mio dolce amore;* the movement has a barrel-organ perfunctoriness that is foreign to Mozart even in his weakest moments.

The work is a parody. The first movement is a two-part theme with four variations: when the flute, the violin, the viola, and finally even the violoncello have had their little say, it is all over. The minuet is of the briefest and most conventional type. By means of parody Mozart vented his scorn and rage at the insipidities with which one could achieve fame and wealth as a 'foreign' musician. The target of his anger was probably Giuseppe Cambini, and the material object, the 'Quatuor d'airs dialogués' cultivated by Cambini. Mozart had met Cambini shortly before in a brief artistic-social encounter. (It should be mentioned here that M. de Saint-Foix has recently assigned the little work to the year 1786-7 and believes it originated in the Jacquin circle: evidence for this view is the provenance of the autograph and the fact that Paisiello's melody cannot be shown to have existed before 1786. I confess that I am unable to render a decision without a re-examination of the autograph. The parodistic character of the whole work, however, remains certain.)

The Oboe Quartet (in F major, K. 370), an ambitious work composed by Mozart for the oboist Friedrich Ramm at Munich in January or February 1781—the period of *Idomeneo*—is another matter. Ramm was, as Gerber had asserted in his *Tonkünstler-Lexicon* (Vol. II, p. 232), 'among the finest living oboists,' and, as Lipowsky says in his *Baierisches Musik-Lexikon,*

it is not too much to say that no one has yet been able to approach him in beauty, roundness, softness and trueness of tone on the oboe, combined with the trumpet-like depth of his *forte*. He plays, for the rest, with a delicacy, a lightness, and a power of expression that enchant the listener; he handles this instrument wisely, according to its true, individual nature, and with a practical skill possessed by few oboists; in an Adagio his interpretation is full of feeling, but he also knows how to express spirit and fire, if the effect and the inspiration demand them.

This description is applicable to the proper performance of Mozart's Quartet also, except for the 'trumpet-like depth of his *forte*.' It is the counterpart of the first Flute Quartet, in D, but on a higher artistic and spiritual level. It, too, is somewhat *concertante*, and even supplies an opportunity for a small cadenza in the Adagio (in D minor); the rondo-finale contains a device that is very rare in Mozart: while the three stringed instruments proceed along their somewhat easy-going way in 6/8 time, the wind-instrument has *cantilene* and figurations in 4/4 time, only to return afterwards to the general chorus in the most natural manner. This is a masterwork, which in its combination of the con-*certante* and chamber-music spirits can be compared only with Mozart's own later Clarinet Quintet.

The six string quartets that followed the 'Vienna Quartets' of 1773 after so long an interval are also Vienna quartets, but in an entirely new sense; as Op. X they are dedicated to Joseph Haydn, with a cele-brated letter of dedication written in Italian—to Haydn, the famous composer, but at the same time the friend, who had already expressed his satisfaction with these quartets. They could not have been dedi-cated to anyone but Haydn. The latter had not written any quartets for nine years, between the 'Sun Quartets' of 1772 and the six quartets Op. 33 of 1781, dedicated to the Grand Duke Paul (hence, 'Russian Quartets'). These were composed, as Haydn himself emphasized, 'in an entirely new and special manner,' and when Haydn makes a statement of this sort, it means something. The crisis in his creative activity as a quartet-composer is surmounted. He no longer writes fugal finales. He has 'an entirely new and special manner' of giving all four instruments a share in the musical discourse: thematic development. It is no longer merely in the development section that 'working out' takes place; from now on the smallest motive, the faintest hint of a rhythm, is significant, and there is no longer any question of predominance or subordination of any voice in the ensemble, except in a few slow movements, such as the 'scena *cantante*' of Op. 33, No. 5, or the 'Serenade' of Op. 33, No. 6. For Haydn does not relinquish any of his gains, not even the construc-tion of sturdy, forceful, and compact minuets, even though he now marks them 'Scherzo' or 'Scherzando.' (But in spite of the marking, the 'Scherzo' of Op. 33, No. 4, is a true minuet.) Nothing is lost and all is won. These quartets, in their combination of originality and spirit, are a great achievement of human invention, quite apart from their his-torical significance. 'Learning' is replaced by the principle of obbligato voice-leading, and one ventures to say that were it not for these quartets, such an ideal instance of obbligato writing as the first movement of the *Eroica* would not have been possible. Beethoven was quite right when he said that he 'came into the world as an obbligato composer'; but he forgot to add, 'thanks to Joseph Haydn.'

The impression made by these quartets of Haydn's was one of the profoundest Mozart experienced in his artistic life. But this time he did

From a portrait by (?) Cignaroli, painted in Verona
MOZART (January 1770)

not allow himself to be overcome. This time he learned as a master from a master; he did not imitate; he yielded nothing of his own personality. If he wrote a series of variations as the finale of the D minor Quartet, K. 421, as Haydn did in Op. 33, No. 5, it was only in ostensible 'homage,' despite the noticeable relation of the themes.

But we have already remarked that Mozart's theme was also an 'homage' to Gluck, and, despite the relation, what a difference between G major and D minor! The amiable Haydn's easy-going half-cadence; Mozart's uncanny concealed chromaticism—Mozart affirms his complete independence. While Haydn deliberately avoids the strict forms in Op. 33, Mozart stresses them in the finale of the very first quartet, which begins as a 'fugue,' and he plays with the contrast between 'learned' and galant, as he does later in the finale of the C major Symphony. Mozart does not allow himself to be led by Haydn into continuing to write 'serenades' as middle movements, any more than into calling his minuets 'Scherzi.' These minuets become not wittier, or more surprising in dynamics and rhythm, but rather more serious and sometimes more moving than an Adagio, like the fatalistic one in D minor with the chromatically descending bass, or the melancholy one in A major, despite its supposedly 'sunny' key. Here too the keys and modes have a different significance for Mozart than for Haydn, even though both composers employ the minor mode only once in six quartets and though Haydn here chooses keys for the slow movements that are more closely related than usual to the principal keys. Mozart never imitates the shirt-sleeve joviality of which the finale of Op. 33, No. 4, may serve as an example:

Ex. 33 *Presto*

At the end of the rondo Haydn humorously plays a trump-card by pre-
senting this theme in simplified form and *pizzicato*; Mozart, on the
other hand, becomes more serious in the finale, or with an enchanting
and lovable gesture leaves the listener deeply stirred. Haydn's development section leans heavily on wit; he always plays with the *fausse reprise*, and only afterwards romps about with the thematic material. One
cannot help laughing when the *fausse reprise* enters after only eight
measures, in the first movement of Op. 33, No. 5—a masterpiece of
spirit and humor. Mozart does not stress such matters, just as he much
less frequently plans the recapitulation to come as a surprise. Haydn
takes an irrepressible delight in mystifying the listener—a South-German
form of banter, quite different from Philipp Emanuel Bach's tendency
to do something unexpected. There is another difference: Haydn sometimes favors the first violin unduly, and gives it—especially in the repetitions in slow movements—rich and fine *fioriture*. Mozart does not care
for such things; they are not simple enough, not spontaneous enough.
In the dedication to Haydn he does indeed speak of these six quartets
as the fruit of long and wearisome labor—'Essi sono, è vero, il frutto di
una lunga, e laboriosa fatica'—and this is certainly a true statement.
Evidence of its truth may be found on almost every page of the autograph; hardly another manuscript of Mozart's shows so many erasures,
improvements, and discarded beginnings. But the 'wearisome labor'
must not be noticed in the finished work. The beginning of K. 458 is
an illustration of Mozart's wisdom in art. Originally, he had written:

Ex. 34 *Prestissimo*

But he very soon saw that this beginning in imitation would anticipate an effect that should be reserved for the development, and he purified it of all 'working out,' of all 'sweat.' This is the difference between the three somewhat later quartets (K. 458, 464, 465) and the earlier half of the group (K. 387, 421, 428): the improvement, if one may venture to speak of improvement here. Leopold opined (in a letter to his daughter, 14-16 February 1785) that the three later quartets were 'somewhat lighter, but at the same time excellent compositions.' It is astonishing that he did not criticize the Introduction of the C major Quartet, which has set so many pens in motion, and which with all its harmonic audacity seems so legitimate to us. But Leopold was right: they are lighter, their art is more concealed, their gaiety seems more innocent, as for example in the first movements of the B-flat major and A major Quartets. But it only seems so: to this very A major Quartet Mozart gave a troubled conclusion that never clears up and that leaves the hearer in a very pensive mood. This movement is one of the few by Mozart that made a deep impression upon Beethoven, though its effect may be seen not in his finales (for Beethoven is an optimist) but in his first movements.

Mozart had completely found himself; scarcely any works of his are more personal than these six quartets. What divides them most sharply from Haydn's quartets is that they are 'music made of music,' 'filtered' art. A quartet like Haydn's Op. 33, No. 3, the so-called 'Bird Quartet,' remains quite alien to Mozart. It is composed, so to speak, if not in the open air, then at least at an open window. It cannot be imitated. On the other hand Haydn cannot imitate Mozart, his inner tension. What sounds chromatically troubled in Mozart:

achieves an undisturbed diatonic clarity in Haydn (Op. 64, No. 6):

Mozart's themes are complete in themselves; Haydn's are material for future development.

The six quartets Op. X are Mozart's principal productions in this field. They were followed by the so-called 'Hoffmeister' Quartet, which stands alone, and half of a new series, the three Prussian Quartets, Op. XVIII, which were published in a miserable edition a few days before his death. The lone Quartet, K. 499, in D major, composed in August 1786, a year and a half after the C major Quartet, is worthy of its solitary position. If Mozart in creating this work wished to pay a debt to his friend and publisher, Hoffmeister, at least he did not make it easy for himself. It can be considered a synthesis of the three 'more difficult' and the three 'lighter' quartets of Op. X; and one may regard its beginning as a symbol of the spirit of the whole composition: first an easy comfortable unison; then a dialogue carried on now by one pair of instruments, now by the other; a turn towards seriousness in minor; then resolution of the tension, but in a canon between first violin and violoncello—an instance of 'learnedness' that no one feels to be learned. The quartet is at once strict and easy; and in many enchanting passages it anticipates Schubert. The minuet is unique. In the main section each voice seems to enact its role unconcerned with the others; the trio, in minor, is a piece of musical wizardry. The Adagio speaks of past sorrow with a heretofore unheard-of depth; and the finale is another of those uncanny movements in which the major mode seems to reverse its character—it is not gay, but despairing, or rather it is despairing under a mask of gaiety—despite the resoluteness of the conclusion.

The Prussian Quartets, K. 575, 589, and 590, form a group, since they are dedicated to King Friedrich Wilhelm in Berlin, who played the violoncello—or at least they were written with an eye towards such a dedication, for the first edition bears no dedication at all. The royal virtuosity had to be taken into account, and so in almost every movement of the three works the violoncello has a predominant part, while the second violin and viola retreat into the background. The quartets are slightly *concertante*, and yet they are purest chamber music. Mozart sometimes completely forgets his royal patron—as for instance in the minuet of the last Quartet. These are three works that originated under the most dreadful spiritual oppression, and yet they rise to heights of pure felicity. This is especially true of the first, in D major, in which Mozart employed for the first and second movements incipits from the happy Milan period, and concluded in a spirit at once youthful and mature. The Minuet, with the 'royal' solo in the trio, and the finale are new; the finale is a new kind of rondo in which the theme is enriched each time it returns—a triumph of art and the soul. Sometimes, as for example in the finale of the B-flat major Quartet, there is a reminiscence of the Haydn of the Russian Quartets:

And the slow movement of this Quartet is also of slenderer proportions. On the other hand, the Minuet achieves a scope and a virtuoso quality that fifteen years previously would have assured it the character of a finale. The last work, in F, attains a complete equality of all the movements—it is like a Mozartean farewell to Haydn, and, in the Andante, one of the most sensitive movements in the whole literature of chamber music, it seems to mingle the bliss and sorrow of a farewell to life. How beautiful life has been! How sad! How brief!

To the period of the composition of the ten 'great' quartets belong three chamber-music works for smaller combinations: two Duos for violin and viola (K. 423 and 424) and a Divertimento for string trio (K. 563)—the first two dating from the beginning of this period and the other from the end. But the fact that they call for fewer instruments is no indication of the value of these works. They are on a plane with the quartets, even though they are not nearly so well known.

There is an anecdote about the origin of the two Duos that is at least not beyond the bounds of credibility. In the summer of 1783 Mozart was visiting in Salzburg when Michael Haydn was prevented by illness from completing a series of six duos apparently ordered by Colloredo—only four had been finished.

The invalid gave his condition as an excuse, but the Archbishop, who did not like excuses, immediately ordered Haydn's salary to be withheld, as the surest means of hastening the convalescence of a man who had only his salary with which to pay the doctor and chemist. Mozart, who visited the sick man every day, found him much disturbed and, upon inquiring, was told of the Archbishop's decree. He was not in the habit of taking refuge in consoling words when there was anything he could do to help. Without saying a word to his poor friend, he went home and two days later brought him the Duets fully written out in a fair copy. Nothing more was needed, except the name of Michael Haydn on the first page, for them to be delivered to the Archbishop.

This anecdote, which originated with two pupils of Michael's, G. Schinn and Fr. J. Otter, may be true to the extent that during Mozart's stay at Salzburg his relations with Michael Haydn really became friendlier; in fact he even borrowed a symphony from him at that time and furnished it with an Introduction. The part of 'ogre' that is again imputed to Colloredo is probably invented: it is difficult to see why six duos would have to be finished by a certain day—duos, by the way, that were never published by Michael Haydn. It is true that the honest Gerber (*Neues Lexicon*, 1, 533) mentions six sonatas for violin and viola that, 'it was announced in 1794, were to be brought out shortly in two instalments by Gombart in Augsburg,' but they apparently never were published. Whether the four duos by Michael that have survived in manuscript (in C, D, E, and F) are identical with those of 1783 is not certain. In any event Mozart had not renounced his rights in the two he composed, for on 6 and 24 December 1783 he asked his father to return them. Probably he had been simply struck by a desire to try his hand at this form, too.

Nowhere else is his genius, his unsought superiority over Michael and even over Joseph Haydn, shown more clearly than in these two works. That there is a relation between Mozart's Duos and those of the Haydns is well known. All of these works, the four by Michael, and six by Joseph (in C, A, E-flat, F, D, and B-flat), which appeared in the 1770's, are in three movements, with a not too extended slow movement in the middle and a rondo or *Tempo di Minuetto* at the end. With Joseph these minuets are nothing more than simple two-part themes with a few variations. And it is only in the first of Joseph's duos that one may speak of a true duet character; all the others, including Michael's, are rather violin solos with obbligato accompaniment by the viola. How little the viola has to do sometimes may be seen in the fact that in Joseph Haydn's sixth duo, which begins and ends with variations, it always merely repeats the theme without even a trace of altered figuration. Nevertheless Mozart takes these works as a starting-point. That he probably knew Joseph's duos is indicated by the following parallels:

Like Haydn, Mozart concludes the second of his duos with a set of variations; like him, he keeps the slow movements short, offering opportunities for a cadenza. These instrumental duos are a curious form that goes back deep into the sixteenth century: curious in their mixture of virtuosity, a didactic, étude-like air, and occasional strict, 'learned' moments. Mozart conserved all this, the virtuosity, the instructiveness, the 'strictness'—how delightful the canon in the development section of the first movement of Duo No. 1!—and yet created art-works of the finest sort, of a freshness, a humor, and an appropriateness for the instruments that make these works unique of their kind. A witticism serves as the introduction to the second Duo, in the most pompous symphonic style; but the following Allegro, in the development section, makes something serious out of the symphonic element. When Mozart composed these pieces he was surely not thinking of Archbishop Colloredo; and, just as surely, he had completely forgotten Michael Haydn.

Unique in a more literal sense is the String Trio, K. 563, completed on 27 September 1788—midway between the 'Hoffmeister' Quartet and the first of the 'Prussian' Quartets. It is the only string-trio Mozart ever wrote. The four preludes to Bach fugues or the Divertimento, K. 205, of 1773 (which is really only a string trio with obbligato horns) may be considered its predecessors, in a way, but its only true predecessor is the fragment K. Anh. 66, in G major, which probably served as a 'springboard' for K. 563. But the framework of this fragment was too small for him; he apparently wanted to write something more important for his friend and brother-Mason, Michael Puchberg, who had helped him out of embarrassment so often, as well as for posterity or eternity. In the following spring he had K. 563 repeated in Dresden, but was not entirely satisfied with the performance, as is implied in his remark (letter of 16 April 1789): '. . . it was played quite decently.'

This is not a trio like the four-movement string trios, Op. 9, later written by Beethoven, but a divertimento 'in six movements' (*di sei pezzi*). On the other hand it is not a divertimento like Beethoven's Serenade for flute, violin, and viola, Op. 25, of which an open-air performance is easily conceivable but which rather brings an echo of open-air music into the drawing-room. Mozart's E-flat major Trio is a true chamber-music work, and grew to such large proportions only because it was intended to offer the hearer something special in the way of art, invention, and good spirits. Thus the minuet is followed by another, slower movement, variations on a folk-like theme; and a second minuet with two trios. But the three principal movements, the first Allegro, the Adagio in A-flat, and the final Rondo, are of full chamber-music stature. Mozart wrote few development sections of such grim seriousness as that of the first movement, few adagios of such breadth, few finales of such lovableness and intimacy; and even the 'gay' movements—the minuets and the Andante variations—have a power and depth found only in a work calculated to please connoisseurs. Only a connoisseur can evaluate properly the well-wrought dialogue of this apparently so modest work: each instrument is *primus inter pares*; every note is significant, every note is a contribution to spiritual and sensuous fulfilment in sound. It seems to me that one does not compliment a masterwork like this by saying that it sounds 'like a quartet.' Would it be a compliment, then, to say of a quartet that it sounds like a quintet or a symphony? No, it sounds like a trio—like the finest, most perfect trio ever heard.

Mozart's first quintet, written long before the others, must be considered by itself. It was composed at Salzburg in the spring of 1773, and in December of that year Mozart replaced the trio of the minuet by a new one and revised the finale so radically that one may almost regard this as a new piece too. The immediate occasion for the writing of this work (in B-flat major, K. 174) is unknown, unless it was the desire to compete with a Quintet in C by Michael Haydn; and Wyzewa and Saint-Foix have shown that the later version of the work was very probably occasioned by a new Quintet in G by Michael. Joseph Haydn could not have offered a model this time because he never wrote any quintets. When he was asked why he had neglected to do so, he is said to have answered that no one had ever commissioned one from him. But another reason might have well influenced him also, namely that there already existed an internationally celebrated composer of quintets, Luigi Boccherini of Lucca, the fame of whose quintets began to spread through the world in the late 1760's. Boccherini cannot have been wholly unknown to Mozart even as early as 1770, and perhaps his influence had something to do with the origin of Mozart's later, Vienna quintets. Meanwhile Mozart held to a model nearer home—Michael's. And there arose a singular work that is not easily pigeonholed. The category of the quintet with two violas was, about 1770, rather closer to the symphony than to the true quintet—one cannot help recalling that in many symphonies of this period Mozart divided the violas. (It may be mentioned in passing that Boccherini himself apparently did not write quintets for any other combination of strings: he does indeed call the second viola 'alto violoncello,' but its part is notated in the viola clef throughout and is almost unplayable on the violoncello. And Beethoven follows both Boccherini and Mozart; Schubert was the first to make the change to the greater sonority afforded by two violoncellos.) In addition, however, the category is close to *concertante* chamber music—a chamber music that is not true chamber music. I cannot boast that I know all of Boccherini's 113 quintets; but in those I do know the first violin and 'alto violoncello' always dominate and relegate the other three participants to the position of accompanying instruments. And so the string quintet of this period acquires something of the character of the divertimento, even of the serenade, or 'notturno' —one can easily imagine it played under starry skies.

Mozart's early quintet is a mixture of all these things. The first movement has the character of chamber music, and the development section especially, with its agitated triplets (an agitation in which the violoncello joins only at the end) would be too serious in a serenade; but on the other hand it does not lack *concertante* dialogue between first violin and first viola. The intimate Adagio is full of concealed echo-effects; the Minuet (especially the Trio), full of unconcealed ones: in the Trio the second violin could easily be played 'off-stage.' And, with all this, the work has one of the longest finales in sonata form that Mozart ever wrote: contrapuntal or rather combinative, with a positively exhibitionistic emphasizing of all possible combinations of the thematic material; including even a *fausse reprise*—so very rare in Mozart—and an elaborate coda. The movement would be astonishing if we did not know what kind of polyphonist Mozart really was; as it is, the movement strikes us as 'premature' and the whole work as a stylistically uneven experiment.

It is only in the last Vienna years that Mozart returns to the category of the quintet—or rather makes a fresh start with it. It is difficult to say what caused him to do so. An external inducement was perhaps the death of Frederick the Great and the accession to the throne in Berlin of a violoncello-playing dilettante. On 21 January 1786, Boccherini had received the title of Prussian Court composer, and Mozart habitually took careful note of lucrative appointments of that sort. We have evidence that in the following year Boccherini visited Berlin and Breslau, and perhaps also Vienna, where his brother Giovanni-Antonio-Gastone, a librettist, lived. (Gastone was closely connected with Salieri, which probably accounts for the fact that he is never mentioned in Mozart's letters.) This external inducement is perhaps the most plausible explanation. From April 1787 to April 1791 Mozart wrote four string quintets, probably intending to dedicate them to the King as soon as he had completed a set of six; to hasten the achievement of that goal he even arranged one of his own wind serenades as a quintet— surely against his artistic conscience. It should not be objected that if Mozart had the new King in mind he would have written quintets with two 'celli. Not at all; the Royal part suffered no rivals. Mozart probably began with a fragment, K. Anh. 80, which is carried out up to the beginning of the development section. It is a sketch of great value, discarded only because Mozart became aware that he had devoted too little attention to the 'cello. And then he began a new quintet, with a dialogue not between first viola and first violin but between 'cello and violin:

Ex. 39.

This was no accident. But Mozart would not have been Mozart if he had not later forgotten the predominant role of the 'cello, as he sometimes did in the Prussian Quartets also. In April 1788, poverty forced him to offer on a subscription basis the three quintets that were completed—those in C major and G minor, and the transcription in C minor.

The first of these (in C, K. 515) is to be compared only with the Quartet in the same key, except that its beginning is not striving or yearning, like the Allegro of the Quartet, but proud and regal and pregnant with fate. Several statements of the first subject are required before the second is reached, and it is again a long time before the friendly closing theme of the exposition arrives. Then begins a development section of the greatest richness, not only in instrumental combinations but also in dramatic expression—one holds one's breath until the organ-point that prepares the recapitulation is reached. Again Mozart writes a worked-out coda, *stretto*-like in character. The following Minuet is more of a *tempo di minuetto*, with a Trio in the subdominant, which itself grows into complete song-form. For the slow movement we have a sketch of an Andante in 6/8 time, which Mozart discarded after 10 measures as too light, in favor of a new one that has a depth of longing and tranquillity, serving as an enchanting embodiment of the flight from the demonism and fatalism of *Don Giovanni* (on which Mozart was working at the same time) into a purer and more blessed world of humanity. One cannot imagine this Andante being addressed to such characters as either Donna Anna or Donna Elvira. Completely forgotten, also, was the fat Prussian King: the dialogue between the lovers is carried on by viola and first violin; and the oneness of the two souls is complete. The finale is full of the most blissful harmony—harmony in the technical sense and harmony too between homophony and counterpoint, *galanterie* and 'learnedness'—once more one of those movements 'full of the art that remains hidden.' When Mozart is fortunate in his art he finds an idea at once godlike and childlike, an idea that has that 'second naïveté' of which only maturity and mastery are capable:

Ex. 40 [*Allegro*]

The sombre counterpart to this Quintet is the one that immediately follows (in G minor, K. 516), which is related to it as the G minor Symphony is related to the so-called 'Jupiter'—except that in the order of the symphonies Mozart goes from darkness to light. Mozart had at first begun a Quintet in A minor, but abandoned this key, which is apt to take on a weeping, 'exotic' sound, in favor of the key that was more familiar to him in such cases. What takes place here can be compared perhaps only with the scene in the Garden of Gethsemane. The chalice with its bitter potion must be emptied, and the disciples sleep. Compare the (rare) movements in minor in Haydn, who—in the C minor Symphony, in the *Reiter* Quartet, in the D minor Quartet Op. 76, No. 5, in the D minor Symphony No. 80—cannot bring himself to remain in gloomy darkness, but writes the recapitulations in the major. Mozart concludes the exposition in the relative major, but in the recapitulation returns inexorably to the minor. There is no escape. And the Minuet says nothing else than: 'Not as I will, but as thou wilt.' In the Trio a ray of divine consolation falls from the clouds, but the return to the main section is of course inevitable. The *Adagio non troppo* is a prayer—the prayer of a lonely one surrounded on all sides by the walls of a deep chasm: the many 'solos,' the enharmonic change before the return to the tonic, are symbolic. The final movement is introduced by a kind of darkly heroic cavatina of the first violin and then turns to G major, but it is the disconsolate major that Mozart utilizes in so many of his last works. The theme of this Rondo seems somewhat too trivial to serve as the resolution of the three preceding movements, and creates a slight shock each time it reappears after the 'episodes.'

The two last string quintets followed in December 1790 and April 1791, supposedly on commission from a Hungarian said to be the wholesale merchant Johann Tost of Ungarisch-Hrodisch in Moravia, himself an excellent violinist, and the bearer of the dedications of two series of quartets by Haydn of 1789 (51-56) and 1790 (57-62). Since Tost had recently become wealthy by marriage, perhaps Mozart was well paid for these two works, at least.

He should have been; both bear all the earmarks of compositions intended for a connoisseur. The first, in D major, K. 593, begins with a Larghetto, which juxtaposes the 'cello (Mozart has not completely forgotten the King of Prussia) and the group of higher instruments; question and answer are repeated at once on a higher step of the scale— a typical beginning for the great instrumental works of the last period (the Piano Sonata in D, K. 576, the fragments of movements for piano, K. Anh. 29 and 30, the Quartet, K. 590, etc.) and a procedure of which Beethoven took careful note, as we see in the String Quartet Op. 59, No. 2, for example. This Larghetto returns at the end of the following Allegro, and leads to a quite short, abrupt conclusion—consisting simply of the eight opening measures of the Allegro. Thus this whole Allegro itself has a somewhat groping, combinative character, with an impetuous development section in two parts, the first marchlike, the second warlike. The recapitulation achieves its effect by means of intensified polyphony. It is a very unusual movement for Mozart, being definitely introductory in character. It leads to a deeply felt Adagio, related to the slow movement of the 'Jupiter' Symphony, with three-part responses as in the five-part madrigals of the sixteenth century, and containing the finest polyphonic development. The Minuet is a bit Haydnish—manly, with a concluding canon as a 'trump card' and a 'spiccato' Trio. The Rondo, finally, is of the richest maturity, with its playful theme, its *fugati* in which 'learnedness' takes on wit and charm without forfeiting any of its earnestness. The beginning of the theme, originally a chromatically descending fifth, gains grace and character by means of a single stroke:

The last of the quintets, in E-flat (K. 614), is by no means to be regarded as a 'farewell.' An *Allegro di molto* gains its individual, peculiarly busy character especially from the trills of the principal motive, from an accompanying motive in agile sixteenth-notes, and from its contrapuntal tendencies—so that only a relatively short development is needed. Again Mozart has not entirely forgotten the King of Prussia, especially in the second theme, in which the violin is answered by the 'cello. The Andante, on the other hand, represents a pinnacle of achievement in the combination of *concertante* and chamber-music elements— it seems like a piece for the middle movement of a piano concerto, treated in chamber-music style: brilliance, workmanship, repose, and joy in creation all together. The Minuet has a bagpipe-trio and is full of Haydnish straightforwardness; and quite Haydnish, like an act of thanksgiving for the only great contemporary in the field of chamber music, is the finale—even the long and contrapuntally inclined development section is Haydnish.

Such other quintets as there are by Mozart are of a very different sort.

It will be better to speak of the transcribing of the Wind Serenade in C minor (K. 388) into a String Quintet (K. 406) when we discuss the original version; the transcription was made for purely 'business' reasons. A Quintet for horn, violin, two (!) violas, and 'cello does not really belong to chamber music. Mozart wrote it in Vienna at the end of 1782 for the Salzburg horn-player Ignatz Leitgeb and, like all the works written for this butt of Mozart's jokes, it is to be taken half humorously. One might take it wholly so if it were not that the middle movement, an Andante, is a deeply felt piece, a little love duet between horn and violin. The first and last movements make sport of the limitations of the solo instrument—listen especially to the humorous fanfare-motive in the Rondo-Finale. The work is a rudimentary concerto with chamber-music accompaniment, and even includes opportunities for cadenzas. André and Artaria tried in vain to stamp it as chamber music by interpolating one of the two Minuets from the Serenade K. 375— but this only results in a loss of unified character. Quite another matter is the true Quintet for clarinet and string quartet of the last Vienna period, the so-called Stadler Quintet, K. 581, dating from the end of September 1789. Mozart himself called it (8 April 1790) 'Stadler's Quintet.' Here is a chamber-music work of the finest kind, even though the clarinet predominates as *primus inter pares* and is treated as if Mozart were the first to discover its charm, its 'soft, sweet breath,' its clear depth, its agility. There is no dualism here between solo and accompaniment, only fraternal rivalry. The term 'fraternal' is used advisedly— clarinets and basset horns acquired for Mozart a Masonic character, if perhaps only for external reasons: it seems that at the less solemn meetings of his lodge, only wind instruments were used. The development section has a *concertante* air about it, but for all five participants. The *cantabile* character of the second theme is resumed in the Larghetto and nursed into full flower. The Minuet contains one Trio in minor for the string quartet alone, and another, a *Ländler*, in which the clarinet becomes the rustic instrument that it was and has remained in South Bavaria and in the other Alpine provinces. The Finale is an Allegretto with variations; brief and amusing with all its variety and richness, serious and lovable. Mozart had originally begun a finale (K. Anh. 88) that anticipates almost note for note Ferrando's aria in *Così fan tutte* (No. 24) to the text *Ah, lo veggio, quell'anima bella al mio pianto resister non sà*—the acme of joyfulness. But this 89-measure beginning turned out to be too *concertante* and may have seemed over-cheerful to Mozart. At any rate he discarded it. A quintet-fragment in F major for clarinet, basset horn, and string trio (K. *Anh.* 90) was perhaps another and even more elaborated study for the Stadler Quintet; but it would necessarily have turned out still more *concertante* in style.

12. *Divertimento, Cassation, Serenade*

OZART was born into a period in which the line between chamber music and symphony, between music intended for the theater or concert hall, on the one hand, or for the concert hall and palace courtyard or garden, on the other, was not as sharply drawn as it became about 1800. A symphony for string orchestra could find its way into Haydn's Quartets Op. 1 without offending chamber-music players very much; an overture of Handel's could be performed now in the Haymarket or Lincoln's Inn Fields and now in Westminster Abbey, or a 'sinfonia' of Paisiello's now at the opera and now at the Concerts Spirituels. Thus there is a whole series of works by Mozart that seem to occupy a place between chamber music and symphony, between the concert hall and the 'open air,' between the symphonic and the *concertante*, between a solo and a symphonic treatment of the strings—any exact or strict distinction seems impossible. It may perhaps be said that all these works owe their origin to some festive occasion, and that they consequently have more of a light, social character, that they are less 'eternal' and more 'eighteenth-century' than the true string quartets and concert-symphonies. This is true enough in a general way, but not always in individual cases. There are many symphonies by Mozart in the Italian style that are inferior in workmanship and seriousness to a serenade; and there are many serenades—for example the two written in Vienna for wind-instruments (K. 375 and 388)—that rise above the purely 'social.' The second of these is one of Mozart's most intense works in a minor key, and Mozart himself transformed it from 'open-air music' to chamber music, even though it lost much thereby in power and beauty. Every one of such works must be considered by itself and the attempt must be made to determine in which group it belongs. For there are groups. One must separate them; one should not follow the 'Complete Works' edition, which, in Series 9, Part 2, unmercifully lumps together in one volume unpretentious wind sextets, music for equestrian ballets, and the finest chamber music, simply because they all bear the title *Divertimento*.

A forerunner of this chamber music of the finest type is the Divertimento K. 205, which Mozart wrote in Vienna in the autumn of 1773 for a garden party in one of the houses frequented at that time by father and son, perhaps for the Mesmer family. There are six movements: the first Allegro is introduced by a brief Largo; the Adagio is framed by two Minuets; and a short March (K. 290) precedes the whole work and follows the presto Finale. The setting: string trio and two horns; the 'cello is doubled by a bassoon, whose part is not even written out separately. One imagines that the five or six instrumentalists made their entrance and exit playing the March, and performed the Divertimento proper in a candle-lit arbor. Here there could be no probing of depths; art must remain inconspicuous and must clothe itself in charm. But virtuosity could be displayed: the first violin is always, or almost always, a *violino principale*, which has the right to predominate and to call forth applause. Thus the orchestral serenades will include a violin concerto; and thus Mozart's true violin concertos will always retain something of the character of a serenade, and can never be placed together with his clavier concertos in one series. Is it not significant that Mozart in Vienna no longer felt the urge to compose a violin concerto, although there was no lack of occasions to do so? It is true that the violinists who participated in Mozart's 'academies' used to bring their own concertos, but he must have been tempted often enough to replace these sometimes very questionable products by works of his own—as he actually did at least once, for a concerto by Viotti. But divertimenti, serenades, and violin concertos were for him more a Salzburg affair, an affair of youth, of a desire to please, even of artistic conciliation. They incline towards the cheerful side. The slow movements are mostly in the friendly dominant of the principal key; the keys themselves are always those nearest at hand, so to speak. Where Mozart goes beyond what lies nearest at hand—and he does that often, because, being Mozart, he cannot do otherwise—he is careful not to let his procedure become too startling for the client. Thus, in this first 'Vienna' Divertimento we find, in the Trio of the first Minuet, a four-measure canon between viola and violin in which one voice enters immediately after the other— in the sixteenth century it would have been called a *canon ad minimam* —a device hardly to be expected in so light a form. The whole little work, dependent in a hundred touches on similar works by Joseph Haydn, is nevertheless more intimate than the Haydn pieces. Even where, as in the Trio of the second Minuet, the horns perform a solo, it abstains from the more robust humor of Haydn. Mozart toys with 'popular' music in these serenades, cassations, and concertos, but it is a different concept for him from what it is for Haydn; we shall return to this point a little later.

Mozart began a similar work (K. 288), for the same instruments, about four years later. Only a fragment has survived—77 measures of the first movement. It is difficult to determine whether it once existed complete or whether it is only a beginning that Mozart abandoned in favor of another work, as was his habit. I incline towards the latter hypothesis; it seems to me that Mozart wished at first to write this 'String Trio with Horns' for Countess Lodron but then preferred the fuller setting of the Divertimento K. 247. The same relation seems to exist between the fragment K. 246b and the Divertimento K. 334. Here, too, the beginning of a first movement, extending to the development section, may have been discarded in favor of K. 334.

What is hinted at in this early Vienna 'String Trio with Three Wind-Instruments' is fully worked out in four compositions written in Salzburg between 1776 and 1779: K. 247, 251, 287, and 334. The first and third of these were composed for the Lodron family and the last for the Robinig family. K. 251 is supposed to have been composed for Nannerl's twenty-fifth birthday, in July 1776, which is quite credible; it is written somewhat more hastily and carelessly than the other three, and 'for seven instruments,' namely, oboe, two horns, and string quartet. The other three, however, which could be called simply string quartets with two obbligato horns, are among the purest, gayest, most satisfying, and most perfect that ever assumed musical form; and there are people who would trade a whole act of *Tannhäuser* or *Lohengrin* for one of these works, a lost paradise of music.

The first of these Divertimenti, in F, written in June 1776, introduced and concluded with a graceful March (K. 248), firmly establishes the tone and style of these works not only for Salzburg but also for the later Vienna period. The first of the two slow movements foreshadows the *Romanze* of the *Kleine Nachtmusik*, which we hardly need to quote for comparison with this *Andante grazioso*:

The piquant antagonism between the *concertante violino principale* and many motives whose existence and character are determined by the horns governs the outer movements—as for example the incipit of the Finale-Allegro, or the omnipresent, gruff and yet contented motive of the first movement:

A slow movement in serenade style, in which the first violin indulges its amorous feelings, is typical; as is the short sustained introduction to the Finale (Beethoven was to retain it for his Septet). The stylistic basis of the whole work is like that of a quartet—chamber-music character, but slightly *concertante*, without 'higher obligations,' and consequently so much the more cheerful, charming, and lovable.

The Septet (K. 251) for Nannerl's birthday (30 July 1776) does not quite belong in the series, especially because of its employment of the oboe, which vies with the first violin for leadership. Thus Mozart renounces the charm of the *violino principale* with its little coquetries; the whole piece sounds quite like chamber music, even though 'seriousness' is almost completely avoided. Why the oboe? Because the 'hautbois' is so French. Just as Egmont, in Goethe's drama, once wished to visit his Klärchen as a 'Spaniard'—that is, in a Spanish costume—so Wolfgang wished to come to his sister as a 'Frenchman,' perhaps in memory of their days together in Paris ten years earlier, in 1764 and 1766. The opening and concluding March bears the superscription *Marcia alla francese*, and is French, with its jagged rhythms; and one has the strong impression that the prototypes of all the themes of this Divertimento were to be found in the French *chanson*. It is as if Mozart were anticipating here the themes of his Parisian ballet music *Les petits riens*, written in the summer of 1778—the theme, for example, of the *Pantomime* in that work:

In February 1777 Mozart wrote a new *Divertimento a 6 stromenti,*
that is, a string quartet with two obbligato horns, K. 287, once more
for Countess Lodron. This is a masterwork *sui generis*—even though
Wyzewa and Saint-Foix have shown how much it owes to a string
quintet by Michael Haydn—and is to be compared only with its earlier
and later sister-works, K. 247 and 334. It contains the same mixture as
the first Lodron Divertimento, but perhaps a somewhat more intimate
one, more like chamber music. Since it is a work written for the winter
and not the summer, there is naturally no introductory and concluding
March. We are at the Carnival; and so in the first slow movement, an
Andante grazioso, the theme dons six different character-masks—none
of them tragic. The first movement ventures into a more impetuous
discourse than usual, with dialogues between strings and horns and a
more general participation of all the instruments, in eighth-notes and
triplets. The second Adagio becomes a true, deeply felt, violin-concerto
slow movement; while the Minuets, in maturity and character, anticipate the last Vienna period. And the Finale is no longer a mere 'last
dance of the evening' but has become a grand, crowning closing movement; the fact is not without significance that Beethoven's name occurred to the two French investigators in their analysis of this movement. For its counterpart is found perhaps only in the Finale of
Beethoven's last Trio, also in B-flat major, with its jolly and straightforward theme. But Mozart is subtler and gayer than Beethoven. His
theme is the South-German popular song *D'Bäuerin hat d' Katz verlorn,*
weiss nit wo's is', and in order to make the joke quite clear he introduces it with an exaggeratedly pathetic recitative. This sporting with

a popular song, however, is not parody or coarse mockery, but wit; and if Mozart, in a true yodeler's theme:

Ex. 45 [*Allegro molto*]

seems to be quoting an Alpine maid, she is an apple-cheeked lass, to be sure, but a dainty one. Shortly before the close, the recitative appears again, in shortened form but with even more comic effect.

The last of these three string quartets with two obbligato horns is the Divertimento in D major, K. 334, written in the summer of 1779—the *Musique vom Robinig*, as Mozart himself called it. Frau von Robinig, especially, was a family friend of the Mozarts, and had accompanied Nannerl to Munich in 1774-5 in the days of *La Finta giardiniera*. Now, while the later Lodron Divertimento transfigures into music, with wit and humor, a quality typical of Salzburg: the ideal harmony of city, landscape, and happy people, a blend that found its actual embodiment perhaps only in a beautiful woman, the Robinig Divertimento does the same thing with 'tenderness,' which is not free of fleeting shadows of melancholy. The Andante, a theme with six variations, would have achieved the intensity of the finale of the D minor String Quartet if a divertimento could have aspired to the same seriousness as a quartet. The mixture of the chamber-music and *concertante* styles is here carried to perfection; and Mozart avoids the seriousness of the quartet either through the sweet sensuousness that appears at its purest in the concluding Rondo, or through a tendency towards the *Ländler*, variants of which are presented in both Minuets. The second slow movement, in A major, is that ideal of a 'serenade,' a concerto movement for the violin, in which the solo instrument voices all the personal sentiments and the accompaniment nevertheless does not sink into insignificance. Here too a graceful March forms the beginning and conclusion.

Divertimenti of a quite different sort are those for three or four pairs of wind-instruments—oboes, horns, bassoons, and, where possible, clarinets; works that are truly 'open-air music' and that lack marches for the entrance and exit of the players; for they were written, not for chamber-music performers, whom one invites into the salon and then dismisses with respect, but for pipers who have to remain outside, beneath the window. Wind-instrument players are always more primitive musicians than fiddlers, at least Mozart so treated them, and in fact in those days the step from servant to horn-player or bassoonist was an easier matter than from servant to violinist or 'cellist. Mozart began to write such works as early as the spring of 1773, when he composed in or for Milan two works for five pairs of wind-instruments—oboes, clarinets, English horns, horns, and bassoons (K. 186 and 166). Whenever he employed clarinets before 1781 it is certain that he was writing 'for abroad,' for these noble instruments were not yet available in Salzburg. Thus two such works, K. Anh. 226 and 227, for oboes, clarinets, horns, and bassoons—formerly considered of doubtful authenticity—cannot have been written in and for Salzburg; they probably originated in Munich at the time of *La Finta giardiniera*, for they are too primitive for the later Vienna period. The Viennese demanded other qualities. For Salzburg two oboes, two horns, and two bassoons sufficed: K. 213 (1775), K. 240, 252, 253 (all 1776), and K. 270 and 289 (1777).

We need not consider these Divertimenti for winds in detail: They are true garden-music; the sonata-like movements are as simple as possible, and to the minuet are added other dances—a *contredanse en rondeau*, a polonaise. Pastorales mix with fanfare-like phrases for the horns, and, despite the fact that the voices usually proceed in pairs, in thirds or sixths, there is the most sensitive feeling for the sound of the whole and of the individual instruments. The form is toyed with, without contrivance and without strain; it is songlike and yet never vulgar. If any works characterize Mozart as an eighteenth-century composer, it is these; they are 'innocent' in every sense, written as it were before the fall from grace—the French Revolution—written for summer nights under the light of torches and lamps, to be heard close by and from afar; and it is from afar that they sound most beautiful. Mozart remembered such sounds of wind-instruments in *Don Giovanni* and in *Così fan tutte*, in the former as table music, in the latter as garden music. Two groups of wind pieces—for flutes, trumpets, and timpani—that do not belong in this series seem to have been written more for everyday use; these are more a military (specifically, a cavalry) project, for Mozart probably had to write them for two productions in the Salzburg Riding School, at the foot of the Mönchberg, and he executed the commission without much enthusiasm.

But at the end of even this unpretentious series there are three works so amazing, inspired with such ambition and seriousness, that they must be regarded as the peak not only of the series but of the whole category. They have had scarcely any successors; we have, dating from Beethoven's youth and early manhood, the Rondino for four pairs of winds, the Sextet for wind-instruments Op. 71, and the Trio for two oboes and English horn Op. 87, but in general the category was left to be cultivated by minor talents, and in the nineteenth century was replaced by arrangements for military band. To be sure, the mischief had already begun in Haydn's and Mozart's time, when whole operas were transcribed for wind ensembles; the Italian libraries, especially, are full of such arrangements for 'banda.'

Now the first of these three works by Mozart, the Serenade in B-flat major for 13 wind-instruments, K. 361, is far from an arrangement. He had begun it in Munich at the beginning of 1781, at the time of the performance of *Idomeneo*, and completed it in Vienna, at the time of his most strenuous efforts to escape from the bonds of Salzburg. In composing it he probably had in mind the excellent wind-players of Munich, as well as the intention of once more trying to insinuate himself into the favor of Carl Theodor by means of an extraordinary piece. We have no evidence that the 13 players ever actually came together in Vienna; there exists an arrangement of this work for the four customary pairs of winds (K. Anh. 182), which may very well have been Mozart's own idea. The contra-bassoon is not named in the autograph: Mozart calls for a double bass. But this in no way contradicts the 'open-air' character of the extraordinary work, which, in any case, rises above any question of purpose into ideal regions. Whether the title *Gran Partita*, which perhaps hints at performance in the open, was affixed by Mozart himself, is uncertain—the authenticity of the handwriting of this title in the autograph is doubtful.

The fascination of the work emanates from its sheer sound. There is a continuous alternation between tutti and soli, in which the part of the soli is usually allotted to the two clarinets; a constant reveling in new combinations: a quartet of clarinets and basset horns, a sextet of oboes, basset horns, and bassoons over the supporting double bass; oboe, basset horn, and bassoon in unison, with accompaniment—a mixture of timbres and transparent clarity at the same time; an 'overlapping' of all the tone-colors, especially in the development section of the first movement. No instrument is treated in true *concertante* fashion, but each one can, and strives to, distinguish itself; and just as in a *buffo finale* by Mozart each person is true to his own character, so each instrument here is true to its own character—the oboe to its aptness for cantabile melodies, the bassoon likewise and also, in chattering triplets, to its comic properties. The two pairs of horns furnish the basic tone-color; but the fact that Mozart uses only the first pair in the first slow movement, a *Notturno*, is an indication of his supreme taste and skill: this is a scene from *Romeo* under starry skies, a scene in which longing, grief, and love are wrung like a distillation from the beating hearts of the lovers. The counterpart to this lyricism is found in a 'Romance' whose sentimentality is carried towards the point of absurdity by means of an oddly burlesque Allegretto, an 'alternativo.' A third slow movement, an Andantino with variations, has an episodic effect, each variation, however, offering new evidence of mastery. The same is true of the two Minuets, the second Trio of the one being in G minor, and the first Trio of the other in B-flat minor, and all the sections differing in character. A somewhat noisy Rondo forms the conclusion; one might call it a Rondo *alla turca*, for the theme of which Mozart seems to have recalled the Finale of his youthful four-hand clavier sonata. The Theme and Variations are taken from the Mannheim Flute Quartet K. *Anh.* 171—if this movement is authentic. But it probably is; very possibly, after the exertion and outpouring of invention of the first five movements, Mozart was willing to permit himself a little relaxation.

Mozart himself has given us precise information concerning the origin of the second work and the identity of the person for whom it was written. It is the Serenade in E-flat K. 375 for pairs of clarinets, horns, and bassoons.

I wrote it for St. Theresa's Day, for Frau von Hickel's sister, or rather the sister-in-law of Herr von Hickel, court painter, at whose house it was performed [15 October 1781] for the first time. The six gentlemen who executed it are poor beggars who, however, play quite well together, particularly the first clarinet and the two horns. But the chief reason why I composed it was in order to let Herr von Strack, who goes there every day, hear something of my composition; so I wrote it rather carefully. It has won great applause too and on St. Theresa's Night it was performed in three different places; for as soon as they finished playing it in one place, they were taken off somewhere else and paid to play it . . .

The six poor devils had the decency to render their thanks to Mozart himself on his name-day, 31 October:

At eleven o'clock at night I was treated to a serenade performed by two clarinets, two horns, and two bassoons—and that too of my own composition . . . these musicians asked that the street door might be opened and, placing themselves in the center of the courtyard, surprised me, just as I was about to undress, in the most pleasant fashion imaginable with the first chord in E♭. [Letter to his father, 3 November 1781.]

He probably dressed again and entertained the six musicians in princely fashion—that is, paid for his own composition, which would have been quite in Mozartean style. However, Herr von Strack, the Emperor's chamberlain, did nothing of any consequence for Mozart; Mozart considered him a patron, but nevertheless held (letter of 23 January 1782) that 'these court flunkeys are never to be trusted.'

If Mozart says of one of his works that he 'wrote it rather carefully,' it should be accorded special attention. The Serenade was originally scored for clarinets, horns, and bassoons, and only in the following year did he enlarge the sextet to an octet by adding oboes, perhaps for Prince Aloys Liechtenstein, who wished to organize or actually did organize a wind ensemble. As in all of these works, a march is lacking; but the first movement is itself an idealized march in sonata-form, full of vital melody and figuration for each individual instrument—what a joy to play it! In the Adagio—which remains in the principal key—there begins a graceful game of question and answer, a gay consorting together of the instruments. Mozart had no wish to go deeper here. This game takes on sturdier character in the two Minuets; in the Finale, the main theme of which seems a compliment to Haydn, there is as much depth and workmanship as the category and the festive occasion allow.

The last and most important of these works is shrouded in mystery. Mozart, in a letter to his father (27 July 1782), says only this about it: '. . . I have had to compose in a great hurry a serenade, but only for wind-instruments . . .," so that the work could not be used for a local Salzburg festivity in the home of the Haffners. But he is silent about the fact that its whole character is not at all suitable for a festivity. We know nothing about the occasion, nothing about the person who commissioned it, nothing about whether this client desired so explosive a serenade or whether that is simply what poured forth from Mozart's soul. Is it really a *Nacht-Musique* for the open air? There are only the customary four movements—no first minuet, no second slow movement, no introductions for the outer movements, no march. The dark tonality of C minor is unique in Mozart's 'social' music. If G minor is the fatalistic key for Mozart, then C minor is the dramatic one, the key of contrasts between aggressive unisons and lyric passages. The lyric quality is always overtaken by gloomy outbursts. The first movement points the way to the Piano Concerto in C minor, as well as to Beethoven's Fifth Symphony—Mozart's development section already employs Beethoven's fundamental rhythm. The Andante, in E-flat, breathes true devoutness, not hypocritical piety, with which Mozart never had anything to do. The Minuet is a contrapuntal display-piece, with all sorts of canonic effects, and yet it is not a mere display-piece, since the counterpoint is not a subject for gaiety, a means for expressing wit, good humor, or cleverness, as in Haydn, but is taken very seriously. The Finale begins with impassioned and sombre variations in minor, anticipating the spirit of the Finale of the C minor Concerto, and seems about to end in minor also, when the E-flat of the horns falls like a gentle beam of light and is extended by the bassoons to a six-four chord; because of this passage alone Mozart should never have arranged the work as a quintet for strings, for these horn-fifths really require horn-tone. (In the sextet of the second act of *Don Giovanni*, when it suddenly becomes light, the same motive returns, but this time with scenic as well as psychological effect.) Victory is achieved, even though C minor returns with intensified vehemence; the theme changes to major; and the conclusion is and remains C major. The speed with which Mozart had to work results not in carelessness but in intensified concentration; the lessons in Bachian polyphony have borne fruit. This final Serenade is not merely 'rather carefully' written. The 'carelessness,' the higher wisdom, that governs the creation of every great masterwork played a part here to an extent that can never be completely accounted for.

This was Mozart's last true serenade. Apparently no further commissions came, not even from young Prince Liechtenstein, in whom Mozart had placed such great hopes. There followed only the Serenade for strings, which, under its original title, *Eine kleine Nachtmusik* (K. 525), has become one of Mozart's best-known works. The truth is that it is one of the most enigmatic. We do not know how it came into existence—it was written while Mozart was working on the second act of *Don Giovanni*, and completed 10 August 1787—nor have we any knowledge of its being performed. We know it only in the coarse form it has acquired through performances with from five to nine double basses and a corresponding multiplication of the other string parts, but Mozart and the work itself surely call for not more than one bass— if any—and a double string quartet. We know it only in the version with four movements, but it originally had five: Mozart writes clearly in his thematic catalogue: '*Eine kleine Nachtmusik*, consisting of an Allegro, Minuet and Trio.—Romance, Minuet and Trio and Finale.' I do not know who suppressed the first Minuet. My guess is that the Minuet of the half-apocryphal Clavier Sonata K. *Anh.* 136, originally doubtless a quartet movement, should be transposed back to G major and interpolated in the Serenade; we would then surely have the Serenade once more in its original form.

All the riddles presented by this work would be solved by the assumption that Mozart wrote it for himself, to satisfy an inner need, and that it served as a corrective counterpart to the *Musikalischer Spass*, which he had written seven or eight weeks previously. To create that satire on clumsy composing must have been an endless pleasure to him, but at the same time a kind of self-mortification that did violence to nature. A pair of ears so sensitive as his required that the mistakes be corrected; for him, as for Bach, every false note was an offense against the cosmic system. There is a delightful anecdote about Bach: while lying in bed he heard Friedemann, at the clavier, break off before the cadence. He sprang up, played the cadence, and then gave his son a mighty box on the ear. This tale could be told also of Mozart and Süssmayr. After Mozart had disturbed the cosmic system by the *Musikalischer Spass*, he set it to rights again with the *Kleine Nachtmusik*. The four (or five) movements are quite short, but not a note could be added to them. Nothing very personal is said—not even in the *Romanze*, which could be dubbed '*Andante innocente*'; only in the middle section in C minor does the prevailing innocence give way to a mild unrest. The Minuet is as short and regular as it can be, robust in the principal section, tender in the Trio. This is supreme mastery in the smallest possible frame.

There remains of the works of a serenade-like character only a small March, which has been lost (K. 544, of 26 June 1788). It was scored for string trio, flute, and horn, and must accordingly have been intended for a divertimento similar to the one Mozart composed in the summer of 1776 for his sister's birthday. But this March does not fit any of his own works. Perhaps he wrote it for the 'chamber serenade' of a composer-friend.

When we turn to the final category of Mozart's serenade compositions, we approach both the symphony and the violin concerto. The best-known example of this category is the so-called 'Haffner' Serenade. Here we have no longer chamber music with two horns, or wind music or *Harmonie* (band-music), but an orchestral, symphonic style with a tendency towards the *concertante*. There are intermediate steps: for example, a Divertimento in E-flat, K. 113, written in the early Milan days (November 1771) and entitled *Concerto o sia Divertimento*, for strings, clarinets, and horns, to which Mozart added later (probably in 1777) two oboes, two English horns, and two bassoons. This work occupies a place between Mozart's wind serenades and his early, Italianate symphonies; strings and winds are contrasted in symphonic fashion, but the work as a whole definitely leans towards the open-air style; it is ideal garden-music. Another example is a Notturno for four orchestras (K. 286)—or rather for one orchestra consisting of strings and horns, answered by three other orchestras in a triple echo. If we did not have reason to believe that it was composed for New Year's Day 1777, we should say that it was the proper nocturnal music for the baroque curiosities at Mirabell Garden, near Salzburg. But Mozart was fond of conjuring up summertime in the winter. There is another *Serenata notturna* (K. 239), of January 1776, for a *concertino* of two *concertante* violins, viola, and double bass, and a *concerto grosso* of string orchestra with timpani. From the standpoint of sound and melody it is one of the most enchanting of Mozart's early works; it consists of a March in 'majestic' tempo, a Minuet, with Trio for the *concertino* alone, and a Rondo with a graceful, Gallic theme—and one does not feel that any additional movements are required. The Rondo contains two intermezzi: a short Adagio like the stiffest kind of minuet, which has the effect of an introduction to the second, a rustic, primitive Allegro. Both are interpolations and undoubtedly citations that were known to the Salzburg audience; if we knew what they were we should have more definite information about the purpose for which the work was written. These *notturni* and divertimenti have this in common with the violin concertos: in the final rondos Mozart cracks a little joke for himself and his hearers; he condescends for a moment to the level of 'the people' and makes somewhat of a display of his own aristocratic nature when he returns to his wonted style; he points to rude bucolic beauties and then shows off his own splendid raiment. Not without reason were such serenades or cassations called *Final-Musiken;* for everyone looked forward to a musical pleasantry of this sort in the finale.

The admixture of serenade elements may be seen in young Mozart's earliest Salzburg works, the *Final-Musiken* in G (K. 63) and D (K. 100), and the Cassation in B-flat (K. 99)—all three dating from 1769. Here we find the introductory and concluding March; the symphonic style of the rather brilliant or comic first movement, with its short motives linked together (as in K. 99); the two Minuets with contrasting Trios; two slow movements, in one of which the first violin expresses amorous feelings, while the other usually has the character of an intermezzo. This is Salzburg music, basically festive and gay, orchestral music that does not aim at great symphonic seriousness, music full of coloristic and echo effects. A loose relationship lingers on between this music and the *Galimathias musicum,* except that the multiplicity of movements has yielded to a firmly established convention and the coarse Augsburg style has been transformed to the finer, more aristocratic one characteristic of Salzburg. In these works, if anywhere, the aristocracy and the upper bourgeoisie of that festive town, transfigured by Mozart, live on.

After the first return from Italy the dimensions of these serenades increase, and their instrumentation becomes richer and more festive. Thus the one of June 1772 (K. 131), in D like most of the others, wrongly called a divertimento, includes two violas among the strings, three woodwinds, and four horns, treated in *concertante* fashion, and has a quite unexpected, street-song-like final tune in the last movement:

Ex. 46
Allegro assai

Somewhat later these serenades become definitely wedding music, of a festive, exuberant character, with at least eight or nine movements—an introductory and concluding March; a first movement; a slow movement framed by two Minuets; a Finale with a solemn Introduction; and, interpolated between the first movement and the first Minuet, a two-movement violin concerto, always in a key other than the principal one. Sometimes these concerto-intermezzi or intermezzi-concertos are as virtuoso in style as Mozart's true violin concertos. The first of these works is the so-called *Andretter-Musik*, written in Vienna at the beginning of August 1773 for the wedding of the older son of Johann Ernst von Andretter, Military Councillor to the Salzburg Court, and performed in the composer's absence. Here there is no trace of the uncertainty to be found in the string quartets written about the same time: Mozart had only to follow an established Salzburg tradition. This is an unambitious symphonic style, full of allusions to known melodies and, as was customary at a wedding, full also of erotic allusions that are all too clear. Thus the principal motive of the very first movement of this Serenade is counterpointed at the end of the exposition with unmistakable symbolism:

The audience was perhaps better able to understand things of this sort than the 'tenderness' of the *Andante grazioso* in A, the main slow movement, in which passages from *Figaro* are foreshadowed:

Again and again Mozart rises above what is merely typical of Salzburg, and even the Finale, a sister-composition of the last movement of the A major Symphony K. 201, this time lacks anything that smacks of a quotation. Only the theme of the Allegro of the interpolated violin concerto seems to contain some local allusion we cannot trace.

In 1774, 1775, and 1779, each time in the month of August, Mozart wrote three additional Serenades of this sort, all in D major. We do not know the occasions that prompted their composition. Niemtschek reports of the first that it was composed for Archbishop Colloredo's name-day. But this day did not come until 30 September, and Mozart was not in the habit of fulfilling such obligations so far in advance, especially when they concerned his hated patron. It must have been, then, that his father compelled him to finish the disagreeable task quickly. Noteworthy in this first Serenade (K. 203) is the thematic relation between the March belonging to it (K. 237) and the *Andante maestoso* that introduces the first Allegro. The fact that a more important occasion than a wedding may have been concerned is indicated by the more serious character of the development section of this Allegro, and by the avoidance of any traits smacking of Salzburg; even the interpolated violin concerto, this time in B-flat major and in three movements instead of two, is fully developed and is an actual work within a work, not a mere episode. One cannot help thinking of a similar phenomenon in the history of opera: the interpolation of an *opera buffa* or an *intermezzo* between the acts of an *opera seria*. In the first movement of the concerto there is another remarkably prophetic passage: the contrast here between the principal melody and the babbling interjections by oboes and violas foreshadowing the contrast in the B-flat major quartet of *Don Giovanni* between Donna Anna and Don Ottavio, on the one hand, and Donna Elvira and Don Giovanni, on the other; even the key is the same:

The interpolation of this concerto in B-flat, the middle movement of which—a minuet—is in F, the key-relations in the two Minuets of the 'symphonic' frame (one Trio is in A major and the other in D minor), and the G major of the second slow movement, result in a brilliant coloring that may have seemed overdone to Mozart the conservative, for it is in this very Andante that he used again the chord-motive of the March and the Introduction. Happy the time when one could hear such a work as a unity and in its proper place, as occasional music; as music that fulfilled all the demands made of it and even surpassed them! For us it has become 'pure music' in a vacuum.

The key-relations are simpler in the Serenade of the next year (K. 204, of August 1775): the interpolated concerto is in A major and has only two movements; yet, in the Trio of the first Minuet, high notes again provide the soloist with an opportunity to shine. The first movement has no Introduction, but has instead a very aggressive and daring development section. For the rest, this work is easy-going and good-humored, and in the last Allegro, in which an Andantino alternates with an Allegro, there is no longer any trace of pomp and circumstance. It is easy to imagine that the work was performed at the end of a *Pölzel-Schiessen*.*

In the last of these Serenades composed in Salzburg (K. 320, of 1779), Mozart was even more cautious in his choice of keys: the interpolated 'concertante' is in G major and consists of only two movements, an *Andante grazioso* and a *Rondeau*; and since G major had already been thus used, the slow movement of the work proper, an Andantino, is in D minor. It is possible that this pretentious work has some connection with Colloredo, for in the first movement the relation between Mozart and the Archbishop is painted in a manner that is only musical and symbolic, to be sure, but nevertheless obvious and humorous. The introductory, six-measure *Adagio maestoso*, which returns *in tempo* in the recapitulation, announces with extreme tension a highly aggressive *Allegro con spirito*, the beginning of which must be classified as a forerunner of the beginning of the first movement of the 'Prague' Symphony—except that this opening is fundamentally *galant* and not yet 'contrapuntal.' With the second theme the conflict develops into a complete contrast: the Archbishop counters all of Wolfgang's pleas with an icy 'No':

* A game in which darts are blown, or shot from an air-gun, at a target.

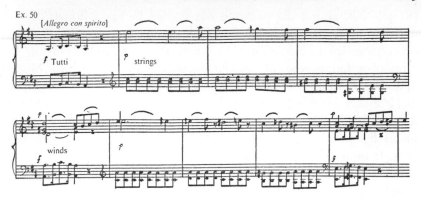

It is quite in line with Mozart's character for him to permit the un-
heeding Archbishop to hear this, and to exact an idealized vengeance
with such a portrait; and the portrait becomes complete in an orchestral
crescendo, so rare with Mozart, a true 'Mannheim' crescendo, a device
Mozart was as a rule much too distinguished a composer to stoop to.
The most extreme dynamic contrast plays a part in the following Minuet also. In the *concertante*, however, it is not the *violino principale*
that predominates this time but the winds—flutes, oboes, bassoons, and
horns: they even have an extended and worked-out cadenza in the
Andante, and in the Rondo there is a short one for the first flute and
oboe. This *concertante* is the sister-work to the Paris *Sinfonia concertante* (K. Anh. 9), the original version of which is lost: the instrumentation is the same, except that it is not for solo winds, as in the
Sinfonia, but for pairs of winds, and consequently that much richer and
more brilliant. And Mozart employs three of these pairs (omitting the
flutes) as soloists in the following D minor Andantino, as a transition
to the main body of the symphony, the homophonic-contrapuntal
finale of which also anticipates, in a way, that of the 'Prague' Symphony. Two new instruments are introduced in the Trios of the second
Minuet: a piccolo, which doubles the violins two octaves higher, and
a *Posthorn*, whose primitive natural tones humorously express Wolfgang's longing to get away from Salzburg.

It was only after he had settled in Vienna that Mozart once more
occupied himself with a festive composition of this sort: the so-called
'Haffner Symphony,' which he composed in the greatest haste and sent
piecemeal to Salzburg at the end of July and the beginning of August
1782. This work, written at his father's request to celebrate the raising
of Sigmund Haffner to the nobility, began and ended with a March

(K. 408, No. 2) and the Andante was framed by two Minuets, one of which seems to have been lost; no attempt was made to write a *Sinfonia concertante* for interpolation. We know the work today only in the form of a four-movement symphony, in the form in which Mozart himself performed it in Vienna on 23 March 1783, after adding flutes and clarinets. He had lost all recollection of it by the time Leopold sent it back to him (letter of 15 February 1783): 'My new Haffner symphony has positively amazed me, for I had forgotten every single note of it. It must surely produce a good effect . . .'

It certainly does. But though Mozart himself classed it among his symphonies, it nevertheless still bears the marks of its origin as a serenade and is a somewhat amphibious work. Not that the first movement, an *Allegro con spirito*, with all its pomp of trumpets and drums, lacks seriousness. The lordly principal motive, which is first stated in unison, is made the basis of rich contrapuntal weaving and contrast; but there is something showy and emphatic about it, as if it were always calling attention to how useful it is and how much it is used. The Andante, graceful and 'innocent' as it is, points backward towards the two Andantinos of the Paris Symphony, rather than forward to the undying perfection of the Andante of the 'Prague' Symphony, and similarly with the final Presto. The outstanding movement is the Minuet, which already expresses, in D major, approximately what the Minuet of the E-flat major Symphony was to express later: strength, festivity, and masculinity in the main section, and the most delicate grace in the Trio. The derivation from the serenade, the contrast with the later Vienna symphonies, appear perhaps most clearly when one considers the problem of how to use the work: the great Vienna symphonies must form the principal constituents of a program, while this Haffner Symphony is best employed as an opening or closing piece. As such it will be surest to 'produce a good effect.'

13. *The Symphony*

OZART wrote more than fifty symphonies, of which only a few, dating from his youth, have disappeared or have not yet been found. When one compares this number with the nine symphonies of Beethoven, or the four of Brahms, it becomes clear that the word 'symphony' did not have quite the same meaning for Mozart that it had for Beethoven and Brahms. In Beethoven's sense of the word—an orchestral work addressed, above and beyond any occasion for its composition, to an ideal public, to humanity—Mozart, too, wrote only four or five symphonies. But if we use the word in its eighteenth-century sense, we must compare Mozart's symphonic production with that of Haydn, who wrote at least 104 symphonies; and we must remember that these 104 symphonies of Haydn's were written over a period of about 40 years; that Haydn wrote his first symphony at the age of twenty-seven and Mozart his at the age of nine; and that Haydn's first symphony thus preceded Mozart's first by only five or six years. The path that leads from Mozart's innocent first symphony, K. 16, to the C major symphony known as the 'Jupiter' is longer than that from Haydn's first work in the form to the last of his London Symphonies, even though these latter were not written until after Mozart's death, and reflected the influence of Mozart and the stimulation of his example. Beethoven's conception of the monumental symphony found its greatest historical and spiritual stimulus in Mozart's 'Prague' Symphony and the three great symphonies of 1788. The art of the great symphony is the achievement of both Mozart and Haydn, and their share in it is difficult to apportion, for neither one would have made the decisive step towards monumentality without the influence of the other. Both took the Italian *sinfonia* as their point of departure, and in no aspect of music history is the miraculous power of personality more striking than in the fact that there is no Italian art of the symphony in a higher sense, and never was one. For where are the successors of Sammartini and Piantanida, of Sarti, Anfossi, and Galuppi? The only Italian symphonist who could possibly influence Beethoven was Luigi Cherubini. But it is really a joke on the part of music history that Florence was Cherubini's birthplace.

We may characterize briefly the path of the symphony, as Mozart handled the form, from 1764 to 1788, as the path away from a concert-piece intended to open or close a program, away from a work whose purpose was to furnish the frame for solo performances or concertos, to one forming the principal composition, the center and climax of a musical program. It is an advance from the decorative to the expressive, from the external to the internal, from mere ceremonial to spiritual avowal. Gradually the center of gravity among the various movements shifted, because the character of these movements themselves changed. About 1765, when Mozart began, the center of gravity lay in an exciting first movement. Then came a little *cantabile* movement, usually for strings alone or at most with a solo oboe or flute, followed by a finale in very quick tempo and in 'short' meter—$\frac{2}{4}$, $\frac{3}{8}$, or perhaps even $\frac{6}{8}$— or at times simply by a minuet. The slow middle movement was always an andante or an *andantino grazioso* or *amoroso*, for the ceremonial character of the work as a whole could not bear any heavier burden than that. Whether these three movements are connected or separated by full cadences and pauses is not very important; when the movements are connected, the works are called overtures, and when Mozart writes overtures of this sort one may always ask what dramatic or operatic work they were intended for. Sometimes he writes just the first two movements, and in the place of the third there comes a chorus, a ballet, or an aria of the operatic work itself. He usually rescues such works for concert use afterwards by adding a newly composed finale. We shall call such a work an 'Italian symphony,' in the interests of both accuracy and historical justice, for its inventors were Italians— apparently Neapolitans in particular, although all Italy, including Milan, Venice, and Rome shared no less than Naples in the development of the form. Germany was at first nothing but an Italian province, musically speaking, and Germany took over the spirit of this type of symphony without really understanding it. Nor was it a very important event when, about 1760, the Germans, particularly the Viennese, began to insert a minuet between the slow movement and the finale, thereby achieving the four-movement symphony. Mozart on several occasions expanded an Italian symphony for German use by the insertion of a minuet, without changing the spirit of the work thereby. We shall call such a symphony, in order to make a distinction, a 'Viennese symphony'; but our distinction would be trifling indeed if the increase in the number of movements to four had not made necessary a gradual increase in the significance of the movements themselves. Thus the path of Mozart's symphonic art may be described as one from the Italian symphony to the Viennese. But in this distinction the spirit is more important than the letter: the 'Prague' Symphony of 1786 has only three movements, but it is far from the Italian symphonies of an earlier period.

What is the spirit of Italian symphonic art? It is the spirit of the *opera buffa*. The change to this spirit from the early classic *sinfonia* or *overtura*, with its solemnity and *grandezza*, its pathos, its elegiac greatness in the slow movements, its contrapuntal dignity, its *soli obbligati*, is as complete as possible. Music history sometimes moves from one extreme to another. When a Neapolitan symphony begins importantly, it does so with chords repeated rhythmically, but it continues with charming little birdlike motives and melodic piquancies, and when it reaches the dominant (in major) or the mediant (in minor) there comes a bit of nothingness still more charming, if possible, though perhaps at the same time more lyric—the lady in her décolleté gown with the hoop-skirt, escorted by the cavalier with his sword of gallantry—or perhaps the innocent country-maid beside the elegant Abbé. The tension, if any, between these two little figures can never be very tragic, and the solution of the conflict—the so-called reprise—can hardly be anything but light, playful, and conventional. The second movement is usually a serenade, the third a gay farewell or a graceful dance.

Even before Haydn and Mozart began to write symphonies, there already existed a Viennese and Bohemian species of this Italian symphony which included a large number of rich and finely wrought works. And the Bohemian species, usually called the 'Mannheim' symphony, already made use of very considerable and varied dynamic shadings, which Haydn and Mozart adopted with so much hesitation and reserve that they may almost be said to have rejected them. But this art is and remains basically Italian and *buffo* in character. To any one who knows this character, the one-movement *sinfonia* of Gluck's *Orfeo ed Euridice* will seem a very serious work, superficial as it may appear to the historically uninformed modern listener. And if we wish to appreciate the nature of the task of raising this symphonic art to a more dignified and more exalted style, we should contemplate the overture to Ignaz Holzbauer's patriotic opera *Günther von Schwarzburg* (1776), which Mozart still had in mind when he wrote the Overture to *Die Zauberflöte*. We shall then not be able to withhold our sympathy from Holzbauer. When the eighteenth century wished to express earnestness and tragedy, it was always bound by convention; but in the symphony, over and above this, it was bound by the specific tradition of the *buffo* style. Remembering this, we can truly appraise the tremendous achievement represented by the G minor Symphony and by the *Andante cantabile* and Finale of the 'Jupiter,' as well as the power of the creative spirit that could accomplish this development, without any 'revolution,' in the space of twenty-five years. At the same time we shall not forget that the achievement was made possible partly by the support of Haydn, for whom the task was easier because he was a more solitary and 'original' figure than Mozart, and had less reverence for tradition.

As a symphonic composer, Mozart began altogether in the Italian style; but it seems symbolic that he learned the form and spirit of the symphony not from an Italian but from an Italianized German— Johann Christian Bach. Whatever elements might be considered German in Johann Christian are very personal in nature: an enchanting grace and amiability of feeling that distinguishes him not only from the Italians but also from his colleague and comrade Carl Friedrich Abel. In these qualities he was very closely related to Mozart. Johann Christian never plumbed the depths, but he never remained wholly on the surface either, as Boccherini, for example, so often did. The symphony was to him a ceremonial form, but he never entirely renounced excursions into the field of quiet, intimate sentiment. It is significant that in his Op. III (1765, containing his first published symphonies, in D, C, E-flat, B-flat, F, and G) two of the middle movements are in minor. In his Op. VI, dating presumably from 1770, there is a whole three-movement symphony in minor. Mozart at the age of eight or nine succumbed without resistance to Johann Christian's influence, and this influence remained for a considerable period the dominating one in his symphonic writing, however much it may have been moderated, varied, or enriched by other impressions. As a symphonic composer, he at first simply could not think or invent along different lines from those on which Johann Christian had worked. A favorite device of Johann Christian was to achieve a contrast of *forte* and *piano* within the very first few tones of the head of the theme:

Mozart adopted the device and made it almost the principle of his symphonic invention:

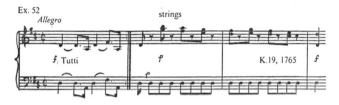

To this principle he held fast up to and including the 'Jupiter' Symphony. The dualism involved in this device is Italian, and Mozart was confirmed in his use of it by other symphonic writers in the Italian style, such as Misliveczek. Nor was the principle unknown to Joseph Haydn, although it was much less frequently employed by him. Haydn was fonder of beginning with a more complete contrast between the tutti and a smaller orchestra ensemble—and this principle, too, did not altogether escape Mozart's attention. But, to continue with the relations of Mozart to Johann Christian: in the works of both men the development section consists of modulatory activity rather than of any real conflict between themes and motives. Johann Christian's Op. III gave the boy courage to include in his very first symphony (K. 16) a deeply felt middle movement in C minor, while in the Finale he even exaggerates the *buffo* character of Bach's last movements:

Still it would be entirely wrong to take Mozart for a mere imitator or amalgamator of other men's styles, or to ask whether he surpassed his prototypes or failed to reach their level. After 1765, Johann Christian went through a development that Mozart did not follow, although he cannot have been unaware of it. There is, for example, no piece of Mozart's to correspond to Johann Christian's brilliant symphonies for double orchestra. Mozart's later relation to Haydn was similar: he adopted and assimilated only those things that were truly congenial to him, rejecting the rest completely. Uncannily retentive as his memory was for everything he heard, his faithfulness to himself was even stronger. An example from the first finale of *Figaro* will illustrate, first, how early the *buffo* character of Mozart's symphonies was established, and second, how well he still remembered in 1786 one of his first symphonies, written in 1765:

When Mozart wrote a symphony, his fancy moved at first along conventional lines: Chordal motives, dotted rhythms, scale-passages, definite alternation of tutti and solo treatment, an early turn towards the dominant, etc. Sometimes, nevertheless, a greater originality is evident —an originality that Mozart seems to exhibit almost in spite of himself. In the same symphony from which the last quotation was taken, the one written in The Hague in 1765 (K. 22), there is an Andante in G minor that is consistently chromatic in a way that had almost no precedent in the works of any other symphonist. The stay in Vienna in the fall of 1767 was productive of new impressions, resulting in a more pompous manner and in richer treatment of the strings, achieved by the use of two violas, and providing the occasion for the first symphonies containing minuets. The four symphonies of 1768—one of which, K. 45, was used with some changes as the overture to *La Finta semplice*—show here and there increased intensity. But the basic character of the music remains; it is always social, ceremonial, *buffo*, Italian. Mozart wrote symphonies so as to have them in his portfolio on the forthcoming trips to Italy, where he would need them to open and close concert programs. The year 1770 saw the birth of five symphonies; 1771, seven; 1772, eight; and 1773—after the return from these tours, but not without hope of further such journeys—seven more. Then this productivity fell off, for in the meantime Mozart had developed a new conception of the symphony, a conception that precluded the writing of a whole series of symphonies, and made each one an individual work.

We need not follow in detail Mozart's development in these years or the various impressions he received or withstood. The account of these impressions is one of the great achievements of Wyzewa and Saint-Foix, even though at times that account seems perhaps a little too rationalistically worked out. The development did not always follow in a straight line. It included sudden spurts and equally sudden reversals, as, for example, in the G major symphony, written in May 1772 (K. 129), the first movement of which could perfectly well have been written under the influence of Johann Christian in London or The Hague, while the second and third movements already breathe the spirit of Haydn. A conspicuous leap ahead, on the other hand, is the accentuation of the development in one of the symphonies of 1771 (F major, K. 75), by the use of singing polyphony as a contrast to the *buffo* character of the themes. There are several types, for instance a splendidly operatic one, usually in D major or C major, with trumpets and kettle-drums, and 'virtuoso' violins: an example of this type is K. 96, of which one can say with certainty that the minuet was inserted later. But in general the signs of increasing depth grow from year to year, as does the change towards greater freedom and individuality in the use of the instruments, the development of figuration in the direction of more singing character, and the perfection of the technique of imitation. Mozart at times threatens to burst out of the framework of the conventional symphonic style. In the quiet of Salzburg he is apt to forget the social purpose of these symphonies; his fancy roams more freely and his invention becomes more personal. Strangely enough, there is at the same time, in the last movements—at least, in those in rondo form—a return to Johann Christian, who liked to flirt with the French *goût*, and liked to slip in an episode in minor before one of the returns of the theme (for example K. 132).

The balance between the movements of Mozart's symphonies gradually shifts, as in the works of Haydn and not without their influence, in favor of the finale. Some of the symphonies of 1772 are already definitely 'finale-symphonies' (K. 129, 130, 132, 133); and especially in the incredibly facile invention of the finale of K. 132 we see a combination of 'French' influence with that of Haydn. But the same Symphony contains a slow movement so full of personal spiritual unrest and rebellion that the term *andante* hardly fits it any more; Mozart himself wrote hardly any other piece as 'expressionistic' as this—any other, that is, in which the expression seems to have left all considerations of traditional form so far behind. And although the Symphony K. 133 begins in what seems a conventional enough fashion, it soon produces a series of surprises, such, for example, as the fact that the initial motive reappears for the first time in the coda and not in the reprise. The choirs of the orchestra seem to go their independent ways, and the symphonic structure takes on more and more the form of a dialogue, both in the large and in detail. Thus the strings may predominate while the winds accompany in the form of a body of rhythmic sound, as in the finale of this symphony. The use of two violins, in unison or in octaves with the oboes, a device of which Mozart is fond, proves a means of orchestral mixture. In the symphony K. 134, dating from August 1772—a conspicuously 'coquettish' symphony altogether—we see a new type of singing character and at the same time a finer feeling for imitation.

The great change takes place in the following year, 1773. Three of the seven symphonies written in this year (K. 199, 181, 182) belong to the 'Italian' type, and may have been written in anticipation of an expected opera commission. Another work of the same sort is K. 184 in E-flat major—distinctly an overture, but written for large orchestra, and with so imposingly concerto-like a first movement and such subtle and sensitively executed dialogue in the Andante (in C minor) that it would have to be counted among the early masterpieces, if the Finale were not perhaps a little too light for the rest of the work. But then there comes a triad of symphonies which exhibit the same perfection as the final triad of 1788, though on a lower rung of the ladder, and within narrower limits. These are the symphonies in C (K. 200, November 1773), G minor (K. 183, end of 1773), and A major (K. 201, beginning of 1774). In the first movement of the C major Symphony one feels a new agitation in place of the old ceremonial character, a finer development of the thematic material, and at the same time new articulations in the structure, which had been relatively undeveloped until this point: it is significant that all these works have codas. The slow movement, in its sustained character, is already on the way to the adagio; and the minuet, with its conspicuous horn, is no longer a mere interlude or interpolation. As for the Finale, it is a milestone in Mozart's development. He could have used this *presto*, with its dialogue between soli (the two violins) and tutti, and with its furious orchestra crescendo at the end, as the overture for his *Entführung*, if the quality of its invention had not still been of the Italian *buffo* type.

The miracle of these G minor and A major symphonies has been truly appreciated only in recent times. In the former, Mozart's first symphony in a minor key, the choice of key alone transcends the boundaries of simply 'social' music, and even contradicts the nature of such music. What purpose of the day can this document of impetuous expression have served? There are Passion symphonies of this period, which are all written in minor; but in this G minor symphony of Mozart's, the inner agitation of the orchestra, with its restless syncopation at the beginning—foreshadowing the piano concerto in D minor; the extreme contrast of dynamics—the outbreak of the *fortissimo* after the dying away of the *pianissimo*; the up-beats wildly rushing forward, the sharp accents, the *tremoli* in the strings: all these things have to do not with pious thoughts of the Mount of Olives and the Crucifixion but rather with quite personal suffering. The Andante is a short but concentrated movement, its melodies characterized by an abundance of suspensions, and the resulting agitation brings about a brief cadenza before the reprise. And the dark fatalistic determination of the minuet is mated to a trio for wind instruments alone which is full of a typically G major sweetness. In the Finale, there is not only a new thematic unity but also, in syncopated formations and accents, a new thematic relation to the first movement, which is not so much to be observed on the surface as to be dimly felt. But the form of the symphony gains a new unity through it.

As for the A major symphony, which has the most modest instrumentation, consisting of strings, oboes, and horns, we need only observe how the beginning in the strings (and what a beginning!) is repeated by the entire orchestra:

There is here a new feeling for the necessity of intensifying the symphony through imitation, and of rescuing it from the domain of the purely decorative through a refinement of detail such as is characteristic of chamber music. The instruments change character: the strings become wittier, the winds lose everything that is simply noisy, the figuration drops everything merely conventional. The new spirit shows itself in all the movements: in the Andante, which has the delicate formation of a string-quartet movement, enriched by the two pairs of wind instruments; in the Minuet, with its contrasts of grace and almost Beethovenlike violence; in the Finale, an *allegro con spirito* that is really *con spirito*, and which contains the richest and most dramatic development section Mozart had written up to this time. It is understandable that these symphonies satisfied Mozart even in his Vienna period, and that he produced them at his 'academies' with only slight changes in the scoring. What an immense distance he had traveled from the Italian *sinfonia!* Who in Italy would have written such a work, and where would it have found its audience?

A few months later, in May 1774, Mozart wrote another symphony (in D, K. 202), the last before the beginning of his journey to Paris. This one he never revived in Vienna, and that, too, is understandable. For it is not a finale-symphony; the last movement is not much more than a *Kehraus* (last dance of the evening), whose only remarkable characteristic is that it has a thematic relation with the first movement; the *Andantino con moto*, for strings alone, could have appeared in one of the Vienna quartets in the style of Haydn; the minuet is not very characteristic; and the first movement, which is the most important, simply applies the technique gained in the G minor and A major symphonies to material to which it is not wholly appropriate. Just as in the Vienna quartets, so in this symphony Joseph Haydn had upset Mozart's thinking: there are instances in which even Mozart's receptive spirit was not strong enough to assimilate an impression and make it fully his own.

Then for a period of more than four years, lasting until June 1778, Mozart did not write a single symphony. How is this to be explained, after the rich productivity of the preceding years? There are external reasons: no trip to Italy or Vienna was in prospect, and for the trip to Munich, on the occasion of the first performance of *La Finta giardiniera*, the manuscripts already on hand sufficed. But there were inner reasons as well. What Mozart had accomplished in the three symphonies in C major, G minor, and A major represented a peak of achievement that could not be surpassed, so he turned to other fields, in which the symphonic principle could be treated with a lighter hand. The years in Salzburg before the journey to Paris were devoted to serenades and divertimenti, and above all to Mozart's first achievements in the field of the concerto—apart from masses and other church works, clavier sonatas, and operatic pieces. Not that symphonic compositions were entirely lacking. There were the overtures to *La Finta giardiniera* and to the festival opera *Il Rè pastore*—the first consisting of an *allegro molto* and an *andantino grazioso*, the second of a *molto allegro*. Mozart later made a symphony out of the *Finta giardiniera* overture by adding a finale to it (K. 121), and there is also a finale for the one for *Il Rè pastore* (K. 102), but this finale must have served to conclude a serenade. The symphony he made out of the *Finta giardiniera* overture is a finale-symphony by virtue of the mere fact that the first two movements are very short. The whole work is important for its confirmation of the *buffo* nature of the species, in that it shows how the overture of an *opera buffa* could be made into a symphony simply by addition. The rondo for the overture of *Il Rè pastore*, a *contredanse en rondeau*, is a first-class work; if it really once served as conclusion for a *Finalmusik* of the same freshness, delicacy, and grace, then we have lost a masterpiece.

In the summer of 1778, in Paris, Mozart received from Le Gros, the director of the Concerts Spirituels, a commission to compose a symphony for the opening of the Corpus Christi program. This confronted him with a new task, for the work naturally had to be in Parisian style

and for the largest orchestra. Accordingly, the autograph bears the unusual caption: *Sinfonia à 10 instrumenti*. The instruments were flutes,
oboes, clarinets, bassoons, horns, trumpets, timpani, and a large body
of strings; thus this was Mozart's first symphony to include clarinets.
In composing the work he had to keep in mind not only a new and
richer body of sound but also new dimensions for the movements—at
least for the opening and closing movements. Even Leopold was concerned with the question of how Wolfgang would meet the difficulties
of the task (letter of 29 June 1778):

To judge by the Stamitz symphonies which have been engraved in
Paris, the Parisians must be fond of noisy music. For these are nothing
but noise. Apart from this they are a hodgepodge, with here and there
a good idea, but introduced very awkwardly and in quite the wrong
place . . .

It is not quite clear whether in this criticism Leopold was speaking of
Johann Stamitz, the founder of the so-called Mannheim symphonic
school (and accordingly of the Parisian as well), or of Johann's son
Karl. However that may be, to anyone who knows the best achievements of that school—above all the symphonies of the elder Stamitz
himself, but also those of Franz Xaver Richter, Filtz, Karl Stamitz,
Eichner, and Franz Beck—the judgment is as brilliant as it is unjust.
The two best orchestras of the world in this period—the Mannheim
orchestra, which really was unsurpassed, and the Paris orchestra, which
at any rate claimed to be—to some extent owed their development to
the symphonic works of Johann Stamitz, while to some extent the
works in turn owed their origin to the existence of these orchestras.
And it is true that the symphonies of the 'Mannheim School' were
concerned above all with exhibiting the qualities of the Mannheim
orchestra: its precision, its skill in making the most sudden changes in
expression, its excellence in passages bringing out particular groups of
wind instruments, and finally its famous crescendo which consisted in
raising a motive from the level of *pianissimo* to that of *fortissimo*, until
it finally exploded in a noisy tutti. The beginning of the Allegro of
Beethoven's *Leonore* Overture and the Scherzo of his Fifth Symphony
are the purest, most idealized, and most meaningful examples of the
Mannheim crescendo. In Mannheim and in Paris the crescendo was
seldom meaningful: Thus, for example, the symphony by Ignaz Holzbauer (Op. 4, III) that ends with a *tempesta del mare* (storm at sea),

the occasion for a veritable orgy of *crescendi* and *decrescendi*, is typical of the Mannheim attitude. But the opportunity offered by so rich and highly developed a body of sound led to innumerable new mixtures of colors, as well as to the broadening of the dimensions of individual movements and to the longer spinning out of the development of motives. Mozart had been well prepared for his Paris commission by his stay in Mannheim. There he had undoubtedly opened his ears very attentively to the symphonies of Holzbauer, Christian Cannabich, and Giuseppe Toëschi, just as he undoubtedly did in Paris when he had the opportunity not only to examine but also to hear symphonies by Gossec and Sterkel, and overtures by old Rameau.

The symphony he wrote for Le Gros (K. 297) is characteristic of the Mannheim-Paris style. In the first movement it even parodies that style to a slight degree. It begins with the *fortissimo-unisono*, precision in which was a great point of pride with the Paris orchestra. Mozart made fun of this pride in the letter of 12 June 1778:

I have been careful not to neglect *le premier coup d'archet*—and that is quite sufficient. What a fuss the oxen here make of this trick! The devil take me if I can see any difference! They all begin together, just as they do in other places.

He continues with the pompous runs in the strings characteristic of the French overture, and does not forget to write impressive unison passages for the strings against sustained tones in the winds. But that is where the parody, or the connivance to please the French taste, ends. Mozart's ambition was far too great, and there was too much dependent on the success of the work, for him not to take it seriously. The fact that the last of the three movements was the most successful does honor to the taste of the Parisians. The second theme of this movement is a *fugato*, supplying the natural material for development; it does not return in the recapitulation- one of the strokes of genius in this masterful movement, which hovers continually between brilliant tumult and graceful seriousness. Mozart had to make two versions of the slow movement. The first one, printed in the Complete Works, was too long for Le Gros, and Mozart accordingly composed a shorter andante, which is to be found only in the first edition, printed in Paris. Although Mozart himself did not wish to express a preference between the two versions, the earlier one—longer, more serious, less pastoral— is without question superior; it alone conforms to the new dimensions of this first 'great' symphony of Mozart's. Le Gros was probably right when he said that 'this was the best symphony' ever written for the Concerts Spirituels. But we, looking back from the standpoint of posterity, are right in feeling that this Paris symphony lacks something of the charm, the amiability, and the unconscious depths of many a shorter and less pretentious Salzburg symphony.

Mozart wrote another symphony for Le Gros, but I do not believe it has survived. Early in the nineteenth century, the Imprimerie du Conservatoire printed an *Ouverture à grand orchestre par Mozart*, consisting of a short *Andante pastorale* and a long *Allegro spiritoso* (K. Anh. 8), a work so lacking in individuality, so crude and fanfare-like in its treatment of the wind instruments, that Mozart's reputation should not be burdened with it. What an authentic Mozart overture is like we may see from the one in G major (K. 318), which Mozart wrote shortly after his return to Salzburg, in April 1779, for large orchestra, with trumpets, timpani, and two pairs of horns. There is no doubt that this work was intended as the overture to the *Singspiel à la française*, the fragment dubbed by the nineteenth century 'Zaide.' When we realize this, we see in the thematic dualism—the commanding *forte* of the tutti and the pleading *piano* of the strings—a programmatic significance: in the one, Sultan Soliman; in the other Zaide. An andante built into the sonata-form movement, in the main key, characterizes or symbolizes the love idyll of the *Singspiel*. Finally, to clinch the matter, Mozart indicated the 'Turkish' character of the opera in the final measures of the overture just as clearly as he did later in *Die Entführung*. Nor are episodes for the wind instruments, or crescendi and other appurtenances of the Mannheim-Paris style lacking; the only direction in which Mozart makes no display, since he has no concert audience in mind, is that of combination of themes.

Mozart wrote only two more symphonies in Salzburg: one in B-flat (K. 319), in July 1779, and one in C (K. 338), in August 1780. He revived both works in Vienna, and added a minuet to the original three movements of each. And this time the 'Italian' symphonies really became Viennese symphonies: the content and the dimensions of the individual movements had now grown to such proportions that they not only could very well stand this addition but almost needed it. This is true even of the first, with its very simple orchestration, using only oboes, horns, and bassoons with the strings; the only advanced feature of the writing is that the bassoons are independent of the basses. We have already indicated that Beethoven took Mozart's finale as the point of departure for the finale of his Eighth Symphony, but there is a similar relation between the first movements of the two symphonies as well. In Mozart we already find, if not the exuberance, at least the energy, high spirits, passion, and intense seriousness of Beethoven. We hardly know whether to be surprised or not when at the beginning of the development section Mozart's 'motto'—the four-note motive that is to have its apotheosis in the 'Jupiter' Symphony—is interpolated in the debate. The *Andante moderato* (the *moderato* is a significant addition) is filled with a new intimacy of feeling, and the Finale represents a new combination of *buffo* elements with those of the march and the pastorale, united by a personal power of imagination. The minuet, composed later, approaches the minuets of the late Vienna period: terse, concentrated, with a *Ländler*-like trio. If we did not know that it had been composed in 1782, we should have to place it among the *Teutschen*, the *Redouten-Tänze* of 1790 or 1791.

The C major Symphony, in which Mozart returns to the large orchestra, fulfils what the 'Paris' Symphony, in French terms, had prophesied. The form of the first movement is the same in both works: the material expected at the beginning of the recapitulation appears instead in the form of a Coda. But all thought of assuming a foreign style has vanished. Here Mozart is completely himself. The work is full of *buffo* elements and, at the same time, of deepest earnestness; the neutral key of C major is constantly colored by changes to the minor or to E minor or A-flat major; the work is an expression of high spirits, energy, and passion. The *Andante di molto*, scored for strings with divided violas, with bassoons * as the sole representatives of the wind choir, is an animated song from beginning to end. The Finale is a presto—not casual or superficial, but full of wit, tenderness, and roguish humor. The minuet that Mozart later added (K. 409) is one of the most pretentious he ever wrote, with solo display passages for the winds in the trio. Now, too, in Vienna, he thought of the flutes, which had not been included in the original score, and wrote flute parts for the opening and closing movements, and perhaps for the Andante as well.

For the ten years in Vienna between 1781 and 1791, only five symphonies remain, if we exclude the 'Haffner Symphony' of 1782, which is really nothing but a second Haffner serenade. For his first 'academies'

* Köchel (even the Third Edition!) to the contrary notwithstanding, the score includes bassoons.

Mozart used partly his earlier symphonies, while the *pièces de résistance* of these programs were his piano concertos, which were not to be overshadowed by too impressive proportions in the one or more symphonies that such programs customarily included. Mozart himself tells us, in a letter to his father, dated 29 March 1783, what the program of such a concert was like:

Our program was as follows:

(1) The new Haffner symphony. [More exactly: the first three movements.]

(2) Madame Lange sang the aria *Se il padre perdei* from my Munich opera, accompanied by four instruments.

(3) I played the third of my subscription concertos.

(4) Adamberger sang the scena that I composed for Countess Baumgarten.

(5) The short *concertante* symphony from my last *Finalmusik*.

(6) I played my concerto in D major, which is such a favorite here, and of which I sent you the rondo with variations.

(7) Mlle Teiber sang the scena *Parto, m'affretto* out of my last Milan opera.

(8) I played alone a short fugue (because the Emperor was present) and then variations on an air from an opera called *Die Philosophen*, which were encored. So I played variations on the air *Unser dummer Pöbel meint* from Gluck's *Pilgrimme von Mekka*.

(9) Madame Lange sang my new rondo.

(10) The last movement of the first symphony.

It is clear that none of Mozart's last four symphonies could have been used in such fashion. The composition of symphonies had become a very responsible task, and they could no longer be written in half-dozens, or even in quarter-dozens. Their importance had been increased not only by Mozart but also by Joseph Haydn.

The first of the truly Viennese symphonies (K. 425), written in November 1783, in Linz, on the way home from Salzburg to Vienna, shows how greatly Mozart had come under Haydn's influence, not only as a quartet composer, but also as the creator of symphonies.

In this work, for the first time in a symphony, he prefaces the first movement with a solemn introduction—like Haydn, who had already done so a dozen times, and this with particular emphasis in the years immediately preceding the Mozart work, 1780 to 1782. There is a small sheet of paper on which the openings of three Haydn symphonies are notated, in Mozart's handwriting (K. 387 d), and among them is one with an introductory Grave dating from the year 1782 (No. 75). But Haydn had not up to this time written any slow introduction like this one of Mozart's, with its heroic beginning and the play of light and shade that follows, leading from the most tender longing to the most intense agitation. The succeeding *Allegro spiritoso* is not free of a certain academic quality, of which the curious 'Turkish' features (tutti in E minor), and even a particularly conspicuous development in solo-dialogue texture, do not wholly relieve it. Mozart always feels a little cramped when he is too close to his model and when, as in this case, he has to work with excessive speed—that is, without considerable forethought. He wrote from Linz to his father, on 31 October 1783:

On Tuesday, 4 November, I am giving a concert in the theater here and, as I have not a single symphony with me, I am writing a new one at breakneck speed, which must be finished by that time . . .

For the slow movement—*Poco Adagio*—too, he took as his point of departure a type very frequent in Haydn's works, in ⅜ meter, such as the Adagio of Haydn's 'Maria Theresa' Symphony of 1772 (No. 48). The Minuet and the Finale would be equally Haydnish if it were not that they contain in every measure typically Mozartean chromaticism, agitation, and pliancy—qualities quite foreign to Haydn, but which Mozart could not avoid even when he composed 'at breakneck speed.'

For the same occasion in Linz, a concert for Count Thun, and at equally breakneck speed, he composed a short and 'majestic' introduction (K. 444) to a G major symphony written by Michael Haydn only a few months earlier (23 May 1783). This symphony, though capable in its workmanship, is an excellent demonstration of how solitary and aristocratic a figure Mozart was, even among the more gifted of his Austrian contemporaries.

He waited more than three years before writing another symphony— the so-called 'Prague' symphony (K. 504), which he finished on 6 December 1786, in Vienna, no doubt with a view to his forthcoming trip to Prague, where it received its first performance on 19 January 1787. This work is also known as the symphony 'without a minuet,' and this nickname is more appropriate than those who have used it realize. For the work is, as we have already suggested, not a return to the Italian symphony type, but rather a full-scale Viennese symphony, which happens to lack a minuet simply because it says everything it has to say in three movements. This is Mozart's last symphony in D major, and it is the synthesis, upon the highest level, of what he had expressed in the 'Haffner' Symphony and the one written in Paris, both also in D. In those works, the first movement is to a certain extent a display piece, and an exhibition of contrapuntal skill. In this one, after the eloquent tension of the slow introduction—how proudly it begins and what conflicts lie behind this apparent assurance!—there comes a movement saturated with polyphony, even though the naive listener would not be aware of it. The thematic material, stated in the first thirty-five measures, seems quite heterogeneous, and yet it forms a wonderful unity. An important part is played by a motive that anticipates the *fugato* of the Overture to *Die Zauberflöte;* our worthy friend Muzio Clementi might here already have accused Mozart of plagiarism:

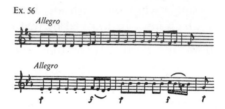

Ex. 56

We have already referred to a sketch in which Mozart experiments with the combination of the motives of this movement—one of the few pages that give us a glimpse into Mozart's workshop. For the development section he reserves a feature of increased intensity: canonic treatment. This development section is one of the greatest, most serious, most aggressive in all Mozart's works. In it, characteristically, the second theme cannot take part, but must remain untouched. The slow movement is marked only 'andante' again, but what a deepening of the concept andante is here! This is no longer a mere intermezzo between two animated movements; it has its own inner animation, and it embodies the most complete combination of a singing quality and polyphonic character. There is a relation between this movement in G major and the aria *Dalla sua pace*, which Mozart wrote as an interpolation for Don Ottavio to sing in the Vienna performance of *Don Giovanni*. The only difference is that what the text prevents from coming to full realization in an aria may flow forth without hindrance in a symphonic movement. The finale is one of those rare D major movements of Mozart's, which, despite all their appearance of cheerfulness, and despite their genuine perfection and feeling of completeness, leave a wound in the soul: beauty is wedded to death. To this as much as to any work of art apply the verses of the German poet Platen, expressing the danger inherent in all perfection:

> Wer die Schönheit angeschaut mit Augen
> Ist dem Tode schon anheimgegeben,
> Wird für keinen Dienst auf Erden taugen,
> Und doch wird er vor dem Tode beben.
> Wer die Schönheit angeschaut mit Augen!

> Ewig währt für ihn der Schmerz der Liebe,
> Denn ein Tor nur kann auf Erden hoffen,
> Zu genügen einem solchen Triebe:
> Wen der Pfeil des Schönen je getroffen,
> Ewig währt für ihn der Schmerz der Liebe!

> Ach, er möchte wie ein Quell versiechen,
> Jedem Hauch der Luft ein Gift entsaugen
> Und den Tod aus jeder Blume riechen:
> Wer die Schönheit angeschaut mit Augen,
> Ach, er möchte wie ein Quell versiechen!
> (January 1825) *

It was only five years after the creation of the 'Prague' Symphony and one year after the completion of that other work in D major, the String Quintet K. 593, that Mozart died.

> * Who hath gazed full in the face of beauty
> Doth himself so unto death deliver;
> Now unfit for any earthly duty,
> Yet at thought of death with fear shall quiver—
> Who hath gazed full in the face of beauty.

> Ever shall he languish with desire;
> None but fools on earth hope to discover
> Limpid water fit to quench such fire.
> Whom beauty's arrow hath made beauty's lover,
> Ever shall he languish with desire.

> He shall waste away as the spring torrent,
> Ev'ry breath he draws a poison'd duty,
> Death in ev'ry flow'r and bloom abhorrent;
> Who hath gazed full in the face of beauty,
> He shall waste away as the spring torrent.

This is similar in idea to the couplet by E. A. Poe ('A Romance,' first version):

> I could not love, except where Death
> Was mingling his with Beauty's breath.

To the summer of 1788 belong the three last symphonies Mozart wrote, in E-flat (K. 543), G minor (K. 550), and C major (K. 551)—all composed within the unbelievably short space of about two months. We know nothing about the occasion for writing these works. It is strange that Mozart should have written symphonies during the summer. Perhaps he hoped to be able to give some 'academies' during the winter of 1788-9, and these plans fell through just as those for the following years did. He had to play his last piano concerto (K. 595) during a concert given by the clarinetist Bähr, in March 1791, in the concert hall of the Court Caterer Jahn in the Himmelpfortgasse. It is possible that Mozart never conducted these three symphonies and never heard them.

But this is perhaps symbolic of their position in the history of music and of human endeavor, representing no occasion, no immediate purpose, but an appeal to eternity. Do they form a cycle? Was Mozart following not only an inner impulse but a 'program'? Does their order follow a purposeful plan? I believe not. Even if Mozart had begun with the 'Jupiter' Symphony, and written either the E-flat or the G minor last, it would not take much ingenuity to find some meaning in their sequence. But in the first of the three, finished on 26 June 1788, we can hardly avoid the assumption of some secret Masonic meaning—less in a 'programmatic' sense than simply to find some way of explaining and characterizing this mysterious work. E-flat major is the key of the trio Mozart dedicated to his friend and helper, Puchberg. It is the key of *Die Zauberflöte*. And just as in the overture to that work the adept knocks at the gate and waits anxiously in the dark, so he does here again, until the six-four chord brings the light. The unusual song-theme of the Allegro, too, is full of those 'ties' that symbolize the brotherhood of the Freemasons. Is it impossible to interpret the Andante in A-flat in the sense of that letter of 4 April 1787, addressed to Leopold, which we have quoted, with its thoughts of death, 'that best and truest friend of man,' of which the thought 'is not only no longer terrifying to me, but is indeed very soothing and consoling'? Does not this program suit well the festive character of the minuet and the cheerfulness of the Finale—a cheerfulness that reminds us only very slightly of Haydn?

The three Symphonies are very different in their use of wind instruments. The 'Jupiter' Symphony has no clarinets and the E-flat has no oboes. The G minor Symphony originally had no clarinets and Mozart added them only afterwards, making slight changes in the oboe parts. This symphony lacks trumpets and timpani, while on the other hand the two horns, one in B-flat and the other in G, are treated not as a pair but quite individually. This is the symphony without drums and trumpets; what would those festive instruments be doing in this fatalistic piece of chamber music? Nowhere does Mozart's independence of Haydn show itself so strikingly as in this work. His inexorableness contrasts sharply with the cheerful optimism of Haydn, who never stuck to the key of D minor or C minor, say, through even one whole first movement, let alone three whole movements, including the Finale. Even the turn to B-flat major in the exposition of the first movement has something both fierce and weary about it, and when, in the recapitulation, the flute, bassoon, and strings return to the minor, they do so with the finality of the pronouncement of Minos. The same is true of the last movement; the finality of both is the result of their developments, which are unlike any Haydn ever wrote. For these developments are plunges into the abyss of the soul, symbolized in modulations so bold that to Mozart's contemporaries they must have seemed to lose their way entirely, and so distant that only Mozart himself could find the path back from them into the light of day. It is strange how easily the world has accepted such a work and has even been able to think of it as a document of 'Grecian lightness and grace' —a characterization that could apply at best only to the divine tranquillity of the Andante or to the trio of the Minuet, otherwise so heroically tragic.

The amalgamation of the *galant* and the 'learned,' which in a thousand features of the Symphonies in E-flat and G minor is more hidden than displayed, is revealed in the Finale of the 'Jupiter' Symphony. This work has been somewhat mistakenly called the symphony with the fugue-finale. For that movement is not a fugue, but simply a sonata movement with fugato passages in the exposition, the development, and the coda, like the finale of the great G major Quartet. The complete fusion of the *galant* and 'learned' styles here achieved constitutes a moment unique in the history of music. The *sinfonia*—once a subsidiary form, intended to induce the audience to stop their conversation before the beginning of an act, or to open or close a concert—had now become the very center of a concert program. The slow movement —once an intermezzo—was now a broad and deep outpouring of the soul; not yet an adagio or a largo, as in the works of Beethoven, but nevertheless an *andante cantabile*. The symphonic style—once, even in Mozart's own work, and not more than a few years earlier, full of the *buffo* spirit—still had something of the *buffo* character: it is significant that Mozart used in the closing theme of the first movement a motive from his arietta *Un bacio di mano* (K. 541). But the symphonic style was now also clearly stamped with what Mozart felt to be the most serious element in music: the contrapuntal. In this work of the utmost harmony and balance, there is tension, too, but it nowhere 'loses its way.' And perhaps it is most appropriate, after all, that this work should be the third of those composed in 1788, and the last symphony Mozart wrote.

14. The Clavier

MOZART was, as we know, a great clavier player, one of the greatest clavier virtuosi of his time, although not a virtuoso in the sense that term came to have in the following generation. He lived long enough to begin to know that type and to reject it—in the person of Clementi. His judgment of Clementi, with whom he had to compete late in 1781 or early in 1782 before the Emperor Joseph, was very harsh (letter of 16 January 1782):

He is an excellent cembalo-player, but that is all. He has great facility with his right hand. His star passages are thirds. Apart from this, he has not a farthing's worth of taste or feeling; he is a mere *mechanicus*.

Now, Clementi was much more than a mere 'mechanicus,' and in many important respects he was the prototype of a whole generation of pianists and composers for the piano, the generation to which Beethoven belonged. Mozart would have had to pronounce the same verdict if Beethoven had played one of his own sonatas à la Clementi (as he may have done on the occasion of their famous meeting in 1787)—such for example as the C major sonata, Op. 2, No. 3. Perhaps on that occasion Mozart did not credit even Beethoven with either taste or feeling. The ideals of his clavier style were very different from those of the early nineteenth century. Yet it should be noted that he wrote for the same instrument as Beethoven, Weber, or Chopin—not for the clavichord or the harpsichord, but for the pianoforte, although of course not for the powerful instrument we know in the products of Erard or Steinway. The only works that can have been conceived and written for harpsichord are the early concerto arrangements after Johann Christian Bach and minor 'French' composers (K. 107, and K. 37, 39, 40, 41). One must not be misled by the fact that even in the last years of Mozart's life he used the word *cembalo* to indicate the clavier part in his scores—or because some famous harpsichordist gains ovations by playing the *Rondo alla turca* from the A major Sonata on his or her instrument. In the Mozart household there were one or more piano-fortes constructed by the Regensburg clavier-builder, Franz Jacob Späth, but when Mozart made the acquaintance of the instruments of Johann Andreas Stein of Augsburg (who was to become the father-in-law and teacher of Johann Andreas Streicher, who worked for Bee-thoven), the latter became his favorites. He gave his reasons in detail (letter of 17 October 1777):

This time I shall begin at once with Stein's pianofortes. Before I had seen any of his make, Späth's claviers had always been my favorites. But now I much prefer Stein's, for they damp ever so much better than the Regensburg instruments. When I strike hard, I can keep my finger on the note or raise it, but the sound ceases the moment I have pro-duced it. In whatever way I touch the keys, the tone is always even. It never jars, it is never stronger or weaker or entirely absent; in a word, it is always even. It is true that he does not sell a pianoforte of this kind for less than three hundred gulden, but the trouble and the labor that Stein puts into the making of it cannot be paid for. His instruments have this splendid advantage over others, that they are made with escape action. Only one maker in a hundred bothers about this. But without an escapement it is impossible to avoid jangling and vibration after the note is struck. When you touch the keys, the hammers fall back again the moment after they have struck the strings, whether you hold down the keys or release them.

It was for such an instrument that Mozart wrote his sonatas, variations, and concertos.

What Mozart did for the development of this instrument can be appreciated only when one remembers that while certain virtuosi played the instrument, it was in general use mainly by amateurs. And this fact had a considerable influence on the music written for it. A work for piano, or for a group of instruments including piano, was, as we have observed, usually not taken so seriously as a quartet or quintet for strings, which was intended for performance by professional musi-cians or by the more serious type of amateurs. A work for quartet or quintet of strings had four movements, while a piano sonata had only three. A string quartet was for connoisseurs (*Kenner*); a piano sonata, a sonata for piano and violin, a piano trio or piano quartet was for amateurs (*Liebhaber*), masculine or feminine. 'For piano and violin,' not 'for violin and piano': the striking fact, from the point of view of the nineteenth or twentieth century, is that in these works the keyboard instrument has the dominant role, and thus is responsible for their lighter character. From about 1750 on, the role of the keyboard instrument became very different from what it had been previously. In an early classic work—say, a 'solo sonata' for violin and harpsichord—everything of importance was in the violin part, which was at times even written in chordal or polyphonic form, and the harpsichord part was relatively unimportant, containing only the bass-line, the support or accompaniment for a solo instrument. But after 1750 the keyboard instrument became the dominant partner, and the violin part became so insignificant, so completely *ad libitum*, that in most cases it could actually be omitted without much loss. Before 1750 there were violin sonatas with *basso-continuo*; after 1750 came clavier sonatas with accompanying violin part. It was a long time before the violin was again treated in truly obbligato fashion, so that both instruments were essential to the musical whole, as we know them to be in the violin-and-piano sonatas of Beethoven; and it was Mozart first and foremost who achieved a balance between the two instruments and created a true dialogue between them.

Mozart and Beethoven were both great pianists and great creators, but the piano does not assume the central position in Mozart's early work that it does in Beethoven's. Beethoven's Opp. 1, 2, 5, 6, 7, 10, 11, 12, 13, 14, 15, 16, 17, and 19 are piano works. But Mozart, in his early years, did not need to write out piano sonatas or variations—he improvised them. Thus his variations K. 24 and 25, which were engraved early in 1766 at The Hague, are nothing but published documents of the child-prodigy's improvisations. A few sonatas dating from a little later period, once in the possession of his sister, have disappeared. The pieces that were written down, because they had to be, were a few four-hand sonatas: K. 19 d (1765), K. 381 (1772), and K. 358 (1774), all three intended for performance by Wolfgang and his sister, sitting at the piano as we see them in the family portrait of 1780. A few sets of variations also were written out, partly because Mozart needed them to use with his pupils, and partly because they might easily be taken up by publishers. But Mozart did not begin to write out his piano sonatas until the summer of 1774, when he was in his nineteenth year, and had hopes of the commission for *La Finta giardiniera* in Munich. Between then and the beginning of 1775 he wrote six sonatas (K. 279-284), five in Salzburg and one in Munich, intended from the beginning to form a series for publication—as we should see, even without other evidence, from the sequence of the keys in which they are written: C, F, B-flat, E-flat, G, D. Mozart first proceeds downwards from C three fifths in succession and then, again from C, upwards two. But of these six sonatas he later published only one, the last. We shall understand why when we look back upon them from the point of view of the ideal of Mozart's piano sonatas, as realized for example in the later sonatas in B-flat (K. 333), C minor (K. 457), B-flat (K. 570), and D (K. 576), and also when we reflect on the constellation of Mozart's models. This constellation may be summed up in the four words: Italy, Paris, Hamburg, and London; that is, the Italians, the 'Frenchmen,' Carl Philipp Emanuel Bach, and Johann Christian Bach. The boy received his first impressions of clavier sonatas from the collections that the Nuremberg lutenist and publisher, Johann Ulrich Haffner, 'made public in particularly fine engraving' (Gerber, 'Altes' *Lexicon*) about 1760—a collection in twelve parts, all of which were presumably present in the Mozart household. Chiefly represented in this collection were the Italians: Galuppi, Pampani, Perotti, Pescetti, Rutini, Serini, Paganelli, Paladini, Sales, Chiarini, Sammartini, G. Scarlatti; only in the later volumes do we come to German names, like Krafft, Fasch, Krause, Marpurg, Kirnberger, Rackemann, Roth, and above all Philipp Emanuel Bach. Mozart's preference was all in favor of the Italians, whose works offered a light, charming, uninhibited art, pure rococo, full of cheerfulness and graceful figuration. This came to an end when Mozart made the acquaintance of Schobert and his Parisian colleagues, for the music-lovers one had to write for in Paris, London, Berlin, and Vienna were quite different from those in Italy. Rutini, whose works are mentioned with approval in the Mozart correspondence, succumbs about 1770 to 'simplicity'—which is in reality nothing but shallowness—perhaps under the influence of Rousseau's 'Return to Nature.' Nothing better characterizes the style of these works than the letter written by Pietro Metastasio on 18 February 1771, an acknowledgment of a copy of Rutini's Op. VII:

Monsieur,

I thank the amiable Mr. Rutini for his kind attention in acquainting me with his most charming sonatas for harpsichord in which not only have I enjoyed their clear, noble and correct harmony and their uncommon inventive fantasy, but I have particularly admired the judicious dexterity with which he has been able to combine charm and grace with ease of execution so as to attract the pupil with material for study that is full of pleasure, hiding the difficulties which might frighten him . . . *

Mozart does not write 'easy' sonatas of this sort (at least when he does, he identifies them as such, like the 'little clavier sonata for beginners,' K. 545, written in 1788), although his sonatas are nowadays misused as material for teaching beginners. Metastasio's praise applies in a much deeper sense to Mozart's sonatas than to Rutini's; but for this combination of 'grace and charm' with easy execution, Mozart found his model not in Rutini or any other Italian, and not in Carl Philipp Emanuel Bach, whose nature was fundamentally alien to his own, but in Johann Christian Bach.

Now, it is strange, and from a pedagogical point of view unfortunate, that the six piano sonatas of 1774-5, with which young pianists customarily begin their acquaintance with Mozart, do not give a unified or true picture of their composer. They are a microcosm of feeling and of subtlety of form, but a very complicated one. It is as if one were to begin one's acquaintance with Wagner not with *Lohengrin* but with *Die Feen*, or *Das Liebesverbot*, supplemented by the *Faust* Overture. True, Mozart is represented much more faithfully in these six sonatas than Wagner in his early works. But they are in a sense a straying from his orbit, as are also, say, the Vienna series of string quartets of 1773; and the man who is responsible for both divagations is Joseph Haydn, or perhaps it would be more clear to say Philipp Emanuel Bach through Haydn. Haydn had written six sonatas in 1773, which had appeared in print in the following year as Op. 13, but Mozart may very well have come to know them during his stay in Vienna. Thus, for the Sonata in F (K. 280) a sonata by Haydn in the same key served as model; and in the Sonata in E-flat (K. 282) not only is the finale quite Haydnish, but the irregularity and the subjectivity shown in the sequence of the movements reflect Haydn's influence. Mozart is not entirely himself; he needs to find himself again. On the other hand, even where he is not entirely himself, there is always this difference: Mozart was a born

* 'Monsieur,
Riconosco l'amabile mio Sig. Rutini nella obbligante attenzione di farmi parte delle sue vaghissime sonate da gravicembalo, nelle quali non mi sono solo compiaciuto della loro chiara, nobile, e corretta armonia, e della non comune inventrice fantasia. Ma o particolarmente ammirato la giudiziosa destrezza con la quale à saputo congiungere l'allettamento alla facilità dell'esecuzione, per innamorar lo scolare d'uno studio dilettevole, dissimulandogli le difficoltà, che potrebbero sgomentarlo . . .'

pianist, while Haydn always thought in terms of the quartet or the orchestra. How often in Haydn's piano style one feels the translation from another instrumental sphere, while in Mozart everything flows smoothly under the hand. Thus it seems to me that the first sonata of the series, the one in C major (K. 279), must have been written before the 'divagation.' It gives the impression of an improvisation; the tones of the instrument sound in direct response to Mozart's imagination; this is how he must have played when he was in the vein and improvised a sonata. When other composers have displayed their ideas, one after the other, they repeat them in the recapitulation. But in this work nothing is mechanical; Mozart's fantasy is continually active in every detail. In the Andante, which is otherwise thoroughly Italian, this fact shows itself in the dynamics. And in the B-flat major Sonata (K. 281), of which the first two movements seem more like Haydn than Haydn himself, we are suddenly faced, in the Finale, with Mozart at his most characteristic and individual. Haydn and even Johann Christian are forgotten. If the date of this rondo, with its air of a modest concerto and its melodic grace, were not so definitely fixed, we should certainly place it ten years later, in the Vienna period. In the fifth sonata, in G major (K. 283), Mozart is at least far enough along the road back to his own style to show more influence of Johann Christian than of Philipp Emanuel; and the *presto Finale* is a pianistic inspiration such as is to be found very seldom, if ever, in Haydn.

Quite unique among the sonatas of this series is the one in D (K. 284), composed in February or March 1775 in Munich for a music-lover of that city, Baron Thaddäus von Dürnitz. The beginning of the first movement survives in an earlier version, appropriately in the style of the other works of this series, but Dürnitz must have stated that he wished something different, more brilliant, in the 'French style'—or Mozart himself must have had a personal or musical experience that suddenly lifted him to a new and higher level. What was this experience? We do not know; but shall we not simply assume that a miracle had taken place, in one of those fortunate hours of inspiration, without which no advances in art would be possible? However that may be, the first movement of this sonata, which is still 'Italian,' is followed by a *Polonaise en Rondeau*, in which the theme returns in ever more elaborate texture, and then there comes, for the first time in a Mozart piano sonata, a *tema con variazioni*—all this, including the second version of the first movement, having a sensuous richness and a concerto-

like animation, which is a perpetual source of wonder. Particularly remarkable is the sonority and the unity of the variations. Mozart had
written out piano variations in the preceding years: those on an arietta
by Salieri (K. 180) in 1773, and the so-called Fischer variations (K. 179)
in 1774, which he used for a long time as a virtuoso display piece. But
they are merely charming or brilliant in comparison to the rich flow
of invention in these later variations, in which there is included, for
the first time, the *minore*, a variation in minor lending its chromaticism
to the variety of the whole. Not even the somewhat old-fashioned and
lengthy adagio variation interrupts the flow of the creative imagination.

These six sonatas provided Mozart for an astonishingly long time
with all he needed for his repertoire as a virtuoso. He played them all
frequently, including the weaker ones, on the grand tour to Mannheim
and Paris in the years 1777-8. But it was in Mannheim that he felt the
need of expanding this repertoire, and so between November 1777 and
the end of the summer of 1778 he wrote seven new sonatas no less
varied and kaleidoscopic than the series written before he went to
Munich. Two of these later sonatas, the one in C (K. 309) and the one
in D (K. 311), must be called Mannheim sonatas, since both were
either written out or completed in Mannheim. We are particularly well
informed about the circumstances attending the composition of the
first one. Mozart had improvised it in his last concert in Augsburg, on
22 October; or, to be more accurate, he had improvised the first and
last movements, with a different slow movement. 'I then played . . .
all of a sudden a magnificent sonata in C major, out of my head, with
a rondo at the end—full of din and sound,' he wrote in a letter of 24
October 1777. The characterization applies to both the first and last
movements, particularly the passages in the rondo that have the thirty-
second-note tremoli; but Mozart forgot to mention the subtlety with
which he had brought this movement, 'full of din and sound,' to a
pianissimo ending. Both movements are full of pianistic brilliance, the
first being like the transcription of a C major Salzburg symphony for a
Stein piano. But the middle movement, an *Andante un poco adagio*,
was not simply written down from memory in Mannheim, but rather
freshly composed, for in it Mozart sought to paint the character of
Mlle Cannabich, daughter of his new friend, the Kapellmeister Cannabich. Since we know nothing of this young lady's character, we cannot judge whether the portrait is a faithful one or not. The movement
is a 'tender' and 'sensitive' andante, containing ever more richly orna-

mented repetitions of the theme. How little Mozart was concerned with realism may be inferred from the fact that the slow movement of the other Mannheim sonata—an *Andante con espressione*, very child-like, very innocent—has also been taken to be the portrait of the young Rose Cannabich. This whole sonata is in a way a companion-piece to the sonata in C. Just as in the first movement of that work, the repetition of the initial motive is here avoided in the recapitulation and appears only as a surprise in the coda. (This touch of subtlety was not new; it is to be found in works written as early as 1776, e.g. the *Divertimento* K. 247.) In both sonatas the middle register of the instrument is cultivated in a new way; in both, the left hand no longer furnishes a mere accompaniment, but becomes a real partner in the dialogue; both works are showy. Mozart counted them among his more difficult piano sonatas—and rightly so, although even the apparently simplest clavier pieces by Mozart are difficult.

If these two Mannheim sonatas are twins, the five written in Paris are as varied as possible. All of them, as well as a series of sets of variations—of which the most delightful is the one on *Ah, vous dirais-je, Maman* (K. 265), with its intentionally childlike humor—were written in the tragic summer of 1778. Indeed, the first one, in A minor (K. 310), is really a tragic sonata, a counterpart to the violin-and-piano Sonata in E minor (K. 304), written just previously. But if the E minor Sonata is lyric, and not without rays of heavenly light, this sonata is dramatic and full of unrelieved darkness; not even the turn towards C major at the end of the exposition section of the first movement can brighten the mood of this work. In the slow movement, *con espressione*, the development does begin somewhat consolingly, but the whole impression is governed by the uncanny agitation that comes just before the recapitulation. Uncanny, too, is the shadowy Presto, from beginning to end—despite the interpolation of a melody that begins in musette style. The key of A minor—and sometimes A major as well—is for Mozart the key of despair. No trace of 'sociability' is left in this sonata. It is a most personal expression; one may look in vain in all the works of other composers of this period for anything similar. And it is easy to understand the astonishment of M. de Saint-Foix over the fact that the public of Paris, the city of criticism, where the work appeared in 1782, greeted it silently and without comment.

As if to regain an inner freedom, Mozart wrote not only the charming variations on a children's tune, mentioned above, but also the C major Sonata, K. 330. There is even a thematic connection between the theme of the A minor sonata and a particle of the second theme of the C major sonata.

Ex. 57

K.310

K.330

The sonata appears 'lighter' than the preceding one, but it is just as much a masterpiece, in which every note 'belongs'—one of the most lovable works Mozart ever wrote. In it the shadows of the *Andante cantabile* give place to an unclouded purity; a particularly delightful feature is the way the second part of the Finale begins with a simple little song.

Next comes the sonata in A major (K. 331), which has become a favorite—the one with the variations at the beginning, the *Rondo alla turca* at the end, and the minuet (or rather *Tempo di minuetto*) in the middle—the work that has given so many people their first impression of Mozart. It is, however, not typical but exceptional; it is in a way a counterpart to the Munich Dürnitz Sonata in D, but it places the variations at the beginning, and accordingly casts them in briefer and less virtuoso forms; it contains instead of a polonaise the most French of all dance forms; and it ends with a true *scène de ballet*. An ardently German professor has attempted to demonstrate the Teutonic origin of the variation theme, to be sure, and one of the most Teutonic of musicians used it as the basis for a set of orchestra variations. But the theme itself is utterly French, and at the same time utterly Mozartean. Especially Mozartean is the strengthening of the end of the theme with a *forte* passage: a device that is to return with symbolic strength in Mozart's setting of Goethe's *Das Veilchen*. Throughout the work one finds the fullness and sensuous beauty of the Dürnitz Sonata, raised to a higher power, just as A major is an intensification of D major. And the minor of the *Rondo alla turca* does not fail to produce a subsidiary effect of mystery.

We have already spoken of the subsequent work, the next to the last of the Parisian sonatas, in F major, as one of Mozart's most personal creations, with which one should not find fault simply because it is so little like Beethoven. One might say of this work (K. 332), and of the following sonata in B-flat (K. 333), that in them Mozart returns to Johann Christian Bach, and to himself: to Johann Christian especially in the Adagio of the F major Sonata and in the first movement of the B-flat; to himself particularly in the Finale of the B-flat, which seems like an even more perfect version of the rondo of the Sonata K. 281, also in B-flat. Johann Christian had, as a matter of fact, come to Paris early in August 1778, and there can be no question that he introduced Mozart to the sonatas that appeared in print, probably the following year, as his Op. 17. But the Mozart to whom he introduced these works, although a no less sensitive and receptive spirit than in years gone by, was now a mature personality, possessed of a mastery and a selective judgment that caused him to convert every stimulus into something truly Mozartean. We do not know whether Mozart played for his admired senior one of his most recent sonatas for piano, or for piano and violin. He does not mention having done so, in his letters, and it is likely that he was prudent enough to avoid placing this strain upon the warm and paternal friendship which he highly valued.

Six years passed before Mozart again committed a piano sonata to paper, an interval to be explained only by the fact that he had no need of writing out his sonatas. This was the period of his big 'academies,' the period of his piano concertos, his piano-and-wind quintet, his great violin sonatas. When he needed an encore, he improvised variations, as for example those on Gluck's *Unser dummer Pöbel meint* (K. 455), or he improvised freer forms. And although for Mozart Vienna was 'the true land of the clavier,' it was also the land that must be conquered through string quartets and above all through opera. Thus all we have from the early Vienna period is the fragment of an Allegro in B-flat major (K. 400)—complete as far as the recapitulation, so that Abbé Stadler was able to finish it in convincing fashion. This piece is one of Mozart's jokes, which are always to be taken half seriously and which always possess artistic form. It begins with an animated and even stormy play of both hands in sixteenth-note arpeggios and scales, which continue until the development section, in which this motion yields to a somewhat exaggerated and mocking declaration of love addressed to 'Sophie' and 'Constanze,' his future sister-in-law and his future wife. This work dates from the summer of 1781, during which Mozart had 'fooled about and had fun with' both girls, and before things had become grimly serious. When they had become grimly serious, Mozart no longer thought of adding the two further movements the piece would have needed.

Grim seriousness reigns in the following sonata, composed on 14 October 1784 (K. 457) and dedicated as Op. XI to Mozart's pupil Therese von Trattner, the second wife of the printer and publisher, Johann Thomas von Trattner. The instructions for the performance of this Sonata and the 'Fantaisie' that precedes it (K. 475) have been lost; they must have constituted one of the most important documents of Mozart's esthetic practice. Did they perhaps contain more personal matters as well, which had to be hidden from posterity? We do not know, and we cannot peer into the biographical mystery of the work. But it is clear that it represents a moment of great agitation, agitation that could no longer be expressed in the fatalistic A minor key of the Paris sonata, but required the pathetic C minor that was to be Beethoven's favorite key for the expression of similar emotions. It has rightly been said that this work contains a 'Beethovenisme d'avant la lettre.' Indeed it must be stated that this very Sonata contributed a great deal towards making 'Beethovenisme' possible. Contrasting with the concentrated first and last movements, there is a broad concerto-like Adagio in the tranquil key of E-flat major, which, in accordance with the true nature of its creator, who could not seek any easy way out, does not lead to a finale in major; on the contrary, the Finale is just as pathetic as the first movement, and even darker. There is a disproportion in this work. The sonata form of 1784 is too small for the expansion of feeling, although we must admit that one of the most powerful reasons for the effectiveness of the work is precisely the explosive compression and brevity of the first and last movements. Mozart found room for the full expression of his feelings in the concerto form, and it is accordingly only natural that this C minor sonata should be followed by a piano concerto—K. 491, a vessel fully adequate to its content. Mozart himself must have felt the necessity of providing a basis for the explosive quality of the sonata, and justifying it as the product of a particular spiritual state; accordingly, he preceded it with the Fantasy, K. 475 (written on 20 May 1785), and published the two together. This Fantasy, which gives us the truest picture of Mozart's mighty power of improvisation—his ability to indulge in the greatest freedom and boldness of imagination, the most extreme contrast of ideas, the most uninhibited variety of lyric and virtuoso elements, while yet preserving structural logic—this work is so rich that it threatens to eclipse the sonata, without actually doing so. It is the key to an understanding of Mozart's other fantasies. A shorter one, in D minor (K. 397), presumably written in the early Vienna years, contains a final Allegretto of a celestially childlike nature, which is far too short really to complete the work; the whole piece seems rather an introduction to a D major sonata—K. 284, say, or K. 311, or even one of the piano-and-violin sonatas. Mozart observed the old connection of the fantasy with a fugue, in K. 394, in C major; this fantasy seems like a preliminary study for the great one in C minor.

For less important pupils than Frau von Trattner, Mozart wrote rondos, such, for example, as the one of 10 January 1786 for a Fräulein von Würm (or Würben)—the strange one in D major, K. 485, of which we have already spoken as paying homage to both Philipp Emanuel and Johann Christian Bach, and the theme of which was taken from the rondo of the Clavier Quartet, K. 478, in G minor. For another pupil he wrote on 10 June of the same year a 'Little Rondo' in F major (K. 494), which he provided on 3 January 1788 with an Allegro and an Andante (K. 533), the three movements forming a sonata. He owed his friend and publisher Hoffmeister money at the time, and doubtless partly acquitted the debt with this sonata. In doing so he paid no attention to what is called unity of style. These movements composed later have a grandeur of harmonic and polyphonic conception, a depth of feeling, and a harmonic daring such as we find only in his last works; indeed they are conceived for an entirely different and more powerful instrument than the innocent rondo, which is written mostly for the middle register. (For Hoffmeister's engraved edition Mozart added a contrapuntal cadenza and a conclusion in a deeper register.) Yet even this rondo, with its lovely *minore* in three obbligato parts, is so rich and perfect that no uninitiated listener would observe any break in style. It is characteristic of the stodginess of many editors of the nineteenth and twentieth centuries that the rondo and the two preceding movements still appear separately.

While this Rondo, K. 494, could be used as a finale, the one in A minor, K. 511, dated 11 March 1787, could not, and was accordingly published separately by Hoffmeister. The whole depth of its emotion, the perfection of its style, its chiaroscuro of major and minor, will be appreciated when it is compared with the Rondo in A-flat that haunts many editions, with an attribution to Mozart, under the title *Romance* (K. *Anh.* 205)—a pleasing work that is little more than Mozartesque.

In these last years, Mozart's aim, in his piano sonatas as elsewhere, was the fusion of the old and the new, the *galant* and the 'learned'; he sought constantly to give depth to *galanterie* through contrapuntal craftsmanship—but craftsmanship that remains unnoticeable. Thus I regard as an authentic work of Mozart's a sonata movement in B-flat major (K. *Anh.* 136), which the Cantor of the Thomaskirche in Leipzig, August Eberhard Müller, later silently allowed to be put forth as his own, probably because it was too late to admit or explain a partial deception or mystification of the public that had already taken place. The misunderstanding may perhaps have come about somewhat as follows: Constanze, who would have been glad to get rid of the fragmentary works of her husband, had sent one of them—the beginning of this movement—to the publisher Thonus in Leipzig for appraisal; Thonus got Müller to complete the work, and sent it out into the world under Mozart's name with the first minuet of the *Kleine Nachtmusik* (which had been lost and had somehow come into his possession) and two movements by Müller. The movement in question shows Mozart on the way to the last sonata, in D (K. 576). It is an attempt to employ both hands in the service of a texture that combines *galant* and contrapuntal elements—an attempt which, since it is not without effort and a certain doctrinaire purposefulness, it is easy to understand why Mozart abandoned. But that the movement once existed, in some such form as that of the sonata movement K. 400, I have no doubt. Even in the 'Little Sonata for Beginners' (K. 545), written in the 'easiest' key of C major, and (strangely enough) not published during Mozart's lifetime, although it was undoubtedly intended by him for the instruction of beginners, the rondo begins humorously in strict imitation, with a 'canon in the fifth below':

Ex. 58

Allegretto

And the 'Little Sonata' in B-flat major (K. 570), dating from February 1789—perhaps the most completely rounded of them all, the ideal of his piano sonata—also contains counterpoint used humorously in the finale as if in open reference to the secrets of which the work is full.

The year 1789 brought forth one more piano sonata, the last, in D major (K. 576). In the spring, Mozart had been in North Germany, and had apparently expected to discover greater generosity in the Royal Family of Prussia than in Vienna. He had in mind six quartets for the King and six clavier sonatas for the King's eldest daughter, Princess Friederike (letter to Puchberg, 12-14 July 1789): '. . . I am composing six easy piano sonatas for Princess Friederike and six quartets for the King, all of which Kozeluch is engraving at my expense.' But just as only three of the quartets were actually written—appearing, as we know, only a few days before Mozart's death, not engraved by Kozeluch, but in a wretched edition by Artaria—so this was the only one of the piano sonatas actually composed, and it never reached the person for whom it was intended, but was printed posthumously. It is anything but 'easy.' In fact, it is conspicuously contrapuntal, full of duet-like oppositions that recall Johann Sebastian, in which one might see a creative acknowledgment of gratitude to the great master to whom Mozart, passing through Leipzig, had again been brought very close, and to whom, in the album of the Court Organist Engel, he had paid tribute in a masterly little three-voiced Gigue. There is no thought of Princesses of Prussia in the Finale, which combines the sweetness of piano sonorities with the fine detail of a string trio, or in the deep longing and consolation of the Adagio. The only counterpart to this Adagio is another by Mozart, the one in B minor, K. 540, composed 19 March 1788, one of the most perfect, most deeply felt, and most despairing of all his works. About this latter work it is hard to arrive at a definite conclusion. Its major ending indicates that it may have been intended for a sonata in E minor. But such a piece, without any further 'purpose,' may simply have flowed from Mozart's pen in an hour at once tragic and blessed.

In the summer of 1790, Mozart returned to the thought of these piano sonatas (letter to Puchberg, 12 June 1790): '. . . in order to have cash in hand to meet my present difficulties . . . I am now composing some piano sonatas.' But all he accomplished was some openings, each a few measures long, for a sonata in F (K. Anh. 29, 30, and 37). He did indeed finish one complete first movement, the Allegro in G minor, K. 312, which I myself dated quite mistakenly, alas, when I placed it among the 'Munich' sonatas. This is indeed one of those 'easy' movements; but it is realized in a fusion of styles, and with a mastery, of which Mozart in 1774 was by no means yet capable. The fact that no one knows this movement or plays it and that none of the popular editions of the piano works contains it is no argument against it.

15. *Chamber Music Including Clavier*

MOZART did not compose seriously for clavier and violin until his visit to Mannheim, when he was almost twenty-two years old. I say 'seriously' because before the Mannheim sonatas there were essays written in Paris, London, and The Hague—four complete opera containing no less than sixteen sonatas—and while these works are of the greatest interest as far as the musical development of the boy Mozart was concerned, they are hardly more than study sonatas for piano with an accompanying violin. Several of these movements existed originally as pieces for piano alone, and the fact that not only in the violin sonata but also in the piano trio Mozart, until his last years, thought of the piano as the dominating instrument, is demonstrated by the existence of the little sonata for violin and piano, K. 547, in a piano solo version, and by the trio, K. 564, which was conceived purely as a piano sonata. And of the Sonata for piano in B-flat major (K. 570), there is a version with violin that, unpretentious as it is, shows so light a touch that it may very well be Mozart's own.

No violinist can muster any enthusiasm for his part in the early violin sonatas of Mozart. The violin accompanies in thirds or at times performs a purely coloristic function, filling in certain chord tones; it remains modestly in the middle register, below the right hand of the piano part, and one feels that the piano would resent any real attempt by the violin to assume a dominant role. It dares now and then to interject little independent passages, but it rarely takes part in any actual dialogue or assumes any truly 'solo' character, as it does in the *Andante maestoso* of the B-flat major Sonata (K. 15), the last of the London Sonatas. The violin part seems always simply fitted into the texture, even though at times very adroitly so, as in the first Minuet of the very first sonata.

Ex. 59

A similar instance is in the Andante in F minor of K. 13, or in the first Minuet of the same Sonata, in which actually a dialogue of chromatic scale fragments is ventured. But nothing shows the inferior role of the violin more clearly than the six variations of the Hague sonata, K. 31, in which it performs only an accompanying function throughout. Strangely enough, Mozart is even more reserved in this respect than his models. Thus in the Sonata of Friedrich Raupach, formerly attributed to Mozart under the number K. 61, although it is in general cruder and more primitive than Mozart's earliest works, the violin takes over the cantilena in the second of the Variations; and even Mozart's beloved Johann Christian Bach, in his Sonatas, Op. X (which, it is true, did not appear until 1775), is a greater friend of the violin, although he still entitles them: 'Sonatas, for the Harpsichord, or Pianoforte; with an Accompagnament for a Violin.'

For Mozart, the relation between the piano and the violin changes when, in Munich, on the way to Mannheim and Paris, he makes the acquaintance of six sonatas by a certain Schuster—perhaps Joseph Schuster (1748-1812), who since 1772 had been Kapellmeister to the Elector of Saxony (letter of 6 October 1777):

I send my sister herewith six duets for clavicembalo and violin by Schuster, which I have often played here. They are not bad. If I stay on I shall write six myself in the same style, as they are very popular here.

'They are not bad'—that is high praise from Mozart. But despite the popularity of these sonatas in their own time, it has not yet been possible to identify them. For a time I thought that they were identical with the so-called 'Romantic Sonatas,' which had been included in Mozart's works as K. 55-60; but if this had been true, Joseph Schuster— assuming that he was the composer—would have protested the attribution to Mozart when the works were published by Breitkopf & Härtel in 1804. Moreover, these Sonatas only occasionally abandon the principle of the preponderance of the piano (as, for example, in the *Minore* of the Finale of K. 57), while the Schuster sonatas that really served Mozart as models must have clearly emphasized the principle of alternation between piano and violin, for that was what he found new and surprising.

And that is what is new and surprising in the so-called Mannheim Sonatas (K. 301, 296, and 302-306)—better called the Palatinate Sonatas, for Mozart dedicated six of them as Op. I to the wife of the Elector of the Palatinate, Maria Elisabeth, consort of Carl Theodor, and one (K. 296) to the little daughter of his landlord in Mannheim, Therese-Pierron Serrarius. Five of the works were written in Mannheim and two in Paris. Thus we have two groups of works labeled Op. I by Mozart (the first consisting of K. 6 and 7), both sonatas for piano and violin; the first, from his earliest youth, however, called 'Clavier Sonatas with Violin *ad libitum*'; and the second referred to by Mozart himself (in a letter of 14 February 1778) as 'Clavierduetti mit Violin.' He began to work seriously on these Sonatas when he became bored with the compositions ordered by the amateur flutist de Jean. But the autograph makes it seem not improbable that the first movement of K. 301 was originally intended for flute rather than for violin, or for either instrument at will. And M. de Saint-Foix has pointed out with happy insight the flutelike character of K. 303 as well.

However that may be, these are the first really *concertante* sonatas by Mozart for piano and violin. The violin is no longer condemned to occasional interjections or incidental imitations; it now alternates with the piano, and often, as in the beautiful and impressive Rondo in K. 302, quite openly and emphatically doubles the melody an octave higher. This does not prevent it, however, from being given accompaniment figures not really appropriate to it whenever the piano has the melody.

But how great Mozart's respect for tradition was, and how strongly he was inclined to remain within the boundaries of the species, we see from the fact that five of these seven Palatinate Sonatas have only two movements, whereas none of the piano sonatas of the same period has less than three. Two movements had been the rule for Johann Christian, of whom Mozart was reminded at every step he took in Mannheim and Paris, and he stuck to this rule. But now he went far beyond Johann Christian in the organic participation of the two instruments, and it is noticeable at times that he finds himself on new and unex-

plored paths, as for example in the somewhat strange C major Sonata
(K. 303), or in the Rondo of the Sonata in G major (K. 301), which
sounds a little like homemade Haydn. He becomes quite free and quite
spontaneous, however, in two Sonatas—the one in A, K. 305, and the
one in E minor, K. 304—which he put on paper just before the A minor
Piano Sonata, in Paris. The earlier of these two is an ideally untroubled,
'social' duet sonata, full of cheerfulness, freshness, and innocence. But
the second is one of the miracles among Mozart's works; it springs from
the most profound depths of emotion, and goes beyond the alternating
dialogue style to knock at those gates of the great world of drama which
Beethoven was to fling wide open. Mozart does not become pathetic,
and this reserve, this concealment of an inner fire, together with—in
the portion in major of the *Tempo di Minuetto*—a brief glimpse of
bliss, only enhances the mysterious power of this apparently 'little'
sonata. As always when Mozart is deeply in earnest, he has recourse to
'work' (*Arbeit*)—that is, counterpoint; in this Sonata he uses it to ac-
centuate the transitions.

The last of the sonatas written for Maria Elisabeth (K. 306, in D
major) and the one for Mlle Serrarius (K. 296, in C major) have three
movements, like a piano sonata. The one for the little Mannheim
beauty, however, is just the one that contains, in the added slow movement, an *Andante sostenuto*, the strongest reminder of Johann Christian: this movement is an instrumental arietta, of which both the theme
and the character of the accompaniment are taken almost note for note
from an aria by the London master (*Dolci aurette*). But in Johann Christian we find none of the daring modulations of the middle section. This
is a finale-sonata: the Rondo can be compared for freshness and richness of invention only with the B-flat major rondos of the piano sonatas.
K. 306 is simply a great concert sonata in which Mozart tries to
forget that he is writing for amateurs: brilliant, sonorous, and rich in
the first movement; *concertante* in the *Andante cantabile* and the
Finale, which, incidentally, is related to the violin concertos of 1775,
and not in its extended cadenza alone. In the E minor Sonata, Mozart
had reached the boundaries of intimacy; in this one, in D major, he
passes beyond them.

The later sonatas may be divided similarly. First, in Salzburg, early
in 1779, after his sad return, Mozart wrote another sonata (K. 378, in
B-flat), doubtless for Marianne and his father, which may be considered
an enhanced replica of the sonata for the little Serrarius girl: the first

movement very brilliant; the last, with its interlude before the return to the rondo theme, very characteristic of Salzburg; between them a deeply felt slow movement that looks both backward to Johann Christian and forward to *Die Entführung.*

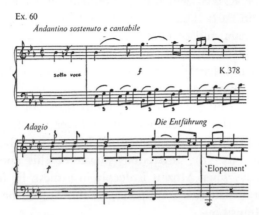

Mozart gathered together one of the three-movement Mannheim sonatas in C (K. 296), this one, and four newly composed sonatas in his Op. II, which Artaria published in November 1781, with the title: *Six Sonates pour le Clavecin ou Pianoforte, avec l'accompagnement d'un Violon,* dedicated to the pianist Josepha von Aurnhammer. Still 'with the accompaniment of a violin'! But how new and surprising they seemed to his contemporaries, at least his North-German contemporaries, we see from an anonymous comment in *Cramer's Magazin* (1, 485):

These sonatas are the only ones of this kind. Rich in new ideas and in evidences of the great musical genius of their author. Very brilliant and suited to the instrument. At the same time the accompaniment of the violin is so artfully combined with the clavier part that both instruments are kept constantly on the alert; so that these sonatas require just as skillful a player on the violin as on the clavier. But it is not possible to give a complete description of this original work. Music lovers and connoisseurs must play them through themselves, and then they will see that we have not exaggerated.

Mozart rarely received criticism like this, which is excellent in every sense. It covers every important point. All that needs to be added is that in the four Sonatas with which he completed his Op. II in the summer of 1781, he found ever more concise and at the same time richer and more melodic formulas, and that in them the relation of the two instruments becomes closer and stronger, so that the concept of 'alternation' gradually changes to that of true dialogue. Two of these Sonatas, composed in direct succession, are in F (K. 376 and 377), and they show again what freedom Mozart felt within a single key. The first of the two is brilliant, with a delicate Andante in B-flat and a graceful Rondo, which, however, is not free of good-natured and rather boisterous unison passages. The second, on the other hand, has a stormy first movement; Variations in D minor, which, in their deep fatalistic brooding, are to be compared only with the Finale of the D minor String Quartet; and a Rondo in the form of a *Tempo di minuetto* that is balsam to the soul. A movement like this last one is really the 'only one of this kind,' not alone in Mozart's time, but among all the music that has come after him as well. Consider the melodic interweaving in the theme of the variations:

Ex. 61

The third and last pair of sonatas in this group (K. 380, in E-flat, and K. 379, in G), also offer a strong contrast: the first is brilliant, with a chromatic and strangely animated Andante in G minor and a Rondo with a hunting-horn theme that could have been used as a finale for a piano concerto; the second has a passionate Allegro in G minor introduced by a solemn Adagio, and concludes with Variations that are perhaps a little too homely and bourgeois. G major is a key that Mozart used again for a similar conclusion—the Finale of the Piano Trio, K. 496. In the Variations of this Sonata there is a 'throwback': in the first variation the violinist drops out entirely, and has to stand by and admire the ostentatiously fleet fingers of the pianist; in fact, the violin tends altogether to fall back into its role of vassal.

The next works for piano and violin, dating from the summer and autumn of 1782, all have in common the fact that they remained unfinished. They are evidence of the spiritual and creative crisis of this summer: the 'struggle for Constanze,' and also the new acquaintance with true polyphony gained in the sessions at Baron van Swieten's house. Mozart writes a two-part Introduction, in the most pompous and ceremonial minuet rhythm (K. 402, A major), to a fugue in A minor, which he does not finish, partly perhaps because he finds the theme a little too archaic and impersonal, partly because he begins to realize that Constanze's love for fugues is not altogether genuine. He follows this work with an even more grandiose Adagio in C minor (K. 396), which goes only as far as the end of the first section; the violin part is barely sketched, and today the work is known only in the version for piano alone. He begins a Sonata for violin and piano in C major (K. 403), as the first in a series written expressly for Constanze: *Sonate Première. Par moi W. A. Mozart pour ma très chère épouse*; but I no longer believe that he would ever have published it. It was intended for Mozart himself as violinist and for Constanze's modest abilities at the keyboard, and written in exactly the style Mozart thought to be his wife's favorite: a little like Bach, in almost pure three-part writing, as in the Preludes for van Swieten. The turn to A-flat in the development section represents an entirely personal event, not altogether understandable from the purely musical point of view. Of the Finale, into which the Andante leads directly, only twenty measures exist. Another 'Sonata,' consisting of an Andante and an Allegretto of only a few measures each (K. 404), is simply a joke—Mozart gently poking fun at his wife.

Three large-scale sonatas represent the last word Mozart had to say in the domain of the sonata for piano and violin. He furnished his father (and us) with information about the composition of the first one, in B-flat, K. 454 in a letter of 24 April 1784:

We now have here the famous Strinasacchi from Mantua, a very good violinist. She has a great deal of taste and feeling in her playing. I am this moment composing a sonata which we are going to play together on Thursday at her concert in the theater. [April 29]

But on the day before the concert Mozart had written out only the violin part, and he played his part from memory, with an empty sheet of music paper before him. We know the repertoire of Regina Strinasacchi, who in 1784 was about twenty years old, from *Cramer's Magazin* (1, 344), in which, incidentally, she is given the first name of Catarina: 'Giarnowick, St. George, Borra, Cambini.' Mozart certainly contributed by far the best piece to this repertoire. One cannot conceive of any more perfect alternation of the two instruments than that in the first Allegro, into which one enters through a proud Largo as through a triumphal arch; or in the Rondo, which in its theme, in its *divertissements*, and in its returns to the theme furnishes ever new and more delightful surprises; nor can we imagine any slow movement—this one is more an Adagio than an Andante—in which feeling and *concertante* brilliance could be more completely fused. There follows, in December 1785, a Sonata in E-flat major (K. 481); we know nothing of the occasion for its composition: perhaps it was written only to get a little money from Hoffmeister, who published it. Mozart never came so close to Beethoven as in the Finale, consisting of six variations on a work-a-day sort of theme, or in the Adagio with its labyrinthine modulations, whose climax comes in an enharmonic change that bares the depths of the soul. All the more Mozartean, in its combination of the lovable with the thoroughly masculine, is the brief and rounded first movement. In the last of these 'great' Sonatas, in A major (K. 526), finished during the composition of *Don Giovanni*, Mozart achieves a perfect reconciliation of styles in this field as he achieved it in others. This work is like Bach, yet thoroughly Mozartean, in three contrapuntal parts, yet *galant* at the same time; and in the slow movement it attains an equilibrium of art and soul that is as if God the Father had brought all motion everywhere to a halt for a moment so that man might savor the bitter sweetness of existence. This sonata has been called a forerunner of Beethoven's 'Kreutzer' Sonata; but it avoids the 'dramatic,' the passionate; it remains within the boundaries of the eighteenth century; and in so doing it is only the more complete.

The only piano and violin works left for discussion are a Sonatina, written on 10 July 1788 (K. 547), and two sets of Variations on French themes dating from the early Vienna years (K. 359 in G major, and K. 360, in G minor)—two very *galant* works. Mozart himself described the Sonatina very well: 'A Little Clavier Sonata for Beginners with a Violin.' For the last two movements, at least—an Allegro and a set of Variations—were undoubtedly written originally for piano alone, since the violin hardly has a chance even to 'alternate' with the piano. Only the first movement, an *Andante cantabile*, is, despite its brevity, a truly *concertante* movement, full of humor, both in its technique and in its ideas; while for the following movements there can hardly have been any thought of beginners—the Variations, above all, are among the masterpieces of Mozart's 'last style.' The most wonderful of these Variations, in minor, exists only for piano—evidence that this was the original medium. This variation is so complete in itself that there was no possibility of adding an accompanying violin part to it. Mozart maintained the same key for all three movements, returning in this respect to his first piano-and-violin sonatas, written in Paris and London.

It is easy to pass from the sonatas for piano and violin to the trios for piano, violin, and violoncello, because the difference is hardly perceptible. The role of the violoncello in these trios is at first so inconspicuous that the earliest work of this species, the Divertimento in B-flat (K. 254, written in August 1776, in Salzburg, about a year before the beginning of the grand tour), ought really to be called a sonata for piano with obbligato violin, and with the addition of a violoncello to reinforce the bass. Only once, in the Rondo of this work, is the violoncello allowed to carry the bass part alone for four whole measures. Mozart's way of writing scores for his piano trios is significantly different from the modern manner: the violin and violoncello are not grouped together above the piano part, but instead the piano part is written between the two string parts. Thus the violoncello seems only to reinforce the left hand of the piano.

The title, *Divertimento*, under which the first clavier trio was published in 1782 by Mme Heina in Paris, as Op. III, is striking. For this is a regular, serious sonata in three movements, and we are not warranted in assuming that the title has to do with the content of the work—that is, that it has any connection with the fact that the first movement, a gay *Allegro assai*, and the last movement, a *Tempo di minuetto* in rondo form, remain within the bounds of polite society music, while only the Adagio strikes a deeper and more personal note. Mozart returned to this species only in Vienna, and only relatively late in his career there. In fact, ten years passed before he began, in July 1786, a series of such works, with the *Terzett für Clavier, Violino und Violoncello* in G (K. 496); 'Terzett,' no longer 'Sonata' or 'Divertimento.' For this is a real trio, in which the violoncello takes part in the dialogue, although somewhat more sparingly than the violin, and is not at all a mere later addition to a work complete without it.*

Mozart seems even to have used red and black ink in the autograph for the purpose of reminding himself not to neglect any of the instru-

---

* This statement represents a revision of the opinion I expressed in my edition of the Köchel *Verzeichnis*, p. 630.

ments. If he had a simple piano sonata in mind at all, he realized the work in that form only in the exposition of the first movement. With the entrance of the development there begins a dramatic use of the instruments such as Beethoven was to carry to its peak. In Mozart, the dramatic element does not burst the bounds of the social nature of music; his contemporaries could still accept it with astonishment and delight—with the same astonishment and delight, in fact, with which they accepted the many miracles of modulation and counterpoint in which particularly the Andante abounds. (This Andante contains a little closing motive that cannot fail to remind the lover of Verdi of Mistress Quickly's 'dalle due alle tre.') The movement intended to serve as finale for this work was presumably the Andante or *Tempo di minuetto* which is usually published as the middle movement of K. 442, but which can hardly have been written as early as 1783, as were the two movements with which it is arbitrarily combined. (All three of the movements are presumably only fragmentary; the D major ending of the movement in D minor is particularly suspect, for it is quite contrary to Mozart's custom.) But perhaps he found this minuet movement too tender or amorous in character, and thus replaced it with variations on a sort of idealized gavotte, in a movement that begins perhaps in somewhat homely fashion, and contains a rather too *galant* adagio variation, but is lifted by the preceding variation in minor and by the concluding section into a region far above homeliness or *galanterie*. Between this work and the two succeeding Piano Trios with violin and violoncello (K. 502 and 542), the great masterworks of the category, there is a Trio with different instrumentation but belonging to the same species: the Trio for piano, clarinet, and viola, in E-flat (K. 498). There are both internal and external grounds for discussing it here: it prepares the way for the two works that are to follow, and it was published by Artaria, doubtless with Mozart's consent, with the usual instrumentation: *Trio per il Clavicembalo o Forte Piano con l'accompagnamento d'un Violino e Viola . . . Opera 14. La parte del Violino si può eseguire anche con un Clarinetto*[!]. But the 'violin part' can and should be played *only* on the clarinet. This work, written for the Jacquin family, or more accurately for the daughter of the family, Francisca, is a work of intimate friendship and love, doubtless intended for Francisca at the clavier, Mozart himself playing the viola, and Anton Stadler the clarinet. No other instrument can realize the melodic savor or the deep, soft accompaniment figures as well as the clarinet. In this work,

E-flat major is not the key of Freemasonry, but the key of intimate friendship, and in the first movement, an Andante full of proud assurance, with a persistent *gruppetto* (separated by an infinite distance from the *gruppetti* of Richard Wagner), the key is continually emphasized by touches of the dominant and subdominant as well as by occasional descents into the more morose region of C minor. This movement is just as unique in Mozart's works as the middle movement, which is at the same time blissful and a little defiant and is another miracle of contrapuntal, 'learned' animation, although its 'learning' is not apparent on the surface. What is one to say of the Finale, a rondo that sings from beginning to end, with a new motive, after the minor episode, which then, gently triumphant, dominates the whole last part of the movement? How well Mozart now understands not only how to end a work but how to close it, with a distillation of melodic and contrapuntal beauty that does not merely satisfy the listener but leaves him enchanted! The last word music can utter as an expression of the feeling of form is here spoken.

This intimate work is followed by one that contains everything of *concertante* display that can be placed within the frame of a piano trio (K. 502, in B-flat). The first movement has a certain relation, not only in key but in thematic material as well, with the Piano Concerto K. 450, of 1784:

The Larghetto sounds like the transcription of a deeply felt slow movement from a piano concerto into the domain of chamber music, and the Finale begins like the rondo of a concerto, as if with a solo passage, *piano*, answered by a tutti passage, *forte*, but without any sacrifice of the finely wrought detail of chamber music. In every measure one finds the freshness, the nobility of invention, and the inspired mastery that synthesize the contrasted elements of brilliance and intimacy, contrapuntal craftsmanship and *galanterie*, into a higher unity. The same is true of the Trio in E major (K. 542), which Mozart wrote just before composing the last three symphonies (June 1788). He announced the completion of this work to his friend and fellow-Mason Puchberg, on 17 June: 'I have composed a new trio!' and sent it with other works to his sister, asking her to invite Michael Haydn to St. Gilgen and play it for him (2 August): 'I am sure he will like the Trio and the Quartet [K. 493].' On 14 April 1789, he played it at the Court of Dresden, which may perhaps indicate that he considered it the climax of his achievement in this field. And so it is, or at least it need dispute that title only with the B-flat major Trio. But the E major has the advantage of the more unusual key, with the radiant turn to B major and the dark-green one to C-sharp minor, and has an *Andante grazioso* as pastoral and full of poetry as a painting by Watteau, and full of the finest and most vital harmonic and contrapuntal workmanship.

The last two Piano Trios are unfortunately not on this level; Mozart's work in this field had no triumphal ending. The last one, in G (K. 564), completed exactly one month after the incomparable String Trio for Puchberg, was originally a piano sonata, obviously intended 'for beginners.' It is simply not big enough to fill the frame of a piano trio, in which, according to Mozart's own standard, the three instruments must carry on a genuine conversation. The work ought to be restored to its original version, so that it might have its full measure of innocent charm, especially in the slow movement, consisting of variations of the same type as those in the Sonata K. 547. More pretentious is the Trio in C (K. 548), dating from July 1788, and finished between the Symphony in E-flat and the one in G minor. But one has almost the impression that Mozart was saving all his powers in the key of C for the 'Jupiter' Symphony. This Trio seems like a rather pale forerunner; it is classic in its mastery, but it does not have the vitality of invention that we find in the three great Trios, or their thematic richness and conciseness, although the *Andante cantabile* is endlessly moving in its soft and delicate religious quality. But the yardstick of perfection against which we measure these two works was put into our hands by Mozart himself.

Towards the end of 1785, or early in 1786, Mozart's friend, colleague, and source of income, Franz Anton Hoffmeister, published a Piano Quartet of Mozart's (K. 478), of which Nissen writes (p. 633) that it was to have been the first of three works agreed upon. 'When, however,' Nissen goes on, 'Hoffmeister complained that the public found the work too difficult and would not buy it, Mozart voluntarily released him from the contract and gave up the project of continuing the series'; * indeed, he claims that Hoffmeister 'made Mozart a present of the advance payment he had already received, on condition that he should not write the two other quartets contracted for . . .' Now, Mozart did write a second Piano Quartet (K. 493), which indeed appeared not under Hoffmeister's imprint, but under that of Artaria. The only striking thing about the whole story is that Artaria should have been more daring than Hoffmeister, who later accepted for publication such difficult works as the Violin Sonatas in E-flat (K. 481), and A (K. 526), the Piano Rondo in A minor (K. 511), and the Fugue for Two Pianos in C minor (K. 426).

Whatever the truth of the story, it is certain that the public, both in Vienna and elsewhere, was little prepared, even by Mozart himself, for such a work. For the species of the piano quartet was practically new, and Mozart's great piano trios are all of later date. We realize how true this is when we remember that Haydn never wrote in this form (among his *Divertimenti für Clavier mit andern Instrumenten* there are, as far as I know, no works with this instrumentation), and that the only such work by Carl Philipp Emanuel Bach is the *Clavier-Sonate mit begleitenden Instrumenten* (Clavier Sonata with Accompanying Instruments), a very modest work, while the only similar piece by Johann Christian is a quintet for assorted instruments with *basso continuo*. A work for clavier with more than two stringed instruments automatically becomes in the hands of Johann Christian or Philipp Emanuel a clavier concerto. Mozart, however, treats it as the purest and most characteristic chamber music, making just as exacting demands on the virtuosity of the pianist, however, as many a concerto of the period, and weaving the string parts into the thematic texture to a degree definitely beyond what amateurs were used to. This quartet in G minor presented performers with the added difficulty of dealing with unwonted earnestness, passion, and depth. For this is no longer in any sense music of mere sociability, which can be listened to superficially and with a smile. G minor is for Mozart the key of fate, as we know from two symphonies and a string quintet; and the wild command that opens the first movement, *unisono*, and stamps the whole movement with its character, remaining threateningly in the background, and bringing the movement to its inexorable close, might be called the 'fate' motive with exactly

---

* *Köchel Verzeichnis*, Third Edition, p. 600.

as much justice as the four-note motive of Beethoven's Fifth Symphony. The Andante, in B-flat major, is a mild companion piece to the first movement, while the Finale, a Rondo in major, full of manly jubilation, completes the balance of the work—for here the major mode has a sense different from that in which it is used in the later String Quintet, in which such balance was no longer attainable. The appearance of that Johann-Christian-like theme, which was later to be the germ of the little Rondo in D (K. 485), represents a moment of perfect bliss—a moment that does not recur, for the theme does not reappear in the course of the whole movement. This is the paradise of Mozart: a melodic blossom that seems to have grown for its own sake alone—a gift from God that must be left untouched.

The only companion-piece to this work, the Piano Quartet in E-flat (K. 493), was finished about three-quarters of a year later, five weeks or so after the completion of *Le Nozze di Figaro*. Perhaps remembering his difficulties with Hoffmeister, Mozart made it technically a little easier, but in its originality, its freshness of invention, and its craftsmanship, it is no less a masterpiece. It is bright in color, but iridescent, with hints of darker shades. The Larghetto, full of delicate echoes, is in A-flat major, and in the same key, now the subdominant, is the melody in the Rondo, sung first by the violin, and then repeated with some elaboration by the piano—the purest, most childlike, and most godlike melody ever sung. The *concertante* element is suggested in all the movements—in the Rondo, for example, by a trill in the piano part substituting for a cadenza—but only to the extent possible within the bounds of chamber music; the sonatas for piano go much further in the same direction. When one listens to such a flawless masterpiece, one can only recall Haydn's remark: 'The highest taste and, what is more, the most profound knowledge of composition.'

The Quintet for Piano, Oboe, Clarinet, Horn, and Bassoon, in E-flat (K. 452), completed on 30 March 1784, was considered by Mozart himself to be 'the best work I have ever composed' (letter to his father, 10 April 1784). Now there must have been some grounds for such an opinion. Beethoven, at any rate, considered it worth while to try to surpass this work in his Piano Quintet, Op. 16, although he did not succeed in doing so. For the delicacy of feeling with which Mozart touches the boundaries of the *concertante* field without overstepping them can only be admired, not surpassed; and the particular charm of this work consists in its feeling for the tonal character of each of the four wind instruments, of which none is disproportionately prominent—not even the clarinet, which shares the leadership in true fraternity with the oboe; and in the fact that none of the instruments is subordinated—not even the horn. The tonal character of the instruments, too, governs the melodic invention: in the majestic Largo; in the pastoral *Allegro moderato* with its short development; in the Larghetto or Andante that begins so innocently and then, just before the recapitulation, plunges with a sudden modulation into the abyss; in the Rondo with its royally high-spirited theme. The rondo includes a *cadenza in tempo*, but the whole work yet remains chamber music, enlivened in every measure by the alternation of the piano and the winds, and by the gentle rivalry of all the instruments. But it is still true that we are on the borders of the *concertante* style; and before proceeding further we must say something about the relations between chamber and symphonic music on the one hand, and *concertante*, polyphonic, and mechanical elements, on the other.

16. Concertante and Mechanical Elements

W E BEGIN our discussion with the simple and obvious observation that a broken-chord or arpeggio is the easiest and most natural tone-pattern at the keyboard, while on string and wind instruments (and in the human voice) it is a much more difficult figure. For the human voice, and all 'singing' instruments, movement in seconds is the most natural. In Mozart's music for piano with other instruments (and of course in that of other composers as well) there is a natural antagonism between the 'mechanical' instrument—for the clavier is to a much greater extent a mechanical instrument than the violin or the clarinet—and the strings or winds. The keyboard lends itself to figurations that stringed instruments cannot execute. Mozart's practice, in his early piano-and-violin sonatas, of giving to the violin in repetitions the same figuration that the piano has previously had, reflects a certain naïveté. 'Murky-basses' and broken chords belong exclusively to the domain of the keyboard.

Keyboard instruments have a certain natural tendency towards the mechanical, even in Mozart. How much of what he uses—apparently naively and without hesitation is pure formula, seemingly lifeless, and well-worn by a hundred hands! This formula, the common property of the period, is a part of his style and of his personality. He has no desire to be revolutionary, but only to use in its proper place whatever is at hand. For a perfect example of how he does this, see the last of the so-called *Sonate da chiesa*, in C major (K. 336), composed in March 1780. These church sonatas were instrumental interpolations in the Mass, between the Gloria and the Credo, or more precisely between the epistle and the gospel, and in Mozart's hands they assume the most varied character and instrumentation, according to the nature of the Mass in which they were used. Usually, however, they took on the form of a miniature sonata movement. For brevity was the one requirement for them all, since the Mass itself had to be as brief as possible—at least under the regime of the last Prince-Bishop of Salzburg. This C major *Sonata da chiesa* (Mozart's last) is a concerto movement for piano and miniature string orchestra—for piano, not organ, since the style is as unsuited to the organ as it can be. Even the opportunity for a virtuoso cadenza is not lacking. The whole movement is a chain, a 'filo,' of formulas that flow along in a natural order from the royal, typically C major opening theme. It contains scales, broken chords, trills—the whole apparatus of *buffo* instrumental music. Mozart must certainly have spent less than an hour composing this movement. In writing it down he had no ambitious aims, although he could not help following his personal bent a little in the recapitulation. But this trifle is authentic Mozart, unmistakable, and incapable of being attributed to any other musician of the period.

Mozart lends charm even to the mechanical. For he allows the mechanical to perform its own function, and the mechanical element is part of the very nature of the *concertante* style. He would have smiled at composers who demand 'expression' in every note; as at those *rubato* players whose left hand 'always follows suit.' For him 'the left hand goes on playing in strict time' (letter of 24 October 1777). Is it not the very secret of his music that it is his own personal language and at the same time a music that is complete in itself, and almost independent of the player? Is this not the same ideal of music which, in its own way, the twentieth century would so much like to realize, although it never succeeds in doing so? Perhaps this is because the twentieth century has no tradition, and therefore cannot make a game of its relations with a tradition, as Mozart did—because its mechanical music is *only* mechanical, and consequently inhuman.

Mozart actually wrote some works for mechanical instruments, and in the bells of *Die Zauberflöte* he imitated a little mechanical instrument with wit and affection. The works of this nature were commissioned by Count Josef Deym, who had a collection full of curiosities. (A few years after Mozart's death he moved to the vicinity of the Rotenturmtor with his collection, to which had been added Mozart's death-mask.) These works are mostly known to the public only in their piano-solo or four-hand versions; but the originals are quite different. One of them, an Andante in rondo form in F major (K. 616), *für eine Walze in eine kleine Orgel* (for a Little Clock-Work Organ) is written on three staves, all in the soprano clef, and it contains little passages of mechanical velocity that Mozart would have written quite differently for the piano. This is really a piece for a magic music-box—the accompaniment for the dance of a tiny fairy princess. The earliest piece of this nature consists of music of mourning, for the exhibition of a wax-figure in a mausoleum also in Deym's collection—the figure of the Field Marshal Laudon, who had died on 14 July 1790. Mozart began it in October en route to the coronation city of Frankfurt, and made very slow progress with it, since he had no pleasure in writing it (letter of 3 October 1790):

I have now made up my mind to compose at once the Adagio for the watchmaker and then to slip a few ducats into the hand of my dear little wife. And this I have done; but as it is a kind of composition which I detest, I have unfortunately not been able to finish it. I compose a bit of it every day—but I have to break off now and then, as I get bored. And indeed I would give the whole thing up, if I had not such an important reason to go on with it. But I still hope that I shall be able to force myself gradually to finish it. If it were for a large instrument and the work would sound like an organ piece, then I might get some fun out of it. But, as it is, the works consist solely of little pipes, which sound too high pitched and too childish for my taste.

I think the piece reveals the fact that Mozart did not enjoy writing it. It is a brooding Adagio in F minor, which is followed by a stormy Allegro in two parts, in major, and then returns at the end in slightly changed form. The Allegro shows that Mozart must have known Handel's organ concertos: he has simply added agitation to the lordly splendor of Handel's allegros. The somber color and excitement of the piece have a certain theatrical quality that is usually quite foreign to Mozart. All the more Mozartean and the more remarkable, then, is an *Orgelstück für eine Uhr* (Organ Piece for a Clock) in the same key (K. 608), which Mozart wrote on 3 March 1791, doubtless for a similar purpose. This piece caught his imagination, whether it was the occasion that interested him or simply the *élan* of his genius applying itself to the task. The first and last sections of this piece, in contrast to the previous one, are allegro, and the middle section andante, but on what a scale, with what depth of feeling, and with what wealth of detail! The heart of the opening and closing section is a fugue, returning as a double fugue with all the tricks of polyphony, and itself preceded and followed by passionate *ritornelli*. The whole piece is an unceasing and mighty flow of melody, alive in every detail, and although many arrangements have been made of it—for the contradiction between its garb and its content was felt long ago—the only appropriate one would be for large orchestra. The function of the polyphony is a grandiose objectivity of expression, a monumental form of mourning that seeks to avoid the slightest trace of sentimentality. It is wholly understandable that the composer of the *Marcia funebre* in the 'Eroica' Symphony should have made a copy of this work; and many points of contact between Mozart and Beethoven may be found in it.

With these pieces belongs the Rondo in C (K. 617), which Mozart wrote on 23 May 1791 for Marianne Kirchgässner and her instrument—the glass-harmonica invented by Benjamin Franklin. The instrument played by the blind virtuoso was not quite the same as the somewhat primitive one of Franklin; it must have had a keyboard and there must have been added to it later, as Gerber reports in his *Neues Lexicon*, an 'elastic sounding board.' Again Mozart was very limited in his use of the lower portions of the gamut, for the instrument did not go below G in the alto register. Nevertheless, this is one of his 'heavenly' works, an instrumental counterpart to the *Ave Verum*, with an unearthly beauty in the Introduction (minor) and the Rondo (major). There are only a few accompanying solo instruments (oboe, flute, viola, violoncello). Doubtless intended for the same virtuoso was a little Adagio in the same key (K. 356). Marianne took the pieces all over Europe and apparently had particular success with them in London.

The purest examples of the *concertante* style are to be found in Mozart's works for piano four hands or for two pianos—all intended for two partners of equal importance. He began very early to write music for four hands. Nissen (1, 102) quotes the following remarks, allegedly from the end of a letter of Leopold, dated London, 9 July 1765: 'In London, little Wolfgang wrote his first piece for four hands. No one had ever written a four-hand sonata before.' The quotation is suspect, since it can hardly come from a London letter, although it might have come from one written later in The Hague. But Leopold was not in the habit of making assertions that contradicted what he knew to be true, and he knew that there had been four-hand sonatas in existence before 1765, including surely some by Johann Christian Bach. In any case, the sonata in question has recently been re-discovered by Saint-Foix, in a Paris edition dating from the last years of Mozart's life. The edition was advertised in Kunzen and Reichardt's *Musikalisches Woch-enblatt* for June 1792 (p. 183), among the 'brand-new musical works engraved in Paris.' And the young Mozart already goes beyond Johann Christian, who in his four-hand sonatas had for the most part been satisfied with an allegro and a minuet, and had remained within the confines of the 'delicate style,' with little echo effects. Mozart's first movement exhibits a definitely concerto-like type of invention, and the Minuet is followed by a Rondo which contains in place of the cadenza a short Adagio, and which is strikingly related in theme to the Rondo of the great Serenade for winds, K. 361. Everything in the work, the alternation and the partnership of the two players, is as primitive and childlike as can be; but perhaps the London public was astonished when, in the Rondo, Nannerl's left hand (she played the *primo*) reached down below the right hand of her brother. The brother and sister are portrayed in a similar position, with the right hand of the *secondo* player reaching above the left hand of the *primo*, in the familiar Salz-burg family portrait of 1780-81.

For himself and his sister, too, Mozart wrote the two following Sonatas for four hands, in D (K. 381) and in B-flat (K. 358). The first, dating probably from the first part of 1772, is best described as a re-duction of an Italian symphony—a symphony in which individual groups of winds and strings, of tutti and soli are quite sharply dis-tinguished. And the Andante contains a genuinely orchestral effect, the melody of the *primo* being doubled two octaves lower by the 'bassoon or 'cello' of the *secondo*. The second of these Sonatas, written a little more than two years later (1774), unfortunately suffers by having a jovial but rather ordinary Finale, which does not even show any par-ticular technical progress, and even the first movement is hardly more than the 'reduction' of an orchestra piece. Only the Adagio exhibits great refinement of melody, and of the voice leading in the accompani-ment, to remind us that the composer of this sonata had already writ-ten the Symphonies in G minor (K. 183) and A major (K. 201).

Not until relatively late in his Vienna period did Mozart think of writing more pieces for four hands. The two Sonatas written in Salz-burg sufficed for a remarkably long time. But when he did, he brought forth the crowning work of its kind (K. 497). This work looks both backwards and forwards: backwards in an unprepossessing contrapuntal motive, such as had already been used in the first movement of the B-flat Sonata; forwards in the refinement of its workmanship, in which it is related to the 'mechanical' pieces in F minor. In this work, at last, the simple alternation of the two players or the subordination of one to the other yields to true dialogue, and the beauty of the melodic lines of this truly pianistic piece has something also of quartet style about it. For what Mozart is concerned with is not massive sonorities, doublings, amplification of the tone, but rather the enrichment of the melody and the fusion of *concertante* and intimate elements. Only the Finale has something of the character of the rondo of a concerto; but there is little to remind us of the 'piano-reduction' style. The four-hand sonata had become for Mozart a special field, in which his fancy had free play, and in which *concertante* and contrapuntal elements, the *galant* and the 'learned,' could be combined and synthesized.

Quite different is the sonata in C major (K. 521), written a year or so later, on 29 May 1787, in the Landstrasse, for Francisca von Jacquin. 'Please be so good as to give the sonata to your sister with my compliments and tell her to tackle it at once, for it is rather difficult,' Mozart wrote to Jacquin on the day on which he finished the work. But later he dedicated it to two young ladies, one of whom was to become Gottfried's sister-in-law—Nanette and Babette Natorp, daughters of the rich merchant Franz Wilhelm Natorp. In this brilliant Sonata, Nanette and Babette are treated quite impartially. It is not without significance that Mozart wrote on the autograph of the two parts *Cembalo primo* and *Cembalo secondo*, for the work would only gain by being performed on two instruments. The two parts are friendly rivals, and the brilliance of the opening and closing movements, in their chivalrous amiability, foreshadows the works of Carl Maria von Weber, though they are without Weber's display of virtuosity. This Sonata would represent the highest ideal of *concertante* style if it were not for a sonata by Mozart for two pianos, to which we shall return presently. Similar in intention to the sonata for the Natorp sisters are the variations in G major for four hands (K. 501), which date from November 1786; these were also originally intended for two pianos, and then, presumably at the desire of Mozart's publisher-friend Hoffmeister, were written for the more usual combination. They are less deep in feeling than the Andante of the Sonata but they are full of charm and in performance are enchanting. Dating from the same period there are also two extended fragments—an Allegro and an Andante—in the same key of G major (K. 357), which strangely enough return almost entirely to the principle of alternation, which Mozart had long since outgrown. There must be some explanation for this work, which is not only unfinished but also strangely immature, although we cannot guess what it is. If the C major Sonata foreshadows the style of Carl Maria von Weber, this one, especially in the Andante, with its middle section in C major, foreshadows the four-hand pieces of Franz Schubert.

Mozart twice yielded to the desire to write for two pianos instead of for four hands at one piano, and we must regret that it was only twice, for in both cases he produced incomparable masterpieces. The first is a Fugue in C minor, completed on 29 December 1783 (K. 426), in which he sums up the fruit of his contrapuntal studies and of everything he had learned from Johann Sebastian Bach. It is a strict, four-voiced fugue, with a deeply serious, 'dualistic' theme—half imperious and half complaining; and it contains all the devices of inversion and *stretto*. Only at the end does it assume a more pianistic bearing, but its relation to the 'objective,' contrapuntal portions of the pieces for mechanical organ is unmistakable. He began a Prelude for this grandiose piece (K. Anh. 44), but did not complete it. In later years (on 26 June 1788), however, he arranged the Fugue for string quartet or for string orchestra, adding to it 'a short *adagio a 2 violini, viola e basso*, for a fugue, which I wrote long ago for two pianos.' It is an introduction that corresponds in significance and weight to the fugue itself.

Quite different in character, but of no less value, is the Sonata in D major (K. 448), written in November 1781 for performance by Fräulein von Aurnhammer and himself. This work is *galant* from beginning to end; it has the form and the thematic material of an ideal *sinfonia* for an *opera buffa*; no cloud obscures its gaiety. But the art with which the two parts are made completely equal, the play of the dialogue, the delicacy and refinement of the figuration, the feeling for sonority in the combination and exploitation of the different registers of the two instruments—all these things exhibit such mastery that this apparently 'superficial' and entertaining work is at the same time one of the most profound and most mature of all Mozart's compositions. No doubt he felt this himself: there is a *Grave* and the beginning of an Allegro for another sonata of the same species, dating from the same period (K. Anh. 42), but of a more pathetic character. However, he did not complete this sonata; the period of the pathetic concerto had not yet arrived, and Mozart doubtless felt that he could hardly set any other piece against the D major work.

When to the competition of two or more instruments the orchestra is added, as another participant in the dazzling tournament—a participant that usually opens the occasion and then retires, leaving the center of attention to the combatants, modestly accompanying or commenting upon their activities, and returning to the foreground only when they are tired and must rest a little—we are squarely in the *concertante* domain. The forerunner of these *concertante* orchestral works of the eighteenth century was the old *concerto grosso* of Corelli and his imitators, in which the *concertino* emerged from the tutti of the *concerto grosso*. In Corelli, the *concertino* always consisted of two solo violins and a violoncello, while in other masters the solo instruments varied. Mozart made a sharp distinction between such works and the symphony, in which he only seldom—far less frequently than Haydn—permitted an instrument to develop along solo lines. There is for instance in all his symphonies no example of a violin solo such as that in the Andante of Haydn's Symphony with the Drum-Roll (No. 103); such a mixture of species seemed to him inconsistent with symphonic style. Unlike Haydn, who had his *Sinfonia Concertante* for violin (flute), oboe, violoncello, bassoon, and orchestra performed as late as 1792, in London (if, indeed, he did not compose it there), Mozart cultivated this form less and less as the years went on. He abandoned the *sinfonia concertante*, and separated its ingredients, developing the symphonic elements in ever purer form in the orchestral symphony, and the *concertante* element in the concerto for a solo instrument, especially for the piano.

He began, early in May 1773, with a *Concertone*, a *concertante* display piece (K. 190) in C major for two solo violins (*violini principali*), oboe, and violoncello—the latter being given little prominence in the first movement, but forming a quartet with the other instruments of the *concertino* in the slow movement, an *Andantino grazioso*, and in the Finale, a quickened *Tempo di minuetto*. But the whole work, including the orchestra with its divided violas, is full of *concertante* zeal, lively figuration, and animated, *galant* imitation, which is not to be confused with any true polyphonic spirit. One is astonished at the formal ability and experience of the boy, barely seventeen years old, who could write a work like this, and at his technical ambition, fully realized in it. Both Leopold and Wolfgang maintained their interest in the work for a long time: 'Could you not have performed in Mannheim your Haffner music, your Concertone, or one of your Lodron Serenades?' asks Leopold, on 11 December 1777, thus indicating the relation between this work and two other 'light,' *galant* forms of Mozart's creative activity. And Mozart himself wrote, three days later: 'I played through my Concertone to Herr Wendling on the piano. He remarked that it was just the thing for Paris. When I play it to Baron Bagge, he's quite beside himself.' (Baron Charles-Ernest de Bagge was one of the famous *melomanes* of his time, and himself an amateur composer.) Indeed, Paris and London, where the orchestras always contained virtuosi, were the places for such works. Johann Christian Bach wrote a whole series of such concertos, in which now a violin and a violoncello, now an oboe and a violoncello, now a flute and a violin, now a bassoon, now an oboe, and once a harpsichord, are featured in an obbligato or *principale* role. I have published one of these *Sinfonie concertanti*, of which a copy was in the possession of this same Baron Bagge.

It was in Paris that Mozart, five years after the *Concertone*, wrote a similar work, the *Sinfonia Concertante*, in E-flat major, for flute, oboe, horn, and bassoon (K. *Anh.* 9), whose composition he announced in a letter to his father dated 5 April 1778: 'I am now going to compose a *sinfonia concertante* for flute, Wendling; oboe, Ramm; horn, Punto; and bassoon, Ritter'—all Mannheim musicians except Punto, who was a traveling virtuoso. The work was intended for performance at the Concerts Spirituels but was never actually performed there; the autograph has disappeared and with it the original instrumentation, so that we know only an arrangement, in which the flute and oboe are replaced by oboe and clarinet. But it is clear that the arranger has not permitted himself any alterations seriously affecting the essential nature of the work. This is a 'Mannheim' work. We know the Mannheim symphonies of Cannabich, Toëschi, and Eichner, works that outdid the Viennese and Italian symphonies in pomp and in general scope, not only through the use of the 'Mannheim crescendo' but also by their exploitation of solo effects; for the virtuosi in this 'first orchestra of Europe' demanded their rights. Now, this Sinfonia Concertante is not a symphony in which four wind instruments have prominent solo parts, nor is it quite a concerto for four wind instruments with orchestral accompaniment. It is between the two; it looks backward to the Salzburg Concertone of 1773, and forward to the Vienna Piano Quintet with winds of 1784. It is planned entirely for brilliance, breadth, and expansiveness; it is quite 'in the long taste,' particularly in the first movement; and in all the movements, especially in the last, it is concerned with exhibiting the abilities of the four wind players. This last movement consists of no less than ten connected variations, one for each of the solo instruments separately and others for various combinations. The highest level is reached in the slow movement (which, strangely enough, is not in B-flat, or A-flat, or C minor, but in the principal key of the work), in which the tutti is more definitely subordinated to the solo quartet than in the opening and closing movements. One is always safe in expecting something extraordinary, when, as in the strings after the unison passage for orchestra, Mozart begins with the 'motto' he carried with him all through his life.

It is one of the ironies of Mozart's creative career that immediately after this concerto for four finished artists he should have written another *Sinfonia Concertante* for two high-born amateurs—the Concerto for Flute and Harp, in the 'easiest' key of C major, composed for the Duc de Guines and his daughter. The Duke, Mozart reports to his father on 14 May 1778, 'plays the flute extremely well,' and the little Duchess 'plays the harp *magnifique*'; nevertheless, he took care to make only moderate demands on their virtuosity. He was not fond of the flute, nor could he see in the harp anything but a very limited form of 'keyboard' instrument, and one has to know his feelings about these instruments in order to realize how successfully he triumphed over them. The work is an example of the finest French salon music—

From a portrait by an unknown artist

Mozart, Wearing the Order of the Golden Spur (1777)

French above all in the Rondo, a *tempo di gavotta*. The orchestra is small, though it includes oboes and horns; the two fashionable instruments are charmingly played off against each other and against the tutti; the Andantino is like a François Boucher, decorative and sensuous but not lacking in deeper emotions. Mozart had to write out the cadenzas for the two aristocratic soloists (he himself described with tragicomic penetration the inability of the harpist as a novice in composition) but both cadenzas have been lost.

On the way home from Paris to Salzburg, in November 1778, in Mannheim, Mozart began a similar work for violin and piano with orchestra (letter of 12 November): 'An Academie des Amateurs, like the one in Paris, is about to be started here. Herr Fränzl is to lead the violins. So at the moment I am composing a concerto for violin and piano.' A *sinfonia concertante* for Fränzl, whom Mozart admired so highly as a violinist, and himself—what a gift to the world this would have been! We can estimate to some extent what we have lost, from the surviving fragment of the first movement (K. *Anh.* 56). The orchestra includes flutes, oboes, horns, trumpets, and timpani; the ritornello is broad and imposing; there is a majestic *Alla marcia*; this would have been a 'Coronation Concerto' before either of the two works we know by that name. But, alas, the plans for the 'academy' came to naught, since a few weeks after the date of the letter quoted, the Mannheim orchestra was no longer in existence. One asks oneself why Mozart did not finish the work in Munich; but Ignaz Fränzl seems to have preferred to stay in Mannheim, and Mozart obviously must have had him and no one else in mind when he began the work. Thus, the smallpox of the Bavarian Elector Max Joseph robbed us of a masterpiece.

Mozart spoke his last word in the form of the *sinfonia concertante* in Salzburg, in a work for violin and viola, in E-flat major (K. 364), the counterpart of an earlier composition in the same key for two pianos (K. 365)—a composition the discussion of which must be reserved for the next chapter. It was his last word because the *Sinfonia concertante* in A major, for violin, viola, and violoncello (K. *Anh.* 104), written about the same time (autumn 1779), remained, like the Mannheim work, only a mighty torso. In the E-flat major *Sinfonia concertante* Mozart summed up what he had accomplished in the *concertante* portions of his serenades, adding what he had learned of the monumental style in Mannheim and Paris, and, most important of all, treating all his materials with the personal and artistic maturity which he had by this time reached. No mere allegro or *allegro spiritoso* opens this work, but rather an *Allegro maestoso*. The motives are no longer *buffo* or simply *galant* in style; they are truly symphonic or singing. Among the singing melodies the subsidiary theme is unforgettable, where the oboes answer the deep seriousness of the strings and at the same time bring in a ray of light, or where, later, the horns and oboes carry on a dialogue against the *pizzicato* of the strings. The powerful orchestra crescendo—a rarity in Mozart's works—is in the Mannheim style; but the living unity of each of the three movements, organic in every detail, and the complete vitality of the whole orchestra, in which every instrument speaks its own language: the oboes, the horns, and all the strings, with the divided violas enhancing the richness and warmth of the texture—all this is truly Mozartean. So is the intimate conversation of the two soloists, rising in the Andante to the level of eloquent dialogue. The Andante is in C minor—a further sign that every trace of *galanterie* has disappeared. The answer of the viola to the muffled plaint of the violin, leading to the gentle key of E-flat major, is a revelation of the deepest feeling. The finale is a *Tempo di contraddanza*, whose gaiety results principally from the fact that in the chain of musical events the unexpected always occurs first, being followed by the expected; the first entrance of the soloists is such a surprise. The viola part is written in D, which means that the instrument is intended to be tuned a half-tone up, and doubtless to be strung with correspondingly finer strings, for it is to sound brighter and clearer than the violas of the tutti. The cadenzas are written out, and are notable alike for their plasticity, their brevity, and their beauty—a model and a warning for posterity.

This double concerto for violin and viola is at the same time Mozart's crowning achievement in the field of the violin concerto. He stopped writing violin concertos entirely in his Vienna period, except for two substitute middle movements, one for a work of his own and one for a work by someone else. Except for the piano concertos and the beautiful one for basset horn or clarinet, all the concertos of the Vienna period are minor works. But the five violin concertos written in Salzburg betwen April and December 1775 (in B-flat, K. 207; D, K. 211; G, K. 216; D, K. 218; and A, K. 219) are in no way minor works. (The so-called 'Adelaide' Concerto, supposed to have been written at Versailles in 1766, is, to put it mildly, a piece of mystification à la Kreisler.) From 27 November 1770 on, Mozart was Konzertmeister to the

Court of the Archbishop of Salzburg, and he had to do something for the instrument with which his service was connected. These concertos are ambitious and serious essays, being less *galant* than the *concertante* movements incorporated in the serenades, or the virtuoso exhibitions occurring in the divertimenti. There is no question that in his father's house Mozart had become thoroughly familiar with concertos of Tartini, Geminiani, and Locatelli, and to these the visits to Italy added the less strict and more sensuous works of a younger generation: Nardini, Pugnani, Ferrari, Boccherini, Borghi. We have yet further evidence of Mozart's respect for tradition, and his tendency to preserve old forms, in the fact that the Violin Concerto in B-flat still contains definite reminiscences of an old ideal of the concerto: qualities of invention that are definitely not *buffo*, figurations of the solo part that might have occurred in Corelli or Vivaldi. Every measure is alive; in fact, there is a surfeit of thematic material, but by virtue of that very fact there are no surprises, there is no play of wit, there is nothing very personal or Mozartean. A year later, in 1776, Mozart replaced the somewhat conventional finale in sonata form with a new and much freer Rondo (K. 269), which does not at all feature virtuosity. (Strangely enough, all five of these concertos make only modest demands on what is called virtuosity, being in this respect far less ambitious than Mozart's own divertimenti. They must certainly have made Paganini smile.) The second Concerto, in D major, written in June 1775, contained from the very beginning a rondo—or rather a French *rondeau*—quite in the style of the later concert rondos of Mozart. The soloist begins, and the orchestra enters with a repetition of the beginning; there is an 'energetic' episode, and one in minor; the theme, one of the most amiable of those in minuet style, returns with perpetual freshness. But the first movement, of which the thematic material is rather short-winded and Haydnesque, and conceived rather in two-quarter meter than in four-quarter, and the Andante, which is a pastoral arioso, like an imitation of an aria sung by some sentimental Sandrina or Celidora in an *opera buffa*, are almost more primitive than the first concerto. There is an almost regular alternation of the solo and the tutti, and the solo part receives mostly a simple accompaniment, usually by the higher string instruments only—another feature that reminds us of Mozart's forerunners, such as Vivaldi.

The same simple sort of accompaniment is also in the other three concertos of the same year, but in them there is no longer anything archaic about it, because they are full of a new spirit—the individual, personal spirit of Mozart. The first two violin concertos are not well known now-a-days by either amateurs or virtuosi, while the last three rightly form a familiar part of the repertoire. What had happened in the three months that separate the second concerto from the third (the latter completed on 12 September)? We do not know. Suddenly there is a new depth and richness to Mozart's whole language: instead of an andante there is an Adagio that seems to have fallen straight from heaven, in which flutes take the place of oboes, and in which the key of D major has a quite new character. All three movements, besides being on a higher level, contain the surprises of which we have previously spoken, and in a double sense: as when, in the Adagio, the solo returns once more to speak with poignant intensity; or when, in the Rondo, the ending comes in the winds, or, in the same movement, humorous or homely and obviously French quotations occur; or when the recapitulation of the magnificent first movement is introduced by an eloquent recitative. Suddenly the whole orchestra begins to speak, and to enter into a new, intimate relation with the solo part. Nothing is more miraculous in Mozart's work than the appearance of this Concerto at this stage in his development; but just as miraculous is the fact that the two concertos that follow, the one in D in October and the one in A in December, are on the same high level. The Concerto in D major is very different from its predecessor in G. It is much more sensuous in sonority, and this quality springs not only from the choice of the more brilliant key, but also from the nature of the model Mozart undoubtedly had in mind. This model is the Violin Concerto in the same key of Boccherini, written about ten years earlier; the two works have almost the same structure, and their thematic relations are palpable.* But the saying *Facile inventis addere* is just as little applicable here as in many another case. It took Mozart to add spirit and wit to the sensuousness of Boccherini's work. The *Andante cantabile* is in reality an uninterrupted song for the violin, and an avowal of love. The Rondo combines Italian and French elements, in that, as in the third concerto, it interpolates little humorous episodes containing references familiar to its listeners: a gavotte, and a musette mentioned several times in the Mozart correspondence as being of Strassburg. This Concerto too ends in a *pianissimo* whisper. It is a work of the spirit, not

---

* Cf. E. von Zschinsky-Troxler, in *Zeitschrift für Musikwissenschaft*, x, 415.

one intended to have a great effect. This is true also of the fifth and last of these Concertos, the one in A. The climax that Mozart has achieved by proceeding from G major through D major to A major, with the middle movements always in the dominant, is not merely external. This Concerto is unsurpassed for brilliance, tenderness, and wit. Even a new middle movement (K. 261), which Mozart wrote late in 1776 'especially' for the violinist Brunetti, 'because he found the other one too studied' (letter of Leopold, 9 October 1777), despite its tenderness and its enchanted, shimmering sonority, cannot match the simplicity and innocence of the original Adagio. The first and last movements are full of surprises: in the first movement, the half improvisatory way in which the violin makes its appearance, possibly inspired by a clavier concerto of Philipp Emanuel Bach in D, published in 1772, and the alternation between gracefulness in march tempo, good-natured roughness, and cajolery; in the last movement, instead of quotations such as had occurred in the rondos of the two preceding works, a humorous outbreak of sound and fury in 'Turkish' style. Mozart borrowed the noisy tutti in A minor of this 'Turkish' intermezzo from himself: it had originally occurred in the ballet *Le Gelosie del serraglio*, which he wrote in 1773 in Milan for his 'Lucio Silla.' It is in duple meter, and contrasts as naturally as it combines with the irresistible *Tempo di minuetto* of the main portion of the movement.

This work, written when Mozart was twenty, is the last of his Violin Concertos that survives in pure and undisputed form. We do possess two later Violin Concertos, one in D (K. 271a), ostensibly written in July 1777, and one in E-flat (K. 268), which was doubtless conceived towards the end of 1780 in Salzburg and Munich. But the first of these is certainly not preserved in the form in which Mozart wrote it—if, in fact, he ever wrote it out as more than a hasty sketch. And the arranger of the second, the youthful Munich violinist Johann Friedrich Eck, can have had before him at best only a sketch of the first movement and perhaps a few opening measures of the Rondo; the middle movement is certainly a crude forgery. We need not concern ourselves with either of these, since this book is not a work of scientific investigation. The first of the two movements for violin and orchestra that Mozart wrote in Vienna, a Rondo in C major (K. 373), dates from the early stormy days in Vienna, when he was still in the service of the Archbishop of Salzburg. It was composed for the violinist Brunetti to play at an evening concert at the home of the father of the hated Archbishop (8 April

1781). Whether it was given as a separate piece, as seems probable, or
as a substitute for the finale of a concerto by someone else, I do not
know. In any case, it is charming, for even where Mozart has only a
routine task to perform he acquits himself in more than a routine way.
The second of these movements, an Andante in A (K. 470), is unfortunately lost except for the four measures Mozart entered in his thematic notebook under date of 1 April 1785. He calls it: 'An Andante
for the violin, for a concerto.' For what sort of concerto? We now know
the answer to this question. It was Giovanni Battista Viotti's Concerto
in E minor, No. 16, which must have been played in Vienna at the
time by a violinist friend of Mozart's, presumably Anton Janitsch, who
belonged to the *Kapelle* of the Wallerstein household. Viotti's original
slow movement is in E major. Mozart not only wrote this Andante,
which begins with canonic imitation, but also made the instrumentation of the opening and closing movements more brilliant by adding
trumpets and timpani. For us it is interesting to note that Mozart knew
and valued Viotti's work (he would not have bothered with it if he
had not valued it); and traces of his familiarity with it are to be found
in his piano concertos, especially the one in C major (K. 467), written
about the same time.

As regards Mozart's concertos for wind instruments, we can deal
with them in short order. They are for the most part occasional works
in the narrower sense, intended to make a pleasant impression, and
since it is in the very nature of wind instruments that their players
must be treated with consideration, all these works are simpler in
structure, and the character of their melodic invention is determined
by the limitations of the instruments. Not that Mozart himself felt in
any way cramped. He always moved comfortably and freely within any
limitations, and turned them into positive advantages. Wind instrument players are usually naive, with something very individual about
them—quite different from violinists or pianists. Accordingly all these
concertos have something special and personal about them, and when
one hears them in a concert hall, which is seldom enough, one has the
feeling that the windows have suddenly been opened and a breath of
fresh air has been let in.

Thus the very first of these concertos, K. 191, written in June 1774,
is a work unmistakably conceived for a wind instrument, a real bassoon

concerto, which could not be arranged, say, for violoncello. (The latter instrument, unfortunately, Mozart treated like a stepchild, or rather he never thought of it at all.) The solo portions are full of leaps, runs, and singing passages completely suited to the instrument. The work was written *con amore* from beginning to end, as is particularly evident in the lively participation of the orchestra. This is even truer of the flute concerto in G major (K. 313), written in Mannheim early in 1778, on commission for the Dutch amateur and patron of music, de Jean. We know that Mozart approached the task of writing it without pleasure, since he did not like the flute. But the longer one knows the work, the less trace one can find of his dislike. The slow movement (in D major) is, in fact, so personal, one might say even so fantastic, so completely individual in character, that the man who had commissioned the work evidently did not know what to do with it. Mozart then presumably had to replace it with a simpler, more pastoral or idyllic Andante in C (K. 315). The Rondo of this G major concerto, a *Tempo di minuetto*, is a veritable fountain of good spirits and fresh invention. Since the Concerto is for flute and not for violin, Mozart naturally renounced any such quotations as had characterized the last Salzburg violin concertos and concerto-like serenade movements, for, as we have seen, he did not like to overstep the bounds of a given species. A second Flute Concerto, in D major (K. 314), apparently written in Mannheim, is almost certainly the same as the Oboe Concerto written for the Salzburg oboist, Giuseppe Ferlendis, in 1777, and often mentioned in the Mozart correspondence. Mozart re-wrote it, out of sheer lack of time and money, for the impatient de Jean, transposing it from C major to D major. (Almost conclusive evidence that the original key was C major is the fact that in the transposition to D the violins never go below the A on the G-string.) The lighter tone of this work, and the fact that it was written earlier than the one in G major, are obvious. It is significant that Mozart later returned to the Rondo theme in composing Blonde's aria *Welche Wonne, welche Lust* in *Die Entführung aus dem Serail*. Early in the Vienna period, Mozart asked his father to send him the original form of this concerto (15 February 1783):

Please send me at once the little book which contains the oboe concerto I wrote for Ramm, or rather for Ferlendis. Prince Esterházy's oboist is giving me three ducats for it, and has offered me six if I will compose a new concerto for him . . .

The oboist referred to was probably Franz Joseph Czerwenka, an excellent player, and two beginnings of oboe concertos have been preserved that are undoubtedly connected with the reference in Mozart's letter, both in F major: a shorter one (K. 416g), and a longer one, of 61 measures (K. 293), of which the former proves to be simply a variant of the entry of the oboe after the tutti in the latter. Why the work was never finished and Mozart never received the six ducats we do not know, but we must regret the fact, for the tutti is full of energy and vitality.

The concertos for horn, with one significant exception, are works intended to please, and nothing more. Mozart wrote them mostly for the Salzburg horn player, Ignaz Leitgeb, who seems to have been the perpetual butt of his good-natured jokes. There are evidences of this in the autographs, as for example in that of the manuscript fragment of the last concerto (K. 495), which is written in a gay variety of blue, red, green, and black inks, to confuse the poor performer; or in another (the Rondo of K. 412), in which the soloist's part bears a succession of remarks such as *adagio—a lei Signor Asino, Animo—presto—su via—da bravo—Coraggio—bestia—o che stonatura—Ahi!—ohime—bravo poveretto*—and at the end: *grazia al Ciel! basta, basta!* The first of these pieces, a Rondo (K. 371), composed in Vienna while Mozart was still in the service of the Archbishop (21 March 1781), survives only in the form of a sketch, although a complete one, and fragments of a first movement to go with it are also preserved. The Rondo is, of course, a comparatively primitive concerto movement, judged from the point of view of the rondos of the piano or violin concertos. But it is full of spontaneity and freshness. Its most striking feature is the appearance of the motive that is to play so great a role in the first finale of *Figaro* (*Susanna, son morta*). A concerto for horn (K. 412) has been made out of two movements, an Allegro and a Rondo in D, which cannot belong altogether if for no better reason than that the bassoons employed in the first of them are missing in the second. Mozart's joking with the soloist, in the first movement, sometimes carries over into the musical invention also; an accompaniment figure like the following one, which occurs in the violins, is not ordinarily to be found in Mozart's works in serious mood:

Ex. 64

The movement is *gemütlich* (homely, comfortable)—undoubtedly fitting the phlegmatic soloist to a *T.* And even the Rondo, which Mozart wrote out again 17 April 1787, changing it considerably on that occasion, has something of the same character, although it was apparently written for a different virtuoso.

The first complete Concerto (K. 417, in E-flat, like all the others) represents Mozart 'taking pity on that ass, ox, and fool of a Leitgeb, in Vienna, 27 May 1783'; it was a work in which, in the *Maestoso* of the first movement (which also ventures into darker regions), in the cantabile of the second, and in the hunting fanfares of the third, Leitgeb could do himself proud. This work has a strange connection with the last two Concertos (K. 447 and K. 495). The later of these, written 'für den Leitgeb' on 26 June 1786, is like a duplicate of the 1783 work but on a higher level, for a work of Mozart's written after a lapse of three years is always on a higher level than its predecessor. The first theme bears a strange relation to the cantata *Die Maurerfreude* (K. 471), dating from the preceding year. This Concerto offers opportunities for cadenzas. The middle movement is a *Romanza*. As for the earlier work, K. 447, one would be tempted to attribute it to a later date if it were conceivable that Mozart should have omitted such a work from his thematic catalogue. It is a unique composition, and makes demands of the soloist that Mozart would not have made of 'that ass Leitgeb.' The instrumentation, too, is unusual and subtler than before: clarinets and bassoons take the place of oboes and horns. It is significant that the middle movement, a *Romanza*, is in the subdominant; here we have a precedent and counterpart for the depth of expression, if not for the length, of the Adagio in the Piano-and-Violin Sonata K. 481. Even in the opening and closing movements, although there is a relation to the 'Leitgeb' style (the Finale being again a hunting scene), there is a depth and earnestness quite different from anything in the earlier works. Perhaps some day the discovery of the autograph will contribute to the solution of this puzzle.

One final wind concerto remains to be discussed—the one for clarinet and orchestra (flutes, bassoons, horns, and strings), K. 622. This is the last concerto of any kind that Mozart wrote. He had originally sketched the first movement (K. 584b) for basset horn, presumably at the end of 1789, and then took it up again in October 1791, transposed it from G to A, and completed it for his clarinetist friend, 'Mr. Stadler, the elder.' The greatness and the transcendent beauty of this work are such as its high Köchel number would lead us to expect. One almost has the impression that Mozart felt impelled to express again, in greater and dramatically animated form, what he had already expressed in more lyric form in the domain of chamber music, in the Stadler Quintet. The first movement is from beginning to end in Mozart's last style, informed throughout by the closest relation between the soloist and the orchestra, and by the utmost possible vitality in the orchestral portion itself, as may be observed by following simply the play of the two violins in dialogue. Significantly, in this work the basses are sometimes separated from the 'cellos: in the Adagio, a counterpart to the Larghetto of the Quintet, there are passages of transparent sonority in which the contrabass is silent. And how all the registers of the solo instrument are exploited, yet without any exhibition of virtuosity! There is no opportunity for free cadenzas. One need only compare this work with similar compositions by another great lover of the clarinet and master in writing for it, Carl Maria von Weber, such as his 'great Quintet,' Op. 34, or his 'great Concertos,' Opp. 73 and 74, to see the difference between the supreme effectiveness of simplicity and mere virtuoso exhibition.

17. *The Synthesis: The Clavier Concerto*

SPLENDID as are the examples of the concerto form for string and wind instruments, it was only in the piano concertos that Mozart achieved his ideal. They are the peak of all his instrumental achievement, at least in the orchestral domain. Mozart cultivated the concerto for violin industriously, but only for a short time; to the concerto for single wind instruments—flute, oboe, bassoon, horn, clarinet—and the *sinfonia concertante*, he devoted only intermittent, though at times very serious, attention; but with the piano concerto he concerned himself from earliest youth until the end, and undoubtedly we should have had more than just two piano concertos dating from the last four or five years of his life—we might have had ten or twelve such masterpieces—if the Vienna public had paid greater attention to Mozart than it did. For of course Mozart wrote no new concertos when he had no opportunity to play them. Of the more than fifty symphonies by Mozart there are, strictly speaking, four that belong among the eternal treasures of music; of the thirty-odd string quartets, ten. But among the twenty-three concertos for piano and orchestra, there is only one that is below the highest level—the concerto for three pianos (K. 242), written to be played not by Mozart himself or any capable soloist, but by three lady amateurs. One reason for the high quality of the piano concertos is the innate superiority of the piano over the other solo instruments, even when these instruments unite to form a *concertino* as in the *Sinfonia Concertante* for four wind instruments or the Double Concerto for violin and viola. Only in the piano concerto are two forces opposed that really balance each other, with neither one necessarily subordinate to the other. The piano is the only instrument that is not at a disadvantage either by reason of its limited tonal volume, like the violin, flute, or clarinet, or because of any limitations in respect to intonation and modulation, like the horn. It is just as powerful as the orchestra, to which it forms a worthy opponent because of the variety

287

of tone production it possesses, as a highly developed percussion instrument. It should be remarked here again that Mozart wrote all his clavier works, including the concertos, not for the harpsichord but for the pianoforte, and that we should banish from the platform all those ladies and gentlemen who would like to claim the C minor Concerto, for example, or the C major, K. 503, for the harpsichord. We should also, of course, banish conductors who accompany a Mozart concerto with a string orchestra padded with ten double basses, forcing the pianist to produce a volume of tone that is possible only on our present-day mammoth instruments.

It was in the piano concerto that Mozart said the last word in respect to the fusion of the *concertante* and symphonic elements—a fusion resulting in a higher unity beyond which no progress was possible, because perfection is imperfectible. The penetrating monograph by C. M. Girdlestone, *Mozart et ses concertos pour piano* (Paris, 1939), rightly emphasizes the fact that the 'emancipation of the orchestra,' often attributed to Beethoven in his concerto-writing, was completely accomplished by Mozart. Beethoven perhaps juxtaposed the two forces more dramatically, and he pursued an ideal of virtuosity different from Mozart's; but at bottom he developed only one type among Mozart's concertos, which we may call for the present the 'military' or 'martial' type. Mozart's concerto form is a vessel of far richer, finer, and more sublime content. It is one of the perfections of Mozart's music that its dramatic element remains latent, and that it contains more profound depths than the struggle between opposing forces. Sometimes the contest in Mozart's works goes very far, but never so far that it could not be called a duality in unity. His piano concerto is really his most characteristic creation. It is the ideal and the realization of that which in some of his piano trios and in the two piano quartets fails of complete expression only because the piano in them is always the more powerful participant, and the strings always remain partially eclipsed by it. Mozart's piano concerto is the apotheosis of the piano—placing the instrument in the broad frame in which it belongs—and at the same time the apotheosis of the *concertante* element is embedded in the symphonic. Or one might even say: the symphonic element creates for itself a protagonist, the piano; it thus creates a dualism that endangers its unity; and then it conquers this danger. Mozart's piano concerto never seems to overstep the bounds of society music—how could it, since it was always intended for performance in public, and thus was prevented from having any quality of intimacy? And yet it always leaves the door open to the expression of the darkest and the brightest, the most serious, the gayest, the deepest feelings. It presses forward from the *galant* world into the symphonic; it lifts the listener to a higher level. Listeners who can really appreciate Mozart's piano concertos are the best audience there is.

Although we have said that the piano concerto is Mozart's most characteristic creation, this does not mean that he did not have any forerunners, or that he did not know them. The form was young, it is true. To its development, the Bach family, including the great father and two of his sons, the second and the youngest, had made the greatest contributions. About 1720 Johann Sebastian Bach adapted the Vivaldi concerto form to works for the clavier. This form consisted of three movements. We may say that it contained, typically, an *allegro maestoso*, an *andante* or *largo*, and a *presto*. The first movement imitated or expanded the form of the *prima parte* of a monumental aria— Aa — dD — a'A'; the capital letters indicate the tutti and the small letters the soli; A indicates the main stream of the thematic material, and D a sort of modulating thematic middle section that takes on more or less the character of a development. The second movement sometimes has the same form, but usually in more singing or melodic style—or, often, simply two-part song form. The third movement is usually a rondeau, and almost always of lower specific gravity than the first movement. Rarely does a concerto have so grand a conclusion as the glorious fugue in Johann Sebastian Bach's C major Concerto for two claviers, or in Philipp Emanuel's famous D minor Concerto of 1748. Now, it is certain that the young Mozart did not know any of Johann Sebastian's clavier concertos, and more than questionable whether he knew any of the forty-seven by Carl Philipp Emanuel. It is possible that in later years he made the acquaintance of the D minor Concerto just mentioned, of which the Finale has a strange but hardly tangible relation to the first movement of his own D minor Concerto. In van Swieten's library, Philipp Emanuel was certainly represented by some clavier concertos. But apart from the fact that Philipp Emanuel's spirit was not congenial to Mozart's, all his clavier concertos were intended specifically for the harpsichord—so completely so, in the nature of their invention and in their dynamics, that at the end of his life, in 1788, Philipp Emanuel could write a double concerto for harpsichord, piano, and orchestra. He was far too ingenious and vital a musician not to give the orchestra its own important role, along with the cembalo, and not to keep varying the concerto form. But Mozart was not influenced by him, or at least not directly so. The composer whose clavier concertos he came to know while still a child was a South-German, Georg Christoph Wagenseil, the old and highly respected teacher of the Hapsburg Archduchesses. His clavier works were shown to Mozart as early as 1764, in London, and a concerto by him for two claviers is expressly mentioned by Leopold as being in the family's possession (November 1767). Wagenseil, the South-German, was an agreeable musician who cultivated a much simpler form of the clavier concerto than Philipp Emanuel, of Berlin. But to Wagenseil's influence was very early added that of Johann Christian Bach. He it was who, in this domain as in so many others, for some time furnished Mozart's fantasy with its greatest stimulus. Or, if this statement seems too categorical, let us say that Mozart's fantasy took Bach's concerto form as its point of departure. For this statement we have documentary evidence. As a ten-year-old boy, in the summer or fall of 1765, Mozart converted three sonatas taken from Johann Christian's Op. V into concertos: *Tre Sonate del Sgr. Giovanni Bach ridotte in Concerti dal Sgr. Amadeo Wolfgango Mozart* (K. 107). These works served Mozart as exercises in the concerto form, with Johann Christian's melodies as material. His procedure was extraordinarily primitive: he distributed the musical material between the two partners, shortening or lengthening the movements of each of the three works by alternating tutti and solo; the tutti consists simply of two violins and bass. But the three works were not intended to be exercises only; they were also to provide material for forthcoming tours. One could find two violins and a bass anywhere (even in the poorest court or the least musical town in Holland, France, or Switzerland) for an appearance by Wolfgang as soloist in a concerto, while most of the concertos of Johann Christian already available required an orchestra including two oboes and two horns. Mozart played the three works not just during his child-prodigy days, but also in later years, as is shown by two cadenzas for the first of the concertos, in D—cadenzas of which the handwriting and the style belong to a much later period. In 1767, in Salzburg, Mozart applied a similar procedure to a series of sonata-movements for the most part by 'Parisian' composers—Hermann Fr. Raupach, Leontzi Honnauer—but

also by Schobert, Eckard, and Philipp Emanuel Bach: a similar procedure, but not the same one, for now the solo part is a little more
pretentious, and the tutti has the usual orchestration, with full strings,
and the two pairs of wind instruments. The unity of style that prevailed in the *galant* period is so striking that until the work of discovery
by Wyzewa and Saint-Foix it was possible to regard these four concertos (K. 37, 39, 40, 41) as 'genuine Mozart.'

It was at the end of 1773 that Mozart wrote his first really original
clavier concerto, in D major (K. 175). In its instrumentation—which
includes not only oboes and horns but trumpets and timpani as well—
in its relation between soloist and orchestra, and in its length, it goes
far beyond Johann Christian Bach, and one has the impression that
Mozart knew this fact and wished to emphasize it. For in the development section, after only six measures of the solo part, the tutti enters
with a so-called 'false recapitulation'—a device Mozart does not usually
greatly emphasize, and one that does not have at all the same significance in his works as in Haydn's. Now, Johann Christian would have
begun the real recapitulation at this point, because in his concertos,
intended as they were for the ornamentation of social functions, an
elegant and ingratiating solo part was more important than any serious
opposition between solo and tutti. Even in the Mozart work the recapitulation comes only twenty-two measures later, but during these
twenty-two measures there are suggestions of perilous and somber
regions, and it is by contrast with them that the royal majesty of the
recapitulation is brought out. There is hardly a measure in the work
in which there is not a lively relation in sound, and often a thematic
relation as well, between the solo and the tutti, although the whole
remains well within the bounds of *galanterie*. The same is true of the
Andante (ma un poco Adagio!) in G major, a deeply felt movement
despite all its *galanterie*. He writes a 'learned,' contrapuntal Finale, as
in a few of the Vienna string quartets of 1773. But here he succeeds
in something that was not quite successful in them. The canonic entrance of the theme in the tutti

Ex. 65
Allegro

is transformed in the following entrance of the solo part:

And this softened, *galant* version of the original 'learned' and somewhat rigid material has been prepared by a subsidiary theme that would not be out of place even in the Finale of the 'Jupiter' Symphony.

The wit and grace in the play of these two contrasting elements are inimitable; in this first attempt, Mozart has not only left Johann Christian and Philipp Emanuel far behind, but has freed himself from them entirely. Did he later become dissatisfied with this movement, or was he no longer sure of its effect on the public? From Mannheim, he reports, diffidently (14 February 1778): 'Then I played my old concerto in D major, because it is still a favorite here'; but for the public of Vienna he replaced the movement in 1782 with a set of Variations (K. 382)—Mozart himself called the new movement a 'rondo'—which is a little miracle of humor when one considers all that is made of the alternation of tonics and dominants (and when one imagines how Mozart must have played it). But as a conclusion for this Concerto it does not maintain the style of the earlier movements. This is the first instance of Mozart's having to write down to the taste of the Vienna public.

For two years thereafter Mozart did not write any piano concertos. The interval, which lasted until January 1776, the date of the Concerto in B-flat (K. 238), was taken up with the composition of a concerto for bassoon, and five for violin. In the second Piano Concerto, more modest in its instrumentation than the first, we feel a certain reflection of the grace of the violin concertos and—in the Rondo, particularly—of the popular element in their finales:

Ex. 68

although there are no real quotations, and no actual changes of meter as in the violin concertos. Mozart considered the piano concerto a higher species, and one of the finest and most expressive motives of the first movement of this Concerto recurred to him later, for Donna Elvira's entrance scene, in a more cajoling and seductive version:

Ex. 69

The next Concerto, in C major (K. 246)—for we shall not concern ourselves further with the purely *galant* Concerto for Three Pianos—is almost a duplicate of its predecessor, except that the Andante is more pastoral and innocent in character, and the Rondo, a *Tempo di min-uetto* with a piquant theme, withholds its trumps until after the cadenza. For this movement, incidentally, although not for the first and second movements, Mozart wrote out the cadenza in the score. The work was composed for Countess Antonia von Lützow, the second wife of the Commandant of the Veste Hohensalzburg, Johann Nepomuk Gottfried Count Lützow. The Countess was a pupil of Leopold's, and Mozart could write for her just as well as for himself, with little need of making concessions to her limitations. At any rate, he played the Concerto himself in Vienna, or wished to play it, for on 10 April 1782, he asked his father to send him the score.

In January 1777, the month in which Mozart celebrated his twenty-first birthday, he wrote a Concerto that is anything but a second replica of the first one (E-flat major, K. 271). He wanted to publish it together with the two preceding works in Paris (letter of 11 September 1778):

As for my three concertos, the one written for Mlle Jeunehomme, the one for Countess Lützow, and the one in B-flat, I shall sell them to the man who engraved my sonatas, provided he pays cash for them.

But the thought of paying cash never occurred to the engraver, Sieber, who was just as good a businessman as he was a musician; and for that fact no doubt this very Concerto for Mlle Jeunehomme (or 'Jenomy,' as Mozart called her) was to blame. Customers who might have liked the two previous concertos would certainly have rejected this one. It is surprising and unique among Mozart's works. Nothing in the products of the year 1776 leads us to expect it, for the Divertimento K. 247, although it is a masterpiece in its own field, is nothing more than a joyous *Final-Musik*. This concerto, on the other hand, is one of Mozart's monumental works, those works in which he is entirely himself, seeking not to ingratiate himself with his public but rather to win them through originality and boldness. He never surpassed it. There are similar bold ventures, full of both youth and maturity, in the works of other great masters: the wedding panel by Titian known as 'Sacred and Profane Love,' Goethe's *Werther*, Beethoven's *Eroica*. This E-flat major Concerto is Mozart's 'Eroica.' It embodies not only a profound contrast, and accordingly a higher unity, among its three movements, but also the most intimate relation of soloist and orchestra; and the orchestra itself is treated with greater vitality and more finely wrought detail than before, in truly symphonic style. The middle movement, an Andantino, is a striking example. It is in C minor, the first minor movement in a Mozart concerto, and thus a forerunner of the C minor Andante of the Sinfonia Concertante of 1779, for violin and viola. The strings are muted, with a canon between Violins I and II. The solo does not repeat the tutti, but rather comments upon it in free singing style. The melody of the whole movement is so eloquent that at any moment it could break into genuine recitative. In the last measures, the mutes disappear, and restraint is cast off in favor of actual recitative. The first and last movements are fitting companions to this slow movement. In the building up of the very first theme, the orchestra and the soloist collaborate. The soloist is in command, in full and proud sovereignty, but, for the first time, he permits himself to accompany a member of the orchestra, the first oboe, in simple chords. What a contrast with the concertos of Johann Christian, in which the solo part does sometimes feature simple chords, while in the orchestra— nothing happens; for in these works the concerto ideal never goes beyond the conception of a solo with accompaniment. The inner agitation responsible for the creation of this concerto brought about a constant succession of surprises, both in the structure and in the smallest details; nothing is left, not even the cadenzas, to chance or routine. The greatest surprise is the interpolation of a real minuet, in A-flat, with four variations, in the midst of the brilliant virtuosity of the *presto Finale*. But this is no excursion into the field of the popular, as in the violin concertos. This minuet is serious, elegant, stately, and expressive, all at once; it reflects the deep agitation of the Andantino, which is still seeking appeasement. There is nowhere any straining for virtuosity; yet this Concerto makes higher demands, technically as well as otherwise, than its predecessors. One would like to know something more about Mlle Jeunehomme, who inspired Mozart to write such a work, but for the present she remains a legendary figure.

In Paris Mozart felt no urge to write a new piano concerto, and for Mannheim, too, both before the visit to Paris and afterwards, the compositions he already had sufficed. But his work on the *Sinfonia Concertante*, the big work for the four wind-instrument players of Mannheim; the concerto for flute and harp written for the Duc de Guines and his daughter; the ambitious project of a double concerto for clavier and violin—all this bore fruit. After his return home, Mozart wrote the Concerto for Two Pianos in E-flat major, for himself and Nannerl (K. 365). It is a companion piece both to the *Sinfonia Concertante* in the same key (K. 364), which it cannot quite equal, and to the Vienna Sonata for Two Pianos, in D major (K. 448, written in 1781), which is likewise not to be matched. But the Concerto contains a brilliant contest between the two players, and the orchestra, with its majestic beginning, enters significantly into this eager dialogue—unforgettably, above all, in a horn call in the cadence of a subsidiary theme.

Ex. 70   a 2

But there is not only a brilliant contest. Side by side with places of what one might call 'mechanical' gaiety, as for example the following:

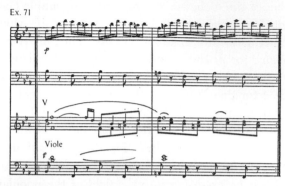

Ex. 71

there is a strange darkening of the mood in the recapitulation. The pastoral Andante, too, quivers with a mood of longing, and has passages of extraordinary luxuriance. And even in the Rondo, which is frankly merry, the middle portion, in C minor, moves into what seem dangerous and mysterious regions—regions, too, of contrapuntal seriousness. But the seriousness is not quite so deep as might appear, as is shown by the fact that Mozart later borrowed one of the C minor passages and put it into the mouth of Papageno, just at the point where the latter's comic anxiety reaches its peak. In general, the Concerto is a work of happiness, gaiety, overflowing richness of invention, and joy in itself, and thus is evidence of how little the secret of creative activity has to do with personal experience, for it was written just after the bitterest disappointments of Mozart's life. In the early years in Vienna he performed it several times with Fräulein Aurnhammer, and for these occasions he enriched the instrumentation of the opening and closing movements by the addition of clarinets, trumpets and timpani. We know the work only in its more modest Salzburg garb, in which the orchestra takes a really active part only in the Rondo.

It seems to me that in this simpler concerto, or rather in the simpler relation of the solo part to the orchestra in it, there are reflections of a musical acquaintance Mozart had made in the summer of 1778, in Paris: the Six Clavier Concertos, Op. III, by Johann Samuel Schröter. 'Write and tell me whether you have Schröter's concertos in Salzburg —and Hüllmandel's sonatas. If not, I should like to buy them and send them to you. Both works are very fine.' Such an estimate by Mozart must be taken seriously. Who was Johann Samuel Schröter? He was the son of a Saxon musician, an oboist in Warsaw, who in 1763 had been seeking a place in his native Saxony for his family of four children. For his daughter Corona, then a girl of twelve, he found a place promptly; Corona Schröter, who later in Weimar set Goethe's heart aflame (among others), needs no further introduction. Johann Samuel, who was probably a little older than his sister Corona, became a clavier virtuoso, and in 1772 went to London, where he made his debut in the Bach-Abel concerts, just as Mozart, six or seven years earlier, had been taken under Johann Christian's wing. In 1782, he became Johann Christian's successor as music master to the Queen, and like Mozart he died young, on 2 November 1788. He retired quite early from public life, that being the condition of his marriage with a pupil, a rich girl from a high-born family. The lady in question later played a romantic role in the life of Joseph Haydn, on the occasion of his first visit to London: she took lessons of Haydn and fell in love with the youthful old man, and Haydn does not seem to have been indifferent to her charms—at least he conscientiously copied out all her love letters.

Now Mozart certainly could not learn anything technically from Schröter. These concertos, Op. III, which are soli with a sparse accompaniment of two violins and bass, are very simple in structure, quite in the style of the concertos of Johann Christian, but even lighter and more primitive. They have, however, the greatest melodic charm and innocence. At times they seem to speak with the voice of Mozart himself, and it seems to me that between the Larghetto of Schroeter's Op. III, No. 6,

and the Andante in the Double Concerto of which we have been speaking,

there is a direct connection. For three of the concertos of Schröter Mozart wrote cadenzas, which is proof that he either played them himself or had his pupils play them.

There is another feature for which Mozart seems to have found the inspiration in Schröter's Op. III—a most characteristic feature. Schröter wrote his clavier concertos for his own performance, but also for amateur performers among the ladies of London, and accordingly he did not bother with any development section in the first movement, or with any organic relation between the solo and the tutti. For this, he substituted a free solo, thematically unrelated to the rest of the movement, which led back to the recapitulation, and was often of great and even enchanting beauty. This made a deep impression on Mozart, who imitated it—not, to be sure, in the first movements of his piano quartets, piano trios, or piano concertos, in which so great and serious a master as he could not renounce development, but in the finales. There have been and will be many occasions, in the course of this book, to speak of the great artistic wisdom and sense of effect displayed by Mozart in such instances.

It seems as if Mozart still had in mind the ideal of the amiable clavier concertos of Schröter when, in the fall of 1782 and the first months of 1783, he wrote his first three Vienna works in this form. Or perhaps it was that he knew his public, and wished to charm them with amiability rather than risk offending them by too aggressive originality. From the very first he was thinking of publication—publication in Paris, where he had made the acquaintance of the Schröter concertos, and where he felt he could hope for a particularly good reception. At first, in January 1783, he offered them in Vienna in manuscript copies at a subscription price of 4 ducats; but as early as 26 April he wrote to the Parisian publisher, J. G. Sieber:

. . . I have three piano concertos ready, which can be performed with full orchestra, that is to say with oboes and horns, or merely a quattro. Artaria wants to engrave them. But I give you, my friend, the first refusal . . .

However, Sieber either replied that he did not wish to pay the thirty louis d'or that Mozart demanded or else did not reply at all, for the three concertos were published by Artaria in Vienna two years later, in March 1785, as Op. IV.

The alternative possibilities provided for by Mozart in these concertos—performance either by full orchestra including oboes and horns (in the third one, in C major, including trumpets and timpani also), or by string quartet—are enough to show that we are not dealing with 'great' concertos. The winds are not essential, as they contribute nothing not fully expressed by the strings; their function is only to lend color or rhythmic emphasis. These works may very well be played as chamber music by a pianist with string quartet accompaniment. No one characterized them better than Mozart himself (letter of 28 December 1782; see page 112). How naive and at the same time how penetrating are his esthetics! And what a high moral standard underlies them: the composer must make things hard for himself and easy for the listener. The fact that Mozart did indeed make things hard for himself is shown by the existence of a second Rondo (K. 386) for the first of the three Concertos (in A major, K. 414), which he left in the form of a sketch so complete that there is no difficulty about supplying the little that is missing. No doubt the reason for abandoning it was that it repeated certain melodic turns of phrase that had appeared in the first movement. To us it seems at least as attractive as the Rondo Mozart used for this work, and perhaps even superior to it. The warmest and most alive movement of this charming little Concerto is the Andante, with its Schubertean *appoggiature* in the cadence:

Ex. 74

and with its romantic, murmuring accompaniment figure in thirds. One has the impression that this movement must have been composed after the Concerto in F (K. 413), which breathes nothing but amiability throughout its three movements, and offers something special to 'connoisseurs' only in the fine contrapuntal writing of the Rondo, a *Tempo di minuetto;* perhaps also in the triple meter of the first movement, triple meter being very unusual in a first movement. Mozart obviously wished to offer three very different types of concertos, contrasting in key, and each typical in its own key. If the first is rather naive and pastoral, and the second more poetic and *amoureux,* the last, in C major, with its trumpets and timpani, is the most brilliant and the most conventional, but it, too, is full of individual details and refinements. Mozart originally wished to write the second movement in C minor, but soon realized that that would make it much too serious for the character of these works, and instead wrote one of the least ambitious slow movements in any of his works. To make up for this, he inserted in the Finale, in which we already hear some of Papageno's ⁶⁄₈ motives, a C minor episode, which, in these surroundings, and with exaggerated ornamentation, is almost comically doleful. The principle of surprise is carried so far in this Finale as to make it almost a *capriccio*.

At any rate, Mozart succeeded in pleasing the taste of the Viennese. We read in a report in *Cramer's Magazin* for 22 March 1783 (I, 578):

Today the celebrated Chevalier Mozart gave a music academy for his own benefit at the National-Theater in which pieces of his own composition, which was already very popular, were performed. The academy was honored by the presence of an extraordinarily large audience and the *two new concertos* and other fantasies which Mr. Mozart played on the Forte Piano were received with the loudest approval. Our Monarch, who contrary to his custom honored the whole academy with his presence, joined in the applause of the public so heartily that one can think of no similar example. The proceeds of the academy are estimated at sixteen hundred gulden.

We do not know which two of the three Concertos Mozart played.

On 9 February 1784, Mozart began to enter in a little notebook of forty-four leaves—perhaps a bit too large to have served as a pocket notebook—all his works as he completed them, giving in each case the date, the type, and the beginning of the work written on two staves. He kept up this book until a few weeks before his death, filling fifty-eight pages. The first work he listed is a Concerto for piano in E-flat major (K. 449), with accompaniment for strings, and oboes and horns *ad libitum*. The fact that the participation of the winds is made optional seems to connect this Concerto with the three written in 1782-3; but the connection is only apparent. Mozart dedicated the work to his pupil Barbara Ployer, the daughter of a fellow-native of Salzburg then living in Vienna, and evidently did not wish to deprive her of the possibility of playing it with a small combination of instruments in a drawing-room. Actually, however, the wind instruments, although they seem sparingly used, can hardly be omitted; and this Concerto is not really a continuation of the type of the Salzburg concertos and the first three composed in Vienna, but a new beginning—the beginning of a new series comprising no less than twelve great Concertos, written between 9 February 1784 and 4 December 1786, and constituting the high-point of Mozart's instrumental composition. This series is followed by only the Coronation Concerto in D major and the last one, in B-flat major, written in January of the year of Mozart's death.

Immediately after the concerto for Fräulein Ployer, he composed two more, in B-flat (K. 450) and in D (K. 451), and then, after the Piano Quintet (K. 452), still another, in G major (K. 453), a miracle of productivity in no way less extraordinary than the miracle of the three symphonies of 1788. For all these works are as different from one another as can be imagined. In an illuminating passage in a letter to his father, dated 26 May 1784, Mozart expressed himself briefly about them. He mentioned the two concertos in B-flat and D, and continued:

I really cannot choose between the two of them, but I regard them both as concertos that are bound to make the performer sweat. From the point of view of difficulty the B♭ concerto beats the one in D. Well, I am very curious to hear which of the three, in B♭, D, and G, you and my sister prefer. The one in E♭ does not belong at all to the same category. It is one of a quite peculiar kind, composed rather for a small orchestra than for a large one . . .

The E-flat Concerto is indeed 'of a quite peculiar kind.' Mozart never wrote another like it, either before or afterwards. Yet, there is a connection between the Finale of this work and the original Finale of Mozart's first Concerto (K. 175). Mozart had in the meantime experienced his contrapuntal crisis, and he wrote a Finale that is full of the contrapuntal spirit:

Ex. 75
Allegro ma non troppo

But what eleven or twelve years earlier had been in some degree contrapuntal display had now become the free play of Mozart's creative gift, his natural idiom, the expression of the most complete mastery, a miracle of the fusion of styles. This work has a thematic variety and unity and an ingenuity of form that reveal the joy of the creative spirit at its highest. The first movement, too, is somewhat exceptional among Mozart's works. It voices an unrest that never tires of inventing contrasting themes. This movement, like the first movement of K. 413, is in ¾ time, and one is tempted to say that it seeks to express in E-flat major what a later movement in the same meter completely realizes— the one in the C minor Piano Concerto, K. 491. The element of unrest intensifies an old tendency in Mozart's language: a leaning towards the use of the chromatic, in both melody and harmony. A deep inner experience, about the exact nature of which we know nothing, is revealed in the more rapid changes of dynamics, the more refined and at the same time bolder chromaticism, the unity of the motives, demonstrable though concealed—in short, in a new degree of sensitiveness. At the same time, and particularly in the slow movement, an Andantino, Mozart seems to have grown simpler, and to be more than ever avoiding pathos and sentimentality. It is characteristic that in a letter to his father he emphasized the fact that none of these concertos has an Adagio. The superficial listener is to have his pleasure in them without noticing the deeper things they contain.

In the next two works, which are twins, in B-flat (K. 450) and D (K. 451), Mozart returns to more familiar paths. He uses a large orchestra, including in K. 451 trumpets and timpani, and in the Finale of K. 450, for the first time in a finale, the flute. The winds are essential, both as soloists and as a body. The orchestra is treated symphonically, with dialogue among its own members, and this leads naturally to a more brilliant treatment of the piano part. One hardly knows whether to call these works, particularly the second, piano concertos with obbligato orchestra or symphonies with obbligato piano solo. Both works are in the highest degree brilliant and personal. Mozart wishes to conquer his public, but without sacrificing anything of his own individuality. The B-flat major Concerto seems quite regular. Even the free fantasy *in tempo*—Mozart calls such a passage *Eingang* (entrance)—which precedes the entry of the theme in the solo part in the first movement, is not an unusual feature. The second movement consists of simple variations on a simple melody, with the repetitions distributed between the soloist and the orchestra, and a free conclusion. The Finale is a hunting scene. The D major Concerto seems like nothing more than a heroic and exuberant quick-march, with a song-like Andante, and a Rondo à la Joseph Haydn. Everything seems familiar and popular; yet at every instant there are surprises, an exuberance of spirit and a feeling of power, and unexpected refinements—like the *piano* passage in the recapitulation of the triumphal and yet passionate first movement, or the contrapuntal climax at the end of the second, or the very serious development section in the Rondo. The nineteenth century gradually lost any understanding for such things, since it had lost the feeling for any definite framework, or any given forms. But Mozart's public included some listeners who could appreciate every subtle divergence from the expected. That is the special quality of these Concertos—the fact that, in Mozart's own phrase, they are 'written for all kinds of ears, not just for the long ones.' Incidentally we may observe that few listeners had better musical ears than Mozart's sister Marianne. She pointed out a passage in the Andante in the D major Concerto that was too bare, and Mozart agreed with her and promised in a letter of 9-12 June 1784 to send her an ornamented variant. This variant survives, and is evidence that Mozart did not always play the solo part in the form in which it has come down to us. We shall return to this problem in connection with the second Coronation Concerto.

Mozart crowned the series of piano concertos written in this astonishing winter of 1784 with one in G major (K. 453), again intended *per la Signora Barbara Ployer*, as the inscription on the autograph tells us. On 10 June there was an 'academy' in the country, at Ployer's house in Döbling—'a concert, where Fräulein Babette is playing her new concerto in G, and I am performing the quintet [K. 452], we are then playing together the grand sonata for two claviers.' This concerto, too, is unique. It is more intimate than its three predecessors; it welds the solo and orchestra parts into a closer unity, its friendly key is full of hidden laughter and hidden sadness. No words can describe the continuous iridescence of feeling of the first movement, or the passionate tenderness of the second. The fact that this C major movement goes as far afield as G-sharp major is only an external sign of its passionate quality. The Finale consists of variations on a naive, birdlike, Papageno sort of theme with a grandiose, polyphonic conclusion. Mr. Girdlestone has rightly remarked that Beethoven's most amiable concerto, in the same key, takes its departure from this work of Mozart's. But the concerto of Beethoven, who could not be naive, is powerful and robust in comparison with the delicate shadings of this unique work, which has no parallel even among Mozart's other compositions.

The year 1784 brought forth two more concertos still, very different from the preceding ones and from each other. The first, again in B-flat (K. 456), which Mozart completed after recovering from a very heavy cold caught at the première of *Il Re Teodoro* by Casti and Paisiello, is distinguished by the fact that he wrote it neither for himself nor for a pupil as talented and close to him as Babette Ployer (for himself or for Babette he would certainly not have chosen B-flat again) but for another Vienna virtuoso, Maria Theresa Paradis. This young lady, who had been blind since childhood, and was at that time twenty-five years old, was the daughter of a State Councilor of Lower Austria, and a godchild of the Empress. She was a pupil of Leopold Kozeluch, and she could play, according to Gerber, 'more than sixty clavier concertos [by Kozeluch] with the greatest accuracy and the finest expression, in every way worthy of her teacher.' It is evidence of Mozart's broad-mindedness, or of his indifference, that he wrote a new concerto for the pupil of his deadly enemy to perform in Paris, whither a concert tour brought her in the autumn of 1784. For Paris, obviously, Koze-luch's concertos did not suffice. Kozeluch was, again quoting Gerber:

without doubt, among young and old, the most generally popular of all composers now living, and that quite rightly. His works are characterized by cheerfulness and grace, the noblest melody combined with the purest harmony and the most pleasing arrangement in respect to rhythm and modulation.

Now Mozart gave even the Parisians, whom he so hated, credit for desiring something more than that. So he harked back a little to Scho-bert, Johann Christian Bach, and Schröter. The relations of the solo part and the orchestra in this work are, to be sure, purely Mozartean, characteristic only of him, and perhaps even closer than ever before; but the solo part has a different, more 'feminine,' more sensuous character than the preceding concertos, and that iridescence of expression characteristic of the second Ployer Concerto is almost completely absent. In the Ployer Concerto there is nothing like the modulation to B minor in this Parisian one, emphasized as it is by the combination of ⁶/₈ and ²/₄ meters. But Schröter, too, had indulged in such pseudo-drama, and the Parisians were fond of that sort of thing. The slow movement consists of variations with coda, in G minor. Their tearful character already has something to do with the loss of Barbarina's pin in *Figaro*; it is very French. The work is full of miracles of sonority, but it contains none of the 'surprises,' great or small, of the great concertos.

The last concerto of 1784, the one in F major (K. 459), finished on 11 December, was surely written with Mozart himself alone in mind. This work exhibits a fine sense of climax. Each of the three movements is more beautiful than the preceding, so that one might almost call it a finale-concerto. The first movement, with its persistent march rhythm, shows more strongly than any other concerto of Mozart's the influence of the violin concertos of Viotti. We know (see p. 282) that Mozart composed a new middle movement for Viotti's 16th Concerto, and this can hardly have been his first acquaintance with the works of the great violinist of Piedmont, who, as Gerber says, had been 'famous since 1783,' and had already toured the entire continent. Now the 'ideal march' is typical of Viotti's first movements; there is hardly one among his twenty-nine concertos that does not have all the characteristics of such an ideal march—the firm step, the dotted rhythms, the military bearing. The seriousness of many of these concertos, too, must have made an impression on Mozart. One of the earlier ones, the 6th, issued in 1782 or 1783, is in D minor. Now the military element had not been foreign to Mozart's concertos even before this, but he had never emphasized it as strongly as in this movement, in which such motives as:

or

are almost everywhere present. Joyful assurance—that is the character of this movement. At the same time, it seems in a way like a festal introduction to the Allegretto in C—not, be it noted, in B-flat—which, in its charming and so often melancholy dreaming, is like an instrumental version, or a projection into the infinite realm of the instrumental, of all the emotions that are later expressed in Susanna's aria *Deh vieni, non tardar.* The last movement exhibits the play of all the spirits of Ariel's troupe, with Colombina, Arlecchino, and Papageno joining them now and again. This is *opera buffa* translated into the domain of instrumental music, and at the same time a masterful play with the 'learned' element, a fusion of homophony and polyphony—one of the few instances in which Mozart uses counterpoint in mocking vein. This Finale contains a few rhythms that are to be found note for note in Mozart's pantomime for the Carnival of 1783 (K. 446).

It is strange to think that Brahms once thought of Viotti's concertos in connection with Mozart's: 'The fact that people in general *do not* understand and *do not* respect the very best things, such as Mozart's concertos and the A minor Concerto by Viotti—that is what permits men like us to live and become famous.' We may hope that Wagner was not thinking of this piece, among others, when he distinguished the 'absolute allegro' from the 'characteristic Beethoven allegro':

What further stamps the Mozartean *absolute Allegro* as specifically belonging to the naive order, is its simple play of *forte* and *piano*, on the side of dynamics, as also, in respect of formal structure, its random juxtaposition [*wahllose Nebeneinanderstellung*] of certain stock melodic–rhythmic forms adapted to the *piano* or the *forte* method, in whose employment (as in the perpetual repetition of the selfsame thunderous half-closes) the master shows an almost more than startling [*eine fast mehr als überraschende*] unconstraint. Yet everything here, even the most heedless use of altogether banal phrases, explains itself by just the character of this Allegro: it has no desire to chain us by a cantilena, but to plunge us into a certain tumult through its restless motion . . . *

Poor 'master'! It is evident that Wagner's 'penetrating' description applies more to Mozart's overtures, but that is not important. For it is not really accurate as applied to the overtures either. One might say on the contrary that no master made less use of formulas than Mozart, and that none did more to transform formulas into expressive material, though not, of course, expressive in the sense of nineteenth-century Romanticism.

On the occasion of the coronation of Leopold II, on 15 October 1790, in Frankfurt-am-Main, Mozart played this Concerto together with the so-called Coronation Concerto (K. 537), with trumpets and timpani in the tutti. The latter were not added for the occasion, but belonged originally to the score. The parts are lost, but they should be prudently restored to the first and last movements: the first movement unquestionably needs them for its 'military' brilliance, and the humor of the Finale would gain here and there in effectiveness.

There could be no greater contrast than exists between this work and the one following, dated 10 February 1785, barely eight or nine weeks later. This is the D minor Concerto, K. 466, Mozart's first piano concerto in the minor mode, and the one best known, one might almost say the only one known, in the nineteenth century. That fact reveals a great deal about the nineteenth century, which did not understand

* *About Conducting*, translated by William Ashton Ellis, IV, 318.

the sublime humor of the F major Concerto, but well understood what distinguished the D minor among all the piano concertos of Mozart: passion, pathos, drama. This Concerto made it possible to stamp Mozart as a forerunner of Beethoven, and it is indeed no accident that for this very Concerto Beethoven wrote cadenzas—a splendid one, fusing the Mozart and Beethoven styles, for the first movement, and a rather weaker one for the last. This is the first work in which the tutti and the solo in the Allegro are sharply contrasted, in a dualism there is no attempt to overcome. The orchestra represents an anonymous threatening power, and the solo instrument voices an eloquent lament. The orchestra never takes over the first theme of the solo part, a *recitativo in tempo*, or the second half of the second theme. The opposition of the two permits of no reconciliation; it is only intensified in the development section. Nor does the reprise offer any solution: the *pianissimo* conclusion of the movement is as if the furies had simply become tired out and had lain down to rest, still grumbling, and ready at any instant to take up the fight again. And they do take it up again, in the middle section (in G minor) of the *Romanza*, which begins and ends in such heavenly tranquillity. Mozart never included stronger contrasts within a single work, contrasts among the three movements as well as within each movement individually. The choice of key for the Andante is revealing: not F major, or D major, but the subdominant of the relative major, just as in the G minor Symphony three years later. The Finale contains chromatically intensified and refined passion and drama, announced at the very beginning in the rocket-like principal motive. But this time Mozart wishes to conquer his pessimism and despair. After the cadenza, he turns towards the major, in a coda of enchanting sweetness, which represents at the same time an affecting ray of light and, in slight degree, a return to the social atmosphere of earlier works, the courtly gesture of a grand seigneur who wishes to leave his guests with a friendly impression. But this is not at all the childlike or grandiose optimism of Haydn or Beethoven.

One cannot say that in the Concerto immediately following this passionate work, the one in C major, K. 467, dated 9 March 1785, Mozart returned to 'normality': normality and classicism in the usual sense are terms that can hardly be applied to Mozart's music, above all in the Vienna period. But what Mozart does return to is the proud, triumphant affirmation of himself, once again symbolized by an ideal march, of which the theme begins:

Ex. 78

This motive waits throughout the entire movement to establish itself. It is symbolized in the fanfares of the winds and in a subsidiary theme of that utmost simplicity of which only great men are capable, men who possess that 'second naïveté,' which is the highest achievement of artistic and human experience. And Mozart returns from dramatic dialogue to symphonic treatment. Up to this time he had written no more imposing counter-melodies than the one in measures 13-20 of the tutti. The passage must be quoted complete and in its full scoring to make its significance clear:

The whole Concerto, but particularly the development, with its modulations through darkness into light, is one of the most beautiful examples of Mozart's iridescent harmony and of the breadth of the domain embraced in his conception of the key of C major. The Finale, which is a *buffo finale* again, is built up entirely on harmony enlivened with chromaticism, and on gay motives entirely lacking, this time, in any 'learned' quality. The Andante, with its muted strings, its quivering triplets, its *pizzicato* accompaniment against the broad arch of the soloist's cantilena, is like an ideal aria freed of all the limitations of the human voice. When one listens to such a work, one understands why Mozart wrote no symphonies in the earlier Vienna years, for these concertos are symphonic in the highest sense, and Mozart did not need to turn to the field of the pure symphony until that of the concerto was closed to him.

During the period of his work on *Le Nozze di Figaro*, in the winter and during the Carnival time of 1785-6, Mozart again completed three piano concertos: in E-flat (K. 482), in A (K. 488), and in C minor (K. 491). The first two give us the impression that he felt he had perhaps gone too far, had given the Viennese public credit for too much, had overstepped the boundaries of 'social' music—or, more simply stated, that he saw the favor of the public waning, and sought to win it back with works that would be sure of success. The first, especially, is a return—a return to the sphere of the earlier E-flat Concertos, the Concerto for Two Claviers and K. 271. The connection is palpable—externally visible, even: in the Allegro, in the motives of the horns (the winds, among which for the first time clarinets replace the oboes, play an enhanced role in this work altogether) or in the Finale, a 'hunting' movement transfigured into a round-dance, in the minuet-like episode in A-flat, which looks backward to the finale of K. 271 and forward to the canon in the second Finale of *Così fan tutte*. Everything reveals a certain routine, not of craftsmanship but of the spirit. But this is true only of the first and last movements. The slow movement, an Andante in C minor, a combination of song and variations, introduces a powerful element: expression unadorned, almost an exhibition of sadness, false consolation, despair, and resignation. Mozart exploits the contrast of major and minor in an entirely new way—that of the nineteenth century. It is significant of the cultural state of Vienna at the time that the public, at a subscription concert of Mozart's on 23 December, understood the direct appeal of the movement and demanded its repetition. Mozart himself was astonished. Leopold wrote to his daughter, on 13 January 1786, that Wolfgang had written him two weeks previously that he had 'composed . . . a new piano concerto in Eb, in which (a rather unusual occurrence!) he had to repeat the Andante.'

In the A major Concerto Mozart again succeeded in meeting his public half-way without sacrificing anything of his own individuality. He never wrote another first movement so simple in its structure, so 'normal' in its thematic relations between tutti and solo, or so clear in its thematic invention, even where it makes excursions into the realm of counterpoint, or contains rhythmic peculiarities. The key of A major is for Mozart the key of many colors. It has the transparency of a stained-glass window. There are relations between the first movement of this Concerto and the Clarinet Quintet. Not without reason are there no trumpets and timpani. But there are also darker shadings and concealed intensities, which the listener interested only in pleasant entertainment misses altogether. Already in this movement there is a threatening touch of F-sharp minor, and the whole Andante is in that key, which Mozart otherwise avoided. The latter movement is short, but it contains the soul of the work. It is the minor counterpart of the Andante of the 'Prague' Symphony, even in the way it dissolves all polyphonic elements in a new style. In this movement there appears in veiled form that passion which in the Andante of the preceding Concerto had revealed itself nakedly; the resignation and the hopelessness are the same. And when Mozart overcomes this impression with the entrance of the rondo theme, he is a true magician. This Presto seems to introduce a breath of fresh air and a ray of sunlight into a dark and musty room. The gaiety of this uninterrupted stream of melody and rhythm is irresistible. But this is no ordinary gaiety. Again, as in the E-flat major Piano Quartet, or the B-flat major Piano Trio, the clarinet introduces one of those 'unrelated' themes (in D major) in which the world seems perfectly balanced, and the scheme of things is fully justified. The work reverses the course of another work in A major, the Violin Sonata K. 526, in which the Andante is the movement of tranquillity, and the Finale sets loose a whole world of demons— another evidence of the breadth of Mozart's conception of the individuality of keys.

The passion that is veiled in the Andante of the A major Concerto breaks out again vehemently in the Concerto in C minor, finished on

24 March 1786, which bears the Köchel number immediately preceding that of *Figaro*. It seems as if Mozart wished to exhaust the key that he had previously, in the Andante of the E-flat major Concerto, used for an effect not quite legitimate, according to his conception of art as a heightened expression of feeling. At the same time there is a secret connection between this great, somber work and the C minor Serenade for Wind Instruments, of 1782. The Concerto is related to *Figaro* as the Serenade is to *Die Entführung*, even though the Serenade was not finished until shortly after the completion of the *Singspiel*. But in March 1786 *Figaro* was also practically finished. In both instances, Mozart evidently needed to indulge in an explosion of the dark, tragic, passionate emotions. There is a connection of a different sort with the Clavier Concerto in D minor, which shows Mozart's concerto form at its most dramatic. This C minor Concerto is another one that is a little Beethovenish; at least Beethoven admired it, and paid a certain homage to it in his own C minor Concerto, Op. 37. But Mozart's C minor Concerto is superior to the one in D minor. It is symphonic rather than simply in dialogue form, and the use of the richest orchestration Mozart had ever employed in a concerto—including both oboes and clarinets and with the wind instruments, both soli and as a body, taking a more prominent part than ever—is only external evidence of this fact. The passion in this work is deeper. Its affirmations of the key—all the modulations, no matter how far they wander, seem only to confirm the principal key—are more inevitable, more inexorable. Even when E-flat major is arrived at, the way remains strait and thorny.

Nothing is left of the ideal march; this first movement is in ¾ meter. Nothing is left of any compromise with social music, as in the Finale of the D minor Concerto; this Finale is an uncanny, revolutionary quick-march consisting of variations with free 'episodes' (actually anything but episodes), which represent glimpses of Elysian fields—but the conclusion is a return to the inevitable.

It is hard to imagine the expression on the faces of the Viennese public when on 7 April 1786 Mozart played this work at one of his subscription concerts. Perhaps they contented themselves with the Larghetto, which moves in regions of the purest and most moving tranquillity, and has a transcendent simplicity of expression.

Mozart closed his great period of concerto writing with a concerto in C major, K. 503, finished on 4 December 1786. He followed it directly with the 'Prague' Symphony—the first of a new and illustrious though brief series—and a few months later turned to a new species, in the C major Quintet, which may be said to have usurped the place of the concerto. For the two piano concertos that were still to come are minor works and not the product of the primary creative urge that had brought forth the great concertos. But the C major Concerto is a grandiose conclusion. It is related both to the C major Concerto, K. 467, and to its immediate predecessor, in C minor: it is an intensification of K. 467, mightier and more exalted, and is a necessary self-affirmation after the desperate passion of the C minor Concerto. In it, victory is attained, symbolized most simply and indisputably in the triumphal march-theme of the first movement, which, significantly, first enters in minor, and needs no *forte*:

Ex. 80

The battle is won. Whatever shadows the work contains are reminiscent only, even in the most passionate and agitated episode of the Rondo, which is not a humorous movement but a serious and self-confident one. No other work of Mozart's has such dimensions, and the dimensions correspond to the power of the symphonic construction and the drastic nature of the modulations. In no other concerto does the relation between the soloist and the orchestra vary so constantly and so unpredictably. The Adagio—for it is an adagio, and not at all, despite the marking, an andante—is to be compared perhaps only to the C major Symphony for its lofty singing character and fullness, and for the vitality of its detail. True, the nobility of the conception is not always quite matched in the execution. At times one has the impression that Mozart was in a hurry, and Mr. Girdlestone rightly points out the comparative indifference displayed by Mozart at the conclusion of the Rondo, a point in the structure at which he usually played his highest trump. But what does that matter when we consider the climaxes of this work in which the concentration of the themes is pushed to the utmost, without any impairment of the forward-driving *élan* of the whole?

To the penultimate concerto, written fourteen months later (24 February 1788; K. 537), in D major, we may quite properly apply the term *hors d'œuvre*. This work is known as the Coronation Concerto, because Mozart played it, along with K. 459, on 15 October 1790 in Frankfurt, during the festivities attending the coronation of Leopold II; and probably, even on that occasion, it had a greater success than the other work, which is much finer, more individual, and more ambitious. It was written for the concerts of Lent, 1788. We do not know whether Mozart ever played it in Vienna, but he took it with him on his trip to Berlin, and played it at Court in Dresden in April 1789. Nor can it be determined whether it was for this occasion or for Frankfurt that he added the trumpets and timpani to the score. But there is no question that it was the proper work for festive occasions. It is very Mozartean, while at the same time it does not express the whole or even the half of Mozart. It is, in fact, so 'Mozartesque' that one might say that in it Mozart imitated himself—no difficult task for him. It is both brilliant and amiable, especially in the slow movement; it is very simple, even primitive, in its relation between the solo and the tutti, and so completely easy to understand that even the nineteenth century always grasped it without difficulty. It has become, along with the D minor, the best known of Mozart's piano concertos. This popularity illustrates once again the strange fact that those works are often held to be particularly characteristic which do not survive in wholly authentic form. For Mozart left the solo part of this concerto in an especially sketchy state. Now, we do not know exactly how he played any of his concertos. Only four were published during his lifetime, and while in his autographs he wrote out the orchestra parts with complete care, he did not do the same with the solo parts; indeed it would have been in his interest not to write them out at all, so as not to lead unscrupulous copyists into temptation. For he knew perfectly well what he had to play. The solo parts in the form in which they survive are always only a suggestion of the actual performance, and a constant invitation to read the breath of life into them. But the solo part of this D major Concerto in particular is no more than a bare sketch, obviously entered into the score by Mozart simply to refresh his memory, consisting mostly of a single line with only the more polyphonic passages written out for both hands. Suffice it to say that only the accompaniment of the rondo theme survives in Mozart's own authentic version. Who was responsible for the version of the solo part that is accepted by pianists without question? I suspect that it was Johann André, who brought out the first edition of the work, in parts, in 1794. For the most part, this version is extremely simple and not too offensive, but at times—for example in the accompaniment of the Larghetto theme—it is very clumsy, and the whole solo part would gain infinitely by revision and refinement in Mozart's own style. No other work—unless it be the score of *Figaro*—shows more clearly how badly we need a new edition of Mozart's works.

Another *hors d'œuvre*, though in quite a different sense, is the Piano Concerto in B-flat (K. 595), Mozart's last, completed on 5 January of the year of which he did not live to see the end. He played it on 4 March 1791—but not in an 'academy' of his own, which the Viennese public would no longer support, but at a concert of the clarinetist Joseph Bähr, in the concert hall of the Court-Caterer Jahn in the Himmelpfortgasse (Gate-of-Heaven Road). Indeed, the work stands 'at the gate of heaven,' at the door of eternity. But when we term this Concerto a work of farewell we do so not at all from sentimentality, or from any misconception of this 'last concerto for clavier.' In the eleven months that remained to him, Mozart wrote a great deal of various kinds of music; it was not in the Requiem that he said his last word, however, but in this work, which belongs to a species in which he also said his greatest. This is the musical counterpart to the confession he made in his letters to the effect that life had lost attraction for him. When he wrote this Concerto, he had two terrible years behind him, years of disappointment in every sense, and 1790 had been even more terrible than 1789. He no longer rebelled against his fate, as he had in the G minor Symphony, to which, not only in key, but in other ways as well, this concerto is a sort of complement. Both these works, and only these, begin with a prefatory measure that established the 'atmosphere' of the key, like the *Eroica* or a symphony by Bruckner. The mood of resignation no longer expresses itself loudly or emphatically; every stirring of energy is rejected or suppressed; and this fact makes all the more uncanny the depths of sadness that are touched in the shadings and modulations of the harmony. The Larghetto is full of a religious, or, as Mr. Girdlestone calls it, a 'Franciscan' mildness; the Finale breathes a veiled joyfulness, as if blessed children were playing in Elysian fields, joyful, but without hate and without love. Mozart used the theme of this Rondo a few days later for a song entitled *Sehnsucht nach dem Frühlinge* (Longing for Spring). The theme has the resigned cheerfulness that comes from the knowledge that this is the last spring. But the most moving thing about it is that in it Mozart received the divine gift of being able *zu sagen was er leide* (to tell the fullness of his suffering). This last Piano Concerto is also a work of the highest mastery in invention—invention that has the quality of that 'second naïveté' of which we have spoken, welding the solo and tutti parts into the richest, closest relation, speaking in the most transparent sonority, and fusing perfectly the *galant* and 'learned' styles. It is so perfect that the question of style has become meaningless. The very act of parting from life achieves immortality.

IV. THE VOCAL WORKS

18. Church Music

WHEN THE ROMANTIC nineteenth century began to discover the Middle Ages, not only the Gothic cathedrals and the Pre-Raphaelites but also what it considered medieval in music—the alleged *a cappella* style of the Gabrielis, Lasso, and Palestrina—the church music of the seventeenth and eighteenth centuries became an object of contempt. Not only the lesser masters were included in this disdain, but also, and particularly, Joseph Haydn and Wolfgang Amadeus Mozart. As early as in Otto Jahn's biography of Mozart, the first in a scientific sense, there was cited and refuted the passage that may be found in *Über Reinheit der Tonkunst* (1824), a singular book by Anton Friedrich Justus Thibaut, jurist, professor at the University of Heidelberg, and Privy Councilor:

Thus our more recent masses and other ecclesiastical compositions have degenerated to the extent that they have become purely amorous and emotional and bear the absolute stamp of secular opera and even of that type of opera which is most in demand, that is, downright vulgar opera [What does Thibaut mean? Opera *buffa*?], in which, to be sure, the crowd feels most at home, and people of quality even more so than the common herd. Even the church music of Mozart and Haydn deserves that reproach, and both masters have even expressed it themselves. Mozart openly smiled at his masses, and several times, when he was commissioned to write a mass, protested, on the ground that he was only made for the opera. But since he was offered 100 louis d'or for each mass, he could not refuse, but explained laughingly that anything good in his masses would be taken out later for use in his operas . . . *

Now Mozart wrote hardly more than two Masses 'on commission': the solemn one in C minor for the consecration of the Waisenhaus-Kirche am Rennweg in Vienna, when he was a lad of thirteen, and the

---

* First ed., Chap. VIII.

Requiem in D minor; and in both cases he neither protested nor smiled, either secretly or openly. His Salzburg church music was written not to order but 'in service,' or out of friendship, or to accommodate someone, and his finest church composition, the great C minor Mass, was composed in fulfilment of a vow. Mozart utilize his Masses for his operas? Mozart, who had the most sensitive feeling for the limitations of forms, for the tradition within those limitations? It is certainly true that ecclesiastical texts were set to music from Mozart's operas, for example from *Così fan tutte*; this was not Mozart's fault, however, but that of the nineteenth century.

The scorn on the part of the nineteenth-century Romantic purists and 'Cecilians' for the church style of Haydn and Mozart is the more comical because their admiration for the church music of the Palestrina period rests upon a historical fallacy. If they had had a better knowledge of the secular music of Palestrina and Lasso and the Gabrielis, they would have had to reject the church music of these masters and their contemporaries also, as being too similar to the secular music and flowing from the same spirit. They regarded as eminently churchly works that in reality were full of an eminently secular symbolism of expression, or at least were full of a symbolism common to both secular and sacred music. If they had known more, nothing would have remained to the Cecilians à la Thibaut but to go back to plainsong or the antiphonal chants of the early Christians. Creative centuries do not think in terms of history. It never occurred to the architects of Chartres or Rheims or Notre Dame to build in the Romanesque style, any more than it occurred to Bramante or Michelangelo to return to the Gothic style for Saint Peter's, although the Gothic style is supposed to be 'more pious' than that of the Renaissance. We have already compared Mozart's Catholicism in his church music with the jubilant Rococo churches in Southern Bavaria and Upper and Lower Austria, which are no less pious and no more secular than San Vitale in Ravenna. If Mozart's church music is to be criticized, then, it must be on the ground not of being too 'worldly,' but because it is not worldly enough. There was no historical reminiscence, no remnant of a heterogeneous past, in the style of those builders who created the Wies-Kirche or the Klosterkirche of Ettal in Upper Bavaria. Unfortunately, in music, and especially in eighteenth-century church music, there was such a remnant: what Mozart's contemporaries called the 'strict' style, the *stile osservato*. Mozart's church works are written partly in a mixed style. As we have seen, tradition demanded that individual sections of the Mass —the *Cum sancto spiritu* or *Et vitam venturi*—and the concluding parts of other liturgical texts be treated 'fugally,' in an archaic, polyphonic style; and Mozart was a traditionalist. As a traditionalist and an ambitious musician he attached particular value to such contrapuntal showpieces, and the more he did so, the more strongly he emphasized the stylistic dualism of his church compositions. Not in all his church compositions; but he never completely overcame this dualism, even in the Requiem—in striking contrast to his success in doing so in his instrumental works and operas. *This* is the esthetic reproach, if any, that may be leveled against his church music.

But not the reproach that this music is too worldly, not devout or Catholic enough; that it does not fit the requirements for ecclesiastical music laid down in the *Motu proprio* of Pope Pius X of 22 November 1903. It surely cannot be called unliturgical. It always employs the full text of the Mass or litany; and only in individual cases does it becloud the understanding of the text by its use of 'polytexture'—that is, by a simultaneous singing of different textual passages that according to liturgical precept should properly follow in succession. Mozart's church music, we repeat, is 'Catholic' in a higher sense—namely, in the sense that it is pious as a work of art, and the piety of an artist can consist only in his desire to give his utmost. Otherwise the devout little pictures, the imitation Lourdes grottoes, the besugared 'Christ-childs' of the religious-goods industry would be more Catholic than Giotto's frescoes or Duccio's panels, and one of the boring 'Nazarene' Masses or hymns by Ett or Aiblinger more Catholic than Mozart's *Misericordias* or *Ave verum.* Furthermore, the Catholic quality of Mozart's church music, in the higher sense, consists not perhaps in any so-called and questionable dignity—a fitness for the interior of a Romanesque or Gothic church—but in its humanity, in its appeal to all devout and childlike hearts, in its directness. If one wishes to be 'pure in style,' one should certainly not perform it in a Gothic church and least of all in a nineteenth- or twentieth-century church; just as one should not perform the Organa of Perotin or the Masses of Obrecht in a Rococo church. One can no more find fault with Mozart for writing Masses, vespers, offertories, motets, litanies, and hymns in the spirit of his time than one can find fault with Giambatista Tiepolo for approaching his church pictures with the same artistic assumptions as those with which he approached his mythological or historical scenes. It was the ultra-cultured and Alexandrian nineteenth century that first cast this stone.

Now, in the eighteenth century, too, there were rationalistic minds that objected to the festive character of the Catholic church music, the discrepancy between words and music, especially in the setting of the *Kyrie* and the *Agnus Dei*. Father Meinrad Spiess, choir director in the Irsee Monastery in Bavaria, complained in his tract on composition (1745 and 1746, p. 133) that logic alone should prevent 'many lightheaded sophomoric composers from setting the *Kyrie eleison* or *Lord, have mercy upon us!* in churches before the most holy sacrament in the style of a dance,' and entreated the ecclesiastical officials and churchwardens to drive such scribblers from the temple. 'It is true! If a modern musical composition is to have the desired effect on the listeners, it requires ideas, spirit, and brilliance . . .' And Johann Bähr, concert-master at the court of Weissenfels, said of the text of the *Kyrie*, in his *Musicalische Discurse* (1719):

This text is a *textus lamentabilis* . . . [and] anyone who pleads for something would come with troubled, not victorious, mien. Even when the trumpets are omitted, most Kyries are set to such merry fugues, themes, and such-like that they are splendid rather than humble, joyful rather than sad—in short, more like dances than like the lamentations of Jeremiah.

(Now, this would be true of Bach too; one need only consider the *Kyrie* of his A major Mass, even though this *Kyrie* was taken from a sacred cantata.) But Bähr wishes

nevertheless to say a few words in defense of [such composers, for] in solemn rites the music is no different from what his garb is to the communicant. May not the communicant be full of devotion, even though he be splendidly attired? The nature of the Kyrie is therefore not altered if it is splendidly intoned and performed . . . *

Yes, Mozart and Haydn and many of their contemporaries were full of devotion, even though they were at the same time 'splendidly attired.' When Mozart composed a Mass, he had splendor in mind, but he never forgot 'expression.' And he began very early to write splendid Masses. His first attempt is a Gallic and songlike *Kyrie* in F (K. 33), which he composed in Paris, 12 June 1766. But only two years later he

---

* Cited after W. Kurthen, 'Studien zu W. A. Mozart's kirchenmusikalischen Jugendwerken' in *Zeitschrift für Musikwissenschaft*, III, 348; and *Kirchenmusikalisches Jahrbuch*, 1889, p. 72 ff.

wrote for an especially ceremonious occasion—the consecration of the Waisenhaus-Kirche am Rennweg—a *Missa solemnis* of considerable dimensions, for a large group of executants: chorus, soloists, strings, two oboes, three trombones, four trumpets, and timpani. This Mass is the problematic and much-discussed C minor Mass, K. 139. I have heretofore considered the Waisenhaus Mass lost (K. 47a) and have attributed the C minor Mass to a somewhat later period; but I must agree with W. Kurthen (*op. cit.*, p. 209 ff.) in regarding it as the one of 7 December 1768. Despite the beginning in C minor, it is not a 'funeral Mass' on the death of Archbishop Sigismund, as Wyzewa and Saint-Foix assume—C minor here is nothing more than an intensification of solemnity; a 'funeral Mass' is a requiem, and we know that the requiem for that occasion—also in C minor—was written by Michael Haydn. An argument on external grounds is provided by the fact that while the lad may have had four trumpets and three trombones at his disposal in Salzburg, he did not have the divided violas—Salzburg church music usually does not indicate the viola at all. Leopold Mozart was extremely proud of the Waisenhaus Mass (letter of 14 December 1768), and it would have been strange if he had not preserved the manuscript; this is another reason to believe that the surviving manuscript and the Waisenhaus Mass are one and the same. As for internal reasons: the lad who had written the *Veni sancte Spiritus* (K. 47), a lofty and imposing work despite its primitiveness, and unquestionably also written in the fall of 1768, and who was to write scarcely a year later the equally authentic Dominicus Mass (K. 66), was quite capable of writing this C minor Mass also.

How did the youthful composer fulfil his task? He followed the standard Italian model, represented by Johann Adolph Hasse, at that time the most influential and respected musician in Vienna, and well disposed towards Mozart. After the repeated solemn invocation, a slow Introduction in C minor, the Kyrie is a cheerful Allegro in major, in three-quarter time, with alternations of soli and tutti, and choral declamation, interrupted or held together by orchestral *ritornelli*, with primitive motives, in a kind of sonata form. The *Christe* is composed anew, in the subdominant, for the soloists alone, and represents approximately the Andantino of a symphony; then the exuberant *Kyrie* is repeated. Ceremony, not expression! The *Gloria* and *Sanctus* are large-scale cantata movements with the traditional construction and traditional stressing of pictorial and symbolic passages in the text. In our

C minor Mass the *Gloria in excelsis Deo et in terra pax hominibus* is presented in pure choral declamation with brilliant orchestration; the *Laudamus te* is a duet in G for soprano and alto, a lovely Andante; the *Gratias* once more a kind of miniature overture, with contrasting tempi —adagio and *vivace*, but with more chromatic melody; the *Domine Deus* a duet for tenor and bass, this time with greater motion and in F. In the center of the *Gloria* is the *Qui tollis*—a choral setting in F minor, Adagio, in the darker regions of harmony, with a solemn accompaniment in triplets. Then a soprano solo in F: *Quoniam tu solus sanctus*, and, in the main key, a triumphant *fugato: Cum sancto Spiritu in gloria Dei patris, Amen.* The *Credo* is treated similarly: the *Incarnatus* is a duet, strangely enough in the same key and with the same time-signature as the later *Incarnatus* in the 'great' C minor Mass of 1783; the *Crucifixus* and *Et Resurrexit* are contrasted with each other, as is fitting; the *Et in Spiritum sanctum* is a friendly tenor solo, and, after the *Et unam sanctam* is sung by the chorus, it concludes with a return of contrapuntal display—this time a double fugue: *Et vitam venturi.* The formation of the three remaining sections of the Mass results automatically. The *Sanctus* bustling, always in the principal key, with the *Pleni sunt* in a more rapid tempo; the *Benedictus* mostly for one or more soloists and mostly in the subdominant, and overlapping with the *Osanna*; the *Agnus Dei* mournful at the beginning but becoming festive and gay with the *Dona nobis* as conclusion and farewell. Thus the tradition, and one submits to it. Church music is not suited to experimentation; one does not give way to subjective feelings, but conducts oneself respectably, in mourning or in rejoicing. There is opportunity enough to display one's personal powers of invention in small, symbolic ways, as for example in the 'pictorial' interpretation of *ascendit* and *descendit*; and the listeners will notice how the contrast between the *Crucifixus* and *Resurrexit* is continued. Such matters did not embarrass Mozart even as a boy, nor was he concerned over the fact that by combining *galant* and 'learned' sections he was creating a style-mixture impossible from the standpoint of the esthetic purist. The more remarkable, therefore, are his treatment of the prose text of the Mass, choosing for it fitting melodies and rhythms, rounding it off with verbal repetitions, and the way in which he joins individual movements into a whole by means of unifying violin-motives—although of the most primitive type.

The sister-work of this C minor Mass is the solemn Mass in C major,

K. 66, which Mozart wrote for the ordination of Cajetan Hagenauer, a
son of Lorenz Hagenauer, the landlord of the Mozart family. Cajetan
had entered the Benedictine monastery of St. Peter while the Mozarts
were on their grand tour, and on 15 October 1769 he celebrated, as
Pater Dominicus, his first solemn high Mass; hence the title 'Dominicus
Mass' for this work. Mozart composed for his friend's ecclesiastical day
of glory not only the Mass, but also the offertory for it, the antiphon
Benedictus sit Deus (K. 117); and so we do not wonder that the Pater
remarked in his diary: 'Duravit Missa supra duo horas . . .' This offertory may have greatly astonished the large congregation ('magna offeren-
tium multitudo'), if they had any understanding of music. It is just
like an Italian *sinfonia*: Allegro—Andante in F—Allegro; but Mozart
constructed the finale in a manner at once original and ecclesiastical,
by employing as a sort of second theme the liturgical psalm-tone:

Ex. 81

Psalmum dicite nomini e - jus. date glo- riam lau-di e - jus.

which he accompanied, however, with a bustling, exceedingly secular
violin figuration. The Mass itself follows closely the model of the
Vienna C minor Mass in its construction, in the disposition of the text
in the Gloria and Credo, and in the distribution of chorus and solo and
galant and 'learned' sections. But, though it is not shorter, it is more
heartfelt and individual in melodic invention than that work performed in the presence of the Empress. The waltz-like entrance of the
solo in the *Kyrie* has always been singled out, or criticized, or apologized
for:

Ex. 82

—a criticism or apology that would be applicable to the childlike themes
of the *Dona nobis* also. But alongside passages like these we find such

maturity of insight and grandeur of conception as may be seen in the *Crucifixus* or the *Miserere nobis*.

Quite different from these big and solemn Masses written for special occasions are the *Missae breves*, which were intended for the ordinary Sunday services. They eschew brilliant accompaniment and content themselves usually with strings only; and above all they do not split up the *Gloria* and *Credo*—the two portions of the Mass containing the longest texts—into numerous independent sections. The solo parts merely emerge from the choral group and return to it; the alternation of the different means of expression is not only more rapid but less noticeable: to be sure, neither the *galant* nor the 'learned' is avoided, but the contrasts of the *stilus mixtus* do not stand out so prominently. Mozart had written two such Masses in his earliest youth—along with the two solemn Masses—one in Vienna in the autumn of 1768 (K. 49, in G) and the other after the return to Salzburg, for performance on 5 February 1769 (K. 65, in D minor). Significantly, the Vienna Mass calls for the viola in the accompaniment, while the Salzburg Mass does not. As early as in the G major Mass Mozart had perceived the principal problem in the composition of the *Gloria* and *Credo*: the unification of these long movements full of contrast; and especially in the *Gloria* he had provided an astounding example of such unification: not by the external means of employing a reiterated violin-figure, but by the relationship of all the melodic motives. An even more astonishing work is the *Missa brevis* in D minor. The unwonted key is explained by the purpose for which the work was written: the opening of the forty-hour prayer in the Salzburg University Church. It is thus a Lenten Mass. The *Gloria* could not be sung, of course, in Lent, but Mozart composed it nevertheless, doubtless for future use. In later years he liked to revive the early Masses: for example, the Dominicus Mass was directed by Leopold in August 1773 in Vienna, and a few years later Mozart even enriched its instrumentation by adding oboes, horns, and another pair of trumpets. Our little D minor Mass, however, despite the *Gloria*, is really well suited to Lent, as is shown especially by the chromatically modulating *Benedictus*, a duet for soprano and alto. The whole work is unusually concentrated, perhaps too much so, for the *Credo* contains already a striking example of the forbidden 'polytexture,' a fact that indicates that this device was permitted or even required under the more lenient Prince-Bishop Sigismund. The work is so concise that the contrasts of the *stilus mixtus* practically disappear:

it is true that the *Cum sancto Spiritu* and *Et vitam venturi* still have the form of short *fugati*, but with what themes! Observe the subject of the *Et vitam*:

Ex. 83

Et vi- tam   ven-tu- ri,   ven-tu-ri   sae-culi, a -   men

There is not much of the 'learned' about a theme like this.

Among the other church pieces written by Mozart as a boy is an offertory *in festo Sancti Benedicti*, which begins *Scande coeli limina* (K. 34), a free motet, or rather a scena for soloists and chorus, droll by reason of the fact that a soprano sings what the chorus should sing and, conversely, the chorus sings what really belongs to a solo bass—a musical counterpart of the Baroque wood carvings of scenes from the Scriptures. It is said to have been composed for the Feast of St. Benedict (21 March 1767) in the Monastery of Seeon at Chiemgau; but the absence of the viola points rather to Salzburg. A *Te Deum* in C with accompaniment for strings alone (once more without viola), dating from the end of 1769 (K. 141), plays approximately the same part in Mozart's church music as the Violin Concerto (K. 218) in D does in his instrumental music. Just as the latter leans on a concerto by Boccherini, so the former leans on a *Te Deum* of 1760 by Michael Haydn, which Mozart follows so closely that the imitation can be shown almost measure for measure. And yet this work is as Mozartean as the Violin Concerto, constructed with a sure hand, enchanting in its choral declamation, and possessed of a certain South-German rustic grandeur even in the concluding double fugue—a worthy conclusion to Mozart's activities as a church composer before setting off on the Italian journeys.

Did the travels in Italy alter Mozart's ideas of church music? Yes and no. On the one hand, what he could observe in Italian churches was a musical 'unchurchliness,' secularization, aria-like quality, even more carefree than in Salzburg or in the dignified Vienna of Maria Theresa; on the other hand, in Bologna he studied with Padre Martini, who still had a true, if somewhat scientific, conception of the purer, higher, more churchly music of the sixteenth century. But we already know that the old *contrappunto osservato* with which Mozart became acquainted in Bologna was for him so much schoolroom dust, which he soon shook off. He could not assimilate this music, a fact that simply indicates the vitality of his mind, the soundness of his productive powers. To be sure, in his 'Italian' years, between 1770 and 1773, he made a few attempts in such a style—a *Miserere* for three voices and instrumental bass (K. 85); a *Missa brevis* for four voices, strings, and organ, of which only the *Kyrie* (K. 116) seems to have survived; another four-part *Kyrie*, with organ (K. 221); and a few fragmentary attempts at other pieces of this sort. Even the *Miserere* was not completed, and the fact that J. A. André, a shrewd businessman, was able to complete it by adding three movements without straying from the style is a clear indication of its impersonal quality, its 'neutrality.' These are just exercises.

When Mozart gave himself up to Italian brilliance or lack of seriousness, he did not entirely forget Salzburg. By Salzburg, we mean his instrumental schooling. The larger and more festive portion of this church music is outspokenly symphonic in conception—the symphonic mixed with the *concertante*. In May 1771 and again in May 1772 Mozart wrote two *Regina coeli*, both for large forces, the one (K. 108, in C) even calling for trumpets, and the other (K. 127, in B-flat) including at least oboes or flutes, and horns. Both, to put it bluntly, are nothing more than three-movement 'Italian' symphonies incorporating a chorus, or solo voices, or a mixture of both. The *Regina coeli* was one—the third—of the four Marian antiphons that could be sung from Holy Saturday to the Saturday in Whitsuntide; that is why both of these works are so festive and *concertante*—the second even more so than the first, although it is more carefully constructed in detail. In January 1773 Mozart wrote at Milan a motet with accompaniment of strings, oboes, horns, and organ, *Exsultate jubilate* (K. 165), for the *castrato* Venanzio Rauzzini, who had sung a principal role in his *Lucio Silla*. It is very well known, since ambitious sopranos like to sing it. Except for the short recitative that introduces the middle movement, it is simply a miniature concerto with an Allegro, an Andante, and a Presto or Vivace, hardly inferior, in brilliance or 'tenderness,' to a true instrumental concerto. Mozart went farthest along the path of Italianate carefreeness in his *Litaniae de venerabili altaris sacramento* of March 1772 (K. 125), in which he took a work by his father as a model and surpassed it. The text actually serves only for private devotions; but Leopold or Wolfgang nevertheless performed the work, or wished to perform it, in Munich in the Hour Service of New Year's Day, 1775. The *Kyrie* is a symphony-movement, or rather, with its Adagio inter-

polated before the chorus enters with the principal theme, a concerto-
movement of the purest water. In the same way, the next movement
(*Panis vivus*), with its soprano solo, is a concerto slow movement. One
wonders why no one has yet had the notion to reconstruct the concerto that underlies a church work of this sort; in our Litany one could
choose as a finale the *Pignus futurae gloriae*, a contrapuntal display-
piece the length and emptiness of which have an almost fatal effect.
In the whole Litany, only the 14 introductory measures of this *Pignus*
(*Viaticum*), in B-flat minor, show signs of any emotion aroused by the
text. For the rest, there is concern for getting the job done quickly, and
for brilliance and festive buoyancy, not for expression. Where would it
lead if one wished always to do justice to the persistent prayer,
'Miserere'! Mozart does it justice several times; but the tenor, in his
solo, *Panis omnipotens*, unblushingly sings the following, among other
passages:

Ex. 84 [*Andante*]

and at the repetition of this passage the trill develops into a veritable
cadenza ad libitum.

But there is another litany, written a year earlier (May 1771), a
Litaniae Lauretanae, also in B-flat major (K. 109). The Lorettine litany
receives its name from the Mary chapel of the Casa Santa in Loreto,
the inscriptions from which are gathered together in its text; this text,
too, is intended to serve primarily for devotions of a private nature.
Now K. 109 is in fact quite intimate; not less Italian, but without
Italian brilliance, and full of Mozartean tenderness. The *Sancta Maria
ora pro nobis* is a wonderful movement, a continuous *arioso* in antiphonal style; and the concluding sigh of the *Agnus Dei* in B-flat minor is
particularly beautiful. A gay and childlike counterpart to this work is
the Offertory *Inter natos mulierum* of June 1771 (K. 72), written for
the feast of John the Baptist, with a pious close—*Ecce Agnus Dei*—
full of poetry. And to this same summer of 1771, belongs the loveliest
church work of Mozart's youth, a *De profundis* in C minor (K. 93)—

the loveliest because it is the simplest. The four voices sing the verses of the 129th Psalm in unadorned declamation, arioso and yet not without accentuations of expression; the conventional doxology at the end turns towards the liturgical style. Mozart originally intended to lend the work a soft instrumental sheen by having two violins, but he discarded them, perhaps deliberately. There is a setting of the same psalm from Gluck's last period, also for four voices, but with a powerful, dark orchestral accompaniment; it seems to me, however, that the lad far surpassed the old giant, if the highest art consists in expressing the most profound things with the simplest means.

There is a polyphonically constructed counterpart to this little homophonic masterwork, the Hymn *Justum deduxit Dominus* (K. 326), unquestionably of the same period. It is a Salzburg piece, not an Italian one. For even in his Italian years Mozart had felt the necessity, despite Padre Martini, of practicing in the strict style, and had taken as models a series of works by Salzburg masters, foremost among them Michael Haydn and Ernst Eberlin. Eberlin (1702-62) was a former Cathedral Kapellmeister and superior of Leopold Mozart. It is South-German, Salzburg, Viennese, J. J. Fuxian counterpoint that he practices here, though one should be careful in using these phrases, for it was at the same time Italian counterpoint. In Italy, too, there was a dignified church style for sections of the Mass, psalms, hymns, and motets for four voices and bass, sometimes with the frugal accompaniment of two violins; a style based on a sometimes rather stylized and archaic but almost honorable and honest polyphony, differing widely from the brilliant, concertante, arioso style of the church works for great occasions. One becomes wary when one knows that a motet of this kind, the Hymn *Adoramus te* (K. 327), which has been ascribed to Mozart's last period, alongside the *Ave verum*, has been shown to be a copy by Mozart of a work by Quirino Gasparini (died 1778). Gasparini was Court and Cathedral Kapellmeister in Turin and, as a member of the Bologna Accademia Filarmonica, a colleague of Mozart's. Mozart could easily have come to know the motet in Bologna and have copied it there. It is a motet for Good Friday, in C minor, of great beauty and in one melodic turn related to the *Ave verum*. And its polyphony is somewhat better balanced than is that of the Salzburg master.

Nevertheless it must be said that Mozart's church compositions written before 1782 were influenced primarily by Salzburg polyphony. The external evidence for this statement is supplied by copies that Mozart made for himself of two fugues by Michael Haydn (fragments from the *Litaniae de venerabili altaris sacramento*), and above all by a notebook containing 19 ecclesiastical works by Michael Haydn and Ernst Eberlin, set down in score from the parts, in an intense zeal for learning. This must have been done in the spring of 1773, shortly after Mozart's return from his final trip to Italy. He had felt the necessity of deepening his church style for Salzburg; and so with these copies there really begins a new chapter in Mozart's activity for the church.

A new chapter begins also partly for external reasons, connected with the accession of the new Archbishop (1772). Hieronymus Colloredo was an impatient ruler and had no love for long Masses, especially if he had to celebrate them himself. Mozart himself characterized the Salzburg church style preferred by Colloredo in the famous letter to Padre Martini (4 September 1776), which he attached to the manuscript of his *Misericordias Domini* (K. 222):

Our church music is very different from that of Italy, since a mass with the whole Kyrie, the Gloria, the Credo, the Epistle sonata, the Offertory or Motet, the Sanctus, and the Agnus Dei must not last longer than three quarters of an hour. This applies even to the most solemn Mass said by the Archbishop himself. So you see that a special study is required for this kind of composition. At the same time, the Mass must have all the instruments—trumpets, drums and so forth . . .

'Very different from that of Italy'! And consequently also very different from the church music of Bologna. The 'Salzburg taste for brevity,' the archiepiscopal desires, could be satisfied in two ways. And Mozart had used both ways at the same time—in the spring of 1773 with the (unfortunately uncompleted) *Missa brevis*, K. 115, and with the so-called *Trinitatis* Mass in C, K. 167. The first, also in C, is a direct result of the studies of Eberlin, Michael Haydn, and Adlgasser. Four voices, with an unpretentious organ accompaniment, proceeding without loss of time in a style contrapuntal in principle, and 'worked-out,' yet without obstructing the path towards a conclusion in simple chordal style; a setting built out of small elements but with enough freedom to broaden out into a double fugue in the *Cum sancto Spiritu*, and with an occasional stressing by musical means of the feeling expressed in the text or of symbolic tone-painting. Thus the symbols for *ascendit*, *descendit*, and *resurrectionem* correspond exactly:

Ex. 85

de- scen- - - - - - - - - - - - - - - - - - - dit

a- scen- - - - - - - - - -·- dit in coe-lum

re- sur-re- - - - - - - - - - - cti-onem

This work may be called a 'motet Mass,' not in the sense of the six-teenth century, but in that of the eighteenth, a period that no longer really knew the freedom and flow of the classic polyphony, and in which polyphony had rigidified somewhat into 'counterpoint'; but in this sense a masterwork by the eighteen-year-old composer. He did not complete it—it breaks off after a few measures of the *Sanctus*—perhaps because the Archbishop demanded brevity but at the same time did not wish to renounce brilliance. And so Mozart wrote his *Trinitatis* Mass, a solemn Mass with the full splendor of the orchestra, with oboes, two pairs of trumpets, timpani, and strings—significantly lacking violas. How was brevity to be attained here? By renouncing all solos; by contracting *Gloria* and *Credo* into unified, symphonic movements; and by forming individual sections of a movement so that they are alike—a relationship that may be called 'correspondence.' Thus in the *Credo* of our Mass the *Genitum non factum*, the *Et ascendit*, and, leaping over a wide area—that is, over the interpolated *Et in Spiritum* in G major—the *Et expecto* 'correspond' to the *Et in unum Dominum*. This is a choral Mass; and the choral setting built into the symphonic structure holds remarkably to a middle path between the contrapuntal and the *concertante*. Only in the *Et vitam venturi* does Mozart permit himself once more to write a contrapuntal display-piece, a fugue that perhaps over-stepped the bounds decreed by Colloredo and to which that gentleman must have listened with impatience and displeasure. For the rest, the Mass, including the 'Epistle sonata' and the Offertory, taken at the proper tempo, actually lasts only forty-five minutes; the problem is solved, the 'special study for this kind of composition' has borne its first fruit.

This is the place once more (cf. p. 267) to say a few words about the 'Epistle sonata,' a category of instrumental pieces of which we possess seventeen examples by Mozart. These *sonate da chiesa* are intended as interpolations between the *Gloria* and the *Credo* or, to put it more precisely, between the Epistle and the Gospel of the Mass. When the duration of the whole Mass is to be only forty-five minutes, such a sonata should be allotted no more than two or three minutes; nor is it ever allotted more than that by Mozart. To help himself keep within the time limit, he writes movements in sonata form *en miniature*, with development sections of a few measures. The instrumentation of these sonatas varies according to that of the Masses to which they belong, and several can definitely be shown to belong to Mozart's own Masses. Thus for his Mass with solo organ (K. 337) he wrote a *Sonata all'epistola*, which is actually a fine first movement of a clavier concerto *en miniature*; on the organ, in the cathedral, it must have seemed strange enough. There is a legend that Colloredo later abolished these instrumental insertions in the Mass and ordered Michael Haydn to replace them with vocal pieces. But if brevity was what was wanted, they could hardly be surpassed.*

As soon as Mozart was able to disregard the Archbishop's desires, he returned at once to a *cantabile* and solo style. Thus in April or May 1774 he wrote for one of the smaller Salzburg churches another *Litaniae Lauretanae* (K. 195), in which he reverted to the forms of the older sister-work, but employed the new tone-language, combining concertante symphonic qualities with finer workmanship. At the risk of being misunderstood, one might call this a combination of 'Pergolesi' and 'Michael Haydn.' The *Sancta Maria* is once more an Andante with solos, bearing the same relation to the *Kyrie* as the slow movement of a symphony to its first movement. The *Salus infirmorum*, again in the relative minor, is a concerto-movement with the most delicate filigree; while the *Regina angelorum* develops into a true *concertone* with soli and tutti. For the *Agnus Dei* Mozart wrote one of the most heavenly of all his Adagio movements, for soprano solo and answering and con-

---

* All 17 *sonate all'epistola* lack the viola, as do some of the Salzburg church music and all of Mozart's dance music. Why this is so has not yet been explained. In my opinion the viola is intended simply to play the bass part an octave higher. But the idiosyncrasy is retained into Mozart's last period, in which he wrote for the carnival a long series of naive and festive dance pieces, some of them rich in invention; they were planned for double use: with two violins and bass alone, or with full wind-orchestra. One can distinguish at a glance a dance-minuet, for example, from a symphony-minuet: a symphony-minuet has a viola and sometimes even two; in a dance-minuet no part is ever written out for viola.

cluding tutti. He returned to this motive ten years later, in the Adagio of the 'Hunt' Quartet (K. 458):

Ex. 86

The statements that such a movement is conceived instrumentally, that the solo would suit a clarinet better than a human voice, and that the style is that of a Neapolitan opera rather than a true and authentic church style may be repeated endlessly, and would be right every time. But aside from the facts that such a judgment would condemn the whole vocal style of the eighteenth century, that singers of today are no longer capable of performing such music, and that Mozart undoubtedly intended the solo part for a neutral *castrato* voice, a Lorettine litany is an intimate devotion, and this piece, softly dying away in the dusk, is enchanting precisely because of its character as a rapturous prayer. The Adagio of the String Quartet is a prayer, too, and, from the highest standpoint, it is difficult to see why, of two most intimately related movements, one should be considered legitimate and the other spurned. At any rate, I do not envy those whose enthusiasm for such a marvel of art and youthful feeling is spoiled by stylistic considerations.

In June and August of the same year (1774) Mozart wrote, for ordinary liturgical use, two short Masses, one in F (K. 192) and one in D (K. 194), both with simple string accompaniment (without viola!), in which he achieved an even greater conciseness. One of the means he employed to this end is simply briefness of duration: in the Mass in F only the *Kyrie* and *Agnus* are provided with an instrumental prelude, while all the other movements begin at once with the voices; and in the Mass in D there are no preludes at all. Other means are the terseness of all the motives, the rapid choral declamation, and the division of lengthy sections of the text among the soloists, who almost interrupt each other, without, however, falling into the forbidden expedient of polytexture. *Gloria* and *Credo* are each held together by unifying violin motives; indeed, in the second Mass the motive of the *Gloria* returns in the *Credo*. It is sometimes impossible not to be reminded of the sections of a *buffo-finale*, which gain their unity by means of the same device of recurrent violin motives. The *Credo* of the Mass in F is also held together by a recurrent principal motive *in the voices*—that four-note theme which attends Mozart throughout his life, up to the finale of the great C major Symphony. In the present work it always asserts, 'I believe,' with ever new counterpoints; and at the end it returns once more, at the *Amen, amen* in a *fugato* with *stretto*. Thanks to this grand and lively movement, this *Missa brevis* is already a true *Credo* Mass, and it deserves this title more than the later Mass in C (K. 257), to which the title has actually been given. In contrast to what occurs in the Mass in F, the *Credo* of the Mass in D is intoned only by the priest, and a special slow movement is interpolated for the *Incarnatus*. The *Dona nobis* of the former Mass is very much like the finale of an Italian *sinfonia*, while that of the latter is more vocal in character, and is trusting and childlike in mood. Between the two Masses, chronologically, are a *Dixit* and *Magnificat* (K. 193, of July 1774), which, with their somewhat more pretentious instrumentation (including trumpets and timpani), must have been written for the vesper service of the eve of a church feast of some importance. These psalm compositions also employ the Mozartean four-note device; the *Magnificat* is even more imposing from the contrapuntal standpoint than the *Dixit*; but both pieces are somewhat too showy.

The extremes of the Salzburg style may be seen in two ecclesiastical compositions written during the period of the *Finta giardiniera* performances in Munich at the beginning of 1775. One is the *Missa brevis* in C (K. 220), which calls for the same forces—except the addition of trumpets and drums—used in the two Masses of 1774. While in all probability it was composed in Munich, it was surely not composed for Munich, though Leopold writes from there to his wife (15 February): 'A short Mass by Wolfgang was performed last Sunday in the court chapel and I conducted it. Next Sunday another is to be performed.' But these were presumably the two *Missae breves* of 1774. For Mozart would hardly have gained much credit in Munich with the new Mass in C. I believe rather that it resulted from a sudden order from Colloredo, who wished thereby to keep his hold on Mozart even from a distance. Mozart filled the order hastily and in such a way as to imply to his patron, 'This is what you wanted and here it is!' The Mass, called 'Sparrow Mass' in the jargon of South-German church musicians, because of the accompanying figure of the violins in the *Credo*, should be entitled *Missa brevissima*. There is not the slightest attempt at a *fugato* as the conclusion of the *Gloria* and *Credo*; the task of setting the text to music is discharged rapidly, chiefly in a homophonic *concertante* style; and there is scarcely more than a hint at anything mystic or emotional. It is as though Mozart wishes to defy the Archbishop when he 'symbolizes' the *Descendit* as follows:

Ex. 87

de-scen-dit, de- scen-dit, de-scen- . . . . . -dit   de coe- - - -lis

The 'symphonic,' *buffo-finale* pattern is emphasized by the return of the *Kyrie* theme in the *Agnus*; it is, so to speak, the thematic coda of the whole Mass. Mozart presented this Mass, along with that in F and the *Misericordias*, to the prelate of the Holy Cross in Augsburg (as he informs his father on 20 November 1777)—which is surprising, for it is surely his weakest, his most Salzburgian, church work.

Salzburgian in a wholly different sense is the Offertory *Misericordias* (K. 222), which has already been mentioned in connection with Mozart's relations with Padre Martini and his attitude towards polyphony (p. 147). It is a contrapuntal teaching- and display-piece in the manner of Eberlin, Adlgasser, and Michael Haydn; and the second of the two themes—one homophonic, one contrapuntal—that Mozart developed in no fewer than 158 measures is even borrowed note for note from that motet by Eberlin (*Benedixisti Domine*) which Mozart copied out for himself in 1773. In this exhibition of his knowledge Mozart is almost as remote from his own poetic church style as in the Munich *Missa brevissima*. Nowhere is the chasm between *galant* and 'learned' more apparent than in these two works, chronologically so close to each other.

As a church musician, Mozart was then silent for over a year. Not until March 1776 did he find himself again composing for the church, with a second *Litaniae de venerabili altaris sacramento* (K. 243), which, strangely enough, differs from that of 1772 (K. 125) in its text. He found himself in another sense also, for this is one of his most personal, most

Mozartean works; only a purist's attitude towards church music can prevent one from marveling at it and loving it. To reject it because of such an attitude would be almost like rejecting the great Last Judgment or the Fall of the Damned of Rubens as painting, simply because some of the female blessed or damned are not at all shy about displaying certain undeniable charms. No true believer of the seventeenth or eighteenth century took offense at this display. Now since Mozart did not have to pay any attention to the Archbishop this time, he was free of musical restrictions. He stretched his wings, he wrote once more extensive arias for the soloists, he allowed himself polyphonic exploits, and built the *Pignus* into a double fugue, for which that of the *Miseri-cordias* seems a mere preliminary study; this is one of his greatest masterworks in the contrapuntal Salzburg style. At the same time he wrote homophonic passages that are so 'modern' that one fancies one could encounter them in such a work as Verdi's Requiem. Such a passage appears in the tutti of the *Hostia sancta*:

Ex. 88 [*Allegro comodo*] Tutti with full orchestra

For whom did Mozart write such things? We have no choice but to imagine that in the audience for such a litany, devoutness was mixed with connoisseurship; it was a concert, given on a liturgical pretext. This is indicated also by the arias with obbligato instruments, rich in coloratura passages; the incredibly rich instrumentation (with two violas); the direct and contrasting succession of the individual movements—what an effect, when the *Tremendum* enters with the three trombones! Once more the *Agnus Dei* borrows from the *Kyrie* for its 'thematic coda.' Surely it was works like this that Mozart had in mind when in his petition to the Municipal Council of Vienna in the spring of 1791 he spoke of his 'thorough knowledge of both the secular and ecclesiastical styles of music.'

It is as though this Litany swept away a dam that obstructed Mozart's writing for the church. In May 1776—this date is fairly certain from both external and internal evidence—there came a new Mass in C (K. 262), called *Missa longa* because of its striking length; and this length as well as the instrumentation show that it was intended not for the cathedral but probably for St. Peter's Church, whose brand-new and profuse Rococo decorations it fitted well. Despite the length of the work it cannot be regarded as belonging in the category of the *Missa solemnis*. It is still a *Missa brevis*, a choral Mass enlivened with solo parts but lacking arias; it is still laid out in individual movements according to a symphonic pattern, but Mozart filled this frame with counterpoint in all its forms and, to conclude the *Gloria* and *Credo*, wrote two display-fugues of the proudest kind. It is as though he then felt that he had done enough, for he made short work of the last three movements of the Mass. The work as a whole has consequently a somewhat empty and divided character; this Mass is perhaps a more respectable, more churchly, composition than the Litanies, but by the same token it is less heartfelt, warm, and personal. And the same is true of *Venite populi* (K. 260), an *Offertorium de venerabili sacramento*, written shortly afterwards, perhaps for Ascension Day in June 1776, for insertion in one of his own litanies or in one by another hand. If for the latter, Mozart was not being very polite, for the piece—in three parts, with an Adagio in the middle, after which there is a brief return to the beginning—requires the lavish apparatus of two four-part choruses, which engage in a contrapuntally enlivened sham fight. Although Mozart was probably unacquainted with the Venetian practice of writing for double choruses, he nevertheless achieved alternations, echo-effects, and overlappings of the two choruses similar to those of Giovanni Gabrieli or Giovanni Croce; and it is not surprising that Brahms, the lover of old music, superintended the first publication of this work in 1873 and that Franz Wüllner published it in his classical *Choral Studies* in an *a cappella* version.

In November and December 1776, Mozart wrote in succession three Masses, all in C (K. 257, 258, and 259). In order to distinguish among them more easily, we shall call them by their popular names: the Credo Mass, the Spaur Mass, and the Organ-Solo Mass.

The first of these Masses is separated from the Offertory for double chorus written in the spring of the same year by so wide a gap that, if one knew only these two works, one would have to attribute them to two different composers. Nowhere is our powerlessness to follow the creative progress of a great master more apparent than here. Nor can any of the works written between these two church compositions—the Haffner Serenade, a few *buffo* arias, a few divertimenti—be regarded as bridging the gap. What had happened? Mozart must have gone through an inner revolution, provoked by some uprooting experience, that caused him to devote himself so exclusively to church music for a time, as well as a revolution in his views about style in church music. He must have pondered over the means of achieving even greater brevity, not for the sake of the Archbishop this time, but for his own benefit. He renounced 'learnedness' completely, without entirely giving up polyphony. But polyphony acquired a new meaning, as did homophony also. Mozart's homophony is no longer *galant*; it is as 'unchurchly' as ever, perhaps even more unchurchly than previously, but it becomes more deeply felt, simpler, more personal. After the 'learned,' the motet-like, the *galant* church music of Mozart, one might speak of a song-like church music—in this instance, of a song Mass. Not that his older music lacked ideas that Mozart could have used as a connecting point; that Verdian passage in the second *Litaniae de venerabili* was one such idea. And in fact this *Missa brevis*, this second *Credo* Mass, stands at the beginning of a development that was completed by Verdi's Requiem. There are in both works the same awe and at the same time the same trusting and childlike fearlessness before God, the same melodic directness, which permit the utmost succinctness and an abundance of invention. The *Credo* device, to which the Mass owes its name, is not constructed with an eye towards contrapuntal use, as is that of the F major Mass of 1774, K. 192 (that mystic four-note device of Mozart's, which here plays a part in the *Sanctus*). It is quite simple and has the effect each time of a childlike outcry. But wherever it appears it has more polyphonic substance than all the 'learnedness' of previous Masses. Mozart had found a new style of expression for his church music.

The two Masses of December 1776 are not on as high a level as is that of November. The Spaur Mass (K. 258)—so called by Leopold in a letter (28 May 1778)—was written probably for the consecration of Friedrich Franz Joseph Count von Spaur, later dean of the cathedral in Salzburg, a ceremony in which the Archbishop, of course, took part.

It is quite as simple and direct in expression as the *Credo* Mass, for the short 'polyphonic' episodes, the suggestion of a *fugato* in the *Gloria*, are not very significant. Mozart shifts the emphasis more and more to the vocal element; at the same time, however, the accompanying motives of the two violins become more and more independent: they stress, as it were, the symphonic unity of the individual movements, without partaking in the expression. Devices for achieving the utmost brevity become ever more complete—this is particularly true of the Organ-Solo Mass (K. 259), the *Credo* of which, comprising 84 measures, perhaps holds the record. Only the *Benedictus*, in both Masses, is a noteworthy exception. In the Spaur Mass it is an extended movement proceeding with solemn motion and continuous alternating, overlapping, and combining of chorus and soli, as though a novice in a sacred rite were being continually entreated by the congregation to take a vow. In the other Mass it is distinguished by the fact that the accompaniment includes an obbligato part for the organ that because of the rapid tempo (*Allegro vivace*) takes on unusual brilliance. Both Masses are full of individual touches and beauties; particularly striking is the reverent 'Lydian' close of the *Dona* in the Spaur Mass—no *buffo-finale*, this.

As a church composer Mozart then fell silent again for almost a year. But in the late summer or fall of 1777 he wrote another Mass (in B-flat major, K. 275), in which he returned so completely to the sincerity, the childlike and songlike character of the first C major Mass of 1776, that the two could be considered sister-works written at the same time if we did not have such definite information about their dates. This B-flat major Mass was performed on 21 December 1777, probably for the first time, for Leopold wrote to his son at Mannheim on the following day: 'I wrote the above yesterday, Sunday, December 21st, on my return home after the Hours Service, when your Mass in B-flat was performed, in which the castrato [Ceccarelli] sang most excellently.' In my opinion it is a votive offering made by Mozart for the fortunate outcome of his long journey—it will be noticed that it was not sung officially until after his departure. If this Mass too were to be provided with a name, it might be called the 'Votive Mass' or, still better, the 'Marian Mass.' It is so intimate, the orchestral apparatus so modest, so lyric, that it has an almost private character, in which the distinction between sacred and secular vanishes. At the same time it has a South-German popular quality, which explains why no other Mass by Mozart may be found in old manuscript copies in so many church music libraries. The *Dona* is a kind of *vaudeville*, such as we find again later, for instance, in the last scene of *Die Entführung*: tutti and soli keep returning to the noble opening melody. At the same time, however, the work is full of fine-grained, unpretentious polyphony and above all of chromatic animation and daring—Mozart remains Mozart, even when he condescends to the people. The title 'Marian Mass' is perhaps justified because an Offertory to the Virgin, *Alma Dei creatoris* (in F, K. 277), very probably belongs to this work. From the standpoint of style it certainly belongs to it: the same forces are used, and the soli and tutti, quite lyric and almost entirely homophonic, are as simple and as heartfelt in the Offertory as in the Mass itself.

Before leaving home, on 9 September 1777, one day before the Feast of the Nativity of Mary, Mozart appealed to the Virgin with the Gradual or Motet *Sancta Maria mater Dei* (K. 273). '. . . Sed ab hac hora singulariter me tuis servitiis devoveo, . . . in vita protege, in mortis discrimine defende . . . ,' he sings. This wonderful piece stands between the *De profundis* of 1771 (K. 93) and the *Ave verum* of 1791; it has in common with the latter the fact that it is written for the same forces—a four part chorus, strings, and organ. And it is perhaps the peer of the *Ave verum*. It is songlike and at the same time a work of consummate skill; it is as profound as it is simple; it preserves humility in the presence of the divine and awe in the presence of the inscrutable, and it is full of trust and purity of feeling—one might say, full of intimacy. And one can scarcely listen to it without thinking of the stage it represents in Mozart's life—youth, the joy of youth, is gone; the disappointments of the journey through life begin. The Holy Virgin did not lend a particularly favorable ear to Mozart.

In Mannheim, at the beginning of 1778, Mozart wanted to write a grand Mass. He was tired of the flute compositions for the Dutch Maecenas: '. . . Hence as a diversion I compose something else, such as duets for clavier and violin, or I work at my Mass . . . If only the Elector were here, I should very quickly finish the Mass . . .' Only a *Kyrie* (in E-flat, K. 322) was completed; it is for large orchestra (including, since this was not Salzburg, the viola), grandly conceived and of the finest workmanship in both the vocal and the instrumental writing. It reminds us of *Die Zauberflöte*, and not only because of the solemn key. Of the other movements of the Mass only the beginning of a *Sanctus* or *Benedictus* has survived. Our knowledge of this work renders

especially regrettable the loss of the eight pieces composed for a
Miserere by Ignaz Holzbauer (Paris, March-April 1778, K. *Anh.* 1). For
Mozart had surely taken pains to match the very serious style of Holz-
bauer and at the same time to surpass it.

In March 1779, after his return home, Mozart wrote a new Mass (K.
317), known as the Coronation Mass because he allegedly composed it,
in fulfilment of a vow, for the miraculous image, crowned in 1751, of
the Virgin Mary on the Plain, near Salzburg. Each year, on the fifth
Sunday after Pentecost, a devotional service commemorating the coronation took place in this holy shrine; and if the legend is true, we
should have here a new Marian Mass by Mozart. But if this were so,
its character would be quite different from that of the B-flat major
Marian Mass of 1777. The apparatus is much more elaborate, the degree of solemnity much greater, the contrasts much stronger. Mozart
seems to have become much less concerned about stressing the symphonic unity, the over-all form, of the Mass: the most striking illustration of this is his employment of the music of the *Descendit de coelis*
for the *Amen* in the *Credo*, or the repetition of the *Kyrie-Andante* for
the *Dona nobis*, which rounds off the whole work. It has often and correctly been remarked that the soprano solo of the *Agnus Dei* foreshadows *Dove sono*, the Countess's aria in *Figaro*; and that the *Benedictus* begins like the rondo of a sonata. There are passages of a popular
nature, for example the solo for soprano and alto in the *Gloria* (notice
also the forbidden polytexture):

Ex. 89

but there are also exquisite and subtle touches, as when, right in the
Maestoso sections of the *Kyrie*, the fanfare motive is given not to the
trumpets but to the violins. New, and perhaps a product of the experiences of the long journey, is Mozart's ability to achieve, by lightning
strokes in the midst of apparently conventional music, a note of seriousness, profundity, and grandeur, while completely preserving the large
outline of the form; the *Credo*, especially, is full of such sudden strokes,
the sorrowful *Crucifixus* being perhaps the most beautiful of them.

With this Mass we have already approached the work that marks the pinnacle of Mozart's activity as a church composer: that magnificent torso, the C minor Mass of 1783. Our proximity to this work becomes even more noticeable when we consider the *Vesperae de Dominica* (K. 321), which, like the Coronation Mass, was written during 1779. (Unfortunately we do not know the occasion for which this work was composed, and are consequently in the dark about its exact date.) The contrasts here are even stronger than in the Mass of the same year; in order to perceive them clearly, one need only observe the keys in which this series of six psalms is written: only the *Dixit Dominus* and *Magnificat*, the first and last parts, are in C major, the principal key; the *Confitebor* is in E minor, the *Beatus vir* in B-flat major, the *Laudate pueri* in F major, and the *Laudate Dominum* in A major. In this work Mozart no longer concerns himself with the accepted notion of ecclesiastical style; the fact that the piece has been called, perhaps apologetically, a kind of oratorio is only another way of saying the same thing. The strongest contrasts succeed each other in the *Laudate pueri* and *Laudate Dominum*—the latter simply a sacred coloratura aria with obbligato organ, the former a choral setting of a thoroughly motet-like character, opening in strict canon *a cappella*, then flowing more and more freely—'laudate pueri'!; one imagines the marble choir boys of Donatello singing it. If Mozart had sent this movement to Padre Martini in Bologna, he might have received greater praise than he did for the Munich *Misericordias*—although that severe gentleman would perhaps have reproved Mozart for using the strictest style only at the beginning and not carrying it through to the end. But by this time Mozart had achieved complete inner independence, and followed his own ideas of style. The youthful sincerity, the song-like quality, of the church music of 1776 has now yielded to an impetuous manliness, a stormy, passionate solemnity. The *Beatus vir* is a good example of this. Chorus and orchestra seem to grow ever more independent of each other; the one becomes more vocal, the other more instrumental; and yet the unity is more complete than ever. The first and last movements are perhaps the most personal. At the end of the first we find once more Mozart's four-note device; and the last, the *Magnificat*, without any change of tempo fuses majesty with the social character of a symphonic Allegro into one incredible whole.

The same quality of stormy solemnity informs the fragment of a *Kyrie* (K. 323) and a *Regina coeli* (K. 276), both in C major, and both written at or just before the end of the Salzburg period. The *Kyrie*, which has the fullest sort of instrumentation, was once complete; since the viola is present and treated as an obbligato instrument, the piece was perhaps intended not for a Mass in the cathedral but as the first movement of a litany, in which Mozart permitted himself a Baroque verve and a magnificent freedom. Maximilian Stadler, the family friend of Mozart and Constanze, completed it in plain and honest fashion, and called it—rightly—a masterpiece. The *Regina coeli*, scored for somewhat smaller forces and perhaps written for a repetition of the Coronation Mass, is a typical example of Mozart's church style at the end of his Salzburg period. The text of the Marian antiphon is gathered together into a powerful whole and not, as in the antiphon settings of 1771 and 1772, distributed among separate contrasting sections. It is a concerto-like Allegro, with the richest sort of inter-relation between tutti and soli; it embodies the finest construction of the various sections, along with the clearest planning of the form; it has the same blend of the sacred and secular as the greatest creations of the architect Fischer von Erlach. For this music would burst asunder the little holy-shrine churches of the Rococo; it has grown too much in scope and breadth.

A year after the Coronation Mass, in March 1780, Mozart composed a new Mass (also in C, K. 337), the last one he wrote in Salzburg. It is traditionally designated a *missa solemnis*, but it is essentially a *missa brevis*, in which the *Gloria* and *Credo* are dealt with as briefly as possible—a Salzburg, archiepiscopal Mass *par excellence*. The fact that the orchestra does not include the viola is simply external evidence that the work was planned for the cathedral and with the Archbishop's attendance at the performance in view. In fact, it seems that Mozart may have received special instructions to be as brief as possible, for the torso of a second *Credo* for this Mass has survived, bearing the unusual inscription *Tempo di Ciaccona*—indicating an attempt to draw the *Incarnatus* and *Crucifixus* into the flow of the movement; the frenzied tempo of the movement is simply slowed down for 19 measures to accommodate them. But in the completed *Credo*, as well as in the *Gloria*, Mozart succeeds in achieving the utmost brevity and conciseness: he returns to the symphonic-symmetrical type of construction, so that the *Et resurrexit*, for example, corresponds to the beginning of the movement, and the *Et vitam venturi* to the *Descendit de coelis*. Perhaps Mozart, by writing the first three movements in forms that would please the Archbishop, wished to lull him into a false sense of security. For the

Benedictus is the most striking and revolutionary movement in all of Mozart's Masses—an extended piece in the harsh key of A minor, in the strictest contrapuntal style; not the usual soft greeting of him 'qui venit in nomine Domini' but rather an expression of grief and a challenge; in a certain sense a very 'churchly' piece indeed, and yet a blasphemous one. And as if to show Colloredo that he always has in mind his duties as archiepiscopal Court Organist, Mozart writes for the *Agnus* a long soprano solo with obbligato organ and solo wind-instruments, abruptly concluded by the tutti. It is quite in line with the rebellious character of Mozart in 1780 that he combined the art of annoying Colloredo with the art of pursuing his own ideals, for this Mass, too, is full of intimate and surprising strokes, such as the symbolism at the *Deum de Deo* in the *Credo*, and the soft close of the *Dona*, which is anything but festive.

Approximately the same relation that exists between this Mass and the Coronation Mass obtains between the *Vesperae solennes de confessore* of 1780 (K. 339; a more exact date cannot be given because the text gives no hint of the identity of the 'confessor' or saint) and the *Vesperae* of the previous year. Mozart has here become, if possible, still freer in his choice of keys (C, E-flat, G, D minor, F, C) and the contrasts clash even more strongly. The *Laudate pueri* here is an archaistic fugue on a theme containing that leap of a diminished seventh which can be traced back through Handel (*The Messiah*, Clavier Fugue), Kuhnau, Buxtehude, and Lubeck, to Pachelbel, and which Mozart himself employed again in the *Kyrie* of his *Requiem*; the *Laudate pueri* is not without an air of 'learnedness,' with its showy inversions and other devices. But immediately thereafter follows the *Laudate Dominum*, a soprano solo floating over a soft choral texture—a piece completely unconcerned with anything churchly, and so enchanting and poetic in its expression that it is difficult to find its counterpart, unless it be Schubert's Serenade, Op. 135, for alto and women's chorus. Only the grand, concluding *Magnificat* is at all churchly, in a purist sense; the three opening psalm verses display the greatest freedom, daring, and earnestness of expression. Anyone who does not know such settings does not know Mozart.

With this work Mozart's ecclesiastical activity for Salzburg came to its inner as well as to its external conclusion. It had become so free, so personal, that it alone would sooner or later have led to a break with the Archbishop—for let no one think that Colloredo, who had occasion to hear the works of other masters also, especially Michael Haydn's, was deaf to the subjectivity or musical rebelliousness of his Court Organist. The last work Mozart wrote while still in Salzburg service, though he did not write it in Salzburg, was a *Kyrie* (K. 341) for four voices accompanied by flutes, oboes, clarinets, bassoons, four horns, trumpets, timpani, strings (including viola), and organ. The mere presence of clarinets and viola precludes the assumption that the work was composed in and intended for Salzburg; it was written for Munich early in 1781, at the time of the production of *Idomeneo*. Mozart wished to offer the Elector, at whose hands he had suffered so many disappointments, one more proof of his ability, not only in the field of *opera seria* but in that of church music:

Be so kind as to send me the scores of the two masses, which I brought away with me—and also the Mass in B♭, for Count Seeau will be telling the Elector something about them shortly. I should also like people to hear some of my compositions in this style . . .

he writes to his father on 13 November 1780. But apparently he found the pieces he had written with the requirements of Salzburg in mind unsatisfactory for Munich; and he wrote, surely not before the completion and performance of *Idomeneo*, this first movement of a new Mass as a sample of his work. It is no longer, like his previous church music— with the apparently youthful exceptions (K. 139 and 65)—in a major key, but in D minor; festivity is superseded by solemnity; the marking *Andante maestoso* refers not to a few introductory measures but to the whole movement. D minor, the key of the Requiem; Mozart is not yet thinking of death, but with all its high solemnity *this* requiem breathes fear of the unknown, and at the same time gentleness, confidence in a delivering Providence; chromaticism always yields to the certainty of the cadence, agitation to tranquillity. The mastery of architectonic construction, the differentiation between the vocal and instrumental groups, the sensitiveness in the working out of detail (observe the treatment of any of the pairs of wind instruments)—they are enough to make one fall to one's knees. The beginning of the vocal part is marked *tutti*, but no soloists emerge from this tutti. Mozart wants to avoid anything that smacks of the *concertante*, of subjectivity. M. de Saint-Foix has made the penetrating remark: 'It would seem impossible to speak of counterpoint or homophony: properly speaking, neither the one nor the other reigns here.' The conflict between the *galant* and the 'learned' is resolved almost before it has arisen; Mozart, in the inscrutable fashion of genius, has anticipated it.

In Vienna, Mozart had no official connection with the church and church music; he was a free lance, and occupied himself at first with sonatas, serenades, piano concertos, and an opera. Four years before his death the Emperor named him Chamber Composer, but gave him no commissions to write for the palace chapel or St. Stephen's Cathedral. But, for all that, Mozart's religious feeling, which in him was almost the same thing as an artistic impulse, did not die out. There are artistic problems the solution of which is possible only in the field of church music. And so the summer of 1782 saw a strange occurrence—Mozart beginning to write a new Mass, in Vienna, not because of any external stimulus but from an inner need, as the fulfilment of a vow whose devoutness we should not wish to submit to a chemical analysis, for it is mixed with too great a proportion of creative urge. Mozart, Constanze's bridegroom, had 'made the promise in his heart of hearts' (letter of 4 January 1783) that when he brought her as his wife to Salzburg, he would have a newly composed Mass performed there; 'the score of half a Mass, which is still lying here waiting to be finished, is the best proof that I really made the promise.' But it waited in vain for completion. When Mozart actually arrived in Salzburg in August 1783, only the *Kyrie*, *Gloria*, *Sanctus*, and *Benedictus* were finished; of the *Credo* we have only the first section and the *Et incarnatus* (the latter in the form of a 'finished sketch'), of the *Agnus Dei* and *Dona*, not a note. Local tradition has it that the work, completed by the addition of movements from Mozart's earlier Masses, was rehearsed 23 August in the chapel and performed 25 August in St. Peter's church—naturally not in the Cathedral—with Constanze singing one or more of the soprano soli. This may or may not be true; what is certain is that Mozart had to produce a complete Mass or none at all, and that if he really did combine a *Credo* and *Agnus* from earlier works—more specifically, from earlier C major Masses—with the new *Kyrie*, *Gloria*, *Sanctus*, and *Benedictus*, he sacrificed his artistic conscience. That he had Constanze in mind in the *Christe* and *Laudamus* (but only there) is also certain: these passages are written for exactly the same voice and the same vocal qualifications as the Solfeggios (K. 393) of August 1782 'per la mia cara consorte.' It is certain, finally, that the Salzburg church musicians must have been skilful and well-routined people if they prepared this giant work in one rehearsal.

The fact that the work was planned for Salzburg is shown by the apparatus called for. It is the old apparatus and yet not the old one. Mozart employs only those instruments that were available in Salzburg (there are consequently no clarinets); but his use of them is different from what it was. As in the *Venite populi* (K. 260), he requires, in the *Qui tollis* of this Mass, an eight-part double chorus; but the movement has a different spirit from that of the decorative piece written in 1776. New in an external sense is the transition from a four-part to a five-part chorus for the *Gratias* and *Sanctus*. Mozart needs two sopranos for certain *concertante* effects, and in the four-part *Benedictus*, for example, he omits the alto, in order to treat the upper voices as one pair and the lower voices as another. Mozart still takes into account all the conditions of performance in Salzburg, but he no longer pays any attention to Salzburg tradition. This work is his entirely personal coming to terms with God and with his art, with what he conceived to be 'true church music.' It has rightly been said that this torso is the only work that stands between the B minor Mass of Bach and the D major Mass of Beethoven. The name of Bach is not used here thoughtlessly. For if it had not been for the crisis that the acquaintance with Bach caused in Mozart's creative career, and the surmounting of that crisis, the C minor Mass would never have taken the shape it did. The *Qui tollis*, for double chorus, in G minor, with the weightiest kind of orchestral accompaniment, in the broadest tempo, is, with its descending chromaticism, quite evidently conceived as a representation of the Saviour, making his way under whiplashes, and bearing the burden of the cross, towards Golgotha. It is a movement that ranks with the *Kyrie* of Bach's B minor Mass and the opening double chorus of the St. Matthew Passion; and the wonder would be only the greater if it could be established that Mozart did not know those works. The mighty invocation of the *Jesu Christe* (which in Bach merely serves to conclude the *Quoniam*) and the fugue on *Cum sancto Spiritu* form movements completely free of Baroque display as well as of the schoolroom dust of counterpoint and 'learnedness.' And this is true in perhaps even greater degree of the *Sanctus* and the double fugue of the *Osanna*. Bach is not the only master who stands behind this work: there are also Handel and the whole eighteenth century, including even the great Italians, such as Alessandro Scarlatti, Caldara, Porpora, Durante; one cannot single out particular names because Mozart sums up his century and transfigures its musical language. Once more we see that a work like this cannot be written without a great artistic heritage—a heritage, however, that the composer must be in a position to accept. The 'Italian' quality is apparent principally in the soprano solo in the *Laudamus*; in the duet of the two sopranos in the *Domine*, with its especially fine contrapuntal-obbligato string accompaniment; and in the concerto-like trio (two sopranos and tenor) of the *Quoniam*, which begins with the same theme as the 'contrapuntal' finale of the Piano Concerto K. 175. Mozart is as little concerned with purity of style as Bach was when he inserted the friendly, dialogue-like *Christe* between the two mighty and unbending *Kyrie* movements of his Mass. The greatest stumbling-block for church-music purists is the *Et incarnatus*, a soprano aria with strings, three obbligato wind instruments, and—this is usually forgotten—obbligato organ, whose part Mozart simply did not get around to writing out. In this movement there is a return to the spirit of the *Incarnatus* of the C minor Mass Mozart wrote when he was a lad; here is reminiscence and, at the same time, mastery. The reminiscence is of Italy—a Christmas song, a representation of the Divine Child lying in the cradle, the adoring Virgin, and, in the background, angels making music—an image of overpowering sweetness and naïveté. If a piece of music like this must be excluded from the church so should the circular panels by Botticelli, depicting the Infant Christ surrounded by Florentine angels; both works are equally profane. We have scarcely any inkling of how the rest of the *Credo* would have turned out: sketches for the *Et in Dominum* and *Crucifixus* show only a few measures. Mozart took the section from the beginning to the *Incarnatus* in one powerful and cantata-like sweep, apparently to leave room for broadening out in the other sections.

About a year and a half later, in March 1785, Mozart participated in one of the Lenten concerts of the Society of Musicians; he was to provide music for the second half of this 'academy.' He employed the *Kyrie* and *Gloria* of this Mass for the purpose; the sacred Latin text was transformed into Italian, and the Mass became an oratorio, *Davidde penitente*. Who supplied the text is not known; but it is a task that could have been done only in close collaboration with Mozart. The name of da Ponte, the librettist for the Italian Opera in Vienna, occurs to one as a likely possibility; Mozart had already known him for some time. Da Ponte, if it was indeed he, came out of the affair very adroitly, as always, and yet this *David* is an extremely self-contradictory work, for Mozart would never have written his powerful music to these words. Whether certain groups of tones resound to the *Kyrie* and *Christe eleison* or to the words 'da mali oppresso' makes a considerable difference; in the latter case the effect of the wonderful, consoling turn from C minor to E-flat major is lost. Despite the similarity of meaning, there is a difference between 'Gloria in excelsis Deo' and 'Cantiam le lodi . . . del Signor amabilissimo.' It is a strange David who sings: 'Se palpitate assai, è tempo da goder.' Mozart must have felt this, and so he did not hesitate to insert an aria for Adamberger, his Belmonte, after the duet 'Sorgi, o Signore' (= Domine Deus), and another for Caterina Cavalieri, the first Constanze in *Die Entführung*, after 'Se vuoi punisci mi' (= the tremendous *Qui tollis*). The first, like 'Martern aller Arten' in *Die Entführung*, is an aria with four *concertante* wind instruments; the second is a true bravura aria with elaborate coloratura passages. Such pieces were wholly admissible within the bounds of the oratorio, the sacred substitute for the opera. But it is to be hoped that no one will have the notion of reviving *Davidde penitente* in place of the Mass, simply because it is a 'final version' by Mozart himself. Let us be content with the *Kyrie* and *Gloria*. Why patch up the noble torso? Even a Michelangelo did not venture to add a head and limbs to the Greek torso in the Belvedere.

Mozart's activity as a church musician now ceased for some years. In place of compositions for the church we have compositions for the Masonic lodge, works in which Mozart felt quite free and for which there were no pre-established requirements to be taken into account. For in musical matters Freemasonry had no ritual. Mozart presumably had to create his own musical symbolism: the rhythm of the three knocks, which later achieved so highly symbolic a significance in *Die Zauberflöte*; and the slurring of two notes, symbolizing the ties of friendship, which plays a part in the very first work Mozart wrote for the lodge—*Gesellenreise* (K. 468), a song with clavier, containing three strophes and serving to greet the brothers upon their accession to the second degree of membership in the order:

Ex. 90

Die ihr   ei- nem   neu- en Gra- de

Another musical symbol of brotherhood is the progressions of parallel thirds that characterize the song 'for adjourning the meeting,' *Lasst uns mit geschlungnen Händen,* in Mozart's last Masonic composition (K. 623). The key, too, has symbolic significance: E-flat major, at once heroic and mild—'humane'—is chosen for *Die Maurerfreude* (K. 471), Mozart's cantata in honor of Ignaz von Born, the director of the Lodge of True Harmony. Otherwise the work is a true *Verein* composition, as is also, unfortunately, the abovementioned more pretentious 'Small Masonic Cantata: consisting of a Chorus, an Aria, two Recitatives, and a Duo for Tenor and Bass,' written in 1791 for the consecration of a Masonic temple. Finally, the choice of timbres—men's voices and, especially, wind instruments—is of course symbolic also; one could call clarinets and basset horns the appropriate Masonic instruments. Thus the two most beautiful Masonic compositions are instrumental works: the Adagio for two clarinets and three basset horns (K. 411) and a piece already mentioned in our biographical section, the *Maurerische Trauermusik* (K. 477), written at the end of 1785 on the death of two brother-Masons of high birth—a work in which the tone is set, and not only in a literal sense, by the oboes, clarinet, basset horn, contra-bassoon, and two horns (or two additional basset horns) that are called for besides the strings. The Adagio was evidently intended for a solemn entrance-procession of the members of the lodge; the Masonic knocking-theme is indicated softly; and the piece is probably an introduction to a complete instrumental lodge ritual to which belong also an Allegro (K. Anh. 95) and a wonderful Adagio (K. Anh. 93), both unfinished, as well as an Adagio for two basset horns and bassoon (K. 410) published as a canon (what a beautiful symbol!).

The *Maurerische Trauermusik* perhaps best justifies our unusual procedure in treating Mozart's Masonic compositions in a chapter on church music. Though it is not a church work, it is a religious composition—the link between the solemn Mass in C minor and the Requiem. The key is the same as that of the Kyrie of the Mass; and what the trombones suggest in the Mass is now openly expressed by the wind instruments in a solemn chorale or march: sorrow, earnestness, resignation, and consolation. If one wished, one could find all the symbols of Masonry in the 69 measures: the parallel thirds and sixths, the slurs, the knocking-rhythm. The thought of death, which had already governed the *Kyrie,* is present here, except that now the ecclesiastical element has been transformed into a Masonic one; but behind both the ecclesiastical and Masonic elements is the same great, human feeling of Mozart. The piece, which in the employment of the chorale goes back to Mozart's studies of Bach, is at the same time a bridge to the noblest scene, the most serious situation, in *Die Zauberflöte*; sacred and secular music flow into one stream.

Mozart's last two church works—the *Ave Verum* for four voices and strings (K. 618) and the Requiem for soli, chorus, and orchestra—also occupy a peculiar position in the church; the one, small and complete, the other large and, in every sense, unfinished. The small Motet, probably composed to be used in the Corpus Christi service by the school-teacher and choir-leader Anton Stoll in Baden near Vienna, a man who also performed Mozart's older church works and who looked out for Constanze a bit, has become one of Mozart's best-known works—so well known that the mastery with which it is fashioned, the 'second' simplicity, the perfection of modulation and voice-leading, lightly introducing polyphony as a final intensification, are no longer perceived. Here, too, ecclesiastical and personal elements flow together. The problem of style is solved.

What shall one say, finally, about the Requiem, not only Mozart's last church work but his last work of any kind? 'Last work'—this is indeed a concept into which are crystallized all possible associations, and especially in this work, which was born in such 'romantic' circumstances and the completion of which was prevented by death. No other work by Mozart has caused so much ink to be spilled, and none has been so unjustly estimated—chiefly by people who knew none of Mozart's other church works, not the C minor Mass, nor the litanies, nor any of the C major Masses of 1776. And in fact it is difficult to remain completely cool and to let the facts speak for themselves.

The Mass was commissioned, but Mozart is said not to have known who ordered it. It was a Count Franz Walsegg zu Stuppach, a musical dilettante, who, to adorn himself with borrowed plumes, liked to perform in his castle and its chapel the works of others, which he gave out to be his own. He had lost his wife some years before and contemplated a requiem for her. In July 1791 he sent his steward Leutgeb to Mozart, with a commission to write such a work. Mozart began and sketched about 40 pages of the score; then he had to lay it aside in order to do *La Clemenza di Tito* and *Die Zauberflöte*. He was able to finish only the *Requiem* and *Kyrie*, and to sketch the eight sections from the *Dies irae* through the *Hostias*—that is, to set down in the score the voice parts, bass, and hints for the instrumentation. The last three movements were completely lacking.

For fear that if the completed manuscript were not handed over to the patron he would not only not pay that portion of the fee which was still due but would demand the return of the portion he had already paid, the widow appealed first to Joseph Eybler and other musicians to finish it, and finally to Süssmayr . . . Süssmayr expressed willingness to do so and first copied everything that Mozart had only sketched and then entered the missing instrumentation in his copy in such a manner as seemed to him best to conform with Mozart's intentions. According to Süssmayr's definite statement, he then composed the close of the *Lacrimosa*, the *Sanctus*, *Benedictus*, and *Agnus Dei*, and repeated the fugue of the *Kyrie* to the words 'Cum sanctis.' The work thus completed was then . . . given to the patron.*

Constanze maintained her version of the affair, a plain fraud, as long as possible, until the honest Süssmayr clarified the situation in a letter (8 February 1800) to Breitkopf & Härtel—but in vain, for the sentimentality of the nineteenth century would have no part of this explanation.

The Requiem, like the great C minor Mass, remained a torso, but in a quite different sense. In the Mass we have the whole *Kyrie*, the whole *Gloria*, the whole *Sanctus* and *Benedictus*, and all of these movements in a version that is authentic down to the smallest detail. In the Requiem small doubts arise as early as in the *Dies irae* and large ones after the first eight measures of the *Lacrimosa*. And yet, with the very first measures of the Introit—*Requiem aeternam dona eis, Domine*—we know definitely Mozart's intention, his attitude towards death. It is no longer entirely ecclesiastical; it is mixed with elements of Masonry. Is it not strange that in this Introit the two pairs of woodwinds—basset horns and bassoons—predominate and the strings are allotted what amounts to only an accompanying role? The mild resignation of the beginning of this movement is not maintained throughout: at the words 'Exaudi orationem meam' the jagged accompanying figure in the orchestra seems to symbolize rebellion rather than prayer. A fugue then develops on *Kyrie*, a fugue based on two themes, one of which contains the leap of a diminished seventh that we have already encountered in the *Laudate pueri* of the Vespers of 1780. This is no academic, 'learned' double fugue; no other master of the time would have dared to venture so deep into the darker regions of harmony. And yet it is not a wholly Mozartean fugue: a residue of Handelian archaism clings to it; it is not

* Köchel, 3rd ed., p. 809.

even one of his own, personal themes that Mozart develops here, but a borrowed one. And Süssmayr made an unfortunate choice in picking just this movement to repeat as the conclusion of the whole work. After the sublime choral setting of the *Dies irae*—sublime because it is at once dramatic and sacred—we encounter doubtful elements again in the *Tuba mirum*, in which the text is divided in *concertante* fashion among the soloists, and in which Süssmayr carries on the solo trombone of the beginning long after it has called all the resurrected before God's throne. But this unquestionably Mozartean solo trombone is itself a painful matter—one cannot shake off the impression that the heavenly player is exhibiting his prowess instead of announcing terribly the terrible moment of the Last Judgment.

In the *Rex tremendae majestatis*, the *Recordare*, the *Confutatis*, and the *Lacrimosa* (unfinished)—four connected movements—Mozart found himself again; they are on the lofty plane of the C minor Mass. The appeal to the Last Judge changes from an outcry to fervent prayer; and in the wonderful setting of the *Recordare* the soloists' beseeching of the 'Mediator' is already heeded; this movement is one of the purest, most skilful, and most enrapturing that Mozart ever wrote. After the dramatic *Confutatis* there follows finally the troubled and awful crescendo of the *Lacrimosa*, with which Mozart breaks off, but which he surely would have developed more broadly than Süssmayr did. Mozart treated the *Domine* and *Hostias* in motet-fashion, the former contrapuntally and the latter homophonically, and concluded each movement with a rather neutral chromatic fugue—*Quam olim Abrahae*—which again is not without an archaistic flavor. We need not concern ourselves with the rest of the work, since it originated with Süssmayr; only for the *Benedictus* did Süssmayr apparently have an indication of Mozart's intentions, in the form of six or eight measures in Mozart's manuscript which Süssmayr developed. He then completely upset the proportions of the work with the *Osanna* fugue, which, quite apart from the insignificance of the theme, is much too short. And yet, by the return of the *Requiem* to the words 'Lux aeternae' the work is rescued once more for Mozart, the self-contradiction of the whole is somewhat—not entirely—overcome. The total impression remains. Death is not a terrible vision but a friend. Only one composer after Mozart was able to soar to the height of this conception: Giuseppe Verdi, in the Requiem for Alessandro Manzoni.

19. *Aria and Song*

*I*N THIS CHAPTER, which is of the nature of an intermezzo, we approach the subject of the final section of our discussion—the opera. But have we ever quite left that subject? Is not almost all the instrumental music of the second half of the eighteenth century in general, and that of Mozart in particular, penetrated through and through with the spirit of the opera—with the spirit of *opera buffa* even more than with that of *opera seria?* Does not Mozart employ the same procedure in joining the *Gloria* and *Credo* movements into musical units as in the construction of the finale of an *opera buffa?* Are not his solemn Masses and his litanies already full of 'profane' arias, hardly to be distinguished from those of an Italian *opera seria?* Nowhere does the purely Italian derivation of Mozart's style show more clearly than in the aria and all other forms that have more or less to do with opera. In the field of instrumental music Mozart could make a certain junction with French style. In Schobert, Eckard, Honnauer, and Raupach, he had French or half-French models, and he imitated them. And when he returned to Paris, in May and June 1778, he wrote for Noverre, the great reformer of the ballet, thirteen or fourteen pieces for a ballet entitled *Les petits riens*, which was interpolated as an entr'acte in the performances of *buffo* operas by Piccinni and Anfossi. They are at the same time Mozartean and very French, this overture and these andantinos, larghettos, and gavottes. And in all Mozart's works there is hardly anything more pointed and Gallic than the *Gavotte joyeuse* in F, a piece of some length, and the shorter *Gavotte gracieuse* in A, or the pastoral pantomime, with its coquettish staccati, trills, *appoggiature*, and rhythmic and melodic piquancies.

But among all Mozart's vocal music we have very few examples of French style. Yes, he wrote two *ariettes* with French text, to which we shall return. But he never tried his hand at French opera, although he was quite sure of his ability to compose one. On many occasions he spoke of his irresistible urge to write opera, whether with German, French, or Italian text: 'French rather than German, Italian rather than French.' But French opera had no arias, in the sense in which Mozart understood the term. When, as a boy, in 1763 or 1764, he visited the Académie Royale, the great opera-house of Paris, both he and Leopold must have felt exactly as old Carlo Goldoni had felt a few years earlier—Goldoni, who thoroughly understood Neapolitan and Venetian *opera buffa* and *opera seria*. His account is so characteristic that it must be quoted:

The orchestra began, and I found the harmony of the instruments of a superior kind, and very accurate in point of execution. But the overture appeared to me cold and languid: I was sure it was not Rameau's; for I had heard his overtures and ballet airs in Italy. [Presumably in Parma, the gate through which French music passed into Italy.]
    The action commenced; and, notwithstanding my favorable situation, I could not hear a word. However, I patiently waited for the airs, in the expectation that I should at least be amused with the music. The dancers made their appearance, and I imagined the act finished, but heard not a single air. I spoke of this to my neighbor, who laughed at me, and assured me that we had had six in the different scenes which I had heard. 'What!' said I, 'I am not deaf; the instruments never ceased accompanying the voices, sometimes more loudly, and sometimes more slowly than usual, but I took the whole for recitative' . . .*

The choruses made more of an impression on Goldoni, but he compares them with the psalms of 'Corelli, Biffi, and Clari,' which is hardly a compliment for theater music. At the end, one of the ladies, accompanied by chorus and ballet, sang a *chaconne*, which had no connection with the opera, and 'this agreeable surprise might have enlivened the piece, but it was a hymn rather than an air.' The author of *Il Burbero benefico*, *La Locandiera*, and *La Bottega del caffè*, usually so amiable, expressed his opinion in the sentence: 'It is a paradise for the eyes, and a hell for the ears.' Now Mozart, brought up in the Italian atmosphere of Salzburg, never let himself be influenced, not even in his *recitativo accompagnato*, by the 'endless recitative' of French opera.

In the spring of 1764 he went to London, and there again breathed the familiar air of Italian opera. He met the composer who was to be his model in so many forms up until the first Vienna years, Johann Christian Bach, and the singer Giovanni Manzuoli, of whose voice and

---

* *Memoirs*, translated by John Black, and published in Boston in 1887, p. 363.

style of performance one needs only to read Burney's description in order to recognize Mozart's ideal: 'the most powerful and voluminous soprano that had been heard on our stage since the time of Farinelli, and his manner of singing was grand and full of taste and dignity.' When Johann Christian and the young Mozart—who later had the good fortune to compose his *Ascanio in Alba* for Manzuoli as the protagonist—had this *castrato* as a model, the vocal portraits they made were almost identical. For the moment, to be sure, the lad was not writing for protagonists. His first essay in stage composition was an aria for a 'secondary,' the tenor Ercole Ciprandi, who at the time was singing the role of a father in Metastasio's *Ezio*—a *pasticcio*, that is, an opera containing arias written by various composers—at the King's Theatre. This was the aria *Va dal furor portata*, K. 21, which had been composed by innumerable others, including, three decades earlier (1732), George Frederic Handel. The text is passionate but concentrated, as befits the secondary role and the dramatic situation: a scheming father calls out reproaches after his too impulsive daughter, who has just left the stage. The young Mozart quite misses the point: he writes a *bravura* aria of the most conventional type, with an accompaniment that, despite its relatively modest orchestration, is overelaborate. The composer who was to write *Don Giovanni* had at this time no conception of dramatic function or of the 'dignity' of an aria, and he obviously wanted to give his singer an occasion for display, as presumably did all the other contributors to the *pasticcio*.

What did the convention of the aria as a form consist in? In its instrumental, 'monumental' character; it was a concerto in miniature, in which the voice replaced the solo instrument. The strange thing about its development, historically speaking, is that the form of the monumental aria was perfected, in the works of Stradella and Alessandro Scarlatti, earlier than the concerto, so that the concerto was actually fashioned after the aria, and not vice versa. But about the middle of the eighteenth century, the aria could truly be called a little concerto for a vocalist with orchestral accompaniment, in which the place of the andantino was usually taken by a very brief *seconda parte*, contrasting with the *prima parte* in key and in its reduced orchestration, and in place of the third movement this *prima parte* was simply repeated. The form of the *prima parte* was just like that of the first movement of the concerto: *ritornello* for the tutti, entry of the soloist, modulation to a neighboring key, with a similar distribution of roles, often with a more animated dialogue between tutti and solo, and finally a reprise, often with coda. At the repetition of this concerto-in-miniature, the singer was expected to heighten the listener's interest in his accomplishments by more elaborate ornamentation. This was an art of musical statics, in which the composer was always in the service of the singer, as the whole institution of opera had been since about the middle of the seventeenth century. The monumental aria is the symbol in operatic history of the triumph of the singer, the *primo uomo*, or the *prima donna*; it is the deadly enemy of the dramatic element. In the concert-hall, or as a part of an oratorio, however, it was a completely legitimate form, and thus we are not surprised that Mozart, all his life long, composed concert arias into which he poured the riches of his vocal invention and his orchestral skill.

The first of these concert arias, composed in The Hague in 1765 and revised in January 1766, is (amusingly enough, after the 'father aria' for Ciprandi) a 'mother aria,' on a text from Metastasio's *Artaserse: Conservati fedele*, K. 23. In it, Mother Mandane warns her parting son: 'Be faithful to me, remember that I remain here, suffering, and think of me now and again; for I, by virtue of my love for thee, will speak with thee whenever I speak with my own heart.' How could such a text be set to music except in the style of the *Andante amoroso* of a divertimento? The aria is much simpler than that for Ciprandi, having string accompaniment only, but in a few chromatic turns of phrases and repetitions, such as 'Ricordati!' (Remember!), it is characteristically Mozartean.

This book does not aim to analyze every aria of Mozart's. On his return to Salzburg Mozart wrote two so-called *licenze*—that is, arias written to follow the end of an opera, in which the most honored guest present is directly addressed. In Vienna, the licenze grew into a miniature scena, in which the whole of Olympus was displayed; but in Salzburg these arias were on a more modest scale. Both the Mozart arias in question, the one for tenor, K. 36, and the other for soprano, K. 70, are just as provincial as they are full of bravura. In Italy, knowing that he would be able to write a whole opera, Mozart then wrote for practice a whole series of arias and scenas the texts of which, apparently, his father sought out in the works of Metastasio—texts that set the most varied problems. In one of the most imposing (K. 88, *Fra cento affanni e cento*), Mozart for the first time omits the full reprise, repeating only the second half of the first section. He always had Manzuoli in mind as the ideal singer, and a comparison of two beginnings may show what kind of model he remembered:

Ex. 91

The second of these incipits is the beginning of an aria sung by Manzuoli in Johann Christian Bach's *Adriano in Siria*, which Mozart had heard in London in 1765. (He later wrote out this particular aria for his beloved Aloysia in Mannheim 'mit ausgesetztem Gusto'—that is, with full notation of the ornaments.) Mozart's own aria, thanks to this admirable model, developed into so remarkable a piece that, if we did not know when it was written, and if it were not for the overloading of the orchestral parts, we should assign it to a much later period.

But since, from the time of *Mitridate* on, Mozart had plentiful opportunities for writing the lengthiest operas—at least *opere serie*, *feste teatrali*, and oratorios—he no longer wrote any arias for practice. All we have are a few discarded earlier versions left over from certain operas, as testimony to the seriousness with which he took the composition of arias. Not until the year 1775, after the performance of *La Finta giardiniera* in Munich, do we again find a few independent arias, this time intended as interpolations or substitutions in *buffo* operas that a touring Italian opera troupe must have brought to Salzburg at this period. For the first two arias of this sort, *Si mostra la sorte* (K. 209), and *Con ossequio, con rispetto* (K. 210), I cannot determine the names of the operas in which they were interpolated. They were both sung by a *tenorino di garbo* (a charming little tenor), a joyful young lover, who was apparently the rival of an influential old fool, a Pantaloon. In the first aria, he sings the praise of purposeful audacity in love; in the second he makes ironic compliments, with humorous asides, to the old addle-pate. Already in these two pieces we see that Mozart, spiritually as well as musically, has more to say in the field of *opera buffa* than in that of *opera seria*, and we see the superiority of the *opera buffa* as the species of the future. In it, from the beginning, there was always an element of parody of the *opera seria*; it was freer, more independent of tradition; it was anti-heroic; it had a direct relation to life, and consequently it always had form, but no set form. And thus the accompaniment was never mere display or decoration, but always wit in tones, at least in Mozart. Consider the *piquanterie* of the interlude that follows the amorous beginning of the first aria:

Ex. 92

In a third *buffo* aria, Voi avete un cor fedele (K. 217), dating from the autumn of the same year, 1775, we are on firmer ground. This was written to substitute for a number in Baldassare Galuppi's *Le Nozze*, one of the great successes since its first performance in Bologna, in 1755, of the amiable 'Buranello,' who may well be called the father of the Venetian *opera buffa*. The leading character in Goldoni's libretto, the chambermaid Dorina, must decide, in accordance with the wishes of her master and mistress, between two lovers, the domestics Titta and Mingone, though she likes neither of them, having long ago secretly given her heart to the 'laughing third party,' the bailiff Masotto. In the original aria, Dorina addresses the two rivals, both of whom she leads around by the nose:

Ex. 93   B. GALUPPI, 1755

Voi a-ve-te un bel vi-set-to,   rotondet-to,   vez-zo-set-to

But the troupe that had come to Salzburg was evidently so reduced in personnel that to represent Titta and Mingone only one lover was available, of whom Dorina accordingly disposes in the most agreeable way:

Ex. 94   MOZART

Voi a-ve-   te un cor te-de- le   K.217

'Your heart may be true,' she says, 'as long as you are passionately in love. But how will it be when we are married? I do not trust you and will not make up my mind!' This rondo-aria, of which the structure may be represented by the symbols A (*Andantino grazioso*)—B (Allegro)—A' (abbreviated and varied form of A)—B'—A'' (still further abbreviated form of A)—C (*Allegro spiritoso*)—exemplifies in itself the superiority and greater subtlety of the *opera buffa* as compared with the *opera seria*: there is no stereotyped return to the beginning, but rather a dramatic development, a musical counterpart of what is happening on the stage. Even the coloratura figuration, which is plentiful even here, has the charm of significant gesture, of psychological clarity, coquetry, humor. No wonder the *opera buffa* involuntarily became more and more the deadly enemy of the *seria*; no wonder it forced the *seria* to imitate it, and ever more clearly exposed the unnaturalness of the highfalutin *aria monumentale*.

In another aria, or rather scena, *Clarice cara mia sposa* (K. 256), dating from the autumn of 1776, Mozart approached not only the *opera buffa* but the *commedia dell'arte*. This was an interpolation or a substitution written for Piccinni's *L'Astratto, ovvero il Giocatore fortunato*. The situation is approximately as follows: Capitan Faccenda (Master Busy-Body) expatiates with incredible volubility upon the virtues that his future wife, Clarice, must possess, while Clarice's father, Don Timoteo, makes feeble attempts to stem the torrent of his words. The two are stock figures of the improvised *commedia*, and thus Mozart, with no attempt to characterize them more profoundly, is satisfied with a simple crescendo, which reminds us at once of Don Bartolo's aria in *Figaro* and of Basilio's calumny aria in Rossini's *Barbiere di Siviglia*. The comic effect is overwhelming. But what is much more interesting is that the dissolution of the stereotyped monumentality of the *aria seria* is already far advanced in a scena Mozart wrote for the alto *castrato* of the traveling opera troupe in 1776: *Ombra felice—Io ti lascio, e questo addio* (K. 255). This singer's name was Francesco Fortini, and the troupe was under the direction of the *Capo Comico* Pietro Rosa. A long and highly dramatic accompanied recitative is followed by a vocal rondo, of which both the text and the structure were borrowed by Mozart from his beloved Johann Christian Bach. The latter had written in 1774 a concert piece for soprano with obbligato oboe and clavier, a work of blooming melodic charm and most delicate treatment; but Mozart in no way yields to him, despite the much simpler orchestra he uses, and fills the piece from beginning to end, despite its considerable length, with dramatic feeling.

Hardly any of the concert arias and interpolations in the operas of other composers that Mozart wrote from this time on are neutral or stereotyped, and it is to be emphasized that in the interpolations he never showed the slightest trace of 'professional ethics,' i.e. he never suited his music to the characteristics of the particular work in which it was to be used—to do which he would usually have had to descend beneath his own level—but always gave his very best. In his purely concert arias he was sometimes more dramatic than in his operas, since the situation had to be supplied by the imagination. This is true of the very first of these arias that is neither exercise nor interpolation, the scena *Ah, lo previdi . . . Ah, t'invola . . . Deh, non varcar* (K. 272), which he wrote in August 1777 for Josefa Duschek (née Hambacher), 'the Bohemian Gabrielli,' wife of the pianist and composer Franz Duschek of Prague. This was his first contact with Josefa, which was to lead to a comradeship of many years; it was in the 'Bertramka' in Smichov near Prague, the country cottage of the Duscheks, that Mozart wrote the last measures of his *Don Giovanni*. The occasion for Josefa Duschek's arrival was a visit to her grandfather Weiser, an artisan who had grown rich, and whose fortune she was later to inherit. At this first meeting there was perhaps on Mozart's side a little more than comradeship; perhaps he was a little in love, for Josefa was young—only a little older than Mozart himself—beautiful, and vivacious. She never went on the stage, being what we should now call a concert and oratorio singer. The judgments of posterity on her personality and her art are various. She was known as the mistress of Count Clam; and it appears that her voice early lost its bloom. The worst opinions about her originated with Leopold Mozart and Friedrich Schiller.

In any case, Mozart almost never wrote anything more ambitious, or containing stronger dramatic feeling, than this aria. The text is from Paisiello's *Andromeda*, first performed in Milan in 1770. Mozart had apparently got hold of a copy of the libretto at that time (it was very likely the work of his own librettist, V. A. Cigna Santi) and the situation represented by the aria had remained in his memory. It is a very complicated text. The lover of Andromeda appears to have received a mortal wound at the hands of her rescuer, Perseus, and the conflict of her emotions rises to the pitch at which extreme pain passes over into a wild but tender ecstasy: Andromeda wishes to die, so as to await her dying lover on the further bank of the river Lethe. When Mozart shortly afterwards was teaching this scena to his Aloysia, he urged on her the greatest dramatic verity (letter of 30 July 1778):

ı advise you to watch the expression marks—to think carefully of the meaning and the force of the words—to put yourself in all seriousness into Andromeda's situation and position!—and to imagine that you really are that very person.

Indeed, this is no scena in the traditional sense, in which two arias of contrasted expression are introduced and connected by recitative. The inspiration, the high quality of the musical invention, the beauty and power of expression with the use of the most modest means—small orchestra, consisting of nothing but strings, oboes, and horns—were never surpassed by Mozart himself. He is so swept up in the genuineness and sincerity of his feeling that he forgets completely what he himself once called 'cut-up noodles'—that is, *coloratura*.

In subsequent arias, written for Aloysia, he unfortunately did not forget this element. For his beloved must display all the facets of her art, and one of the elements of the art of song is coloratura. The first of these arias, *Alcandro, lo confesso . . . Non sò, d'onde viene*, dated 24 February 1778, was originally intended for the tenor Anton Raaff, a famous fixture of the Mannheim opera, for whom Mozart a short time later was to write the role of Idomeneo, and who was already sixty-four years old. The aria was written also to compete with one of Mozart's favorite arias by Johann Christian Bach, which, in the 1765 performance of *Ezio* he had heard sung by the tenor Ciprandi, for whom he had written his own first attempt at an aria. About the origin of no other work of Mozart's do we have such exact information as about this one (letter of 28 February 1778, previously quoted):

For practice I have also set to music the aria *Non sò d'onde viene*, etc. which has been so beautifully composed by Bach . . . At first I had intended it for Raaff; but the beginning seemed to me too high for his voice. Yet I liked it so much that I would not alter it; and from the orchestral accompaniment, too, it seemed to me better suited to a soprano. So I decided to write it for Mlle Weber. Well, I put it aside and started off on the words *Se al labbro* for Raaff. But all in vain! I simply couldn't compose, as the first aria kept on running in my head. So I returned to it and made up my mind to compose it exactly for Mlle Weber's voice. It's an *Andante sostenuto* (preceded by a short recitative); then follows the second part, *Nel seno a destarmi*, and then the *sostenuto* again . . .

The text of the aria, from Metastasio's *Olimpiade*, makes sense only when sung by a man: King Clisthenes beholds an unknown man, who is really the son he has long believed dead, and expresses the strange feelings of sympathy that seize him involuntarily. In Mozart's version, the text becomes a declaration of love: 'I know not whence comes this tender inclination, this agitation that fills my breast, this frost that chills my veins. Such stormy conflicts in my bosom cannot, methinks, arise from sympathy alone.' Now, nothing is more instructive than the comparison of these two arias—the one by Johann Christian and the other by Mozart—to show us what Mozart learned from his model, and what he could not learn from any model. In the external structure of the piece Mozart follows Johann Christian exactly: there is a principal section in ¾ meter, a middle section in duple meter (*allegro assai*), and then a reprise. But despite all its melodic charm, how schematic in form and how neutral in expression throughout is the aria by Johann Christian in comparison with the richness, the subtlety of the transitions, and the throbbing vitality of every detail in the one by Mozart! We understand well how Mozart himself was forced to say: 'This is now the best aria she has . . .' (letter of 28 February 1778). 'The members of the orchestra [consisting, this time, of flutes, clarinets, bassoons, horns, and strings] never ceased praising the aria and talking about it' (letter of 24 March 1778). The piece became in fact a favorite of Aloysia's and remained so even after she moved to Vienna.

Mozart wrote two more concert arias in Mannheim: one, finally, for old Raaff himself (K. 295), and the other, *Basta, vincesti . . . Oh, non lasciarmi, no* (K. 486a), for Dorothea Wendling, wife of the flutist in the Court orchestra, who had formerly been the mistress of the Elector. Mozart gives us very exact information, again, about the composition of the first of these (letter of 28 February 1778):

I was at Raaff's yesterday and brought him an aria which I composed for him the other day. The words are: *Se al labbro mio non credi, bella nemica mia*, etc. I don't think that Metastasio wrote them. He liked it enormously. One must treat a man like Raaff in a particular way. I chose these words on purpose, because I knew that he already had an aria on them: so of course he will sing mine with greater facility and more pleasure. I asked him to tell me candidly if he did not like it or if it did not suit his voice, adding that I would alter it if he wished, or even compose another.

'God forbid,' he said, 'the aria must remain just as it is, for nothing could be finer. But please shorten it a little, for I am no longer able to sustain my notes.' 'Most gladly,' I replied, 'as much as you like. I made it a little long on purpose, for it is always easy to cut down, but not so easy to lengthen.' After he had sung the second part, he took off his spectacles, and looking at me with wide-open eyes, said: 'Beautiful! Beautiful! That is a charming *seconda parte*.' And he sang it three times. When I took leave of him he thanked me most cordially, while I assured him that I would arrange an aria in such a way that it would give him pleasure to sing it. For I like an aria to fit a singer as perfectly as a well-made suit of clothes . . .

We see that Mozart was still very different from later musicians, who cast their melodies upon the air, and counted upon a future generation of ideal singers. Mozart was not limited by his knowledge of his singers and protagonists; on the contrary, he was inspired by it. Thus this aria has become for us a perfect portrait of the voice and style of the famous old tenor, who, as we read in an old source (Lipowsky, *Baierisches Musik-Lexikon*), 'even in his later years sang with feeling and delightful charm.' Keeping within the range of a twelfth, the aria is of a perfect, quiet, lyric, singing character. The middle portion, which pleased Raaff so particularly, is an evidence of Mozart's cunning: it is a little old-fashioned in effect, à la Hasse, for Mozart naturally did not want to shock the old man with any excess of boldness or revolutionary 'modernity.' In the orchestra part every note 'sets' well; what a far cry from Mozart's youthful zeal to make every instrument 'work' as much as possible. Nor is any one of the wind instruments treated in *concertante* fashion; this is an aria without any virtuoso elements.

Very similar, on a smaller scale, is the aria for Dorothea Wendling, which Mozart sketched on 27 February and later himself completed for orchestra (flutes, bassoons, horns, and strings). The text, from Metastasio's *Didone*, had been sought out by the singer herself, and is not inappropriate: Dido, after a scene of simulated scorn or indifference, is suddenly disarmed in a despairing and unrestrained outburst of emotion. Here again, Mozart keeps in mind the conventions of the aria form and the abilities, obviously no longer remarkable, of the singer; but here again it is impossible for him to stick to the conventional scheme. He does not compose a special *seconda parte*, but rather sets the entire eight-line text to a steadily flowing melodic stream and inserts before the repetition, which is greatly intensified, a short, free recitative instead. *Andantino espressivo* reads the heading. The *aria monumentale* has become the scena.

In Paris, in June 1778, Mozart sketched a new grand scena for Aloysia (K. 316), choosing as his model the address of the Queen to the people of Thessaly (*Popoli di Tessaglia . . . Io non chiedo, eterni dei*) in the Italian version of *Alceste* by Calzabigi and Gluck. He did not finish it until 8 January 1779, in Munich, a few weeks after the break with his beloved; perhaps he intended it as a sort of 'double bar,' symbolizing the end of his relationship with her. We may wonder whether he was then still of the opinion expressed in his letter to Aloysia dated 30 July 1778: 'I can only say that of all my compositions of this kind—this scena is the best I have ever composed.' This estimate is perhaps just, as far as the external ascent of the piece is concerned, from the recitative, *Andantino sostenuto e languido*, through the aria, *Andantino sostenuto e cantabile*, to the *stretta* (*Allegro assai*); perhaps, too, in respect to the orchestral treatment, in which a solo oboe and bassoon are added to the strings and horns, for this treatment does indeed represent a high point in delicacy. But the deeper Mozart gets into the work, the more he thinks of the success of his beloved, with her astonishing staccato tones, and the less he thinks of the dramatic situation, and of the queen who is also wife and mother. He far surpasses Gluck in musical quality, in technique, and in invention, but this exhibition piece 'smells of music.' On a far higher level is the scena *Ma, che vi fece, o stelle . . . Sperai vicino il lido*, K. 368, from Metastasio's *Demofoonte*, which he wrote in Munich after completing *Idomeneo*, presumably for Elisabeth Wendling, who had sung the role of Elettra. This work is as full of *bravura* as the one for Aloysia, though written for a fuller and more heroic voice; but every note, including the highest, of this bravura, is full of genuine passion, and the freedom of the form is carried to such lengths that nothing is left of the *aria monumentale*. The form is dictated by the spirit. When the text reads:

> 'E da uno scoglio infido, mentre salvar mi voglio,
> Urto in un' altro scoglio, del primo assai peggio'

(When I seek to avoid one perilous rock I throw myself upon another, far worse than the first) Mozart flings the tonality from cliff to cliff, so that in thirteen measures we are cast violently from E-flat major to A major. This powerful piece is worthy of the other works of the same period, such as the D minor *Kyrie* and the *Gran partita*. Like them, it is a work of inner revolt, far too grand and free for Salzburg.

The last work of this type, and the last work Mozart wrote before his removal to Vienna, dated Munich, 8 March 1781, is a scena from Metastasio's *Ezio: Misera dove son . . . Ah! non son'io che parlo*, K. 369, a courtesy-piece intended to please Carl Theodor's favorite of the moment, the Countess Baumgarten. But despite its modest orchestration it is much more than a courtesy-piece, and in it the dramatic situation is completely grasped. This is the last aria of Fulvia, that passionate lady whom we already know from the Aria K. 21; it is sung in a moment where all seems lost and passion gives way to resignation. In the eighteenth century, when everyone knew the text, since it had been composed a hundred times, the situation was clear. In later times such a piece is almost wasted. Mozart achieved a wonderful balance between the demands of the text and the powers of the high-born singer, of whom he could not demand what he would have demanded of a professional. The Rondo *Or che il cielo a me ti rende* (K. 374), on the other hand, which Mozart wrote for the Salzburg singer Ceccarelli in April 1781, while still in the Archbishop's service, is a pure concert piece for *castrato*. Ceccarelli sang it in an 'academy' on 8 April, and had to repeat it. It is a piece that can be enjoyed like an instrumental rondo, and it is of similar sensuous delicacy and grace, completely passionless, like the Rondo for violin (K. 373) that was played in the same concert by the Salzburg violinist Brunetti—except that the vocal Rondo is introduced by a recitative.

In Vienna there now began an uneven series of arias and other vocal pieces—their unevenness caused by the varying purposes and occasions for which they were composed. There is, for example, a sort of *licenza* in German (K. 383), which Aloysia must have sung in April 1782 at her last appearance on one of the Vienna stages—sentimental and philistine in a way that Mozart very seldom is, and then only when he sets a German text. On the other hand, he devoted his highest talents to a scena, *Mia speranza adorata . . . Ah non sai* (K. 416), a grand scene of farewell, the text presumably taken from a *Zemira* by Anfossi, which had been performed in Venice in the winter of 1781-2. This is the counterpart to that scena written in Mannheim and Munich which Mozart called his best; it is just as full of bravura, but even freer in form and more intense in the quality of its invention, and it reveals clearly that neither the voice nor the artistry of Aloysia—and perhaps not even their possessor—had yet become a matter of complete indifference to Mozart.

He soon had another opportunity to employ his time and talents in her service. At the end of June 1783, the *opera buffa* of Pasquale Anfossi, *Il curioso indiscreto*, was performed for the first time in Vienna by the Italian troupe, but with the two principal roles sung by Germans: Aloysia singing the part of Clorinda and Valentin Adamberger that of the Count. To assure their success, Mozart wrote two arias for Aloysia and one for Adamberger—not interpolations, but substitutions. This, according to Mozart's one-sided account, gave the Italians the opportunity to make unpleasant insinuations, as Salieri did not fail to do, that Adamberger had given up his original aria because he was afraid to sing it. On 2 July Mozart wrote to his father:

Anfossi's opera *Il curioso indiscreto*, in which Madame Lange and Adamberger appeared for the first time, had its first performance the day before yesterday, Monday. It failed completely, with the exception of my two arias, the second of which, a bravura, had to be repeated. Well, I should like you to know that my friends were malicious enough to spread the report beforehand that 'Mozart wanted to improve on Anfossi's opera.' I heard of this and sent a message to Count Rosenberg that I would not hand over my arias unless the following statement were printed in the copies of the libretto, both in German and in Italian:

Notice

The two arias on p. 36 and p. 102 have been set to music by Signor Maestro Mozart to suit Signora Lange, as the arias of Signor Maestro Anfossi were not written for her voice, but for another singer. It is necessary that this should be pointed out so that honor may be given to whom it is due and so that the reputation and the name of the most famous Neapolitan may not suffer in any way whatsoever.

Well, the statement was inserted and I handed out my arias, which did inexpressible honor both to my sister-in-law and to myself. So my enemies were quite confounded!

Mozart's naïveté both as diplomatist and as artist was hardly to be surpassed. For presumably he did not appease any of his 'enemies' by the bow to Anfossi, and in order really to improve the roles sung by

Aloysia and Adamberger he would have had to compose them anew from beginning to end. Paying no heed to the style of Anfossi's opera, which was six years old at the time and had had great success, he wrote for his sister-in-law a scena, *Vorrei spiegarvi* (K. 418), and an aria, *Nò che non sei capace* (K. 419), of contrasting characters: the first, half lyric and half *concertante*, the second, dramatic and full of bravura; the first full of subtle psychological insight, the second a partial return to the stereotyped expression of heroic indignation; but both somewhat external and limited by Mozart's consciousness of the nature of Aloysia's cold virtuosity. The Rondo composed for Adamberger, *Per pietà, non ricercate* (K. 420), which Mozart never heard sung, is on a much higher level. It represents an intensification of emotion from concealed agitation to the most open and passionate excitement. There is hardly another piece in which Mozart used so many tremoli, crescendi and *sforzati* in the strings. If this aria were in *Figaro* or *Don Giovanni*, it would be world famous.

Mozart continued until the end of his life to write arias and ensembles, some of which are closer to the stage and some to the concert hall, and on numerous occasions he repeated the naïveté of letting his Italian colleagues feel his superiority as a musician by writing pieces for insertion in their operas. Thus the aria *Aspri rimorsi atroci*, introduced by a brief recitative *Così dunque tradisci* (K. 432), cannot possibly have been a concert number. It was presumably written for the basso Carl Ludwig Fischer, Mozart's first Osmin, for a performance of Metastasio's *Temistocle*. Strangely enough, it is sung by one of the secondary characters, the trusted but traitorous friend of King Xerxes, as an expression of his qualms of conscience after having been unmasked. For us this is the crassest sort of melodrama; but Mozart took it quite seriously and wrote a somber piece in F minor, which has a power and seriousness not to be found in any of his *opere serie*, and appropriate only to a leading role. Another grand scena dating from the same period, the end of 1783, *Misero! o sogno, o son desto?* (K. 431), might, it seems to me, have been intended for the same occasion, representing Themistocles in prison, if it were not somewhat too lyric and too little heroic in bearing. This is rather the expression of a Florestan or a Manrico, hovering between terror at his plight and gentle thoughts of his beloved, and ending with an explosive outcry against his fate—a work of the most extraordinary invention in both the vocal and orchestral parts.

In March and December 1786, just before the completion of *Figaro* and a few months after it, Mozart set the same text twice in two of his most remarkable concert pieces for voice with an obbligato instrument: the first, a '*Scena con rondo* with violin solo for Baron Pulini and Count Hatzfeldt for my opera *Idomeneo*' (*Non più, tutto ascoltai*, K. 490); the second, in which the introductory *recitativo accompagnato* is changed, the *Recitativo con rondo, composto per la Signora Storace dal suo servo ed amico W. A. Mozart* (*Ch'io mi scordi di te?*, K. 505), with obbligato piano, upon the biographical significance of which we have already commented. Both pieces are the products of the same artistic impulse, and yet they are very different; they might be used equally well to demonstrate how much and how little of a formalist Mozart was. It is puzzling to know just what he had in mind in connection with the first of these arias. In March 1786, he got out his *Idomeneo* again for a private performance at the home of Prince Karl Auersperg, and composed for this occasion a duet for two of the highborn singers, Frau von Pufendorf and Baron Pulini, *Spiegarti non poss'io* (K. 489), to replace the original duet in the twentieth scene of Act II, as well the *Scena con rondo* we are now discussing. But while in the duet Baron Pulini sings tenor, and his part is notated in the tenor clef, in the aria he has a soprano part, which is almost unthinkable for tenor. Was Mozart, when he set this aria down on paper, still thinking of Idamante in his opera—a *castrato* role? Or did he already have Nancy Storace in mind? However that may be, the first aria, which is introduced by a dialogue, seems like a study for the second; it is like a perfect concert piece of rather neutral emotion, compared with the other one, into which Mozart poured his whole soul. In the first version, the violin plays a *concertante* duet with the voice; in the second the voice and piano carry on a dialogue so intimately interwoven and so heartfelt that one feels the particular intention in every measure. And at the same time the aria is so extended that it seems more like a concerto movement than an aria. We have the impression that Mozart wanted to preserve the memory of this voice, no brilliant soprano and not suited to display of virtuosity, but full of warmth and tenderness; and that he wanted to leave with her in the piano part a souvenir of the taste and depth of his playing, and of the depth of his feeling for her:

Ex. 95

Piu non reg - go a tan-te pe-ne l'al - ma mia man - can - do va, man - can- - - - - do va

Few works of art combine such personal expression with such mastery—the intimacy of a letter with the highest grandeur of form. Such a combination may perhaps be found in Goethe—in the *Trilogie der Leidenschaft* say, which is also an eternal farewell.

Once more Mozart followed old paths when, after an interval of ten years, he again set the scena from Metastasio's *Olimpiade* which he had once composed for Aloysia: *Alcandro, lo confesso . . . Non sò, d'onde viene* (K. 512, March 1787). This time he kept in mind the role of the father and the dramatic situation, and composed the aria for the excellent basso Carl Ludwig Fischer, in the grandest style, and with the sharpest contrast of rhythm, harmony, and tempo. In this work the 'monumentality of the aria' achieves an entirely new meaning. A few days later, he wrote another 'father aria' (*Mentre ti lascio, o figlia*, K. 513), for another basso, his young friend Gottfried von Jacquin, even longer than the first, with a wonderful *concertante* orchestra part, which, traversing somber harmonies, swells from pp to ff, in contrast to the questioning aria, with its diminuendo, written for Fischer. Then, in the period of the Prague performance of *Don Giovanni*, late autumn 1787, he produced another piece for Josefa Duschek, *Bella mia fiamma . . . Resta, oh cara*, K. 528, which employs extreme means to represent an extreme situation. This is no piece for the public, but rather what artists call a 'studio piece.' According to an anecdote related by Mozart's son, Mozart wrote it to bring out Josefa's full powers, and this is quite easy to believe. For in the andante section of the Aria there occurs the following passage, which returns later a half-tone lower—a passage very uncomfortable for an eighteenth-century singer:

Ex. 96

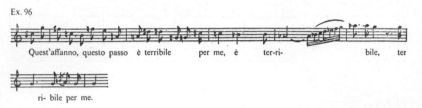

Quest'affanno, questo passo è terribile   per me, è   ter-ri-   bile,   ter ri- bile per me.

The whole aria, from the brooding polyphony of the orchestra in the recitative to the passionate *stretta*, has an atmosphere of intense agitation that is suited to a work written in close proximity to the sinister *Don Giovanni*. A hero, going to his sacrificial death, takes leave of three persons, among whom is his beloved. Perhaps the latter is Proserpina, for the names Cerere and Alfeo, which occur at the end of the recitative, point to a scene in Hades. But we shall not fully understand this grandiose piece until we are able to reconstruct the situation with certainty.

A few months later, on 4 March 1788, Mozart made his final offering to the virtuosity of his sister-in-law Aloysia in the form of an aria, *Ah se in ciel, benigne stelle* (K. 538), the text of which is taken from Metastasio's *Eroe cinese*. This is a vocal concerto, in the creation of which Mozart was only the wonderful *routinier;* and that fact delights us, for it is striking evidence that his emotional relation to the fatal lady was entirely at an end. But when it came to the task of writing an aria for the basso Francesco Albertarelli, who had sung the title role of *Don Giovanni* in the Vienna performance—an aria to be inserted in Anfossi's *Le gelosie fortunate*—his whole heart and soul were in his work again. This *dramma giocoso*, first performed in Venice in 1786, came to Vienna on 2 June 1788. The aria (*Un bacio di mano*, K. 541) belongs

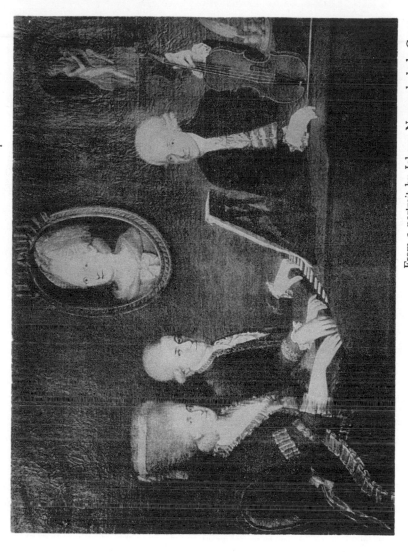

THE MOZART FAMILY (1780-81) Nannerl, Wolfgang, Mother (portrait), Father

From a portrait by Johann Nepomuk de la Croce

to the *buffo* domain of *Così fan tutte*. A witty Frenchman, Monsieur Giraud (Giro), is giving ironic advice to a somewhat stupid lover. This aria has become famous because it anticipates note for note the third theme in the first movement of the 'Jupiter' Symphony, and thereby shows how many *buffo* elements still haunt that most royal of all symphonies. But the aria is also a masterpiece of wit, vitality, brevity, showing a profound knowledge of the theater.

During the dreary remainder of his life, Mozart contented himself in the field of the aria with a few pieces for his singers, intended simply to please. Aloysia was succeeded by her elder sister, Josefa, who had married the violinist Hofer, and who was to be the first Queen of the Night in *Die Zauberflöte*. For her Mozart wrote the *teutsche Aria—Schon lacht der holde Frühling* (K. 580) in September 1789. This piece was intended as an interpolation in a proposed performance of Paisiello's *Barbiere* in German at the Theater auf der Wieden, where Josefa was engaged. But the production was apparently abandoned, which explains the sketchy and unfinished character of Mozart's manuscript. The principal portion of the piece is as much like a composition for Aloysia as two peas in a pod; but there is a middle portion, in G minor, that is conceived for a singer of deeper and more genuine emotion— the same singer who was one day to sing the Larghetto (*Zum Leiden bin ich auserkoren*) in *Die Zauberflöte*. Another German aria (*Ohne Zwang, aus eignem Triebe*, K. 569), written in January 1789, was, to judge from the incipit, a sentimental one, and seems to have been intended for Josefa; it has not survived. A little on the pathetic side, also, is the first of three pieces Mozart wrote for his first Dorabella, Louise Villeneuve (*Alma grande e nobil core*, K. 578, August 1789). This was written for Cimarosa's Intermezzo *I due baroni di Rocca Azzurra*, and it breathes the indignation of a young lady at whom Mozart secretly pokes fun in the orchestra part—a ravishing piece. The other two arias (*Chi sa, chi sa, qual sia*, K. 582, and *Vado, ma dove?*, K. 583) dated October 1789 are interpolations in Vicente Martin's *Il Burbero di buon core*. This was the same 'Martini lo spagnuolo,' as the Italians called him, whom Mozart immortalized also on other occasions. The text of *Il Burbero*, arranged by da Ponte, goes back, of course, to Goldoni's masterpiece, out of which nothing could be made but a half sentimental, half *buffo commedia in musica*. Thus the two arias belong to the sentimental side, and they have in common the syncopated rhythm of agitation in their accompaniments. The second leads into a *tempo di minuetto* of the finest, lyric, singing character. Mademoiselle Louise must have been a charming little person, with a delightful style and a perfection—no empty brilliance—of coloratura.

There remains an aria for basso with obbligato contrabass, *Per questa bella mano* (K. 612), which Mozart wrote at the beginning of 1791, 'for Messrs. Görl and Pischlberger.' Franz Gerl was to be his first Sarastro; Pischlberger, who was a member of the Freihaustheater orchestra, was a virtuoso on his unwieldy instrument, and Mozart entrusted unbelievable things to him. The text, a declaration of love, is possible only when sung by a tenor, and thus the piece, in its comfortable ⅜ rhythm, has willy-nilly a certain air of parody, only intensified by the efforts of the instrumental Behemoth. Mozart's good-natured acquiescence in writing such purely occasional pieces would make us sad if there were not another little aria for basso (*Io ti lascio, o cara, addio*, K. Anh. 245), dating from the time of *La Clemenza di Tito*—an aria of which the authenticity was suspected by Constanze, but which in its heartfelt simplicity completes the chain of Mozart's arias better and more fittingly than any bravura piece could have done.

PROSODY

Did Mozart write any German songs? This question can be answered both yes and no. He certainly set German texts to music, but the question is whether the results were German songs. The two *chansons* he wrote during his visit to Mannheim in 1777-8, for Mademoiselle Gustl (Auguste) Wendling (*Oiseaux, si tous les ans* and *Dans un bois solitaire*, K. 307 and 308), are much more truly French than his *Lieder* are German: French despite all the violence they do to the prosody of the language; French above all in the piquancy of their rhythmic invention; completely alive scenas that would do honor to any score of Philidor or Grétry. For both these scenas are 'through composed,' and the piano follows every turn of the vocal line with commentary that is always alive. Both are performance pieces of the highest type; completely rounded, despite all their freedom—the first by a short prelude and postlude, the second by a return of the melody of the first stanza. The verses, chosen by Auguste Wendling from an anthology, are by Antoine Ferrand and Houdart de la Motte—typical anacreontic verses, especially the second, with the motive descended from late antiquity: 'Wake not, I pray thee, sleeping Cupid!' This *chanson* is Watteau in music—not

Boucher or Lancret, for Mozart is too serious and too passionate for mere dalliance.

Four German songs, or rather twice two, were published by Mozart during his lifetime, and they are called significantly on the title page *deutsche Arien,* and even more specifically *deutsche Arien zum Singen beim Clavier* (German arias to sing at the clavier): not *deutsche Lieder,* and not just simply *Lieder.* Mozart did not write any real *Lied,* if by the term we mean a song like those of Schubert, or even of his lesser forerunners or contemporaries like Zumsteeg, Schulz, or Zelter. In the songs of Schubert, the voice and the accompanying instrument are in complete equilibrium; these songs are neither melodies with piano accompaniment nor piano pieces with voice. Schubert, with his fine sense of poetry, never set worthless doggerel to music, and never used a text simply as an excuse for music. He enhanced the value of the text with his music, without ever doing it violence or obscuring it. Mozart almost never had either the good fortune or the desire to connect his name with the names of great poets, or even of real poets. When one glances through the list of his songs, one finds, with a single exception, none but minor and less than minor versifiers, completely forgotten today: Canitz, Günther, Uz, Weisse, Hermes, Miller, Ratschky, Blumauer, Schmidt, etc. In the face of all these mediocrities one breathes a sigh of relief even when one comes upon the German anacrcontics Hagedorn and Hölty. Mozart cannot be blamed for having had no respect for his text. For him a poem was merely something to hang music upon. All these poems and the very names of the poets would have been long since forgotten if he had not immortalized them. Unlike Schubert, Mozart always wrote a little in aria style. The Schubert song grew up in mysterious ways out of the folksong. Mozart's songs have nothing to do with folksong. They are, like all his works, 'music made out of pure music.' They have much more to do with the Italian *canzonetta* or the French *romance,* both of which grew up out of the soil of the opera or the *opéra-comique.* Moreover, Mozart remained almost completely untouched by the experiments that were being made with the song, not only in North Germany but also in his immediate surroundings. At the end of 1785, his publisher, Artaria, had brought out Gluck's *Oden und Lieder beim Clavier zu singen*—seven songs that had already been in circulation for ten years, and that Mozart must have known. They were the products of an intentionally extreme simplicity, and a complete subordination of the music to the words of the poet, to their antique meter. The only indication that they made any impression on Mozart is in the so-called portrait aria, sung by Tamino, which undoubtedly owes its opening to *Die frühen Gräber* by Klopstock and Gluck. But it was not only his aversion to Klopstock's 'exaggerated' poetry and Gluck's rationalistic method that prevented any possible imitation of them by Mozart. It was, rather, the fact that for Mozart poetry was subordinate to music, and music to him was not German, but rather Italian or French, or, best of all, Mozartean. He insisted on remaining free, even in the song. Mozart had been from the very first a dramatist and an instrumental composer, and both these qualities represented dangers to his song style. It is just because he was a true dramatist that one might say that his German operas—*Bastien und Bastienne, Die Entführung,* and *Die Zauberflöte*—contain his most genuine *Lieder.*

Not that all the stages of development of the song were not represented even in Mozart's examples of the species. It was still young, this species, but its history was already quite complicated. We need not trace it in detail: the first phase was the dance-song, the song conceived from an instrumental point of view; this was the phase in which more or less suitable texts were fitted to minuets, sarabandes, and gigues; and examples of this procedure are particularly plentiful among Mozart's youthful songs: *An die Freude* (K. 53, 1767) is a 'symphonic' andantino, while *O heiliges Band* (K. 148, 1772) is a slow minuet, which, although its text may be interpreted in a Masonic sense, cannot possibly date from the Vienna period. The second and third phases are connected with North Germany, and their names are artificiality and false naïveté. The representative of artificiality—and often of the other phases as well—was Philipp Emanuel Bach, whose music, as we know, was well known in the Mozart household. Leopold had paid tribute to him already in a few songs, and if the three songs on texts by Günther and Canitz (K. 149, 150, and 151) are really by Wolfgang Amadeus and not by Leopold, they show how well Mozart had absorbed the cantatalike song style of Berlin and Hamburg. What could be made out of this style Mozart showed at the end of his Salzburg period, about 1780, in three songs (K. 390, 391, and 392) apparently composed in response to a commission from an almanac publisher, as interpolations in a popular novel of the period, *Sophiens Reise von Memel nach Sachsen,* by J. T. Hermes. The texts are as ungrateful as is the whole novel, and in these songs for once Mozart fell a victim to the 'sensibility' of the time, as even the indications on the songs show: *Gleichgültig* und *zufrieden* (Indifferent and content), *Traurig doch gelassen* (Sad but collected), *Mässig gehend* (*Moderato*, in walking tempo). The essential elements of expression in them—the harmony, the chromaticism, the diminished chords—correspond to these indications. The most concentrated of the songs is *An die Hoffnung* (K. 390, *Ich würd' auf meinem Pfad*), in which Mozart composed not the first stanza but the last, since it is only in the latter that the expression and the sense of the text completely agree—another evidence of Mozart's delicate sense of the dramatic.

In 1781, Mozart went to Vienna, and there, if he became a song composer at all, he became a specifically Viennese song composer. In Vienna, the history of the song had been even shorter than in other German centers, because Vienna was a city of instrumental Italian music and Italian opera. Vienna had no true *Lied* of its own; the populace had its *Gassenhauer* (street tunes), and in cultured circles the *canzonetta* took the place of the *Lied*. Not until 1778 did the first collection of true art songs appear, written by a gifted man, Josef Anton Steffan, who was followed by a series of smaller men: Johann Holzer, Carl Friberth, Leopold Hoffmann, Franz Anton Hoffmeister (Mozart's friend), and others. In 1782 and 1784 appeared Haydn's two collections of *deutsche Lieder*, by which the composer himself mistakenly set great store. Mozart took attentive note of all these collections, and they corresponded, in their mixture of Italianism and instrumentalism, to his own artistic origins. Haydn's songs almost always betray their instrumental ancestry, and songs of a character at once anacreontic and instrumental like Mozart's *Die kleine Spinnerin* (1787, K. 531), or the delicious parody of an antiquated song with *basso continuo*, *Die Alte* (K. 517), show their connection with Haydn's *Eine sehr gewöhnliche Geschichte* or *Die zu späte Ankunft der Mutter* or *Lob der Faulheit*.

Mozart himself placed not the slightest value upon his songs. They were by-products, crumbs from the table of his operas and instrumental works. We have documentary evidence of this fact in the story of Mozart's relation to his young friend Gottfried von Jacquin. From Prague, at the time of the performance of *Don Giovanni*, Mozart writes to Jacquin (9 November 1787): 'It has been a most pleasant surprise to receive your second letter. If the song in question is necessary to prove my friendship for you, you have no further cause to doubt it, for here it is . . .' This passage is preceded by fatherly warnings to Gottfried to give up his butterfly existence in favor of some more serious aim. We know the circle of young ladies and gentlemen in which Jacquin moved; it is the same circle for which Mozart composed his delightful *Gesellige Lieder* (Songs of Good Fellowship), vocal trios usually accompanied by wind trio, on texts chiefly taken from Metastasio (K. 436, 437, 346, 438, 439, 532, 549, 562). And perhaps not only these anacreontic flowers of melody, but also a series of his coarser musical jokes in the form of ensembles and canons, were intended for this young and gay society. Now, the Jacquin family published, under the imprint of Cappi, in Vienna, and giving Gottfried's name as composer, the song mentioned in Mozart's letter (*Das Traumbild*, K. 530) in 1803, together with five songs by Gottfried, who had died in 1792. Mozart had ceded his authorship. There is another similar instance: in a manuscript belonging to the library of the Istituto Musicale in Florence there is a volume containing six songs that once belonged to Gottfried, in which he claimed not only the *Traumbild* (this time with the title *An eine Unbekannte*) but also one of Mozart's most beautiful songs—*Louise, als sie die Briefe ihres ungetreuen Liebhabers verbrannte* (K. 520), which Gottfried expressly dedicated to one of his flames, a Fräulein von Altomonte. The manuscript bears the notation in Mozart's handwriting: '26. *Mai* 1787. *Landstrasse . . . in Herrn Gottfried von Jacquins Zimmer,* (26 May 1787, Landstrasse . . . in Mr. Gottfried von Jacquin's room). Thus Mozart composed it under supervision, so to speak; made a present of it at once to Jacquin; and never published it himself. It is not really a song at all, but a dramatically conceived scena, in which one not only feels the injured mood of the young lady, in the complaining chromaticism in C minor, but also sees the fire on the hearth—a little masterpiece, at once free and perfectly rounded.

But in respect to a few other songs of these middle Vienna years, Mozart did not yield his author's rights. These are, in the first of the two volumes of 1789 we have mentioned, *Abendempfindung* and *An Chloe* (K. 523 and 524), and *Das Veilchen* and *Das Lied der Trennung* (K. 476 and 519). *An Chloe* is a piano rondino with text—very charming but not a song. *Abendempfindung,* on the other hand, is a fine lyric outpouring, possessing a genuine depth of feeling and expression and a singing perfection that make one forget completely whether it is a scena or a song, whether it is Italian or German. Of similar depth and beauty, while of quite different form, is the *Trennungslied* (*Die Engel Gottes weinen*): it is strophic in structure, but beginning with the fifth stanza the melody, the accompaniment, and the expression become steadily freer and fuller, and the tear-drenched sentimentality of the text, quite in the vogue of the period, is completely surmounted.

Das Veilchen represents the only instance in which Mozart encountered a real poem, and even this time it was more by accident than by design, for he found the text in Steffan's *Sammlung deutscher Lieder* of 1778, where it was published not under the name of Goethe but under that of Gleim! This is Mozart's most famous and most familiar song, and rightly so. But is it a song? Perhaps we shall have characterized it best when we have recognized the fact that both the poem and the music must have owed their origins to some quite personal experience. This is an 'occasional' work in the highest sense. The poem is first found in *Erwin und Elmire*, Goethe's first *Singspiel*; he did not include it among his ballads until years later. Now *Erwin und Elmire* mirrors in the light of the springtime of poetry the stormy and painful relation between two lovers, as Goethe had observed it first between his friend Herder and his betrothed, and then between himself and Lili: how a pert and exuberant young girl teases a fine and serious youth, and plays with his affections, even while she loves him. It is from the soul of such a fine and serious youth that *Das Veilchen* springs. And when, in Goethe's *Singspiel*, the repentant beauty sings it reminiscently, she feels, 'every time she ends it, as if she had just drained a cup of poison.'

Mozart's setting of *Das Veilchen* must have had some similar background. This is not a song like any other. In Mozart, Goethe's text found a kindred spirit. *Das Veilchen* is a lyric scena, and the lyric element, the stream of musical feeling, receives equal emphasis with the dramatic element, the depiction of the situation, saturated as the latter is with emotion. How amiably it begins, in the introduction and the first two lines; how manly is the emphasis on the cadence; how daintily, 'with a light step and a gay spirit,' the young shepherdess approaches, and how carefree is her song as it flows over the fields (she has been to the opera, this little beauty)! How modest and heartfelt is the meditation of the violet and how sad and inevitable the approach of the catastrophe! For it is a catastrophe, symbolized in the *fortissimo* chords of the accompaniment and in the bare recitative of the voice. How touching is the final line, added—as has been so often observed— by Mozart himself: 'Das arme Veilchen, es war ein herzigs Veilchen!' (The poor little violet! It was such a dear little violet!) Mozart burst open the form of the song, not arbitrarily, or from any insensitiveness to the words of the poet or the sense of the song form, but from inner necessity. On the basis of this inner necessity we can only speculate. It was rooted in the depths of his personality and experience. Mozart was physically small and unprepossessing, and an incurable disease had long since marked him. Undoubtedly he had suffered deeply despite a keen awareness of his greatness as an artist, because of his unimpressive appearance. However that may be, in this song that is not a song, one genius has struck fire from another. In this field, too, just as in that of the aria, Mozart said the last word, and achieved the ultimate in directness of expression.

V. OPERA

20. *Mozart and Opera*

*T*HE NAIVE, truly inspired artist casts himself with reckless enthusiasm into his art work; and only when this is finished, when it shows itself in all its actuality, does he win from practical experience that genuine force of reflection which preserves him in general from illusions, yet in the specific case of his feeling driven again to art work by his inspiration, loses once more its power over him completely. There is nothing more characteristic of Mozart, in his career of opera-composer, than the unconcernedness wherewith he went to work; it was so far from occurring to him to weigh the pros and cons of the aesthetic problem involved in Opera, that he the rather engaged with utmost unconstraint in setting any and every operatic textbook offered him, almost heedless whether it were a thankful task for him as pure musician. If we piece together all his aesthetic hints and sayings, culled from here and there, we shall find that the sum of his Reflection mounts no higher than his famous definition of his 'nose' . . .

Thus, and further to the same effect, Richard Wagner in Part I of his *Opera and Drama.** We shall have something to say about his further remarks later on. The paragraph above would make one of the most significant quotations in a book still to be written, bearing the title *Mozart and Posterity.* Now, if Wagner's judgment about Mozart were true, then Mozart, who is supposed to have accepted a libretto as naively as a child devours an apple; who could only compose good dramatic music (Wagner says 'beautiful' music) when the poetry met him half-way (Wagner, who could only conceive of the act of opera composition as symbolized by a sexual act, says: 'when to the spirit of divinest Love within him was shewn the object worthy love, the object that in ardent heedlessness of self it could embrace')—Mozart, then, would be disposed of as an opera composer. And it should be noted that Wagner is not talking about Mozart's youthful works, which he did

* Translated by W. A. Ellis, in *Prose Works*, II, 36.

not know, but of his later operas, from *Die Entführung* to *La Clemenza di Tito.*

Actually however this judgment is as wrong as it could possibly be. Or rather, it fails to apply to exactly those works that Wagner had in mind. It is really a judgment *pro domo,* a typical nineteenth-century judgment. In actual fact, what torment Mozart went through with his librettists, from *Idomeneo* to *Tito!* And what discussions must have taken place with da Ponte and Schikaneder, of which we know nothing, before the final forms of *Figaro, Don Giovanni, Così fan tutte,* and *Die Zauberflöte* were arrived at. For what other reasons did Mozart abandon a piece like *Il regno delle Amazoni* (K. 434), after the merest beginning, or fail to finish the setting of libretti like *L'Oca del Cairo* (K. 422), or *Lo Sposo deluso* (K. 430), except that they did not satisfy him as a dramatist? Nothing is more revealing of Mozart's conscientiousness and his dramatic instinct than the letter he wrote his father about the composition of *Die Entführung* (26 September 1781):

I . . . think that it will afford you pleasure if I give you some idea of my opera. As the original text began with a monologue, I asked Herr Stephanie to make a little arietta out of it—and then to put in a duet instead of making the two chatter together after Osmin's short song. As we have given the part of Osmin to Herr Fischer, who certainly has an excellent bass voice (in spite of the fact that the Archbishop told me that he sang too low for a bass and that I assured him that he would sing higher next time), we must take advantage of it, particularly as he has the whole Viennese public on his side. But in the original libretto Osmin has only this short song and nothing else to sing, except in the trio and the finale; so he has been given an aria in Act I, and he is to have another in Act II. I have explained to Stephanie the words I require for this aria—indeed I had finished composing most of the music for it before Stephanie knew anything whatever about it. I am enclosing only the beginning and the end, which is bound to have a good effect. Osmin's rage is rendered comical by the accompaniment of the Turkish music. In working out the aria, I have given full scope now and then to Fischer's beautiful deep notes (in spite of our Salzburg Midas). The passage *Drum beim Barte des Propheten* is indeed in the same tempo, but with quick notes; but as Osmin's rage gradually increases, there comes (just when the aria seems to be at an end) the *allegro assai,* which is in a totally different measure and in a different key; this is bound to be very effective. For just as a man in such a towering rage oversteps all the bounds of order, moderation, and propriety, and completely forgets himself, so must the music too forget itself. But as passions, whether violent or not, must never be expressed in such a way as to excite disgust, and as music, even in the most terrible situations, must never offend the ear, but must please the hearer, or in other words must never cease to be *music*, I have gone from F (the key in which the aria is written), not into a remote key, but into a related one, not, however, into its nearest relative D minor, but into the more remote A minor. Let me now turn to Belmonte's aria in A major, *O wie ängstlich, o wie feurig*. Would you like to know how I have expressed it—and even indicated his throbbing heart? By the two violins playing octaves. This is the favorite aria of all those who have heard it, and it is mine also. I wrote it expressly to suit Adamberger's voice. You feel the trembling—the faltering—you see how his throbbing breast begins to swell; this I have expressed by a crescendo. You hear the whispering and the sighing—which I have indicated by the first violins with mutes and a flute playing in unison.

The Janissary chorus is, as such, all that can be desired, that is, short, lively and written to please the Viennese. I have sacrificed Constanze's aria a little to the flexible throat of Mlle Cavalieri, *Trennung war mein banges Los und nun schwimmt mein Aug' in Tränen*. I have tried to express her feelings, as far as an Italian bravura aria will allow it. I have changed the *Hui* to *schnell*, so it now runs thus—*Doch wie schnell schwand meine Freude*. I really don't know what our German poets are thinking of. Even if they do not understand the theater, or at all events operas, yet they should not make their characters talk as if they were addressing a herd of swine. Hui, sow!

Now for the trio at the close of Act I. Pedrillo has passed off his master as an architect—to give him an opportunity of meeting his Constanze in the garden. Bassa Selim has taken him into his service. Osmin, the steward, knows nothing of this, and being a rude churl and a sworn foe to all strangers, is impertinent and refuses to let them into the garden. It opens quite abruptly—and because the words lend themselves to it, I have made it a fairly respectable piece of real three-part writing. Then the major key begins at once *pianissimo*—it must go very quickly—and wind up with a great deal of noise, which is always appropriate at the end of an act. The more noise the better, and the shorter the better, so that the audience may not have time to cool down with their applause.

I have sent you only fourteen bars of the ouverture, which is very short with alternate *fortes* and *pianos*, the Turkish music always coming in at the *fortes*. The ouverture modulates through different keys; and I doubt whether anyone, even if his previous night has been a sleepless one, could go to sleep over it. Now comes the rub! The first act was finished more than three weeks ago, as was also one aria in Act II and the drunken duet (*per i signori viennesi*) which consists entirely of my Turkish tattoo. But I cannot compose any more, because the whole story is being altered—and, to tell the truth, at my own request. At the beginning of Act III there is a charming quintet or rather finale, but I should prefer to have it at the end of Act II. In order to make this practicable, great changes must be made, in fact an entirely new plot must be introduced—and Stephanie is up to the eyes in other work. So we must have a little patience. Everyone abuses Stephanie. It may be that in my case he is only very friendly to my face. But after all he is arranging the libretto for me—and, what is more, as I want it—exactly—and, by Heaven, I do not ask anything more of him. Well, how I have been chattering to you about my opera! But I cannot help it.

This does not sound like the child with the apple. It is true that Mozart said that 'in an opera the poetry must be altogether the obedient daughter of the music' (letter of 13 October 1781). This is, as we have seen, exactly the inversion of the theory of Gluck and Wagner—Gluck, who in his reform-opera pretended to forget that he was a musician, and Wagner, who saw the curse of opera in the fact, which he had printed in bold type, 'that a means of expression [Music] has been made the end, while the end of expression [the drama] has been made a means.' But in practice Gluck and Wagner agree with Mozart. For what would the poets Calzabigi, du Roullet, and Guillard be without Gluck, and what would the poet Richard Wagner be without Richard Wagner the musician? It would be far more accurate to say that not only in the history of opera but in any individual opera the balance between 'drama' and 'music' is continually shifting, that the scales are only rarely exactly even, and that one side or the other almost always bears the heavier weight. What would the second act of *Tristan*, where the action is at a standstill and we can only gaze at the green half-light on the stage, from which the tones of the love duet soar forth, and there is really nothing to watch—what would this act be without music? No period has the right to impugn the operatic ideals of another period; each should strive to do justice to the other.

But Wagner was not altogether wrong about the Mozart that he did not know. Mozart began his career as an opera composer very early, at the age of twelve or thirteen, and hardly was aware of the problem of opera until *Idomeneo*, written when he was twenty-five. But we can hardly reproach him for that when we remember that Gluck was almost fifty years old before he, not without the help of others, became aware of this problem, and that his *Alceste* was just one year old when Mozart made his first essays in the opera field. The most striking example of Mozart's youthful innocence and respect for the traditional is perhaps his setting of Metastasio's *Betulia liberata*—a work that significantly enough was not set by the musician most devoted and most indebted to Metastasio, Johann Adolf Hasse. It was on his first visit to Italy, after the performance of *Mitridate* in Milan, that Mozart had received the commission to set Metastasio's oratorio to music (Padua, 13 March 1771). Whether it was then sung in Lent, 1772—indeed, whether it was ever sung—is not established. As late as 1784, Mozart asked his father to send him the score, since he must set the text for the Tonkünstler-Societät, and might well be able to use one or another piece from the youthful work. It is even said that at this time he composed a new introductory chorus and a quintet for the work. But I do not believe it. For in 1784, Mozart must have seen after the most cursory examination that this was not a text he could set to music again, either in whole or in part. Now, an Italian oratorio is not an opera, even though it has the form of an opera. An oratorio has two acts, not three like an opera seria; an oratorio emphasizes the role of the chorus; an oratorio relies on the imagination of the listener, and can represent things that would be impossible to present on the stage, as, for example, in Metastasio's oratorio, when Judith displays the bleeding head of Holofernes. But, like the opera, the oratorio was supposed to present happenings and people, in which and in whom the contents of the Bible and of religion and the experience of God were to take on vivid and credible forms. Handel would not have been able to use Metastasio as an oratorio writer, even if the Imperial Court Poet had not been a Catholic. Presumably he dismissed *La Betulia liberata*, of which the subject matter was very congenial to him, and which he probably knew very well, with a scornful smile. For Metastasio, it was not Judith who occupied the center of attention, still less Holofernes, who does not actually appear at all. For him the important theme was the conversion of an Ammonite prince, Achior, who, badly treated by Holofernes, goes over to the Jews, discusses religious questions with

Ozia, the *Principe* of the besieged city, and is moved only by Judith's deed to give up his heathen skepticism.

> Giuditta, Ozia, Popoli, Amici, io credo.
> Vinto son io. Prende un novello aspetto
> Ogni cosa per me. Tutto son pieno,
> Tutto del vostro Dio. Grande, infinito,
> Unico lo confesso . . . *

In the first act, Judith, adorned like a bride, leaves Betulia; in the second act she returns and tells in detail how, filled with the consciousness of her God, she has chopped off the head of the tyrant in two stages, which she describes with the objectivity of a court expert in a murder trial. Achior at first takes Judith's story for mere boasting:

> Inerme, e sola
> Tanto pensar, tanto eseguir potesti!
> E crederti degg'io? †

—and he is thoroughly convinced only by the sight of the bleeding head he knows so well, which Judith draws forth from her sack. Whereupon Judith sings one of Metastasio's famous 'comparison arias' in which she forgives Achior's hesitation, saying that a prisoner just emerging from the darkness of the dungeon must first accustom himself to the light:

> Prigionier, che fa ritorno
>   Dagli orrori al dì sereno,
>   Chiude i lumi a'rai del giorno;
>   E pur tanto il sospirò.
>
> Ma così fra poco arriva
>   A soffrir la chiara luce,
>   Che l'arriva, e lo conduce
>   Lo splendor, che l'abbagliò.‡

---

* Judith, Ozia, People, Friends, I believe.
I am convinced. Behold, everything
Takes on a new aspect for me. I am full,
Full of your God. Great, infinite,
One I acknowledge him.
† Unarmed and alone
Thou couldst plan and perform such a deed?
This thou wouldst have me believe?
‡ The prisoner, when just returning
    From horrid night to light of day,

The young Mozart composed all this nonsense without changing a jot or tittle. Nor was he the only one to do so. A score or more of adult composers both before and after him did likewise. How he composed it is a question that belongs to the history of his development as a musician more than as a dramatist. But his feeling for style, nevertheless, is astounding. He writes a serious three-part *sinfonia*, in Gluck's key of D minor, in which the last section is thematically connected with the first, and the *cantabile* middle section contains more 'workmanship' than the *sinfonia* of an opera; he composes splendid arias in *concertante* style, although, in order to avoid tiring the singers or listeners, they have only abbreviated reprises; for Judith's account of the murderous deed he writes one of his longest and by no means least effective *recitativi accompagnati*; and above all he writes pious choruses, the last a dialogue between Judith and the people, a sort of religious *vaudeville* in which a psalm-tone (*In exitu Israel*) is very ingeniously used. But his musical development affects us in this connection less than his dramatic. And it is part of his greatness as a dramatist that ten years later he would not have composed anything of the same sort—not as a result of theoretical or esthetic reflection, not because he would have wished to burst the traditional frame of the *opera seria*, but because of his developed dramatic instinct, his urge for dramatic truth, his joy in creating real beings, and in giving them musical characterization.

But what we said a moment ago, that in the history of opera the emphasis is continually shifting between music and drama, is not the whole truth. For the emphasis does not shift simply between music and drama. Who was the most important participant in the opera of the seventeenth century? With whom would criticism, if there had been any, have been primarily concerned? The stage designer and mechanic, who was able to display the furies of hell confined upon his stage or the wonders of Alcina's enchanted garden; who sent Mercury, the messenger of the gods, floating down out of the air, or in an apotheosis grouped all the inhabitants of Olympus in a celestial semi-circle. From the beginning of the eighteenth century the most important partici-

> Shuts out the air and sunlight burning,
> The while he breathes so deep a sigh.
>
> 'Tis but a little while before
> He learns the brilliant light to suffer,
> Which comes to him and seems to offer
> The splendor that doth blind him quite.

pant was the singer: more especially the *prima donna*, and above all
the *primo uomo*, the *castrato*. The most famous name in the opera of
the seventeenth century was not Cavalli, Cesti, or Lulli, but the Imperial Court Architect Lodovico Burnacini. The most famous name in
the eighteenth century was not Handel or Hasse, Graun or Gluck, but
the *castrato* Carlo Broschi, known as Farinelli. The composer was in
the service of the singer, and the librettist in the service of the composer. The librettist was thus subordinate to every one; his was the
lowest rung of the ladder. Apostolo Zeno and Pietro Metastasio were no
exceptions. It was very important for musicians that the libretti of
these men so perfectly suited the operatic ideal of the period; but it
was a matter of complete indifference to them that the two Imperial
Court Poets sought to give their libretti poetical or literary value above
and beyond that. It even irked them. In this respect Carlo Goldoni,
after a single unsuccessful attempt, which opened his eyes once and for
all, was a much greater realist. In his libretti for the *opera seria* he served
his composers exactly as they wished to be served, without the slightest
literary ambition. Thus it would be little more than pedantry to apply
a poetic yardstick to a *dramma per musica* of the eighteenth century.
Similarly it would be pedantry to apply a dramatic yardstick to the
operas of the youthful Mozart. The center of gravity for him still lay
in the singers, male and female. Mozart fulfilled the conditions upon
which the success of an opera depended: he served as well as he could
the art of the singer. When he made changes, he did so usually not
for dramatic reasons. For his first opera for Milan, earlier versions have
survived for no less than six arias and one duet—versions that simply
did not meet the wishes of the singers.

What is true of the *opera seria* is even more true of the *opera buffa*.
We are astonished when we learn that Mozart as a boy of twelve or
thirteen wrote an *opera buffa*, *La Finta semplice*. But the cast of an
opera buffa consisted of types, and it was the composer's duty to do
justice to these types. We are still far from character comedy. The connection of the *opera buffa* with the *commedia dell'arte*, with Pantalone
and Zanni, Gratiano and Captain Spaventa, Rosaura and Leandro, is
clear and palpable. This was true not only of the *opera buffa* but also of
the comedy. Not only of the *fiabe* by Carlo Gozzi, but also of Goldoni's
character comedy—even though Goldoni's whole struggle, his purpose,
his mission in the history of literature, seemed to be the dethrone-

ment of the *commedia dell'arte*. The *commedia dell'arte* influenced French comedy as well as Italian. Does not Beaumarchais's *Le Barbier de Séville* stem from the *commedia dell'arte*, with its stock types? Is not Bartholo, 'tuteur de Rosine,' the same as Pantalone? Is not Figaro Arlecchino? Is not Don Basile Graziano? Do we not see Rosaura and Leandro in Rosine and Almaviva? Every member of a troupe of comedians could find in this play his habitual role, and it was for this reason that it was so easy to transform Beaumarchais's comedies into libretti. In the *opera buffa* about 1770, every character simply changed his name and his mask, but not his role. Nothing is more revealing than a letter of Mozart's rival, Giovanni Paisiello, written from Petersburg to his famous friend the Abbé Galiani in Naples, in September 1781. Paisiello, lacking a librettist in Russia, has in despair set again the old *Serva Padrona* by Pergolesi and requests Galiani to obtain for him a libretto by his old helper Giovanni Batista Lorenzi. But Lorenzi is ill, and Galiani suggests a substitute. Thereupon Paisiello formulates his requirements as follows: It must be short—the shorter the better. One act would be better than two, for the whole thing must not last longer than an hour and a half. Only four or five roles,

of which I will explain the character as follows, for these are the ones that are present in the Imperial service:
A *buffo caricato*, excellent in the role of the old man, the father, the jealous guardian, the philosopher.
Another *buffo caricato*.
A lyric tenor—but he can also be used for humorous things and sings well.
We also have a *buffa* who will do justice to any caricature role.
Another lady for *mezzo carattere*, about as good as the first one; and I say that so that the poet will arrange the distribution of numbers to be sung in such a way that no one can say that she has been slighted . . . *

Thus we see the point of view. The drama is arranged according to the categories to which the singers belong, and the composer governs himself according to the singers available. Is it conceivable that the child-prodigy Wolfgang Amadeus Mozart should have composed at the age of thirteen what is, externally and in form, at least, an *opera buffa*? We do not know who gave him the libretto. Its author was sup-

* The letter is reprinted in Andrea della Corte's *Paisiello*, Turin, 1922, p. 70.

posed to be Marco Coltellini, a Tuscan (from Montepulciano), who had been Metastasio's successor in the field of opera *seria* since 1769, and was a reformer in the Gluck and Calzabigi sense. Even Leopold believed that Coltellini was the author. Actually, the libretto was by Goldoni, and it had first been produced at San Moisé in Venice, in 1764, with music by Salvadore Perillo. The original libretto had appeared anonymously at that time. The opera had been a failure, and had not been produced outside Venice. Thus it is quite possible that Coltellini, by agreement with the Imperial impresario of the time, Afflisio, who was a thoroughgoing rascal, had plumed himself with borrowed feathers. He replaced only a few arias with new ones, and changed the third act just enough (and not unsuccessfully, particularly in the Finale) to justify him in adding his name to Goldoni's. The piece was not printed with the name of its real author until 1794, a year after Goldoni's death.

La Finta semplice does the author of La Locandiera little honor; but we must concern ourselves with it to some extent. The cast consists of seven persons:

1. *Don Cassandro*, a rich property-owner of Cremona, a rough and boorish fellow, conceited, stingy, a misogynist.

2. His younger brother, *Don Polidoro*, whom he treats like a dog, in which he is not altogether wrong, since Polidoro is an utter simpleton.

3. Their sister, *Donna Giacinta*, who is in love with

4. *Fracasso*, Hungarian Captain, quartered on Don Cassandro's estate.

5. *Ninetta*, the maid of Donna Giacinta, in love with

6. *Simone*, a Sergeant, servant to Fracasso.

The brothers are opposed to both matches. In order to overcome their opposition, the two couples arrange that

7. *Rosina*, Fracasso's sister, who is expected on a visit, shall cause both brothers to fall in love with her, so as to obtain their consent. This she does by putting on a mask of 'assumed innocence,' and the whole opera consists of a series of burlesque scenes, which are nothing more than variations on similar scenes in the *commedia dell'arte*.

Cassandro and Polidoro are, of course, none other than Pantalone, except that in this case Pantalone has been split into two characters, one to represent his tyrannical traits, and the other his stupid ones. Giacinta is the timid ward, Fracasso is the Captain as lover, Ninetta is Serpina, the chambermaid, Simone is Arlecchino or Zanni in uniform, with the typical trait of gluttony. The only more or less new figure is Rosina, the 'innocent' one, the 'ingénue,' who is descended from Molière's immortal Agnès in *L'Ecole des femmes*, and who here, in infinitely coarsened form and not at all consistently realized, is misused for the most nonsensical situation-jokes, and in the end actually decides to marry the uncouth Cassandro. Some of these situation-jokes are typical scenes of the *commedia dell'arte*: the idiot in love, who wishes to marry his adored one on the spot; the drunken suitor (Cassandro), who is forbidden by the lady in the opposite corner of the room to come near her, and must make himself understood with pantomime gestures; the duel between a bravo and a coward; the explosion of the man-crazy chambermaid, in which one can just recognize Goldoni:

Sono in amore,	With love I am burning,
Voglio marito,	I must have a husband,
Se fosse il primo	Though he be the first one
Che passerà.	That passes by.
Guai chi mi stuzzica	Curst he who trifles,
O mi maltratta:	Or doth ill-use me;
Gli salto agli occhi	I'll spring at his eyes
Come una gatta,	Like any cat,
E l'unghie adopero	And use my fingernails
Con tanto sdegno,	So hard and fiercely,
Che forse il segno	That they will mark him
Gli resterà.	Forever more.

Mozart had to compose this particular aria twice—undoubtedly because the first version did not please the singer, for reasons we do not know, since the boy and composer acquitted himself very well both times. But in general it will be admitted that this is no *dramma giocoso*, no gay drama, no comedy set to music; that there is no psychological insight into character; that all that is required is the realization of certain musical categories. This was all the more difficult for Mozart in this particular work, since most of the arias did not even arise convincingly from the situations and did not even fit the characters—quite apart from the fact that he did not always fully understand the text and (if the Complete Works Edition is correct) at times set utter nonsense. The fool Polidoro sings an aria (No. 7) that Mozart borrowed from *Die Schuldigkeit des ersten Gebotes*, the sacred *Singspiel* of 1767;

all he did was to shorten it. The braggart Fracasso sings a long aria (No. 25) that would fit better into an opera *seria*, but the tenor, Laschi, demanded it. In the Second Act, at the beginning of a change of scene, Rosina sings an aria in E major (No. 15, *Amoretti che ascosi*), which is musically the loveliest piece in the whole work; but it is a typical interpolation. Rosina is in general treated with favoritism, as far as her singing is concerned, and she alone is allowed to indulge her fondness for *coloratura*. The most unified realization of character is achieved in the figure of Giacinta—the anxious, sentimental woman in love. It seems that Mozart must have known already, in addition to a number of works by Galuppi, the epoch-making *Buona figliuola* by Duni or Paisiello (1760 or 1764), in which sentimentality had made its entrance into the field of opera *buffa*. And Giacinta even has an almost too serious and not at all *buffo* aria, in C minor (No. 24, not included in Goldoni's original), which underlines the situation with an excess of drama. In short, Mozart was hampered on every side except the instrumental one (which is why the *sinfonia* is the most charming piece in the whole opera). So he did the best thing he could do in the circumstances: he abandoned himself to his musical fancy, writing neutral pieces where the text offered him no stimulus, and where it did offer him one making the most of it, especially in the scurrilous scenes, which, with his childish inclination for fun and his precocious gift of observation, he well understood. The duel scene is a little masterpiece; the pantomime is full of suggestion; the orchestra takes advantage of every 'descriptive' hint in the text, whether it be witty or rough (No. 8) or poetic— the most poetic passage is in the echo-aria, No. 9. At the same time, the boy knew well what the *buffo* style required: striking terseness, sharp contrasts between the two parts of an aria, avoidance of the stereotyped da capo, invention of piquant motives in the accompaniment. In the ensembles—the conventional quartet of the introduction and the three finales—one was not expected to depict any conflicts of feelings or characters, and the sequence and alternation of different tempi was indicated clearly enough in the poem. Mozart did not yet have any notion of the capacity of music to depict contrasting feelings and conflicting characters simultaneously. Even the famous duel scene is just a dialogue, and not yet a duet. What is very characteristic, and full of little gestures, is the secco recitative, and if our knowledge of the history of the opera *buffa* before 1768 were more comprehensive we could perhaps identify the particular model the boy was following.

But we are not here concerned with the clarification of historical or personal influences or relationships. Nor need we occupy ourselves with the analysis of other dramatic works of Mozart's youth: the sacred *Singspiel* already mentioned: *Die Schuldigkeit des ersten Gebotes* (K. 35); the *Grabmusik* (K. 42); the Latin school-comedy *Apollo et Hyacinthus* (K. 38), in which the young musician shows his indebtedness to the worthy Johann Ernst Eberlin, and pays his tribute to the baroque local tradition of Salzburg. The dramatic musician shows himself not only in how he composes an opera but also in what he deems worthy of composition. *La Finta semplice*, which was never produced in the place for which it was intended, and which was performed only in Salzburg in what must have been a thoroughly provincial production, was not a total loss for Mozart, and was in any case excellent training for him in the *buffo* style. But what distinguishes him from a hundred Italian contemporaries, not excluding the most famous ones, like Paisiello, Piccinni, Guglielmi, Sarti, and Cimarosa, is that once he reaches maturity he does not remain permanently satisfied with dramatic nonsense.

21. Opera Seria

*M*ITRIDATE, *re di Ponto*, Mozart's first *opera seria*, was first performed on 26 December 1770, in Milan. The *scrittura*—the commission to compose it—was the fruit of the admiration the boy had aroused at the beginning of the same year in the house of Count Firmian, Governor-General of Lombardy. Firmian surely did not neglect to obtain from Vienna the Imperial permission to risk the experiment with the child-prodigy, and thus we see that at the outset of his career Mozart did after all receive more significant tokens of favor from the house of Habsburg than mere kisses and second-hand court clothes. I suspect that the recommendation of the boy given by Johann Adolf Hasse, the most famous Italian opera composer of the period, in two letters dated 30 September and 4 October 1769, addressed to the Abbate Ortes in Venice, is connected with this commission. Hasse knew about Leopold's plans for a visit to Italy, and Leopold surely did not keep silent about his desire to obtain for his son the highest triumph that could crown such a tour—a *scrittura*. Doubtless the cautious Vienna court sought assurance from Hasse.

Mozart was in the middle of his fifteenth year when he received the libretto, which had been set two years earlier (1767) by Quirino Gasparini, a musician of Turin. Of musical models he had plenty: Johann Christian Bach, Hasse, Guglielmi, Piccinni, and Jommelli. He heard the latter's *Armida abbandonata* in Naples at a decisive moment, and it at first appealed to him greatly (he wrote, in a letter of 29 May 1770, 'è ben scritta e mi piace veramente' [it is well composed and I really like it]). But a few days later (5 June), presumably under Leopold's influence, although he still held it to be beautiful, he found it 'too serious and old-fashioned for the theater.' Leopold was afraid that his son might stray too far from the popular style and be headstrong about setting too ambitious tasks for the singers.

The story of this first *opera seria* is a strange one. If Mozart, when he wrote *La Finta semplice*, had been ten years older, he would have refused to set such wretched and incoherent nonsense. When it came to *Mitridate*, some persons of judgment—and Leopold, in his blind ambition, was not such a person—should have told him: 'Keep your hands off! This is beyond your powers. Wait until you are more mature, for this is the best libretto for an *opera seria* that you will ever have.' That would have been the truth. The man who made the Italian version, Vittorio Amadeo Cigna-Santi, deserves very little credit for the fact, however. He quite honestly recorded in the libretto, after the *argomento*, his source: 'Veggasi la tragedia del francese Racine, che si è in molte parti imitata.' (See the tragedy by the Frenchman Racine, which has here been imitated to a large extent.) This was not the first time that Racine's *Mithridate*, which, having been written in 1673, was at the time of Mozart's composition almost a hundred years old, had served as the basis for a libretto. Apostolo Zeno had used the material in 1728, and Leopoldo de Villati had re-worked it for Carl Heinrich Graun in 1751. And always something had remained of the nobility, the distinction, the genuine passion, the human truth of the original. The death of Mitridate was not to be avoided, and although it clears the way to a double wedding, there can be no 'happy ending, with the principal character suffering a tragic fate.' Mitridate is an Asiatic despot, but his ill-fated struggle against Rome wins our sympathy, and we cannot blame the aging man when he is not willing simply to give up his betrothed, Aspasia, to his two sons, Sifare and Farnace. The character of Sifare is painted in pure white; Farnace in black—but not unalloyed black, so that the way of repentance is left open for him. The action is simple and logical and—what is most important—almost all the arias are action arias, growing directly out of the situation and not, as in Metastasio, simply finely wrought and sententious expressions that could perfectly well change places with one another. The third act alone is unsuccessful—now dragging (in the moment of greatest danger Mitridate sings an aria, instead of allowing the action to forge ahead) and now over-precipitate. The *opera seria*, from its very beginning, bore a curse of Apollo, which never permitted it, even within its own frame, to approach perfection.

Mozart was too young to take advantage of the virtues of this libretto. He was thinking, of course, of the singers, and he had to do so, since it was his task to win them over. Clearly he first composed all the recitatives and only then all the arias (and *recitativi accompagnati*); accord-

ingly, he must have made a plan of the keys of all the numbers beforehand. He composed stereotyped pieces, of which the most stereotyped,
in the latest Neapolitan style, were those for Mitridate himself, who,
for example, closes the first act with an aria that is almost *buffo* in
style (No. 9). Mozart had to write for four singers of approximately the
same quality—two female sopranos and two *castrati*, one soprano and
one alto—and no matter how characteristic or sensitive the cantilena
he spun, the singers and the listeners were always looking for virtuosity
and coloratura. Mozart had no courage, even in the recitative or in the
orchestral part, which is hardly ever anything but a primitive accompaniment. But along with the concert pieces, along with the arias containing long *ritornelli*, there are pieces in which he embodied a dramatic
spark—pieces in which passion simply will not be kept waiting. Mitridate's entrance aria (No. 7) far transcends mere routine. In it, the
defeated warrior returns to his homeland, weary and sore at heart. This
aria alone is enough to keep one from seeing in him nothing but a stock
theatrical tyrant. Aspasia's aria (No. 4), in G minor, has always been
admired for its explosive directness. The Roman Marzio is well characterized in his single aria (No. 21) with its soldierly march-rhythm,
though the aria is really superfluous. The duet at the end of the second
act is both beautiful and appropriate to its position. The general judgment of connoisseurs may well have been: 'What a lot of superfluous
notes! Any Italian composer would have composed more simply and at
the same time more effectively. But what a talent!'

Between *Mitridate*, the first *opera seria* for Milan, and *Lucio Silla*,
the last, there is a Milan intermezzo. It is called *Ascanio in Alba*, and it
is a *serenata teatrale* or *festa teatrale*, with the composition of which
Count Firmian, on behalf of the Empress, entrusted the boy in connection with the ceremonies attending the wedding of the Archduke
Ferdinand with the Princess Maria Ricciarda Beatrice of Modena. In
earlier times, a serenade of this sort had been interpolated between the
acts of an *opera seria*. On the occasion of an important Imperial wedding, however, it took a whole evening in itself, and the principal opera
for the occasion was left for a later evening. This was Metastasio's *Ruggiero o vero l'eroica gratitudine*, the last opera composed by Hasse.
Leopold Mozart did not miss the opportunity to play off the work of his
son against that of the old master (letter of 19 October 1771): 'It
really distresses me very greatly, but Wolfgang's serenata has completely
killed Hasse's opera . . .'

Mozart composed the work in four weeks, during the month of September 1771: first the *sinfonia*, which is a regular *buffo sinfonia* and leads directly into a ballet; then the recitative and choruses; and finally the arias. The commission was one that wholly suited his age and talent. For the work is a purely decorative creation, in which all that needed to be done was to connect a series of choruses, dances, and recitatives, both *secchi* and *accompagnati*, giving to each the best possible musical investiture. The project made no dramatic demands. The famous Giuseppe Parini, author of the 'Giorno,' who had many enemies and was under the sole protection of Count Firmian, had trouble enough in drawing out the action to the necessary length of a full evening. The Archducal couple saw their own first meeting represented on the stage in a heroic-pastoral masquerade. Ferdinand was Ascanio, the grandson of the goddess Venus, and Maria Beatrice was the shepherdess Silvia, descended from Hercules, offspring of Alcaeus. The only complication in the plot, of which the climax comes when Silvia faints, results from the fact that Venus forbids her grandson to reveal himself at once as the chosen one. No attention is paid to dramatic tempo. The longest aria is sung by the quite superfluous Fauno, a soprano role. For the rest, Mozart was well able to write long and varied *recitativi accompagnati*, and arias in coloratura for the sopranos, and he was free to provide his beloved Manzuoli with an opportunity to exploit his beautiful deep register and to *spianar la voce*. The writing of a *terzetto* presented no difficulties. The only new task was the composition of the choruses of nymphs and shepherds, of which 'five are danced as well as sung.' These choruses are pleasing in sound and almost completely homophonic. One of them (No. 6) has to be repeated until one is tired of it. The whole thing reminds one of a French tapestry, in which the shepherds look like heroes and the heroes like shepherds.

A similar task awaited Mozart a few months later in Salzburg. Hieronymus Colloredo had been appointed Prince-Bishop in March 1772, and for his consecration Wolfgang composed Metastasio's *Sogno di Scipione*, originally written (in 1735) for a quite different occasion— the birthday of the Empress Elisabeth. It is one of the poorest products of the Imperial Court poet's pen, a 'dramatic' version of Cicero's *Somnium Scipionis*. Scipio the Younger has fallen asleep in the palace of Massinissa. In his dream, there appear to him the goddesses of Constancy (Costanza) and Good Fortune (Fortuna), demanding that he choose immediately which of them he will follow for life. Fortuna is especially insistent. Constancy informs him that he is in a part of heaven where his departed ancestors dwell; meanwhile he learns something about the mechanics of the music of the spheres. For the blessed ladies and gentlemen do not neglect the opportunity to join their voices in a chorus. Scipio's foster-father, Scipio Africanus, instructs him about the immortality of the soul and the reward of the virtuous in heaven, and his real father, Aemilianus Paulus, shows him the earth as a mere spark in the celestial spaces, and thus demonstrates to him the insignificance of all that is earthly. Scipio wishes to be taken at once into the company of the blessed, but is informed that he must first perform the duty of saving Rome. He decides, of course, in favor of Costanza, whereupon Fortuna reveals herself in thunder and lightning, as a thoroughgoing fury. Scipio awakes, and a *licenza*—an apostrophizing of the Archbishop—draws the moral of the story.

For Mozart the composition of this wretched piece was simply a matter of routine. The charm of stage-setting was almost completely absent. Accordingly he wrote longer arias than in *Ascanio*, of rather greater (and more provincial) virtuosity, and thought more often of the orchestra, which he knew better than he did the one in Milan. The Chorus of the Blessed Heroes stimulates him to finer work. But there is not the slightest attempt to characterize Fortuna, and everything remains entirely on the level of the decorative. Why he later wrote another setting of the soprano aria of the *licenza*, we do not know, for there is no evidence of a repetition of this occasional work.

Mozart was nearing his seventeenth birthday when he wrote his last opera for Italy, *Lucio Silla*, which was first performed in Milan at Christmas, 1772, and was, like *Ascanio in Alba*, dedicated to the Archduke and his consort. The libretto was by Giovanni de Gamerra, of Leghorn (1743-1803), who had been first an abbé and then a soldier, and was just beginning his literary career. He took the precaution of having his handiwork appraised by Metastasio, who, after making a few suggestions for changes, pronounced his 'full approval.' It would be doing the author too much honor to relate the action in detail. Lucio Silla, the dictator of Rome, desires as his wife Giunia, the daughter of Marius, who is betrothed to the banished Cecilio. Cecilio has secretly returned to Rome; the first act ends with the reunion of the lovers at the grave of Marius. The second act is devoted to a conspiracy against Silla, in which not only Cecilio takes part but also his friend Cinna, who is loved by Silla's sister. The conspiracy fails and

Cecilio is arrested. In the third act, Cecilio is condemned to death—a fate that Giunia is prepared to share with him. But at the end, after a pathetic accusation of Silla by Giunia before the assembled senate and people, Silla, in good Metastasian style, suddenly shows himself to be a man of noble heart, transforms himself from a dictator into a citizen, and gives up any objections to a double wedding.

The libretto contains two arias intended for Silla which Mozart did not set to music—obviously for external reasons. The tenor, Bassano Morgnoni, to whom the principal role of Silla had to be entrusted, was such a novice that Mozart did not dare to give him more than two arias, and even these two are the most conventional in the whole opera. Thus he concentrated his entire forces in the arias for the two first-class singers who took the parts of Giunia and Cecilio: Anna de Amicis and Venanzio Rauzzini. For de Amicis he composed three arias (Nos. 4, 11, and 16) of such brilliance and virtuosity that he revived them in 1777 and 1778 for Aloysia, and even had one of them, the last, sung as late as 1783, in Vienna, by Therese Teyber. But along with these display pieces there is another, in C minor (No. 22), that is quite simple and brief, without any virtuoso display, and so deeply felt that it would do honor to the role of Donna Anna. Rauzzini received a few lyric pieces of similar beauty and for the two together Mozart wrote a duet that, in its sensuous brilliance, anticipates parts of *Così fan tutte*. For these two singers, also, he wrote the most beautiful scene of the opera—their nocturnal meeting at the grave of Marius—including one of the many expressive *recitativi accompagnati* the work contains, and a *lugubre canto* for the chorus. This is one of the rare scenes of the *opera seria* in which the mood of a scene comes alive. Another advance into the realm of tragedy is a trio at the end of the second act, in which the two lovers are united, not only dramatically but musically as well, against the threatening dictator—just as one day Leonore and Manrico are to be united against Count di Luna in a juxtaposition that constitutes the germ of a greater finale. In general, however, the work is thoroughly unsuccessful and uneven. Not because it has too many arias sung by secondary characters (one of whom, the singer of the role of Celia, had definite *buffo* tendencies, and apparently wished to exhibit her brilliance in staccati); not because of the false heroism, which no longer had any meaning for Mozart; but rather because his entire relation to one species had become false. The music he wrote was much too beautiful, too rich, too overladen, too instrumentally conceived. He acquitted himself of a purely musical task. In this work the aria became for him a symphonic movement dominated by the vocal part. Indeed, he could have found the material for a dozen symphonies in the work. His listeners apparently felt this instinctively. Leopold reports at length (2 January 1773) about the unlucky star under which the first performance was given. But the repetitions, too, of which there were apparently more than twenty, had no lasting effect. The work was never produced outside Milan. In 1774, Anfossi wrote a new *Lucio Silla* for Venice, and in 1779 Gamerra made over his text for Michele Mortellari in Turin. Mozart never had an opportunity to compose another opera for Italy.

What is true of *Lucio Silla*—that Mozart could have used the material in the arias for a dozen symphonies—is even more true in the same sense of the *componimento drammatico* he wrote in April 1775, in Salzburg, for the festivities attending the visit of the Archduke Maximilian Franz, the youngest son of the Empress. This was *Il Re pastore*, one of the later works of Metastasio. Although Metastasio wrote to a friend, the Conte di Cervellon, on 6 December 1751, after completing the libretto: 'Non ho mai scritto alcuna delle mie opere con facilità uguale e della quale io abbia meno arrossito.' (None of my works was written with as much facility and about none have I had less occasion to blush)—nevertheless, it is one of his weakest. The two pairs of lovers, who under the patronage of Alexander the Great represent the theme of love *versus* reasons of state, produce veritable torrents of noble sentiments, and words of wisdom about the duties of a ruler drip unceasingly, sweet as syrup. The arias—half heroic, half pastoral—have hardly any connection with the action. There is nothing for Mozart to do but write beautiful music, again instrumentally conceived. But this time it is less in the style of the symphony than in that of the concerto, conceived for three sopranos and two tenors, as *voci principali*. This was the year of the five violin concertos, and many of the arias, in which the second part simply takes over the function of a development, are exactly like concerto-movements in miniature. Others are charming andantinos in which the singing voice takes the part of the solo instrument. Two of the arias employ *concertante* instrumental solos in competition with the voice: a heroic one of Alessandro's, using the flute, and a lyric one of Aminta's (*L'amerò, sarò costante*), the violin. The latter, a rondo, defaced by a tasteless cadenza written in the nineteenth century, has become very well known. The first act closes

with a charming duet; the second with a *vaudeville*—a *tutti-ritornello*
with soli. The distance that separates this work from the Milan operas
and from *La Betulia*, after an interval of hardly two and a half years,
is infinite. If any relation is to be seen, it is with the decorative *Ascanio
in Alba*. But the invention in *Il Re pastore* is of a quite new order—
warmer, more full-blooded, more personal, less stereotyped. Everything
is richer and more concentrated—not simply shorter. It is clear that
Mozart has already tired of the *langer Geschmack* (the taste for length)
of Salzburg. He no longer writes long-winded orchestral *ritornelli*, when
he writes any at all, and he composes his first real, one-movement overture, full of thematic life and variety—an overture that no longer has
anything to do with the *sinfonia*. He performed this overture as late
as February 1778 in Mannheim in an 'academy' at Cannabich's, using
with it presumably the first aria, an andantino, as middle movement,
and composing a finale for the occasion.

For five years—years full of a ceaseless longing to write opera, and
occupied with dramatic essays and the composition of a substitute for
opera—no further operatic commission offered itself. In despair, Mozart even began on his own account to compose a 'German opera' (for
that was the category that had the best prospects of being produced at
the time), 'Zaïde.' Then, after his return from Paris, came the great
opportunity. Carl Theodor ordered for the Munich carnival of 1781
an *opera seria*, and, as the *Münchner Local-Bericht* stated after the performance on 29 January, the work was thoroughly a Salzburg product:
the music was by the Salzburg Court Organist Wolfgang Amadeus
Mozart, the libretto by the Abbate Giambatista Varesco, Colloredo's
Court Chaplain, and the German translation included in the printed
libretto was by Andreas Schachtner, Court Trumpeter in Salzburg and
family friend of the Mozarts.

For the first time there arose a situation that indicates the complete
awakening of Mozart's dramatic instinct: a conflict between the composer and the librettist. The material Varesco had to handle was not
bad, and it was familiar to every one in its Biblical version: the story
of Jephtha, who on his return from the wars makes a vow to offer up
as a sacrifice to God the first living being he meets, and who thereupon
encounters his daughter. In the opera, of course, the story is made
over into a Greek one: Idomeneo, King of Crete, is returning home
from the destruction of Troy, whence he has sent on in advance as a
prisoner, among others, Ilia, the daughter of Priam. Pursued until the

end by the wrath of Poseidon, he makes the fateful vow during the last storm while in sight of his native shores, and thereupon encounters his son Idamante, to whom, after the scene of recognition, he does not dare to reveal the terrible secret. Arbace, his confidant, advises him to let Idamante escape from the danger by allowing him to escort Elektra, the sister of Orestes, to Argos. (Heaven only knows what Elektra is doing on the island of Crete!) But Poseidon is not to be trifled with. At the moment of their departure, he stirs up a new storm and sends a sea-monster who lays low an even greater number of the population of the poor kingdom of Crete than the Minotaur had once done. Idamante vanquishes the mythological beast, but the high priest insists that the nature of the promised sacrifice be stated. Idomeneo has to reveal the dread secret, and is ready to sacrifice his son, when Ilia throws herself between them and offers to take the place of Idamante. This appeases Poseidon, and a subterranean voice commands the abdication of Idomeneo in favor of Idamante, and the marriage of the latter to Ilia. Poor Elektra is left without consolation.

Varesco's model was a *tragédie lyrique* by Antoine Danchet, which had been set to music in 1712 by Campra, and his libretto owes a great deal to its French forebear. As far as its versification is concerned it may be in the style of Metastasio, but not at all as regards its construction or its spirit. Metastasio never offered a musician the opportunity for such an imposing scene as that of the shipwreck of Idomeneo before the eyes of his anxious people; he never worked the chorus so firmly into the story as an active participant; and he would certainly have introduced some male puppet-character so that Elektra should not be left alone at the end. What a typically Metastasian master-stroke it would have been, for example, to unite Elektra and Idomeneo! This is not to say that the libretto is a good one. But Mozart, now twenty-five years old, and with the experiences of Mannheim and Paris behind him, would not have set it to music if he had found it unusable. He sought to make it even more usable, and in doing so he had his troubles with the librettist, as we learn from his letters to his father, beginning with that of 8 November 1780. Varesco was a proud and self-willed fool, and actually succeeded in having the product of his pen appear in unabridged form in its first printing. But Mozart altered it with complete freedom. Brevity was always his motto. He was always complaining: 'It is really far too long!' (as in the letter of 24 November 1780). He considered it of no importance that an aria should necessarily have a *seconda parte*: '. . . we do not need a second part—which is all the better' (letter of 29 November). He never dreamed of setting to music all the stanzas Varesco provided for the chorus numbers. His careful attention extended to the smallest detail, such as the placing of resonant vowels, as well as to the most important matters, such as scenic convenience and the total scenic effect.

It has been observed that Mozart in *Idomeneo* approached French opera in general and Gluck in particular, and there is no denying that the important participation of the chorus, the conclusion of the first act with a *chaconne*, a great decorative choral scene, the introduction of marches, and the ballet-music are 'French'; or that Mozart introduces a subterranean voice accompanied by trombones just as Gluck includes pronouncements of the oracle in his *Alceste*. But at bottom Mozart was never more independent than in *Idomeneo*. He wrote this work in a burst of musical inspiration. This was his first opportunity to exert his full powers; this was the first time he had written an opera for which he could count on all the resources of opera. The singers were not a cause of unalloyed pleasure. Old Raaff, for whom Idomeneo was the last role of his career, had to be handled with care; Panzacchi, who sang Arbace, was also an old *routinier*; and the *castrato* del Prato, who sang Idamante, was a rank beginner and as stiff as a board. But with the ladies, Dorothea and Liesel Wendling, who sang Ilia and Elektra, he had not the slightest difficulties. And above all, he had the best orchestra in the world: 'Do come soon, and hear and admire the orchestra!' he wrote, just after his arrival in Munich (8 November 1780), to his father. Thus we find in this score, which one never tires of studying, and which will always remain a source of delight to every true musician, a veritable explosion of the power of musical invention—and not only of musical, but of musico-dramatic as well. We no longer notice that fact simply because the *opera seria* has become an alien form. But *Idomeneo* hardly preserves anything in common with the earlier *opere serie* or *feste teatrali* of Mozart. It is true that he did not turn his back entirely on the whole species. If he had, he might have done without Elektra; but then he would have lost the opportunity for some of the most beautiful arias, such as the aria of rage, in C minor (No. 29), which is not unworthy of the Queen of the Night. He would then also have had to eliminate the superfluous role of Arbace—Arbace who among other things has to sing the following, in a mood of ominous foreboding of the fate of Crete:

Se colà ne'fati è scritto,	If there in the fates it is written,
Creta, o Dei, s'è rea, or cada,	That Crete, O Gods, if guilty, must fall,
Paghi il fio del suo delitto,	Then must she pay the price of her crime.
Ma salvate il prence, il rè	But save the prince, the King,
Deh d'un sol vi plachi il sangue,	Ah, be content with a single life,
Ecco il mio, se il mio v'aggrada,	Here is mine own, if mine ye accept,
E il bel regno che già langue,	And on this glorious Kingdom, already failing,
Giusti Dei! abbia mercè.	Just Gods! have mercy.

If a violoncello were substituted for the voice in this aria, we should have one of the most beautiful concerto andantes that Mozart ever wrote.

But only a few numbers in the opera are as instrumental or as formal in conception as this one. In fact, the distinguishing quality of the whole work is that it contains nothing merely traditional or conventional or stereotyped. For Raaff, Mozart wrote a heroic aria (*Fuor del mar*, No. 12) in the old style, which nevertheless became a display piece of unparalleled brilliance. The orchestra follows the vocal parts with an elasticity, an attention to detail, and a sensuousness that are a never-ending object for our admiration. Sometimes Mozart brings forward the soloists in the orchestra, as, for example, in Ilia's aria *Se il padre perdei* (No. 11), the flute, oboe, bassoon, and horn. The richness of some scenes has perhaps been equalled only by Berlioz: the last scene in the second act, for example, which begins with a barcarole-idyll in E major, includes a wonderful *terzetto*, and ends with the storm and the curse of the people, in D minor. Mozart is not afraid of anything, even of the shipwreck scene, with its two contrasting choruses, one on the stage and one in the distance. The Quartet, No. 21, in which Idamante takes his leave, did not altogether please Raaff; but Mozart succeeded in making of it perhaps the most deeply felt and most stirring piece in the whole opera. It is the first really great ensemble in the history of the *opera seria*. Mozart no longer wrote any every-day numbers. To us it seems as if in *Idomeneo* he had brought a series of his best vocal concert numbers—*recitativi accompagnati*, arias, and ensembles—into a dramatic connection and united them by means of an imposing and uncanny overture, choral scenes, and instrumental pieces. Yet for its period *Idomeneo* was, in operatic form, a drama of unprecedented freedom and daring.

But *Idomeneo* is one of those works that even a genius of the highest rank, like Mozart, could write only once in his life. It is an *opera seria* unlike any other. It was not taken up in other cities simply because at the time only Munich could produce such a work. Mozart wished to transplant it to Vienna, and had in mind a performance in German translation, following the precedent of Gluck with some of his operas; but he had to give up the idea. In 1786, the work seems to have had a concert performance in private for which Mozart added some purely concert pieces to it (K. 489 and 490). As always, he did only infinite harm to his own work, just as he later did when he made changes in *Don Giovanni* and *Figaro*. Only the elimination of the role of Arbace was perhaps an improvement. But even in Vienna, five years after its original composition, and when Mozart was five years older and more mature, he found nothing to change as far as the essence of the music was concerned. It is said that he valued and loved *Idomeneo* most among all his works, and this any true musician can easily understand.

For ten years then, Mozart did not write another opera *seria*. Vienna, despite Gluck or perhaps because of him, had ceased to be a home of serious Italian opera. Gluck virtually had to force his *Alceste* on the Viennese. The weight of his personality and of his continent-wide reputation was such in the early 'eighties that he could produce his Paris operas in German, but the place where they made a really deep impression was not Vienna but North Germany, especially Berlin. At the Imperial Court there were no longer many festal occasions to celebrate. The Empress Mother, Maria Theresa, had been dead since 1780, and the Emperor, widowed and childless, was far too parsimonious to indulge in opera *seria* with its lavish stage-settings and its *castrati*.

Then, in the summer of his last year, Mozart received one more commission. The Bohemian Estates extended to him, through the impresario Guardasoni, an invitation to write a festival opera for the coronation of Leopold II as King of Bohemia. He had four weeks in which to execute the commission. The libretto was prescribed—*La Clemenza di Tito*, by Metastasio, one of the oldest tributes of loyalty from the pen of the imperial poet. (He had written it in 1734.) The first performance took place on 6 September 1791; it was not a success, either among the Imperial Highnesses or with the public. The categorical judgment of the Empress has been recorded: *una porcheria tedesca* (German rubbish). The Prague reporter for Kunzen and Reichardt's *Studien für Tonkünstler und Musik-Freunde* (IX, p. 70) stated:

The grand Italian opera *La Clemenza di Tito* composed by the Herr Capellmeister Mozart, produced in connection with the coronation ceremonies, did not have the success that the composer, who has always been so popular here, had a right to expect.

But this was true only of the first performance. On 7 October, Mozart was able to write to Constanze, probably relying on reports of the Duscheks or of the clarinettist Stadler:

. . . *Tito* was given in Prague for the last time [30 September] with tremendous applause. Bedini sang better than ever. The little duet in A major which the two maidens sing was repeated; and had not the audience wished to spare Madame Marchetti, a repetition of the rondo would have been very welcome. Cries of 'Bravo' were shouted at Stodla [= Stadler, for the arias Nos. 9 and 23] from the parterre and even from the orchestra . . .

It is customary to speak disparagingly of *La Clemenza di Tito* and to dismiss it as the product of haste and fatigue. A product of haste it certainly was. There was so little time that Süssmayr had to take over the composition of the secco recitatives; his authorship of them quickly became known: the Prague correspondent previously quoted already knew of it, and Niemtschek (p. 74) confirmed it. But not of fatigue. *Die Zauberflöte* and the *Requiem*, on which Mozart was working at the same time, show little sign of fatigue. Mozart's contemporaries and the composer himself had a quite different opinion of *La Clemenza di Tito*. Its success constantly increased during the rest of the century, and of all Mozart's operas this was the first to reach London, and the only one that did not have to suffer the mutilations to which the others, until very recent times, continued to be subjected there. As for Mozart himself, he entered in his catalogue: 'La Clemenza di Tito . . . ridotta a vera opera dal Signore Mazzolà, Poeta di S:A:S:l'Elettore di Sassonia' (made into a real opera by Signor Mazzolà, court poet to His Serene Highness, the Elector of Saxony). This was an honor he did not pay to da Ponte even for *Figaro*, *Don Giovanni*, or *Così fan tutte*; only for

Die Zauberflöte did he again remember to mention the librettist, Schikaneder.

The feeling of gratitude that Mozart apparently felt towards Caterino Mazzolà was not unjustified. He would certainly have been unable in 1791 to compose a libretto by Metastasio just as it stood, as he had done in his youth with *La Betulia liberata*, *Il Sogno di Scipione*, and *Il Re pastore*, or as Caldara, Hasse, Gluck, Galuppi, Jommelli, Giuseppe Scarlatti, Anfossi, and many others had already done with *La Clemenza di Tito*. Metastasio's libretto for this opera is, in accordance with the practice of the *opera seria* in 1734, nothing but a chain of exit arias, joined together by long recitatives; there is no provision even for the smallest duet. What Mazzolà did with this libretto is evidence not of lack of respect but of courage and ingenuity.

The three acts of the original are condensed into two, the endless secco recitatives are shortened, many of the old arias are replaced by others, newly written, and offering more favorable opportunities to the composer, and finally all the ensemble pieces—the three duets, the three trios, the final quintet of the first act, and the final sextet of the second act—are added.*

We may add that Mazzolà provided Mozart with the opportunity for the musically and scenically grandiose conclusion of the first act, the burning of the Capitol and the chorus of the outraged people in the distance. Naturally Mazzolà could not make a masterpiece out of Metastasio's court libretto. Tito is nothing but a mere puppet representing magnanimity, renouncing his chosen brides when he learns that they are already promised, and tearing up death sentences that he has already signed. Vitellia, who secretly loves Tito, and, because she believes herself scorned by him, incites the conspiracy against him, is similarly nothing but a puppet representing the thirst for revenge and the pangs of conscience. Sesto, who loves her and is used by her as a tool in the attempted assassination, is a mere puppet representing the state of being in love and emotions of repentance. There are two more puppets, Servilia, Sesto's sister, and Annio—with whom she is in love—the friend of Tito and Sesto. And there is of course the inevitable Publio, commander of the Praetorean Guards and confidant of Tito. These puppets cannot be made into real people merely by simplifying the machinery of the action or by shortening the dialogue. Mazzolà, as a matter of

* *Revisions-Bericht* in Complete Works Edition, v, iii.

fact, at times roughly disturbed the mechanism of the action, which in Metastasio's original, as always in his works, runs on finely greased wheels. But he made the libretto a hundred times more effective.

This libretto has the form, but of course not the spirit, of an *opera buffa*. It has two acts like an *opera buffa*, and the end of the first act is planned exactly on the principle of an *opera buffa*, that is, leaving the action quite up in the air, and the issue quite undecided. There are ensembles instead of arias, rapid progress in the action, and the expression of conflicting feelings in the ensembles. Brevity was Mazzolà's motto as well as Mozart's. (Perhaps it was even required by the Court.) Thus Mozart composed only two extended arias: Sesto's (No. 19), the most famous one in the work, and the rondo-aria of Vitellia (No. 23), which—very effectively—leads directly into the fatal *marche de supplice*, the final scene. The need for brevity was so compelling that Mozart apparently suppressed entirely an aria of Tito's between Scenes VII and VIII of the second act. The famous Duettino (No. 3) for Sesto and Annio, twenty-four measures long, is a little ditty—something unheard of in an *opera seria*. The arias contain no *ritornelli*; they seldom have any return of the first part; and they are almost all constructed on the pattern of a rapid increase in intensity. The ensembles are all built on psychological contrasts. In one trio (No. 10), Vitellia, chosen by Tito to be his bride, expresses her bewilderment while the two witnesses, Annio and Publio, completely misinterpret her feelings. Even more beautiful is the later trio (No. 14), in which Sesto, arrested by Publio, takes leave of Vitellia, while the bailiff tries to hurry him along but cannot suppress his own sympathy for him. All the decorative portions, too—the marches and choruses—are short but very vivid and striking. The shortness of the time in which the commission had to be executed restricted Mozart to the greatest simplicity, even in the orchestra, and even in the *concertante* elements. Only Stadler, in the two arias mentioned, was richly provided for in parts for the clarinet and basset horn. The Overture has become a sister work to the Overture to *Die Zauberflöte*: it is both festal and characteristic.

Mozart did what he could. Let us state once again that he was not a revolutionary and had no desire to burst open the framework of the *opera seria*; but what he did do was to expand that form to its uttermost limits. He had Gluck's model before him but he did not follow it, since he did not wish to sacrifice musical considerations to the extent to which Gluck, making a virtue of his limitations, was ready to sacrifice them. But why should we make apologies for Mozart for not having left us any such immortal work in the domain of the *opera seria* as *Figaro* or *Die Zauberflöte?* Who else in the eighteenth century created any such works in this field? What opera of Gluck's is still really alive— so alive that we can enjoy it even without any historical sense and without putting ourselves into a special frame of mind? The *opera seria* in 1790 was already an artifact, a fossil relic of earlier cultural strata. It needed to be transformed; and it was transformed, becoming, first 'grand heroic opera' as in Spontini, and then simply 'grand opera,' as in Weber's *Euryanthe*, Auber's *Masaniello*, Rossini's *Guillaume Tell*, the operas of Meyerbeer, and Wagner's *Rienzi*. And only truly great musicians and personalities, such as Wagner and Verdi, succeeded in making it at all human.

22. Opera Buffa

*I*N LATE SUMMER, 1774, Mozart received the commission to write an *opera buffa* for Munich—not yet for the splendid Munich of the Elector Carl Theodor, for whom he was later to compose *Idomeneo*, but for the more modest court of the Elector Maximilian Joseph, who three years later was to state that he had 'no vacancy' for him. Mozart composed *La Finta giardiniera* half in Salzburg, and half in Munich, between September 1774 and January 1775, and the first performance took place on 13 January. Mozart wrote home to his mother on the following day:

Thank God! My opera was performed yesterday, the 13th, for the first time and was such a success that it is impossible for me to describe the applause to Mamma. In the first place, the whole theater was so packed that a great many people were turned away. Then after each aria there was a terrific noise, clapping of hands and cries of 'Viva Maestro.' Her Highness the Electress and the Dowager Electress (who were sitting opposite me) also called out 'Bravo' to me. After the opera was over and during the pause when there is usually silence until the ballet begins, people kept on clapping all the time and shouting 'Bravo'; now stopping, now beginning again and so on . . .

Actually, however, the work was not a success, any more than *Lucio Silla* had been, two years earlier. No Italian opera house interested itself in the work, and it was only in 1779 that a wandering German troupe, that of Böhm, which was then in Salzburg, took it over and carried it, in the form of a German *Singspiel*—that is, with spoken dialogue replacing the recitatives—in a very adroit and faithful translation by the actor Stierle, all over southern and western Germany. (This was how the autograph of the first of the three acts was lost; but fortunately we are able to reconstruct the text completely.) As late as 1789, *Das verstellte Gärtnermädchen* was produced in Frankfurt-am-Main as a 'comic opera.' At one of the performances in Munich, the Swabian poet, journalist, and musician, Christian Friedrich Daniel Schubart, was present, and he gives the following account in his *Deutsche Chronik* under the date of 27 April 1775:

I also heard an *opera buffa* by the wonderful genius Mozart; it is called *La Finta giardiniera*. There were flames of genius flickering here and there, but they did not combine to make that still, small altar fire that rises in clouds of incense to heaven and makes a fragrance pleasing to the gods . . .

Schubart apparently took Mozart for a *Sturm und Drang* artist. Or he simply could not follow the abundance of music that Mozart poured into his work. But the effect upon Schubart was the one Mozart's music generally had upon his contemporaries.

In *La Finta semplice*, written in 1768, Mozart had been four years behind the latest developments in libretto writing; in *La Finta giardiniera*, he had fully caught up with them. The text, anonymous, but presumably by Calzabigi, who had been Gluck's collaborator, had been set to music by Pasquale Anfossi only half a year before Mozart began his work. Anfossi's opera, first performed in the Teatro delle Dame in Rome, had had a great success. By 1775 it had spread not only all over Italy but as far north as Dresden. Naturally, Mozart knew Anfossi's score very well. And he would have been a fool if he had not taken it without hesitation as a springboard for his own work. He followed it, as a comparison shows, in every step; but he gave his wonderful Mozartean gift of musical invention free play, where Anfossi had provided very little more than routine material. He seized the opportunity to write for better singers and for a better orchestra than were ordinarily available to the Italian *buffo* writers.

Mozart's score contains such bewitching things that some people have believed he must have changed much of it after 1775, while others have looked upon it as a preparation for *Figaro* or *Don Giovanni*. Both views are incorrect. Not a single piece in the whole work, except for a few recitatives for the German version, was added or changed later. And the work is not yet a companion of *Figaro* but rather, despite all its qualities, of *La Finta semplice*. Mozart was still in a state of utter innocence, so to speak, when he wrote it. A few years were to pass before he would throw such a text out the window. He was still so possessed with music that once more he unhesitatingly accepted what was offered him.

This text belongs to a type quite different from that of *La Finta semplice*. In the printed version of the libretto there is a strange division of the roles, which is worth quoting verbatim:

Parti serie

Arminda Gentildonna Milanese Amante del Cav. Ramiro, ed ora promessa sposa al Contino Belfiore.
Il Cavaliere *Ramiro* Amante di Arminda, dalla stessa abbandonato.

Parti buffe

La Marchesa *Violante* Amante del Contino Belfiore creduta morta sotto nome di *Sandrina* in abito di Giardiniera.
Il *Contino Belfiore* primo amante di Violante, ed ora d'Arminda.
Serpetta Cameriera del Podestà innamorata del medesimo.
Don Anchise Podestà di Lagonero, Amante di Sandrina.
Roberto servo di Violante, che si finge suo cugino sotto nome di *Nardo* da Giardiniero, Amante di Serpetta da lei non corrisposto.*

This division into *seria* and *buffa* parts points to a new development in the *opera buffa*. *La Finta semplice* had been nothing but a direct descendant of the *commedia dell'arte*. But in *La Finta giardiniera*, tragic and *buffa* elements were mixed—if we may misuse the term tragic by applying it to the *opera buffa*. The *Podestà* is of course our old friend Pantalone: the old fool, who still falls in love with young girls; embodying, as an official, a *magistrato*, inflated self-importance; he is a caricature. And the chambermaid, Serpetta, who would be happy to become the wife of the *Podestà*, coquettish, heartless, shameless, is of

---

* Seria Parts

Arminda, a gentlewoman of Milan, in love with the cavalier *Ramiro*, but now the promised bride of the Contino Belfiore.
The cavalier *Ramiro*, lover of Arminda, who has abandoned him.

Buffa Parts

The *Marchesa Violante*, in love with the Contino Belfiore, believed dead, but appearing under the name of Sandrina in the garb of a gardener-maid.
The *Contino Belfiore*, formerly the lover of Violante, now of Arminda.
Serpetta, maid-servant of the Podestà, in love with the same.
Don Anchise, Podestà of Lagonero, lover of Sandrina.
Roberto, servant of Violante, who pretends to be her cousin under the name of *Nardo*, the gardener, in love with Serpetta, but not loved by her.

course a descendant of the *Serva padrona*, and is more a type than a person; just as Nardo represents the Pulcinella type, except that here he is rather an honest lout. But what of the four other roles? What of the Contino, who in a fit of jealousy has sorely wounded his betrothed, Violante, and believes her dead? What of Sandrina, who still loves the 'murderer,' and who tries, by disguising herself as the gardener-maid in the service of the *Podestà*, to find out where he has fled to? It is no amusing situation in which she finds herself having to repel the advances of the old fool and bear the hatred of the chambermaid. She really belongs much more in the category of the *seria* parts than Arminda, the niece of the *Podestà*, a proud, willful, malicious, and brutal person, who prefers the Contino to her old lover Ramiro, and causes her rival, Sandrina, to be put aside. Ramiro is in the category where he belongs, for he is a constant, faithful, and despairing lover.

We see that the division is not based on the essentially tragic or comic character of the roles, but on convention, and on the categories to which the singers who took those roles belonged. It is regrettable but true that Mozart respected these categories without hesitation. He saw before him the singers and the conventions, instead of looking into the hearts of his characters. Sandrina sings an aria, *Noi donne poverine*, No. 4, in rondo form, with a second allegro part appended (Mozart loves this form), which belongs in the domain of a soubrette like Zerlina. The Contino, who has attempted murder out of jealousy, sings a burlesque aria (*Da scirocco a tramontana*, No. 8) in which he counts up his noble ancestors, who go back to Caracalla and Numa. Even the *Podestà* does not take this fool seriously. Another aria sung by the Count (*Care pupille*, No. 15) begins in an amorous and heartfelt tone, but must end on a note of burlesque. One effective scene occurs in the second act. Ramiro brings the *Podestà* a letter from Milan, in which the Contino is named as the murderer of Violante-Sandrina; the *Podestà* is compelled to arraign the Count, which he does in a very comic *recitativo secco*, and on this occasion the Count conducts himself as pathetically as a pickpocket caught in the act. Sandrina saves him by declaring that she is really Violante and that she has only been wounded, not killed, whereupon the delighted Count declares his love for her anew. The action could be over at this point, but Sandrina once again denies her identity and thrusts her unhappy lover from her, which drives him nearly to madness. The end of the second act and the beginning of the third are full of actual mad-scenes of the two lovers: in the Finale of the second act they believe themselves to be shepherds, then Medusa and Hercules; then they propose a dance; and all this before the astonished eyes of the five other characters. Not until the third act is their madness dispelled. In this connection we must remember that the eighteenth century found all evidences of madness extremely funny—even in Gluck's *Rencontre imprévue*, the figure of a mad painter, Vertigo, provides comic relief which we find repulsive. And everyone knows how interesting the early nineteenth century found the mad scenes of the coloratura singers in such *opere serie* as *Lucia di Lammermoor* and *I Puritani*.

There is a strange mixture of the *seria* and the *buffa* in this *opera buffa*—an impossible mixture. In *Don Giovanni*, when Donna Elvira is placed in a comic situation, as when she wastes all her tenderness on Leporello, who is masquerading as Don Giovanni, we find her doubly tragic. In *La Finta giardiniera* such situations are simply shocking. And since there are no really defined characters, Mozart cannot write any grand ensembles; as a matter of fact, the only opportunities to do so are in the Introduction and in the Finales, for, except for a duet and a trio, *La Finta giardiniera* consists exclusively of exit arias, and thus belongs, in the technical, dramatic sense, to an outmoded genre. The Introduction and the Finales are in dialogue form, not contrapuntal, like the Finales of the three great *opere buffe* written in Vienna. But Mozart already tries to bring together the individual scenes of which they consist by the use of persistent motives in the accompaniment; and one number, in the first Finale, attains symphonic stature.

Ex. 97

Sandrina: Ah che, so- lo io son ca- pa-ce Di tor- men -to e di do- lor

Contino: Ah che so- lo io son ca- pa- ce di tor- men- to

Each character speaks, as far as may be, in his own style, but one after the other; and it is only in the second Finale that the two groups are set off against each other.

But when one has stated the basic error of this opera, which is that Mozart composed it at all, one must express delight at how he composed it. What wit there is in the caricature arias: the one of the *Podestà* (*Dentro il mio petto*, No. 3), which grows into a game of in-strumentation; or *Una damina*, No. 17, which, in its inflated self-importance, seems like a study for Bartolo's great aria in *Figaro*; or Nardo's imitations of the Italian, French, and English styles (No. 14)! What a wealth of invention in the 'grand' arias, such as Arminda's in G minor (*Vorrei punirti indegno*, No. 13)! What heartfelt emotion in the pieces in which Mozart's soul is stirred: Sandrina's tender aria *Geme la tortorella* (No. 11), or her grand scena *Crudele fermati* (No. 21), in C major and A minor, which is worthy of any opera seria, or rather of any true grand opera! For the musician who knows the basis of this work, and accepts the fact of its essential weakness, it is a de-light from beginning to end.

Not until Vienna did Mozart again approach the field of opera buffa. It is fortunate that he did not do so until he was fully mature, so that he did not waste his genius any further on mediocre materials. He had *Idomeneo* and *Die Entführung aus dem Serail* behind him. After com-pleting *Die Entführung*, he applied himself at first to the composition of another German opera, of which only fragments are preserved (K. 433 and 435), and which must have been much more broadly burlesque in character—a sort of opera buffa in German. But he soon abandoned it, and he seems to have had the prospect of placing a true opera buffa with a new Italian troupe in Vienna. In any case, his urge to create such a work became so powerful that despite all his experiences in working on *Idomeneo* he again set his hopes on the Court Chaplain of Salzburg, after he had in vain

looked through at least a hundred libretti and more, but I have hardly found a single one with which I am satisfied; that is to say, so many alterations would have to be made here and there, that even if a poet would undertake to make them, it would be easier for him to write a completely new text—which indeed it is always best to do . . .

So I have been thinking that unless Varesco is still very much an-noyed with us about the Munich opera, he might write me a new libretto for seven characters. Basta! You will know best if this can be arranged. In the meantime he could jot down a few ideas, and when I come to Salzburg we could then work them out together. The most essential thing is that on the whole the story should be really comic; and, if possible, he ought to introduce two equally good female parts, one of these to be seria, the other mezzo carattere, but both parts equal *in importance and excellence.* The third female character, however, may be entirely buffa, and so may all the male ones, if necessary.*

It looks as if Mozart were still thinking in categories, in typical roles, for which typical protagonists were available in Vienna. But among these protagonists was Benucci, who was later to be Mozart's Figaro, and who was far more than a mere Arlecchino or Pantalone. It is unfortunate that Mozart approached Varesco with demands that could have been satisfied by the libretto for a second *Finta giardiniera*. And that is how they were satisfied—or rather in much worse fashion. When Mozart came to Salzburg in the summer of 1783, he talked over the plan of the whole opera with Varesco. Varesco completed the first act, and Mozart, in his blind eagerness, set himself immediately at composing it, so that he could take sketches of a part of this act with him to Vienna. Then he began to have his doubts. On 6 December he wrote to his father:

I have only three more arias to compose and then the first act of my opera will be finished. I can really say that I am quite satisfied with the aria buffa, the quartet and the finale and am looking forward to their performance. I should therefore be sorry to have written this music to no purpose, I mean, if we do not secure what is absolutely necessary . . .

Then follows a series of proposals for basic changes—proposals that Mozart supplemented in two further letters, dated 10 and 24 December. The astonishing thing is that he still did not see how impossible Varesco's whole handiwork was, although already on 6 December he admitted to his father: 'I must tell you that my only reason for not objecting to this goose story altogether was because two people of greater insight and judgment than myself have not disapproved of it, I mean yourself and Varesco.' But the true reason was that Mozart had a pre-conceived idea of the opera buffa: 'The more comic an Italian opera is the better!' (December 6.) 'I am very curious to see how you carry out your capital idea of bringing Biondello into the tower. Provided it is diverting, I shall raise no objection, even if it is a little unnatural.' (December 24.) And then nothing further is said of the work. Varesco was either not in a position, or not willing, to carry out Mozart's proposals, or else Mozart himself came to the conclusion, after further reflection on the plot, that he was wasting his efforts on a

---

* Letter to his father, 7 May 1783.

piece of nonsense. If Constanze had not destroyed Leopold's replies, we should presumably know the truth of the matter.

We need not analyze in detail Varesco's libretto, of which the complete plan survives. Again the list of the eight roles will suffice:

Don Pippo Marchese di Ripasecca innamorato di Lavina, e credutosi vedovo di
Donna Pantea sotto nome di *Sandra*, sua moglie.
Celidora loro unica figlia destinata sposa al Conte Lionetto di Casavuota, Amante di
Biondello, Gentiluomo ricco di Ripasecca.
Calandrino Nipote di Pantea, Amico di Biondello, ed Amante corrisposto di
Lavina, Compagna di Celidora.
Chichibio, Maestro di casa di Don Pippo, Amante di
Auretta, Cameriera di Donna Pantea.*

The kernel of the plot is a wager, as it was later to be—but with what a difference—in *Così fan tutte*. The old fool Don Pippo holds his daughter Celidora, with her companion Lavina, locked in a tower, and promises her to Biondello as his wife, if Biondello can succeed in getting into the tower within a year. The attempt to enter the tower by means of a bridge fails: Don Pippo surprises the lovers at the last moment (Finale I). Then Biondello's friend, Calandrino, an ingenious mechanic, who is himself in love with Lavina, secretly devises an artificial goose, and sends it over the water to Pantea, who is to come to Ripasecca disguised and exhibit the marvel at the fair. The plan is to hide Biondello in it. Don Pippo, so the conspirators believe, will not refuse to let the poor girls in the tower have the curio, and thus Biondello will win the wager. After a hundred nonsensical and ridiculous complications, the plan succeeds, and at the end we are confronted with four more or less happy couples. Such is 'The Goose of Cairo'—*L'Oca del Cairo*.

---

* *Don Pippo*, Marchese of Ripasecca, in love with Lavina, and believing that he has been widowed by the death of
Donna Pantea, going under the name of *Sandra*, his wife.
Celidora, their only daughter, betrothed to Count Lionetto di Casavuota, but in love with
Biondello, a rich gentleman of Ripasecca.
Calandrino, nephew of Pantea, friend of Biondello, and the lover of
Lavina, companion of Celidora, who returns his love.
Chichibio, major domo of Don Pippo, the lover of
Auretta, the servant of Donna Pantea.

Mozart sketched two duets, some arias (and even, for one of Don Pippo's that is not preserved in full, the introductory recitative), a quartet, and the Finale of the first act, writing out the vocal parts and the bass so explicitly that it would have taken him only a few days to fill the empty staves in the orchestra part. He was right in being satisfied with his work. The introductory Duet, a scene of jealousy and reconciliation between Auretta and Chichibio, would be worthy, in its freshness and charm, of Susanna and Figaro. It is clear that Mozart had Benucci in mind for Chichibio, and thus his aria *Ogni momento* (No. 3) is a masterpiece of lingual agility—one cannot help thinking of Rossini's *Barbiere*. The Quartet, two sopranos and two tenors, depicts the amorous unity of hopeful and determined pairs of lovers, and it is full of inner life. And the Finale, in which all seven persons take part (Pantea, of course, has not yet appeared), should be contemplated with respect: it is Mozart's first great *buffo* finale, masterfully designed, and increasing in intensity steadily to the end, even culminating in a chorus. It shows the sharpest juxtaposition of the two groups: on the one hand the irate Don Pippo with his aides, on the other the three couples, each of which has its own characterization. When one reads through these pieces and the other surviving sketches of the work, one begins to hesitate about saying how fortunate it is that Mozart did not complete the opera.

Doubtless one of the reasons why he did not finish it was that he had meanwhile received another libretto (or actually taken it along with him secretly to Salzburg): *Lo Sposo deluso—o sia La rivalità di tre donne per un solo amante* (The Husband Deceived, or The Rivalry of Three Ladies for One Lover). The identity of the author of this libretto has hitherto been unknown, but almost certainly it was the product of none other than Lorenzo da Ponte. This was Mozart's first connection with the librettist of *Figaro, Don Giovanni,* and *Così fan tutte*—three works that conferred immortality upon that poet along with Mozart.

Da Ponte was seven years older than Mozart. He was born in 1749 in the Ghetto at Ceneda (now Vittorio Veneto), in the province of Venice. His real name was Emmanuele Conegliano. His father, Geremia, was a tanner of cordovan leather; his mother's maiden name was Ghella (Rachel) Pincherle, and she died in 1754 probably after the birth of a younger brother of Emmanuele-Lorenzo. On 29 August 1763, the father went with his sons, Emmanuele, Baruch, and Anania to be baptized by the Bishop of Ceneda, Lorenzo da Ponte. Geremia became Gasparo; and Emmanuele, Baruch, and Anania became Lorenzo, Girolamo, and Luigi; while the surname of Conegliano was changed, in accordance with a custom of long standing, to da Ponte. The Bishop assumed the expenses of educating the three boys, and his help was needed, for a few days after the baptism the father entered into a second marriage with a Christian woman who was to bear him ten more children—three sons and seven daughters. Lorenzo attended the priests' seminaries at Ceneda and Portogruaro, took lower orders in 1770 and 1771, and read his first Mass on 27 March 1773. He was now an abbé; he held a few teaching positions in Portogruaro, and came to Venice in the autumn of 1773, presumably not for the first time; in the following year he was named professor *di grammatica inferiore* in Treviso, and he continued in this post almost two years. Then he was dismissed and went to Venice, where he devoted himself to affairs of literature and gallantry, and was as much at home in the muddy waters of the corrupt republic as a fish in the sea. Anyone interested in following his adventures should read his Memoirs, preferably in the original, but also consulting the corrections in the excellent German edition of Gustav Gugitz (Dresden, 1924); they will not be found boring. For three years da Ponte was able to continue this sort of life until the scandal caused by his affair with a married woman forced him to flee in haste: he was banished from Venice and its territories for fifteen years, on pain of confinement in a dungeon for seven years if he should be discovered there. The latter possibility did not appeal to him at all, and he turned to the Austrian provinces, staying for a few months in Görz and prudently avoiding Vienna until a few days after the death of Maria Theresa (December 1780), who would undoubtedly have sent him packing just as quickly as she had his friend Casanova. He gladly seized the opportunity to write a respectful sonnet on her death, which was printed by the ennobled von Trattner. But Vienna was not yet the place for him to establish himself permanently. In the winter of 1780 to 1781 he was in Dresden, under the protection of the Court Poet Mazzolà, who initiated him into the 'dramaturgy of opera.' Then he returned to Vienna, perhaps in the hope of succeeding to the position of Metastasio, whom he did not fail to visit, and who died in April 1782. This would have been a strange succession, of which not even the great reformer Joseph II would have approved. But another prospect opened for da Ponte. The revival of the Italian Opera in Vienna, which opened on 12 April 1783 with Salieri's *La Scuola de' gelosi*, aroused in him the same hopes as it did in Mozart. Salieri recommended him, and thus, on 1 March 1783, the Abbé Lorenzo da Ponte was engaged as the poet of the theater with the salary of 600 gulden. One of his first accomplishments was to furnish an Italian translation of Gluck's *Iphigénie en Tauride*—which was printed with Alxinger's German translation—for the benefit of those members of the Vienna audience who could not read the German. Da Ponte's first libretto was of course for Salieri: *Il Ricco d'un giorno* (1784), which was a failure.

Mozart wrote to his father, on 7 May 1783:

Our poet here is now a certain Abbate Da Ponte. He has an enormous amount to do in revising pieces for the theater and he has to write *per obbligo* an entirely new libretto for Salieri, which will take him two months. He has promised after that to write a new libretto for me. But who knows whether he will be able to keep his word—or will want to? For, as you are aware, these Italian gentlemen are very civil to your face. Enough, we know them! If he is in league with Salieri, I shall never get anything out of him.

Nevertheless, da Ponte seems to have kept his word, and if he really set to work immediately after finishing the libretto of *Il Ricco d'un giorno*, Mozart must have had *Lo Sposo deluso* in his hands upon his return from Salzburg in the autumn. The fact that he does not mention anything about it in his letter to his father in the month of December is understandable, for Varesco would have refused at once to continue his work on *L'Oca del Cairo* if he had learned that Mozart was working on another libretto. Nor is it any great mystery that da Ponte in his own Mémoirs fails to mention his first collaboration with Mozart. Quite apart from the fact that his Mémoirs, which were written in his very old age (1823-7), are full of omissions and inaccuracies, both intentional and unintentional, *Lo Sposo deluso* is no fine feather in his cap. It may be objected that there are other libretti by da Ponte which do him no honor: but he was not without literary ambition. Once again we can form the best conception of this strange *opera buffa* from the cast of characters, to which Mozart appended in his own handwriting the names of the singers he had in mind for the various roles:

Primo buffo caricato: *Sempronio*, uomo sciocco e facoltoso, promesso
in marito ad Emilia.
Signore Benucci.

Prima buffa: *Emilia*, giovane Romana di nobili natali, alquanto capric-
ciosa e promessa in consorte a Sempronio, ma fida amante di
Annibale.
Signora Fischer.

Primo mezzo carattere: *Annibale*, uffiziale Toscano, molto coraggioso ed
amante di Emilia.
Signore Mandini.

Seconda buffa: *Laurina*, nipote di Sempronio, ragazza vana, ed innamorata di Annibale.
Signora Cavalieri.

Secondo buffo caricato: *Fernando*, sprezzator delle donne ed amico di
Sempronio.
Signore Bussani.

Secondo buffo mezzo carattere: *Geronzio*, tutore di Emilia, che poi
innamorasi di Metilde.
Signore Pugnetti.

Terza buffa: *Metilde*, virtuosa di canto e ballo, anch'essa innamorata di
Annibale e finta amica di Laurina.
Signora Teyber.*

What a play Shakespeare could have made with these seven characters! The central figures are Emilia and Annibale, two proud and
passionate beings who have been separated by a misunderstanding—
and Emilia is led to believe that Annibale is dead. Forced to become

---

* First buffo caricato: *Sempronio*, a rich and stupid man, engaged to marry Emilia.
Signor Benucci.

Prima buffa: *Emilia*, young Roman woman of noble birth, of somewhat capricious
temperament, engaged to marry Sempronio, but really in love with Annibale.
Signora Fischer [= Nancy Storace].

Primo mezzo carattere: *Annibale*, a Tuscan official, very courageous, and in love
with Emilia.
Signor Mandini.

Seconda buffa: *Laurina*, niece of Sempronio, a vain girl, in love with Annibale.
Signora Cavalieri.

Secondo buffo caricato: *Fernando*, friend of Sempronio, who scorns women.
Signor Bussani.

Secondo buffo mezzo carattere: *Geronzio*, tutor of Emilia, who falls in love with
Metilde.
Signor Pugnetti.

Terza buffa: *Metilde*, virtuoso singer and dancer, also in love with Annibale and
pretended friend of Laurina.
Signora Teyber.

the unwilling bride of the old fop Sempronio, in Leghorn, she encounters Annibale again, but now he is being sought as a husband by the stupid Laurina and the sly actress Metilde. Here are opportunities for the most plentiful scenes of jealousy. Fernando corresponds exactly to Benedict in *Much Ado about Nothing*. But what da Ponte produced is nothing more than a compromise between the *commedia dell'arte* and a play of intrigue, at the end of which, of course, poor Sempronio has become the deceived husband (*Lo sposo deluso*) and Annibale, the object of the rivalry of three women, has chosen the proper one. But Laurina and Metilde are also satisfied, the first with the misogynist, and the second with old Geronzio. As always in da Ponte's libretti, the first act is the best. It contains a charming scene: the proud Roman woman, Emilia, arriving in the little provincial town of Leghorn, does not receive the reception she considers due her, and she expresses her chagrin in an aria (*Nacqui all'aura trionfale*), which Mozart sketched beautifully in the pseudo-heroic style, something like Fiordiligi's 'Rock Aria' in *Così fan tutte*. After this aria she haughtily overlooks the wretched idiot Sempronio, and prefers to believe that any other man she sees is her betrothed husband. We discover this idiot, when the curtain rises, completing his toilet, and being made fun of by Laurina, Annibale, and Fernando, in a grand Quartet of the finest workmanship, though perhaps somewhat overextended. This Quartet, after an enchanting and genuinely moving andantino, takes up the triumphal allegro of the overture. Then there comes the ironic aria (which survives in sketched form) sung by the scorner of women, Fernando—a unique piece, which one could imagine as being sung by a young Basilio: and then, again in complete form, a Trio for Annibale, Emilia, and Sempronio, which is another piece of the first rank. Emilia and Annibale, after their unhoped for reunion, seek to master their feelings, while the old bridegroom expresses his helplessness, anticipating a melody of Bartolo's at one point note for note. The piece is at once passionate and comic, brief and dramatic, and all three characters are sharply drawn.

But Mozart must have realized as soon as he had finished these four pieces that he could not continue in this direction, and that he was on the wrong track with his idea of the 'buffonesque.' He followed it only once again, when he composed the introduction of a libretto by Giuseppe Petrosellini, *Il Regno delle Amazzoni*, which had been performed at the end of December 1783, in Parma and later in Florence, in a setting by Agostino Accorimboni. This piece shows how desperate he was, for Petrosellini's text is if possible even more nonsensical than that of *Lo Sposo deluso*. We need contemplate only the opening scene, a quintet, in which a lover resigns himself unwillingly to the company of two old fools, an archaeologist and a meteorologist. Mozart begins the scene in *concertante* style and with real fire; but we are relieved when he breaks off after a hundred measures, before the five voices have all entered.

This brings us to a decisive point. Mozart's unlimited musical resources have long since taken the measure of the forms that represent the peak of success in *opera buffa*; the ensembles, the trios, quartets, and finales, in which every participating character expresses himself in his own distinctive way, and in which Mozart can display his contrapuntal art. But still he has not found the proper material. Now comes a lucky accident, comparable only to his making the acquaintance of the works of Bach, two years earlier, through Baron van Swicten: on 23 August 1784, *Il Re Teodoro in Venezia* by the Abbate Giovanni Battista Casti, with music by Paisiello, was produced at the Burgtheater. Mozart attended the first performance. It precipitated no crisis in his creative career similar to that produced by his acquaintance with *The Well-Tempered Clavier* and *The Art of the Fugue*. Nevertheless, it did produce a severe malady—perhaps not 'just a cold,' but rather the result of mastering the excitement Casti's libretto must have aroused in him.

About Casti very little has been written, and that little grudgingly, in Italian dictionaries and histories of literature. Only the latest edition of the *Enciclopedia italiana* closes its article on him with the suggestion that perhaps he was better than his reputation would indicate. The libraries preserve his works in their 'reserved' sections, and it is easier to form an idea of the life work of the dullest poet who has received the stamp of approval from the authorities on the history of literature than of one of the most alive and penetrating minds of eighteenth-century Italy. The eighteenth century was less prudish than the nineteenth, and Goethe, for example, enjoyed with a smile the reading aloud of one of this poet's *Novelle galanti*. Da Ponte both hated and admired Casti, for he could not fail to see in him the superior intelligence which stood in his way. Externally there was little difference between the two, except for the fact that Casti was about twenty-five years the elder. He, too, was an *abbate*, but his vows proved no more of a hindrance than da Ponte's to his becoming the lover of a marchesa. But he was of quite different calibre as a personality than da Ponte, and had the advantage over him of many years of experience as a poet and man of the world. In 1764 he became Court Poet to the Archduke Leopold in Florence; in 1769, Joseph II, delighted with his conversation, called him to Vienna, where he became the friend and traveling companion of the younger Kaunitz, son of the all-powerful Prime Minister; in 1778 he went for a few years to St. Petersburg as the spoiled favorite of Catherine the Great—which did not prevent him from exposing her in the most ruthless way in his *Poema tartaro*, as a result of which he lost the protection of the Emperor Joseph. From 1782 to 1786 he was in Vienna again, returning then to Italy as the traveling companion of the Count Fries to whom Beethoven was to dedicate his C major Quintet, Op. 29. In 1790, after a journey in the Levant, he came back to Vienna, and, thanks to the favor of Leopold and of Count Rosenberg, he became the true successor of Metastasio, as *Poeta Cesareo*. But in 1796 he too was banished from Vienna, and he spent his last days in Paris, where he finished his principal work, *Gli Animali parlanti*, and died on 7 February 1803. Not all his libretti were printed or survived. The best and wittiest is perhaps an *opera buffa*, *Catilina*, which—with Cicero in the role of a political nitwit—anticipates all the parody effects of Offenbach. He explicitly reciprocated da Ponte's hatred: in one of his *Novelle galanti* ('Novella quarta') there are three bitingly sarcastic stanzas about *Don Giovanni*.

For his *Re Teodoro*, Casti had borrowed from Voltaire's *Candide* the chapter in which Candide and his old friend Martin are dining with no less than half a dozen dethroned monarchs. The hero is Baron Theodor von Neuhoff, a Westphalian, who for a time was really the chosen King of Corsica, and ended his life confined in a tower. (His tombstone is still to be seen in London, at St. Anne's, Soho.) Casti depicts the beginning of his tragi-comic end, as, despite the efforts of his faithful major domo to arrange a marriage for him with the rich daughter of an innkeeper, he finds himself in the prison tower in Venice, and bemoans his fate. In this libretto, which, in spite of many minor shortcomings, is a masterful one, there are no puppets; all the characters are real, although they are not entirely free of elements of caricature. The tragi-comic ex-King, forced to play the role of lover; the stiff but faithful Master of the Household; the Venetian innkeeper, who is inordinately proud of the prospect of becoming father-in-law of a king; the unwilling daughter, and her enraged lover who succeeds in having his rival jailed for debts; and with these the minor characters—a phlegmatic pasha, likewise dethroned, who is spending his years in exile in Venice as pleasantly as possible, and Theodor's sister, who has become a courtesan and is at the moment the beloved of the pasha, an intelligent and sympathetic character—these were quite other figures than the old idiots, the impertinent chambermaids, the disguised gardener-maids and country ingénues, the geese of Cairo, with which Mozart had had the misfortune to have to deal until now. The work must have struck both him and da Ponte like a bolt of lightning.

Nor was it the only bolt to strike him. On 25 November 1785, there was produced in Vienna *La Villanella rapita*, an *opera buffa* by Francesco Bianchi of Cremona, one of the many 'international' *buffo* composers of the time, which had first seen the light of day in the autumn of 1783 at San Moisè in Venice, and had had an exceptional success. The libretto was by Giovanni Bertati, whose name should not be mentioned without respect by any admirer of Mozart or Cimarosa, for without him we should not possess either *Don Giovanni* or *Il Matrimonio segreto*. In age he was between Casti and da Ponte; he was born in 1735 and died in 1815. Starting out, as did Casti and da Ponte, to be a priest, he preferred like them the career of librettist, and furnished the products of his pen chiefly to the Teatro Giustiniani di San Moisè. Fate willed that he should become da Ponte's successor as the poet for the Italian opera in Vienna; he held this post only a few years (1791-4), and then returned to Venice.

Bertati's biographer and bibliographer, Albert Schatz, has summed up his work as follows: * 'Sixty-six libretti in thirty-five years, which served as the basis for ninety-one operas by forty-five composers—including the most famous of their time.' Of these operas forty-one 'were taken up outside the borders of their native cities, but only three achieved a real place in the repertoire . . .' One of these operas was *La Villanella rapita*, which owed its success certainly not to the music of Bianchi but to the libretto, which in the boldness of its social criticism hardly yields to other 'heralds of the Revolution.' Such a work was doubly remarkable in the field of *opera buffa*. On the other hand, precisely in this field it was possible to say a good deal that, if it had been said in pamphlets and books, would have put the author behind prison bars. In the opera there is a count who has cast his eyes on a peasant maiden of his domain, Mandina, daughter of Biagio, and engaged to the peasant youth Pippo, who watches over

* In the *Vierteljahrsschrift für Musikwissenschaft*, v, 270.

his beloved with a jealous eye. The Count decides to steal Mandina on the day of her wedding. He puts drugs into the drinks of the wedding company, and takes the semi-conscious bride into his castle, where she awakens the next morning in a rich bed, with the clothing of a lady laid out beside her. But Pippo and Biagio are not disposed simply to accept the aristocrat's misdeed. They get into the castle, Pippo in disguise, and in turn steal the girl away. The threats of the Count in the second Finale are of no effect, for Pippo and Mandina have been married in the meantime. Here we see already figures from *Figaro* and *Don Giovanni* on the horizon. Bertati's Count is a close relative of Almaviva, except that he is even cruder and more ruthless; Pippo is the prototype of Masetto; Mandina, of Zerlina, than whom she is no less naive and no less easily led astray. And in the dialogue of the peasants one feels already a hint of that subterranean grumbling which was to lead to the eruption of 1789.

For the Vienna production of *La Villanella rapita*, Mozart composed for the charming singer Celeste Coltellini (who was the daughter of the poet Marco Coltellini, and who later in Naples became the wife of the rich Swiss banker Meuricoffre) two interpolated scenes: a Trio (K. 480, *Mandina amabile*) and a Quartet (*Dite almeno, in che mancai*, K. 479). The first is, properly speaking, a duet that expands into a trio: the Count is making a present of money to the pretty girl, who in her innocence can hardly contain herself at so much kindness, but Pippo interrupts the tender scene, and the Trio develops the varied feelings of the participants: Mandina's bewilderment, the Count's secret triumph, and Pippo's frantic mistrust. The Quartet, which similarly begins as a trio and expands into a quartet, depicts the scene in which the father and the bridegroom, who have forced their way into the castle the next morning, find Mandina in her suspicious situation. There are reproaches and weeping self-justification; insults and threats on the part of the Count, whose attention has been attracted by all the noise; and finally unanimous agreement to postpone any decision until a quieter moment. As usual, Mozart did not pay the slightest heed to Bianchi. Both ensembles have a fascinating abundance of musical invention and a mastery in characterization that belong to Mozart alone. The Duet between Mandina and the Count, like the better-known duet between Zerlina and Don Giovanni, is in A major, and is full of the same seductive sweetness:

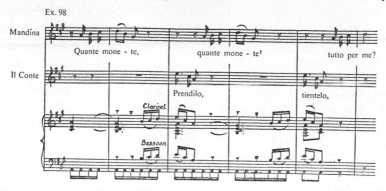

Ex. 98

All Mozart's musical forces were gathering for an outburst. All he needed was the grand opportunity, and it came with Beaumarchais's *Le Mariage de Figaro*, which had reached the stage, not without having triumphed over considerable obstacles, in 1784, and had caused powerful reverberations throughout Europe. Let it not be objected that Beaumarchais's *Le Barbier de Séville* had been available since 1775, and had been set to music as an *opera buffa* by Paisiello in St. Petersburg (with apologies for his boldness). *Le Barbier de Séville* was a predestined *opera buffa*, and had indeed originally been conceived by Beaumarchais as an *opéra-comique*. The cheated old man who wishes to marry his ward, the noble lover in disguise, the wily servant, this time in the guise of a barber—these are typical figures of the *commedia dell'arte*, and Rossini's genius, his diabolic buffoonery, was needed to rescue them for operatic immortality. What might have distinguished *Le Barbier de Séville* from the usual *opera buffa* would have been the conservation of the striking, witty, sparkling original; but this original was essentially weakened and destroyed by Paisiello's literary hack, Giuseppe Petrosellini.

But *Le Mariage de Figaro* is quite another affair. It has been observed with truth that in Susanna there is a bit of Colombina left, in Figaro of Arlecchino; that Don Bartolo and Marcellina are pure *buffo* figures. But the Countess? The Count? Cherubino? The tiny roles of Barbarina and her father, the gardener Antonio? Basilio the schemer? It took courage to see the *opera buffa* possibilities in this work and to realize them—courage that Mozart and da Ponte can have gathered only from pieces like those of Bertati and Casti. They were fully conscious of what they were doing. Nothing was more common in opera libretti than perfunctory dedications to members of the nobility and crowned heads; nothing, on the other hand, was rarer than prefaces. But da Ponte provided the original libretto (which has now become a rarity; I know of only two copies) with the following introductory remarks:

The duration prescribed for a stage performance by general usage, and the given number of roles to which one is confined by the same, as well as several other considerations of prudence, of costume, place, and public constituted the reasons for which I have not made a translation of that excellent comedy [the Beaumarchais original], but rather an imitation, or let us say an extract.

For these reasons I was compelled to reduce the sixteen original characters to eleven, two of which can be played by a single actor, and to omit in addition to one whole act, many highly effective scenes and many witty sayings, with which the original teems. For these I have had to substitute *canzonette*, arias, choruses, and other thoughts and words susceptible of being set to music—things that can be handled only with the help of poetry and never with prose. In spite, however, of all the zeal and care on the part of both the composer and myself to be brief, the opera will not be one of the shortest that has been performed on our stages. We hope that our excuse will be the variety of development of this drama, the length and scope of the same, the number of musical pieces necessary in order not to keep the performers idle, to avoid the boredom and monotony of the long recitatives, to paint faithfully and in full color the divers passions that are aroused, and to realize our special purpose, which was to offer a new type of spectacle, as it were, to a public of such refined taste and such assured understanding.

The Poet.

An 'imitation'—an 'extract'! Da Ponte did not use the right word for his form of arrangement. We should call it a transfiguration of the Beaumarchais original. It is a simplification, which sacrifices none of the life of the original, and which transplants it into a new, purer, richer, and more ideal soil—that of music. I do not know whether it would be possible to drag Victor Hugo's *Le Roi s'amuse* out of its Romantic storeroom, now that Verdi's *Rigoletto* is in existence. But just as Shakespeare's *Othello* and *The Merry Wives of Windsor* maintain their own existence beside the two works of Verdi's old age, so Beaumarchais's *Figaro* holds its own beside Mozart's. It survives for its revolutionary tendency, for its wit and aptness of expression. The work by Mozart and da Ponte is something different; a *Commedia per musica*, as the title reads (no longer *opera buffa*), a play in which social

undertones are by no means lacking, but one that is gayer, more unconcerned, more human, and more inspired. It was in truth a 'new
type of spectacle,' for the Viennese. The success of the work on 1 May
1786 does not seem to have been overwhelming, despite the brilliance
of the cast, which included Storace (Susanna), Laschi (Contessa),
Benucci (Figaro), and Mandini (Conte). It did not really take hold
until it was produced in Prague. The demands it made upon its listeners were too unusual; in Florence, in 1788, the work was performed in
two successive evenings, and at the first Italian performance, which
took place in Monza, near Milan, in the autumn of 1787, the Archduke
had the third and fourth acts newly composed by Angelo Tarchi, undoubtedly because he found them too long. Let us not be too shocked
by this fact, for when the work was taken up again in the late summer
of 1789, in Vienna, Mozart himself handled it very roughly, just as he
later maltreated *Don Giovanni* when that work was produced in
Vienna. In Mozart's operas the rule is always: the original version is
the best.

We know from the Memoirs of the Irish tenor Michael Kelly, who
sang Basilio and Don Curzio in the first performance, which number
in the opera was Mozart's own favorite: it was the Sextet in the third
act, in which Don Bartolo and Marcellina reveal themselves as Figaro's
father and mother, and are transformed from deadly enemies into
guardian angels. Susanna, knowing nothing of all this, and bursting in
upon the family embraces, misunderstands the situation until it is explained to her, when she joins in the bliss of the other three over the
untying of the knot. In this bliss, only the Count and Don Curzio do
not join. We have here a typical *buffo* scene—the finding of the long-
lost child—as old as the comedies of Plautus and Terence, and repeated
and varied a thousand times in a thousand comedies. Two of the participants, Bartolo and Marcellina, have been up to this point mere cari-
catures—particularly Bartolo, with his 'Profession Aria' (*La vendetta*,
No. 4), which is the crowning piece among all *buffo* arias. But at this
point they both become human beings. Two lovers give voice to genuine happiness, two newly revealed parents express their genuine good-
will, and the Count, who has been led around by the nose, utters his
genuine spite. The historical significance of *Le Nozze di Figaro* is that,
thanks to da Ponte's skill and Mozart's greatness, it no longer belongs
to the category of the *opera buffa*, but rather, to use a favorite word of
Wagner's, 'redeems' the *opera buffa* and makes of it a comedy in music.

No longer is anything of *buffo* style that is sung by any of the principal characters. The recitative and aria of the Count (*Vedrò, mentr'io sospiro*, No. 17) is an outbreak of passion at the thought that a servant is to enjoy a piece of good fortune denied to him, the nobleman. What a moving figure is the Countess, in all her utterances! And Figaro, who in his first aria (the cavatina *Se vuol ballare*) sounds the note of the entire opera, 'cunning against force,' and this with unprecedented brevity and directness, and the most amusing symbolism, brings the act to a glorious close with his military aria. Susanna—what an intelligent, lovable, little creature she is! Cherubino, of whom someone—I believe it was Kierkegaard—has rightly said that he is Don Giovanni as a boy, with all his feelings for the whole race of women in all its representatives compressed into two immortal arias! The unique greatness of Mozart becomes clear only when one imagines how an Italian would have composed these two arias, especially the second, an arietta, *Voi che sapete*. An Italian composer always had the possibility of using folk-tunes and for such purposes he would have found something Neapolitan or Venetian. But Mozart had to get along without such references; the source of all he used was in himself. It is significant that except for the fandango in the third act, Mozart renounced any Spanish flavor, any local color: he did not need it.

Our admiration mounts when we contemplate the ensembles. The Letter Duet of Susanna and the Countess, with its sublime 'echo'; the little *prestissimo* of Susanna and Cherubino before the boy jumps out of the window; the Introduction, in which the two lovers are occupied with the preparation for their wedding and their married life, in ways that are even musically so sharply differentiated; the Duet of Susanna and the Count, in which Susanna, anticipating Freudian psychology, gives such irrelevant answers to the Count's importunate questions. But the numbers that constitute Mozart's greatest triumph are the larger ensembles and the two great Finales; above all the first one, which in a thousand measures expands from a duet into a septet—a septet in which not alone two groups are juxtaposed (the Countess, Susanna, and Figaro on one side, and the Count, Marcellina, Bartolo, and Basilio on the other), but in which also every individual is subtly characterized. This piece exhibits a mastery of the counterpoint of characterization, and of the expression of feeling, such as has been attained by few and surpassed by none. Let the attempt be made in the Quintet of *Die Meistersinger* to separate Magdalena and David from

the general G-flat major bliss at the end of the scene: it will not succeed. Mozart never made such mistakes, never sacrificed a character.
And where the treatment of the voice is neutral, the flexible orchestra
offers the finest commentary. This commentary sometimes passes beyond the framework of the scenic into the deeply personal, or even into
the metaphysical. Before Susanna emerges from the closet, in the first
Finale, Mozart slips in a measure—*molto andante*—of contemplation, a
moment of mourning for the world and its people, of sadness at the
nothingness of all things. Is this too much to say? I do not think so,
even though of course such matters can only be felt, and never proved.

Da Ponte suggests the care he and Mozart took to achieve brief and
pregnant expression. And they succeeded: *Figaro*, big as the score is,
is not too long. Only two arias can be omitted—the ones for Marcellina
and for Basilio at the beginning of the fourth act, which Mozart wrote
for the sake of the two 'secondaries.' The second (*In quegl' anni*, No.
25) is a very curious one, of which up to now hardly any explanation
has been forthcoming. Apart from this, the whole work, and each of
its four (or rather two-times-two) acts, is a unity built up of arias, ensembles, recitatives, choruses, the splendid pompous march that ends
the third act, and the Overture that introduces the 'mad day' with a
prestissimo. When the curtain falls on the fourth act with its *quid pro
quo*—the act that has brought Susanna's *Deh vieni non tardar*, and the
recognition scene of the two lovers—we are still by no means satisfied
in regard to the future marital happiness of the poor Countess, but we
know that in this work Mozart has added to the world's understanding
of people and to its lightness of spirit.

Don Giovanni is the fruit of the success *Figaro* had had in Prague.
Even Mozart's *Entführung aus dem Serail* had reached Prague, in 1783,
not long after its first Vienna performance; and in December 1786,
only a few months behind Vienna, the public of Prague had made the
acquaintance of *Figaro* in a production by the Bondini company, and
had given it a reception such as no other operatic work had ever had:

The enthusiasm . . . was without precedent; people never got tired
of hearing it . . . Figaro's songs resounded in the streets and gardens,
and even the harpist at the Bierbank had to strike up *Non più andrai* if
he wanted people to listen . . . *

* Niemtschek, p. 26.

It is understandable that Mozart, who at the first performances of *Figaro* had by no means been spoiled by the public of Vienna, wished to enjoy his triumph to the full, and accepted an invitation of Bondini's to come to Prague. From 11 January 1787 until well into February he stayed there with Constanze, and made a contract with Bondini to write a new opera for the coming season, for 100 ducats.

Time was pressing. Mozart and da Ponte seized on one of the oldest subjects, which happened to come into their hands in a brand-new version—*Il Convitato di pietra* (The Stone Guest) by Giovanni Bertati, which had just been produced in Venice as the second carnival opera, with music by Giuseppe Gazzaniga. It must have come over Mozart in a flash that this was the proper material, not only for himself, but also for da Ponte, who had to work at two other libretti at the same time as *Don Giovanni*. For in working on the new Mozart opera he could lean to a great extent on Bertati. To say that he stole from Bertati in the most shameless manner would be both true and untrue. Da Ponte actually used Bertati's text as a model as far as he could; but eighteenth-century notions of property in ideas were different from those of today, and da Ponte actually went far beyond Bertati in his *Don Giovanni*.

We can best appreciate Mozart's boldness in deciding to set *Don Giovanni* to music not by drawing for our knowledge upon Sören Kierkegaard's fantasies on 'Don Juan,' say, or other books of the nineteenth and twentieth centuries, but only by considering the attitude of the eighteenth century towards this subject. Goldoni summed up that attitude as follows:

Tout le monde connoît cette mauvaise Pièce espagnole, que les Italiens appellent *il Convitato di Pietra*, et les François le *Festin de Pierre*.

Je l'ai toujours regardée, en Italie, avec horreur, et je ne pouvois pas concevoir comment cette farce avoit pu se soutenir pendant si long-tems, attirer le monde en foule, et faire les delices d'un pays policé.

Les Comédiens Italiens en étoient étonnés eux-mêmes; et soit par plaisanterie, soit par ignorance, quelques-uns disoient que l'Auteur du *Festin de Pierre* avoit contracté un engagement avec le diable pour le soutenir.

Je n'aurois jamais songé a travailler sur cet Ouvrage; mais ayant appris assez de françois pour le lire, et voyant que Molière et Thomas Corneille s'en étoient occupés, j'entrepris aussi de regaler ma Patrie de ce même sujet, afin de tenir parole au diable avec un peu plus de décence.

Il est vray que je ne pouvois pas lui donner le même titre; car, dans ma Pièce, la Statue du Commandeur ne parle pas, ne marche pas et ne va pas souper en ville; je l'ai intitulée *Don Jouan*, comme Molière, en y ajoutant, *ou le Dissolu*.

Je crus ne devoir pas supprimer la foudre qui écrase Don Jouan, parce que l'homme méchant doit être puni; mais je ménageai cet événement de manière que ce pouvait être un effet immédiat de la colère de Dieu, et qu'il pouvoit provenir aussi d'une combinaison de causes secondes, dirigées toujours par les loix de la Providence.

Comme dans cette Comédie, qui est en cinq actes et en vers blancs, je n'avois pas employé d'Arlequin, ni d'autres masques Italiens, je remplaçai le comique par un Berger et une Bergère . . . *

This 'tragicommedia' *Don Giovanni Tenorio*, by Goldoni, which was produced at San Samuele to close the carnival of 1736, is probably the lowest point reached by any arrangements of the material, and that just because Goldoni wished to 'redeem' it. In Spain it had originally been what is called a *Commedia di cappa e spada*, that is, an improvised piece teeming with amorous adventures, duels, and murders, out of which

---

* *Mémoires* 1787, I, 39:

'Everyone knows this bad Spanish play, which the Italians call *Il Convitato di Pietra*, and the French *Le Festin de Pierre*.

I have always regarded it, in Italy, with horror, and I have never been able to understand how this farce could hold its own for such a long time, could draw crowds, and could be the delight of a cultivated nation.

Italian comedians were astonished themselves; and, whether simply as a joke or in ignorance, some of them said that the author of *Le Festin de Pierre* had made a contract with the devil to support him.

I should never have thought of working on this piece; but having learned enough French to read it, and seeing that Molière and Thomas Corneille had occupied themselves with it, I undertook to regale my own country with the same subject, in order to fulfill the contract with the devil a little more fittingly.

It is true that I could not give it the same title; for, in my play, the statue of the commander does not speak, or walk, or go into town to supper; I called it *Don Jouan*, as Molière did, adding the words: *ou le Dissolu* (or, The Rake).

I did not consider it permissible to do away with the bolt of lightning that strikes down Don Jouan, because the wicked man must be punished; but I arranged this event in such a way that it could be the immediate effect of the wrath of God, and that it could also arise from a combination of secondary causes always governed by the laws of providence.

Since in this comedy, which is in five acts, and in blank verse, I did not employ any Arlecchino, or other Italian stock characters, I replaced them with a shepherd and a shepherdess to furnish the comic element . . .'

the figure of Don Juan crystallized as the hero. At the same time, however, it was full of religious pathos. The hero rises to such heights of infernal frivolity and such vast audacity that earthly justice cannot deal with him, and the powers of heaven must intervene, in the form of Don Juan's victim, the Governor, whose statue accepts the impulsive invitation of the murderer to a nocturnal dinner, and delivers him over to hell: *Il Convitato di pietra*, The Stone Guest. When the subject is transplanted to Italy and France it loses some of its moral and religious character, and adds burlesque scenes, provided by Don Juan's servant: Pasquariello, Arlecchino, Leporello, Molière's Sganarelle—a mixture of wit, impertinence, cowardice, gluttony, and a hundred other characteristics of the typical 'servant,' who was one of the oldest stock characters of comedy.

Such a subject, too, addresses itself to the primary instincts of the theatergoer: his delight in the bold frivolity of the aristocrat, in the reactions of his feminine victims, and in the impertinence of his servant, as well as his shudders at the intervention of superhuman forces of justice, ending with an abduction to hell, employing every conceivable theatrical effect. Goldoni, as well as a certain number of the cultured public of the century of enlightenment, considered the tale food for the theatrical rabble. Gluck used it as a subject for a ballet (1761), which is a masterpiece of stylization, and which of course entirely avoids the comic element. It is reduced to the simplest dramatic formula, but, despite its simplicity, not to the most ingenious: the Stone Guest appears twice, the first time to no particular purpose. Mozart knew Gluck's ballet very well, but its influence upon him was more musical than dramatic. However, in a ballet much could be dared that was not possible in more pretentious dramatic forms. At any rate, Bertati and Gazzaniga presented their *Convitato di pietra* with an apology. They preceded their one-act play with a dramatic *capriccio*, which introduces the audience into the midst of a group of players (a favorite device of the Italian *commedia* since Marcello's satire *Il teatro alla moda*). The troupe's affairs are in a bad state, they are facing ruin; thereupon the shrewd impresario suggests to his actors that they revive the old story of the Stone Guest, which has always drawn audiences. And that is what they do.

All this suggests what courage and insight into the inherent power of the material it took to make *Don Giovanni* into a grand opera *buffa*.

Painted by Josef Lange

AN UNFINISHED PORTRAIT OF MOZART (1782)

Da Ponte at first stuck close to Bertati. His dependence on the latter is evident in a comparison of the two arias in which Don Giovanni's servant lists his master's conquests:

Madamina, il catalogo è questo
Delle belle che amò il padron mio,
Un catalogo egli è che ho fatto io
Osservate, leggete con me.

Dell 'Italia, ed Allemagna
Ve ne ho scritto cento, c tante.
Della Francia, e della Spagna
Ve ne sono non sò quante:

In Italia sei cento e quaranta
In Lamagna due cento e trent' una,
Cento in Francia, in Turchia novant'una,
Ma in Ispagna son già mille e trè.

Fra Madame, Cittadine,
Artigiane, Contadine,
Cameriere, Cuoche, e Guattere;
Purchè basta che sian femmine,
Per doverle amoreggiar.

V'han fra queste contadine,
Camerierc, cittadine,
Marchesane, principesse,
E v'han donne d'ogni grado,
D'ogni forma, d'ogni età.

Vi dirò ch'è un'uomo tale,
Se attendesse alle promesse,
Che il marito universale
Un dì avrebbe a diventar.
Vi dirò ch'egli ama tutte,
Che sian belle, o che sian brutte:
Delle vecchie solamente
Non si sente ad infiammar.

Nella bionda egli ha l'usanza
Di lodar la gentilezza,
Nella bruna la costanza,
Nella bianca la dolcezza;
Vuol d'inverno la grassotta,
Vuol d'estate la magrotta;
È la grande maestosa,
La piccina è ognor vezzosa,
Delle vecchie fa conquista,
Pel piacer di porle in lista:
Ma passion predominante
È la giovin principiante.
Non si picca se sia ricca,
Se sia brutta, se sia bella:
Purche porti la gonella,
Voi sapete quel che fa! *

* For translation, see footnote on following page.

Quite apart from the fact that in Bertati's version the aria leads to a duet, which leaves the listener less crushed than he would be otherwise, the relation of the two is that of a sketch to a finished work of art. True, da Ponte leans heavily upon Bertati; but the comparison shows us that there is not a single line to which he has not given wittier, more striking, more trenchant form, and that he has conceived every figure more sharply, with greater subtlety and more plasticity. At the same time, Mozart's collaboration is evident. But for Mozart, this aria would

---

Milady, here is the catalogue:
Of the beauties that my lord has loved
I have made a list of every one;
Come and scan it, read it with me.

* Now, from Italy and Germany,
A hundred-odd I've listed here
And then I don't know how many
From France and from Iberia:

In Italy six hundred and forty,
In Germany, two hundred thirty-one,
A hundred in France, in Turkey
  ninety-one,
While in Spain already a thousand and
  three!

There were ladies, there were citizens,
There were countesses and artisans
Servants, cooks, and scullery-maids,
Needing only to be women
For him to love them, every one.

Now, among them there were
  countesses,
Servant-girls and citizens,
Princesses and marchionesses,
There were ladies of every station,
  Every form, and every age.

Such a lover, I must tell you,
Were he to keep all his promises,
Some day'd find himself becoming
Husband to the whole wide world.
I must tell you, he'll have any,
Be they plump or be they skinny,
Since 'tis none except the old ones
Fail to set his heart aflame.

With the blondes it is his custom
To commend their gentle manners,
With the brunettes, constancy,
With the fair ones, their sweet ways.
He wants plump ones in December,
But in June they must be slender,
While the tall ones must be stately
And the small ones must be spritely.
Old ones, too, he has not missed,
Just to have them on his list;
But his favorite form of sinning
Is with one who's just beginning.
Whether they be rich or poor,
Fair or ugly, one thing's sure:
Just provided they are women,
You know well what happens then!

For purposes of comparison, these translations have been made quite literal. But we have borrowed from Edward J. Dent's version of the da Ponte text—made to be sung and so, in general, freer than ours—two lines that are both literal and particularly fortunate.—*Translators.*

never have contained the two lines about innocence betrayed, which are spoken to an uncanny *pianissimo*. We are reminded again of the proverb *Facile inventis addere*; but it is facile only for a facile hand. A still more fortunate stroke is the reduction of the number of characters by Mozart and da Ponte from ten to eight. In Bertati's version, another lady, Donna Ximena, becomes a victim of Don Giovanni, and he has a second servant, the cook Lanterna. Bondini had only seven singers, so that Masetto and the Governor had to be sung by the same man. But the real achievement in the transformation of the libretto was the creation of Donna Anna. In Bertati's version, she withdraws after the murder of her father into the darkness of the cloister, and does not reappear. In the version of da Ponte and Mozart, she is the chief of the three feminine characters and hers is actually the counter-role to Don Giovanni himself. No character in the opera was as badly misunderstood in the nineteenth century as Donna Anna. On the one hand she was considered cold and unlovable; on the other, the German romantic poet E. T. A. Hoffmann, for example, believed he had found her secret: she loves Don Giovanni! This is, of course, nonsense; but what is true is that she is one of the hero's victims, that Don Giovanni in the dark of night, disguised as Don Ottavio, has reached the summit of his desires, and that the curtain rises at the moment when Donna Anna has come to the realization of the terrible truth of her betrayal. In the eighteenth century no one misunderstood this. It goes without saying that in the famous *recitativo accompagnato* in which she designates Don Giovanni to her betrothed as the murderer of her father, she cannot tell Don Ottavio the whole truth; and his *respiro* has always had a tragi-comic flavor for every understanding listener. This explains everything: Don Giovanni's indifference to her, since he has possessed her just as he has Donna Elvira; her insistence that Don Ottavio must avenge her (even in Spain there was the Holy Hermandad to prosecute murderers); her refusal to become his, although she loves him; and in the Finale, after her seducer is dead, her putting off of Ottavio for another year. Da Ponte must have found a suggestion for the figure of Donna Anna even in Goldoni's wretched *tragicommedia*, lacking as it is in insight. For the strangest theme in Goldoni's play is the fact that Donna Anna detests the man who is forced upon her as her betrothed, Don Ottavio. A comparison of the maxims with which the two pieces end also shows that Goldoni's play cannot have been unknown to da Ponte.

Che l'uom muore qual visse, e il giusto cielo
Gli empi punisce, e i dissoluti abhorre.

[For man dies as he has lived, and a just heaven
Will punish the sinner, abhorring all debauchers.]—Goldoni

Questo è il fin di chi fa mal,
E de' perfidi la morte
Alla vita è sempre ugual.

[This is the end of the evil-doer,
And the dying of the wicked
Ever suits the way they lived.]—Da Ponte

In one important respect, in the transformation of Bertati's one-act libretto to the great two-act opera *buffa*, da Ponte and Mozart had to stand on their own feet. In Bertati, the rescue of Zerlina from the clutches of her seducer by Donna Elvira is followed immediately by the cemetery scene and the nocturnal feast, with Don Giovanni's end. Not alone the great Finale of the first act is da Ponte's invention; he had to fill out more than half of the second act with action. We know how he did it, by resorting to a series of trivialities and dramatic postponements. The second seduction of Elvira, with the change of costume under the balcony; the chastisement of Masetto; the unmasking of Leporello: all clumsy expedients. But they were not clumsy expedients for Mozart. Without them we should not have the wonderful Trio in A major, Don Giovanni's immortal Serenade, Zerlina's *Vedrai carino*, which ends the conflict of Masetto and Zerlina once and for all, or the grandiose Sextet, in which so much of grief and of dignity finds expression in music. Mozart was not afraid of such dramatic weaknesses. Here we see an overflowing of pure, non-functional beauty; he seems to bid us 'stay awhile.' At such moments the proceedings on the stage lose their air of reality and become mere play-acting. For this is opera, and in opera 'poetry must be the obedient daughter of music.'

This is not to say that Mozart's goal was not the highest dramatic verity. *Don Giovanni* still contains two numbers that are arias in the old style: Don Ottavio's *Il mio tesoro* and Donna Anna's *Non mi dir*, with its great introductory recitative. Mozart himself omitted the first of these in the Vienna version, and satisfied the tenor by giving him a shorter number at another place—the wonderful *Dalla sua pace*—this is the only change he made for Vienna that may be called an improvement. But probably no one has ever been bored by any of the most prominent pieces in *Don Giovanni*. The two Finales are miracles of rapidity: the second exceptionally simple, in three or four connected scenes; the first full of excitement, Leporello's invitation, the festal dance with the three orchestras, the explosion—and in the middle the solemn cæsura of the Masked Trio. The question of tempo in the opera is here a burning one. It is the question of reconciling music and action, to which there are several answers. In the *opera seria* it is just as simple as in the Wagnerian music-drama. In the former there is a clear division between the aria, in which the music lingers and spreads out, and the *recitativo secco*, in which it is pushed forward. And Wagner has the symphonic orchestra under cover of which the voice can, when necessary, declaim as rapidly as desired. Mozart found the golden mean, which is a rarity in the history of opera. His *Introduzione* has always seemed to me one of the wonders of the world: Leporello's striding back and forth beneath Donna Anna's window, his remarks on the passionate dialogue-duet between the seducer and his victim, the entrance of the Governor, the duel and its tragic issue. Then, without transition, the whisper of the *recitativo secco*, and the outcry of Donna Anna when she returns. There is not a second or a measure too many or too few. In a spoken drama of *Don Giovanni* the director would have to determine the tempo; in the opera, Mozart establishes it so perfectly that both dramatic and musical needs are fully satisfied. Nor is his secret simply brevity; it is fullness in brevity. And this fullness in brevity increases in the second Finale to an almost explosive degree in Elvira's last attempt to rescue Don Giovanni and the terrible D minor scene in which the Governor pronounces the judgment of heaven—a scene that has always been looked upon as the peak of dramatic and theatrical force.

In this tragic scene, in which Don Giovanni, whatever else he may be, rises to the full stature of his character, Leporello is permitted a few bits of drollery, as when he warns his master from under the table ('dite di nò, dite di nò') not to accept the invitation of the Governor. There has been much dispute about the style of this opera, and performances in our own time have tended now more to the gay side and now more to the tragic. In one production the final Sextet, which draws the moral from Don Giovanni's fate, is respected; in another it is omitted. Mozart himself sanctioned this uncertainty by closing his own Vienna version of the work, as produced in 1788, with Don Giovanni's descent to hell. The libretto is subtitled *Dramma giocoso* (gay drama), but this does not mean much, since many librettists of the period gave the same title to the most nonsensical farces. Mozart himself, in his thematic catalogue, called it simply 'opera buffa in due atti.' For us, historically speaking, the work presents no riddle: it is an *opera buffa* with *seria* roles—for instance, those of Donna Anna and Don Ottavio—and *buffa* roles. But a merely historical point of view is inadequate for such a work. Is there any reason, however, to rack our brains further over the problem? Where material like this is concerned, in which, as in *Faust,* such dark, primeval, and demonic forces are inextricably combined, analysis can never be complete. The work is *sui generis,* incomparable and enigmatic from the evening of its first performance to the present day.

That evening was 29 October 1787. Mozart had gone to Prague late in the summer, taking with him the greater part of the score, for time was again pressing: the première was planned for 14 October as a gala performance on the occasion of the visit of the Archduchess Maria Theresa, who was to pass through on her way to visit her betrothed, a Saxon prince. Probably Mozart and da Ponte took special pains to upset this plan, as we may infer from a surviving libretto printed in Vienna, 1787. Apparently the office of the Court Chamberlain had required that the text be submitted beforehand, which must have frightened both the librettist and the composer not a little. Accordingly they had an incomplete text printed, omitting all the passages that might offend: the whole second half of the first act, which breaks off in the middle of the Quartet (No. 9). But even so Mozart's fears do not seem to have been quieted. He speaks in his letters of the intrigues of a noble lady. And here we have the explanation also of the anecdote—probably true —about the writing out of the overture on the evening before the performance. Mozart had purposely postponed doing this until the Archduchess, who had had to be satisfied with *Figaro,* had turned her back on Prague again. Among the witnesses of the first performance was old Casanova, who had come over from the near-by town of Dux, and who must have had a strange experience in listening to the aria about the *mille e trè,* even though his arts of seduction were based on methods different from those of Don Giovanni. He seems not to have been entirely satisfied with da Ponte, for among his papers there is preserved a new version for the text of the Sextet in the second act.

There was now an interval of more than two years without any operatic commission for Mozart—an interval during which he might have enriched us and posterity with three or four dramatic works. Finally, in the autumn of 1789, he received another commission. It appears that the success of the revival of *Figaro*, in August 1789, induced Emperor Joseph II to order a new *opera buffa* from Mozart and da Ponte. It appears, further, that the subject for this *opera buffa* had been provided by an actual happening among the Vienna aristocracy: a wager between an old cynic and two young officers that the young ladies to whom the latter were betrothed, and upon whose fidelity they were ready to take an oath, could be induced to betray them within twenty-four hours—each by the betrothed of the other. The conditions were that the two officers should disguise themselves so as to be unrecognizable, and should follow unquestioningly the strategy prescribed by the old man. The old man wins the wager: *Così fan tutte* (They are all the same!). *Eine macht's wie die andre, oder die Schule der Liebhaber* was the German title of the work, which, being very successful, was quickly translated.

No work of Mozart's has experienced such opposition and occasioned so many attempts to 'rescue' it as *Così fan tutte*. The composer of *Fidelio*, who regarded the libretto of *Don Giovanni*, even, as scandalous, is said to have rejected it because of the frivolity of its subject matter. The composer of *Tannhäuser* and *Lohengrin* disapproved on other grounds. His thesis was that it was impossible to write as good music to a poor libretto as to a good one, since drama was the masculine element in opera and music the feminine:

The noble, straightforward simplicity of his [Mozart's] purely musical instinct, for instance his instinctive penetration into the arcana of his art, made it wellnigh impossible to him there to bring forth magical effects, as Composer, where the Poem was flat and meaningless. How little did this richest-gifted of all musicians understand our modern music-maker's trick of building gaudy towers of music upon a hollow, valueless foundation, and playing the rapt and the inspired where all the poetaster's botch is void and flimsy, the better to show that the Musician is the jack in office and can go to any length he pleases, even to making something out of nothing—the same as the good God! O how doubly dear and above all honor is Mozart to me, that it was not possible to him to invent music for *Tito* like that of *Don Giovanni*, for

Così fan tutte like that of *Figaro!* How shamefully would it have dese-
crated Music! *

Here we have Wagner the theorist in all his glory as a counterfeiter
of esthetics and history. His testimony would have been somewhat
more justified if he had applied it to the *Euryanthe* of his idol Carl
Maria von Weber, and had compared this work with *Der Freischütz.*
But da Ponte's libretto for *Così fan tutte* is, as far as craftsmanship
goes, his best work—better than that for *Figaro* or *Don Giovanni.* Quite
apart from the fact that it was his own independent creation, and accordingly gives the lie to those who consider da Ponte only an arranger
and literary freebooter, this libretto does not contain a single dead spot.
The entire action develops gaily and logically, and at the end we have
the esthetic satisfaction that we get from a chess problem well solved,
or a trick of magic. The trick is all the harder, and the solution all the
more satisfying, because da Ponte had only six characters to work with.
Fiordiligi is the more 'heroic' of the two ladies, while Dorabella is the
more light-hearted; of the officers, Guglielmo, the baritone, is the more
determined, while Ferrando, the tenor, has a softer and more lyric role.
The threads of the action are all gathered in the hands of the old cynic,
or worldly-wise man, as the eighteenth century called him, and the
maid, Despina.

But the important thing is that Mozart's music for *Così fan tutte* is
not in any way poorer than that for *Figaro.* It is simply different.
Mozart was at the peak of his creative ability, and he wrote the work
con amore. On 29 December 1789, he invited his fellow-Masons Puchberg and Joseph Haydn to a 'little opera rehearsal' in his lodgings, and
on 20 January 1790, to the 'first instrumental rehearsal in the theater,'
which he would not have done if he had felt his work to be in any
way inferior.

There are two ways of approaching *Così fan tutte,* and perhaps even
more, for every work of art has its inexhaustible secrets and resists every
attempt to treat it categorically. One way is to forget the moralistic
point of view of the nineteenth and twentieth centuries, and not to let
oneself be shocked by the 'trashy' plot. The other approach is the historical. Goldoni again gives us the key. He writes:

C'étoit un usage invétéré parmi les Comédiens Italiens, que les Sou-
brettes donnassent tous les ans, et à plusieurs reprises, des Pièces qu'on

---

* Translated by William Ashton Ellis, *Richard Wagner's Prose Works,* II, 36.

appelloit de transformations, comme *l'Esprit follet*, la *Suivante Magi-cienne*, et d'autres du même genre, dans lesquelles l'Actrice paroissant sous différentes formes, elle changeoit plusieurs fois de costume, jouoit plusieurs personnages, et parloit différens langages.*

Here we have the explanation for the figure of Despina, who in the Finale of the first act appears as a doctor, effecting miraculous magnetic cures, and in the second act as a notary. Once we understand this fig-ure, we understand the others as well. They are not at all mere marion-ettes, whose movements are accomplished merely by pulling wires. They do not have the same 'reality' as Tosca and Scarpia, but, to remain within the field of comic opera, they do have the same as Eva and Beckmesser, Mistress Alice Ford and Sir John Falstaff—that is to say an operatic reality. Anyone who cannot put himself into the mood to accept this operatic reality should not go to the theater at all.

That Mozart's purpose was genuine 'drama' is proved by evidence that survives. For Guglielmo, the baritone, he had composed the high-spirited burlesque aria, *Rivolgete a lui lo sguardo* (K. 584), in such ex-tended form that it seemed to him to interrupt the flow of the first act. Accordingly, he replaced it with a shorter one (*Non siate ritrosi*, No. 15) and entered the original aria in his thematic catalogue as: 'an aria which was intended for Così fan tutte; for Benucci.' It may confidently be said that this is the most remarkable *buffo* aria ever written. But in this thoroughly *buffo* opera Mozart was not concerned simply with buf-foonery. There are, of course, typical *buffo* pieces in this score, among which are the arias of Despina, and the whole mad Finale of the first act. But Mozart reserves the liberty to change his attitude continually. When the two lovers have taken their military farewell, Dorabella, the more impulsive of the two ladies, voices her state of mind in an aria (*Smanie implacabili*, No. 11) that would do credit to any fury robbed of her serpents. When the first attempt is made on the fidelity of the young ladies, Fiordiligi responds with an aria (*Come scoglio*, No. 14) that would be perfectly fitting in the most pathetic opera seria. It is pure parody. But not everything is parody. When things become serious,

* 'It was an established custom amongst the Italian actors, for the waiting-maids [soubrettes] to give several times every year pieces which were called transformations, as *The Hobgoblin*, *The Female Magician*, and others of the same description, in which the actress, appearing under different forms, was obliged to change her dress frequently, to act different characters and speak various languages.' (*Mémoires*, 1, 43. Translated by John Black, Boston, 1877.)

Mozart adopts quite another tone. In the first act, Ferrando sings an Arietta in praise of the constancy of his beloved (*Un'aura amorosa*, No. 17, in A major), the lyric tenderness of which corresponds completely to the sensuous atmosphere of the whole act. But when he has evidence of Dorabella's unfaithfulness, he sings the Arietta *Tradito, schernito* (No. 27, in C minor), in which the expression of his anguish is as genuine as it is brief. Consider the complete appropriateness of the tonalities, in relation to C major. When Fiordiligi makes the heroic decision to follow her beloved into the field she sings a Rondo in E major (*Per pietà, ben mio, perdona*, No. 25), which voices a genuine struggle with herself, repentance, and joy at having come to a decision. It is no accident that Beethoven imitated this aria in Leonore's great aria, with the difference that instead of Mozart's two obbligato horns Beethoven naturally used three.

This opera is iridescent, like a glorious soap-bubble, with the colors of buffoonery, parody, and both genuine and simulated emotion. To this, moreover, is added the color of pure beauty. We have already mentioned, as a moment of such pure beauty, the Quartet in A-flat in the second Finale: three of the lovers sing in canon, while the fourth, Guglielmo, who cannot reconcile himself to defeat, grumbles a wrathful commentary. Another piece of this sort is the Farewell Quintet in the first act (*Di scrivermi ogni giorno*, No. 9). What was Mozart to do at this point? The two young ladies were weeping real tears, while the officers knew that there was no occasion to do so. Mozart raises the banner of pure beauty, without forgetting the old cynic in the background, 'laughing himself to death.' There is an evening glow over this whole score. Mozart is full of sympathy for his two victims, the representatives of frail femininity, unlike the old Verdi of *Falstaff*, who observes the gyrations of his characters as disinterestedly and ruthlessly as an Olympian. There is a touch of melancholy in the moral of the burlesque incident, and we can hear it already in the andante of the overture:

Ex. 99

Anyone who has ears to hear will not fail to realize Mozart's personal sympathy with his creatures even in this most *buffa* of all his *opere buffe*. And consequently no one will take even this apparently most Italian of all his operas to be truly Italian—not because Mozart was a German, but because he was a great dramatist, and not just a great *melodista*. For Paisiello and Cimarosa were great melodists too.

23. The German Opera

Of the dramatic forms in which Mozart wrote, the national one, the *Singspiel* or German operetta, was the youngest. The *opera seria* could look back on a development of at least 170 years, and the *opera buffa* on one of 50 or 60, while the *Singspiel* was still in its 'teens. Its origins were certainly not German. They went back to the French *opéra-comique*, whose repertory—small, more or less innocent, more or less bucolic comedies with interpolated musical pieces—had been favorably received in Vienna since 1752. *Opéra-comique* had started about the beginning of the century as a parody of grand opera, without, however, ever attaining in Paris the high level of satire and social criticism reached by *The Beggar's Opera* in London; later it attempted, by granting music a more and more important place, to rival the Italian *buffo* opera. There always remained, however, this distinction: the Italian buffoonists were singers who could also act, while the performers of *opéra-comique* were actors who could also sing a bit.

Count Durazzo, the Imperial Intendant in Vienna, established this French product there; its ingredients and scope are recognizable even from the titles: *Le Déguisement pastoral*; *Les Amours champêtres*; *Le chinois poli en France*; *Tirsis et Doristée*. And Gluck had added to these imported wares a series of delightful miniatures: *L'Isle de Merlin* (1758), *La Fausse esclave* (1758), *L'Arbre enchanté* (1759), *La Cythère assiegée* (1759), *L'Ivrogne corrigé* (1760), *Le Cadi dupé* (1761)—dramatic miniatures, which he augmented in 1762 with a grand comic opera, *La Rencontre imprévue* or *Les Pèlerins de la Mecque*, which is scarcely less significant in its field than *Orfeo* is in the field of *opera seria*. For this was no parodistic, pastoral, gently frivolous, or lightly socio-critical trifle, but rather a French counterpart to the *opera buffa*, and reform was just as much a part of its purpose as it was of that of *Orfeo*. Although the work was intended for the French stage, it had a much greater effect on the German; the former had its own masters of opéra-comique in Duni, Philidor, Monsigny and Grétry. From 1770 on, it spread, under the title *Die Pilgrimme von Mekka* and in a German translation, through all the German theaters, large and small. We know how familiar Mozart was with it from his variations on *Unser dummer Pöbel meint.*

For a time Mozart did not venture to imitate so ambitious a work. Perhaps melodies and miniatures of Philidor and Monsigny and Duni were still ringing in his ears when, in 1768, Dr. Anton Mesmer commissioned him to compose the German *Singspiel, Bastien und Bastienne,* as a more modest counterpart to *La Finta semplice.* Unlike *La Finta semplice,* this work achieved a performance in Vienna, in the garden theater of Dr. Mesmer, who at that time held open house at his home in the Landstrasse district and who later became world famous as a hypnotist. Opera students still like to perform *Bastien und Bastienne* today, and audiences are always astonished to discover that in the *Intrada,* the brief prelude, young Mozart anticipated the opening theme of Beethoven's *Eroica.* The little work was to have been repeated in Salzburg, with an alto singing the part of Colas; for this performance, which did not materialize, we have a few *secco* recitatives. But it is clear that the simple little piece could not sustain so close an approach to *opera buffa* and that Mozart himself probably realized that it would be best to restrict himself to spoken dialogue.

The material of the piece stemmed from no less a person than Jean-Jacques Rousseau. Rousseau, passionate defender of *opera buffa,* especially of Pergolesi's *La Serva padrona,* and originator of the cry 'Back to Nature,' had written the text and composed the music (if we may call it composed) of *Le Devin du village* in 1752; and, like all very successful pieces, *Le Devin du village* was immediately parodied. As *Les Amours de Bastien et Bastienne,* Rousseau's pastoral play, altered by Favart into something more peasant-like, was produced in Paris in 1753. This parody was introduced in Vienna by Friedrich Wilhelm Weiskern (1710-68), the son of a Saxon riding-master and one of the most successful comedians of the Viennese stage; and the work even achieved publication, beginning in 1764. A certain Johann Müller wrote the texts of three additional arias (Nos. 11, 12, and 13) for Mozart.

This is a long history for so simple a piece. There are only three characters: the pair of lovers, Bastien and Bastienne, and the old shepherd, Colas. Bastienne bemoans Bastien's inconstancy and is advised by Colas that an effective cure would be for her to pretend to be equally fickle. Bastien also comes to seek Colas's advice. Colas summons Bastienne, seemingly by means of magic, and, after further quarreling, the two lovers are reconciled. That is all, and it is all so childlike, so well suited to the age and genius of the lad composing the music for it, that it became a charming little piece with sufficient vitality to keep it alive up to the present. For Bastien and Bastienne, Mozart wrote simple little songs and songlike duets, always in simple duple or triple meter and often of great melodic charm; for Colas, a coarse piece of rustic music as an entrance-scene and a droll conjuring aria in the here menacing key of C minor; everything remains within the frame of the *Singspiel* form. A sensitive critic would perhaps even then have noticed two different traits that pointed towards the future: the assurance with which the small orchestra (consisting only of strings, two oboes [flutes], and two horns) is handled; and the dramatic instinct—shown, for example, in the jovial beginning of the final trio, when Colas surprises the lovers in a warm embrace.

No two of Mozart's operas are alike: *Figaro, Don Giovanni,* and *Così fan tutte* are all *opere buffe,* but each work is so different from the others that it seems to be *sui generis.* The same is true of his German operas—*Bastien und Bastienne; Die Entführung;* and *Die Zauberflöte*—three quite different examples of the form. And each of these works has its special historical background. For *Die Entführung* and *Die Zauberflöte,* however, Mozart creates his own 'springboard' or historical background: for *Die Entführung,* in the *Singspiel* that posterity christened *Zaide;* for *Die Zauberflöte,* in the choruses and entr'actes he wrote for the play, *Thamos, König in Ägypten* by Tobias Philipp Baron von Gebler.

Of these two 'springboards,' the music for the Baron's 'heroic drama' was written first. Most of it goes back to the sojourn of Leopold and Wolfgang in Vienna in 1773. The poet, who was Privy Councillor and Vice Chancellor of the Imperial Bohemian Court Chancery, had at first entrusted the composition of the two big choral scenes, in Acts I and V of his drama, to a Master Johann Tobias Sattler, whose work he then had Gluck examine. This music does not seem to have satisfied the Baron, however, and he commissioned Mozart to write new music for his work. Mozart composed at that time the two choruses and five instrumental pieces; Gebler, who was anxious that his work be performed in Berlin, wrote on 13 December 1773 to the Berlin writer Nicolai: '[I] enclose the music of *Thamos,* recently composed by a certain Sigr. Mozzart. He wrote it according to his own ideas and the first chorus is very beautiful.' Later, for Böhm's troupe, who visited Salzburg in 1779, Mozart revised both of the choral scenes, the second one drastically, and added a third chorus, the text of which is not in Gebler's drama. Presumably he also revised the five instrumental entr'-actes on this occasion. Böhm then used all of these pieces for performances of a play by Karl Martin Plümicke called *Lanassa*, which stems from A.-M. Lemierre's *La Veuve de Malabar*, a drama evidently on an Indian subject. Mozart also permitted Böhm to use one of his more richly orchestrated symphonies of 1773 (K. 184) as an overture to the play. In this form Mozart's music for *König Thamos* was carried throughout South and West Germany, and when Mozart was in Frankfurt at the end of September 1790 for the coronation of the Emperor, he had the opportunity to hear it himself. He was not fated to hear it in the original version. At the beginning of 1783 Leopold sent some of Mozart's manuscripts, including *Thamos*, to him at Vienna. Mozart replied (15 February):

I am extremely sorry that I shall not be able to use the music of *Thamos*, but this piece, which failed to please here, is now among the rejected works which are no longer performed. For the sake of the music alone it might possibly be given again, but that is not likely. Certainly it is a pity!

He was right. If his choruses and instrumental pieces were actually performed in the original instrumentation, they must have smothered Gebler's or Plümicke's clumsy work. The first chorus, especially, accompanied by a large orchestral apparatus (flutes, oboes, bassoons, horns, trumpets, timpani, three trombones, and strings), can be compared only with some of the greatest choral pieces by Mozart himself—the D minor *Kyrie* or movements from the C minor Mass. It is worthy of note that already in Gebler's 'Egyptian' drama, as later in *Die Zauberflöte*, the symbolic contrast between darkness and light plays an important part. Thus, this first chorus is a mighty morning hymn, a greeting to the sun, with a solemn tutti returning in rondo fashion, and division of the chorus into men's and women's voices—music of the finest workmanship and, at the same time, striking effect. The same is true of the even more extensive and more complex chorus in Act V, a song of thanksgiving whose patriotic jubilation has something so hymn-like about it that one instinctively recalls the choral finale of the Ninth

Symphony. And when the last chorus, composed later—another song of prayer and thanksgiving—is introduced by a bass solo exhorting in priestly fashion, one fancies one already hears the voice of Sarastro.

The instrumental pieces, which lead from one act to the next, reveal Mozart as a composer of program music. 'The first act closes with the agreement between Pheron and Mirza [the conspirators of the drama] to place Pheron on the throne.' It is a two-part Allegro movement in a savage C minor, introduced, as in the Overture to *Die Zauberflöte*, by three solemn chords. 'Thamos's good character shows itself at the end of the second act . . .' contrasted with 'Pheron's false character.' This is a tender Andante in E-flat, in the bright light of which Pheron's shadow is scarcely perceptible. The transition from the third act to the fourth is music to accompany a pantomime, scarcely comprehensible in itself but very expressive in its proper frame; the one from the fourth act to the fifth paints 'the general confusion' in an *Allegro vivace assai* beginning in D minor; the piece that concludes the fifth act depicts, in a storm-scene, 'Pheron's despair, blasphemy, and death.' When, in the Vienna Carnival of 1783, Mozart with his wife and friends performed a little pantomime, costumed as the characters of the *commedia dell'arte*, he offered the comic counterpart of this heroic pantomime in his music for it—music so striking, so droll, that one must greatly regret it has survived only in fragmentary form.

If *König Thamos* (K. 345) is a distant ancestor of *Die Zauberflöte*, the German operetta known as *Zaide* (K. 344) is a very close one of *Die Entführung aus dem Serail*. *Zaide* has a remarkable history. The autograph of the work turned up in 1798 in Mozart's estate as a German *Singspiel* with not much of the music lacking, and seeming to require only the connective text to be revived and used by Constanze as a business property. Constanze—with whom Mozart, significantly, had never discussed the work—therefore published in the *Allgemeine Musicalische Zeitung* a request that 'anyone who knows the title of this *Singspiel* or, if it has been published, knows where it was issued, inform the publishers of this periodical.' Evidently there was no reply. J. Anton André, who shortly thereafter purchased the whole treasure of Mozart's manuscripts, including the autograph of the still nameless work, eventually published it in 1838, under the title of *Zaide*. The librettist was the Salzburg trumpeter Andreas Schachtner, who played so friendly a part in the story of Mozart's childhood and who was later to translate the text of *Idomeneo*. His source had been a miserable

Singspiel entitled *Das Serail, oder: Die unvermittelte* [= unvermutete] *Zusammenkunft in der Sclaverei zwischen Vater, Tochter und Sohn* (*The Seraglio, or: The Unexpected Encounter in Slavery of Father, Daughter, and Son*), which, with music by Joseph von Friebert, was produced in Bozen in 1779. Schachtner presumably retained the title *Das Serail*. Mozart wrote the work at the end of 1779 for Böhm's traveling company, with a view towards performance in Vienna—it was one of his many attempts to gain a foothold somewhere outside the hated Salzburg. But on 29 November 1780, the Empress died, and so Leopold was forced to report to his son at Munich (11 December): 'As for Schachtner's drama, it is impossible to do anything at the moment, as the theaters are closed and there is nothing to be got out of the Emperor . . . It is better to let things be, as the music is not finished . . .' Whereupon Mozart begged his father at least to bring 'Schachtner's operetta' with him to Munich: '. . . there are some people who come to the Cannabichs, who might just as well hear a thing of this kind.' There is no further mention of the work, which probably lacked only a final chorus (with soli) and an overture.

We know why, now. It was a 'Turkish opera,' and it was an opera about virtue and benevolence, and Mozart was obviously attracted to it by the possibilities of musical coloring offered by the scene of the action as well as by its 'sentimental' dénouement. We learn what was expected of a 'sentimental comedy' in those days from the poet Jean-Pierre Claris de Florian, who, as a creator of such plays, knew whereof he spoke:

I understand by the comedy of sentiment . . . one that places before the eyes of the spectator characters who are virtuous and persecuted; as well as an interesting situation in which passion struggles against duty, or honor triumphs over self-interest; one, finally, that instructs us without boring us, moves us without saddening us, and causes gentle tears to fall, the first requirement of a sensitive heart.*

All this was present here. The 'virtuous and persecuted characters': the noble Gomatz, who is taken prisoner and made a slave to the Sultan; the favorite, Zaide, who contemplates the sleeping Gomatz with sympathy, secretly gives him money, and determines to fly with him; and the renegade in the Sultan's service, who, seized by involuntary sympathy for the pair, facilitates their escape. The plans miscarry, of course,

* *Théâtre*, Tome 1, Paris, 1797.

and all three are sentenced to death. The Sultan seems adamant. Then the renegade—he is called Allazim in Mozart's work and is in reality the Prince Ruggiero—proves that he had saved the Tyrant's life fifteen years earlier, and, at the last moment, it is revealed that Gomatz and Zaide are the renegade's son and daughter. The Sultan frees them all, not without pointing out that 'not only Europe but Asia also can produce virtuous souls.' One might trace this dénouement to Lessing's *Nathan der Weise*—in which all the characters also turn out at the end to be brothers and sisters or otherwise related—if it were not for the fact that *Nathan* was also written in 1779, and if it were thought fitting to establish a relationship between a work of the broadest religious and human tolerance and the little, provincial, South-German *Singspiel*.

Zaide or, as we should like to rename it, *Das Serail*, is a 'serious operetta.' Humor is represented only by the subordinate role of the overseer of the slaves, Osmin, who in a *prestissimo*, a 'laughing aria,' delivers himself of some practical philosophy about the fools who do not know how to profit by their good fortune; the aria has approximately the same meaning as Goethe's songs from the *Gross-Kophta*, which Hugo Wolf set to music in so masterly a fashion. Filled with a fine humor, in a higher sense, is Gomatz's aria (No. 6); *Herr und Freund! wie dank ich dir*. Gomatz feels the need both to thank the renegade for his help and at the same time to inform Zaide of the sudden shift in their fortunes; and Mozart expressed this conflict most delightfully. Otherwise the work is much on the side of 'sensibility.' Zaide sings over the sleeping Gomatz a melodically full-blown 'slumber aria' (No. 3); she tries to mollify the Sultan by comparing herself to a nightingale in a cage, who can also not be blamed for seeking to escape—this in No. 12, a charming piece in A major accompanied only by strings; she berates him in G minor (No. 13) and, in the middle section, a larghetto, mournfully recalls the loved one. Gomatz has a kind of 'portrait aria' anticipating the one in *Die Zauberflöte*, a notably exalted piece (No. 4); and brother and sister have a short, restrained duet of joy (No. 5). Allazim, in two somewhat neutral pieces (Nos. 7 and 14), is characterized as prince and sage, and Soliman, in his two arias (Nos. 9 and 11), as a despot. A small chorus of criminals breaking stones introduces the first act and gives Gomatz the occasion for one of the two pieces that are, from a historical standpoint, the most remarkable in the score: the melodrama in which Gomatz bemoans his fate, from whose unbearable sorrow he seeks surcease in sleep. The other, introducing the second act, is the Sultan's vehement diatribe against the female sex. Mozart had encountered the melodrama, a new form, in a performance by the Seiler troupe in Mannheim:

. . . I saw a piece of this kind performed twice and was absolutely delighted. Indeed, nothing has ever surprised me so much, for I had always imagined that such a piece would be quite ineffective! You know, of course, that there is no singing in it, only recitation, to which the music is like a sort of obbligato accompaniment to a recitative. Now and then words are spoken while the music goes on, and this produces the finest effect. The piece I saw was Benda's *Medea*. He has composed another one, *Ariadne auf Naxos*, and both are really excellent. [Letter of 12 November 1778.]

His enthusiasm was so great that it seemed to him desirable to replace *recitativo accompagnato* entirely by melodramatic treatment of the text, and he decided to write a whole melodrama himself—*Semiramis*, to a text by Baron von Gemmingen. Fortunately he did not carry out his intention; we say fortunately, because melodrama is a doubtful, mongrel form; here in the *Singspiel*, however, it happens to be a happy intermediary between spoken dialogue and aria, and the two pieces are an arsenal of expressive Mozartean formulas.

The loveliest pieces in the score, however, are the two ensembles: a trio in E major closing the first act, and a great quartet in the second, before the dénouement. To begin with the quartet, all four characters are ruled by different emotions: Zaide desires only to die for Gomatz; Gomatz bids her take courage; the renegade, already pardoned, laments the fate of the two victims; and the Sultan continues to affirm his relentless intention. All this is realized clearly and with feeling in the pure and flowing music. The trio is even more beautiful. The three captives, prepared to escape, stand at dawn before the open sea, thunder receding in the distance, a rainbow in the dark sky. Bliss fills their hearts; only Zaide sees in the distant lightning an omen of approaching disaster. But everything is resolved in an Allegro containing the smoothest melody and the finest workmanship. For this piece alone it might be worth while to rescue the work from oblivion. But Mozart himself prevented this: three years after *Das Serail* he composed *Die Entführung aus dem Serail*, and this greater, Vienna sister-work overshadows for all time its more modest Salzburg forerunner.

A certain person by the name of Mozart, in Vienna, has had the audacity to misuse my drama *Belmont und Constanze* as an opera-text.

I hereby protest most solemnly against this infringement of my rights and reserve the right to take further measures. Christoph Friedrich Bretzner, author of *Das Räuschchen*.

This notice was published by Bretzner, a bookkeeper by profession, in the *Leipziger Zeitung* for 1782. The opera-text in which Bretzner's mediocre work was 'misused' was called *Die Entführung aus dem Serail* and had already appeared on the boards in Berlin a year previously as a *Singspiel* with music by Johann André. Mozart was unable to use it as it was; with the help of Gottlieb Stephanie, an actor at the National-theater who provided Vienna with all sorts of translations and theatrical pieces, he attempted to arrange it to suit his purpose. We have seen with how keen an eye for the nature of his characters, with what an instinct for the stage, he set to work. And the result was quite a good libretto; indeed, the text even contains, alongside extremely awkward passages, a few poetic ones: when Belmonte and Constanze see death facing them, they find some extremely moving words. And I cannot agree with the criticism that the escape of the two couples should have taken place at the end of the second act: the third act gains extraordinary tension and richness by virtue of the fact that it concentrates within a small space the attempted escape, its failure, the imminent punishment, and the happy solution. What belongs at the end of an act in an operetta is music, not a dramatic cæsura, and Mozart offered music in an immortal quartet that is one of his greatest masterworks.

The content of the work has already been indicated to some extent by what we have said. It is almost the same as that of *Zaide*, except that *Die Entführung* is related to *Zaide* as a rich variation is to a simple theme. Instead of Zaide and her brother Gomatz, we have a truly noble pair of lovers, Constanze and Belmonte; in place of the despotic Sultan Soliman, who becomes generous only at the end, we have the speaking part of the Pasha Selim, a renegade, who behaves nobly from the very beginning and who wishes to possess the captive Constanze only with her own consent. These are the three 'serious' parts. But whereas in *Zaide* practically all the parts had been serious, *Die Entführung* is enriched by *buffo* roles as well: Constanze's maid, Blonde; Belmonte's servant, Pedrillo, captured with the two women by pirates and sold to the Pasha; and especially Osmin, guardian of the Pasha's harem and in love with Blonde. The action is very simple. Act I: Belmonte enters disguised before the palace of the Pasha; he is roughly turned away by Osmin; he achieves contact with Pedrillo, who introduces him as an architect to the Pasha; and thus he gains entrance to the palace. Act II: Osmin renews his attempts, as clumsy as they are vain, to win Blonde's favor; the Pasha makes equally vain attempts, not without threats, to win Constanze's; Pedrillo informs Blonde of Belmonte's arrival, and renders Osmin harmless by plying him with wine; Belmonte appears and joins in a quartet—at first a double duet—in which the plan of escape is agreed upon; the men doubt the women's constancy; reaction of the women; reconciliation and hymn to love. Act III: Heroic aria of Belmonte; serenade of Pedrillo, which serves as a signal that all is ready; flight and discovery. The two couples, brought in by Osmin in triumph, are in fear of imminent death; but the Pasha, although he recognizes in Belmonte the son of his deadly enemy, forgives them and grants them freedom; song of thanksgiving in the form of a *vaudeville*, and chorus of jubilation.

Several circumstances combined to render Mozart's *Die Entführung* an epoch-making work. It was a German *Singspiel*, but of a special kind, as Goethe realized when he concluded his own attempts in this field as a provider of texts for the minor musicians of Weimar: the appearance of *Die Entführung* 'ruined everything,' as he put it. In the course of the 1760's the *Singspiel* of North and Central Germany had, like the *opéra-comique* and in imitation of it, granted more and more room to music. It was especially Johann Adam Hiller, later cantor of St. Thomas's in Leipzig, who in his own way introduced in the 'German operetta' the division of characters into 'serious' and *buffo* parts, and made greater demands on the vocal abilities of the performers. Gerber, in his *Altes Lexicon* (1790), calls Hiller 'the man who did most for our time,' and means by this 'that he taught us Germans how to *sing* as we should sing.' He goes so far as to maintain that Hiller

gave us German operetta at a time when a singer had never yet been seen in a German theater, operetta that . . . is greatly to be preferred to that of the Italians and French in correctness of declamation, in truth of expression, in clear-cut delineation of the different characters, in appropriateness of the music—now playful, now bold and fiery, but always noble—in scrupulous purity of harmony, and in wit, humor, and variety . . .

If this description does not apply to Hiller and his many imitators, such as Benda, Koch, Neefe, etc., it certainly does to *Die Entführung*. The

Viennese demanded much more than the North Germans in respect to music, singing technique, and richness of orchestration. And Mozart gave it to them; he dipped deep into the paint-pot. 'Too beautiful for our ears, and far too many notes, my dear Mozart,' Joseph II is supposed to have said after the first performance, on 16 July 1782; whereupon Mozart is said to have replied, 'Exactly as many, Your Majesty, as are needed.' Mozart had clarinets again, as in Paris and Mannheim and Munich, and how he used them! Mozart had 'Turkish music': piccolo, trumpets and timpani, triangle and cymbals; and what color they lend to the Overture, to the Janissary choruses, to Osmin's outbursts of anger, to the drinking duet!—a coloration at once exotic, gay, and menacing.

The other and even more important reason for the epoch-making effect of *Die Entführung* is that Mozart, to put it bluntly, for the first time did justice to the drama. In *Idomeneo* there had still been a superfluity of music, which was not unsuited to the *opera seria* with its traditional proportion of text to music. In *Die Entführung* Mozart no longer thinks in terms of 'categories.' Belmonte is not a tenor singing arias but a noble youth of the same type as Tamino, tender-hearted, energetic, and heroic. Constanze is a similar character; and only once did Mozart sacrifice the dramatic truth of her character to 'the agile throat of Cavalieri' (the first singer of the role), when he wrote for her the great C major aria with *concertante* flute, oboe, violin, and 'cello (No. 11, *Martern aller Arten*), a long piece of heroic virtuosity to which the poor Pasha simply is compelled to listen. But otherwise every piece grows out of the dramatic situation, every character is hit off with striking justice: Blonde's jubilation (No. 12, *Welche Wonne, welche Lust*); Pedrillo's shaky attempt to talk himself into a mood of courage (No. 13, *Frisch zum Kampfe*); Belmonte's joyful expectation (No. 1, *Hier soll ich dich denn sehen*), taken from the Overture, but changed from minor to major; his and Constanze's 'sentimental' arias, perhaps the loveliest of which are Belmonte's *O wie ängstlich* (No. 4) and Constanze's *Traurigkeit ward mir zum Lose* (No. 10), both introduced by recitatives full of the finest nuances. The directness of expression in these arias is doubly intensified in the recitative and duet *Welch ein Geschick* in the last act (No. 20). Mozart's greatest creation in this work is the figure of Osmin. This is no *basso buffo caricato* who happens to sing in German, no caricature, but as realistic a rogue as Falstaff: coarse, irascible, infinitely comical as a spiteful friend of women and wine, but infinitely dangerous. With strokes of color and of chromaticism in melody and harmony, Mozart makes real his paroxysms of rage and sadism: his *Erst geköpft, dann gehangen* is the counterpart of Don Giovanni's drinking aria; the G minor of the little song with which he enters characterizes the barbarian.

A German operetta does not have finales like an *opera buffa* but it does have ensembles. And the remarkable thing about the ensembles in *Die Entführung* is the fact that they sustain the dramatic action, develop it, and drive it forward in a continuous flow. No one stands on the stage merely to sing. Belmonte's encounter with Osmin (No. 2), Blonde's matrimonial instruction of Osmin (No. 9), the trio of the three men at the end of the first act, and the quartet at the end of the second—all carry the action forward. The quartet has always been particularly admired, and rightly so: each of the two tenors expresses in his own way his reflections about the integrity of the two women, and each of the women reacts in her own way—it is like the combination of two two-part canons, one serious and the other comic. Any other composer would have maintained the harmonious mood of the vaudeville at the end, but Mozart interrupts it with a new and final outburst of rage from Osmin and thus intensifies its stirring and touching effect. This dramatic agitation is matched by the agility of the orchestra. It seems to me that in *Die Entführung* more than anywhere else Mozart follows the suggestions of the text—Belmonte's heart-beats, the trembling of Pedrillo's limbs, Constanze's sighs, and so on. This orchestra speaks a new language, new also as regards dynamics, which are here of infinitely fine gradations. The whole work marks the complete emergence of Mozart's personality as a dramatic composer. He had taken extreme pains with it: none of his other opera scores is so full of deletions, condensations, and alterations as *Die Entführung*; for none of them did he require so long a time—almost a full year. But from now on he could write nothing in which the drama would be indifferently treated. And the work was a great success. Cramer's *Magazin* (1, 352) reports from Vienna in December 1782: '. . . *Die Entführung aus dem Serail* is full of beauties . . . and surpassed the expectations of the public, and the author's taste and new ideas, which were enchanting, received the fullest and most general applause.'

Mozart collaborated with Stephanie once more, when Joseph II arranged a 'pleasure festival' in Schönbrunn in honor of the Governor

General of the Netherlands, Duke Albert of Saxe-Teschen, and his wife, the Archduchess Christine. The result of the collaboration was 'Der *Schauspiel-Director*, a Comedy with Music, consisting of an Overture, two Arias, a Trio, and *Vaudeville*' (K. 486), as Mozart himself listed it in his thematic catalogue on 3 February 1786. It was presented before the princely audience at Schönbrunn on 7 February and repeated publicly on the 18th and 25th. The subject of the work is the experiences of a theater director who, after having made a fiasco with a good repertory, has received permission to gather together a new troupe for Salzburg. Some stage folk present themselves to him—first some actors, then two sopranos and a tenor. Each of the sopranos offers a sample of her ability, the one (Madame Herz = Aloysia Lange), a 'sentimental' aria; the other (Madame Silberklang = Caterina Cavalieri), a more naive rondo; then they come to blows, because each one thinks she deserves a higher salary than the other, and they try to out-sing each other in a trio, in which the tenor (Monsieur Vogelsang = Adamberger, Mozart's Belmonte) attempts to quiet them. Harmony is finally achieved in a *vaudeville* like the finale of *Die Entführung;* here the *buffo* of the troupe, who had given the poor theater-director appropriate counsel, also has a little solo—only to prove that he can *not* sing. The material of the piece is old and had already been very cleverly treated as an intermezzo by Metastasio in *L'Impresario delle Canarie;* and after Metastasio a hundred other comedy-writers (Goldoni, for example, in *L'Impresario delle Smirne*) and a hundred other librettists (Bertati, for example, in *Il Capriccio*) had used it for more or less sanguinary theater and opera satires. The best of all these pieces is Calzabigi's *Opera seria;* and among the most uncouth surely belongs the *Schauspiel-Director* of our Stephanie the younger: his language was as free as he dared to make it before so exalted an audience, and the character of the banker, who is keeping one of the actresses, is daring enough. At the same court festivity Salieri was again the more fortunate: he was permitted to compose Casti's dramatic prank *Prima la musica e poi le parole,* a quite different masterpiece of apt opera-satire.

Mozart had written two very grateful arias 'to measure' for his sopranos and remained as uncouth in the *vaudeville* as the text demanded. 'Every artist strives for honor—wants to be the only one'—these words were not inspiring. The trio is very gay and is not unrelated to the comic trios that Mozart sometimes tossed off for use at home. The finest piece in this occasional work is the witty Overture, which is in purest *buffo* style and of which the form is full of surprises; it towers far above the occasion for which it was written.

When Mozart wrote the interpolations for *Der Schauspiel-Director* he had long been working on *Figaro*; and for the next three or four years he became entirely an Italian *buffo* composer. But after *Così fan tutte* he could hardly count on an Imperial commission to compose an opera; Leopold II was not fond of him. Then, in the last year of his life, the course of his dramatic activity was again affected by an old acquaintance who had meanwhile gained fresh influence over him as a lodge-brother—the director of the Freihaus-Theater auf der Wieden, Emanuel Schikaneder. The Mozart family's acquaintance with Schikaneder had been concluded in 1780-81, when he and his troupe played a five months' engagement in Salzburg, and when Mozart had, while in the midst of his work on *Idomeneo*, written an aria (K. Anh. 11a, now lost) for one of Schikaneder's singers, Mademoiselle Ballo.

Schikaneder was completely a man of the theater. He was born of poor parents in 1748 at Regensburg, but his name points to a Tyrolean origin rather than to a Bavarian. After the early death of his father he became a strolling musician, but soon (in 1773) joined a troupe of actors and in 1777 became a prominent member of the 'Electoral Bavarian Privileged Moser Company,' which provided all South Germany with dramatic art in every form: comedies, tragedies, *Singspiele*, and ballets. Schikaneder's best role, in which he was supported by his wife, was in those days that of the youthful lover and hero; we know that he was one of the first German Hamlets. In the following year, however, he became the leading actor of the company and was especially successful in Stuttgart, Nuremberg, Augsburg, and Regensburg. His successes were not always attained by the loftiest means in the art of the theater, for Schikaneder was fond of mechanical contrivances, extravagant decorations, brilliant settings, mass-scenes, thunder and lightning, and graves and ghosts, and was always ready to cater to the coarsest desires of his public. After the engagement in Salzburg he extended the field of his activity, without neglecting South Germany, to the Austrian possessions; in 1786 he was in Vienna, where the Emperor even granted him the privilege of erecting a new suburban theater. In 1789, at his wife's request, he returned to Vienna and settled there, taking over the direction of the Freihaus-Theater in the suburb of Wieden, which had been opened shortly before (1787) and at once commenced with acumen to present *Singspiele* and German operas there. Nothing is more significant of his tendencies than the two pieces with which he began. The first was a farce with songs, *Der dumme Gärtner aus dem Gebirge, oder die zwei Anton* (The Stupid Gardener from the Mountains, or the Two Antons), in which he reserved for himself the Punch-like role of the foolish Anton. Its success was so great that Schikaneder presented six sequels. The second piece was a big romantic-comic opera, *Oberon, König der Elfen*, after Wieland's epic, the text by the comedian Carl Ludwig Gieseke, the music by Paul Wranitzky, a pupil of Haydn. This work, too, was so successful that Schikaneder followed it with several pieces of the same or similar character, as for example his own *Stein der Weisen*, produced in September 1790, or *Die Zauberinsel*, the material of which he took from Wieland's collection of fairy-tales, *Dschinnistan*.

Mozart followed these events with interest. From one of the sequels to *Der dumme Gärtner* he borrowed the theme for a set of piano variations (K. 613, *Ein Weib ist das herrlichste Ding auf der Welt*), not his best, although they are his last. For *Der Stein der Weisen* he orchestrated a comic duet, *Nun, liebes Weibchen, ziehst mit mir*, the composer of which was probably Benedict Schack. The characters of Lubano and Lubanara correspond exactly to those of Papageno and Papagena and were sung by the same performers—Schikaneder himself and Madame Gerl. Mozart could not have been very much surprised when Schikaneder approached him in the spring of 1791 with the request that he write an opera similar to *Der Stein der Weisen* or *Die Zauberinsel*— namely, *Die Zauberflöte*. The problem of where Schikaneder got the material for this work is very difficult to solve in detail; it is perhaps sufficient for us to know that it was taken, in the main, from Wieland's fairy-tale collection, especially the tale called *Lulu oder die Zauberflöte*.

The origin of *Die Zauberflöte*, like that of the Requiem, is covered with a web of legends. Mozart is supposed to have rescued Schikaneder, by means of this work, from financial difficulties; Schikaneder is said to have kept him in good humor during its composition by giving him wine and oysters and to have kept him locked up in a garden-house near the theater. This house was brought to the Capuziner-Berg near Salzburg in 1874, as the Santa Casa to Loreto, and every board in it is presumably as authentic as every one in the Santa Casa itself. Mozart is supposed to have hesitated to accept the proposal for fear of a fiasco, for 'he had not yet composed a magic opera.' All this is nonsense, of course. The work was produced on 30 September and its success grew with every repetition. Schikaneder could really have become rich from the work he wrote in collaboration with Mozart. But he was a happy-go-lucky comedian, a spendthrift, and a petticoat-chaser. In 1802 he lost the license for his theater to a wealthy lodge-brother, and returned to a diminutive castle in Nussdorf, which eventually he was compelled to sell. Towards the end of his life he became insane. He died in 1812, and, like Mozart, was buried in a pauper's grave.

One's judgment of the libretto of *Die Zauberflöte* is a criterion of one's dramatic, or rather dramatico-musical, understanding. Many critics find it so good that they deny its authorship to poor Schikaneder and ascribe it to the actor Carl Ludwig Gieseke, whose real name was Johann Georg Metzler, who had added the study of mineralogy to that of law, and in 1783 had become a comedian and joined Schikaneder's company. In 1801 he bade farewell to the stage, became Royal Director of Mines in Denmark and, in 1814, Professor of Mineralogy and Chemistry at the University of Dublin, where he died. When he visited Vienna again about 1818 or 1819 he is supposed to have claimed the authorship of the entire text of *Die Zauberflöte*. But if he wrote any of it at all, it was at most Tamino's discourse with the Speaker, the diction of which is somewhat above Schikaneder's powers.

For the weakness of the libretto—a small weakness, easily overcome—lies only in the diction. It contains a great number of unskilful, childish, vulgar turns of speech. But the critics who therefore decide that the whole libretto is childish and preposterous deceive themselves. At any rate Goethe did not so consider it when he wrote a 'Zauberflöte Part II,' unfortunately unfinished, but full of fairy-tale radiance, poetic fantasy, and profound thought. In the dramaturgic sense Schikaneder's work is masterly. The dialogue could be shortened and improved, but not a stone in the structure of these two acts and of the work as a whole could be removed or replaced, quite apart from the fact that any change would demolish Mozart's carefully thought out and organic succession of keys.

Nor can I find the slightest evidence for the claim that Schikaneder, after finishing the first half of his libretto, changed the course and characters of his opera because of the production of a competing opera at the Leopoldstädter theater. Sarastro, the representative of light, goodness, and humanity, has an enemy in the Queen of the Night; Sarastro holds her daughter Pamina captive, in order to guard her from her mother's influence. The Queen believes that she sees in Tamino, who has come by chance into her domain, the instrument for freeing Pamina and avenging herself upon Sarastro. She appears to Tamino, who is aflame with love for Pamina from having seen a mere portrait of her, gives him Papageno, a child of nature, as a companion, and provides both with helpful magic instruments, Tamino with a flute, Papageno with a glockenspiel. But, though she gains a traitor to Sarastro in the Moor Monostatos, who pursues Pamina lecherously, her plan miscarries. Tamino wanders into the benevolent power of Sarastro and his followers. In order to be taken into their circle he submits to the severest tests, in which Papageno participates somewhat less successfully, and the second act ends with the union of the lovers and their acceptance into the community, and with the defeat of the Queen. All this is enacted in a fairy-tale atmosphere: three genii float down to make reports, to impart instruction, and to ward off catastrophes; two men in armor stand before the portal through which Pamina and Tamino pass to undergo the final test, that of fire and water; Papagena, the mate intended for Papageno, appears to him at first in the guise of a wrinkled hag; Tamino's flute allures and tames all the beasts of the wilderness; Papageno's glockenspiel drives Monostatos and his black constabulary into a frenzied dance. This all seems merely a fantastic entertainment, intended to amuse suburban audiences by means of machines and decorations, a bright and variegated mixture of marvelous events and coarse jests. It is such an entertainment, to a certain extent; but it is much more, or rather it is something quite different, thanks to Mozart. *Die Zauberflöte* is one of those pieces that can enchant a child at the same time that it moves the most worldly of men to tears, and transports the wisest. Each individual and each generation finds something different in it; only to the merely 'cultured' or the pure barbarian does it have nothing to say. Its sensational success with its first audiences in Vienna arose from political reasons, based on the subject-matter. Mozart and Schikaneder were Freemasons: Mozart an enthusiastic one, and Schikaneder surely a crafty and active one. The latter used the symbols of Freemasonry quite openly in the libretto. The first edition of the libretto contained something rare in such books— two copperplate engravings, one showing Schikaneder-Papageno in his costume of feathers, but the other showing the portal to the 'inner rooms,' the great pyramid with hieroglyphics, and a series of emblems: five-pointed star, square and trowel, hour-glass and overthrown pillars and plinths. Everyone understood this. After a period of tolerance for the 'brothers' under Joseph II, a reaction had set in with Leopold II, and there had begun again secret persecutions and repressions. The Queen of the Night was Maria Theresa, Leopold's mother; and I am convinced that the black traitor Monostatos also was intended to represent a particular personage. Under the cloak of symbolism *Die Zauberflöte* was a work of rebellion, consolation, and hope. Sarastro and his priests represent hope in the victory of light, of humanity, of the brotherhood of man. Mozart took care, by means of rhythm, melody, and orchestral color, to make the significance of the opera, an open secret, still clearer. He began and ended the work in E-flat major, the Masonic key. The slow introduction of the Overture begins with the three chords, symbolizing the candidate knocking three times on the portal; and then in the climactic scene Tamino knocks on three different doors. A thrice-played chord follows Sarastro's opening of the ceremonies in the temple. Woodwinds—the typical instruments of the Viennese lodges—play a prominent part; the timbre of the trombones, heretofore used by Mozart—in *Idomeneo*, in *Don Giovanni*—only for dramatic intensification, now takes on symbolic force.

These Masonic elements had little meaning for the 'uninitiated' and have had even less for later generations. What remains is the eternal charm of the naive story, the pleasure in Schikaneder's skill—what a master-stroke, to bring the lovers together in full sight of everyone in the finale of Act I!—and the wondering awe at Mozart's music. The work is at once childlike and godlike, filled at the same time with the utmost simplicity and the greatest mastery. The most astonishing thing about it is its unity. The *Singspiel*, the 'German opera,' had been from its very beginning a mixture of the most heterogeneous ingredients: French *chanson* or *romance*, Italian *aria* or *cavatina*, *buffo* ensembles, and—the only thing German in it, aside from the language—simple songs. This is true of *Die Zauberflöte* also. The Queen of the Night's great scena (No. 4, *O zittre nicht, mein lieber Sohn*) and aria (No. 14, *Der Hölle Rache kocht in meinem Herzen*), written for Mozart's sister-in-law Josefa Hofer, are pieces in purest *opera-seria* style, stirring, or full of passionate force, with elaborate coloratura passages; but the coloratura also serves to characterize the blind passion of the direful Queen. At the other extreme is Papageno's little entrance song (No. 2, *Der Vogelfänger bin ich ja*), which would have been a street song if Mozart had not ennobled it with his wit and the genius of his instrumentation; or Papageno's magic song with the glockenspiel (No. 20, *Ein Mädchen oder Weibchen*); or his burlesque suicide scene and the droll ensuing duet (*pa . . . pa . . . pa . . .*) with Papagena. Between the two extremes are the pieces sung by Tamino, Pamina, and Sarastro— Tamino's 'Portrait Aria' (No. 3); Pamina's moving plaint in G minor, when Tamino can answer her questions only with sighs (No. 17, *Ach, ich fühl's, es ist verschwunden*); Sarastro's famous exhortation (No. 15, *In diesen heil'gen Hallen*); and the little duet between Pamina and Papageno (No. 7, *Bei Männern, welche Liebe fühlen*), which is a song in two strophes. Are they Italian; are they German? One can say only that they are Mozartean, in their combination of purest expression with purest melody; they are *cantabile* but not Italian; they are simple, but much too rich in expression, far from simple enough, much too sensitive in every turn of the voice part, every shading of the accompaniment, to fit into the category of the German *Lied*. Similarly with the relation of the ensembles and the two great finales to opera *buffa*. Where would a place have been found in opera *buffa* (opera *seria* does not enter into consideration at all here) for the trios of the three boys, which, in their transparent shimmer, seem drawn from a new domain of music, the domain of Ariel; or for the scenes of the three ladies, which are so humanly amusing and at the same time so imperious. But above all there was no place in opera *buffa* for the chorus, with which Mozart achieves the loveliest and most imposing effects in his work.

The most imposing effects! The mixture and fusion of the most heterogeneous elements in *Die Zauberflöte* are truly incredible. Papageno, with a padlock on his prattling lips, may make desperate signs to the three ladies; or Monostatos, to a pianissimo accompaniment of the orchestra, may perform his grotesque phallic dance before the sleeping Pamina—but no sooner does Mozart strike the mood of intense seriousness than we are in the true, innermost magic circle of the work. The March of the Priests and Sarastro's invocation (No. 10, *O Isis und Osiris*) introduced a new sound to opera, far removed from churchliness: it might be called a kind of secular awe. Two pieces particularly contribute to this new sound. In the first act it is the beginning of the finale, with the trombones, muted trumpets, sustained notes in the woodwinds, and the luminous voices of the trio of boys—the solemn introduction to Tamino's dialogue with the old priest. We are at one of the central points of the work: when Tamino, after this grave dialogue, asks himself:

O ew'ge Nacht! Wann wirst Du schwinden?
Wann wird das Licht mein Auge finden?

[O endless night! hast thou no breaking?
When dawns the day mine eyes are seeking?] *

and the invisible choir answers him consolingly, we sense the dawn of a better world. In the second act it is the final test of the lovers, the 'test of fire and water,' for which Mozart called into play every musical means at his disposal and for which he ordained extreme simplicity, extreme mastery; the scene of the men in armor, which he constructed in the form of a chorale prelude, building up a solemn *fugato* around the chorale *Ach Gott vom Himmel sieh' darein;* the blissful and serious duet between Tamino and Pamina, which grows into a quartet; the muted slow march of the wind instruments to Tamino's flute; the C major jubilation that greets the successful conclusion of the test.

There are two ways of approaching *Die Zauberflöte.* Mozart had occasion to observe both of them in reactions of contemporaries. At one of the early performances some acquaintances from Bavaria sat near his box:

The ——'s had a box this evening and applauded *everything* most heartily. But he, the know-all, showed himself to be such a thorough *Bavarian* that I could not remain or I should have had to call him an ass. Unfortunately I was there just when the second act began, that is, at the solemn scene. He made fun of everything. At first I was patient enough to draw his attention to a few passages. But he laughed at everything. Well, I could stand it no longer. I called him a Papageno and cleared out. But I don't think that the idiot understood my remark. [Letter of 8/9 October 1791.]

But a few days later he brought Salieri and Mme Cavalieri to the opera and 'you can hardly imagine how charming they were and how much they liked not only my music, but the libretto and everything. They both said that it was an *operone*, worthy to be performed for the grandest festival and before the greatest monarch . . .'

An 'operone,' a 'grand opera.' Yes, that is what this machine-play for a wretched Viennese suburban theater became in Mozart's hands. The growing acclaim with every performance delighted him. 'But what always gives me most pleasure is the *silent* approval. You can see how this opera is becoming more and more popular . . .' It was his bequest

* Translation by Edward J. Dent.

to mankind, his appeal to the ideals of humanity. His last work is not *Tito* or the Requiem; it is *Die Zauberflöte*. Into the Overture, which is anything but a *Singspiel* overture, he compressed the struggle and victory of mankind, using the symbolic means of polyphony: working out, laborious working out in the development section; struggle and triumph.

24. Conclusion

NINE WEEKS after the first performance of *Die Zauberflöte* Mozart died. His influence began to be felt at once, to such an extraordinary extent—precisely because of *Die Zauberflöte*—that it immediately evoked protests. In the 18th issue of the *Berliner Musik-Zeitung* of 1793 Johann Friedrich Reichardt, Prussian Court *Kapellmeister*, published a short article on the subject of 'vogue-composers,' which states, in part:

To what injustices [against the music of Johann Friedrich Reichardt, for example], therefore, can the defense of the latest fashion in music not lead! Mozart, for example, deserves to be honored, of course; he was a great genius and sometimes wrote excellent things, as for instance his *Zauberflöte* and some of his overtures and quartets. But of inordinate fuss about Mozart there is now scarcely an end . . .

Which did not prevent this aggrieved or envious man from imitating Mozart as much as possible in *Die Geisterinsel*, his own *Singspiel*, after Shakespeare's *Tempest*. But, not to be unjust to North Germany, let us also quote the report of Johann Baptist Schaul, Court Musician of Württemberg, who, in his *Briefe über den Geschmack in der Musik* (1809, and still in 1818), said of Mozart's works in general that 'they contain good things, moderately good things, bad things, and very bad things, so that they in no way deserve such to-do as his admirers make about them'; and, of the arias in particular, that Mozart was never fortunate in them and that Tamino's 'Portrait Aria' was a street-song. It is true that such judgments dwindled in the course of the nineteenth century, and it was not often that a creative musician still had the courage to express openly his extreme aversion to Mozart, as Frederick Delius did, although there were many anti-Mozarteans—a fact that tells us little about Mozart but much about the anti-Mozarteans.

As we have already indicated, the definitive work on Mozart's effect on musical history has not yet been written. The Haydn of the London symphonies, the two oratorios, and the late Masses was just as profoundly influenced by him, though in a different way, as the young—and middle-aged and older—Beethoven, or as the young Schubert. Despite Beethoven, many musicians of the generation following Mozart—like his personal pupil Johann Nepomuk Hummel, or like Louis Spohr—remained lifelong Mozarteans. Mozart was recommended to North-German early Romanticism by the literary standard-bearer of the Romantic movement, E. T. A. Hoffmann, who, as a musician, was unable to escape from the Mozart style even when dealing with the most Romantic material, as in his opera *Undine*. Romanticism proper did everything possible to misinterpret Mozart in terms of itself, since it could not deny his existence; but a few Romantic musicians nevertheless understood how to amalgamate some part of the essential Mozart with their work. Such were Mendelssohn, who at least possessed some feeling for Mozart's inspired perfection of form; Chopin, whose work contains flashes of Bach, Mozart—and Rossini, sometimes side by side, sometimes fused and sublimated; Brahms, to whom Mozart's innocence of feeling and purity and transparency of technique remained an object of eternal envy; Busoni, who loved Mozart and found beautiful things to say about his art. It must be remembered that the nineteenth century came into possession of Mozart's complete work only gradually, and that many of his works only became available at all with their publication in the Complete Edition. Mozart the opera-composer exerted influence before Mozart the instrumental composer; the Masses and some of the other church works, loved and understood in South Germany, have always remained a closed book to North Germany. But one ought not to generalize even about the historical effect of the operas. The Italian *opere buffe* have had no successors; historically speaking, Mozart wrote them in vain. Germany was unable to fructify them, and the Italians—despite Rossini's admiration of them—scarcely noticed them, Rossini least of all. But *Die Zauberflöte* became the starting-point of German opera; without it there would have been perhaps no *Freischütz* or *Oberon*, no *Vampyr* or *Hans Heiling*, and consequently no *Tannhäuser* or *Lohengrin* or anything else that followed these.

But Mozart's influence transcends history. Each generation sees something different in his work. The situation can perhaps be explained in the words of a poet. Eduard Mörike once presented as a wedding gift

to friends an unpretentious earthen pot which bore the following inscription:

> Doch, Freunde, lacht so viel ihr wollt
> Ihr werdet Wunder noch erfahren:
> Denn wisst, von heut in fünfzig Jahren
> Verwandl' ich mich in pures Gold.

> [A marvel will to you unfold,
> Friends, though you now be filled with laughter:
> For this day fifty summers after
> I shall be turned to purest gold.]

And so it is. Mozart's music, which to so many of his contemporaries
still seemed to have the brittleness of clay, has long since been transformed into gold, gleaming in the light, though it takes on a different
luster for each new generation. Without it each generation would be
infinitely poorer. No earthly remains of Mozart survived save a few
wretched portraits, no two of which are alike; the fact that all the re-
productions of his death-mask, which would have shown him as he
really was, have crumbled to bits seems symbolic. It is as though the
world-spirit wished to show that here is pure sound, conforming to a
weightless cosmos, triumphant over all chaotic earthliness, spirit of the
world-spirit.

Catalogue of Works

K.52 Song, 'Daphne deine Rosenwangen'

K.53 Song, 'Freude, Königin der Weisen,' 376

K.54 Variations for Piano in F

K.55 Sonata for Piano and Violin (dubious) in F, 253

K.56 Sonata for Piano and Violin (dubious) in C, 253

K.57 Sonata for Piano and Violin (dubious) in F, 253, 257

K.58 Sonata for Piano and Violin (dubious) in E flat, 253

K.59 Sonata for Piano and Violin (dubious) in C minor, 253

K.60 Sonata for Piano and Violin (dubious), in E minor, 253

K.61 Sonata for Piano and Violin (by Raupach), 253

K.61^g Two Minuets, 1 for Orchestra, 11 for Piano

K.61^h Six Minuets for Orchestra

K.62 Cassation in D

K.63 Serenade in G, 145, 146, 209

K.64 Minuet for Orchestra in D

K.65 Missa brevis in D minor, 326, 346

K.65^a Seven Minuets for Two Violins and Bass

K.66 Missa ('Dominicus') in C, 323, 324, 326

K.67 Sonata da Chiesa in E flat, 332

K.68 Sonata da Chiesa in B flat, 332

K.69 Sonata da Chiesa in D, 332

K.70 Recitative and Aria for Soprano, 'A Berenice,' 358

K.71 Aria for Tenor, 'Ah, più tremar'

K.72 Offertorium pro Festo Sti. Joannis Baptistae, 329

K.73 Symphony in C

K.74 Symphony in G

K.74^g (Anh. 216) Symphony in B flat

K.75 Symphony in F, 221

K.76 Symphony in F

K.77 Recitative and Aria for Soprano, 'Misero me,' 359

K.78 Aria for Soprano, 'Per pietà, bell' idol mio'

K.79 Recitative and Aria for Soprano, 'O temerario Arbace'

K.80 Quartet for Strings in G, 168, 171

K.81 Symphony in D

K.82 Aria for Soprano, 'Se ardire, e speranza'

K.83 Aria for Soprano, 'Se tutti i mali miei'

K.84 Symphony in D

K.85 Miserere, 328

K.86 Antiphon, 'Quaerite primum,' 146, 147

K.87 Mitridate, opera seria, 125, 359, 387, 390, 396

K.88 Aria for Soprano, 'Fra cento affanni,' 358

K.89 Kyrie in G

K.90 Kyrie in D minor

K.91 Kyrie in D

K.92 Salve Regina

K.93 Psalm, 'De profundis,' 329, 341

K.94 Minuet for Piano (?) in D

K.95 Symphony in D

K.96 Symphony in C, 221

K.97 Symphony in D

K.98 Symphony in F (dubious)

K.99 Cassation in B flat, 209

K.100 Serenade in D, 209

K.101 Serenade (Contredanse) in F

K.102 Finale of a Symphony in C, 225, 403

K.103 Nineteen Minuets for Orchestra

K.104 Six Minuets for Orchestra

K.105 Six Minuets for Orchestra

K.106 Overture and three Contredanses

K.107 Three Concertos after J. Chr. Bach, 237, 290

K.108 Regina Coeli, 328

K.109 Litaniae de B.M.V., 329

K.110 Symphony in G, 146

K.111 Ascanio in Alba, serenata (festa teatrale), 32, 125, 357, 398, 400, 403

K.112 Symphony in F

K.113 Divertimento in E flat, 208

K.114 Symphony in A

K.115 Missa brevis in C, 331

K.116 Missa brevis in F, 328

K.117 Offertory, 'Benedictus sit Deus' in C, 325

K.118 La Betulia liberata, oratorio, 109, 387, 403, 409

K.119 Aria for Soprano, 'Der Liebe himmlisches Gefühl'

K.120 Finale of a Symphony in D

K.121 Finale of a Symphony in D, 225

K.122 Minuet for Orchestra in E flat

K.123 Contredanse for Orchestra in B flat

K.124 Symphony in G

K.125 Litaniae de venerabili altaris sacramento, 328, 336

Index of Names